USING THIS BOOK

Where to stay...?

Over 800 answers to the age-old question!

Revised annually, this is the most comprehensive guide to bed and breakfast establishments in Scotland.

Every property in the guide has been graded and classified by VisitScotland inspectors. See page VI for details

How to find accommodation

This book split into eight areas of Scotland:

Accommodation

The map on page XIX shows these areas. Within each area section you will find accommodation listed alphabetically by location.

Alternatively there is an index at the back of this book listing alphabetically all accommodation locations in Scotland.

USING THIS BOOK

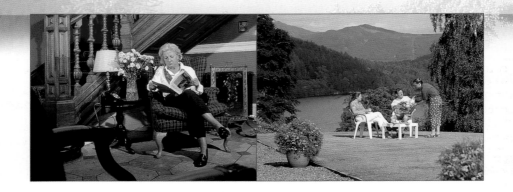

LEARN to use the symbols in each entry – They contain a mine of information! **There is a key to symbols on the back flap.**

Naturally, it is always advisable to confirm with the establishment that a particular facility is still available.

Prices in the guide are quoted per person and represent the minimum and maximum charges expected to apply to most rooms in the establishment. They include VAT at the appropriate rate and service charges where applicable.

The prices of accommodation, services and facilities are supplied to us by the operators and were, to the best of our knowledge, correct at the time of going to press. However, prices can change at any time during the lifetime of the publication, and you should check again when you book.

Bookings can be made direct to the establishment, through a travel agent, or through a local Tourist Information Centre.

Remember, when you accept accommodation by telephone or in writing, you are entering a legally binding contract which must be fulfilled on both sides. Should you fail to take up accommodation, you may not only forfeit any deposit already paid, but may also have to compensate the establishment if the accommodation cannot be re-let.

Introduction

Hotels & Guest Houses

Where to Stay Guide 2002

Accommodation

Scotland is split into eight tourist areas.
You will find accommodation listed
alphabetically by location
within each of these areas.
There is an index at the back of this book
which may also help you.

Appendix

Welcome to Scotland
Hotels & Guest Houses

FROM world-famous hotels to friendly guest houses, you'll find all the variety of Scotland reflected in the wide choice available in this guide.

Hundreds of hotels in all kinds of locations, are listed each with their own special character and atmosphere.

There are city hotels, located within walking distance of all the main attractions, which also offer the high-tech and sophisticated facilities for the business traveller, as well as some of the best conference and function facilities in Europe. Outwith the city, there is an exciting range of country retreats, where you can relax in luxurious and peaceful surroundings, which are ideal for a spot of golf, fishing or stress-relieving spa treatments.

Scotland also provides numerous friendly and welcoming family hotels, with sports, activities and entertainment for all ages, and excellent value for weekend breaks. Many of these large hotels have modern leisure complexes, for a work-out, swim or sun-tan, whatever the weather.

Staying in one of Scotland's hotels or guest houses give you the ideal opportunity to tempt your taste-buds with the distinctive quality of Scottish produce. In addition, these guest houses are friendly and economical, and almost all are family-run to provide great value and comfort in a homely atmosphere.

From the furthest-flung islands to the busy hub of Scotland's capital, there is something to suit everyone's taste – so go out and experience the very best of Scotland's traditional welcome and hospitality!

USING THIS BOOK

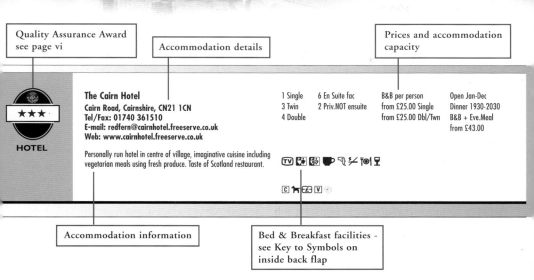

Quality Assurance Award
see page vi

Accommodation details

Prices and accommodation
capacity

The Cairn Hotel
Cairn Road, Cairnshire, CN21 1CN
Tel/Fax: 01740 361510
E-mail: redfern@cairnhotel.freeserve.co.uk
Web: www.cairnhotel.freeserve.co.uk

★★★
HOTEL

Personally run hotel in centre of village, imaginative cuisine including
vegetarian meals using fresh produce. Taste of Scotland restaurant.

1 Single   6 En Suite fac
3 Twin   2 Priv.NOT ensuite
4 Double

B&B per person
from £25.00 Single
from £25.00 Dbl/Twn

Open Jan-Dec
Dinner 1930-2030
B&B + Eve.Meal
from £43.00

Accommodation information

Bed & Breakfast facilities -
see Key to Symbols on
inside back flap

Disclaimer

VisitScotland has published this guide in good faith to reflect information submitted to it by the proprietors of the premises listed who have paid for their entries to be included. Although VisitScotland has taken reasonable steps to confirm the information contained in the guide at the time of going to press, it cannot guarantee that the information published is and remains accurate. Accordingly, VisitScotland recommends that all information is checked with the proprietor of the premises prior to booking to ensure that the accommodation, its price and all other aspects of the premises are satisfactory. VisitScotland accepts no responsibility for any error or misrepresentation contained in the guide and excludes all liability for loss or damage caused by any reliance placed on the information contained in the guide. VisitScotland also cannot accept any liability for loss caused by the bankruptcy, or liquidation, or insolvency, or cessation of trade of any company, firm or individual contained in this guide.

Follow the stars and you won't be disappointed when you get to the inn.

THE VisitScotland Star System is a world-first. Quality is what determines our star awards, not a checklist of facilities. We've made your priorities our priorities.

Quality makes or breaks a visit. This is why the most important aspect of your stay; the warmth of welcome, efficiency and friendliness of service, the quality of the food and the cleanliness and condition of the furnishings, fittings and decor earn VisitScotland Stars, not the size of the accommodation or the range of available facilities.

This easy to understand system tells you at a glance the quality standard of all types and sizes of accommodation from the smallest B&B and self-catering cottage to the largest countryside and city centre hotels.

Look out for this distinctive sign of Quality Assured Accommodation

Please note, although VisitScotland is the new name for what was formerly called the Scottish Tourist Board, we will continue to use 'Scottish Tourist Board' throughout 2002 for our Quality Assurance schemes.

Quality Assurance awards correct at end September 2001

SIGNS YOU NEED TO KNOW
Quality Grading

The standards you can expect:

★★★★★ **Exceptional**
★★★★ **Excellent**
★★★ **Very good**
★★ **Good**
★ **Fair and Acceptable**

A trained VisitScotland Quality Advisor grades each property every year to give you the reassurance that you can choose accommodation of the quality standard you want.

To help you further in your choice the VisitScotland System also tells you the type of accommodation and the range of facilities and services available.

Please turn over for details.

For further information call into any Tourist Information Centre, or contact VisitScotland.

More details available from:

Quality Assurance Department
VisitScotland
Thistle House
Beechwood Park North
INVERNESS
IV2 3ED

Tel: **01463 723040**
Fax: **01463 717244**
Email: **qa@visitscotland.com**

If you have a complaint about your accommodation, make it known to the management as soon as possible so that they can take action to investigate and resolve the problem. You should not feel reluctant to complain if you are dissatisfied with some aspect of your accommodation. Indeed, it is always the best policy to draw attention to the problem on the spot. Proprietors and their staff want you to return and for you to recommend what they provide to your friends. If you let them know what displeases you at the time they have an opportunity to put matters right. However, if you do have a problem with one of our Quality Assured properties which has not been resolved by the proprietor, please write to Quality Assurance, VisitScotland, Beechwood Park North, Inverness, IV2 3ED; or email on qa@visitscotland.com.

Accommodation Types

Self Catering
A house, cottage, apartment, chalet or similar accommodation which is let normally on a weekly basis to individuals where facilities are provided to cater for yourselves.

Serviced Apartments
Serviced apartments are essentially self catering apartments where services such as a cleaning service is available and meals and drinks may be available. Meals and drinks would normally be provided to each apartment or in a restaurant and/or bar which is on site.

Guest House
A guest house is usually a commercial business and will normally have a minimum of 4 letting bedrooms, of which some will have ensuite or private facilities. Breakfast will be available and evening meals may be provided.

B&B
Accommodation offering bed and breakfast, usually in a private house. B&B's will normally accommodate no more than 6 guests, and may or may not serve an evening meal.

Hotel
A hotel will normally have a minimum of twenty letting bedrooms, of which the majority must have ensuite or private bathroom facilities. A hotel will normally have a drinks licence (may be a restricted licence) and will serve breakfast, dinner and normally lunch.

Small Hotel
A small hotel will normally have a maximum of twenty letting bedrooms and a minimum of six. The majority of the bedrooms will have ensuite or private facilities. A small hotel will be licenced (may be a restricted licence) and will serve breakfast, dinner and normally lunch. It will normally be run by owner(s) and reflect their style and personal input.

International Resort Hotel
A hotel achieving a 5 Star quality award which owns and offers a range of leisure and sporting facilities including an 18 hole golf course, swimming and leisure centre and country pursuits.

Lodge
Primarily purpose-built overnight accommodation, often situated close to a major road or in a city centre. Reception hours may be restricted and payment may be required on check in. There may be associated restaurant facilities.

Inn
Bed and breakfast accommodation provided within a traditional inn or pub environment. A restaurant and bar will be open to non-residents and will provide restaurant or bar food at lunchtime and in the evening.

Restaurant with Rooms
In a restaurant with rooms, the restaurant is the most significant part of the business. It is usually open to non-residents. Accommodation is available, and breakfast is usually provided.

Campus Accommodation
Campus accommodation is provided by colleges and universities for their students and is made available-with meals-for individuals, families or groups at certain times of the year. These typically include the main Summer holiday period as well as Easter and Christmas.

SIGNS YOU NEED TO KNOW
Quality Grading

Serviced Accommodation
Facility and Service Symbols

TV in bedrooms

Satellite/cable TV

Tea/coffee making facilities in bedrooms

Telephone in bedrooms

Hairdryer in bedrooms

Evening meal available

Room service

Restaurant

Leisure facilities

Indoor swimming pool

Laundry service

Porterage

Lounge

TV Lounge

Full alcohol drinks licence

Restricted alcohol drinks licence

Non-smoking establishment

Smoking restricted

Payphone provided

Washbasin in bedrooms

Ensuite bath and/or shower for all bedrooms

Ensuite bath and/or shower for some bedrooms

Private bath and/or shower for all bedrooms

Private bath and/or shower for some bedrooms

Private parking

Limited parking

No TV

SIGNS YOU NEED TO KNOW
For a Quality Destination

YOU not only want to be sure of the standard of accommodation you choose to stay in, which ever type it may be, you want to be sure you make the most of your time.

VisitScotland not only grades every type of accommodation every year, but also a wide range of visitor attractions every second year to grade the standard of customer care provided for visitors.

The grading scheme for visitor attractions provides you with the assurance that an attraction has been assessed for the condition and standard of the facilities and services provided – the warmth of welcome, efficiency of service, level of cleanliness, standard of visitor interpretation and of the toilets, restaurant and shop, if provided.

A large world famous castle, or small local museum can attain high grades if their services for the visitor are of a high standard.

The Standards You Can Expect:

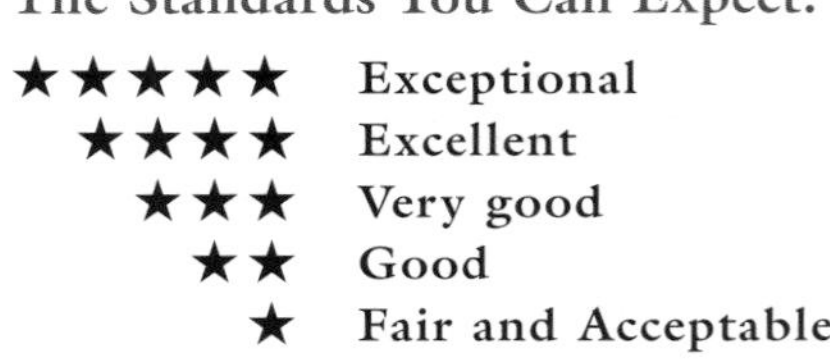

★ ★ ★ ★ ★   **Exceptional**
★ ★ ★ ★   **Excellent**
★ ★ ★   **Very good**
★ ★   **Good**
★   **Fair and Acceptable**

In addition to the star grades, every attraction is categorised under one of the following types to help give the visitor an indication of the type of experience on offer:

Visitor Attraction
Castle
Historic Attraction
Museum
Tour
Garden
Activity Centre
Tourist Shop
Leisure Centre
Arts Venue
Historic House

Look for the VisitScotland/Scottish Tourist Board sign of quality:

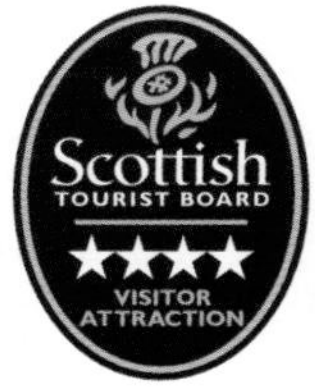

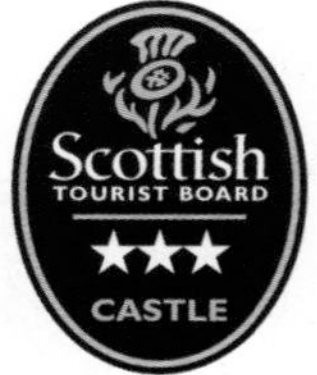

SIGNS YOU NEED TO KNOW
Mobility Needs

Visitors with particular mobility needs must be able to be secure in the knowledge that suitable accommodation is available to match these requirements. Advance knowledge of accessible entrances, bedrooms and facilities is important to enable visitors to enjoy their stay.

Along with the quality awards which apply to all the establishments in this, and every VisitScotland guide, we operate a national accessibility scheme. By inspecting establishments to set criteria, we can identify and promote places that meet the requirements of visitors with mobility needs.

The three categories of accessibility – drawn up in close consultation with specialist organisations are:

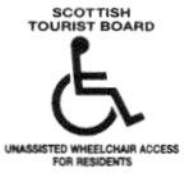

 Unassisted wheelchair access for residents

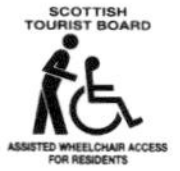

 Assisted wheelchair access for residents

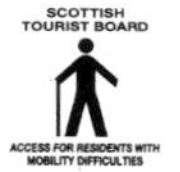

 Access for residents with mobility difficulties

Look out for these symbols in establishments, in advertising and brochures. They assure you that entrances, ramps, passageways, doors, restaurant facilities, bathrooms and toilets, as well as kitchens in self catering properties, have been inspected with reference to the needs of wheelchair users, and those with mobility difficulties. Write or telephone for details of the standards in each category – address on page VII.

For more information about travel, specialist organisations who can provide information and a list of all the Scottish accommodation which has had the access inspection write to VisitScotland (or ask at a Tourist Information Centre) for the VisitScotland booklet "Accessible Scotland".

Holiday Care
2nd Floor
Imperial Buildings
Victoria Road
Horley
Surrey RH6 7PZ
Tel: **01293 774535**
Fax: **01293 784647**
Email: **holiday.care@virgin.net**
Web: **www.holidaycare.org.uk**

In addition, a referral service to put enquirers in touch with local disability advice centres is:

Update
27 Beaverhall Road
Edinburgh
EH7 4JE
Tel: **0131 558 5200**
Email: **info@update.org.uk**
Web: **www.update.org.uk**

OVER 900 quality assured accommodation providers are offering an extra warm welcome for visitors who are cycling or walking for all, or part, of their holiday in Scotland.

As well as having had the quality of the welcome, service, food and comfort assessed by VisitScotland, they will be able to offer the following:-

★ hot drink on arrival
★ packed lunch/flask filling option
★ late evening meal option
★ early breakfast option
★ drying facilities for wet clothes
★ local walking and/or cycling information
★ daily weather forecast
★ local public transport information
★ secure, lockable, covered area for bike storage
★ details of local cycle specialists

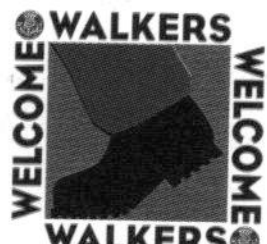

Walkers Welcome Scheme

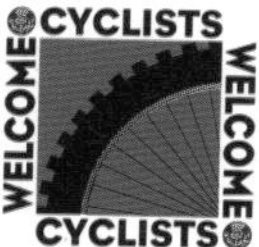

Cyclists Welcome Scheme

Look out for the logos in this guide and other accommodation listings.

Green Tourism

In response to the increasing need for businesses throughout the world to operate in an environmentally friendly way, VisitScotland has developed the Green Tourism Business Scheme.

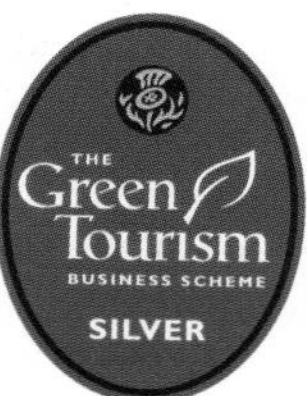

Where tourism businesses are taking steps to reduce waste and pollution, to recycle and to be efficient with resources they are credited in this Scheme with a "Green Award". In our assessment of the degree of environmental good practice the business is demonstrating they are awarded one of the following;

Bronze award   BRONZE

for achieving a satisfactory level

Silver award   SILVER

for achieving a good level

Gold award   GOLD

for achieving a very good level

SIGNS YOU NEED TO KNOW
Taste of Scotland
The Scotch Beef Club

FROM Scotland's natural larder comes a wealth of fine flavours. The sea yields crab and lobster, mussels and oysters, haddock and herring to be eaten fresh or smoked. From the lochs and rivers come salmon and trout.

Scotch beef and lamb, venison and game are of prime quality, often adventurously combined with local vegetables or with wild fruits such as redcurrants and brambles. Raspberries and strawberries are cultivated to add their sweetness to trifles and shortcakes, and to the home-made jams that are an essential part of Scottish afternoon tea.

The Scots have a sweet tooth, and love all kinds of baking – rich, crisp shortbread, scones, fruit cakes and gingerbreads. Crumbly oatcakes make the ideal partner for Scottish cheeses, which continue to develop from their ancient farming origins into new – and very successful – styles.

And in over a hundred distilleries, barley, yeast and pure spring water come together miraculously to create malt whisky – the water of life.

Many Scottish hotels and restaurants pride themselves on the use they make of these superb natural ingredients – around 400 are members of the Taste of Scotland Scheme which encourages the highest culinary standards, use of Scottish produce and a warm welcome to visitors. Look for the Stockpot symbol at establishments, or write to Taste of Scotland for a copy of their guide.

In Shops		£8.99
By Post:	UK	£9.50
	Europe	£10.50
	US	£12.00

Taste of Scotland Scheme
33 Melville Street
Edinburgh, EH3 7JF
Tel: **0131 220 1900**
Fax: **0131 220 6102**
E-mail: **tastescotland@sol.co.uk**
Web: **www.taste-of-scotland.com**

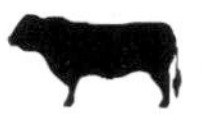

The Scotch Beef Club is an international association of restaurants of considerable repute.

The membership profile is wide and varied – ranging from intimate establishments, through beautiful country houses, to city centre hotels. The membership includes 5 Star golf resorts, former vicarages, cottages, a bakehouse and even a station. Their styles are individual but what they all have in common is a recognised excellence and a commitment to using only the finest quality produce in their award winning kitchens. This commitment is demonstrated by their choice of beef – Scotch Beef.

Give yourself a treat and try one of the Scotch Beef dishes on the menu at a Scotch Beef Club member.

SCOTLAND has some of the finest food products in the world.

Our seafood, beef, lamb, venison, vegetables and soft fruit are renowned for their high quality. These fine indigenous raw materials and a wide assortment of international food products are skillfully combined by cooks and chefs into the vast range of cuisine available in Scotland.

As you travel throughout the country you will find an excellent standard of cooking in all sorts of establishments from restaurants with imaginative menus to tea rooms with simple wholesome home-baking.

You will find some of these culinary gems by reading of their reputation in newspapers and magazines, from advice given by Tourist Information Centre staff, by looking for the Taste of Scotland logo, or by using your own instinct to discover them yourself.

VisitScotland has recognised that it would be helpful to you, the visitor, to have some assurance of the standards of food available in every different type of eating establishment; and indeed to be able to find a consistent standard of food in every place you choose to eat.

We launched The Natural Cooking of Scotland as a long-term initiative to encourage eating places to follow the lead of those who are best in their field in providing a consistently high standard of catering.

We have harnessed the skills of chefs, the experience of restaurateurs and the expertise of catering trainers to introduce a series of cooking skills courses which will encourage the use of fresh, local produce, cooked in a simple and satisfying way. We are providing advice and guidance to eating places throughout Scotland on high quality catering and the skills involved in efficient food service and customer care. Many more initiatives are being planned to support this enhancement of Scottish cooking standards and a high dependency on the food available on our own doorsteps.

Whilst you will appreciate the food experiences you will find in eating your way around Scotland this year, the Natural Cooking of Scotland will ensure that the profile of fine Scottish cooking is even greater in future years.

Look out for the new VisitScotland food grading scheme where the quality of food, as well as service and ambience are assessed on a scale of one to five stars.

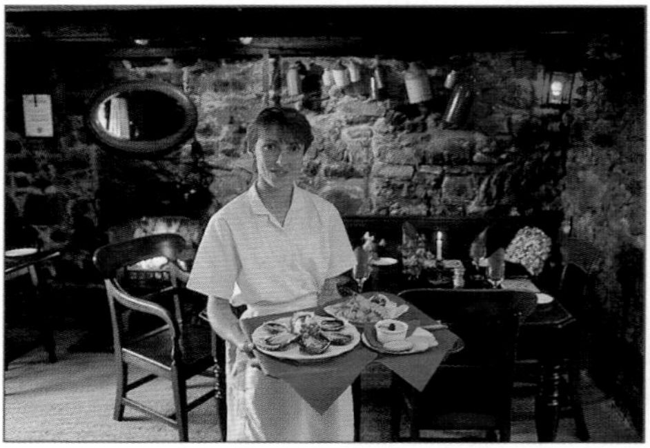

TRAVELLER'S TIPS
Getting Around

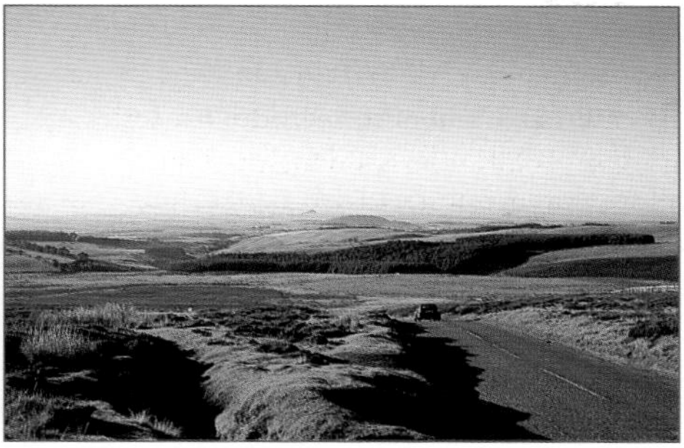

SCOTLAND is a small country and travel is easy. There are direct air links with UK cities, Europe and North America. There is also an internal air network bringing the islands of the North and West within easy reach.

Scotland's rail network not only includes excellent cross-border services but also a good internal network. All major towns are linked by rail and there are also links to the western seaboard at Mallaig and Kyle of Lochalsh (for ferry connections from Skye and the Western Isles) and to Inverness, Thurso and Wick for ferries to Orkney and Shetland.

All the usual discount cards are valid but there are also ScotRail Rovers (multi journey tickets allowing you to save on rail fares) and the Freedom of Scotland Travelpass, a combined rail and ferry pass allowing unlimited travel on Caledonian MacBrayne ferry services to the islands and all of the rail network. In addition Travelpass also offers discounts on bus services.

Cross-border rail services are available from all major centres, for example: Birmingham, Carlisle, Crewe, Manchester, Newcastle, Penzance, Peterborough, Preston, Plymouth, York and many others.

There are frequent rail departures from Kings Cross and Euston stations to Edinburgh and Glasgow. The journey time from Kings Cross to Edinburgh is around 4 hours and from Euston to Glasgow around 5 hours.

COACH connections include express services to Scotland from all over the UK; local bus companies in Scotland offer explorer tickets and discount cards. Postbuses (normally minibuses) take passengers on over 130 rural routes throughout Scotland.

Ferries to and around the islands are regular and reliable, most ferries carry vehicles, although some travelling to smaller islands convey only passengers.

Contact the Information Department, VisitScotland, 23 Ravelston Terrace, Edinburgh, EH4 3TP, or any Tourist Information Centre, for details of travel and transport.

Many visitors choose to see Scotland by road – distances are short and driving on the quiet roads of the Highlands is a new and different experience. In remoter areas, some roads are still single track, and passing places must be used. When vehicles approach from different directions, the car nearest to a passing place must stop in or opposite it. Please do not use passing places to park in!

Speed limits on Scottish roads: Dual carriageways 70mph/112kph; single carriageways 60mph/96kph; built-up areas 30mph/48kph.

The driver and front-seat passenger in a car must wear seatbelts; rear seatbelts, if fitted, must be used. Small children and babies must at all times be restrained in a child seat or carrier.

Opening Times

Public holidays: Christmas and New Year's Day are holidays in Scotland, taken by almost everyone. Scottish banks, and many offices close in 2002 on 1st and 2nd January, 29th March, 1st April, 6th May, 3rd and 4th June, 26th August, 25th and 26th December. Scottish towns also take Spring and Autumn holidays which may vary from place to place, but are usually on a Monday.

Banking hours: In general, banks open Monday to Friday, 0930 to 1700, with some closing later on a Thursday. Banks in cities, particularly in or near the main shopping centres, may be open at weekends. Cash machines in hundreds of branches allow you to withdraw cash outside banking hours, using the appropriate cards.

Pubs and restaurants: Pubs and restaurants are allowed to serve alcoholic drinks between 1100 hours and 2300 hours Monday through to Saturday; Sundays 1230 hours until 1430 hours then again from 1830 hours until 2300 hours.

Residents in hotels may have drinks served at any time, subject to the proprietors discretion.

Extended licensing hours are subject to local council applications.

Telephone codes

If you are calling from abroad, first dial your own country's international access code (usually 00, but do please check). Next, dial the UK code, 44, then the area code except for the first 0, then the remainder of the number as normal.

Bring your pet

The Pet Travel Scheme (PETS) means you are able to bring your dog or cat into the United Kingdom from certain countries and territories without it first having to go into Quarantine, provided the rules of the scheme are met. PETS only operates on certain air, rail and sea routes and your own government should be able to provide you with details. Alternatively you may wish to obtain detailed information from:

**Department of Environment,
Food and Rural Affairs
1a Page Street
London
SW1P 4PQ**

Tel: **0870 241 1710**
Fax: **0207 904 6834**
E-mail: **pets.helpline@defra.gsi.gov.uk**
Web: **www.defra.gov.uk/animalh/
            quarantine**

Scotland on the net
Visit our web site at:
www.visitscotland.com

66 VisitScotland is committed to ensuring that our natural environment, upon which our tourism is so dependant, is safeguarded for future generations to enjoy. **99**

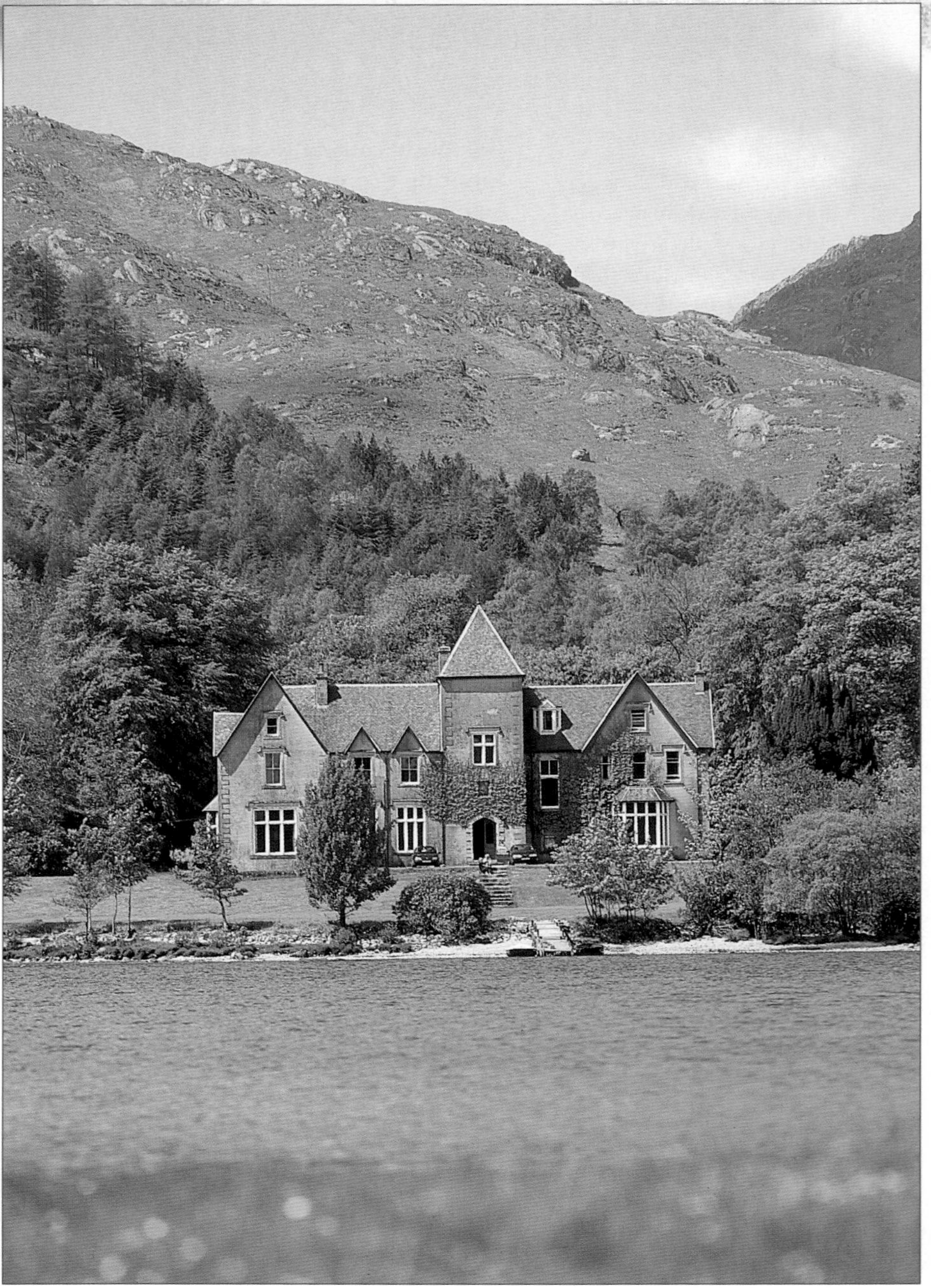

MAPS
Scotland's tourist areas

Accommodation

MAP 5

Lerwick

MAP 3 H

Kirkwall

MAP 4

Stornoway

Inverness

G

F

Fort William

Aberdeen

MAP 1

E

MAP 2

D

Glasgow

B
Edinburgh

C

A

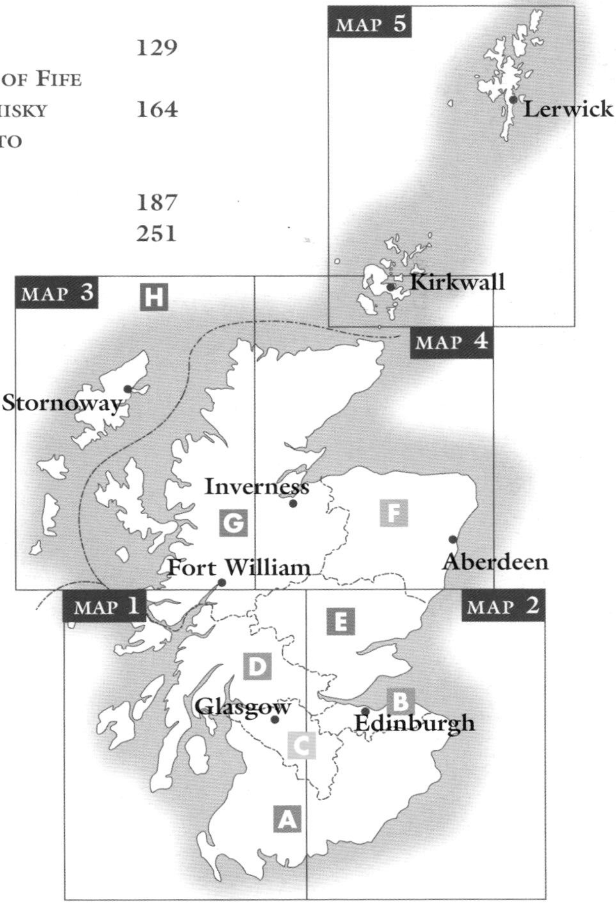

MAP 1

Grid columns: A B C D E F G H
Grid rows: 1–12

Row 1: Arinagour, COLL, Kilchoan, Tobermory, Strontian, Glencoe, Kentallen, Ballachulish, Glen Duror, Calgary, Dervaig, Appin, Bridge of Orchy, Ardeon, Ki Ra

Row 2: Scarinish, TIREE, Isle of Tiree, Killiechronan, Fishnish, Lochaline, Lismore, Barcaldine, Ardchattan, Connel, Craignure, MULL, Tyndrum, Killin, Loch Tay, Ardgeon

Row 3: Isle of Iona, Fionnphort, Pennyghael, Lerags, Oban, Dalmally, Crianlarich, Lochearnhead, Balquhidder, Bunessan, Uisken, Kilninver, Kilchrenan, Ardlui, Strathyre, Clachan Seil, Inveraray, Cairndow, Tarbet, Port of Menteith, D, Call

Row 4: COLONSAY, Arduaine, Kilmelford, Strachur, Lochgoilhead, Rowardennan, Aber, Ardfern, JURA, Inverbeg, Luss, Loch Lomond, Scalasaig, Crinan, Lochgair, Rhu, Drymen, Gartocharn, Fintry, Lochgilphead, Ardrishaig, Helensburgh, Balloch

Row 5: Port Askaig, Feolin, Sandbank, Dunoon, Duntocher, Bishopb, ISLAY, Ballygrant, Craighouse, Rhubodach, Colintraive, Inverkip, Wemyss Bay, Glasgow Airport, Clydeba, Tighnabruaich, Bridgend, Bowmore, Tarbert, Portavadie, Paisley, Renfrew, Port Charlotte, Rothesay, Largs, Howwood, GLASG, Kennacraig, BUTE, Claonaig, Cumbrae, E, Kilbri

Row 6: Isle of Gigha, Lochranza, Millport, Uplawmoor, Port Ellen, Ardminish, Seamill, CUMBRAE, Tayinloan, Corrie, Ardrossan, Kilwinning, Kilmarnock, Carradale, ARRAN, Irvine

Row 7: ATLANTIC OCEAN, Blackwaterfoot, Brodick, Firth of Clyde, Troon, Monkton, Lamlash, Prestwick, Campbeltown, Whiting Bay, Ayr, Dalrymple

Row 8: Turnberry, Girvan

Row 9: New Gallow

Row 10: Cairnryan, Newton Stewart, Gateho of F, Stranraer, Glenluce, Portpatrick, Luce Bay, Sorbie

Row 11: Port William, Isle of Whitho

Row 12: BELFAST, To Douglas, Isle of Man, To Liverpool

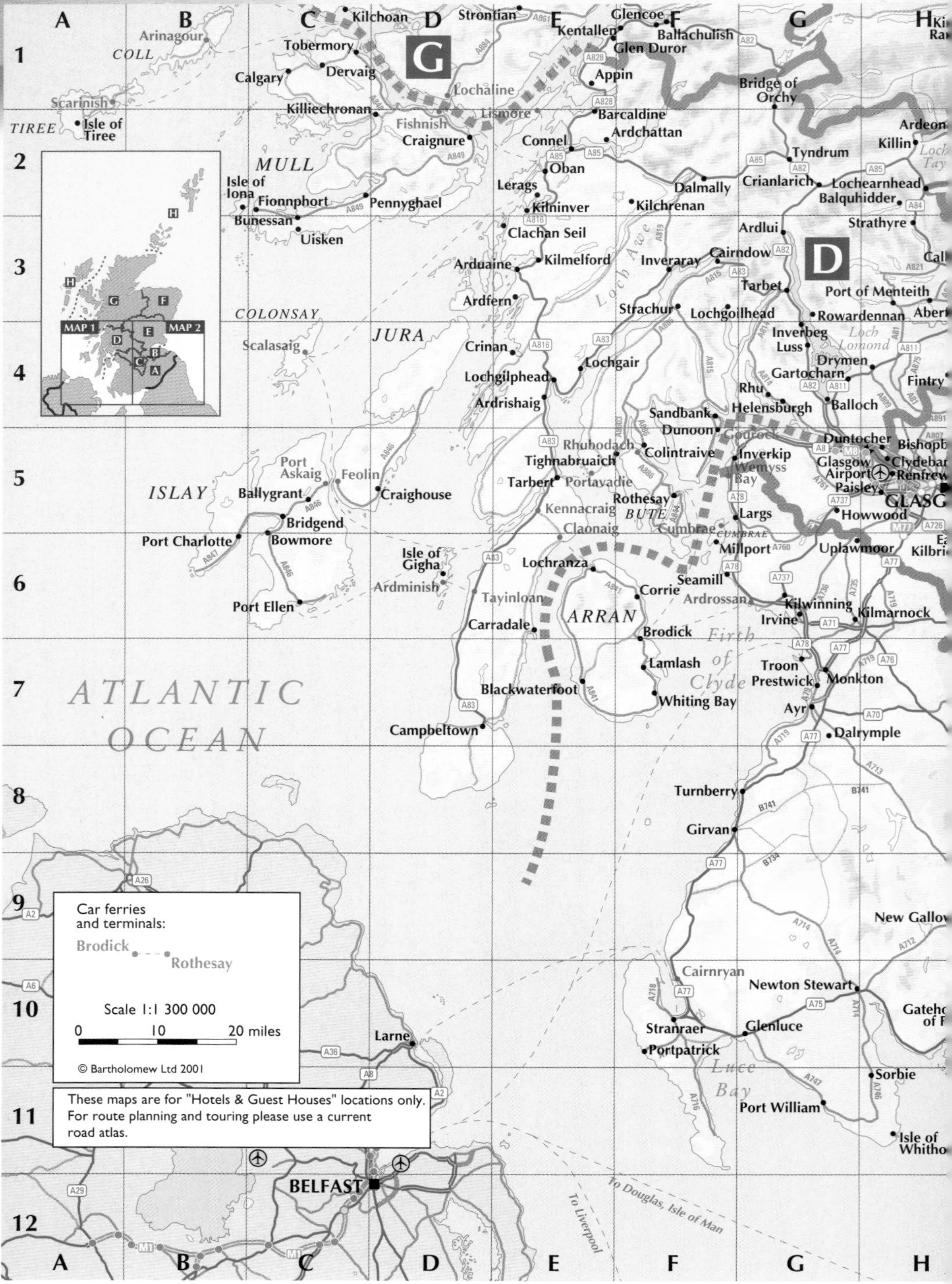

Car ferries and terminals:
Brodick — Rothesay

Scale 1:1 300 000
0 — 10 — 20 miles

© Bartholomew Ltd 2001

These maps are for "Hotels & Guest Houses" locations only.
For route planning and touring please use a current
road atlas.

MAP 2

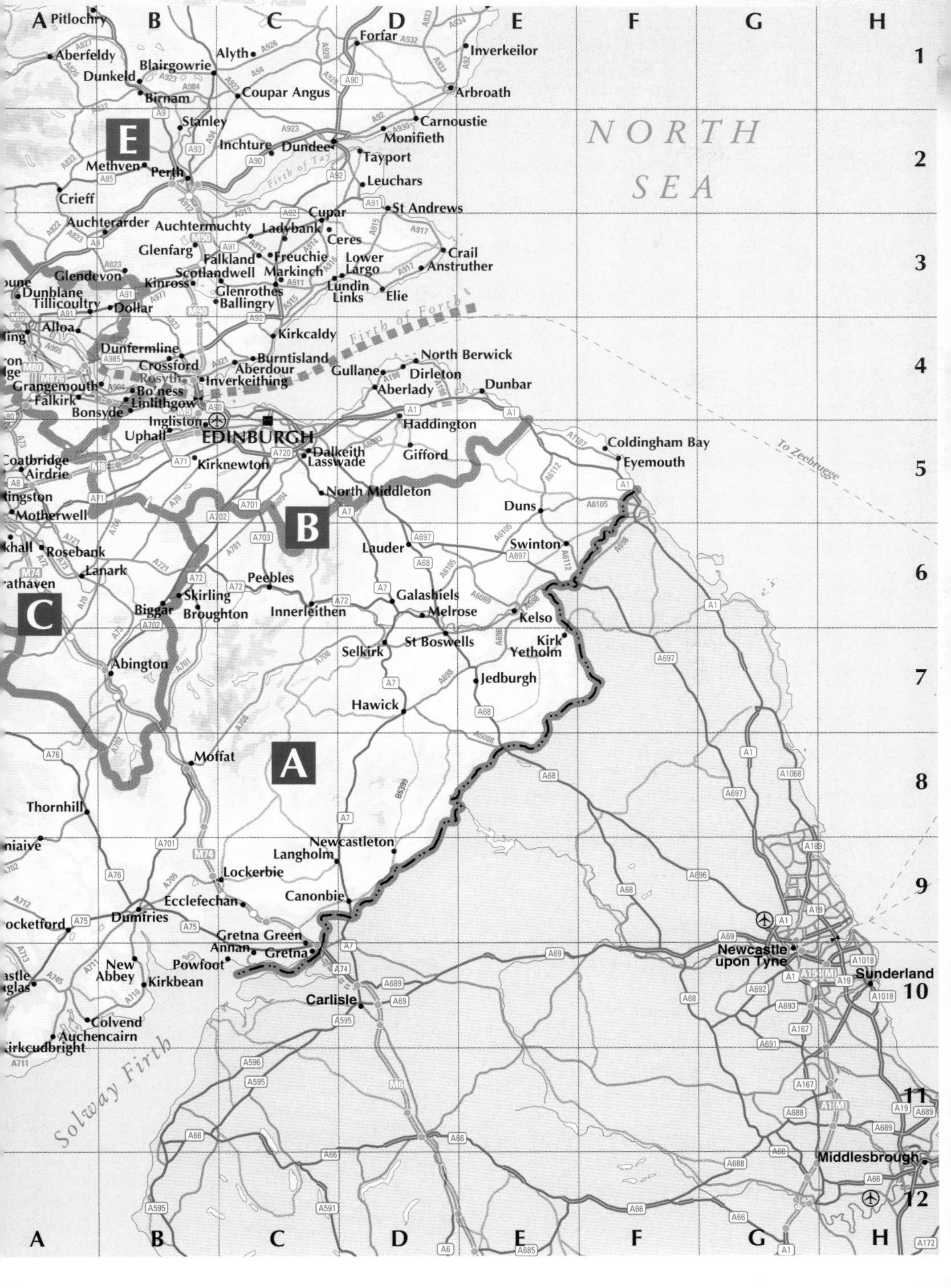

North Sea region / Southern Scotland and Northern England map

Grid columns: A B C D E F G H
Grid rows: 1 2 3 4 5 6 7 8 9 10 11 12

NORTH SEA

Firth of Tay
Firth of Forth
Solway Firth

To Zeebrugge

Place names:

Pitlochry, Aberfeldy, Dunkeld, Blairgowrie, Birnam, Alyth, Stanley, Coupar Angus, Forfar, Inverkeilor, Arbroath, Carnoustie, Monifieth, Methven, Perth, Inchture, Dundee, Tayport, Leuchars, Crieff, Auchterarder, Auchtermuchty, Cupar, St Andrews, Glenfarg, Ladybank, Ceres, Crail, Anstruther, Kinross, Falkland, Freuchie, Lower Largo, Glendevon, Scotlandwell, Markinch, Lundin Links, Elie, Dunblane, Glenrothes, Tillicoultry, Dollar, Ballingry, Alloa, Kirkcaldy, Dunfermline, Burntisland, North Berwick, Crossford, Aberdour, Gullane, Dirleton, Rosyth, Inverkeithing, Aberlady, Dunbar, Grangemouth, Bo'ness, Falkirk, Bonsyde, Linlithgow, Uphall, Ingliston, Haddington, EDINBURGH, Dalkeith, Gifford, Coldingham Bay, Kirknewton, Lasswade, Eyemouth, Coatbridge, Airdrie, North Middleton, Duns, Motherwell, Lauder, Swinton, Rosebank, Peebles, Galashiels, Kelso, Lanark, Skirling, Broughton, Innerleithen, Melrose, Biggar, Selkirk, St Boswells, Kirk Yetholm, Abington, Jedburgh, Hawick, Moffat, Thornhill, Newcastleton, Langholm, Lockerbie, Canonbie, Ecclefechan, Dumfries, Gretna Green, Annan, Gretna, New Abbey, Powfoot, Kirkbean, Carlisle, Colvend, Auchencairn, Kirkcudbright, Newcastle upon Tyne, Sunderland, Middlesbrough

Boxed region labels: A, B, C, E

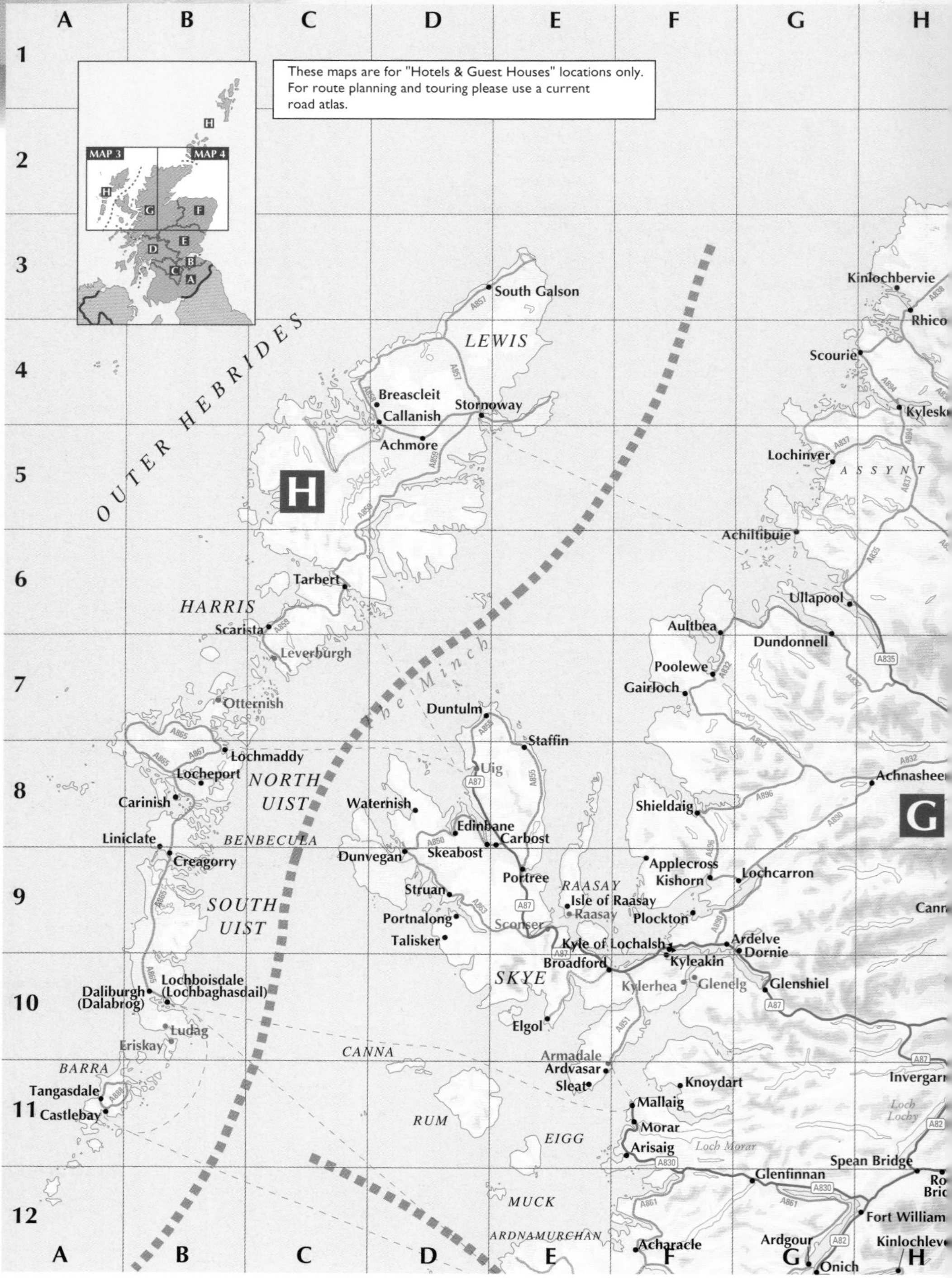

These maps are for "Hotels & Guest Houses" locations only. For route planning and touring please use a current road atlas.

MAP 4

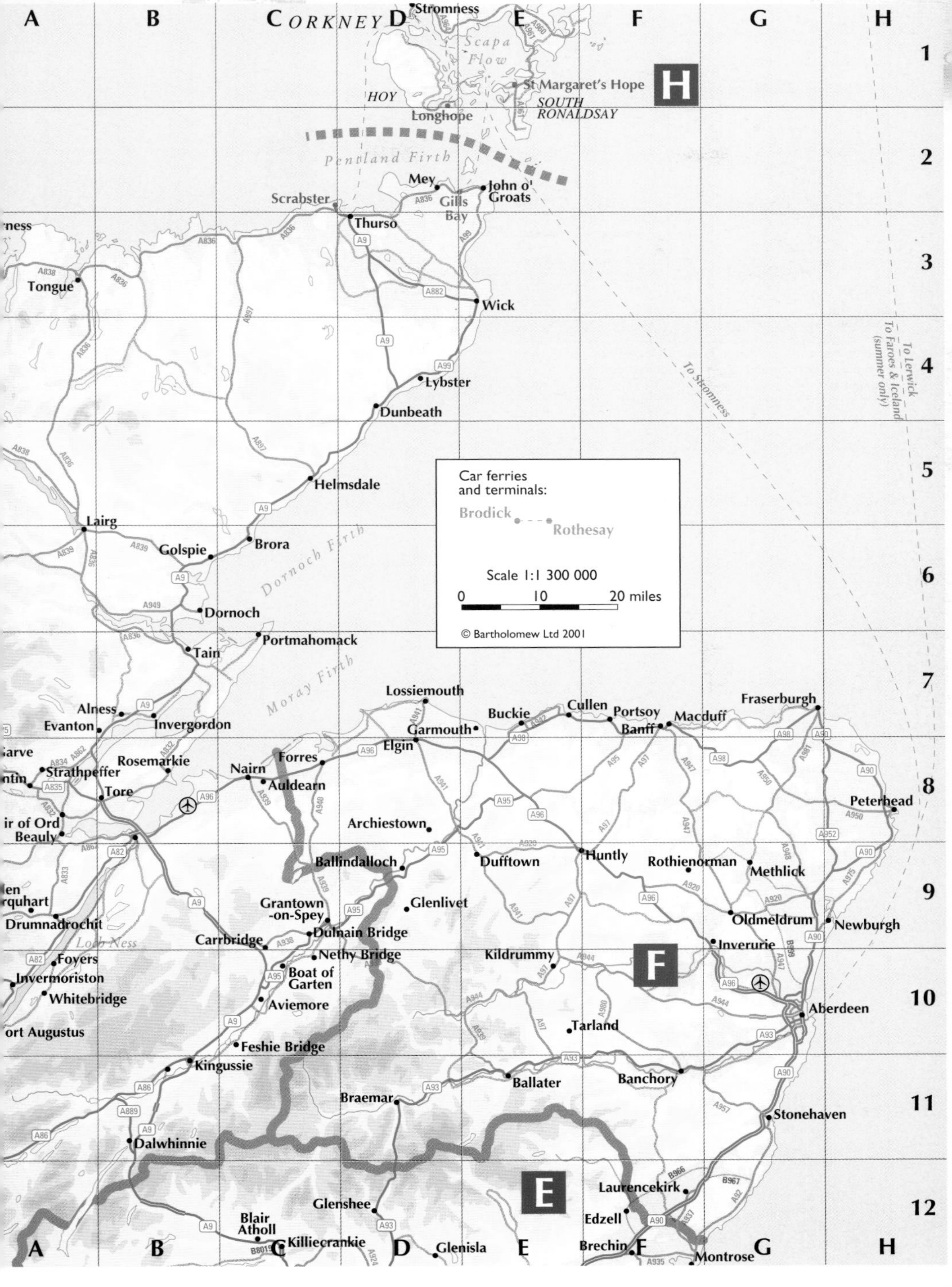

A B C *ORKNEY* D E F G H

1 Stromness

Scapa Flow

H

HOY St Margaret's Hope
Longhope *SOUTH RONALDSAY*

2 *Pentland Firth*

Mey
Scrabster Gills John o'
Bay Groats
3 Thurso

ness Tongue

Wick

4 Lybster

Dunbeath

To Stromness

To Lerwick
To Faroes & Iceland
(summer only)

5 Helmsdale

Car ferries
and terminals:

Brodick • – – • Rothesay

6 Lairg
Golspie Brora

Dornoch Firth

Dornoch

Scale 1:1 300 000

0   10   20 miles

Portmahomack

© Bartholomew Ltd 2001

Tain

7 Lossiemouth Fraserburgh
Alness *Moray Firth* Buckie Cullen
Evanton Garmouth Portsoy Macduff
arve Forres Banff
ntin Rosemarkie Nairn Elgin
8 Strathpeffer Auldearn Peterhead
Tore
ir of Ord Archiestown
Beauly
Ballindalloch Dufftown Huntly Rothienorman Methlick
9 *en* Grantown Glenlivet
rquhart -on-Spey Oldmeldrum Newburgh
Drumnadrochit Carrbridge Dulnain Bridge Inverurie
Loch Ness Nethy Bridge Kildrummy
10 Foyers Boat of
Invermoriston Garten **F**
Whitebridge Aviemore
ort Augustus Tarland Aberdeen
Feshie Bridge
Kingussie
11 Banchory
Braemar Ballater
A889 Stonehaven
Dalwhinnie
E
12 Glenshee Laurencekirk
Blair Edzell
Atholl Killiecrankie Glenisla Brechin **F** Montrose

A B C D E F G H

Invergordon

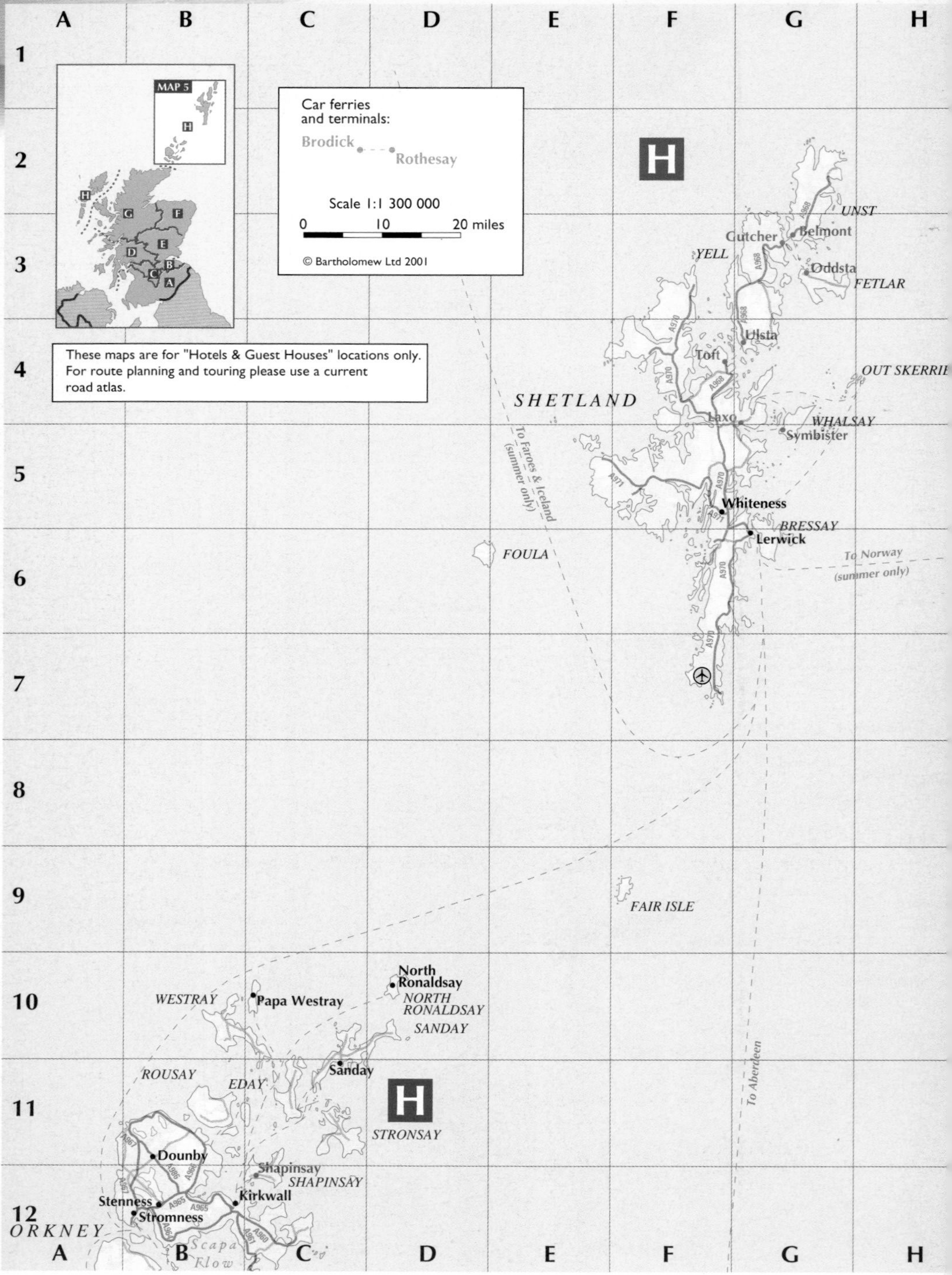

Car ferries
and terminals:

Brodick •····• Rothesay

Scale 1:1 300 000

0   10   20 miles

© Bartholomew Ltd 2001

These maps are for "Hotels & Guest Houses" locations only.
For route planning and touring please use a current
road atlas.

H

UNST

Gutcher • Belmont

YELL • Oddsta

FETLAR

Ulsta

OUT SKERRIE

Toft

SHETLAND

Laxo

WHALSAY

Symbister

Whiteness

BRESSAY

Lerwick

To Faroes & Iceland
(summer only)

FOULA

To Norway
(summer only)

FAIR ISLE

To Aberdeen

North
Ronaldsay

NORTH
RONALDSAY

WESTRAY • Papa Westray

SANDAY

ROUSAY

EDAY

Sanday

H

STRONSAY

Shapinsay

SHAPINSAY

• Dounby

Stenness • Kirkwall

ORKNEY Stromness

Scapa
Flow

Scotland

Bed & Breakfast

The official Where to Stay Guide 2002

welcome to scotland

SOUTH OF SCOTLAND:
Ayrshire and Arran, Dumfries and Galloway, Scottish Borders

Scotland's south west offers a beautiful and uncrowded landscape where you can enjoy a real feeling of space.

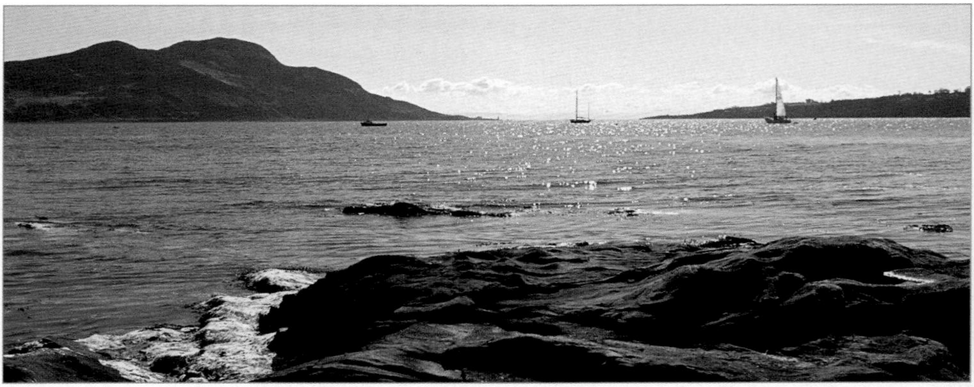

Looking across to Holy Island from Lamlash Bay, Isle of Arran

HERE you will find over 400 miles of the National Cycle network plus superb golf courses. There is also great walking country to be found, including the 212 mile coast-to-coast Southern Upland Way. This long-distance footpath begins in Portpatrick, goes through the Galloway Forest Park – the largest in Britain – then it crosses the Moffat Hills before it heads into the Scottish Borders. Back on the south-west coast, the tidal mudflats and sandy beaches of the Solway Firth are dotted with attractive villages and seaside towns including Kirkcudbright, with its long artistic tradition as well as a thriving current arts scene. Dumfries is the main town in the region. Sometimes known as the Queen of the South, this handsome red sandstone town has strong associations with Robert Burns. Some of the many attractions to visit include Caerlaverock Castle with four bird

reserves nearby, Gretna Green and the Famous Old Blacksmith's Shop Visitor Centre, Threave Gardens and its new Countryside Centre, Wigtown (now a celebrated 'Book Town') and Sweetheart Abbey.

The Ayrshire coast has some excellent holiday attractions for all the family, including Vikingar! in Largs, Culzean Castle and The Big Idea and the Magnum Leisure Centre both at Irvine Harbourside. For those interested in Scotland's national poet, Robert Burns, you can visit many attractions including his birthplace in Alloway. And you can relive some of his dramatic life at the Tam O' Shanter Experience. Less than an hour's sail will take you to the Isle of Arran which offers fine mountains, quiet beaches, the famous Brodick Castle and the Isle of Arran Distillery. For those who prefer a sporting holiday, the region offers horse-

SOUTH OF SCOTLAND:
Ayrshire and Arran, Dumfries and Galloway, Scottish Borders

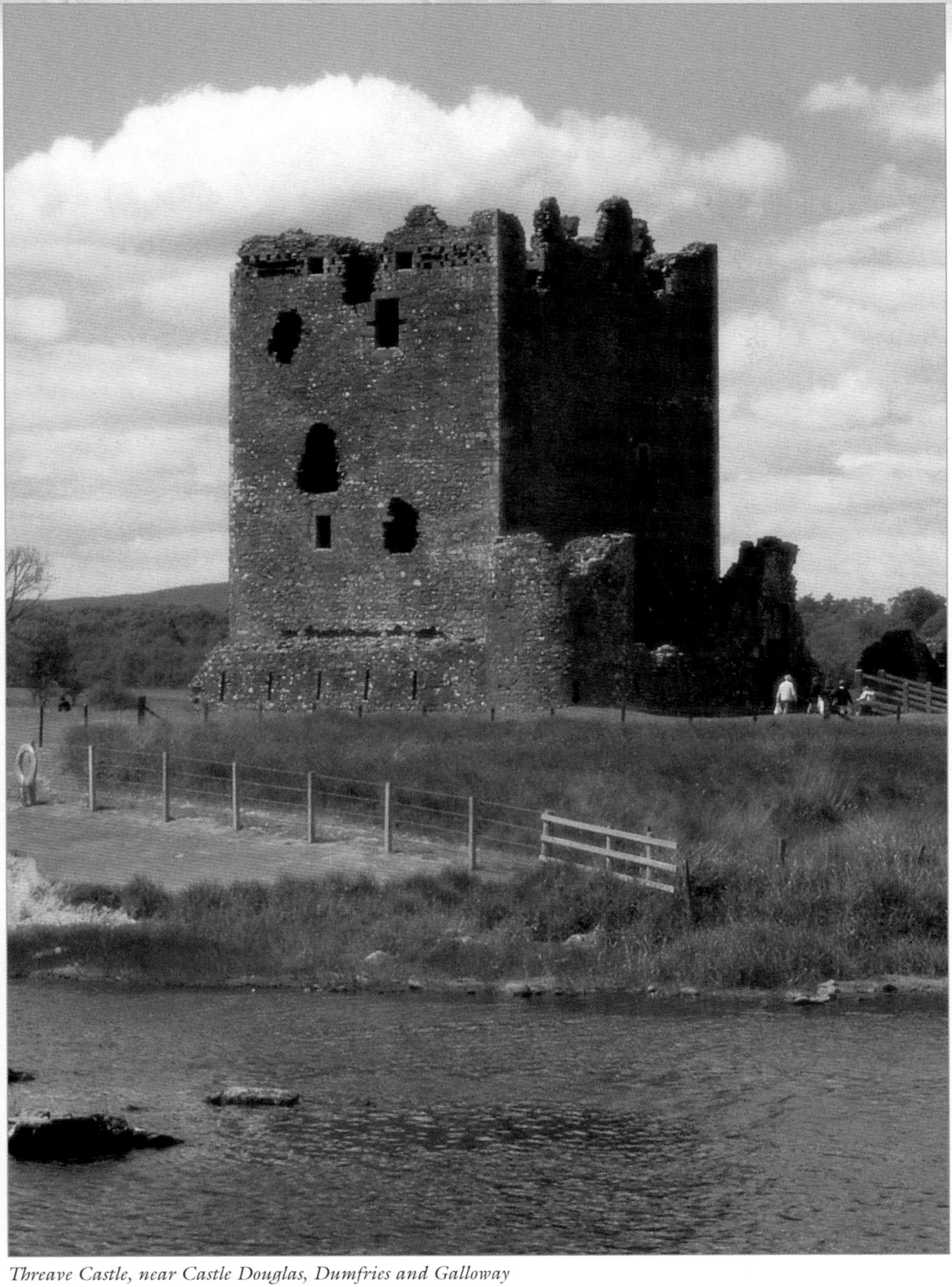

Threave Castle, near Castle Douglas, Dumfries and Galloway

SOUTH OF SCOTLAND:
Ayrshire and Arran, Dumfries and Galloway, Scottish Borders

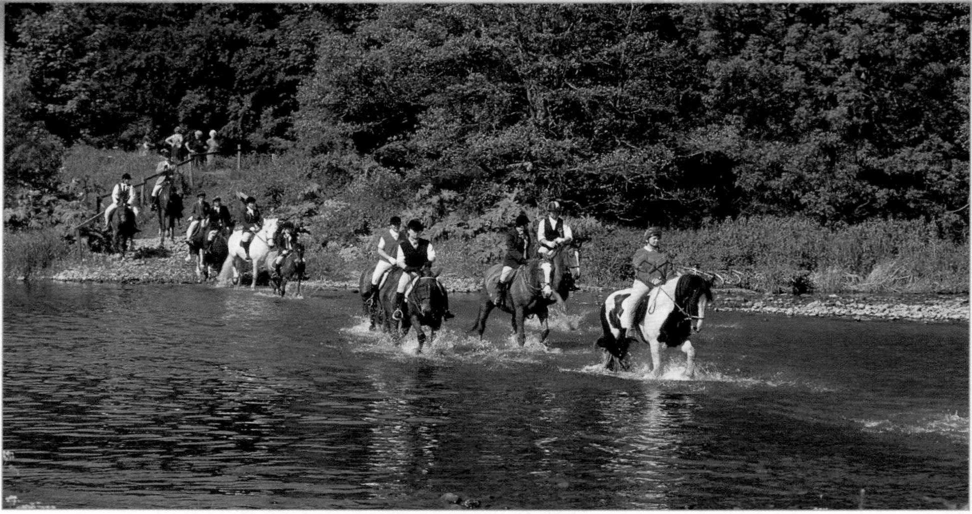

Common Riding near Selkirk, Scottish Borders

racing and football, while with over forty golf courses, golf is one of the biggest attractions. There are world famous courses at Troon, Turnberry and Prestwick.

First impressions of the Scottish Borders are of a surprisingly wild area, though river valleys with their woodlands and farms soon give a softer appearance. These borderlands were fought over until the 17th century and as a result there are many magnificent ruined abbeys and towered castles to visit. There are also many grand stately homes such as the magnificent Edwardian mansion of Manderston and the superb Georgian house of Mellerstain. Market towns such as Kelso, Selkirk, Hawick and Melrose offer good shopping and accommodation facilities. In the centre of Melrose you'll find the magnificent ruins of Melrose Abbey and the distinctive triple peaks of the Eildon Hills, a landmark for miles around. Below is the Tweed, one of Scotland's most famous salmon-fishing rivers. Sir Walter Scott's

fascinating home of Abbotsford and the secluded Dryburgh Abbey where he is buried are just a few of the fascinating historical sites throughout this region. The colourful past of the border towns is brought to life each year when the local residents re-enact the Common Ridings by dressing up in period costume and riding around the burgh boundaries. The landscape to the east is a beautiful mosaic of farmland and finally ends at the dramatic cliffs of St Abbs, a favourite place for bird watching.

The South of Scotland offers plenty of scope for those who want an active holiday. Cycling along quiet country lanes, trekking and riding, walking and fishing are just some of the activities widely available.

EVENTS
SOUTH OF SCOTLAND:
Ayrshire and Arran, Dumfries and Galloway, Scottish Borders

* 22-31 MARCH
Festival of Folk Music, Arts and Crafts
Gatehouse of Fleet,
Various venues
Contact:
George McCulloch
Tel: 01557 814030
Web:
www.gatehouse-festival.co.uk

19-20 APRIL
Scottish Grand National
Ayr, Ayr Racecourse
The highlight of the
Scottish horseracing year.
Contact: Ayr Racecourse
Tel: 01292 264179
Web:
www.ayr-racecourse.co.uk

24 MAY-1 JUNE
Dumfries & Galloway Arts Festival
Dumfries and Galloway,
Various Venues
A ten-day festival covering a
wide range of art forms.
Contact:
Gracefield Arts Centre
Tel: 01387 267447

8-15 JUNE
Guid Nychburris Week
Dumfries, Various Venues
A week of festivities
including processions, music
and tournaments.
Contact: Stanley McEwen
Tel: 01387 254952

14 JUNE
Selkirk Common Riding
Selkirk, Town Centre
Traditional ceremony
marking the town
boundaries.
Contact: Allan Douglas
Tel: 01750 21954

9-12 JULY
Ayrshire Golf Classic
Ayrshire, Various Venues
A four-day amateur event
played over four of
Scotland's finest courses.
Contact: Scottish Golf
Classics
Tel: 0800 027 1070 (UK)
or 01292 671500
Web:
www.scottishgolfclassics.com

3-4 AUGUST
Traquair Fair
Innerleithen,
Traquair House
A weekend of entertainment
including music and street
performers, workshops and
crafts.
Contact: Traquair House
Tel: 01896 830323
Web: www.traquair.co.uk

* 4-6 OCTOBER
Moffat Walking Festival
Moffat, Various Venues
Discover the pleasure of
walking in the hills around
Moffat.
Contact: Andy Armstrong
Tel: 01683 220059

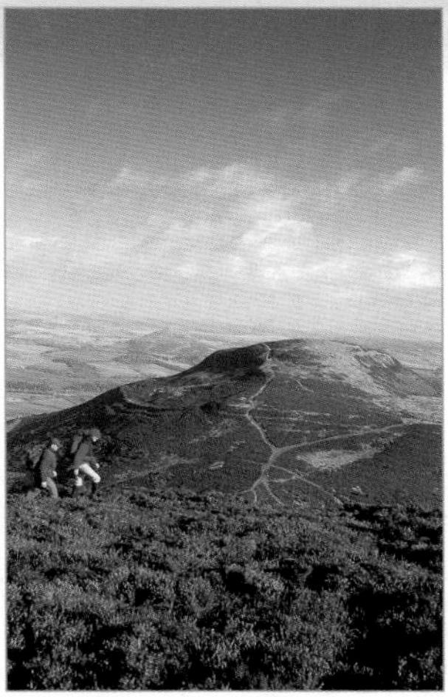

11-18 OCTOBER
Royal National Mod
Largs, Various Venues
The premier festival of
Gaelic arts and culture
featuring the best of Gaelic
song, dancing, piping,
drama and literature.
Contact:
Royal National Mod
Tel: 01463 709705
Web: www.the-mod.co.uk

** denotes provisional date,
please check before attending.*

Area Tourist Boards
South of Scotland:
Ayrshire and Arran, Dumfries and Galloway, Scottish Borders

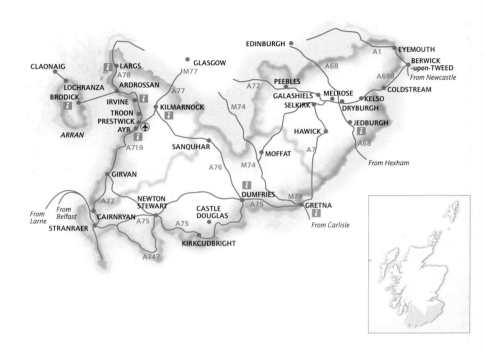

AYRSHIRE AND ARRAN TOURIST BOARD
Customer Information
Centre
15 Skye Road
Prestwick
KA9 2TA

Tel: 01292 678100
Fax: 01292 471832
E-mail:
info@ayrshire-arran.com
Web: www.ayrshire-arran.com

DUMFRIES AND GALLOWAY TOURIST BOARD
64 Whitesands
Dumfries
DG1 2RS

Tel: 01387 25 38 62
Fax: 01387 24 55 31
E-mail: info@dgtb.ossian.net
Web:
www.dumfriesandgalloway.
co.uk

SCOTTISH BORDERS TOURIST BOARD
Shepherd's Mill
Whinfield Road
Selkirk
TD7 5DT

Tel: 0870 6080404
Fax: 01750 21886
E-mail:
info@scot-borders.co.uk
Web:
www.scot-borders.co.uk

Tourist Information Centres
South of Scotland:
Ayrshire and Arran, Dumfries and Galloway, Scottish Borders

Ayrshire and Arran Tourist Board

Ayr
22 Sandgate
Tel: (01292) 678100
Jan-Dec

Brodick
The Pier
Isle of Arran
Tel: (01770) 302140
Jan-Dec

Girvan
Bridge Street
Tel: (01292) 678100
Easter-Oct

Irvine
New Street
Tel: (01292) 678100
Easter-Oct

Largs
The Railway Station
Main St
Tel: (01292) 678100
Easter-Oct

Millport
28 Stuart Street
Isle of Cumbrae
Tel: (01292) 678100
Easter-Oct

Dumfries and Galloway Tourist Board

Castle Douglas
Markethill Car Park
Tel: (01556) 502611
Easter-Oct

Dumfries
Whitesands
Tel: (01387) 253862
Jan-Dec

Gatehouse of Fleet
Car Park
Tel: (01557) 814212
Easter-Oct

Gretna Green
Old Blacksmith's Shop
Tel: (01461) 337834

Kirkcudbright
Harbour Square
Tel: (01557) 330494
Easter-end Oct

Moffat
Ladyknowe
Tel: (01683) 220620
Easter-end Oct

Newton Stewart
Dashwood Square
Tel: (01671) 402431
Easter-Oct

Stranraer
Burns House
28 Harbour Street
Tel: (01776) 702595
Jan-Dec

Scottish Borders Tourist Board

Coldstream
High Street
Tel: (0870) 6080404
Easter-Oct (Winter hours as library)

Eyemouth
Auld Kirk, Manse Road
Tel: (0870) 6080404
April-Oct

Galashiels
St John Street
Tel: (0870) 6080404
April-Oct

Hawick
Drumlanrig's Tower
Tel: (0870) 6080404
April-Oct

Jedburgh
Murray's Green
Tel: (0870) 6080404
info@scot-borders.co.uk
Jan-Dec

Kelso
Town House, The Square
Tel: (0870) 6080404
Jan-Dec

Melrose
Abbey House
Tel: (0870) 6080404
Easter-Oct

Peebles
High Street
Tel: (0870) 6080404
info@scot-borders.co.uk
Jan-Dec

Selkirk
Halliwell's House
Tel: (0870) 6080404
April-Oct

Blackwaterfoot, Isle of Arran | Map Ref: 1E7

SMALL HOTEL

Blackwaterfoot Lodge
Blackwaterfoot, Isle of Arran, KA27 8EU
Tel/Fax: 01770 860202
E-mail: info@blackwaterfoot-lodge.co.uk
Web: www.blackwaterfoot-lodge.co.uk

Situated 50 yards from the picturesque harbour at Blackwaterfoot, this family run hotel provides a warm & welcoming home during your holiday. Creature comforts on the windswept west coast. With a small bistro style restaurant and traditional ale from Arran Breweries in the fully licensed bar.

1 Single	7 En Suite fac	B&B per person	Open Jan-Dec
4 Twin	1 Pub Bath/Show	from £25.00 Single	B&B + Eve.Meal
2 Double		from £35.00 Dbl/Twn	from £45.00
2 Family		Room only from £20.00	

HOTEL

Kinloch Hotel
Blackwaterfoot, Isle of Arran, KA27 8ET
Tel: 01770 860444 Fax: 01770 860447
E-mail: kinloch@cqm.co.uk
Web: www.kinloch-arran.com

On the sea front with views of the Mull of Kintyre. Extensive leisure facilities, indoor pool. Ideal for families and open to non-residents. All day food.

13 Single	All En Suite	B&B per person	Open Jan-Dec
20		from £36.00 Single	B&B + Eve.Meal
Double/T		from £72.00 Dbl/Twn	from £55.00
win		Room only from £40.00	

Brodick, Isle of Arran | Map Ref: 1F7

GUEST HOUSE

Allandale House
Brodick, Isle of Arran, KA27 8BJ
Tel/Fax: 01770 302278

Comfortable guest house in south facing postion with well laid out garden, on the outskirts of Brodick. Only a few minutes walk from the ferry and Brodick centre yet in a peaceful location. Some ground floor annexe accommodation.

1 Single	5 En Suite fac	B&B per person	Open 20 Jan-31 Oct
2 Twin	1 Priv.NOT ensuite	£20.00-£26.00 Single	B&B + Eve.Meal
2 Double		£20.00-£26.00 Dbl/Twn	£34.00-£38.00
1 Family			

HOTEL

Auchrannie Country House Hotel
Brodick, Isle of Arran, KA27 8BZ
Tel: 01770 302234 Fax: 01770 302812
Web: www.auchrannie.co.uk

The hospitality offered at Auchrannie confirms its popular reputation as Arran's flagship hotel. Close to Brodick village, beach and golf course, Auchrannie offers a choice of cuisine from award winning garden restaurant to informal dining. The extensive leisure club incorporates superb 20 m swimming pool, sauna/steam, gym, solariums, aromatherapy and snooker room.

10 Twin	All En Suite	B&B per person	Open Jan-Dec
16 Double		from £42.00	B&B + Eve.Meal
2 Family		Single Supplement £10	from £50.00

GUEST HOUSE

Dunvegan House
Shore Road, Brodick, Isle of Arran, KA27 8AJ
Tel/Fax: 01770 302811
Web: www.dunveganhouse-arran.co.uk

Superb sea and mountain views, conveniently situated for ferry terminal. Licensed. Dinner using fresh local produce when available. Private parking. Ground floor bedrooms available.

2 Single	8 En Suite fac	B&B per person from	Open Jan-Dec excl
3 Twin	1 Priv.Bath/Show	£35.00 Single	Xmas/New Year
6 Double		£29.00 Dbl/Twn	B&B + Eve.Meal
			from £45.00

Important: Prices stated are estimates and may be subject to amendments

Brodick, Isle of Arran | Map Ref: 1F7

Glen Cloy Farmhouse
Glen Cloy Road, Brodick, Isle of Arran, KA27 8DA
Tel: 01770 302351
E-mail: mvpglencloy@compuserve.com
Web: www.SmoothHound.co.uk/hotels/glencloy.html

GUEST HOUSE

Farmhouse full of character set in peaceful glen with views of hills and sea. Within easy reach of Brodick ferry. Mark and Vicki produce memorable breakfasts with homemade jams and bread, and eggs from their own hens. Embroidery courses held in spring and autumn.

1 Single	2 En Suite fac	B&B per person	Open Jan-Dec excl
2 Twin	1 Pub Bath/Show	£22.00	Xmas/New Year
2 Double			

Kilmichael Country House Hotel
Brodick, Isle of Arran, KA27 8BY
Tel: 01770 302219 Fax:01770 302068
E-mail: enquiries@kilmichael.com
Web: www.kilmichael.com

SMALL HOTEL

A small historic country house, set in acres of beautiful wooded ground in peaceful Glen Cloy. Taste of Scotland award winner.

1 Twin	All En Suite	B&B per person	Open Mar-Oct
6 Double		from £60.00 Dbl/Twn	B&B + Eve.Meal from £89.50

The Auchrannie Spa Resort
Brodick, Isle of Arran, KA27 8BZ
Tel: 01770 302234 Fax: 01770 303300
E-mail: resort@auchrannie.co.uk
Web: www.auchrannie.co.uk

LODGE

12 Twin	All En Suite	Room only per person	Open Jan-Dec
24 Double		from £39.95	

Lochranza, Isle of Arran | Map Ref: 1E6

Apple Lodge
Lochranza, Isle of Arran, KA27 8HJ
Tel/Fax: 01770 830229
E-mail: applelodge@easicom.com

GUEST HOUSE

A charming intimate country house set amidst spectacular scenery where deer and eagles are often sighted. Taste of Scotland.

1 Twin	All En Suite	B&B per person	Open Jan-Dec excl
2 Double		from £46.00 Single	Xmas/New Year
1 Suite		from £31.00 Dbl/Twn	B&B + Eve.Meal from £50.00

Auchencairn, by Castle Douglas, Kirkcudbrightshire | Map Ref: 2A10

Old Smugglers Inn
Main Street, Auchencairn,
Dumfries & Galloway, DG7 1QU
Tel: 01556 640331

INN

Cosy Inn dating from 17th Century located in picturesque village on Solway Coast. Secluded Beer Garden with children's play area and burn running through it. Extensive menu with daily specials using fresh local produce.

1 Single	All En Suite	B&B per person	Open all year
1 Twin		from £20.00 Dbl/Twn	
2 Double			
1 Family			

All properties graded by VisitScotland, formerly known as the Scottish Tourist Board.   **Key to symbols is on back flap.**

Auchencairn, by Castle Douglas, Kirkcudbrightshire | Map Ref: 2A10

Balcary Bay Hotel

Auchencairn, near Castle Douglas, Dumfries & Galloway DG7 1QZ
Telephone: 01556 640217/640311 Fax: 01556 640272
e.mail: reservations@balcary-bay-hotel.co.uk
Web: www.balcary-bay-hotel.co.uk
Family-run country house in three acres of garden. A magnificent and
peaceful setting on the shores of the bay. Ideal base for all leisure facilities or
a relaxing holiday with warm hospitality, good food and wine.
AA/RAC ★★★. One of Scotland's Hotels of Distinction.

★★★★ HOTEL

★★★★

HOTEL

Balcary Bay Hotel
Shore Road, Auchencairn, nr Castle Douglas,
Dumfries & Galloway, DG7 1QZ
Tel: 01556 640217 Fax: 01556 640272
E-mail: reservations@balcary-bay-hotel.co.uk
Web: www.balcary-bay-hotel.co.uk

A lovely country house hotel, with past smuggling associations dating
back to 1625. Stands in over 3 acres of garden in a secluded and
enchanting situation on the shores of the bay. Cuisine based on local
delicacies: Galloway beef, lamb, lobster and of course, Balcary Bay
salmon.

3 Single	All En Suite	B&B per person
8 Twin		from £61.00 Single
8 Double		from £54.00 Dbl/Twn
1 Family		

Open Mar-Nov
B&B + Eve.Meal
from £79.00

Ayr | Map Ref: 1G7

★★

SMALL
HOTEL

Belleisle House Hotel
Belleisle Park, Doonfoot Road, Ayr, KA7 4DU
Tel: 01292 442331 Fax: 01292 445325

Set in the heart of Burns Country, the immediate surrounds include two
parkland golf courses, an aviary, a deer park and many beautiful walks.
The house is only two miles from the centre of Ayr. Recently refurbished
Fountainebleu Restaurant.

2 Single	B&B per person
6 Twin	from £25.00 Single
2 Double	from £37.50 Dbl/Twn
4 Family	

Open Jan-Dec
B&B + Eve.Meal from
£45.00

★★

GUEST
HOUSE

Belmont Guest House
Belmont Guest House, 15 Park Circus, Ayr, KA7 2DJ
Tel: 01292 265588 Fax: 01292 290303
E-mail: belmontguesthouse@btinternet.com
Web: www.belmontguesthouse.co.uk

Victorian townhouse in a quiet tree lined conservation area, within easy
walking distance of town centre. Ground-floor bedrooms, all with ensuite
facilities. Guest lounge with extensive book collection. On street and
private car parking. Credit/Debit cards are now accepted.

1 Twin	All En Suite	B&B per person
2 Double		from £23.00 Single
2 Family		from £20.00 Dbl/Twn
		Room only from £15.00

Open Jan-Dec

★★

SMALL
HOTEL

Carrick Lodge Hotel
46 Carrick Road, Ayr, KA7 2RE
Tel: 01292 262846 Fax: 01292 611106
E-mail: margaret@carricklodgehotel.co.uk
Web: www.carricklodgehotel.co.uk

The Carrick Lodge Hotel offers comfortable accommodation of an exceptional
standard. It is centrally situated for easy access to the town, beach and Burns
Heritage Trail with Glasgow Prestwick Airport only 15 minutes away. All bedrooms
are equipped with TV, radio/alarm, hairdryers and hospitality trays and if you
want to experience the best local produce, cooked to perfection with the warmest
of Scottish welcomes then the Carrick Lodge is the perfect choice.

1 Single	All En Suite	B&B per person
2 Twin		from £40.00 Single
2 Double		£30.00-£40.00 Double
3 Family		

Open Jan-Dec

Important: Prices stated are estimates and may be subject to amendments

Ayr

Map Ref: 1G7

The Ivy House

2 Alloway, Ayr, KA7 4NL
Tel: 01292 442336 Fax: 01292 445572
e.mail: enquiries@theivyhouse.uk.com
Web: www.theivyhouse.uk.com

Set in the heart of Burns Country, The Ivy House offers the very highest standards of Scottish hospitality and food. Personally run, the emphasis is on quality throughout, from the individually designed bedrooms to the freshly cooked Scottish produce and our friendly and highly professional staff.

★★★★

The Ivy House

2 Alloway, Ayr, KA7 4NL
Tel: 01292 442336 Fax: 01292 445572
E-mail: enquiries@theivyhouse.uk.com
Web: www.theivyhouse.uk.com

The Ivy House is a relaxed country house with views across the golf course. The public areas are bright and light, the food really rather good, the hospitality warm and the five bedrooms have been refurbished to the highest level of comfort. A jewel in the Ayrshire crown.

1 Twin	All En Suite	B&B per person	Open Jan-Dec
4 Double		from £100.00 Dbl/Twn	B&B + Eve.Meal
			from £120.00

★★★

SMALL HOTEL

The Pickwick Hotel

19 Racecourse Road, Ayr, KA7 2TD
Tel: 01292 260111 Fax: 01292 285348
E-mail: info@pickwickhotel.freeserve.co.uk

18 Century Villa House Hotel set in its own lanscaped gardens. Themed throughout on Charles Dickens there is the Mr Micawber Restaurant and all rooms are named after Charles Dickens characters. Short walk from town centre and seafront.

2 Single	All En Suite	B&B per person	Open Jan-Dec
9 Twin		from £39.50 Single	B&B + Eve.Meal from
4 Double		from £70.00 Dbl/Twn	£45.00 Single

★★★

GUEST HOUSE

The Richmond

38 Park Circus, Ayr, Ayrshire, KA7 2DL
Tel: 01292 265153 Fax: 01292 288816
E-mail: Richmond38@btinternet.com
Web: www.richmond-guest-house.co.uk

Traditional stone built town house with many period features. Easy walking distance to sea front and town centre with all its amenities including a variety of eating establishments.

2 Double	5 En Suite fac	B&B per person	Open Jan-Dec
4 Family	1 Priv.NOT ensuite	from £25.00 Single	
		from £22.00 Double	

★★

SMALL HOTEL

St Andrews Hotel

7 Prestwick Road, Ayr, Ayrshire, KA8 8LD
Tel: 01292 263211 Fax: 01292 290738
E-mail: st_andrews_ayr@yahoo.com

St Andrews is a family run hotel, recently upgraded. The hotel has a lounge bar, public bar, games room and a newly fitted dining room. The hotel is close to Ayr town centre, railway station and Prestwick Airport. Private parking.

1 Single	3 En Suite fac	B&B per person	Open Jan-Dec excl
3 Double	2 Pub Bath/Show	from £20.00 Single	Xmas/New Year
3 Family		from £20.00 Dbl/Twn	

All properties graded by VisitScotland, formerly known as the Scottish Tourist Board. | *Key to symbols is on back flap.* |

Ayr
Map Ref: 1G7

B&B ★★★

Tramore Guest House
17 Eglinton Terrace, Ayr, Ayrshire, KA7 1JJ
Tel/Fax: 01292 266019
E-mail: tramoreguesthouse@amserve.net

2 Twin	1 Pub Bath/Show	B&B per person	Open Jan-Dec
1 Double		from £18.00 Single	B&B + Eve.Meal
		from £17.00 Dbl/Twn	from £24.00

Set in a quiet conservation area in a Victorian terraced house - a two minute walk from either town centre or beach. Evening meals available.

GUEST HOUSE ★★

Windsor Hotel
6 Alloway Place, Ayr, KA7 2AA
Tel: 01292 264689

2 Single	7 En Suite fac	B&B per person	Open Jan-Dec excl
1 Twin	1 Pub Bath/Show	from £23.00 Single	Xmas/New Year
3 Double	1 Priv.NOT ensuite	from £23.00 Dbl/Twn	B&B + Eve.Meal from
4 Family			£35.00

Victorian house near centre of Ayr and the promenade with its long sandy beach. Lounge and three ensuite bedrooms with sea views. Home cooked evening meals by prior arrangement. Ground floor ensuite bedrooms.

Broughton, by Biggar, Peeblesshire
Map Ref: 2B6

GUEST HOUSE ★★★

The Glenholm Centre
Broughton, by Biggar, Tweeddale, ML12 6JF
Tel/Fax: 01899 830408
E-mail: glenholm@dircon.co.uk
Web: www.glenholm.dircon.co.uk

2 Twin	All En Suite	B&B per person	Open Feb-Dec
1 Double		from £25.20 Single	
1 Family		from £22.50 Dbl/Twn	

A warm welcome awaits you at our family run guest house set on a farm at The Heart of Glenholm in the Scottish Borders. Close to Broughton, 30 miles South of Edinburgh - it is the perfect location to come to unwind and enjoy the hills, glens, nature and history of the valley. Full board available.

Canonbie, Dumfriesshire
Map Ref: 2D9

HOTEL ★★★

Cross Keys Hotel
Canonbie, Dumfriesshire, DG14 0SY
Tel: 013873 71205 Fax: 013873 71878
Web: www.gretnaweddings.com/crosskeys.html

2 Single	9 En Suite fac	B&B per person	Open Jan-Dec
4 Twin	1 Priv.NOT ensuite	from £30.00 Single	B&B + Eve.Meal from
3 Double		from £27.50 Dbl/Twn	£40.00
1 Family			

An 'Olde Worlde' 17th century coaching inn situated in the centre of the picturesque village of Canonbie just off the main A7 road to Edinburgh. Ideal for those seeking peace and solitude backed up by the comfort, service and hospitality of a traditional coaching inn.

Carrutherstown, Dumfriesshire
Map Ref: 2B9

HOTEL ★★★

Hetland Hall Hotel
Carrutherstown, Dumfriesshire, DG1 4JX
Tel: 01387 840201

5 Single	All En Suite	B&B per person	Open Jan-Dec
10 Twin		from £60.00 Single	
10 Double		from £40.00 Dbl/Twn	
5 Family			

Elegant 19c country mansion set in 27 acres of sweeping landscaped grounds with fine views over the Solway Firth. Recently refurbished to a high standard. All bedrooms en-suite. Wide range of leisure facilities including indoor pool, sauna and gym. Conference and wedding package facilities available.

Important: Prices stated are estimates and may be subject to amendments

Castle Douglas, Kirkcudbrightshire	Map Ref: 2A10

★★★

SMALL HOTEL

Imperial Hotel
35 King Street, Castle Douglas, Kirkcudbrightshire, DG7 1AA
Tel: 01556 502086 Fax: 01556 503009
E-mail: david@thegolfhotel.co.uk
Web: www.thegolfhotel.co.uk

Privately owned hotel in market town, close to local leisure facilities. Ideal base for touring Galloway. Golfing holidays. Private secure parking.

2 Single / 5 Twin / 5 Double — All En Suite

B&B per person
£35.00-£45.00 Single
£56.00-£60.00 Dbl/Twn

Open Jan-Dec excl Xmas/New Year
B&B + Eve.Meal £37.50-£45.00

★★

SMALL HOTEL

The Kings Arms Hotel
St Andrews Street, Castle Douglas, Kirkcudbrightshire, DG7 1EL
Tel: 01556 502626 Fax: 502097
E-mail: david@galloway-golf.co.uk
Web: www.galloway-golf.co.uk

Former coaching inn in town centre. Ideal for touring Galloway. Private secure parking.

2 Single / 5 Twin / 2 Double / 1 Family — All En Suite

B&B per person
from £35.00-£45.00 Single
from £56.00-£60.00 Dbl/Twn

Open Jan-Dec excl Xmas/New Year
B&B + Eve.Meal £37.50-£45.00

★★★

GUEST HOUSE

Rose Cottage Guest House
Gelston, Castle Douglas
Kirkcudbrightshire, DG7 1SH
Tel/Fax: 01556 502513

Friendly welcome in personally run guest house, situated in quiet village. Ideal for walkers and birdwatchers. Ample private parking. All rooms on ground floor. 1 ½ miles from Threave Gardens - National Trust for Scotland.

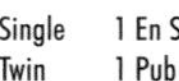

1 Single / 1 Twin / 2 Double — 1 En Suite fac / 1 Pub Bath/Show

B&B per person
from £20.00 Single
from £18.00 Dbl/Twn

Open Jan-Nov excl New Year
B&B + Eve.Meal from £29.00

★★★★

B&B

Smithy House
The Buchan, Castle Douglas, Kirkcudbrightshire, DG7 1TH
Tel: 01556 503841
E-mail: enquiries@smithyhouse.co.uk
Web: www.smithyhouse.co.uk

A warm welcome awaits at our home, a traditional old Galloway cottage, carefully extended and renovated with en-suite facilities and a comfortable guest sitting room. Beautiful views over Carlingwark loch to the hills and a gentle stroll into town and Threave Gardens. Centrally situated for exploring Galloway's coast and countryside; weekly rates available. Non smoking.

1 Twin / 2 Double — 2 En Suite fac / 1 Priv.NOT ensuite

B&B per person
from £30.00 Single
from £22.50 Dbl/Twn

Open Jan-Dec

★★

SMALL HOTEL

The Urr Valley Hotel
Ernespie Road, Castle Douglas, Dumfries & Galloway, DG7 3JG
Tel: 01556 502188 Fax: 01556 504055
E-mail: info@urrvalleyhotel.co.uk

Friendly welcome in a family run hotel with fine views, in a peaceful rural setting. 1 mile (1.5km) from town centre.

4 Single / 4 Twin / 6 Double / 5 Family — All En Suite / 2 Priv.NOT ensuite

B&B per person
£32.00-£50.00 Single
£30.00 Dbl/Twn

Open Jan-Dec
B&B + Eve.Meal from £50.00

All properties graded by VisitScotland, formerly known as the Scottish Tourist Board.   Key to symbols is on back flap.

by Castle Douglas, Kirkcudbrightshire

Map Ref: 2A10

★★★

**GUEST
HOUSE**

Airds Farm

**Crossmichael, Castle Douglas, Kirkcudbrightshire, DG7 3BG
Tel/Fax: 01556 670418
E-mail: tricia@airds.com
Web: www.airds.com**

A warm welcome over Loch Ken and the picturesque village and church of Crossmichael will delight visitors to this traditional farmhouse. Lovers of nature will enjoy walking through the wooded glen and pastures nearby or relaxing in the conservatory. Gardens, castles and other attractions are within easy reach, fishing, boating and watersports are available on the loch. A warm welcome, in a comfortable and relaxing home.

1 Single	2 En Suite fac	B&B per person	Open Jan-Dec
1 Twin	1 Pub Bath/Show	from £23.00 Single	
2 Double		from £18.00 Dbl/Twn	
1 Family			

Crocketford, Dumfriesshire

Map Ref: 2A9

★★

HOTEL

Galloway Arms Hotel

**Crocketford, Near Dumfries, Dumfriesshire, DG2 8RA
Tel: 01556 690248 Fax: 01556 690266
E-mail: info@gallowayarmshotel.co.uk
Web: www.gallowayarmshotel.co.uk**

Historic Coaching Inn ideally situated on A75 only 9 miles from Dumfries. A perfect location for touring "The Land O'Burns" and the beautiful Solway coastline through which runs the Burns Heritage Trail.

3 Single	8 En Suite fac	B&B per person	Open all year
5 Twin	2 Pub Bath/Show	from £35.00 Single	Xmas and New Year
4 Double	5 Priv.NOT ensuite	from £27.50 Dbl/Twn	
2 Family		Room only from £22.50	

Millport, Isle of Cumbrae

Map Ref: 1F6

★

**GUEST
HOUSE**

College of the Holy Spirit

**The College, Millport, Isle of Cumbrae, KA28 0HE
Tel: 01475 530353 Fax: 01475 530204
E-mail: tccumbrae@argyll.anglican.org
Web: www.argyll.anglican.org**

Unique opportunity to stay in the smallest working cathedral in Europe. Refectory style dining. Library. All the buildings are grade 'A' listed.

4 Single	5 Pub Bath/Show	B&B per person	Open Jan-Dec excl
7 Twin		from £17.50 Single	Xmas/New Year
5 Double		from £35.00 Dbl/Twn	B&B + Eve.Meal
3 Family		Room only per person	from £27.00
		from £12.50	

Dumfries

Map Ref: 2B9

Cairndale Hotel and Leisure Club

**English Street, Dumfries DG1 2DF
Tel: 01387 254111 Fax: 01387 250555
e.mail: sales@cairndale.fsnet.co.uk   Web: www.cairndalehotel.co.uk**

Regular entertainment in this popular hotel includes dinner dances (Saturdays), ceilidhs (Sundays, May to October) and cabaret evenings throughout the year. Superb leisure facilities including heated indoor pool and spa. Leisure breaks from £45 pp D,B&B. Golf, inclusive rate from £69.50 pp. 'Twixmas', Christmas, Hogmanay, Valentines and Easter packages also available.

★★★

HOTEL

Cairndale Hotel and Leisure Club

**English Street, Dumfries, DG1 2DF
Tel: 01387 254111 Fax: 01387 250555
E-mail: sales@cairndalehotel.fsnet.co.uk
Web: www.cairndalehotel.co.uk**

Family run hotel in town centre. Executive rooms with jacuzzis. Extensive leisure facilities. Range of dining options.

14 Single	All En Suite	B&B per person	Open Jan-Dec
15 Twin		from £55.00 Single	B&B + Eve.Meal
38 Double		from £52.50 Dbl/Twn	from £52.50
22 Family			
2 Suites			

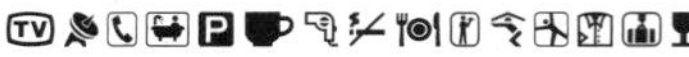

Important: Prices stated are estimates and may be subject to amendments

Eyemouth, Berwickshire

Map Ref: 2F5

★★★★
HOTEL

Churches Hotel
Albert Road, Eyemouth, Berwickshire, TD14 5DB
Tel: 01890 750401 Fax: 01890 750747
E-mail: bookings@churcheshotel.co.uk
Web: www.churcheshotel.co.uk

Unique privately owned hotel overlooking busy harbour in this picturesque fishing port. Four star cuisine, specialising in seafood.

2 Twin
4 Double

All En Suite

B&B per person
from £60.00 Single
from £40.00 Dbl/Twn

Open Jan-Dec excl New Year
B&B + Eve.Meal from £65.00

Galashiels, Selkirkshire

Map Ref: 2D6

★★
**SMALL
HOTEL**

Abbotsford Arms Hotel
63 Stirling Street, Galashiels, Selkirkshire,
TD1 1BY
Tel: 01896 752517 Fax: 01896 750744

Family run hotel, with both bar and restaurant meals, food available all day. Good base for touring the Borders and golfing. Convenient town centre location and just 1 hour to Edinburgh.

2 Single
4 Twin
5 Double
3 Family

All En Suite

B&B per person
from £40.00 Single
from £60.00 Dbl/Twn

Open Jan-Dec excl Xmas/New Year

★★
**SMALL
HOTEL**

King's Hotel
56 Market Street, Galashiels, TD1 3AN
Tel/Fax: 01896 755497
E-mail: kingshotel@talk21.com
Web: www.kingshotel.co.uk

Family run hotel with bedrooms non-smoking centrally situated in the heart of market town. Restaurant offers traditional Scottish fayre with emphasis on fresh local produce.

1 Single
4 Twin
3 Double
2 Family

All En Suite

B&B per person
from £35.00 Single
from £25.00 Dbl/Twn

Open Jan-Dec excl Xmas/New Year
B&B + Eve.Meal from £40.00

★★★
HOTEL

Kingsknowes Hotel
1 Selkirk Road, Galashiels, Selkirkshire, TD1 3HY
Tel: 01896 758375 Fax: 01896 750377
E-mail: enquiries@kingsknowes.co.uk
Web: www.kingsknowes.co.uk

Family owned and run hotel, built 1869 overlooking the River Tweed and Eildon Hills. 10 minutes walk from centre of town. Winners of the "Good Food Award 2001" as voted for by the readers of the Border Telegraph. Golf, fishing, shooting and riding can all be arranged.

11 Single
9 Twin
7 Double
3 Family

All En Suite

B&B per person
from £49.00 Single
from £74.00 Dbl/Twn

Open Jan-Dec
B&B + Eve.Meal from £42.00

---

by Galashiels, Selkirkshire

Map Ref: 2D6

★★
INN

Clovenfords Hotel
1 Vine Street, Clovenfords, by Galashiels,
Selkirkshire, TD1 3LU
Tel/Fax: 01896 850203
E-mail: clovenhotel@barbox.net

18c Coaching Inn situated in small village 3 miles from Galashiels. Busy bars, popular locally, serve Real Ales as available with entertainment often provided. Bar meals are home made. Golfing, fishing, walking, clay pigeon shooting and stalking can be arranged. Conveniently located for visiting many visitor attractions in the Borders.

2 Twin
2 Double
1 Family

All En Suite

B&B per person
from £25.00 Single
from £25.00 Dbl/Twn

Open Jan-Dec

All properties graded by VisitScotland, formerly known as the Scottish Tourist Board.   **Key to symbols is on back flap.**

Gatehouse of Fleet, Kirkcudbrightshire — Map Ref: 1H10

B&B

The Bay Horse
9 Ann Street, Gatehouse of Fleet, DG7 2HU
Tel: 01557 814073 Mobile: 07808 130269

1 Single	2 En Suite fac	B&B per person	Open Mar-Oct
1 Twin	1 Pub Bath/Show	from £18.00 Single	
2 Double	1 Priv.NOT ensuite	£20.00-£25.00 Dbl/Twn	
1 Family			

The Bay Horse provides quiet and comfortable accommodation overlooking gardens and parkland yet convenient to hotels, restaurants and gift shops. Gatehouse of Fleet is an ideal location for touring Galloway and the many local attractions include sandy beaches, sailing, walking, fishing, golf etc.

Girvan, Ayrshire — Map Ref: 1F8

HOTEL

Westcliffe Hotel
15-17 Louisa Drive, Girvan, Ayrshire, KA26 9AH
Tel/Fax: 01465 712128
E-mail: hotel@westcliffe-girvan.fsnet.co.uk
Web: www.smoothhound.co.uk

3 Single	All En Suite	B&B per person	Open Jan-Dec
9 Twin		from £28.00 Single	B&B + Eve.Meal
5 Double		from £24.00 Dbl/Twn	from £34.00
7 Family			

A family hotel, run by the Jardine family for 35 years, on the seafront overlooking the promenade, putting green and boating lake. Views across the Firth of Clyde to Ailsa Craig, Isle of Arran, Kintyre and Irish coast. Ground floor accommodation. Relax after a days sightseeing, golfing, fishing or walking in the whirlpool spa, steam room, toning table or exercise gym. Limited secure private parking, unrestricted street parking.

Gretna, Dumfriesshire — Map Ref: 2C10

HOTEL

The Gables Hotel
1 Annan Road, Gretna, Dumfriesshire, DG16 5DQ
Tel/Fax: 01461 338300
E-mail: info@gables-hotel-gretna.co.uk
Web: www.gables-hotel-gretna.co.uk

2 Twin	All En Suite	B&B per person	Open Jan-Dec excl
8 Double		from £50.00 Single	Xmas/New Year
2 Family		from £42.50 Dbl/Twn	

Turn of the century Grade II listed building retaining many of its original architectural features. Well kept gardens with spacious lawns sheltered by trees and shrubs. Located 300 yards from Gretna village centre and within easy reach of many of the areas attractions.

**SMALL
HOTEL**

Gretna Chase Hotel
Sark Bridge, Gretna, DG16 5JB
Tel: 01461 337517 Fax: 01461 337766
E-mail: enquiries@gretnachase.co.uk
Web: www.gretnachase.co.uk

2 Twin	All En Suite	B&B per person	Open Jan-Dec excl
8 Double		from £65.00 Single	Xmas/New Year
9 Family		from £79.00 Dbl/Twn	

Family run hotel originally built in 1856 for eloping couples and their guests.New 9 bedroom wing added (2001) to a high standard. Original rooms now modernised yet retaining much of the hotels original character. 2 acres of award winning gardens. Several rooms with 4 poster beds.

HOTEL

Solway Lodge Hotel
97-99 Annan Road, Gretna, Dumfriesshire, DG16 5DN
Tel: 01461 338266 Fax: 01461 337791
E-mail: gduncan@btconnect.com
Web: www.solwaylodge.co.uk

4 Twin	All En Suite	B&B per person	Open Jan-Dec excl
6 Double		from £41.50 Single	Xmas/New Year
		from £29.50 Dbl/Twn	
		Room only per person	
		from £26.00	

Family run hotel situated in gateway village to Scotland. Some superior rooms fitted with whirlpool baths. Some annexe accommodation.

Important: Prices stated are estimates and may be subject to amendments

A

nr Gretna Green, Dumfriesshire

Map Ref: 2C10

★★★

LODGE

The Mill

Grahamshill, Kirkpatrick Fleming, Dumfriesshire,
DG11 3BQ
Tel: 01461 800344 Fax: 01461 800255

Converted farm steading and mill with stone built chalet style, en-suite accommodation. Just off the M74 near Gretna Green. Fully licensed bar /restaurant and function room. Purpose built, churchlike Forge building for marriage ceremonies in attractive grounds.

2 Single
12 Dbl/Twn
9 Family
4 Bridal

All En Suite

B&B per person
from £24.00 Single
from £34.00 Dbl/Twn

Open Jan-Dec

Hawick, Roxburghshire

Map Ref: 2D7

★★

SMALL HOTEL

Elm House Hotel

17 North Bridge Street, Hawick, Roxburghshire, TD9 9BD
Tel: 01450 372866 Fax: 01450 374175
E-mail: forbes@elmhouse-hawick.fsnet.co.uk
Web: www.elmhouse-hawick.fsnet.co.uk

Family run, centrally situated in old town. Ideal base for touring the Borders. Fishing, bowling, golfing and shooting available. 8 annexe bedrooms.

2 Single
6 Twin
4 Double
3 Family

All En Suite

B&B per person
from £30.00 Single
from £46.00 Dbl/Twn

Open Jan-Dec

★★

B&B

Hopehill House

Hopehill, off Mayfield Drive, Hawick, TD9 7EH
Tel/Fax: 01450 375042
E-mail: anne.borthwick@btinternet.com

Detached Victorian house in large secluded gardens. Near centre of town, with panoramic views of hills from bedrooms. Private parking available.

1 Double
2 Family

3 En Suite facs
1 Limited ensuite

B&B per person
from £18.00 Single
from £20.00 Dbl/Twn

Open Jan-Dec

Innerleithen, Peeblesshire

Map Ref: 2C6

★★★★

SMALL HOTEL

Caddon View

14 Pirn Road, Innerleithen, Peeblesshire, EH44 6HH
Tel: 01896 830208
E-mail: caddonview@aol.com
Web: www.caddonview.co.uk

A warm welcome and excellent fine dining at this substantial Victorian house, with many period features. Ideal for touring the Borders. Two en-suite rooms on ground floor.

1 Single
2 Twin
2 Double
1 Family

All En Suite

B&B per person
from £38.00 Single
from £30.00 Dbl/Twn

Open Apr-Feb
B&B + Eve.Meal
from £48.00

All properties graded by VisitScotland, formerly known as the Scottish Tourist Board. | *Key to symbols is on back flap.*

Irvine, Ayrshire — Map Ref: 1G6

HOTEL
★★★

Annfield House Hotel
6 Castle Street, Irvine, Ayrshire, KA12 8RJ
Tel: 01294 278903 Fax: 01294 278904

2 Single
1 Twin
6 Double

All En Suite

B&B per person
from £49.50 Single
from £35.00 Dbl/Twn

Open Jan-Dec excl
Xmas/New Year

Country house in residential area near town centre. Overlooking River Irvine and Clyde and Arran hills beyond.

Isle of Whithorn, Wigtownshire — Map Ref: 1H11

INN
★

Steam Packet Inn
Harbour Row, Isle of Whithorn, Wigtownshire, DG8 8LL
Tel: 01988 500334 Fax: 01988 500627
E-mail: steampacketinn@btconnect.com
Web: www.steampacketinn.com

1 Twin
5 Double
1 Family

All En Suite

B&B per person
from £22.50 Single
from £22.50 Dbl/Twn

Open Jan-Dec excl
Xmas

Personally run, on harbour front. Sea fishing. Access to walks, birdwatching and archaeological sites. Children and dogs welcome. Excellent value food with the emphasis on fresh local seafood, meat and game. Separate children's menu. Extensive wine list and range of malt whiskies. Real ales. Traditional Sunday lunches and buffet. Lunches served 12-2pm. Bar meals and restaurant 7-9.30pm. Conservatory and beer garden. No smoking areas. Open fires.

Jedburgh, Roxburghshire — Map Ref: 2E7

GUEST HOUSE
★★★

Glenfriars House
The Friars, Jedburgh, Roxburghshire, TD8 6BN
Tel: 01835 862000 Fax: 01835 862112
E-mail: glenfriars@edenroad.demon.co.uk
Web: www.edenroad.demon.co.uk

2 Single
2 Twin
2 Double
1 Family

All En Suite

B&B per person
£30.00 Single
£50.00 Dbl/Twn

Open Jan-Dec excl
Xmas/New Year
B&B + Eve.Meal
from £42.50

Large Georgian house set above Jedburgh and centrally situated for touring the Borders. Special deals available on short breaks. Some four poster beds. All ensuite.

SMALL HOTEL
★★★★

Jedforest Hotel
Camptown, Jedburgh, TD8 6PJ
Tel: 01835 840222 Fax: 01835 840226
E-mail: mail@jedforesthotel.freeserve.co.uk
Web: www.jedforesthotel.freeserve.co.uk

2 Twin
6 Double

All En Suite

B&B per person
from £57.50 Single
from £42.50 Dbl/Twn

Open Jan-Dec
B&B + Eve.Meal
from £77.00

First hotel in Scotland on A68 route. High quality accommodation. All rooms en-suite. Taste of Scotland restaurant. Country setting, in 35 acres of grounds with 1 mile of trout fishing on the Jed Water. Scottish hospitality with a continental flavour.

GUEST HOUSE
★★★

Willow Court
The Friars, Jedburgh, Roxburghshire, TD8 6BN
Tel/Fax: 01835 863702
E-mail: mike@willowcourtjedburgh.co.uk
Web: www.willowcourtjedburgh.co.uk

1 Twin
2 Double
1 Family

3 En Suite
1 Priv.NOT ensuite

B&B per person
from £25.00 Single
from £19.00 Dbl/Twn
Room only per person
from £18.00

Open Jan-Dec

Set in 2 acres of garden above the town, with excellent views. Peaceful setting, yet close to all amenities including Abbey, Castle and a good selection of restaurants. All rooms are either ensuite or with private bathroom or shower-room. Most rooms are on the ground floor.

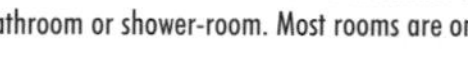

Important: Prices stated are estimates and may be subject to amendments

by Jedburgh, Roxburghshire

Map Ref: 2E7

★

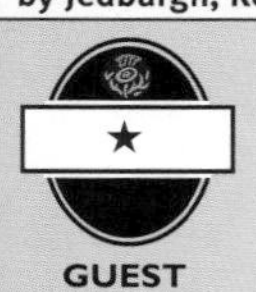

GUEST HOUSE

Ferniehirst Mill Lodge
by Jedburgh, Roxburghshire, TD8 6PQ
Tel/Fax: 01835 863279

1 Single	All En Suite	B&B per person	Open Jan-Dec
4 Twin	1 Pub Bath/Show	from £23.00 Single	B&B + Eve.Meal
3 Double		from £23.00 Dbl/Twn	from £37.00
1 Family		Room only per person	
		from £20.00	

Personally run, modern guest house, all rooms ensuite. Secluded riverside location, just two and a half miles South of Jedburgh. Haven for bird watchers and walkers. Specialists in home cooking using local produce. Trail riding centre.

Kelso, Roxburghshire

Map Ref: 2E6

★★

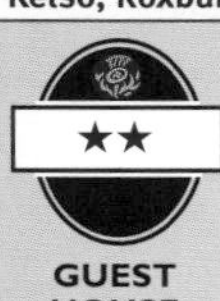

GUEST HOUSE

White Swan Inn
Abbey Row, Kelso, TD5 7AT
Tel: 01573 225800
Web: www.whiteswan-kelso.com

2 Twin	B&B per person	Open Jan-Dec excl
1 Double	from £30.00 Single	Xmas/New Year
2 Family	£50.00 Twin	

Over 300 years old, all ensuite or private bathrooms. Listed Georgian town house. Close to Abbey and said to have been used by Bonnie Prince Charlie. Convenient for shops and restaurants.

---

by Kelso, Roxburghshire

Map Ref: 2E6

The Roxburghe
Hotel & Golf Course

HEITON, BY KELSO, ROXBURGHSHIRE TD5 8JZ
Tel: 01573 450331 Fax: 01573 450611
e.mail: hotel@roxburghe.net
Web: www.roxburghe.net

Majestically set in the Scottish Borders, The Roxburghe Hotel, under the careful ownership of The Duke and Duchess of Roxburghe, boasts superb cuisine and delightfully individual rooms. Open fires, oil paintings and four-poster beds, combined with attentive service, add to the unique atmosphere of The Roxburghe. One hour from Edinburgh and Newcastle, this luxury hotel stands in a beautiful 200-acre estate on the banks of the River Teviot. Facilities include an all-weather tennis court, croquet lawn, trout pond, shooting school, luxury beauty salon and 18-hole championship Roxburghe Golf Course designed by Dave Thomas. Home of the Scottish Seniors Open.

★★★★

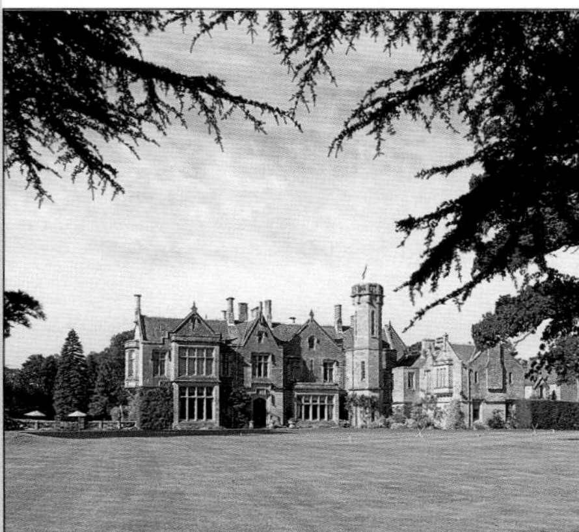

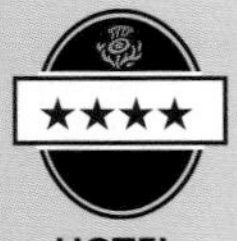

HOTEL

The Roxburghe Hotel & Golf Course
Heiton, by Kelso, Roxburghshire, TD5 8JZ
Tel: 01573 450331 Fax: 01573 450611
Web: www.roxburghe.net

2 Single	All En Suite	B&B per person	Open Jan-Dec excl
7 Twin		from £120.00 Single	Xmas
7 Double		from £62.50 Dbl/Twn	B&B + Eve.Meal
4 Family			from £89.50

Country house hotel owned by the Duke and Duchess of Roxburghe. Set in two hundred acres of woodland and park. Log fires and fresh produce. Shooting school, fishing and eighteen hole championship golf course.

All properties graded by VisitScotland, formerly known as the Scottish Tourist Board.   *Key to symbols is on back flap.*

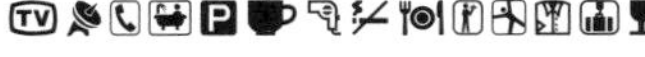

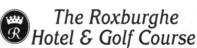

Kilmarnock, Ayrshire
Map Ref: 1G6

**GUEST
HOUSE**

Burnside Hotel
18 London Road, Kilmarnock, Ayrshire, KA3 7AQ
Tel: 01563 522952 Fax: 01563 573381
E-mail: djd@burnsidehotel.co.uk
Web: www.burnsidehotel.co.uk

Early 19th century private hotel, conveniently located for town centre.
Private parking. Opposite museum and art gallery. No pets.

3 Single	5 En Suite fac
4 Twin	2 Pub Bath/Show
2 Double	
1 Family	

B&B per person
from £25.00 Single
from £24.00 Dbl/Twn

Open Jan-Dec
B&B + Eve.Meal
from £38.00

Kilwinning, Ayrshire
Map Ref: 1G6

B&B

Blairholme
45 Byres Road, Kilwinning, KA13 6JU
Tel: 01294 552023
E-mail: t.cully@nationwideisp.net

Turn of the century, semi detached bungalow with one bedroom on
ground floor level, and the other upstairs. Close to town centre and only
2 mins walk to The Railway Station, 15 mins by Train/Car to Prestwick
Airport.

1 Double	1 Priv.NOT ensuite
1 Family	

B&B per person
£15.00-£20.00 Single
£15.00-£20.00 Dbl/Twn

Open Jan-Dec excl
Xmas/New Year

nr Kilwinning, Ayrshire
Map Ref: 1G6

HOTEL

Montgreenan Mansion House Hotel
Montgreenan Estate, nr Kilwinning, Ayrshire, KA13 7QZ
Tel: 01294 557733 Fax: 01294 850397
E-mail: info@montgreenanhotel.com
Web: www.montgreenanhotel.com

Country house in 48 acres of garden. Near championship golf courses -
Royal Troon, Old Prestwick and Turnberry. Tennis courts and 4 hole
practice golf course. Billiard room. Ideal base for touring Burns Country,
Arran and the Isles. Extensive refurbishment in last 2 years.

2 Single	All En Suite
8 Twin	
7 Double	
4 Family	

B&B per person
from £80.00 Single
from £115.00 Dbl/Twn
Room only from £72.50

Open Jan-Dec
B&B + Eve.Meal
from £159.00

Langholm, Dumfriesshire
Map Ref: 2D9

HOTEL

Crown Hotel
High Street, Langholm, Dumfriesshire, DG13 0JH
Tel: 013873 80247 Fax: 013873 81128
E-mail: ashleybarrie@compuserve.com

18C Coaching Inn steeped in history and tradition. Centrally located for
all amenities. Warm welcome and traditional Scottish fare.

2 Single	
3 Twin	
2 Double	
1 Family	

B&B per person
from £20.00 Single
from £19.00 Dbl/Twn
Room only from £15.00

Open Jan-Dec
B&B + Eve.Meal from
£28.00

INN

The Reivers Rest
81 High Street, Langholm, Dumfriesshire, DG13 0DJ
Tel: 013873 81343
E-mail: paul@reivers-rest.demon.co.uk

Small family run Inn. Centre of the historic Borders town of Langholm.
Personally managed by the proprietors Paul and Betty Hayhoe. There is
always a warm welcome and the very best in Borders hospitality, locally
brewed real ale, extensive wine list, innovative, informal menu using
fresh local produce wherever possible. Open fire. Ample public car
parking in the immediate vicinity. The area is steeped in history and
there is plenty to see and do.

2 Single	All En Suite
2 Twin	
3 Double	
1 Family	

B&B per person
from £35.00 Single
from £29.00 Dbl/Twn

Open Jan-Dec excl Xmas
B&B + Eve.Meal
from £44.00

Important: Prices stated are estimates and may be subject to amendments

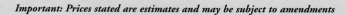

Largs, Ayrshire | Map Ref: 1F5

★★★★

B&B

Stonehaven Guest House
8 Netherpark Crescent, Largs, KA30 8QB
Tel: 01475 673319
E-mail: stonehaven.martin@virgin.net

Situated in quiet residential area in front of Routenburn Golf Course, overlooking the Largs Bay, Isle of Cumbrae with the Isle of Arran and Ailsa Craig in the distance.

1 Single	1 Pub Bath/Show	B&B per person	Open Jan-Dec excl
1 Twin	1 En Suite	from £20.00 Single	Xmas/New Year
1 Double		from £23.00 Dbl/Twn	

★★★

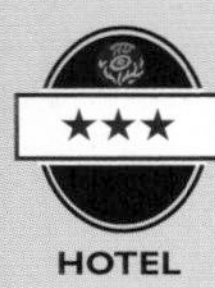

HOTEL

Willow Bank Hotel
96 Greenock Road, Largs, Ayrshire, KA30 8PG
Tel: 01475 672311 Fax: 01475 689027
E-mail: iain@willowbankhotellargs.freeserve.co.uk

Modern hotel offering bedrooms on ground floor and 1st floor only, in tree-lined location on edge of town. Mid week and weekend entertainment. Bar meals, high teas and dinner available daily.

3 Single	All En Suite	B&B per person	Open Jan-Dec
14 Twin		from £54.00 Single	B&B + Eve.Meal from
7 Double		from £44.00 Dbl/Twn	£56.00
4 Family			

---

by Lauder, Berwickshire | Map Ref: 2D6

★★★★

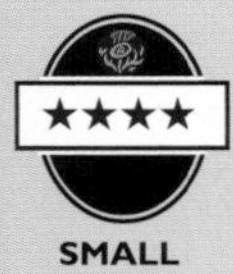

**SMALL
HOTEL**

The Lodge, Carfraemill
Lauder, Berwickshire, TD2 6RA
Tel: 01578 750750 Fax: 01578 750751
E-mail: enquiries@carfraemill.co.uk
Web: www.cafraemill.co.uk

A former coaching Inn offering friendly hospitality and bistro/restaurant meals. Situated in rural Lauderdale at the junction of the A697/A68. Ideally situated for both Edinburgh and the Borders.

2 Twin	All En Suite	B&B per person	Open Jan-Dec
6 Double		from £48.00 Single	B&B + Eve.Meal
2 Family		from £35.00 Dbl/Twn	from £50.00

Lockerbie, Dumfriesshire | Map Ref: 2C9

★★

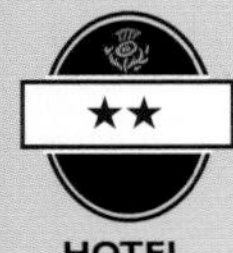

HOTEL

Dinwoodie Lodge Hotel
Johnstonebridge, Lockerbie, DG11 2SL
Tel/Fax: 01576 470289
E-mail: dinwoodielodge@tinyworld.com

Personally run, fully licensed with extensive bar food menu. Situated 6 miles North of Lockerbie just off the M74 (junction 16). Ground floor en-suite room with disabled facilities. Ample parking. All bedrooms ensuite.

1 Single	5 En Suite fac	B&B per person	Open Jan-Dec excl
3 Twin	1 Priv.NOT ensuite	from £37.50 Single	Xmas/New Year
2 Double		from £29.50 Dbl/Twn	
1 Family			

All properties graded by VisitScotland, formerly known as the Scottish Tourist Board. | *Key to symbols is on back flap.*

Lockerbie, Dumfriesshire   Map Ref: 2C9

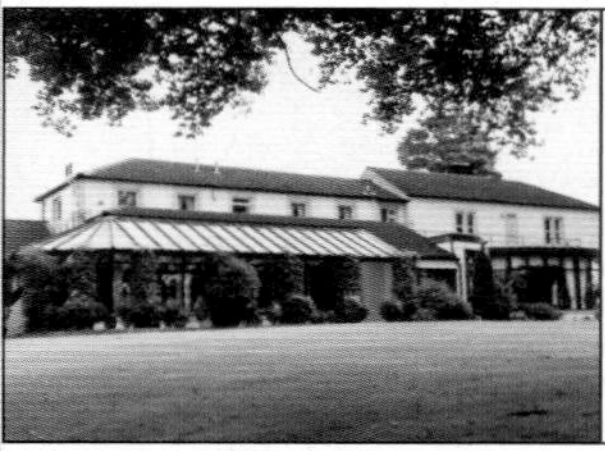

The Dryfesdale Country House Hotel

Dryfebridge, Lockerbie, Dumfriesshire DG11 2SF
Tel: 01576 202427 Fax: 01576 204187
e.mail: reception@DryfesdaleHotel.co.uk
web: www.dryfesdalehotel.co.uk
A relaxing family run hotel only 4 minutes drive and clearly seen from J17 of the M74. The hotel nestles in an elevated position with superb views over rolling countryside. The bedrooms are all luxurious and well-equipped. Our award winning rosetted restaurant looks forward to welcoming you.

HOTEL

Dryfesdale Country House Hotel
Dryfebridge, Lockerbie, Dumfriesshire, DG11 2SF
Tel: 01576 202427 Fax: 01576 204187
E-mail: reception@dryfesdalehotel.co.uk
Web: www.dryfesdalehotel.co.uk

Family run country house in 5 acres of ground, yet close to M74. Award winning restaurant serving fresh local produce. Ideal for business or pleasure. Ground floor rooms available and all rooms en-suite.

4 Single	All En Suite	B&B per person	Open Jan-Dec
4 Twin		from £55.00 Single	B&B + Eve.Meal from
7 Double		from £42.50 Dbl/Twn	£61.00
1 Family		Room only per person	
		£32.50	

HOTEL

Kings Arms Hotel
29 High Street, Lockerbie, Dumfriesshire, DG11 2JL
Tel/Fax: 01576 202410
E-mail: reception@kingsarmshotel.co.uk
Web: www.kingsarmshotel.co.uk

17c coaching inn situated in centre of Lockerbie. Ideal stopover en-route whilst travelling north or south.

3 Single	All En Suite	B&B per person	Open Jan-Dec
3 Twin		from £35.00 Single	B&B + Eve.Meal from
5 Double		from £30.00 Dbl/Twn	£45.00
2 Family		Room only from £25.00	

SMALL HOTEL

Ravenshill House Hotel
12 Dumfries Road, Lockerbie, Dumfriesshire, DG11 2EF
Tel/Fax: 01576 202882
E-mail: enquiries@ravenshillhotellockerbie.co.uk
Web: www.ravenshillhotellockerbie.co.uk

A family run hotel set in 2.5 acres of garden in a quiet residential area, yet convenient for town centre and M6/M74. With a chef proprietor the hotel enjoys a reputation for good food, comfortable accommodation and friendly service. Weekend, short and golfing breaks.

3 Twin	7 En Suite fac	B&B per person	Open Jan-Dec excl
3 Double	1 Priv.NOT ensuite	from £37.00 Single	Xmas/New Year
2 Family		from £27.00 Dbl/Twn	B&B + Eve.Meal
			from £34.00

GUEST HOUSE

Rosehill Guest House
9 Carlisle Road, Lockerbie, Dumfriesshire,
DG11 2DR
Tel/Fax: 01576 202378

Attractive Victorian villa with large well stocked garden in residential area, within walking distance of the town centre and with a choice of restaurants. Private parking.

1 Single	3 En Suite fac	B&B per person	Open Jan-Dec excl
2 Twin	2 Priv.NOT ensuite	from £20.00 Single	Xmas/New Year
1 Double		from £20.00 Dbl/Twn	
1 Family			

Important: Prices stated are estimates and may be subject to amendments

A

Melrose, Roxburghshire | **Map Ref: 2D6**

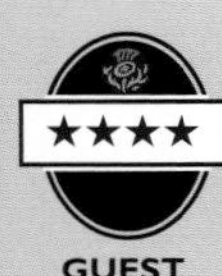

**SMALL
HOTEL**

Burts Hotel
Market Square, Melrose, Scottish Borders, TD6 9PL
Tel: 01896 822285 Fax: 01896 822870
E-mail: burtshotel@aol.com
Web: www.burtshotel.co.uk

Family owned and run town house hotel in the heart of the Scottish
Borders specialising in imaginative food in award winning Taste of
Scotland restaurant. Scottish Borders chef of the year 2000.

7 Single	All En Suite
9 Twin	
4 Double	

B&B per person
from £52.00 Single
from £46.00 Dbl/Twn

Open Jan-Dec
B&B + Eve.Meal
from £65.00

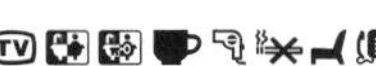

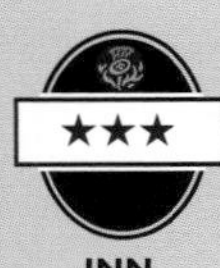

**GUEST
HOUSE**

Dunfermline House
Buccleuch Street, Melrose, TD6 9LB
Tel/Fax: 01896 822148
E-mail: bestaccom@dunmel.freeserve.co.uk
Web: www.dunmel.freeserve.co.uk

Overlooking Melrose Abbey. A highly respected and well established
guest house offering very high standards. All rooms (except one) with ensuite facilities, the single room has a private bathroom. Traditional
Scottish breakfasts with interesting variations. Non-smoking house.

1 Single	4 En Suite fac
2 Twin	1 Priv.NOT ensuite
2 Double	

B&B per person
from £20.00 Single
from £20.00 Dbl/Twn

Open Jan-Dec

Kings Arms Hotel
High Street, Melrose, Roxburghshire, TD6 9PB
Tel: 01896 822143 Fax: 01896 823812
E-mail: enquiries@kingsarmsmelrose.co.uk
Web: www.kingsarmsmelrose.co.uk

Former coaching Inn dating back some 300 years, in centre of historic
Border town. Cosy lounge bar with open fires.

INN

1 Single	All En Suite
3 Twin	
1 Double	
2 Family	

B&B per person
from £36.50 Single
from £28.75 Dbl/Twn

Open Jan-Dec
B&B + Eve.Meal from
£37.50

Waverley Castle Hotel
Skirmish Hill, Waverley Road, Melrose, TD6 9AA
Tel: 01786 436600 Fax: 01786 436650
E-mail: l.graig@shearingsholidays.co.uk
Web: www.shearingsholidays.com

HOTEL

26 Single	All En Suite
22 Twin	
29 Double	
4 Family	

Open Feb-Dec

---

by Melrose, Roxburghshire | **Map Ref: 2D6**

B&B

Whitehouse
St Boswells, Melrose, Roxburghshire, TD6 0ED
Tel: 01573 460343 Fax: 01573 460361
E-mail: tyrer.whitehouse@lineone.net
Web: www.aboutscotland.com/south/whitehouse.html

Spacious former Dower house, decorated to a high standard. Full of
character, relaxed atmosphere, log fires, home cooked dinners, baking
and preserves. Kelso, Dryburgh and Melrose within 10 minuites.

2 Twin	All En Suite
1 Double	

B&B per person
from £35.00 Single
from £30.00 Dbl/Twn

Open Jan-Dec
B&B + Eve.Meal
from £50.00

All properties graded by VisitScotland, formerly known as the Scottish Tourist Board. | *Key to symbols is on back flap.*

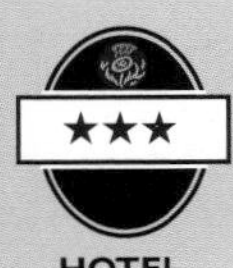

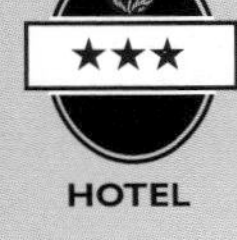

Moffat, Dumfriesshire | Map Ref: 2B8

★★

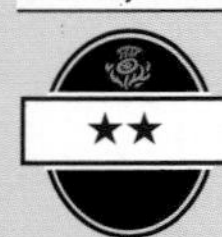

GUEST HOUSE

Barnhill Springs Country Guest House
Moffat, Dumfriesshire, DG10 9QS
Tel: 01683 220580

2 Twin	1 Priv.NOT ensuite	B&B per person	Open Jan-Dec
2 Double	2 Pub Bath/Show	from £23.00 Single	B&B + Eve.Meal
1 Family		from £23.00 Dbl/Twn	from £38.00

Barnhill Springs is an early Victorian country house standing in its own grounds overlooking upper Annandale. It is a quiet family run guest house situated ¹/₂ a mile from the A74/M at the Moffat junction no.15. Barnhill Springs is ideally situated as a centre for touring Southern Scotland, for walking and cycling on the Southern Upland Way or for a relaxing overnight stop for holiday makers heading North or South.

★★★★

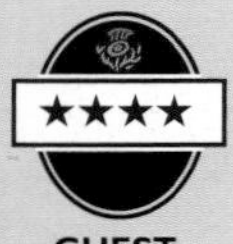

GUEST HOUSE

Hartfell House
Hartfell Crescent, Moffat, Dumfriesshire, DG10 9AL
Tel: 01683 220153
E-mail: robert.white@virgin.net
Web: http://freespace.virgin.net/robert.white/

1 Single	7 En Suite fac	B&B per person	Open Jan-Dec
2 Twin	1 Priv.NOT ensuite	£28.00 Single	B&B + Eve.Meal
4 Double		£24.00 Dbl/Twn	from £37.50
1 Family			

Family run, in rural setting, within walking distance of the town centre. Large, well maintained garden and fine views. Evening meals by prior arrangement.

★★★

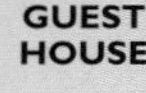

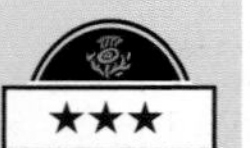

HOTEL

Moffat House Hotel
High Street, Moffat, Dumfriesshire, DG10 9HL
Tel: 01683 220039 Fax: 01683 221288
E-mail: moffat@talk21.com
Web: www.moffathouse.co.uk

3 Single	All En Suite	B&B per person	Open Jan-Dec excl
8 Twin		£50.00-£60.00 Single	Xmas/New Year
8 Double		£35.00-£47.00 Dbl/Twn	
2 Family			

18c Adam mansion with magnificent staircase, set in own grounds with country views to rear, yet in the centre of the award winning 'Scotland in Bloom' village of Moffat. All rooms en suite, ground floor rooms available including a self contained cottage. Lounge food plus fine dining in Hopetown's Restaurant.

★★★★

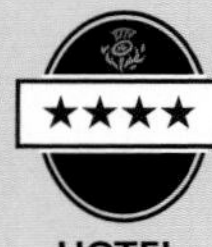

HOTEL

Well View Hotel
Ballplay Road, Moffat, Dumfriesshire, DG10 9JU
Tel: 01683 220184 Fax: 01683 220088
E-mail: info@wellview.co.uk
Web: www.wellview.co.uk

2 Twin	All En Suite	B&B per person	Open Jan-Dec
4 Double		from £55.00 Single	B&B + Eve.Meal
		from £75.00 Dbl/Twn	from £66.00

Mid Victorian house converted to comfortable, family run hotel. Overlooking town and surrounding hills, with its own large garden. Innovative and original use of fresh local ingredients, in our attractive award winning restaurant.

Moniaive, Dumfriesshire | Map Ref: 2A9

★★

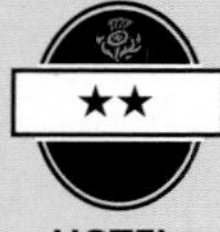

HOTEL

Woodlea Hotel
Moniaive, Dumfriesshire, DG3 4EN
Tel: 01848 200209
E-mail: robin@woodlea43.freeserve.co.uk
Web: www.woodlea-hotel.co.uk

1 Single	All En Suite	B&B per person	Open Apr-Oct
1 Twin		from £30.00 Single	B&B + Eve.Meal
2 Double		from £60.00 Dbl/Twn	from £45.00 pp
8 Family		Room only from £24.00	

Friendly country hotel with indoor swimming pool, sauna, bowls, putting, croquet, tennis, badminton, clay pigeon shooting, bikes, golf, horse riding and sailing available close by.

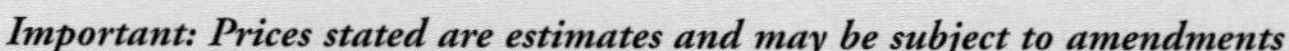

Important: Prices stated are estimates and may be subject to amendments

New Abbey, by Dumfries, Dumfriesshire — Map Ref: 2B10

★★

INN

Abbey Arms Hotel
1 The Square, New Abbey, Dumfries, DG2 8BX
Tel: 01387 850489 Fax: 01387 850501

3 Twin	4 En Suite fac	B&B per person	Open Jan-Dec
2 Double	1 Priv.NOT ensuite	from £23.00 Single	
2 Family		from £23.00 Dbl/Twn	
		Room only from £19.00	

Cosy Inn with en-suite situated in the picturesque and historical village of New Abbey. It makes a perfect first stop along the Solway Coast Heritage Trail and for visiting Sweetheart Abbey and Shambellie House Museum of Costume.

Newton Stewart, Wigtownshire — Map Ref: 1G10

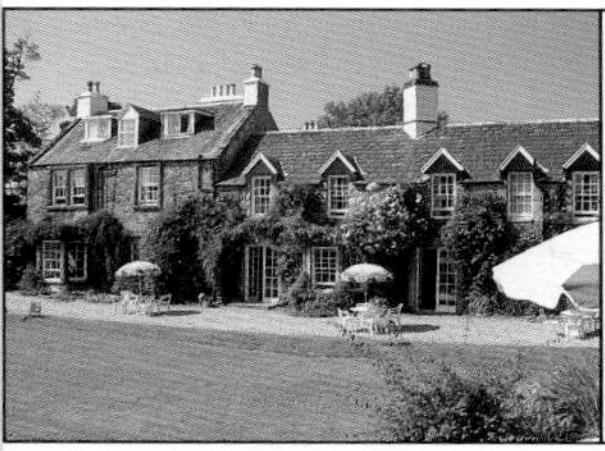

Creebridge House Hotel
Newton Stewart, Dumfries and Galloway DG8 6NP
Tel: 01671 402121   Fax: 01671 403258
e.mail: info@creebridge.co.uk Web: www.creebridge.co.uk

Country house hotel with award-winning cuisine. 19 bedrooms, choice of two restaurants, log fires, elegant public lounges. Ideal base for exploring the south west of Scotland. Golf, salmon fishing, walking, mountain biking all arranged. Come and unwind, slow down and enjoy our renowned hospitality at an unhurried pace.

★★★

SMALL HOTEL

Creebridge House Hotel
Newton Stewart, Dumfries and Galloway, DG8 6NP
Tel: 01671 402121 Fax: 01671 403258
E-mail: info@creebridge.co.uk Web: www.creebridge.co.uk

2 Single	All En Suite	B&B per person	Open Jan-Dec
6 Twin		£49.50-£59.50 Single	Dinner, B&B
9 Double		£39.50-£49.50 Dbl/Twn	£55.00-£70.00
2 Family			

Delightful Country House Hotel set in three acres, only a short walk away from the market town of Newton Stewart. Award winning modern Scottish cuisine served in the garden restaurant or brasserie. Fishing and golf breaks arranged.

★★★

GUEST HOUSE

Flowerbank Guest House
Millcroft Road, Minnigaff, Newton Stewart,
Wigtownshire, DG8 6PJ   Tel: 01671 402629
E-mail: flowerbankgh@btopenworld.com
Web: www.flowerbankgh.com

1 Twin	4 En Suite fac	B&B per person	Open Jan-Dec excl
2 Double	1 Priv.NOT ensuite	from £19.00 Dbl/Twn	Xmas/New Year
2 Family			B&B + Eve.Meal
			from £29.00

Geoff and Linda Inker welcome you to Flowerbank, a charming 18th century house where the River Cree runs alongside our 1 acre landscaped gardens, just 1/2 mile from Newton Stewart. Warm, comfortable, non-smoking accommodation with colour TVs, tea/coffee, lounge with log fire and ample parking. Spacious dining room, separate tables, good home cooking. Quiet and friendly - a warm welcome awaits you.

All properties graded by VisitScotland, formerly known as the Scottish Tourist Board. | *Key to symbols is on back flap.*

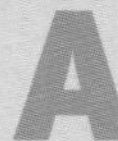

Newton Stewart, Wigtownshire				Map Ref: 1G10

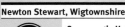

Greenmantle Hotel
Mochrum, nr Port William, Newton Stewart, DG8 9LY
Tel/Fax: 01988 700357

SMALL
HOTEL

1 Single   All En Suite
1 Twin
3 Family

B&B per person
from £22.00 Single
from £24.00 Dbl/Twn

Open Jan-Dec

Personally run hotel in village of Mochrum just 1.5 miles from shores of Luce Bay. Ideal base to explore the peace and beauty of the Wigtownshire countryside.

TV 🅱 P 🍵 🍴 ♟

C 🐕 £ W V

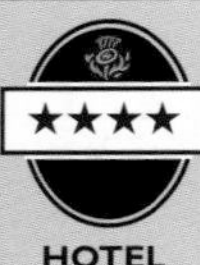

Peebles				Map Ref: 2C6

Cringletie House Hotel
Eddleston, Peebles, Peebles-shire, EH45 8PL
Tel: 01721 730233 Fax: 01721 730244
E-mail: enquiries@cringletie.com
Web: www.cringletie.com
A member of the Wren's Group

HOTEL

1 Single   All En Suite
6 Twin
7 Double

B&B per person
from £75.00 Single
from £75.00 Dbl/Twn

Open Jan-Dec
B&B + Eve.Meal
£100.00

Group owned and personally run Scottish Baronial mansion house set in 28 acres of garden and woodland.

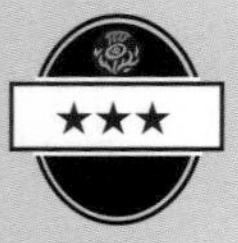

TV 📞 🅱 P 🍵 ♟ 🍴 ⓘ 💷 ♟

C 🐕 £ W V 🐂 🗲

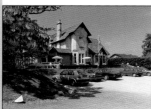

Kingsmuir Hotel
SPRINGHILL ROAD, PEEBLES, BORDERS EH45 9EP
Telephone: 01721 720151   Fax: 01721 721795
e.mail: enquiries@kingsmuir.com
Web: www.kingsmuir.com   ★★★ SMALL HOTEL

Kingsmuir is a charming 1850's style country mansion in leafy grounds. Resident proprietors specialise in traditional Scottish cooking and have won many awards. All bedrooms are tastefully decorated with private bathrooms, TV and telephone. Peebles is a Royal and Ancient Burgh famous for Tweeds and Woollens, golf, fishing, walking and mountain biking.

Kingsmuir Hotel
Springhill Road, Peebles, EH45 9EP
Tel: 01721 720151 Fax: 01721 721795
E-mail: enquiries@kingsmuir.com
Web: www.kingsmuir.com

SMALL
HOTEL

1 Single   All En Suite
7 Twin
1 Double
1 Family

B&B per person
from £36.00 Single
from £32.00 Dbl/Twn

Open Jan-Dec
B&B + Eve.Meal
from £46.00

A 19c mansion in its own grounds with ample parking, situated in a quiet corner of Peebles near the River Tweed. A warm welcome and friendly service are a feature of this personally run hotel. Restaurant and bar meals available.

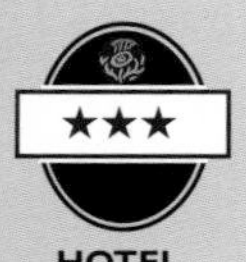

TV 📞 🅱 P 🍵 ♟ 🗲 🍴 ♟

£ W V

Park Hotel
Innerleithen Road, Peebles, EH45 8BA
Tel: 01721 720451 Fax: 01721 723510
E-mail: reserve@parkpeebles.co.uk
Web: www.parkpeebles.co.uk

HOTEL

4 Single   All En Suite
10 Twin
10 Double

B&B per person
from £56.00 Single
from £50.00 Dbl/Twn

Open Jan-Dec
B&B + Eve.Meal
from £66.00

Quiet and comfortable, with extensive gardens and fine hill views. Ideal touring centre, and only 22 miles (35kms) from Edinburgh.

TV 📞 🅱 P 🍵 ♟ 🗲 🍴 ⓘ 💷 ♟

C 🐕 £ W V

Important: Prices stated are estimates and may be subject to amendments

Portpatrick, Wigtownshire

Map Ref: 1F10

★★

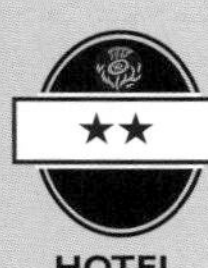

GUEST
HOUSE

Braefield Guest House
Portpatrick, Wigtownshire, DG9 8TA
Tel: 01776 810255

1 Single	5 En Suite fac	B&B per person	Open Jan-Dec
2 Twin	1 Pub Bath/Show	from £20.00 Single	
3 Double		from £20.00 Dbl/Twn	
1 Family			

A warm friendly welcome awaits you at Braefield Guest House, which is a large detached Victorian house in an excellent position overlooking the harbour, with extensive sea views. A short walk takes you to the centre of the village with its variety of eating places, bowling and putting greens and tennis courts, 100 yds from the golf course.

★★

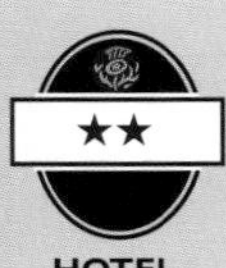

HOTEL

Downshire Arms Hotel
Main Street, Portpatrick, by Stranraer, Wigtownshire,
DG9 8JJ
Tel: 01776 810300 Fax: 01776 810620
E-mail: info@downshire-arms-hotel.co.uk
Web: www.downshire-arms-hotel.co.uk

2 Single	14 En Suite fac	B&B per person	Open Jan-Dec
8 Twin		from £35.00 Single	B&B + Eve.Meal
8 Double		from £35.00 Dbl/Twn	from £50.00
5 Family		Room only per person	
		from £30.00	

This family run hotel is conveniently situated only 75 yards from the sea front of this picturesque harbour village. Shops and amenities nearby. Fully refurbished public areas and bedrooms for the 2000 season. Most bedrooms have sea views. With a chef/proprietor the hotel offers a choice of menus using fresh local produce when available. Friendly Scottish hospitality. CAMRA Good Beer Guide. Golf parties our speciality.

★★

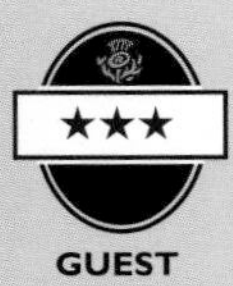

HOTEL

Portpatrick Hotel
Heugh Road, Portpatrick, Dumfries & Galloway, DG9 8TQ
Tel: 01786 436600 Fax: 01786 436650
E-mail: l.graig@shearingsholidays.co.uk
Web: www.shearingsholidays.com

8 Single	All En Suite		Open Feb-Dec
25 Twin			
23 Double			
1 Family			

A family and golfing hotel situated above picturesque village and giving panoramic views over the harbour and beyond. Par 3 golf course, snooker room, lawn tennis.

★★★

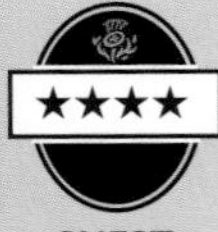

GUEST
HOUSE

Rickwood Hotel
Heugh Road, Portpatrick, Stranraer, DG9 8TD
Tel: 01776 810270
E-mail: MaggieFindlay@aol.com
Web: www.rickwood.sageweb.co.uk

2 Twin	4 En Suite fac	B&B per person	Open Jan-Dec
2 Double	1 Priv.NOT ensuite	from £24.00 Single	B&B + Eve.Meal from
1 Family		from £22.50 Dbl/Twn	£33.50

Detached Edwardian house in mature gardens, overlooking village and sea, close to golf course. Reductions for stays of 3 and 7 nights.

Prestwick, Ayrshire

Map Ref: 1G7

★★★★

GUEST
HOUSE

The Fairways
19 Links Road, Prestwick, Ayrshire, KA9 1QG
Tel/Fax: 01292 470396
E-mail: anne@thefairways.co.uk
Web: www.thefairways.co.uk

2 Single	4 En Suite fac	B&B per person	Open Jan-Dec excl
3 Twin	1 Priv.NOT ensuite	from £27.00 Single	Xmas/New Year
		from £28.00 Dbl/Twn	

Impressive Victorian house with private parking in quiet location overlooking Prestwick Golf Course. Close to town centre amenities, railway station and Prestwick International Airport.

All properties graded by VisitScotland, formerly known as the Scottish Tourist Board.   **Key to symbols is on back flap.**

B&B

★★★

Fionn Fraoch
64 Ayr Road, Prestwick, Ayrshire, KA9 1RR
Tel: 01292 478029

1 Twin	2 En Suite fac	B&B per person	Open Jan-Dec
1 Double	1 Pub Bath/Show	£18.00-£25.00 Single	
1 Family		£18.00-£23.00 Dbl/Twn	
		Room only £18.00-£20.00	

Comfortable and homely accommodation close to Prestwick Airport with pick up/drop off facilities. Within walking distance of Ice Rink, swimming pool, bowling, golf courses and sea front. Numerous restaurants and bars nearby. Pets by arrangement. Non smoking B & B.

St Boswells, Roxburghshire   Map Ref: 2D7

HOTEL

★★★

Buccleuch Arms Hotel
The Green, St Boswells, Roxburghshire, TD6 0EW
Tel: 01835 822243 Fax: 01835 823965
E-mail: bucchotel@aol.com
Web: www.buccleucharms.co.uk

5 Single	All En Suite	B&B per person	Open Jan-Dec
8 Twin		£35.00-£50.00 Single	
6 Double		£30.00-£42.00 Dbl/Twn	

A former 17c coaching inn, situated on the main A68. Ideally located for business or pleasure, with function facilities for up to 100 guests. Good restaurant plus bar food served all day.

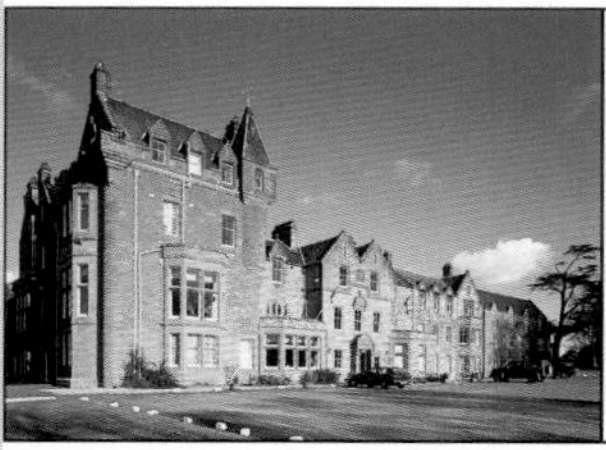

Dryburgh Abbey Hotel

St Boswells, Melrose TD6 0RQ Tel: 01835 822261 Fax: 01835 823945
e.mail: enquiries@dryburgh.co.uk Web: www.dryburgh.co.uk

Peacefully set in 10 acres of grounds and gardens, the Dryburgh Abbey Hotel stands on the banks of the River Tweed adjacent to the historic ruins of Dryburgh Abbey. This splendid baronial mansion is owned and managed by the Grose family who have over 100 years experience in providing hospitality. An ideal base for all manner of country pursuits. We offer excellent service, award winning cuisine and extensive wine list.

HOTEL

★★★★

Dryburgh Abbey Hotel
St Boswells, Roxburghshire, TD6 0RQ
Tel: 01835 822261 Fax: 01835 823945
E-mail: enquiries@dryburgh.co.uk
Web: www.dryburgh.co.uk

6 Single	All En Suite	B&B per person	Open Jan-Dec
25 Twin		from £45.00 Single	B&B + Eve.Meal
3 Double		from £90.00 Dbl/Twn	from £60.00
4 Family			

Country house hotel on banks of River Tweed overlooked by 12c Dryburgh Abbey. Ideal base for fishing, shooting or exploring this historic area. Indoor pool, putting green and mountain bikes, trout rights on the Tweed.

Seamill, Ayrshire   Map Ref: 1F6

HOTEL

★★★

Seamill Hydro
Ardrossan Road, Seamill, Ayrshire, KA23 9NB
Tel: 01294 822217 Fax: 01294 823939
E-mail: seamillhydro@bun.com
Web: www.seamillhydro.co.uk

6 Single	All En Suite	B&B per person	Open Jan-Dec
17 Twin		from £55.00 Single	B&B + Eve.Meal
27 Double		from £42.50 Dbl/Twn	from £55.00
30 Family			

Family-owned hotel, overlooking Firth of Clyde to Arran. Access to the beach. Swimming pool and leisure facilities. Some annexe accommodation.

Important: Prices stated are estimates and may be subject to amendments

Selkirk

Map Ref: 2D7

★★★

SMALL HOTEL

The Glen Hotel

Yarrow Terrace, Selkirk, TD7 5AS
Tel/Fax: 01750 20259
E-mail: glenhotel@hotmail.com
Web: www.glenhotel.co.uk

Spacious family run Victorian house in pleasant gardens, set high above the A707, with views over the River Ettrick. Half mile to town centre.

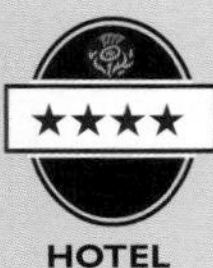

1 Single	All En Suite	B&B per person	Open Jan-Dec
2 Twin	1 Pub Bath/Show	from £40.00 Single	B&B + Eve.Meal from
4 Double		from £32.00 Dbl/Twn	£42.00
1 Family			

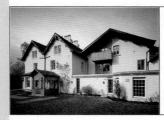

PHILIPBURN COUNTRY HOUSE HOTEL

Linglie Road, Selkirk TD7 5LS
Tel: 01750 20747   Fax: 01750 21690
e.mail: info@philipburnhousehotel.co.uk
Web: www.philipburnhousehotel.co.uk

★★★★
HOTEL

Philipburn Country House Hotel re-opened after complete refurbishment in May 1998, the resulting hotel can only be described as stunning. Situated in the beautiful Scottish borders, the hotel is perfect for an activity based holiday or merely for relaxing. Our dining areas – Charlie's Bar and Bistro and '1745' cater for all tastes.

★★★★

HOTEL

Philipburn Country House Hotel

Selkirk, TD7 5LS
Tel: 01750 20747 Fax: 01750 21690
E-mail: info@philipburnhousehotel.co.uk
Web: www.philipburnhousehotel.co.uk

Set amidst beautiful Borders scenery. Unique, tasteful accommodation in historic manor house. Recently refurbished. Innovative and interesting cuisine. Also garden rooms available by outdoor heated pool.

1 Single	All En Suite	B&B per person	Open Jan-Dec
4 Twin		from £75.00 Single	B&B + Eve.Meal
9 Double		from £50.00 Dbl/Twn	from £77.50

---

by Selkirk

Map Ref: 2D7

★★

INN

Tibbie Shiels Inn

St Mary's Loch, Selkirkshire, TD7 5LH
Tel: 01750 42231

Historical coaching inn on the shores of beautiful St Marys Loch. Fishing, sailing, walking and birdwatching. Imaginative cooking.

1 Twin	All En Suite	B&B per person	Open Jan-Dec excl Xmas
2 Double		to £30.00 Single	Mon-Wed Nov-Mar
2 Family		to £26.00 Dbl/Twn	

Sorbie, Wigtownshire

Map Ref: 1H11

★★★★

GUEST HOUSE

Birchtrees Guesthouse

Reiffer Park Road, Sorbie, Newton Stewart, Wigtownshire, DG8 8EH
Tel: 01988 850391

Pauline and John welcome you to Birchtrees which is an attractive bungalow set in a 1/2 acre garden in a peaceful location amidst beautiful scenery in the heart of Galloway countryside. 12 miles south of Newton Stewart, 6 miles from Wigtown, Scotland's book town. Non smoking home.

2 Twin	All En Suite	B&B per person	Open Jan-Oct excl
		from £24.00 Single	Xmas/New Year
		from £24.00 Dbl/Twn	B&B + Eve.Meal
			from £32.00

All properties graded by VisitScotland, formerly known as the Scottish Tourist Board.   **Key to symbols is on back flap.**

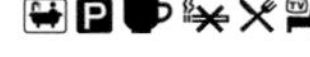

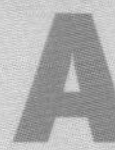

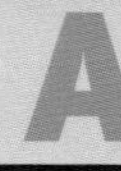

Stranraer, Wigtownshire — Map Ref: 1F10

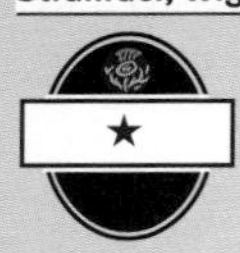

INN ★

County Hotel
Stoney Kirk, Stranraer, Wigtownshire, DG9 9DH
Tel: 01776 830431

5 Twin	8 En Suite fac	B&B per person	Open Jan-Dec
4 Family	1 Priv.NOT ensuite	from £22.00 Single	B&B + Eve.Meal from
		from £20.00 Dbl/Twn	£30.00
		Room only from £17.50	

En-suite rooms available at this inn, conveniently only a few miles from Stranraer and Port Patrick. Plenty of golf courses nearby. Country and Western music at weekends. Irish bands.

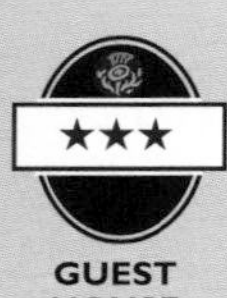

GUEST HOUSE ★★★

Harbour Guest House
11 Market Street, Stranraer, Wigtownshire, DG9 7RF
Tel/Fax: 01776 704626
E-mail: reservations@harbourguesthouse.com
Web: www.harbourguesthouse.com

1 Twin	All En Suite fac	B&B per person	Open Jan-Dec excl
1 Double	2 Pub Bath/Show	from £25.00 Single	Xmas/New Year
2 Dbl/Twin		from £23.00 Twin	
		Room only per person	
		from £20.00	

This refurbished guest house now with full ensuite facilities is ideally situated on harbour front in the centre of Stranraer. Convenient for train station and ferry terminals. Street parking or limited yet secure private parking available. Totally non smoking house. Late Victorian listed building.

---

nr Stranraer, Wigtownshire — Map Ref: 1F10

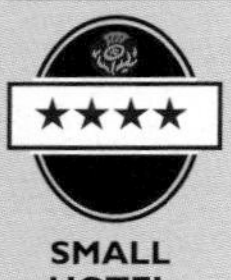

SMALL HOTEL ★★★★

Corsewall Lighthouse Hotel
Kirkcolm, Stranraer, DG9 0QG
Tel: 01776 853220 Fax: 01776 854231
E-mail: corsewall_lighthouse@msn.com
Web: www.lighthousehotel.co.uk

7 Double	8 En Suite fac	B&B per person	Open Jan-Dec
2 Family	1 Priv.NOT ensuite	£80.00-£120.00 Single	B&B + Eve.Meal
		£50.00-£100.00	from £50.00
		Dbl/Twn	

Corsewell Lighthouse Hotel offers the charm and romance of an 1815 functional lighthouse with its cosy bedrooms each individually furnished. Spectacular sea views. The award winning restaurant caters for a wide range of tastes including local beef, lamb, seafood and vegetarian dishes. Additionally there are 3 properties in the grounds.

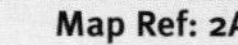

Thornhill, Dumfriesshire — Map Ref: 2A8

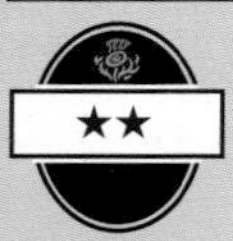

HOTEL ★★

Buccleuch & Queensberry Hotel
112 Drumlanrig Street, Thornhill, Dumfriesshire, DG3 5LU
Tel/Fax: 01848 330215
E-mail: naomi@buccleuchhotel.co.uk
Web: www.buccleuchhotel.co.uk

6 Twin	B&B per person	Open Jan-Dec
3 Double	from £34.00 Single	
3 Family	from £50.00 Dbl/Twn	

Built in 1856 as a coaching inn, the hotel stands in the centre of this picturesque conservation village. The traditional bar offers a friendly team of staff serving cask ale, fine wines and a variety of bar and restaurant meals. Close to Drumlairig Castle and the River Nith, famous for its salmon fishing. The Buccleuch is an ideal haven for families, fishermen and country pursuits.

Troon, Ayrshire — Map Ref: 1G7

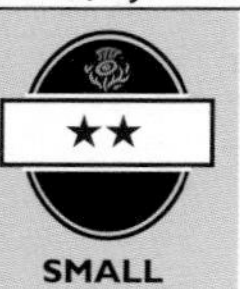

SMALL HOTEL ★★

Anchorage Hotel
149 Templehill, Troon, KA10 6BR
Tel: 01292 317448 Fax: 01292 318508
E-mail: anchor1812@aol.com
Web: www.theanchoragehotel.com

2 Single	All En Suite	B&B per person	Open Jan-Dec excl
10 Twin		from £39.00 Single	Xmas/New Year
4 Double		from £52.00 Dbl/Twn	B&B + Eve.Meal from
2 Family		Room only from £33.00	£49.00

Coaching Inn built in 1812, tastefully restored. Conveniently situated near town centre and marina.

Important: Prices stated are estimates and may be subject to amendments

Troon, Ayrshire

Map Ref: 1G7

SMALL HOTEL ★★

Ardneil Hotel
51 St Meddans Street, Toon, Ayrshire, KA10 6NU
Tel: 01292 311611 Fax: 01292 318111

14 Twin	17 En Suite fac	B&B per person	Open Jan-Dec
4 Double	2 Priv.NOT ensuite	from £40.00 Single	
2 Family		from £60.00 Dbl/Twn	

Family owned friendly hotel with extensive restaurant and bar facilities. Close to railway station and 5 minutes walk from the town centre.

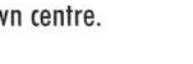

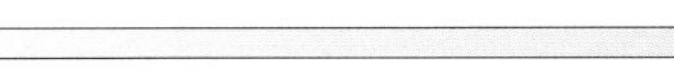

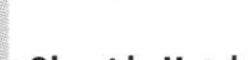

GUEST HOUSE ★★★

Glenside Hotel
2 Darley Place, Troon, Ayrshire, KA10 6JG
Tel/Fax: 01292 313677

3 Twin	All En Suite	B&B per person	Open Jan-Dec
1 Family		from £30.00 Single	
		from £27.50 Dbl/Twn	

Victorian stone built house. Accent on warm hospitality and comfort. Ideal touring centre - Glasgow 32 miles (51kms). Six golf courses including Royal Troon nearby. Non smoking establishment.

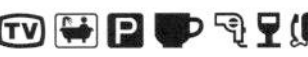

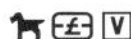

HOTEL ★★★★

Marine Hotel
Crosbie Road, Troon, Ayrshire, KA10 6HE
Tel: 01292 314444 Fax: 01292 316922
E-mail: marie@paramount-hotels.co.uk
Web: www.paramount-hotels.co.uk

16 Single	All En Suite	B&B per person	Open Jan-Dec
31 Twin	Suites avail	from £96.00 Single	
25 Double		from £80.00 Dbl/Twn	

The Marine Hotel is located overlooking to Royal Troon Golf Course with views out to sea and the Isle of Arran. The hotel offers Fairways Restaurant & the Arran Lounge for lunch, dinner and snacks. There are five Conference & Banqueting Centre with parking for 200 cars. Residents also have the use of Bodysense Health & Leisure Club boasting pool, jacuzzi, steam & Sauna, squash court, techno gym and treatment room.

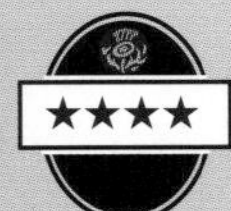

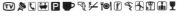

HOTEL ★★★★

Piersland House Hotel
15 Craigend Road, Troon, Ayrshire, KA10 6HD
Tel: 01292 314747 Fax: 01292 315613
E-mail: reservations@piersland.co.uk
Web: www.piersland.co.uk

1 Single	All En Suite	B&B per person	Open Jan-Dec
21 Twin		£62.50-£90.00 Single	B&B + Eve.Meal
6 Double		£59.50-£82.50 Dbl/Twn	£79.50 Single
			£102.50 Dbl/Twn

Unique and historic house built for Sir Alexander Walker with 13 cottage suites set in beautifully landscaped grounds and situated on the Southwest Coast - a haven for golfers. Family owned hotel. Many historic attractions including Robert Burns Cottage and Culzean Castle nearby.

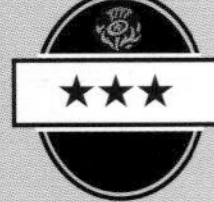

HOTEL ★★★

South Beach Hotel
73 South Beach, Troon, Ayrshire, KA10 6EG
Tel: 01292 312033 Fax: 01292 318438
E-mail: info@southbeach.co.uk
Web: www.southbeach.co.uk

4 Single	All En Suite	B&B per person	Open Jan-Dec
21 Twin		from £40.00 Single	B&B + Eve.Meal
6 Double		from £30.00 Dbl/Twn	from £45.00
3 Family			

Privately owned hotel facing the sea on main road and about 0.5 miles (1km) from town centre. Convenient for Troon championship golf course.

All properties graded by VisitScotland, formerly known as the Scottish Tourist Board. | Key to symbols is on back flap. |

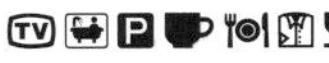

MALIN COURT

TURNBERRY, AYRSHIRE KA26 9PB
Telephone: 01655 331457   Fax: 01655 331072
e.mail: info@malincourt.co.uk Web: www.malincourt.co.uk

Malin Court is situated in the heart of Burns Country, close to Culzean Castle, overlooking Turnberry's famous Open Championship golf course and the Firth of Clyde. It offers a perfect blend of informality, congeniality, the best of local produce cooked to perfection and the warmest of Scottish welcomes.

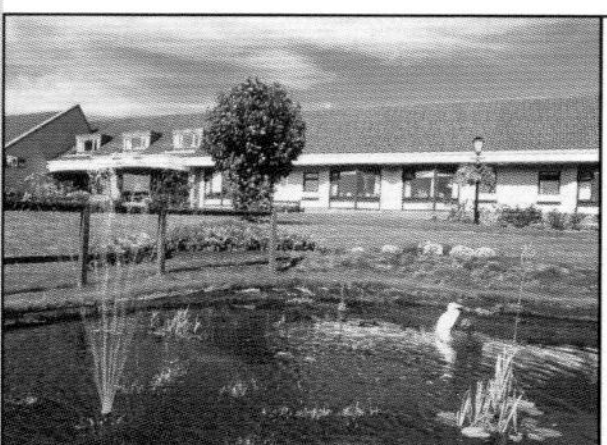

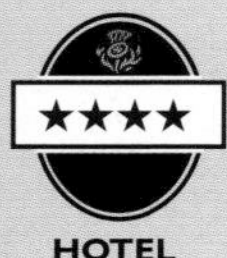

HOTEL

Malin Court
Turnberry, Ayrshire, KA26 9PB
Tel: 01655 331457 Fax: 01655 331072
E-mail: info@malincourt.co.uk
Web: www.malincourt.co.uk

Totally refurbished modern hotel with views over Turnberry Golf Course and Ailsa Craig, near Culzean Castle. Patio garden. AA 2 rosettes restaurant.

7 Twin	All En Suite
3 Double	
7 Family	
1 Suite	

B&B per person
£72.00-£82.00 Single
£52.00-£62.00 Dbl/Twn

Open Jan-Dec
B&B + Eve.Meal
from £85.00 Sgl
from £65.00 Dbl

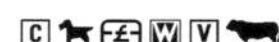

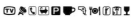

welcome to scotland

EDINBURGH AND LOTHIANS

With a city skyline every bit as spectacular as the postcards suggest, Scotland's capital is simply outstanding in world terms.

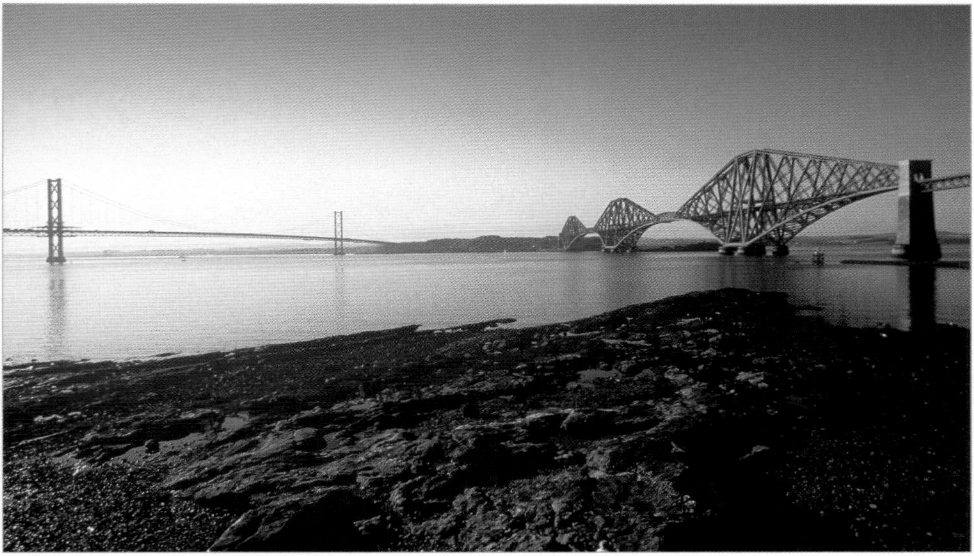

The Forth Bridges viewed from South Queensferry

THE Scottish Parliament has brought a buzz to the city. Edinburgh Castle is one of the most famous symbols of Scotland, but it is only one of a whole range of attractions stretching down the Royal Mile in the heart of the Old Town. The city is steeped in history and culture, from the Palace of Holyroodhouse, where the tragic story of Mary Queen of Scots unfolded, to the striking architecture of the Museum of Scotland which tells the nation's story from its geological beginnings to the present day. The Royal Yacht Britannia and Our Dynamic Earth are just two of the city's other visitor attractions.

The most famous events the city host are the spectacular International Festival and the Festival Fringe, but it remains the liveliest of cities all year round with other events such as the Science Festival, Film Festival and the biggest New Year street party in the world – Edinburgh's Hogmanay. As a major cultural centre, Edinburgh has many art galleries, theatres and cinemas. There are many street cafés and restaurants specialising in both international and modern Scottish cuisine, while over 700 bars in the city offer fine locally brewed beers and, of course, a wide range of malt whiskies.

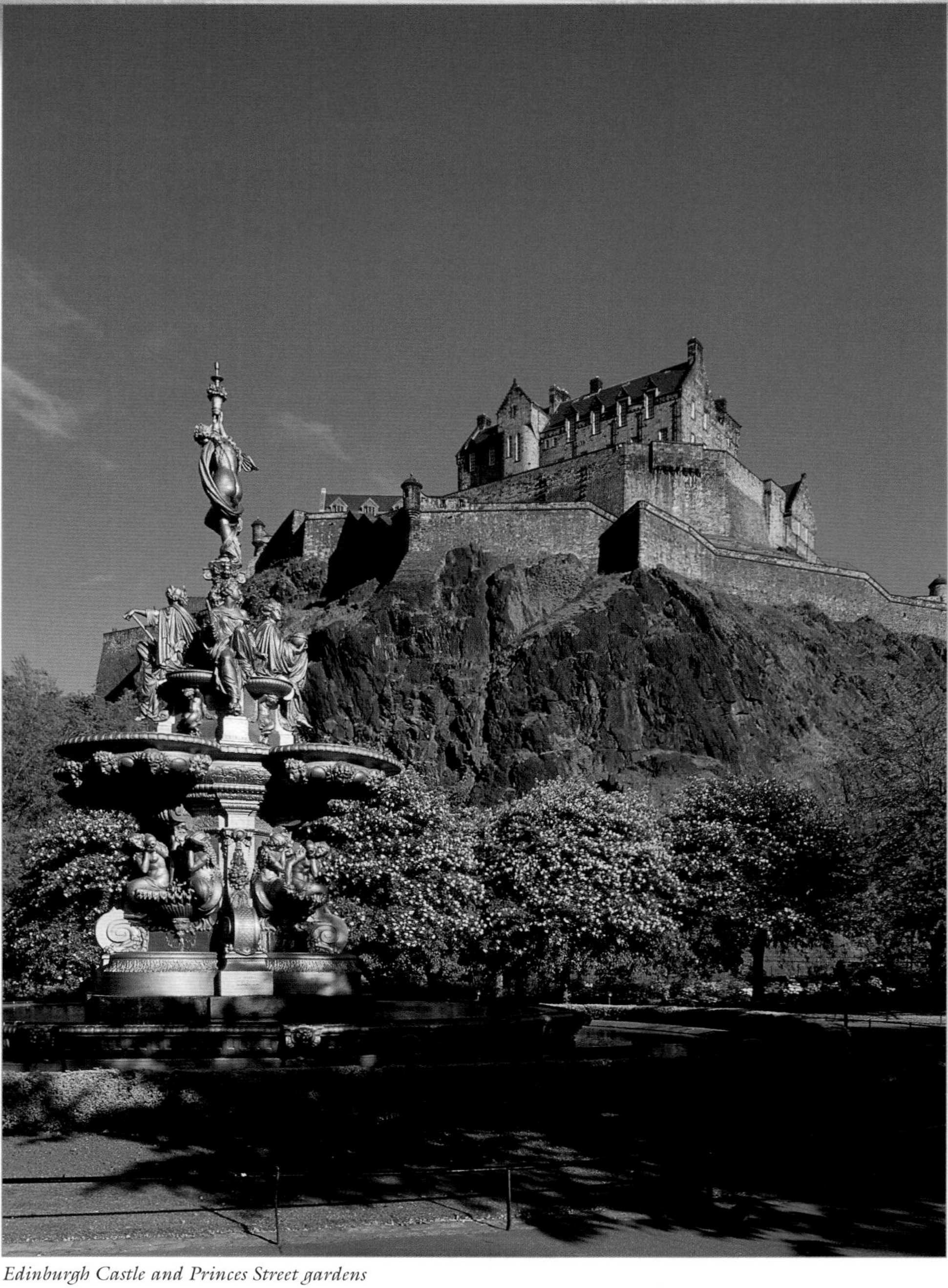

Edinburgh Castle and Princes Street gardens

EDINBURGH AND LOTHIANS

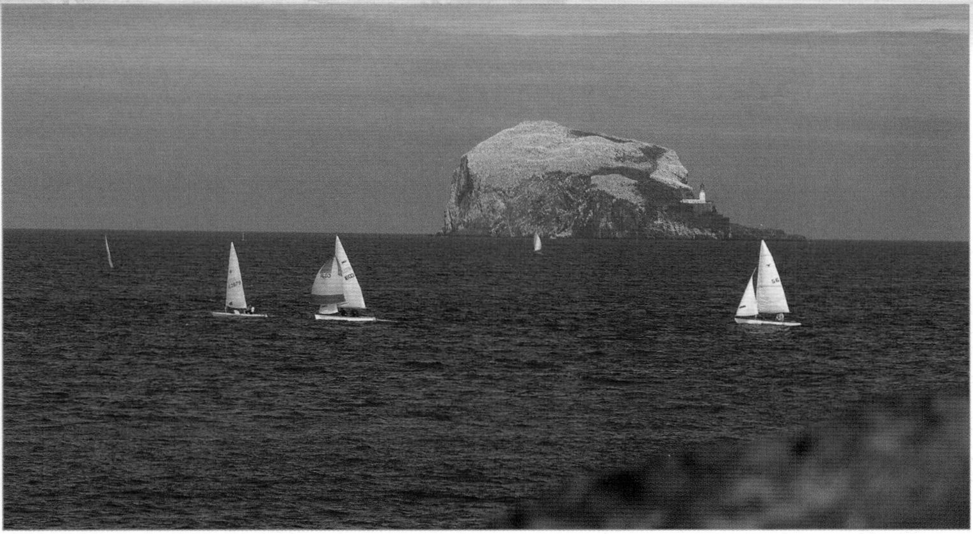

Sailing on the Firth of Forth, near Bass Rock

This fast-paced and cosmopolitan city offers superb shopping in the many department stores along the famous thoroughfare of Princes Street as well as Princes Mall and the many designer shops along elegantly proportioned George Street in the heart of the 18-century New Town. The village-like suburbs of Stockbridge and Bruntsfield offer small shops where a friendly welcome is guaranteed. A relaxing alternative within the bustling city are the many quiet green spaces including Holyrood Park, Calton Hill, the Dean Village and the Royal Botanic Garden, which features Britain's tallest palm house and the world-famous Rock Garden.

Within a few miles of the city centre are the Lothians. This is soft rolling farmland with splendid hill-walking in the surrounding Pentland, Moorfoot and Lammermuir Hills. There are almost 70 miles of coastline along the Firth of Forth combining nature reserves, sandy beaches and seaside resorts. Dunbar has been officially recorded as Scotland's driest and sunniest town. The award-winning Scottish Seabird Centre in North Berwick uses the latest technology to allow all the family to view the famous gannet colony on the nearby Bass Rock. To the west, South Queensferry is set in a dramatic location immediately below the gigantic structures of the famous Forth Bridges.

Experience and enjoy one of Europe's most exciting regions, by combining city and countryside. With easy access by air, rail and road, Edinburgh and the Lothians is a year-round destination for everyone.

EVENTS
EDINBURGH AND LOTHIANS

1-31 JANUARY
Turner Exhibition
Edinburgh,
National Gallery of Scotland
Annual show of Turner
watercolours.
Contact: National Gallery of
Scotland
Tel: 0131 624 6200
Web: www.natgalscot.ac.uk

6-16 APRIL
*Edinburgh's International
Science Festival*
Edinburgh, Various Venues
The world's largest event
devoted to the celebration
of science.
Contact: Edinburgh
International Science
Festival
Tel: 0131 530 2001
Web:
www.edinburghfestivals.
co.uk/science

20-23 JUNE
Royal Highland Show
Edinburgh,
Royal Highland Centre
The highlight of Scotland's
country calendar with a food
exhibition, pedigree
livestock and more.
Contact:
Royal Highland Centre
Tel: 0131 335 6200
Web: www.rhass.org.uk

18-21 JULY
Open Golf Championship
Muirfield, East Lothian
The 131st Open Golf
Championship in Scotland,
the 'Home of Golf'.
Contact:
Royal & Ancient Golf Club
Tel: 01334 460010
Web: www.opengolf.com

2-24 AUGUST
Edinburgh Military Tattoo
Edinburgh,
Edinburgh Castle
The Capital's annual
military extravaganza.
Contact: Tattoo Office
Tel: 0131 225 1188
Web: www.edintattoo.co.uk

4-26 AUGUST
Edinburgh Festival Fringe
Edinburgh, Various Venues
The largest arts festival in
the world, including theatre,
comedy, music and magic.
Contact: Fringe Office
Tel: 0131 226 5257
Web: www.edfringe.com

9-25 AUGUST
*Edinburgh International
Book Festival*
Edinburgh,
Charlotte Square
The world's biggest book
festival with leading
international and Scottish
authors.
Contact: EIBF
Tel: 0131 228 5444
Web: www.edbookfest.co.uk

* 11-25 AUGUST
*Edinburgh International
Film Festival*
Various Venues, Edinburgh
A two week celebration of
cinema with gala premieres
and talks from visiting
directors.
Contact: EIFF
Tel: 0131 467 5200
Web: www.eif.co.uk

11-31 AUGUST
*Edinburgh International
Festival*
Edinburgh, Various Venues
One of the world's most
prestigious arts festivals
offering the very best in
international opera, theatre,
dance and music.
Contact: The Hub
Tel: 0131 473 2001
Web: www.eif.co.uk

** denotes provisional date,
please check before attending.*

AREA TOURIST BOARDS
EDINBURGH AND LOTHIANS

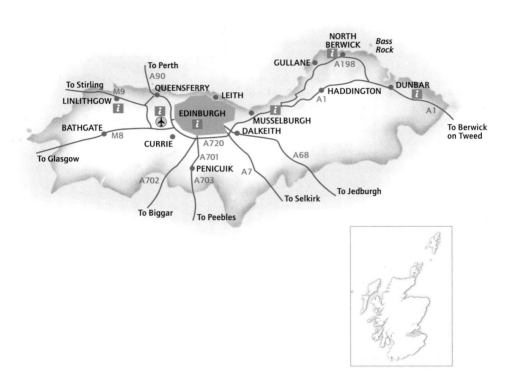

EDINBURGH AND
LOTHIANS TOURIST
BOARD
Edinburgh and Scotland
Information Centre
3 Princes Street
Edinburgh
EH2 2QP

Tel: 0131 473 3800
Fax: 0131 473 3881
E-mail: esic@eltb.org
Web: www.edinburgh.org

TOURIST INFORMATION CENTRES
EDINBURGH AND LOTHIANS

**EDINBURGH AND
LOTHIANS TOURIST
BOARD**

Dunbar
143 High Street
Tel: (0131) 473 3800
esic@eltb.org
Jan-Dec

Edinburgh
Edinburgh and Scotland
Information Centre
3 Princes Street
Tel: (0131) 473 3800
esic@eltb.org
Jan-Dec

Edinburgh Airport
Tourist Information Desk
Tel: (0131) 473 3800
esic@eltb.org
Jan-Dec

Newtongrange
Scottish Mining Museum
Lady Victoria Colliery
Tel: (0131) 473 3800
esic@eltb.org
Easter-Oct

North Berwick
Quality Street
Tel: (0131) 473 3800
esic@eltb.org
Jan-Dec

Old Craighall
Granada Service Area
A1
Musselburgh
Tel: (0131) 473 3800
esic@eltb.org
Jan-Dec

Penicuik
Edinburgh Crystal
Visitor Centre
Eastfield
Tel: (0131) 473 3800
esic@eltb.org
Easter-Sept

Bonsyde, by Linlithgow, West Lothian

Map Ref: 2B4

★★

HOTEL

Bonsyde House Hotel
Bonsyde, Linlithgow, West Lothian, EH49 7NU
Tel: 01506 842229 Fax: 01506 846233
E-mail: info@bonsyde.co.uk
Web: www.bonsydehouse.co.uk

B listed Georgian house in elevated position overlooking Linlithgow Palace and Loch. Brasserie restaurant with emphasis on fresh produce in relaxed environment.

1 Single	8 En Suite fac	B&B per person	Open Jan-Dec
3 Twin		from £30.00 Single	
6 Double		from £20.00 Dbl/Twn	
2 Family			

by Dalkeith, Midlothian

Map Ref: 2C5

★★

INN

Laird & Dog Hotel
5 High Street, Lasswade, Midlothian, EH18 1NA
Tel/Fax: 0131 663 9219
E-mail: lairdanddog.btinternet.co.uk
Web: www.lairdanddog.btinternet.co.uk

Old Coaching Inn (est. 1740) 0.5 mile from City Bypass with excellent bus service to Edinburgh. New conservatory restaurant, à la carte and bar meals, large car park, olde worlde bar and newly discovered historical well. All bedrooms en suite.

1 Single	All En Suite	B&B per person	Open Jan-Dec
4 Twin		from £25.00 Single	
3 Double		from £22.00 Dbl/Twn	
1 Family			

Dirleton, East Lothian

Map Ref: 2D4

★★★★

**SMALL
HOTEL**

The Open Arms Hotel
Dirleton, East Lothian, EH39 5EG
Tel: 01620 850241 Fax: 01620 850570
E-mail: openarms@clara.co.uk
Web: www.openarmshotel.com

Dating from 1185, this family run hotel stands at the foot of the village green overlooking the 13th Century Castle. Quiet lounges with open fires add to the warmth of personal welcome. All bedrooms are highly decorated, and as one would expect of a building of this age variety in size and style. Dine in Deveau's Brasserie or the intimate Library restaurant.

2 Single	All En Suite	B&B per person	Open Jan-Dec
5 Twin		from £50.00 Single	B&B + Eve.Meal from
2 Double		from £35.00 Dbl/Twn	£45.00
1 Family			

Dunbar, East Lothian

Map Ref: 2E4

★

**SMALL
HOTEL**

Hillside Hotel
3 Queens Road, Dunbar, East Lothian, EH42 1LA
Tel/Fax: 01368 862071

Personally run hotel with a reputation for good food using fresh local produce. Ideal for golf and touring East Lothian.

4 Single	11 En Suite fac	B&B per person	Open Jan-Dec
3 Twin	2 Pub Bath/Show	from £40.50 Single	
4 Double		from £31.50 Dbl/Twn	
3 Family			

★★

**SMALL
HOTEL**

Royal Mackintosh Hotel
Station Road, Dunbar, East Lothian, EH42 1JY
Tel: 01386 863231 Fax: 01368 865200

Family run hotel ideally situated at centre of this coastal town. Restaurant has original carved panelling from the 'Mauretania' liner.

1 Single	All En Suite	B&B per person	Open Jan-Dec excl Xmas
5 Twin		from £37.50 Single	B&B + Eve.Meal from
7 Double		from £49.50 Dbl/Twn	£49.50
3 Family		Room only from £30.00	

All properties graded by VisitScotland, formerly known as the Scottish Tourist Board. | **Key to symbols is on back flap.**

B

Dunbar, East Lothian

Map Ref: 2E4

GUEST HOUSE
★★

Springfield Guest House
Belhaven Road, Dunbar, East Lothian, EH42 1NH
Tel/Fax: 01368 862502
E-mail: smeed@tesco.net

An elegant 19c villa with attractive garden. Family run with home-cooking. Ideal base for families, golf and touring.

1 Single	2 Priv.NOT ensuite
1 Twin	1 Pub Bath/Show
1 Double	
2 Family	

B&B per person
from £22.00 Single
from £20.00 Dbl/Twn

Open Jan-Nov excl
New Year
B&B + Eve.Meal from
£30.00

Edinburgh

Map Ref: 2C5

B&B
★★★

11 Belford Place
Edinburgh, Midlothian, EH4 3DH
Tel: 0131 332 9704

Peacefully situated on a private road beside the Water of Leith Valley, the Kinross family (and Isla the dog) give a warm welcome to all who come to share the relaxed atmosphere and warm hospitality of their home.

1 Single
1 Twin

B&B per person
£30.00-£40.00 Single
£30.00-£40.00 Dbl/Twn

Open Jan-Dec excl
Xmas/New Year

GUEST HOUSE
★★★★

Aaron Guest House
16 Hartington Gardens, Edinburgh, EH10 4LD
Tel/Fax: 0131 229 6459
E-mail: aaron.guest.house@blueyonder.co.uk
Web: www.aaron-gh.com

Quality service in a thoughtfully restored 19th century Victorian house located in a quiet cul-de-sac in residential area in central Edinburgh with private parking. Within walking distance of all major attractions. Ground floor accommodation available. Non smoking establishment.

1 Single	All En Suite
2 Twin	
5 Double	
2 Family	

B&B per person
from £35.00 Single
from £30.00 Dbl/Twn

Open Jan-Dec

GUEST HOUSE
★★★★

Acorn Lodge Guest House
26 Pilrig Street, Edinburgh, EH6 5AJ
Tel: 0131 555 1557 Fax: 0131 555 4475
E-mail: info@acornlodge.co.uk
Web: www.acornlodge.co.uk

Refurbished Georgian town house centrally situated for all amenities. Personal attention assured. Extensive breakfast menu. Non smoking house.

2 Single	All En Suite
3 Twin	
4 Double	
1 Family	

B&B per person
£30.00-£75.00 Single
£60.00-£150.00
Dbl/Twn

Open Jan-Dec

GUEST HOUSE
★★★

Adria Hotel
11-12 Royal Terrace, Edinburgh, EH7 5AB
Tel: 0131 556 7875 Fax: 0131 558 7782
E-mail: manager@adriahotel.co.uk
Web: www.adriahotel.co.uk

Friendly family run private hotel in quiet Georgian terrace. Spacious bedrooms. Ten minutes walk from centre.

2 Single	9 En Suite fac
6 Twin	6 Pub Bath/Show
9 Double	1 Priv.NOT ensuite
6 Family	

B&B per person
£25.00-£40.00 Single
£21.00-£35.00 Dbl/Twn

Open Feb-Nov

Important: Prices stated are estimates and may be subject to amendments

Edinburgh

Map Ref: 2C5

GUEST HOUSE ★★

Afton Guest House
1 Hartington Garden, Edinburgh, EH10 4LD
Tel/Fax: 0131 229 1019
E-mail: ronmarie@afton-g-house.co.uk
Web: www.afton-g-house.co.uk

End terraced Victorian house in residential area but near main bus route to city centre. Variety of restaurants nearby.

2 Single	2 En Suite fac	B&B per person	Open Jan-Dec
1 Twin	5 Pub Bath/Show	from £16.00-£28.00	
1 Double		Standard	
3 Family		from £18.00-£30.00	
		Suite	

Ailsa Craig Hotel
24 Royal Terrace, Edinburgh EH7 5AH
Tel: 0131-556 1022/6055 Fax: 0131-556 6055
e.mail: ailsacraighotel@ednet.co.uk Web: www.townhousehotels.co.uk

Elegant Georgian townhouse hotel ideally situated in the city centre within walking distance to Princes Street, Waverley train station, Edinburgh Castle and the Playhouse Theatre. Combining traditional features with modern facilities, the hotel offers superb views, private gardens and friendly atmosphere together providing the perfect blend of history and hospitality.

SMALL HOTEL ★★★

Ailsa Craig Hotel
24 Royal Terrace, Edinburgh, EH7 5AH
Tel: 0131 556 1022/6055 Fax: 0131 556 6055
E-mail: ailsacraighotel@ednet.co.uk
Web: www.townhousehotels.co.uk

Elegant Georgian town house in city centre with tastefully decorated bedrooms, situated in quiet residential area overlooking landscaped public gardens. Front facing top floor bedrooms have views across Edinburgh to the Firth of Forth and the Fife Coast, architectural building. Meals on request.

3 Single	15 En Suite fac	B&B per person	Open Jan-Dec
5 Twin	1 Priv.NOT ensuite	from £22.50 Single	B&B + Eve.Meal
4 Double	2 Pub Bath/Show	from £22.50 Dbl/Twn	from £34.50
6 Family		Room only from £22.50	

HOTEL ★★★★

The Albany Town House Hotel
39 Albany Street, Edinburgh EH1 3QY
Tel: 0131-556 0397 Fax: 0131-557 6633
e.mail: info@albanyhoteledinburgh.co.uk
Web: www.albanyhoteledinburgh.co.uk

You will find the Albany Town House Hotel in the famous New Town less than 10 minutes' walk from the town centre. We have renovated the hotel so that you can enjoy superb comfort in a traditional environment, where you will be spoilt by our attentive and caring team.

HOTEL ★★★★

Albany Hotel
39/43 Albany Street, Edinburgh, EH1 3QY
Tel: 0131 556 0397 Fax: 0131 557 6633
E-mail: info@albanyhoteledinburgh.co.uk
Web: www.albanyhoteledinburgh.co.uk

An elegant Georgian terrace town house situated in a quiet street in Edinburgh's New Town. Retaining many original features and refurbished to a high standard of comfort. A charming intimate restaurant and county house lounge. All main visitor attractions within walking distance.

5 Single	All En Suite	B&B per person	Open Jan-Dec
8 Twin		from £75.00 Single	B&B + Eve.Meal from
8 Double		from £72.50 Dbl/Twn	£115.00

All properties graded by VisitScotland, formerly known as the Scottish Tourist Board. | Key to symbols is on back flap.

B

Map Ref: 2C5

GUEST HOUSE
★★★★

The Alexander Guest House
35 Mayfield Gardens, Edinburgh, EH9 2BX
Tel: 0131 258 4028 Fax: 0131 258 1247
E-mail: alexander@guest68.freeserve.co.uk
Web: www.thealexanderguesthouse.co.uk

Elegantly furnished four star Victorian villa situated one mile from Edinburgh's famous Royal Mile, Castle and Holyrood. Every detail has been thought of in our recently refurbished bedrooms, to make your stay a memorable one. Breakfast time is special at the Alexander with a wide variety of dishes on offer.

2 Single	4 En Suite fac	B&B per person	Open Jan-Dec
2 Twin	1 Pub Bath/Show	from £20.00 Single	
4 Double	1 Limited ensuite	from £20.00 Dbl/Twn	
1 Family		Room only from £20.00	

GUEST HOUSE
★★

Alness Guest House
27 Pilrig Street, Edinburgh, EH6 5AN
Tel: 0131 554 1187

Friendly family run guest house. On main bus route, 1 mile (2kms) from Princes Street and Castle. Close to Port of Leith and Britannia.

1 Single	1 En Suite fac	B&B per person	Open Jan-Dec
1 Twin	2 Pub Bath/Show	£20.00-£25.00 Single	
2 Double	1 Priv.NOT ensuite	£18.00-£26.00 Dbl/Twn	
3 Family		Room only from £15.00	

HOTEL
★★★

Apex European Hotel
90 Haymarket Terrace, Edinburgh, EH9 2NN
Tel: 0131 474 3456 Fax: 0131 220 5345
E-mail: european@apexhotels.co.uk
Web: www.apexhotels.co.uk

Sister hotel to Apex International conveniently situated in the city centre with easy access to Edinburgh airport and especially suited to the business traveller. Small cosmopolitan restaurant specialising in food with a Mediterranean feel.

21 Twin	All En Suite	B&B per person	Open Jan-Dec
46 Double		£60.00-£120.00 Single	
		45.00-£70.00 Dbl/Twn	

HOTEL
★★★

Apex International Hotel
31-35 Grassmarket, Edinburgh, EH1 2HS
Tel: 0131 300 3456 Fax: 0131 220 5345
E-mail: international@apexhotels.co.uk
Web: www.apexhotels.co.uk

Modern hotel in city centre with views towards Edinburgh Castle. Roof top restaurant with spectacular views of the castle. Private car parking. Ideal location for visitors to city without a car.

99 Twin/	All En Suite	B&B per person	Open Jan-Dec
Family		£70.00-£130.00 Single	
76 Double		£50.00-£80.00 Dbl/Twn	

GUEST HOUSE
♿
🖼🖼

Ardgarth Guest House
1 St Mary's Place, Portobello, Edinburgh, EH15 2QF
Tel: 0131 669 3021 Fax: 0131 468 1221
E-mail: rooms@ardgarth.demon.co.uk
Web: www.ardgarth.demon.co.uk

Comfortable accommodation in friendly guest house. Close to sea. Special diets catered for, full ensuite disabled facilities. French spoken. On street parking available.

3 Single	4 En Suite fac	B&B per person	Open Jan-Dec
4 Twin	2 Pub Bath/Show	from £16.00 Single	
3 Family		from £32.00 Dbl/Twn	

Important: Prices stated are estimates and may be subject to amendments

Edinburgh	Map Ref: 2C5

SMALL HOTEL ★★

Ardmillan Hotel
9-10 Ardmillan Terrace, Edinburgh, EH11 2JW
Tel: 0131 337 9588 Fax: 0131 346 1895
E-mail: hotelardmillan@hotmail.com
Web: www.ardmillanhotel.com

Small family run hotel, with recently refurbished popular locals bar. Located on bus route to city centre and only 10 minutes to Princes Street. Murrayfield Leisure and Tynecastle Stadium close-by.

4 Single	12 En Suite fac	B&B per person	Open Jan-Dec
6 Twin	3 Priv.NOT ensuite	from £30.00 Single	B&B + Eve.Meal from
3 Double		from £30.00 Dbl/Twn	£45.00
2 Family		Room only from £50.00	

GUEST HOUSE ★★★

Ard Thor
10 Mentone Terrace, Newington, Edinburgh, EH9 2DG
Tel: 0131 667 1647

Victorian semi-detached villa in quiet residential area. Friendly and family run. Easy access to city centre by car and public transport.

1 Double	2 Pub Bath/Show	B&B per person	Open Jan-Dec excl
1 Family		from £26.00 Single	Xmas
		from £21.00 Dbl/Twn	

GUEST HOUSE ★★★

Arthur's View Guest House
10 Mayfield Gardens, Edinburgh, EH9 2BZ
Tel: 0131 667 3468 Fax: 0131 662 4232
E-mail: arthursview@aol.com
Web: www.arthursview.com

Friendly hotel, personally run by owners, 1.5 miles (3kms) from Royal Mile. Own private parking. On main bus routes.

1 Single	All En Suite	B&B per person	Open Jan-Dec
3 Twin		from £25.00-£40.00	
3 Double			
2 Family			
1 Triple			

GUEST HOUSE ★★★★

Ashlyn Guest House
42 Inverleith Row, Edinburgh, EH5 5PV
Tel/Fax: 0131 552 2954
E-mail: reservations@ashlyn-edinburgh.com

Semi-detached Georgian family home, only 5 minutes walk from the beautiful Botanical Gardens. This listed building retains many original features with ornate cornicing and period fireplaces. 20 minute walk to Princes Street and the Castle with frequent bus service on the door step. Unrestricted free street parking nearby. Self Catering facilities also available.

2 Single	5 Ensuite fac	B&B per person	Open Jan-Dec excl
2 Twin	2 Pub Bath/Show	from £25.00 Single	Xmas
3 Double	2 Priv.NOT ensuite	from £25.00 Dbl/Twn	
1 Family		Room only from £23.00	

GUEST HOUSE ★★★

Auld Reekie Guest House
16 Mayfield Gardens, Edinburgh, EH9 2BZ
Tel: 0131 667 6177 Fax: 0131 662 0033
E-mail: rhona@auldreekiegh.freeserve.co.uk
Web: www.auldreekiegh.freeserve.co.uk

Family run stone built house on south side of city centre. On main bus route to Princes Street.

1 Single	All En Suite	B&B per person	Open Jan-Dec
2 Twin		from £25.00 Single	
2 Double		from £20.00 Dbl/Twn	
2 Family			

All properties graded by VisitScotland, formerly known as the Scottish Tourist Board. | Key to symbols is on back flap. |

Edinburgh | Map Ref: 2C5

HOTEL

The Balmoral Edinburgh
1 Princes Street, Edinburgh, EH2 2EQ
Tel: 0131 556 2414 Fax: 0131 557 8740
E-mail: reservations@thebalmoralhotel.com
Web: www.roccofortehotels.com

Edinburgh's landmark hotel, completely refurbished to international standard.

49 Twin | All En Suite | Room only per person | Open Jan-Dec
119 | | from £175.00 Single | B&B + Eve.Meal from
Double | | from £200.00 Dbl/Twn | £220.00
20 Suites

GUEST HOUSE

Balquhidder Guest House
94 Pilrig Street, Edinburgh, EH6 5AY
Tel: 0131 554 3377
E-mail: enquiries@balquhidderguesthouse.co.uk
Web: www.olstravel.com/guest/balquhid/

Detached house built in 1857, and a former church manse, in its own grounds overlooking public park and on bus routes to the city centre.

1 Single | 5 En Suite fac | B&B per person | Open Jan-Dec excl
2 Twin | 1 Pub Bath/Show | £20.00-£30.00 Single | Xmas/New Year
2 Double | 1 Limited ensuite | £25.00-£30.00 Dbl/Twn
1 Family

GUEST HOUSE

Barony House
23 Mayfield Gardens, Edinburgh, EH9 2BX
Tel/Fax: 0131 667 5806 Fax: 0131 667 6833
E-mail: susieb@baronyhouse.co.uk
Web: www.baronyhouse.co.uk

An impressive detached Victorian villa with off road private parking. Beautifully restored to a very high standard with decorative plasterwork and period cornices. Very comfortable spacious accommodation, all en-suite. Easy access to city centre via main bus route.

2 Single | All En Suite | B&B per person | Open Jan-Dec
2 Twin | | from £35.00 Single | B&B + Eve.Meal from
5 Double | | from £30.00 Dbl/Twn | £44.00
1 Family

GUEST HOUSE

Ben Craig House
3 Craigmillar Park, Edinburgh, EH16 5PG
Tel: 0131 667 2593 Fax: 0131 667 1109
E-mail: bencraighouse@dial.pipex.com
Web: www.bencraighouse.co.uk

Traditional detached sandstone Victorian villa with quiet gardens. Family run, chef proprietor also runs a well known Edinburgh restaurant. On main route for city centre. (1.5 miles south of Princes Street.) Tastefully restored and decorated to high standard. All bedrooms en-suite.

1 Twin | All En Suite | B&B per person | Open Jan-Dec excl Xmas
3 Double | | £25.00-£45.00 Single
1 Family | | £25.00-£45.00 Dbl/Twn
| | Room only £25.00-
| | £38.00

GUEST HOUSE

Ben Cruachan
17 McDonald Road, Edinburgh, EH7 4LX
Tel: 0131 556 3709
E-mail: nan@bencruachan.com
Web: www.bencruachan.com

Centrally located, personally run, terraced house 0.5 mile (1 km) to Princes St. All en-suite bedrooms. Unrestricted street parking. Excellent selection of restaurants nearby Playhouse Theatre, 0.25 mile.

1 Twin | All En Suite | B&B per person | Open Apr-Oct
1 Double | | from £25.00 Dbl/Twn
1 Family

Important: Prices stated are estimates and may be subject to amendments

Edinburgh

Map Ref: 2C5

★★★★

GUEST HOUSE

Ben Doran
11 Mayfield Gardens, Edinburgh, EH9 2AX
Tel: 0131 667 8488 Fax: 0131 667 0076
E-mail: info@bendoran.com
Web: www.bendoran.com

Very comfortable listed Georgian townhouse, beautifully refurbished.
Central, on bus routes, close to city centre and Edinburgh attractions.
Lovely city and hillside views and a warm welcome.

1 Single	6 En Suite fac	B&B per person	Open Jan-Dec
2 Twin	4 Priv.NOT ensuite	from £35.00 Single	B&B + Eve.Meal
4 Double	3 Pub Bath/Show	from £30.00 Dbl/Twn	from £50.00
3 Family			

☑ 🖭 🅿 ⅙✕ (📠

🏤 Ⓦ Ⓥ

BERESFORD HOTEL
32 COATES GARDENS, EDINBURGH EH12 5LE
TEL: 0131 337 0850 FAX: 0131 538 7123
E.MAIL: bookings@beresford-edinburgh.com
WEB: www.beresford-edinburgh.com

Relax in this recently refurbished Victorian town-house. In a prime location only 1/2 mile from Princes Street and all city centre amenities, an ideal base for your visit to Edinburgh. En-suite rooms with direct-dial phones and some with fridges. Children most welcome.

★★★

GUEST HOUSE

Beresford Hotel
32 Coates Gardens, Edinburgh, EH12 5LE
Tel: 0131 337 0850 Fax: 0131 538 7123
E-mail: bookings@beresford-edinburgh.com
Web: www.beresford-edinburgh.com

Family run establishment close to city centre and Haymarket station. Most rooms en-suite. Children most welcome.

3 Twin	10 En Suite	B&B per person	Open Jan-Dec
4 Double	2 Pub Show/Toilet	from £25.00 Single	
5 Family		from £20.00 Dbl/Twn	

☑ 📞 🖭 🍵 🕾 ◢ (📠

Ⓒ 🏤 Ⓥ

★★

GUEST HOUSE

Blossom House
8 Minto Street, Edinburgh, EH9 1RG
Tel: 0131 667 5353 Fax: 0131 667 2813
E-mail: blossom_house@hotmail.com
Web: www.blossomguesthouse.co.uk

Comfortable, family run guest house. City centre within walking distance.
Excellent bus service. Private car park. Close to commonwealth pool.

2 Twin	En Suite fac	B&B per person	Open Jan-Dec
3 Double	Pub Bath/Show	from £20.00 Single	
3 Family		from £17.00 Dbl/Twn	
		Room only from £15.00	

☑ 🖭 🅿 🍵 ⅙✕ (📠

Ⓒ 🏤 Ⓥ

All properties graded by VisitScotland, formerly known as the Scottish Tourist Board.   Key to symbols is on back flap.

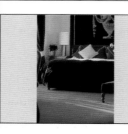

THE

B O N H A M

35 Drumsheugh Gardens,
Edinburgh, EH3 7RN
Tel: 0131 623 6060
Fax: 0131 226 6080
e.mail: reserve@thebonham.com
Web: www.thebonham.com

The Bonham is an award winning, contemporary boutique townhouse. Each of
the 48 spacious rooms has an individual design, using rich bold colours,
maintaining the original Victorian features. Overlooking tree-lined gardens,
situated in Edinburgh's West End, the hotel is just a short walk from the city's
shops and tourist attractions.

★★★★

HOTEL

The Bonham
35 Drumsheugh Gardens, Edinburgh, EH3 7RN
Tel: 0131 623 6060 Fax: 0131 226 6080
E-mail: reserve@thebonham.com
Web: www.thebonham.com

At Edinburgh's West End lies The Bonham designed in rich, bold colours
to give a contemporary feel of the highest quality. All 48 bedrooms are
fitted with the latest in modern equipment including Internet, E-mail,
DVD and CD. The restaurant offers wholesome European dishes using
Scottish produce.

10 Single	All En Suite	B&B per person	Open Jan-Dec
36 Dbl/Twn		from £135.00 Single	
2 Suites		from £165.00 Dbl/Twn	

★★★

GUEST
HOUSE

Brodies Guest House
22 East Claremont Street, Edinburgh, EH7 4JP
Tel: 0131 556 4032 Fax: 0131 556 9739
E-mail: info@brodiesguesthouse.co.uk
Web: www.brodiesguesthouse.co.uk

Small, friendly, family run Victorian town house in a cobbled street
within ¹/₂ mile of Princes Street. Convenient for bus/railway station,
Playhouse theatre, pubs and restaurants nearby. Scottish breakfasts a
speciality.

1 Single	3 En Suite fac	B&B per person	Open Jan-Dec
1 Twin	2 Pub Bath/Show	from £25.00 Single	
1 Double		from £25.00 Dbl/Twn	
2 Family			

★★★★

HOTEL

Bruntsfield Hotel
69 Bruntsfield Place, Edinburgh, EH10 4HH
Tel: 0131 229 1393 Fax: 0131 229 5634
E-mail: bruntsfield@queensferry-hotels.co.uk
Web: www.thebruntsfield.co.uk

Overlooking a park close to the city centre, the Bruntsfield is a well
appointed townhouse hotel with friendly & professional service. The 75
comfortably furnished bedrooms offer all facilities & services required by
both business & leisure travellers. The Potting Shed Restaurant serves
modern Scottish cuisine in an elegant but informal atmosphere. A relaxing
lounge & stylish bar add to the distinctive character of The Bruntsfield.

14 Single	All En Suite	B&B per person	Open Jan-Dec
29 Twin		from £79.00 Single	B&B + Eve.Meal
27 Double		from £55.00 Dbl/Twn	from £59.50
5 Family			

Important: Prices stated are estimates and may be subject to amendments

Caledonian Hilton

PRINCES STREET, EDINBURGH EH1 2AB
Tel: 0131 222 8888   Fax: 0131 222 8889
e.mail: ednchhirm@hilton.com
Web: www.hilton.com

Situated in the heart of the city in the shadow of Edinburgh Castle, The Caledonian Hilton provides the finest possible base from which to explore Scotland's historic capital. The hotel's elegant decor and it's long tradition of attentive and friendly service have charmed guests from around the world for almost a century. The Caledonian Hilton stands as a proud symbol of Scottish hospitality.

★ ★ ★ ★ ★ **HOTEL**

Caledonian Hilton

HOTEL

The Caledonian

Princes Street, Edinburgh, EH1 2AB
Tel: 0131 222 8888 fax: 0131 222 8889
E-mail: ednchhirm@hilton.com

Traditional hotel with friendly atmosphere, elegantly furnished. Situated on world famous Princes Street, affording spectacular views of the castle.

43 Single	All En Suite	B&B per person	Open Jan-Dec
101 Twin		£170.00-£190.00	
82 Double		Single	
23 Suites		£85.00-£170.00	
		Dbl/Twn	

★ ★ ★ ★

GUEST HOUSE

Cameron Toll Guest House

299 Dalkeith Road, Edinburgh, EH16 5JX
Tel: 0131 667 2950 Fax: 0131 662 1987
E-mail: camerontoll@msn.com
Web: www.edinbed.com

Andrew and Mary offer you a cosy bedroom in our friendly guest house with some private parking. Situated on the A7, there is a frequent bus service to the city centre. The Commonwealth Pool is nearby. Scottish hospitality to ensure a memorable stay. Gold award for environmental management.

3 Single	10 En Suite fac	B&B per person	Open Jan-Dec
2 Twin	1 Priv.NOT ensuite	from £26.00 Single	B&B + Eve.Meal
3 Double		from £21.00 Dbl/Twn	from £31.00
3 Family			

PPP

B

Caravel Guest House

30 London Street, Edinburgh, EH3 6NA
Tel: 0131 556 4444 Fax: 0131 557 3615
e.mail: caravelguest@hotmail.com
Web: www.hotels.co.uk/caravel.htm

Family-run hotel within city centre. Caravel Guest House where good hospitality and a warm welcome still exist. Children most welcome. B&B from £20-£30 per person per night.

GUEST HOUSE

Caravel Guest House
30 London Street, Edinburgh, EH3 6NA
Tel: 0131 556 4444 Fax: 0131 557 3615
E-mail: caravelguest@hotmail.com
Web: www.hotels.co.uk/caravel.htm

A warm welcome at this guest house with spacious, en-suite bedrooms. Own restaurant serving many home made specialities. This Georgian house is situated in the heart of Edinburgh's New Town only a few minutes walk from Princes Street and close to Waverley Station and the bus station.

2 Single	with shared fac	B&B per person	Open Jan-Dec
2 Twin	All other rooms	from £25.00 Single	B&B + Eve.Meal from
3 Double	with private fac	from £20.00 Dbl/Twn	£30.00
2 Family		Room only from £20.00	

HOTEL

Carlton Hotel
North Bridge, Edinburgh, EH1 1SD
Tel: 0131 472 3001 Fax: 0131 556 2691
E-mail: carlton@paramount-hotels.co.uk
Web: www.paramount-hotels.co.uk

Central, spacious, hotel refurbished in contemporary style with modern amenities. Leisure complex including squash, aerobics, gym and swimming.

17 Single	All En Suite	B&B per person	Open Jan-Dec
40 Twin		from £50.00 Single	B&B + Eve.Meal
132		from £95.00 Dbl/Twn	from £65.00
Double		Room only from £95.00	

GUEST HOUSE

Carrington Guest House
38 Pilrig Street, Edinburgh, EH6 5AL
Tel: 0131 554 4769

Large family run guest house convenient for all city centre attractions. On street parking.

3 Twin	4 En Suite fac	B&B per person	Open Jan-Dec
2 Double	3 Pub Bath/Show	£22.00-£35.00	
2 Family			

GUEST HOUSE

Castle Park Guest House
75 Gilmore Place, Edinburgh, EH3 9NU
Tel: 0131 229 1215 Fax: 0131 229 1223

Family run guest house close to city centre. Convenient for Kings Theatre and Conference Hall. A variety of local restaurants and bistros. Children welcome.

2 Single	4 En Suite fac	B&B per person	Open Jan-Dec excl
3 Twin		from £17.50 Single	Xmas/New Year
3 Double		from £20.00 Dbl/Twn	
1 Family		Room only per person	
		from £15.00	

Important: Prices stated are estimates and may be subject to amendments

Edinburgh

Map Ref: 2C5

GUEST HOUSE

Castle View Guest House

30 Castle Street, Edinburgh, EH2 3HT
Tel: 0131 226 5784 Fax: 0131 226 1603
E-mail: coranne@castleviewgh.co.uk
Web: www.castleviewgh.co.uk

Spacious Georgian 3rd floor apartment with comfortable lounge area offering views to Castle and the Forth. Ideally positioned approximately 100 metres from Princes St yet a haven above the bustle of the city. Within walking distance of rail and bus stations, and International Conference Centre.

2 Single	5 En Suite fac	B&B per person	Open Jan-Dec excl Xmas
2 Double	1 Priv.NOT ensuite	£30.00-£45.00 Single	
2 Family		£28.00-£42.00 Dbl/Twn	

CHANNINGS
15 South Learmonth Gardens, Edinburgh EH4 1EZ
Tel: 0131 332 3232 Fax: 0131 332 9631
e.mail: reserve@channings.co.uk Web: www.channings.co.uk
Channings is just a few minutes walk from the centre of Edinburgh, providing easy access to shops and Edinburgh Castle. Originally five Edwardian townhouses and facing onto a quiet cobbled street, Channings has 46 individually designed en-suite bedrooms all with traditional, restored period features, providing relaxing and comfortable surroundings.

HOTEL

Channings

15 South Learmonth Gardens, Edinburgh, EH4 1EZ
Tel: 0131 332 3232 Fax: 0131 332 9631
E-mail: reserve@channings.co.uk
Web: www.channings.co.uk

On a peaceful street close to the city centre Channings is a stylish transformation of 5 Edwardian townhouses into an hotel of character and charm. A relaxed ambience pervades from restful firelit lounges to the 46 individually designed guest rooms. Channings Restaurant serves distinctive contemporary Scottish cooking in elegant informal surroundings with terraced gardens and a new conservatory and wine bar creating a welcoming atmosphere.

5 Single	All En Suite	B&B per person	Open Jan-Dec excl
38		from £125.00 Single	Xmas
Dbl/Twn		from £155.00 Dbl/Twn	
3 Suites			

Christopher North House Hotel
★★★
SMALL HOTEL
6 Gloucester Place, Edinburgh EH3 6EF
Tel: 0131 225 2720 Fax: 0131 220 4706
e.mail: reservations@christophernorth.co.uk
Web: www.christophernorth.co.uk

Within the city centre set amid magnificent architecture, the Christopher North House Hotel exudes an air of grace that favours all who delight in the finer things in life. All our rooms and facilities will have you waxing lyrical long after your visit.

SMALL HOTEL

Christopher North House Hotel

6 Gloucester Place, Edinburgh, EH3 6EF
Tel: 0131 225 2720 Fax: 0131 220 4706
E-mail: reservations@christophernorth.co.uk
Web: www.christophernorth.co.uk

Georgian town house hotel situated in Edinburgh's city centre. Convenient for Princes Street and all city centre amenities. The historic nature of the building precludes the provision of a lift. All rooms en-suite. Bar, bistro and leisure facilities available.

1 Single	All En Suite	B&B per person	Open Jan-Dec
4 Twin		from £58.00 Single	
4 Double		from £45.00 Dbl/Twn	
6 Family			

All properties graded by VisitScotland, formerly known as the Scottish Tourist Board. | *Key to symbols is on back flap.*

| Edinburgh | | Map Ref: 2C5 | | |

GUEST HOUSE
★★

Claymore Guest House
68 Pilrig Street, Edinburgh, EH6 5AS
Tel/Fax: 0131 554 2500
E-mail: enquirehere@blueyonder.co.uk

Red sandstone Victorian terraced villa, a former manse. Centrally situated with close proximity to all Edinburgh's main attractions. 10 minutes to Playhouse Theatre.

2 Twin 3 En Suite fac
2 Double 1 Pub Bath/Show
2 Family 1 Priv.NOT ensuite

B&B per person
from £20.00 Dbl/Twn

Open Jan-Dec excl Xmas

GUEST HOUSE
★★★★

Craigelachie Hotel
21 Murrayfield Avenue, Edinburgh, EH12 6AU
Tel: 0131 337 4076 Fax: 0131 313 3304
E-mail: craig01@globalnet.co.uk
Web: http://come.to/edinburgh

Victorian terraced house in a quiet residential area with ample street parking. Near Murrayfield Stadium and bus services to the city centre.

3 Single All En Suite
1 Twin
2 Double
2 Family

B&B per person
from £30.00 Single
from £60.00 Dbl/Twn
Room only from £60.00

Open Jan-Dec

GUEST HOUSE
★★★

Crioch Guest House
23 East Hermitage Place, Edinburgh, EH6 8AD
Tel/Fax: 0131 554 5494
E-mail: welcome@crioch.com
Web: www.crioch.com

Only 10 minutes from the city centre, Crioch overlooks the leafy park of Leith Links. Our recent major refurbishment means that all rooms now have ensuite shower or private bathroom, and you still receive the same warm welcome. Free parking and a frequent bus service leaves you to enjoy Edinburgh's sights on foot, and later a short stroll takes you to Leith's fine cafes, bars and restaurants.

1 Single 5 Ensuite fac
1 Twin 1 Priv.NOT ensuite
2 Double
2 Family

B&B per person
from £22.00 Single
from £22.00 Dbl/Twn
Room only from £19.50

Open Jan-Dec

GUEST HOUSE
★★★

Cruachan Guest House
53 Gilmore Place, Edinburgh, EH3 9NT
Tel/Fax: 0131 229 6219
E-mail: janette@cruachan9.freeserve co.uk
Web: www.cruachan9.freeserve.co.uk

Janette & Graham promise you a warm welcome at this very homely, non-smoking guest house. Situated close to the heart of our beautiful city. We are only 10 minutes walking distance from Castle, Conference Centre, theatres and Princes Street. Private parking 400 yards.

2 Single 4 En Suite
1 Twin 1 Pub Bath/Shower
2 Double
1 Family

B&B per person
£22.00-£35.00 Single
£22.00-£35.00 Dbl/Twn
Family Room £18.00-£30.00 pppn

Open Jan-Dec

Dalhousie Castle and Spa
Bonnyrigg, Nr Edinburgh, Midlothian EH19 3JB
Tel: 01875 820153 Fax: 01875 821936
e.mail: res@dalhousiecastle.co.uk
Web: www.dalhousiecastle.co.uk

Only 20 minutes from Edinburgh city centre this 13th century castle offers whole-hearted Scottish hospitality. 13 of the 32 en-suite bedrooms are historically themed including Robert the Bruce. The Aqueous Hydrotherapy Spa and Orangery, an alternative dining area to the Dungeon restaurant complete the unique services of the castle.

★★★★

HOTEL

Dalhousie Castle and Spa
Bonnyrigg, Edinburgh, Midlothian, EH19 3JB
Tel: 01875 820153 Fax: 01875 821936
E-mail: res@dalhousiecastle.co.uk
Web: www.dalhousiecastle.co.uk

13c Castle set in own parkland. 8 miles (12kms) from the centre of Edinburgh. Orangery and Dungeon Restaurants. New health spa. Helipad. 5 bedrooms in lodge 3 minutes from castle.

2 Single	All En Suite	B&B per person from £80.00 Single	Open mid Jan-Dec
14 Twin		from £52.50 Dbl/Twn	B&B + Eve.Meal
15 Double		Room only per person	from £78.00
3 Family		from £42.00	

📺 ⚡ 📞 🖥 🅿 💷 ⌇ ⚔ 🍴 🛅 🛄 ♿ 🍷

🅲 🐾 ♿ 🅦 🆅

★★

SMALL HOTEL

Dean Hotel
10 Clarendon Crescent, Edinburgh, EH4 1PT
Tel: 0131 332 0308 Fax: 0131 315 4089
E-mail: deanhotel@aol.com
Web: www.deanhotel.co.uk

Personally run hotel in traditional Edinburgh terrace. Close to West End and all amenities. Comfortable and popular lounge bar. No evening meal available, choice of eating places within 200 metres distance. Private garden by Water of Leith available to guests on request. Street parking available (free overnight Mon-Fri and at weekends).

4 Single	5 En Suite fac	B&B per person from £39.00 Single	Open Jan-Dec
3 Twin	2 Pub Bath/Show	from £35.00 Dbl/Twn	
1 Double	4 Priv.NOT ensuite	Room only from £30.00	
1 Family			

📺 📞 🍴 💷 ⚔ 🍷

🅲 🐾 ♿ 🆅

★★★

GUEST HOUSE

Dene Guest House
7 Eyre Place, off Dundas Street, Edinburgh, EH3 5ES
Tel: 0131 556 2700 Fax: 0131 557 9876
E-mail: deneguesthouse@yahoo.co.uk
Web: www.deneguesthouse.com

Charming Georgian townhouse offering friendly service and a relaxed atmosphere. Perfectly located in city centre to experience Edinburgh's culture, history, restaurants and bars.

3 Single	5 En Suite fac	B&B per person from £19.50 Single	Open Jan-Dec
2 Twin	2 Pub Bath/Show	from £19.50 Dbl/Twn	
4 Double			
2 Family			

📺 🍴 💷 📱

🐾 ♿ 🆅

Edinburgh   Map Ref: 2C5

GUEST HOUSE

★★★★

Dorstan Private Hotel
7 Priestfield Road, Edinburgh, EH16 5HJ
Tel: 0131 667 6721 Fax: 0131 668 4644
E-mail: reservations@dorstan-hotel.demon.co.uk
Web: www.dorstan-hotel.demon.co.uk

5 Single	9 En Suite fac	B&B per person	Open Jan-Dec excl New
1 Twin	2 Limited ensuite	£32.00 Single	Year
4 Double	2 Pub Bath/Show	£36.00 Dbl/Twn	
2 Family			

Victorian villa in quiet residential area. Own car parking. 1 mile (2 kms) on main bus route from city centre. Most rooms en suite. Golf course adjacent. Ideal for visiting tourist attractions and surrounding area.

GUEST HOUSE

★★

Dunedin Private House
21-23 Colinton Road, Edinburgh, EH10 5DR
Tel: 0131 447 0679 Fax: 0131 446 9358
E-mail: enquiries@dunedinprivatehouse.com
Web: www.dunedinprivatehouse.com

1 Single	6 En Suite fac	B&B per person	Open Jan-Dec excl Hols
3 Twin	1 Priv.NOT ensuite	from £23.00 Single	
2 Double	2 Limited en suite	from £46.00 Dbl/Twn	
3 Family			

Listed Victorian town house retaining period ambience. Princes St. is approximately 15 minutes walk and close to the regular bus route. A bed and breakfast with basement annexe accommodation with independent front door entrance.

DUNSTANE HOUSE HOTEL
4 West Coates, Haymarket, Edinburgh EH12 5JQ
Tel: 0131 337 6169 Fax: 0131 337 6060
e.mail: reservations@dunstanehousehotel.co.uk
Web: www.dunstanehousehotel.co.uk
Impressive Victorian mansion dating 1850's retaining spectacular original features. All rooms luxuriously refurbished. Four poster deluxe rooms available. Unique bar and restaurant themed on the Scottish islands. Excellent range of malt whiskies stocked. Located in the heart of the city, only minutes from Princes Street, the Castle, conference centre and Edinburgh Airport. Private car park.

SMALL HOTEL

★★★★

Dunstane House Hotel
4 West Coates, Edinburgh, EH12 5JQ
Tel: 0131 337 6169 Fax: 0131 337 6060
E-mail: reservations@dunstanehousehotel.co.uk

4 Single	All En Suite	B&B per person	Open Jan-Dec
2 Twin		from £40.00 Single	
5 Double		from £35.00 Dbl/Twn	
5 Family			

Impressive Listed Victorian mansion retaining many original features enjoying imposing position within large grounds on the A8 airport road (major bus route). 10 mins walk from city centre. Close to Edinburgh Conference Centre, Murrayfield and Edinburgh Zoo. Private secluded car park. Lounge bar. Seafood restaurant. Newly opened bar and restaurant themed on the Scottish Islands.

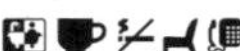

Duthus Lodge Hotel

5 West Coates, Edinburgh EH12 5JG

Tel: 0131-337 6876   e.mail: Duthus.Lodge@ukgateway.net
Fax: 0131-313 2264   Web: www.duthuslodgehotel.com

Splendid detached family-run Victorian establishment offering bed and breakfast
in tastefully decorated and comfortable surroundings. The perfect base to
explore Edinburgh. All rooms ensuite. Ten minutes from city centre, close to
International Conference Centre and Murrayfield stadium. Private parking.

★★★

**GUEST
HOUSE**

Duthus Lodge Hotel

5 West Coates, Edinburgh, EH12 5JG
Tel: 0131 337 6876 Fax: 0131 313 2264
E-mail: Duthus.Lodge@ukgateway.net
Web: www.duthuslodgehotel.com

Detached Victorian sandstone villa with attractive walled gardens. All
rooms with garden or city outlook. Some with views to the Pentland Hills.
Ideal base for exploring Edinburgh's historical attractions. Close to zoo,
Murrayfield Stadium and Conference Centre. On main bus route to city
centre.

1 Single	All En Suite
2 Twin	
2 Double	
2 Family	

B&B per person
£35.00-£45.00 Single
£25.00-£40.00 Dbl/Twn

Open Jan-Dec
Evening meals on
request

Edinburgh First, University of Edinburgh

18 Holyrood Park Road, Edinburgh EH16 5AY
Tel: 0800 028 7118   Fax: 0131-667 7271
e.mail: Edinburgh.First@ed.ac.uk   Web: www.EdinburghFirst.com

Beautiful location only 10 minutes from Princes Street, Edinburgh First's
Pollock Halls are one of Edinburgh's most popular accommodation
centres for people of all ages. With 1,200 modern rooms (500 en-suite),
restaurant, shop, bar, meeting facilities and free parking. Edinburgh First
offers a complete centre in the heart of Edinburgh.

★★

**HOTEL &
CAMPUS**

Edinburgh First

**The University of Edinburgh, 18 Holyrood Park Road, Edinburgh,
EH16 5AY**
Tel: 0800 028 7118 Fax: 0131 667 7271
E-mail: edinburgh.first@ed.ac.uk
Web: www.EdinburghFirst.com

On campus in Holyrood Park beside Arthur's Seat. Close to Royal
Commonwealth Pool, 3 km from city centre. In beautiful surroundings,
we offer comfortable accommodation with en-suite facilities. Particularly
suitable for groups. Alternative annexe accommodation available.
Conference and meeting facilities.

1140 Single	470 En Suite fac
123 Double	

B&B per person
from £27.00 Single
from £69.00 Dbl/Twn

Open Jun-Sept

★★★

HOTEL

Edinburgh Marriott (Royal Scot)

111 Glasgow Road, Edinburgh, EH12 8NF
Tel: 0131 334 9191 Fax: 0131 316 4507
E-mail: edinburgh@marriotthotels.co.uk
Web: www.marriotthotels.co.uk

Modern hotel in outskirts of city and only 5 minutes drive from
Edinburgh Airport.

64 Twin	All En Suite
152 Double	
25 Family	

B&B per person
from £90.00 Single
from £90.00 Dbl/Twn
Room only per person
from £90.00

Open Jan-Dec
B&B + Eve.Meal from
£120.00

All properties graded by VisitScotland, formerly known as the Scottish Tourist Board. | *Key to symbols is on back flap.* |

Edinburgh	Map Ref: 2C5

SERVICED APARTMENTS

The Edinburgh Residence
7 Rothesay Terrace, Edinburgh, EH3 7RY
Tel: 0870 055 0016
E-mail: reservations@residenceinternational.com

New tastefully furnished, quality serviced apartments, in the centre of Edinburgh. Private, secure parking for each apartment on site. Excellent location for castle, theatres and restaurants.

5 Twin
21 Double
8 Family

All En Suite

B&B per person
from £175.00 Single
from £175.00 Dbl/Twn

Open Jan-Dec

HOTEL

Edinburgh's Minto Hotel
16-18 Minto Street, Edinburgh, EH9 9RQ
Tel: 0131 668 1234 Fax: 0131 662 4870

Family run hotel on main A701 road south, with private car park. On main bus route to city centre (10 minutes). Easy access to theatre and Commonwealth Pool.

5 Single
5 Twin
10 Double
3 Family

All En Suite

B&B per person
from £35.00 Single
from £35.00 Dbl/Twn

Open Jan-Dec

GUEST HOUSE

Elder York Guest House
38 Elder Street, Edinburgh, EH1 3DX
Tel: 0131 556 1926 Fax: 0131 624 7140
E-mail: elder-york@eyork.fsbusiness.co.uk

Guest house in centre of city, short walk from Princes St, rail and bus station. Close to car park.

3 Single
3 Twin
6 Double
1 Family

6 En Suite facs
2 Pub Shower

B&B per person
from £27.00 Single
from £25.00 Dbl/Twn

Open Jan-Dec

GUEST HOUSE

Ellesmere House
11 Glengyle Terrace, Edinburgh, EH3 9LN
Tel: 0131 229 4823 Fax: 0131 229 5285
E-mail: celia@edinburghbandb.co.uk
Web: www.edinburghbandb.co.uk

City centre Victorian terraced house in quiet location overlooking Bruntsfield Links with frontage overlooking golf links. Kings Theatre, Conference Centre and all amenities within walking distance. All rooms en suite. Full Scottish Breakfast.

1 Single
2 Twin
2 Double
1 Family

All En Suite

B&B per person
from £28.00 Single
from £56.00 Dbl/Twn

Open Jan-Dec

Important: Prices stated are estimates and may be subject to amendments

EMERALD GUEST HOUSE
3 Drum Street, Gilmerton, Edinburgh EH17 8QQ
Tel: 0131 664 5918 or 664 1920
Fax: 0131 664 1920 Mobile: 07930 889598

Family run Victorian villa within easy reach of city centre.
Convenient to city by-pass for all national routes.
Private parking. Good bus route. Warm welcome assured.

★★

B&B

Emerald Guest House
3 Drum Street, Gilmerton, Edinburgh. EH17 8QQ
Tel: 0131 664 5918
Fax: 0131 664 1920

Family run bed and breakfast located on convenient bus route to city centre. Private parking available.

3 Twin	
2 Double	1 Pub Bath/Show
1 Family	

B&B per person
£25.00-£35.00 Single
£20.00-£35.00 Dbl/Twn

Open Jan-Dec

★★★

HOTEL

Express by Holiday Inn
Britannia Way, Ocean Drive, Edinburgh, EH6 6LA
Tel: 0131 555 4422 Fax: 0131 555 4646
E-mail: info@hiex-edinburgh.com
Web: www.hiex-edinburgh.com

New quality hotel, 1.5 miles from city centre, overlooking Royal Yacht Britannia. Continental breakfast included in room price. Children stay free. Ample parking. In-house bar, power showers, in-room telephones, movies and Sky TV.

36 Twin	All En Suite
30 Double	
36 Family	

B&B per person
from £55.00 Single
from £55.00 Dbl/Twn

Open Jan-Dec excl
Xmas/New Year

★★★

GUEST HOUSE

Fairholme Guest House
13 Moston Terrace, off Mayfield Gardens, Edinburgh, EH9 2DE
Tel: 0131 667 8645 Fax: 0131 668 2435
E-mail: STB@fairholme.co.uk Web: www.fairholme.co.uk

Look no further... Nestled away from noisy traffic yet close to the city centre Fairholme provides facilities for restful relaxation after an eventful day sightseeing. Unwind in an elegant home of comfort, charm and character. Start the day refreshed and replenished after indulging in our traditional Scottish breakfast. You'll be glad you did! Unrestricted parking. Special winter breaks offer.

1 Single	4 En Suite fac
1 Twin	1 Priv.NOT ensuite
2 Double	
1 Family	

B&B per person
from £25.00 Single
from £24.00 Dbl/Twn
Room only per person
from £20.00

Open Jan-Dec excl
Xmas/New Year

★

GUEST HOUSE

Falcon Crest Guest House
70 South Trinity Road, Edinburgh, EH5 3NX
Tel: 0131 552 5294

Victorian terraced family home in attractive residential area, near main bus route to city centre. Free on street parking.

1 Single	3 En Suite fac
2 Twin	2 Pub Bath/Show
2 Double	
1 Family	

B&B per person
from £17.00 Single
from £16.00 Dbl/Twn
Room only per person
from £15.00

Open Jan-Dec

All properties graded by VisitScotland, formerly known as the Scottish Tourist Board. | *Key to symbols is on back flap.* |

Frederick House Hotel

42 Frederick St, Edinburgh, EH2 1EX
Tel: 0131 226 1999 Fax: 0131 624 7064
e.mail: frederickhouse@ednet.co.uk Web: www.townhousehotels.co.uk

Newly opened and tastefully refurbished, Frederick House Hotel offers an atmosphere of comfort and tradition situated in the very heart of Edinburgh city centre with Princes Street practically on our door step. All 45 rooms have en-suite, satellite TV, telephone/modem, refrigerators, tea/coffee, trouser press, hairdryers. We aim to make your stay comfortable.

★★★

LODGE

Frederick House Hotel
42 Frederick Street, Edinburgh, EH2 1EX
Tel: 0131 226 1999 Fax: 0131 624 7064
E-mail: frederickhouse@ednet.co.uk
Web: www.townhousehotels.co.uk

4 Single	All En Suite	B&B per person
9 Twin		from £30.00 Single
16 Double		from £25.00 Dbl/Twn
15 Family		Room only per person
		from £20.00

Open Jan-Dec

Situated in the heart of Edinburgh close to all city centre amenities and with a wide variety of restaurants and bars in the immediate vicinity. Georgian building with all rooms recently refurbished to a high standard with en-suite facilities, fridges and modem points. Princes Street just 50 yards away. Street parking.

★★★

GUEST HOUSE

Galloway
22 Dean Park Crescent, Edinburgh, EH4 1PH
Tel/Fax: 0131 332 3672

2 Single	6 En Suite fac	B&B per person
2 Twin	3 Pub/Bath Show	from £30.00 Single
2 Double	1 Priv.NOT ensuite	from £20.00 Dbl/Twn
4 Family		

Open Jan-Dec excl
Xmas/New Year

Friendly, family run guest house, beautifully restored and situated in a residential area, 10 minutes walk from Princes Street and convenient for Edinburgh International Conference Centre. Free street parking.

★★★★

HOTEL

The George Inter-Continental Hotel
19-21 George Street, Edinburgh, EH2 2PB
Tel: 0131 225 1251 Fax: 0131 226 5644
E-mail: edinburgh@interconti.com
Web: www.edinburgh.interconti.com

51 Single	All En Suite	B&B per person
94 Twin		from £85.00 Single
47 Double		from £65.00 Dbl/Twn
3 Suites		Room only from £80.00

Open Jan-Dec

Located in heart of business and commercial centre of city. The hotel offers extensive Scottish and French cuisine in classically elegant surroundings.

★★★★

GUEST HOUSE

Gifford House
103 Dalkeith Road, Edinburgh, EH16 5AJ
Tel/Fax: 0131 667 4688
E-mail: giffordhotel@btinternet.com

1 Single	All En Suite	B&B per person
2 Twin		from £22.00 Single
2 Double		from £20.00 Dbl/Twn
2 Family		Room only per person
		from £18.00

Open Jan-Dec

A well appointed Victorian stone built house situated on one of the main routes into Edinburgh. Close to Holyrood Park and Arthur's Seat and only 300 metres from Royal Commonwealth Swimming Pool. Regular bus services to all city amenities. Well positioned for conference centre.

Important: Prices stated are estimates and may be subject to amendments

Edinburgh

Map Ref: 2C5

★★★

GUEST HOUSE

Gil-Dun Guest House

9 Spence Street, Edinburgh, EH16 5AG
Tel: 0131 667 1368 Fax: 0131 668 4989
E-mail: gildun.edin@btinternet.com

1 Single	5 En Suite fac	B&B per person	Open Jan-Dec
1 Twin	2 Pub Bath/Show	£18.00-£35.00 Single	
1 Double	1 Priv.NOT ensuite	£18.00-£35.00 Dbl/Twn	
5 Family			

A warm and freindly run guest house situated in cul de sac with private parking. Close to Commonwealth Pool and bus route to city centre. Cameron Toll Shopping Centre nearby and situated near University Halls of Residence. A variety of eating establishments within walking distance.

★★★

GUEST HOUSE

Glenorchy Guest House

22 Glenorchy Terrace, Edinburgh, EH9 2DH
Tel: 0131 667 5708 Fax: 0131 667 1201

2 Twin	B&B per person	Open Jan-Dec
3 Double	from £20.00 Dbl/Twn	
1 Family		

Privately owned Victorian house situated in quiet residential area, convenient for bus routes to city centre. Unrestricted parking. Non smoking throughout.

Greenside Hotel
9 Royal Terrace, Edinburgh EH7 5AB
TEL: 0131-557 0022/0121   FAX: 0131-557 0022
e.mail: greensidehotel@ednet.co.uk   Web: www.townhousehotels.co.uk
Elegant Georgian Townhouse hotel ideally situated in the city centre within walking distance to Princes Street, Waverley train station, Edinburgh Castle and The Playhouse Theatre combining traditional features with modern facilities, the hotel offers superb views, private gardens and friendly atmosphere together providing the perfect blend of history and hospitality.

★★★

SMALL HOTEL

Greenside Hotel

9 Royal Terrace, Edinburgh, EH7 5AB
Tel: 0131 557 0022/0121 Fax: 0131 557 0022
E-mail: greensidehotel@ednet.co.uk
Web: www.townhousehotels.co.uk

3 Single	All En Suite	B&B per person	Open Jan-Dec
4 Twin		from £22.50 Single	B&B + Eve.Meal
5 Double		from £22.50 Dbl/Twn	from £34.50
4 Family		Room only from £22.50	

Personally run hotel in traditional Georgian terraced house. Quiet location, close to Princes Street and all amenities. 10 minutes walk from Waverley Station and Princes Street. Excellent selection of restaurants in immediate vicinity. Building of architectural interest. Evening meals on request.

★

GUEST HOUSE

Halcyon Hotel

8 Royal Terrace, Edinburgh, EH7 5AB
Tel: 0131 556 1033/2
E-mail: patricia@halcyon-hotel.com
Web: www.halcyon-hotel.com

4 Single	14 Ensuite fac	B&B per person	Open Jan-Dec
4 Twin	2 Pub Bath/Show	Min £35.00 -	
4 Double	2 Priv.NOT ensuite	Max £45.00 inclusive	
4 Family	2 Limited ensuite	pppn	

Within walking distance of Princes Street, Georgian terrace property in quiet area. 5 minutes walk from bus station, 10 minutes walk from Waverly Station. Metered street parking available.

All properties graded by VisitScotland, formerly known as the Scottish Tourist Board.   **Key to symbols is on back flap.**

Edinburgh   Map Ref: 2C5

GUEST HOUSE ★★★

Hanover House Hotel
26 Windsor Street, Edinburgh, EH7 5JR
Tel: 0131 556 1325 Fax: 0131 556 1325
E-mail: enquiries@hanoverhousehotel.co.uk
Web: www.hanoverhousehotel.co.uk

1 Twin	All En Suite
3 Double	
1 Family	

B&B per person
£40.00-£50.00 Single
£25.00-£35.00 Dbl/Twn

Open Jan-Dec excl Xmas

A recently refurbished family run Guest House offering comfortable accommodation in quiet area near to free on street parking.

GUEST HOUSE ★

Harvest Guest House
33 Straiton Place, Portobello, Edinburgh, EH15 2BA
Tel: 0131 657 3160 Fax: 0131 468 7028
E-mail: sadol@blueyonder.co.uk
Web: www.harvestguesthouse.co.uk

1 Single	2 En Suite fac
1 Twin	1 Pub Bath/Show
3 Double	
2 Family	

B&B per person per
night from £16.00-
£25.00 Single
from £15.00-£24.00
Dbl/Twn

Open Jan-Dec

Terraced house in quiet residential area with garden giving direct access to beach and promenade. Front bedrooms have super views of the Firth of Forth. Some private and street parking. Variety of eating establishments locally. Frequent bus service provides easy access to city centre.

SMALL HOTEL ★★★

Haymarket Hotel
1 Coates Gardens, Edinburgh, EH12 5LG
Tel: 0131 337 1045/1775 Fax: 0131 313 0330
E-mail: ritchie@haymarket-hotel.co.uk
Web: www.haymarket-hotel.co.uk

2 Single	All En Suite
2 Twin	
4 Double	
4 Family	

B&B per person
from £37.50 Single
from £27.50 Dbl/Twn
Room only from £25.00

Open Jan-Dec
B&B + Eve.Meal
from £65.00

Personally run, privately owned hotel within a short walking distance of Haymarket railway station and west end of Princes Street. Evening meal by prior arrangement. Large screen TV in lounge bar. Free on-street parking (6.30pm-8.30am).

HOTEL ★★

Herald House Hotel
70 Grove Street, Edinburgh, EH3 8AP
Tel: 0131 228 2323 Fax: 0131 228 3101
E-mail: info@heraldhousehotel.co.uk
Web: www.heraldhousehotel.co.uk

8 Single	All En Suite
16 Twin	
14 Double	
7 Family	

B&B per person
from £42.00 Single
from £28.00 Dbl/Twn

Open Jan-Dec excl
Xmas

Traditional Victorian stone faced building located close to city centre. Fully modernised but small enough to give individual attention. 500m from Edinburgh Conference Centre. Limited street parking (free 6.30pm - 8.30am & all day Sunday) off street parking near by. Dinner is not available but there are many restaurants within walking distance.

GUEST HOUSE ★★★

Hermitage Guest House
16 East Hermitage Place, Leith Links, Edinburgh, EH6 8AB
Tel: 0131 555 4868 Fax: 0870 1249537
Web: www.guesthouse-edinburgh.com

1 Single	5 En Suite fac
2 Twin	1 Priv.NOT ensuite
2 Double	
1 Family	

B&B per person
from £20.00 Single
from £20.00 Dbl/Twn

Open Jan-Dec

Brenda extends a warm and friendly welcome to you at her Victorian Terraced House overlooking historic Leith Links. Excellent restaurants nearby or city centre only 10 minutes journey by bus. Unrestricted street parking. Business support service available on request.

Important: Prices stated are estimates and may be subject to amendments

Edinburgh   Map Ref: 2C5

HOTEL

Holyrood Hotel
Holyrood Road, Edinburgh, EH8 6AE
Tel: 0131 550 4500

57 Twin	All En Suite	Room only per person	Open Jan-Dec
100		from £90.00 Single	
Double		from £120.00 Dbl/Twn	

City centre hotel, situated close to the new Scottish Parliament, Dynamic Earth and the Palace of Holyrood House. Leisure facilities including pool; valet parking available.

SMALL HOTEL

The Howard
34 Great King Street, Edinburgh, EH3 6QH
Tel: 0131 315 2220 Fax: 0131 557 6515
E-mail: reserve@thehoward.com
Web: www.thehoward.com

5 Twin	All En Suite	B&B per person	Open Jan-Dec excl
8 Double		£175.00 Single	Xmas
5 Suites		£255.00 Dbl/Twn	

Restored Georgian Town House situated in the New Town, within easy walking distance of Princes St. Small conference/wedding suite available. Parking available.

GUEST HOUSE

International Guest House
37 Mayfield Gardens, Edinburgh, EH9 2BX
Tel: 0131 667 2511 Fax: 0131 667 1112
E-mail: intergh@easynet.co.uk
Web: www.accommodation-edinburgh.com

4 Single	All En Suite	B&B per person	Open Jan-Dec
2 Twin		from £25.00 Single	
2 Double		from £20.00 Dbl/Twn	
1 Family			

Stone built Victorian house in residential area with regular bus service to city centre. All rooms have ensuite facilities. Some private parking and on-street parking. Ground floor room available for persons with limited mobility.

The Inverleith Hotel
5 Inverleith Terrace, Edinburgh, EH3 5NS
Tel: 0131 556 2745 Fax: 0131 557 0433
E-mail: info@inverleithhotel.co.uk
Web: www.inverleithhotel.co.uk

SMALL HOTEL

2 Single	All En Suite	B&B per person	Open Jan-Dec excl
2 Twin		from £28.00 Single	Xmas/New Year
2 Double		from £55.00 Dbl/Twn	
2 Family		Room only per person	
		from £25.00	

Under new ownership this townhouse is situated a short walk from city centre. Excellent bus service. Free on-street parking. Close to botanical gardens. Group discount.

Jewel and Esk Valley College

24 MILTON ROAD EAST, EDINBURGH EH15 2PP
TEL: 0131 657 7252 FAX: 0131 657 7253
e.mail: tgilchri@jevc.ac.uk Web: www.jewel-esk.ac.uk
Student halls of residence in quiet suburb, 4 miles east of city centre
(frequent bus service takes 15 mins). Easy access to bypass and motorways.
Rooms have washbasin and tea/coffee tray. Limited access to on-site
leisure/swimming facilities. Ample parking. Open Jan-Nov.

★

**CAMPUS
ACCOMMODATION**

Jewel & Esk Valley College
24 Milton Road East, Edinburgh, EH15 2PP
Tel: 0131 657 7252 Fax: 0131 657 7253
E-mail: tgilchri@jevc.ac.uk

Student halls of residence in quiet residential suburb on excellent bus
route to city centre. Ample parking. Limited access to indoor pool.

100	42 Pub Bath/Show	B&B per person	Open Jan-Nov
Single		from £23.50 Single	
2 Twin		from £47.00 Dbl/Twn	
2 Double			

★★★

HOTEL

&

Jurys Inn
43 Jeffrey Street, Edinburgh, EH1 1DG
Tel: 0131 200 3300 Fax: 0131 200 0400
E-mail: bookings@jurysdoyle.com
Web: www.jurysdoyle.com

Jury's Inn's superb city centre location (adjacent to Royal Mile, Princes
Street and Waverley Station) is combined with incredible value for
money. For a fixed rate your room can accommodate up to 3 adults or 2
adults and 2 children. All rooms are ensuite and have direct dial phone,
satellite TV, hairdryer, modem and tea and coffee making facilities.
Warm welcome and friendly prices in the Inn Pub and Arches restaurant.

5 Single	All En Suite	B&B per person	Open Jan-Dec excl Xmas
91 Twin		from £50.00 Single	B&B + Eve.Meal from
90 Double		from £35.00 Dbl/Twn	£50.00
		Room only from £30.00	

★★

**GUEST
HOUSE**

Kariba Guest House
10 Granville Terrace, Edinburgh, EH10 4PQ
Tel: 0131 229 3773 Fax: 0131 229 4968
E-mail: karibaguesthouse@hotmail.com

A Victorian house on major bus route to city centre about 10 minutes
away. Restaurants, theatres and International Conference Centre all
within easy reach. Private car parking.

3 Twin	6 En Suite fac	B&B per person	Open Jan-Dec
4 Double	1 Priv.NOT ensuite	from £20.00 Single	
2 Family	2 Pub Bath/Show	from £18.00 Dbl/Twn	
	1 Limited ensuite	Room only from £18.00	

Important: Prices stated are estimates and may be subject to amendments

KENVIE GUEST HOUSE

16 Kilmaurs Road, Edinburgh EH16 5DA
Tel: 0131 668 1964 Fax: 0131 668 1926
e.mail: dorothy@kenvie.co.uk Web: www.kenvie.co.uk

Quiet and comfortable house situated in a residential area with easy access to City Centre on an excellent bus route. All rooms have tea and coffee-making facilities and TVs. Central heating throughout. *A warm and friendly welcome is guaranteed.*

★★★

**GUEST
HOUSE**

Kenvie Guest House

16 Kilmaurs Road, Edinburgh, EH16 5DA
Tel: 0131 668 1964 Fax: 0131 668 1926
E-mail: dorothy@kenvie.co.uk
Web: www.kenvie.co.uk

A charming, comfortable, warm, friendly family run Victorian town house in a quiet residential street. Very close to bus routes and the city by-pass. We offer for your comfort, lots of caring touches including complimentary tea / coffee, colour TV and no-smoking rooms. En-suite available and vegetarians catered for. You are guaranteed a warm welcome from Richard and Dorothy.

2 Twin	3 En Suite fac	B&B per person	Open Jan-Dec
2 Double	2 Pub Bath/Show	from £20.00 Dbl/Twn	
1 Family		Room only from £18.00	

★★★★

**SMALL
HOTEL**

Kew House

1 Kew Terrace, Murrayfield, Edinburgh, EH12 5JE
Tel: 0131 313 0700 Fax: 0131 313 0747
E-mail: kewhouse@ednet.co.uk
Web: www.kewhouse.com

We offer comfort in a contemporary style and cater for both business and tourist customers alike. Our immaculately decorated ensuite rooms have all the essentials you require for a comfortable stay. We are just a short walk or brief bus trip from the city centre and on the main road from the airport. We have a residents drinks license and serve light meals. Hot breakfast is included in the tariff.

1 Single	All En Suite	B&B per person	Open Jan-Dec
1 Twin		from £50.00 Single	
3 Double		from £66.00 Dbl/Twn	
1 Family			

★★★

**GUEST
HOUSE**

Kingsley Guest House

30 Craigmillar Park, Edinburgh, EH16 5PS
Tel: 0131 667 3177 Tel/Fax: 0131 667 8439
E-mail: accom.kingsley@virgin.net
Web: www.kingsleyguesthouse.co.uk

Friendly, comfortable family run Victorian villa with own private car park. Excellent bus service for all major attractions in the city. Close to university area and Commonwealth Pool.

1 Twin	4 En Suite fac	B&B per person	Open Jan-Dec
2 Double	1 Priv.NOT ensuite	from £22.00 Single	
2 Family		from £20.00 Dbl/Twn	

★★

**GUEST
HOUSE**

Kingsview Guest House

28 Gilmore Place, Edinburgh, EH3 9NQ
Tel/Fax: 0131 229 8004
E-mail: kingsviewguesthouse@talk21.com
Web: www.kingsviewguesthouse.com

Family run, city centre guest house conveniently situated near the Kings Theatre. Close to all main bus routes.

1 Single	3 En Suite fac	B&B per person	Open Jan-Dec
2 Twin	1 Pub Shower	from £18.00 Single	
2 Double	1 Limited Ensuite	from £18.00 Dbl/Twn	
4 Family			

All properties graded by VisitScotland, formerly known as the Scottish Tourist Board. | *Key to symbols is on back flap.*

King's Manor Hotel

100 Milton Road East, Edinburgh EH15 2NP
Tel: 0131 669 0444 Fax: 0131 669 6650
e.mail: reservations@kingsmanor.com Web: www.kingsmanor.com

Family owned and managed hotel in suburbs of Edinburgh.
70 well-appointed bedrooms. Two bars, full-service restaurant and bistro.
New extensive leisure club with 20-metre pool, sauna, solarium and full gym.
Short breaks and special interest holidays. Open to non-residents.

HOTEL

Kings Manor Hotel
100 Milton Road East, Edinburgh, EH15 2NP
Tel: 0131 669 0444 Fax: 0131 669 6650
E-mail: reservations@kingsmanor.com
Web: www.kingsmanor.com

Family run hotel 4 miles (6kms) east of city centre, handy for beach and all major road routes. Extensive modern leisure facilities.

11 Single	All En Suite
38 Twin	
14 Double	
2 Family	

B&B per person
from £35.00 Single
from £70.00 Dbl/Twn

Open Jan-Dec
B&B + Eve.Meal
from £50.00

GUEST HOUSE

Kingsway
5 East Mayfield, Edinburgh, EH9 1SD
Tel: 0131 667 5029 Fax: 0131 662 4635
E-mail: room@edinburgh-guesthouse.com
Web: www.edinburgh-guesthouse.com

Friendly family run guest house in Victorian terrace in quiet residential area near bus routes and 1 mile (1.5 kms) from Princes Street. Private car park. Choice of restaurants nearby.

1 Single	4 En Suite facs
2 Twin	2 Pub Shower/WC
2 Double	1 Priv.NOT ensuite
2 Family	

B&B per person
from £35.00 Single
from £40.00 Dbl/Twn

Open Jan-Dec

GUEST HOUSE

The Lairg
11 Coates Gardens, Edinburgh, EH12 5LG
Tel: 0131 337 1050 Fax: 0131 346 2167
E-mail: info@thelairghotel.co.uk
Web: www.thelairghotel.co.uk

A warm welcome at this personally run guest house within easy access to city centre and all tourist attractions.

1 Single	All En Suite
3 Twin	
2 Double	
3 Family	

B&B per person
from £28.00 Single
from £25.00 Dbl/Twn

Open Jan-Dec excl
Xmas/New Year

GUEST HOUSE

Lauderville House
52 Mayfield Road, Edinburgh, EH9 2NH
Tel: 0131 667 7788 Fax: 0131 667 2636
E-mail: res@laudervilleguesthouse.co.uk
Web: www.LaudervilleGuestHouse.co.uk

Brian and Yvonne Marriott welcome visitors to their restored Victorian Town House, centrally situated with easy access to city centre. Comfortable rooms, excellent breakfast, including vegetarian. Some secure private parking available. Totally non smoking house.

1 Single	All En Suite
2 Twin	
6 Double	
1 Family	

B&B per person
£28.00-£45.00 Single
£25.00-£40.00 Dbl/Twn

Open Jan-Dec

Important: Prices stated are estimates and may be subject to amendments

Edinburgh

Map Ref: 2C5

GUEST HOUSE

Lindsay Guest House
108 Polwarth Terrace, Edinburgh, EH11 1NN
Tel: 0131 337 1580 Fax: 0131 337 9174
E-mail: bill@lindsay-polwarth.demon.co.uk

1 Single	3 En Suite fac	B&B per person	Open Jan-Dec excl
2 Twin	2 Pub Bath/Show	from £20.00 Single	Xmas/New Year
2 Double		from £25.00 Dbl/Twn	
2 Family			

Listed semi-detached sandstone house in residential area on bus route to city centre. 1.5 miles (3 kms) from Princes St. Car parking. TVs in all bedrooms.

GUEST HOUSE

Lorne Villa Guest House
9 East Mayfield, Edinburgh, EH9 1SD
Tel/Fax: 0131 667 7159
E-mail: lornevilla@cableinet.co.uk

1 Single	3 En Suite fac	B&B per person	Open Jan-Dec
3 Twin	1 Priv.NOT ensuite	£18.00-£36.00 Single	B&B + Eve.Meal
2 Double	1 Pub Bath/Show	£18.00-£36.00 Dbl/Twn	from £28.00
1 Family			

Personally run guest house conveniently situated for city centre bus route with off street parking. Ground floor ensuite bedroom. Dinner available on request.

THE LODGE HOTEL
6 Hampton Terrace, West Coates, Edinburgh, EH12 5JD
TEL: 0131 337 3682 FAX: 0131 313 1700
E.MAIL: thelodgehotel@btconnect.com WEB: www.thelodgehotel.co.uk

Elegant West End hotel beautifully appointed throughout offering guests the highest quality of service and accommodations. Ideally situated close to city and conference centres with easy access from airport and railway station. Car parking available. Ask about our special spring and winter tariffs from £29 per person per night.

SMALL HOTEL

The Lodge Hotel
6 Hampton Terrace, West Coates, Edinburgh, EH12 5JD
Tel: 0131 337 3682 Fax: 0131 313 1700
E-mail: thelodgehotel@btconnect.com
Web: www.thelodgehotel.co.uk

1 Single	All En Suite	B&B per person	Open Jan-Dec
2 Twin		from £38.00 Single	
7 Double		from £58.00 Dbl/Twn	

The Lodge Hotel is a private hotel which has been extended and refurbished yet has retained many features of an elegant Georgian residence. The lodge is situated on the main A8 Edinburgh to Glasgow road convenient for the city centre, conference centre and airport. Guests can relax in the cocktail bar before enjoying a freshly prepared dinner with emphasis on fresh local produce when available. Non smoking house. Private car park.

GUEST HOUSE

Mackenzie Guest House
2 East Hermitage Place, Edinburgh, EH6 8AA
Tel: 0131 554 3763
Fax: 0131 554 0853
E-mail: mackenzie.house@virgin.net
Web: www.mackenzieguesthouse.co.uk

1 Single	2 En Suite fac	B&B per person	Open Jan-Dec
2 Twin	2 Pub Bath/Show	£25.00-£35.00 Single	
2 Double	1 Priv.NOT ensuite	£22.00-£35.00 Dbl/Twn	
3 Family			

A warm friendly welcome awaits you at this family run Victorian terraced home overlooking Leith Links. Within easy walking distance of Royal Yacht Britannia, restaurants and bars at the waterfront of Leith. Street parking. 1.5 miles to city centre on main bus route. Non smoking.

All properties graded by VisitScotland, formerly known as the Scottish Tourist Board.   Key to symbols is on back flap.

Edinburgh | Map Ref: 2C5

GUEST HOUSE

Meriden Guest House
1 Hermitage Terrace, Morningside, Edinburgh, EH10 4RP
Tel: 0131 447 5152
E-mail: info@meridenguesthouse.co.uk
Web: www.meridenguesthouse.co.uk

Stone built Victorian terraced house in quiet residential area. Theatres, restaurants, shops and universities nearby. Central location with bus service to city centre. Completely non-smoking. Dogs welcome.

2 Twin
2 Double
1 Family

1 En Suite fac
2 Pub Bath/Show

B&B per person
£28.00-£35.00 Single
£20.00-£30.00 Dbl/Twn
Room only £26.00-£30.00

Open Jan-Dec

GUEST HOUSE

Milton House
24 Duddingston Crescent, Edinburgh, EH15 3AT
Tel: 0131 669 4072
E-mail: milton-house@blueyonder.co.uk

Friendly family atmosphere with off street parking and easy access to the city centre. Adjacent to 9 hole golf course. Dog friendly household.

1 Twin
3 Double

2 En Suite

B&B per person
from £18.00 Single
from £18.00 Dbl/Twn
Room only from £18.00

Open Jan-Dec

GUEST HOUSE

Newington Guest House
18 Newington Road, Edinburgh, EH9 1QS
Tel: 0131 667 3356 Fax: 0131 667 8307
E-mail: newington.guesthouse@dial.pipex.com
Web: www.newington-gh.co.uk

Interestingly furnished Victorian house on main road into city from south. Easy access to centre. Most rooms double glazed.

1 Single
2 Twin
3 Double
3 Family

6 Ensuite fac
1 Pub Bath/Show
3 Limited ensuite

B&B per person
from £35.00 Single
from £23.50 Dbl/Twn

Open Jan-Dec excl Xmas

B&B

Mrs D R Frackelton
17 Hope Park Terrace, Edinburgh, EH8 9LZ
Tel: 0131 667 7963

Ground floor flat 15 minutes walk to Princes Street (1 mile) 10 mins. Royal mile, 7 mins University and Royal College of Surgeons. Central to all attractions.

2 Double

1 Pub Bath/Show

B&B per person
from £23.00 Double

Open Apr-Oct

HOTEL

Old Waverley Hotel
43 Princes Street, Edinburgh, EH2 2BY
Tel: 0131 556 4648 Fax: 0131 557 5791

City centre hotel overlooking Princes Street Gardens within 100 yards of Waverley station. Views of Castle and Scott Monument. Use of leisure facilities of sister hotel on North Bridge.

11 Single
32 Twin
20 Double
3 Family

All En Suite

B&B per person
from £70.00 Single
from £120.00 Dbl/Twn

Open Jan-Dec

Important: Prices stated are estimates and may be subject to amendments

Osbourne Hotel

51-59 York Place, Edinburgh EH1 3JD

Tel: 0131 556 5577   Fax: 0131 556 1012
e.mail: reservations@osbourne-hotel.com
Web: www.osbourne-hotel.com

Ideal city centre location within easy
walking distance of Edinburgh's main
attractions and rail and coach stations.
With 46 ensuite rooms, restaurant, bar, lift,
night porter, etc. Start your holiday with
us. Low season £36; high season £56 per
ensuite single including fully cooked buffet
breakfasts. We book tickets and tours.
Friendly service and reasonable rates.

★

HOTEL

Osbourne Hotel
51-59 York Place, Edinburgh, EH1 3JD
Tel: 0131 556 5577 Fax: 0131 556 1012
E-mail: reservations@osbourne-hotel.com
Web: www.osbourne-hotel.com

Personally run hotel close to city centre and all amenities. Short distance from railway and bus stations.

10 Single	All En Suite	B&B per person	Open Jan-Dec
9 Twin		from £36.00 Single	B&B + Eve.Meal from
10 Double		from £72.00 Dbl/Twn	£46.00
7 Family		Room only from £36.00	

📺 📞 🛗 🍴 🔟 🏆

C £ V

★★★

**GUEST
HOUSE**

Parklands Guest House
20 Mayfield Gardens, Edinburgh, EH9 2BZ
Tel: 0131 667 7184 Fax: 0131 667 2011
E-mail: parklands_guesthouse@yahoo.com

Look forward to a warm welcome at this late Victorian house with fine woodwork and ceilings. Situated on the south side, on main bus routes to city centre. Close to University.

2 Twin	5 En Suite fac	B&B per person	Open Jan-Dec
3 Double	1 Priv.NOT ensuite	from £22.00 Single	
1 Family		from £20.00 Dbl/Twn	

📺 🛗 📶 🅿️ 🍴 🔌 ✂️ 📞

HOTEL

Parliament House Hotel
15 Calton Hill, Edinburgh, EH1 3BJ
Tel: 0131 478 4000 Fax: 0131 478 4001
E-mail: phhadams@aol.com
Web: www.scotland-hotels.co.uk

New town house hotel in city centre location and situated on historic Calton Hill a few minutes walk from Princes Street and the Playhouse Theatre. 3 minutes walk from Waverley Train Station. Discounts Parking at nearby Greenside Multi-storey. "MP's" Bistro available for dinner and non-residents welcome.

2 Single	All En Suite	B&B per person	Open Jan-Dec
10 Twin		from £50.00 Single	
40 Double		from £35.00 Dbl/Twn	
1 Family			

📺 📞 🛗 📶 🔌 🍴 🔟 🏆

£ W V

All properties graded by VisitScotland, formerly known as the Scottish Tourist Board. | Key to symbols is on back flap.

Edinburgh   **Map Ref: 2C5**

HOTEL ★★

Piries Hotel
4-8 Coates Gardens, Edinburgh, EH12 5LB
Tel: 0131 337 1108 Fax: 0131 346 0279
E-mail: regvarma@aol.com

4 Single	All En Suite	B&B per person	Open Jan-Dec
10 Twin		from £29.00 Single	
10 Double		from £20.00 Dbl/Twn	
6 Family			

Comfortably furnished privately owned, stone terraced building in West End of city. City centre location, within walking distance of Princes Street, and EICC. Selection of bar meals available.

HOTEL ★★★

Point Hotel
34 Bread Street, Edinburgh, EH3 9AF
Tel: 0131 221 5555 Fax: 0131 221 9929
E-mail: sales@point-hotel.co.uk
Web: www.point-hotel.co.uk

87 Twin	All En Suite	B&B per person	Open Jan-Dec excl Xmas
41 Double		from £95.00 Single	
8 Family		from £47.50 Dbl/Twn	

Contemporary and unique hotel with spectacular castle views, Monboddo Bar and superb restaurant. Centrally located, easy walking distance to Royal Mile and Princes Street.

GUEST HOUSE ★★★

Portobello House
2 Pittville Street, Edinburgh, EH15 2BY
Tel: 0131 669 6067 Fax: 0131 657 9194
E-mail: portobello.house@virgin.net
Web: http://freespace.virgin.net/portobello.house/index.htm

2 Single	B&B per person	Open Jan-Dec excl Xmas
1 Twin	from £17.50 Single	
2 Double	from £17.50 Dbl/Twn	
1 Family	Room only from £15.00	

Situated in a quiet residential Cul - De - Sac leading to the sea and sandy beach 100 mts distance. This large Victorian villa offers stylish accommodation in a relaxed ambience attracting all who appreciate quality at reasonable expense. Free parking area, with excellent bus service to city centre 15 mins, 4 miles distance. Mostly organic food served.

Priestville Guest House

10 Priestfield Road, Edinburgh, EH16 5HJ. Tel/Fax: 0131 667 2435
E.mail: priestville@hotmail.com Web: www.priestville.f2s.com

Friendly Scottish hospitality in grandly proportioned Victorian town house. 20 minutes walk from city centre. Vegetarians catered for. Broadband internet access. Pets welcome by arrangement. Colour TV and video in all rooms. Family rooms available. One minute from golf course and two minutes from Royal Commonwealth Pool, gym and fitness centre.

GUEST HOUSE ★★★

Priestville Guest House
10 Priestfield Road, Edinburgh, EH16 5HJ
Tel/Fax: 0131 667 2435
E-mail: priestville@hotmail.com
Web: www.priestville.f2s.com

2 Single	B&B per person	Open Jan-Dec
2 Twin	£23.00-£35.00 Single	
2 Double	£20.00-£32.00 Dbl/Twn	
2 Family	Room only £18.00-£30.00	

Semi detached Victorian villa in quiet residential area but close to main bus routes to city centre, about 15 minutes away. Close to Cameron Toll shopping centre and Holyrood Palace and park.

Important: Prices stated are estimates and may be subject to amendments

Edinburgh

Map Ref: 2C5

HOTEL ★★

Ritz Hotel
14-18 Grosvenor Street, Edinburgh, EH12 5EG
Tel: 0131 337 4315 Fax: 0131 346 0597

3 Single	All En Suite	B&B per person	Open Jan-Dec
19 Twin		from £52.90 Single	
10 Double		from £40.00 Dbl/Twn	
4 Family			

On five floors, each room of individual character, some featuring four poster beds. Within easy walking distance of Haymarket railway station and West End of Princes Street. There is a wide range of restaurants available in the city centre, or evening meals are available by prior arrangement.

SMALL HOTEL ★★★

Rosehall Hotel
101 Dalkeith Road, Edinburgh, EH16 5AJ
Tel/Fax: 0131 667 9372
E-mail: RosehallH@aol.com
Web: www.rosehallhotel.co.uk

2 Single	All En Suite	B&B per person	Open Jan-Dec
2 Twin		from £25.00 Single	B&B + Eve.Meal
2 Double		from £22.00 Dbl/Twn	from £35.00
2 Family			

This small, recently refurbished hotel retains many fine period features restored to their original Victorian splendour. One room has a 4-Poster bed. A cosy lounge bar provides bar suppers. Free on-street parking is available nearby. One room has a private bathroom. The hotel is located around 1.5 miles from Princes Street.

Royal British Hotel
20 Princes Street, Edinburgh EH2 2AN
Tel: 0131 556 4901 Fax: 0131 557 6510
e.mail: royalbritish@hotmail.com

Situated in the heart of the city, on world famous Princes Street – a popular attraction particularly with shoppers – and adjacent to Waverley mainline rail station, the Royal British Hotel provides an ideal location for the business traveller and tourist alike. A warm welcome awaits your arrival.

HOTEL ★★

Royal British Hotel
20 Princes Street, Edinburgh, EH2 2AN
Tel: 0131 556 4901 Fax: 0131 557 6510
E-mail: RoyalBritish@hotmail.com

17 Single	All En Suite	B&B per person	Open Jan-Dec excl
37 Twin		from £99.00 Single	Xmas
9 Double		from £150.00 Dbl/Twn	
9 Family			

City centre hotel situated on Princes Street and 100 yards from Waverley railway station. Ideally situated for shopping, sightseeing, airport, bus terminal and business outlets.

GUEST HOUSE ★★★

The St Valery
36 Coates Gardens, Haymarket, Edinburgh, EH12 5LE
Tel: 0131 337 1893 Fax: 0131 346 8529
E-mail: stvalery@compuserve.com
Web: www.stvalery.com

1 Single	All En Suite	B&B per person	Open Jan-Dec
3 Twin		from £25.00 Single	
3 Double		from £20.00 Dbl/Twn	
4 Family		Room only per person	
		from £20.00	

Traditional guest house, centrally situated in West End of Edinburgh. 1/2 mile from Princes Street. 3 minutes walk from Haymarket Station. Evening meal on request.

All properties graded by VisitScotland, formerly known as the Scottish Tourist Board. | **Key to symbols is on back flap.**

Edinburgh

Map Ref: 2C5

★★★

GUEST HOUSE

Sandaig Guest House

5 East Hermitage Place, Leith Links, Edinburgh, EH6 8AA
Tel: 0131 554 7357 Fax: 0131 467 6389
E-mail: marina-ferbej@email.msn.com
Web: www.smoothhound.co.uk/hotels/sandaig

Marina and Derek personally welcome you to their comfortable Victorian terraced villa overlooking historic Leith Links. Unrestricted street parking. Variety of restaurants nearby or 10 mins by bus or car to Princes Street with all its amenities. Some non-smoking bedrooms.

2 Single	6 En Suite fac	B&B per person	Open Jan-Dec
2 Twin	1 Priv.NOT ensuite	from £25.00 Single	
4 Double	1 Pub Bath/Show	from £20.00 Dbl/Twn	
2 Family		Room only from £20.00	

SHERATON GRAND HOTEL
1 FESTIVAL SQUARE, EDINBURGH EH3 9SR
Telephone: 0131 229 9131   Fax: 0131 229 6254
e.mail: grandedinburgh.sheraton@sheraton.com
Web: www.sheraton.com
Nestling in the shadow of Edinburgh Castle, the Sheraton Grand combines the excellence of an international hotel with a warm luxurious Scottish style and superior modern facilities, including a state-of-the-art spa. Within easy walking distance of theatres, shops, restaurants and visitor attractions!

★★★★★

HOTEL

Sheraton Grand Hotel and Spa Edinburgh

1 Festival Square, Edinburgh, EH3 9SR
Tel: 0131 229 9131 Fax: 0131 229 6254
E-mail: grandedinburgh.sheraton@sheraton.com
Web: www.sheraton.com

5 star luxurious city centre hotel. Situated within walking distance to Edinburgh Castle, visitor attractions, restaurants and theatres. Facilities includes a state-of-the-art spa and gym, three restaurants and on-site car parking.

102 Twin	All En Suite	B&B per person	Open Jan-Dec
130		from £120.00 Single	B&B + Eve.Meal from
Double		from £85.00 Dbl/Twn	£140.00
28 Family		Room only per person	
		from £115.00	

SIMPSONS
79 LAURISTON PLACE, EDINBURGH EH3 9HZ
TEL: 0131 622 7979 FAX: 0131 622 7900
E.MAIL: rez@simpsons-hotel.com WEB: www.simpsons-hotel.com
Situated within the city centre, Simpsons is particularly convenient for Edinburgh Castle, Princes Street and The National Museum of Scotland. Converted to a hotel in 1998 from a historic Victorian building, there is a comfortable blend of the old and the new. 51 highly equipped rooms with en-suite bathrooms. New bar/restaurant opening in 2001.

★★★

HOTEL

Simpsons

79 Lauriston Place, Edinburgh, EH3 9HZ
Tel: 0131 622 7979 Fax: 0131 622 7900
Web: www.simpsons-hotel.com

Formerly Simpsons Memorial maternity hospital, completely refurbished in 1998 to provide 52 rooms and suites furnished to a high standard in a quiet location 0.5 mile from Princes Street. All bedrooms with refrigerators. Metered on street parking adjacent to hotel with more near by, this is free overnight.

7 Single	All En Suite	B&B per person	Open Jan-Dec
14 Twin		from £70.00 Single	B&B + Eve.Meal
24 Double		from £40.00 Dbl/Twn	from £59.50
6 Family			

Important: Prices stated are estimates and may be subject to amendments

B

Edinburgh

Map Ref: 2C5

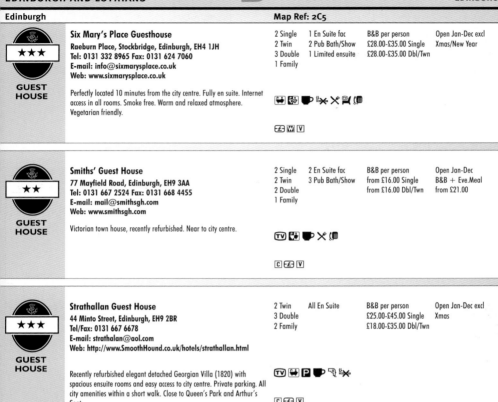

Six Mary's Place Guesthouse
★★★ GUEST HOUSE

Raeburn Place, Stockbridge, Edinburgh, EH4 1JH
Tel: 0131 332 8965 Fax: 0131 624 7060
E-mail: info@sixmarysplace.co.uk
Web: www.sixmarysplace.co.uk

2 Single	1 En Suite fac	B&B per person	Open Jan-Dec excl
2 Twin	2 Pub Bath/Show	£28.00-£35.00 Single	Xmas/New Year
3 Double	1 Limited ensuite	£28.00-£35.00 Dbl/Twn	
1 Family			

Perfectly located 10 minutes from the city centre. Fully en suite. Internet access in all rooms. Smoke free. Warm and relaxed atmosphere. Vegetarian friendly.

Smiths' Guest House
★★ GUEST HOUSE

77 Mayfield Road, Edinburgh, EH9 3AA
Tel: 0131 667 2524 Fax: 0131 668 4455
E-mail: mail@smithsgh.com
Web: www.smithsgh.com

2 Single	2 En Suite fac	B&B per person	Open Jan-Dec
2 Twin	3 Pub Bath/Show	from £16.00 Single	B&B + Eve.Meal
2 Double		from £16.00 Dbl/Twn	from £21.00
1 Family			

Victorian town house, recently refurbished. Near to city centre.

Strathallan Guest House
★★★ GUEST HOUSE

44 Minto Street, Edinburgh, EH9 2BR
Tel/Fax: 0131 667 6678
E-mail: strathalan@aol.com
Web: http://www.SmoothHound.co.uk/hotels/strathallan.html

2 Twin	All En Suite	B&B per person	Open Jan-Dec excl
3 Double		£25.00-£45.00 Single	Xmas
2 Family		£18.00-£35.00 Dbl/Twn	

Recently refurbished elegant detached Georgian Villa (1820) with spacious ensuite rooms and easy access to city centre. Private parking. All city amenities within a short walk. Close to Queen's Park and Arthur's Seat.

Tania Guest House
★ GUEST HOUSE

19 Minto Street, Edinburgh, EH9 1RQ
Tel: 0131 667 4144

1 Single	2 En Suite fac	B&B per person	Open Jan-Dec excl Xmas
1 Twin		from £20.00 Single	
1 Double		from £17.50 Dbl/Twn	
3 Family			

Traditional Guest House, welcoming families, conveniently situated on main bus route, 10 minutes from city centre. Limited private parking. Choice of restaurants available locally.

Terrace Hotel
★★ GUEST HOUSE

37 Royal Terrace, Edinburgh, EH7 5AH
Tel: 0131 556 3423 Fax: 0131 556 2520
E-mail: terracehotel@btinternet.com
Web: www.terracehotel.co.uk

2 Single	11 En Suite fac	B&B per person	Open Jan-Dec
2 Twin	2 Pub Bath/Show	from £29.00 Single	
3 Double		from £25.00 Dbl/Twn	
7 Family			

Personally run guest house in impressive Georgian terrace close to city centre, shopping and all amenities. Excellent views.

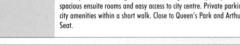

All properties graded by VisitScotland, formerly known as the Scottish Tourist Board. | *Key to symbols is on back flap.*

Edinburgh
Map Ref: 2C5

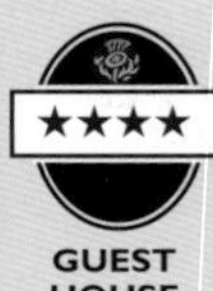

GUEST HOUSE
★★★★

The Town House
65 Gilmore Place, Edinburgh, EH3 9NU
Tel: 0131 229 1985
E-mail: Susan@thetownhouse.com
Web: www.thetownhouse.com

1 Single
1 Twin
2 Double
1 Family

All En Suite

B&B per person
from £30.00 Single
from £30.00 Dbl/Twn

Open Jan-Dec

A Victorian terraced town house c1876 in a residential area. Easy walking distance of West End, Princes Street and Kings Theatre. A skilful mix of modern and period furnishings enhanced by stylish decor makes for a very warm and comfortable stay.

TV ⊟ P ☕ ⏰ ⌇ ✂ ⌁ 📱

C V

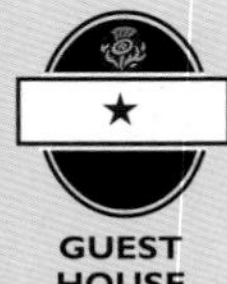

GUEST HOUSE
★★★★

Turret Guest House
8 Kilmaurs Terrace, Edinburgh, EH16 5DR
Tel: 0131 667 6704 Fax: 0131 668 1368
E-mail: turret@clara.net
Web: www.turret.clara.net

1 Single
1 Twin
3 Double
1 Family

4 En Suite fac
1 Priv.NOT ensuite
1 Pub Bath/Show

B&B per person
from £20.00 Single
from £20.00 Dbl/Twn

Open Jan-Dec excl Xmas

Listed Victorian house in quiet residential area, furnished to a high standard. Convenient for buses to city centre. Commonwealth Pool nearby.

TV 👶 👶 ☕ ⏰ ⌇ 📱

W V

GUEST HOUSE
★

Villa Nina
39 Leamington Terrace, Edinburgh, EH10 4JS
Tel/Fax: 0131 229 2644
E-mail: VillaNina@amserve.net

1 Twin
2 Double
1 Family

4 Limited ensuite
2 Pub Bath/Show

B&B per person
from £20.00 Single
from £17.50 Dbl/Twn

Open Jan-Dec excl Xmas/New Year

Good value bed and breakfast accommodation is offered at this friendly guest house in the city centre of Edinburgh. Close to Castle, theatres, International Conference Centre and major attractions.

TV ☕ ✂ 📱

♿ W V

---

by Edinburgh
Map Ref: 2C5

INN
★★★★

Ashcroft Farmhouse
East Calder, nr Edinburgh, EH53 0ET
Tel: 01506 881810 Fax: 01506 884327
E-mail: ashcroft30538@aol.com
Web: www.ashcroftfarmhouse.com

3 Twin
1 Double
2 Family

All En Suite

B&B per person
from £40.00 Single
from £28.00 Dbl/Twn

Open Jan-Dec

A warm Scottish welcome awaits you at this modern bungalow with interesting landscaped garden and quality choice of breakfast. Half an hour by bus to Edinburgh city centre, 5 miles from the airport and within easy access to all major routes. Ample parking. Totally non-smoking.

TV ⊟ P ☕ ⏰ ⌇ ✂ ⌁ 📱

C ♿ W V

Haddington, East Lothian

Map Ref: 2D4

**SMALL
HOTEL**

★★★★

Brown's Hotel
1 West Road, Haddington, East Lothian, EH41 3RD
Tel/Fax: 01620 822254
E-mail: info@browns-hotel.com
Web: www.browns-hotel.com

Regency town house, elegant furnishings and decor with contemporary
Scottish paintings. Restaurant noted in many guides. Easy access to A1,
only 20 minutes by car from Edinburgh on the outskirts of this historic
market town.

1 Single	All En Suite
2 Twin	
2 Double	

B&B per person
from £75.00 Single
from £60.00 Dbl/Twn

Open Jan-Dec
B&B + Eve.Meal
from £90.00

North Berwick, East Lothian

Map Ref: 2D4

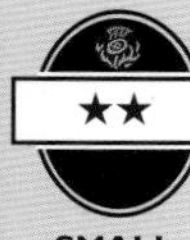

**SMALL
HOTEL**

★★

Belhaven Hotel
28 Westgate, North Berwick, East Lothian, EH39 4AH
Tel: 01620 893009 Fax: 01620 895882
E-mail: enquiries@belhavenhotel.co.uk
Web: www.belhavenhotel.co.uk

Family run hotel overlooking the 18th green and 1st tee of West Links
Golf course. 5 minutes walk from town centre and railway station.
Extensive sea views. Half an hour by road or rail to Edinburgh.

2 Single	5 En Suite fac
5 Twin	4 Pub Bath/Show
2 Triple	

B&B per person
from £22.00 Single
from £22.00 Twin

Open Dec-Oct
B&B + Eve.Meal
from £35.00

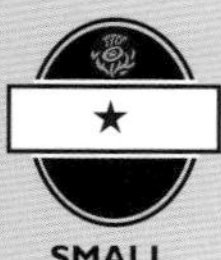

**SMALL
HOTEL**

★

Blenheim House Hotel
14 Westgate, North Berwick, East Lothian, EH39 4AF
Tel: 01620 892385 Fax: 01620 894010
E-mail: blenheimhotel@aol.com
Web: www.blenheimhousehotel.co.uk

Family run, Victorian stone built house on shore of Firth of Forth, 200
yards from first tee of Westlinks Golf Course. 14 golf courses within a half
hour drive. Beer garden available.

2 Single	All En Suite
3 Twin	
6 Family	

B&B per person
£25.00-£37.00 Single
£25.00-£37.00 Dbl/Twn

Open Jan-Dec
B&B + Eve.Meal
£37.00-£49.00

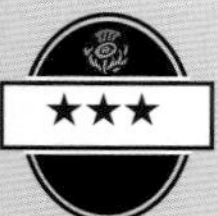

HOTEL

★★★

Marine Hotel
Cromwell Road, North Berwick, East Lothian,
EH39 4LZ
Tel: 0870 400 8129 Fax: 01620 894480
E-mail: heritagehotels_north_berwick.marine@forte-hotels.com
Web: www.heritagehotels.com

Traditional golf and conference hotel, with superb views over golf course
and Firth of Forth. Leisure break and incentive rates.

42 Twin	All En Suite
26 Double	
6 Four	
Posters	
9 Suites	

B&B per person
from £35.00 Single
from £60.00 Dbl/Twn

Open Jan-Dec
B&B + Eve.Meal
from £45.00

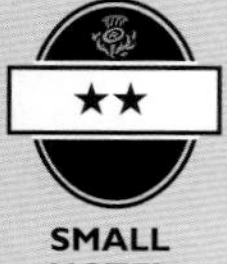

**SMALL
HOTEL**

★★

Nether Abbey Hotel
20 Dirleton Avenue, North Berwick, EH39 4BQ
Tel: 01620 892802 Fax: 01620 895298
E-mail: bookings@netherabbey.co.uk
Web: www.netherabbey.co.uk

Stone built hotel with character, situated in attractive grounds. 2 minutes
walk to sandy beach and west links. 19 golf courses within 10 mile
radius. 30 minute train service to Edinburgh.

4 Twin	All En Suite
4 Double	
6 Family	

B&B per person
from £35.00 Single
from £32.50 Dbl/Twn

Open Jan-Dec

All properties graded by VisitScotland, formerly known as the Scottish Tourist Board. | Key to symbols is on back flap.

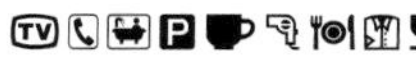

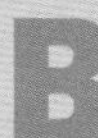

North Middleton, Midlothian

Map Ref: 2C5

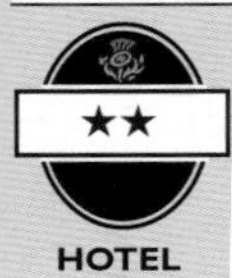

**SMALL
HOTEL**

Borthwick Castle Hotel
North Middleton, Gorebridge, Midlothian
EH23 4QY
Tel: 01875 820514 Fax: 01875 821702

3 Twin	All En Suite	B&B per person	Open Mar-Jan excl
7 Double		from £80.00 Single	Xmas/New Year
		from £67.50 Dbl/Twn	B&B + Eve.Meal
			from £97.50

Unique twin tower fortified keep c.1430 with great hall and state room retaining medieval atmosphere. Dine by log fires and candlelight. Only 12 miles South of Edinburgh in a pastoral valley, this romantic Castle stands on the summit of a knoll.

Penicuik, Midlothian

Map Ref: 2C5

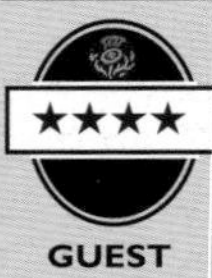

HOTEL

Royal Hotel
34 High Street, Penicuik EH26 8HY
Tel: 01968 676979 Fax: 01968 672944

1 Single	5 En Suite	B&B per person	Open Jan-Dec excl.
3 Twin	1 Pub Bath/Show	from £35.00 Single	Xmas/New Year
1 Double		from £55.00 Dbl/Twn	
1 Family			

Refurbished late 18th century coaching hotel in centre of town. Bar lunches and informal dining. 9 miles south west of Edinburgh.

South Queensferry, by Edinburgh, Midlothian

Map Ref: 2B4

**GUEST
HOUSE**

Priory Lodge
8 The Loan, South Queensferry, EH30 9NS
Tel: 0131 331 4345 Fax: 0131 331 4345
E-mail: calmyn@aol.com
Web: www.queensferry.com
Traditional Scottish hospitality in this friendly family run guest house located in the picturesque village of South Queensferry . Edinburgh city centre 7 miles: Airport / Royal Highland Exhibition grounds 3 miles. Priory Lodge is within walking distance of the village shops, variety of eating establishments, Forth Bridges and Dalmeny train station. Ground floor accommodation. Non-smoking establishment.

1 Twin	All En Suite	B&B per person	Open Jan-Dec
1 Double		from £40.00 Single	
3 Family		from £54.00 Dbl/Twn	

welcome to scotland

GREATER GLASGOW AND CLYDE VALLEY

For sheer excitement, Glasgow is one of the top UK destinations. This forward-thinking and stylish city offers a choice of shopping, entertainment and culture that should not be missed. The legendary Glasgow friendliness is a bonus, while first-time visitors will be struck by the city's panache.

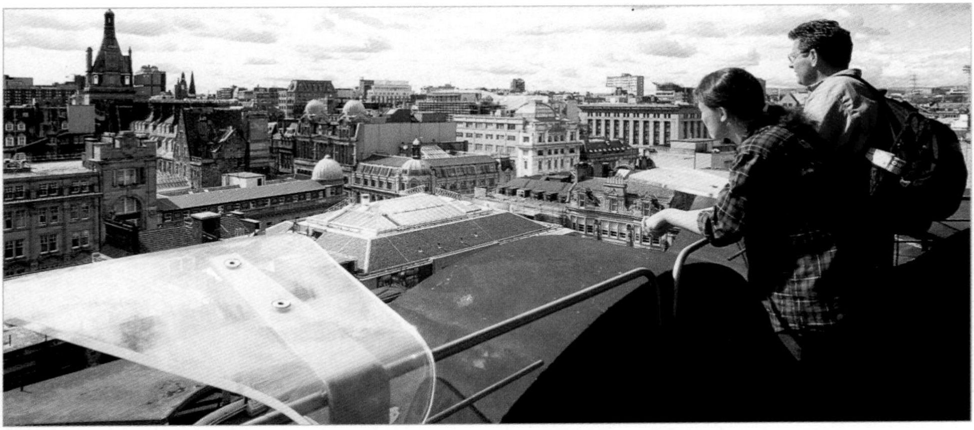

Glasgow skyline viewed from "The Lighthouse"

GLASGOW'S architecture ranges from the magnificent Gothic style of Glasgow Cathedral to the imposing Italian Renaissance of the Victorian City Chambers. As Britain's finest Victorian city, Glasgow offers 19th-century grandeur in its streets, squares and gardens while the fashionable and elegant terraces of the West End have been restored. In the 18th-century Merchant City, you will find cafés and boutiques and the chic Italian Centre with its exclusive designer shops. You can explore the St Enoch's Shopping Centre which is the largest glass-covered building in Europe as well as the Buchanan Galleries and stylish Princes Square. If you have any money left,

head for a bargain in the famous Barras Market.

Glasgow has an unrivalled selection of more than 20 art galleries and museums to discover from the innovative Gallery of Modern Art to the internationally acclaimed Burrell Collection. Throughout the city, the unmistakable influence of two of the city's greatest sons – the architects Charles Rennie Mackintosh and Alexander 'Greek' Thomson can been seen. Visit Mackintosh's outstanding Glasgow School of Art and Thomson's recently restored Holmwood House.

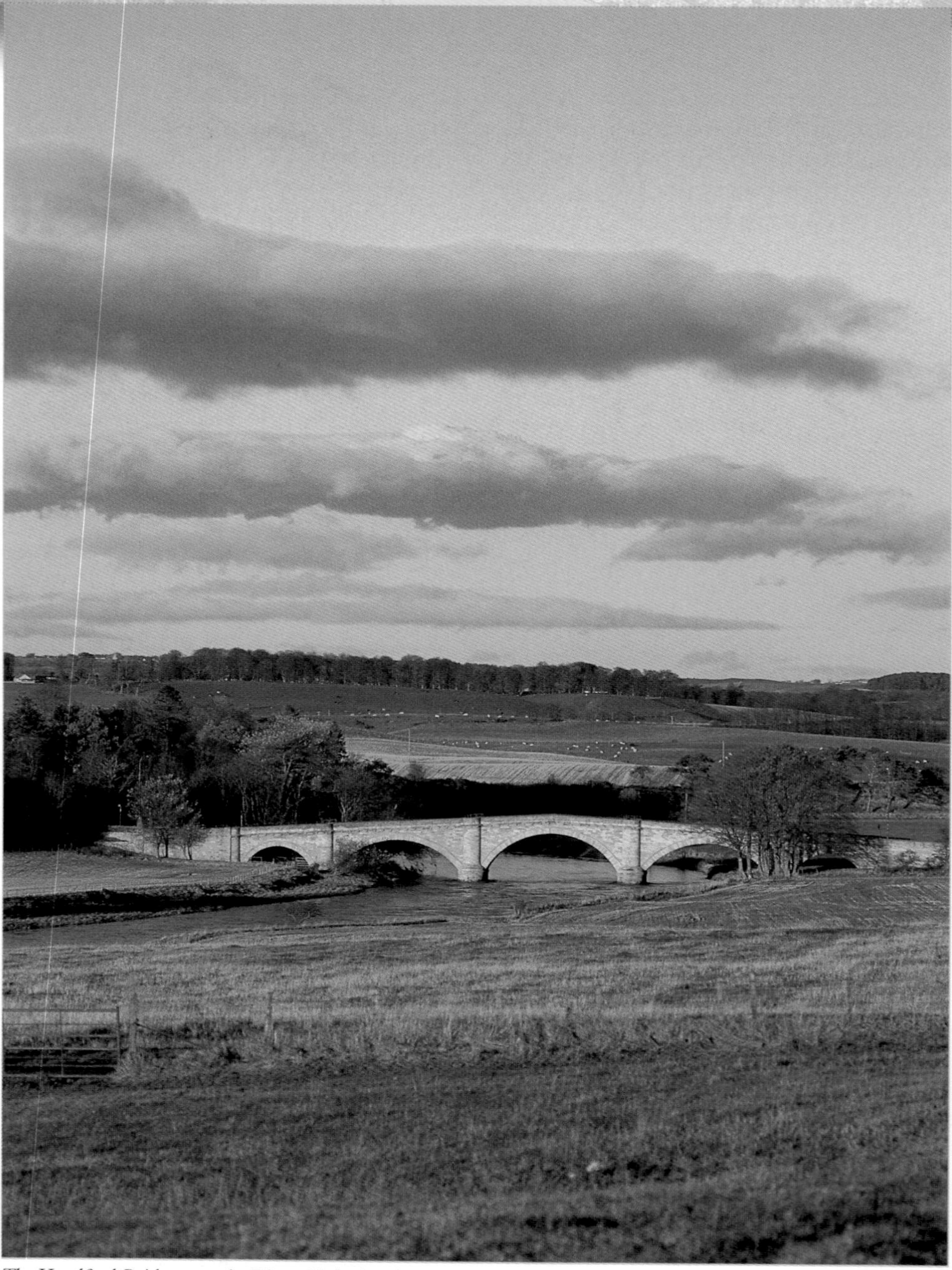

The Hyndford Bridge over the River Clyde, South-east of Lanark

GREATER GLASGOW AND CLYDE VALLEY

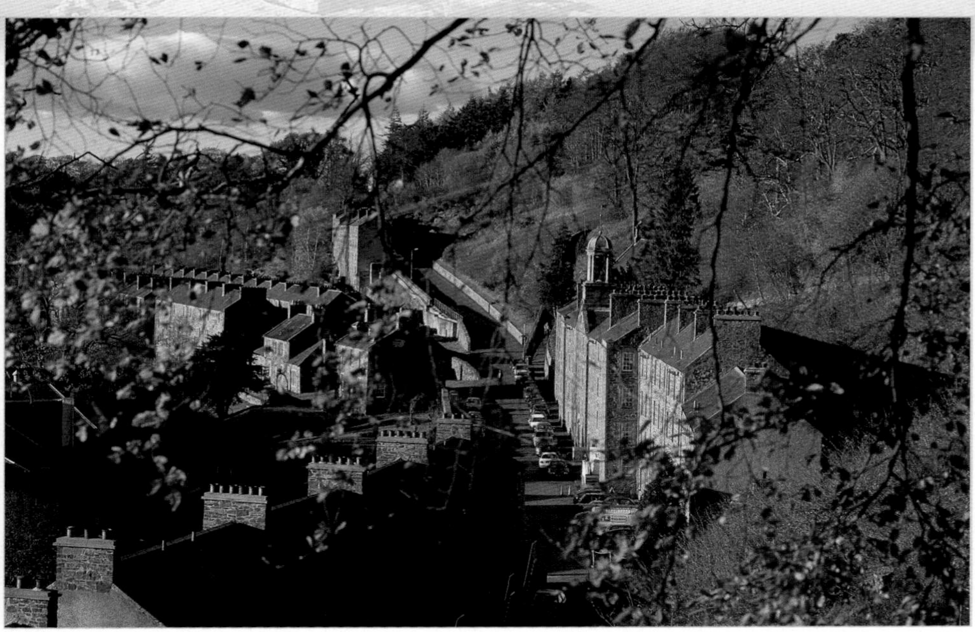

World Heritage Site, New Lanark

Another exciting development is the Glasgow Science Centre – an IMAX theatre, Science Mall and the Glasgow Tower with its 100m high viewing cabin.

A year-round programme of events including Celtic Connections, the Glasgow Folk Festival and the International Jazz Festival complements the arts scene in the city which is also home to Scottish Opera, Scottish Ballet and the Royal Scottish National Orchestra. Glasgow's cafés, bars and nightclubs offer plenty of opportunities to enjoy the friendliness and colourful character of the locals.

From Glasgow, there is easy access to the rolling hills of Renfrewshire, the Inverclyde coastline and the fertile Clyde valley. At Paisley, you can visit the restored 12th-century abbey and learn about the famous Paisley textile pattern at the Paisley Museum and art galleries with their world-famous collection of Paisley shawls. Further upriver and the River Clyde changes its character tumbling over waterfalls into a rocky gorge at New Lanark Industrial Heritage Village, which is now a World Heritage site.

16 JANUARY-3 FEBRUARY
Celtic Connections
Glasgow, Various Venues
Annual celebration of Celtic
music, featuring
international artists.
Contact: Celtic Connections
Tel: 0141 353 8000

5-10 MARCH
*Scottish Curling
Championship*
Renfrew, Braehead
International Arena
The national final of the
men's and ladies curling
championships.
Contact: Royal Caledonian
Curling Club
Tel: 0131 333 3003
Web: www.rccc.org.uk

11-14 APRIL
Glasgow Art Fair 2002
Glasgow, Various Venues
Scotland's national art fair,
the largest and
contemporary art fair
outside London, is now in
its 7th year.
Contact: Marie Christie
Tel: 0141 552 6027
Web: www.glasgowartfair.com

1 JUNE
Shotts Highland Games
Shotts, Hannah Park
Traditional Highland games
with pipe band contests,
Highland dancing, athletics
and heavy events.
Contact: Alex Hamilton
Tel: 01501 820280
Web:
www.shottshighlandgames.
org.uk

* 8-23 JUNE
West End Festival
Glasgow, Various Venues
Celebrates the best of
Glasgow's west end culture.
Contact: Michael Dale
Tel: 0141 341 0844

6 JUNE
*Lanark Lanimer
Celebrations*
Lanark, Town Centre
Traditional procession and
events.
Contact: Mr L Reid
Tel: 01555 663251

* 30 JUNE-8 JULY
*Glasgow International
Jazz Festival*
Glasgow, Various Venues
The UK's premier
international jazz festival
highlighting international
and U.K based artists.
Contact: Glasgow
International Jazz Festival
Tel: 0141 552 3552
Web: www.jazzfest.co.uk

* 10 AUGUST
*World Pipe Band
Championships*
Glasgow, Glasgow Green
The most prestigious event
in the annual pipe band
calendar, attracting some
200 bands from around the
world.
Contact: Royal Scottish
Pipe Band Association
Tel: 0141 221 5414
Web: www.rspba.co.uk

* 1 SEPTEMBER
Victorian Fair
New Lanark,
World Heritage Village
Annual street fair with stalls
and entertainment.
Contact:
World Heritage Village
Tel: 01555 661345
Web: www.newlanark.org

** denotes provisional date,
please check before attending.*

AREA TOURIST BOARDS
GREATER GLASGOW AND CLYDE VALLEY

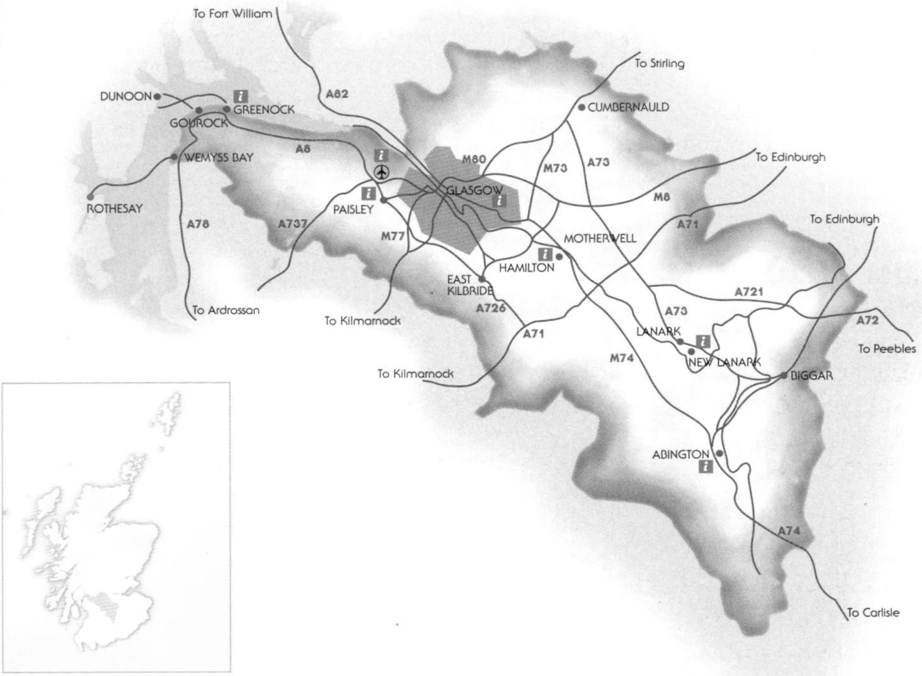

GREATER GLASGOW AND CLYDE VALLEY TOURIST BOARD
11 George Square
Glasgow
G2 1DY

Tel: 0141 204 4400
Fax : 0141 204 4772
E-mail:
enquiries@seeglasgow.com
Web: www.seeglasgow.com

TOURIST INFORMATION CENTRES
GREATER GLASGOW AND CLYDE VALLEY

**GREATER GLASGOW
AND CLYDE VALLEY
TOURIST BOARD**

Abington
Welcome Break Service
Area
Junction 13, M74
Tel: (01864) 502436
abington@seeglasgow.com
Jan-Dec

Biggar
155 High Street
Tel: (01899) 221066
Easter-Sept

Glasgow
11 George Square
Tel: (0141) 204 4400
enquiries@seeglasgow.com
Jan-Dec

Glasgow Airport
Tourist Information Desk
Tel: (0141) 848 4440
airport@seeglasgow.com
Jan-Dec

Hamilton
Road Chef Services
M74 Northbound
Tel: (01698) 285590
hamilton@seeglasgow.com
Jan-Dec

Lanark
Horsemarket
Ladyacre Road
Tel: (01555) 661661
lanark@seeglasgow.com
Jan-Dec

Paisley
9a Gilmour Street
Tel: (0141) 889 0711
paisley@seeglasgow.com
Jan-Dec

Abington, Lanarkshire
Map Ref: 2B7

HOTEL

Abington Hotel
Abington, by Biggar, Lanarkshire, ML12 6SD
Tel: 01864 502467 Fax: 01864 502223
E-mail: info@ab-hotel.com
Web: www.ab-hotel.com

5 Single	All En Suite
6 Twin	
11 Double	
6 Family	

B&B per person
from £45.00 Single
from £32.50 Dbl/Twn

Open Jan-Dec
B&B + Eve.Meal
from £42.00

Personally run family hotel situated in centre of village at the start of the Clyde Valley Tourist Route. All bedrooms en-suite. Easy to find, M74, junction 13. Good touring base for central Scotland - within one hours drive of Glasgow, Stirling, Edinburgh and Ayrshire Coast.

Airdrie, Lanarkshire
Map Ref: 2A5

GUEST HOUSE

Rosslee Guest House
107 Forrest Street, Airdrie, Lanarkshire, ML6 7AR
Tel: 01236 765865 Fax: 01236 748535
E-mail: alanrgh@blue.yonder.co.uk

2 Single	4 En Suite fac
3 Twin	2 Pub Bath/Show
1 Family	

B&B per person
from £20.00 Single
from £20.00 Twn/Fam
Room only per person
from £18.00

Open Jan-Dec

Former church manse, now family run guest house with comfortable rooms. Central situation for Edinburgh or Glasgow.

Bellshill, Lanarkshire
Map Ref: 2A5

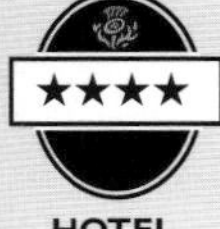

HOTEL

Hilton Strathclyde
Phoenix Crescent, Bellshill, North Lanarkshire, ML4 3JQ
Tel: 01698 395500 Fax: 01698 395511
E-mail: reservations_strathclyde@hilton.com
Web: www.hilton.com

39 Twin	All En Suite
54 Double	
14 Family	

B&B per person
from £135.00 Single
from £155.00 Dbl/Twn
Room only from
£135.00

Open All Year

Modern Hotel on business park close to M8 and M74 motorways giving easy access to both Glasgow and Edinburgh. Hotel offers full range of conference and banqueting facilities. Assured Meeting rooms and business centre and comprehensive leisure facilities including a 20 metre pool and fully equipped gymnasium. Some office bedrooms available.

Bothwell, South Lanarkshire
Map Ref: 2A5

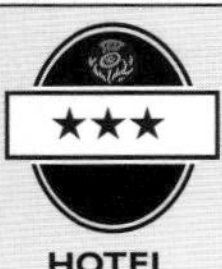

HOTEL

Bothwell Bridge Hotel
89 Main Street, Bothwell, Glasgow, South Lanarkshire, G71 8EH
Tel: 01698 852246 Fax: 01698 854686
Web: www.bothwellbridgehotel.com

76 Double	All En Suite
14 Family	

B&B per person
from £58.00 Single
from £68.00 Dbl/Twn

Open Jan-Dec
B&B + Eve.Meal from
£71.50

Family run hotel, 9 miles (14kms) from Glasgow city centre and convenient for motorway. Business meeting rooms. Ample parking.

Cumbernauld, Glasgow
Map Ref: 2A5

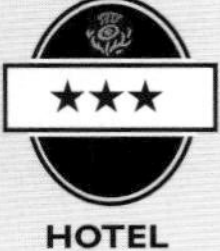

HOTEL

Westerwood Hotel, Golf & Country Club
1 St Andrews Drive, Cumbernauld, G68 0EW
Tel: 01236 457171 Fax: 01236 738478
E-mail: rooms@morton-hotels.com
Web: www.morton-hotels.com

50 Twin	All En Suite
50 Double	

B&B per person
from £40.00 Single

Open Jan-Dec
B&B + Eve.Meal from
£60.00

Modern hotel nestling on edge of Kilsyth Hills. Own championship golf course and leisure complex. Clubhouse and Tipsy Laird restaurant.

All properties graded by VisitScotland, formerly known as the Scottish Tourist Board.   Key to symbols is on back flap.

Glasgow

Map Ref: 1H5

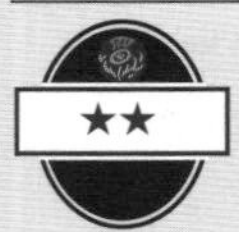

B&B

★★

Alamo Guest House
46 Gray Street, Kelvingrove, Glasgow, G3 7SE
Tel: 0141 339 2395
E-mail: info@alamoguesthouse.com
Web: www.alamoguesthouse.com

Friendly family run Victorian house, in quiet location overlooking park in conservation area. Easy access to city centre and West End within walking distance of SECC, galleries, Transport Museum, Glasgow University and a range of restaurants and pubs. Free on-street parking. Some ensuite rooms available. Tv's in all bedrooms.

2 Single
1 Triple
1 Double
5 Family

2 En Suite fac
1 Priv.NOT ensuite
2 Pub Bath/Show

B&B per person
from £21.00 Single
from £18.00 Dbl/Twn

Open Jan-Dec

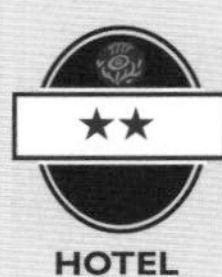

HOTEL

★★

Albion Hotel
405-407 North Woodside Road, Glasgow, G20 6NN
Tel: 0141 339 8620 Fax: 0141 334 8159
E-mail: albion@glasgowhotelsandapartments.co.uk
Web: www.glasgowhotelsandapartments.co.uk

Conveniently located in the heart of Glasgow's highly desirable West End, yet only 1 mile from the City Centre. Ideal for public transport, museums and art galleries. All rooms ensuite'.

6 Single
1 Twin
4 Double
5 Family

All En Suite

B&B per person
from £39.00 Single
from £24.00 Dbl/Twn
Room only from £35.00

Open Jan-Dec

HOTEL

★★★

Ambassador Hotel
7 Kelvin Drive, Glasgow, G20 8QG
Tel: 0141 946 1018 Fax: 0141 945 5377
E-mail: ambassador@glasgowhotelsandapartments.co.uk
Web: www.glasgowhotelsandapartments.co.uk

Small privately run Victorian townhouse quietly located in the bustling West End, convenient for city centre, museums, art galleries and the Botanic Gardens. The ideal base for a business or pleasure stop over in the city. Free onsite car park.

8 Single
4 Twin
4 Double

All En Suite

B&B per person
from £41.00 Single
from £25.00 Dbl/Twn
Room only from £38.00

Open Jan-Dec

GUEST HOUSE

★★

Belgrave Guest House
2 Belgrave Terrace, Hillhead, Glasgow, G12 8SD
Tel: 0141 337 1850 Fax: 0141 337 1741
E-mail: belgraveguesthse@hotmail.com
Web: www.belgraveguesthouse.co.uk

Refurbished guest house, in the West End. Convenient for Botanic Gardens, other local attractions and amenities. 5 minute walk from two tube stations. Many restaurants, cafes and bus a few minutes walk away. Small private car-park to rear. Ensuite rooms available.

3 Single
2 Twin
2 Double
2 Family

2 En Suite fac
3 Pub Bath/Show
3 Priv.NOT ensuite

B&B per person
from £21.00 Single
from £18.00 Dbl/Twn

Open Jan-Dec

HOTEL

★★★

Ewington Hotel
132 Queens Drive, Glasgow, G42 8QW
Tel: 0141 423 1152 Fax: 0141 422 2030
E-mail: info@scotlandhotels.net
Web: www.scotland-hotels.co.uk

Victorian town house hotel situated in residential area overlooking Queens Park, 1 mile south of city centre. Unrestricted on lane parking. Individually designed bedrooms offering all modern day comforts. Minstrels Restaurant offers the discerning diner a true flavour of Scotland. Conference and banqueting facilities available.

8 Single
6 Twin
28 Double
1 Family

All En Suite

B&B per person
from £79.00 Single
from £99.00 Dbl/Twn

Open Jan-Dec

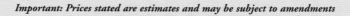

Important: Prices stated are estimates and may be subject to amendments

Glasgow

Map Ref: 1H5

HOTEL

Express by Holiday Inn
Theatreland, 165 West Nile Street, Glasgow, G1 2RL
Tel: 0141 331 6800 Fax: 0141 331 6828
Web: www.hiexpress.com

Situated in the centre of Glasgow. A short walk from the Royal Concert Hall, cinemas, theatres, restaurants and all amenities. There is a bar in the hotel and all rooms have satellite TV, direct dial telephones and tea and coffee making facilities.

45 Twin   All En Suite
38 Double
5 Single

B&B per person
£58.00 per room

Open Jan-Dec

🖵 📶 📞 🖥 ☕ 🍷 🧺 ✂ 🍽

Ⓒ 🐾 🔥 Ⓥ

HOTEL

♿

Hilton Glasgow
1 William Street, Glasgow, G3 8HT
Tel: 0141 204 5555 Fax: 0141 204 5004
E-mail: sales-glasgow@hilton.com
Web: www.hilton.com

Built in 1992, this hotel is a stunning 20 storey landmark offering panoramic views across the city. There are executive art Japanese floors in addition to 5 floors of non-smoking rooms. Enjoy fine dining in Camerons restaurant or dine in the more informal Minskeys. Extensive conference business and leisure facilities.

98 Twin   All En Suite
39 Executive
182 Queen/
King
bedrooms

Room rate
from £160.00

Open Jan-Dec

🖵 📶 📞 🖥 🅿 🍷 🧺 ✂ 🍽 🎁 📶 🔥 🛏 🎱 🏋 🍽

Ⓒ 🐾 🔥 Ⓦ Ⓥ 🐄 🎣

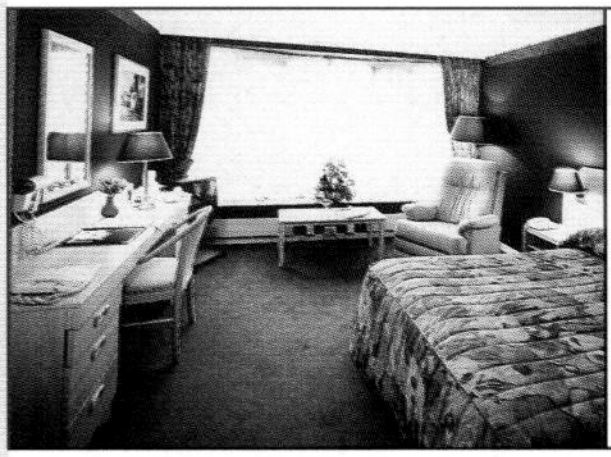

HOLIDAY INN – GLASGOW
161 West Nile Street, Glasgow G1 2RL
Tel: 0141 352 8305 Fax: 0141 352 8311 (Reservations)
E.mail: reservations@higlasgow.com Web: www.higlasgow.com

Ideally located in the heart of the city's theatreland, the Holiday Inn Glasgow offers 113 superbly appointed air conditioned bedrooms including executive rooms and penthouse suites. Recently benefiting from a £2 million reinvestment, the Holiday Inn delivers comfort and relaxation with an undertone of unassuming style and a focus on guest service.

HOTEL

♿

Holiday Inn Glasgow
161 West Nile Street, Glasgow, G1 2RL
Tel: 0141 332 0110 Fax: 0141 332 7447

In the heart of the city, five minutes walk from theatres and transport. Brasserie style restaurant. Penthouse suites now available along with a small mini gym.

32 Twin   All En Suite
60 Double
3
Penthouse
18
Executive

B&B per person
£40.00-£87.00 Dbl/Twn
Room only per person
£30.00-£75.00

Open Jan-Dec   B&B + Eve.Meal
£55.00-£102.00

🖵 📶 📞 🖥 🍷 🧺 ✂ 🍽 🎁 🔥 🏋 🍽

Ⓒ 🔥 Ⓦ Ⓥ

Glasgow | Map Ref: 1H5

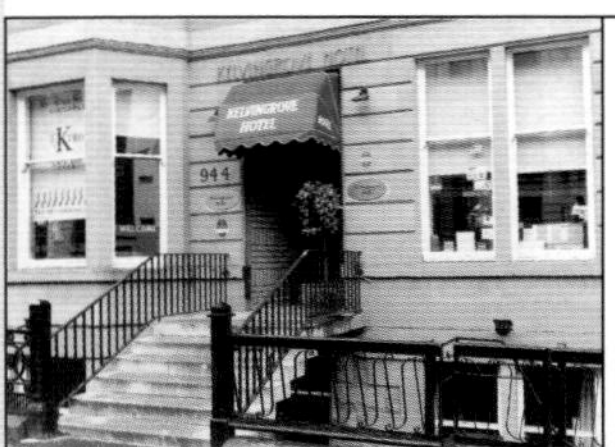

KELVINGROVE HOTEL

944 Sauchiehall Street, Glasgow G3 7TH
Tel: 0141-339 5011/0141-569 1121 Fax: 0141 339 6566
e.mail: kelvingrove.hotel@business.ntl.com
Web: www.kelvingrove-hotel.co.uk

Quality rooms at low prices, fully refurbished, close to S.E.C.C., art gallery, parks, transport museum, university, transport to town takes 5 minutes. Central heating, 23 en-suite rooms, double glazing throughout, colour TV in all rooms, direct dial phone, satellite and cable TV. Tea and coffee making facilities in all rooms. No parking restrictions. 10 mins walk to International Conference Centre. Tremendous value for money.

★★★

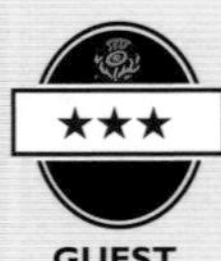

GUEST
HOUSE

Kelvingrove Hotel
944 Sauchiehall Street, Glasgow, G3 7TH
Tel: 0141 339 5011 Fax: 0141 339 6566
E-mail: kelvingrove.hotel@business.ntl.com
Web: www.kelvingrove-hotel.co.uk

City centre hotel with mainly ensuite rooms, TV, tea and coffee facilities. 15 minutes walk to shopping centre. SECC nearby. Kelvingrove Art Gallery, Kelvin Hall, The Western Infirmary and Glasgow University and all a short walk away.

2 Single 23 En Suite fac
3 Twin 2 Pub Shower
13 Double 2 Priv.NOT ensuite
7 Family

B&B per person
from £38.00 Single
from £29.00 Dbl/Twn
Room only per person
from £16.00-£33.00

Open all year excl New Year

★

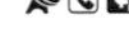

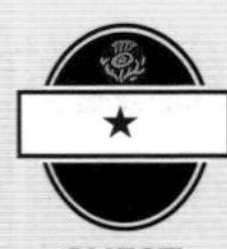

GUEST
HOUSE

McLays Guest House
264-276 Renfrew Street, Glasgow, G3 6TT
Tel: 0141 332 4796 Fax: 0141 353 0422
E-mail: info@mclays.com
Web: www.mclays.com

McLays Guest House situated in the heart of the city was originally 3 townhouses, now interlinked to provide 62 rooms. Of these, 39 have private bathrooms, however all floors have communal bathrooms for guests to use. All our rooms have colour television, satellite channels, tea/coffee making facilities and telephones. You will find our staff members at McLays helpful, warm and friendly. Our reception staff has a depth of local knowledge, which will help ensure that all our guests get the maximum pleasure from their visit to Glasgow.

18 Single 39 En Suite fac
20 Twin 9 Pub Bath/Show
12 Double
12 Family

B&B per person
from £22.00 Single
from £19.00 Dbl/Twn

Open Jan-Dec

★★★★

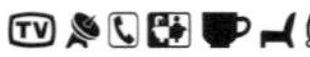

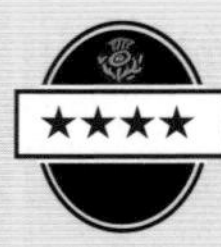

HOTEL

Millennium Hotel
George Square, Glasgow, G2 1DS
Tel: 0141 332 6711 Fax: 0141 332 4264
E-mail: sales.glasgow@mill-cop.com
Web: www.millennium-hotels.com

Recently refurbished landmark hotel in the heart of Scotland's commercial capital. Ideal for city centre attractions and amenities.

15 Single All En Suite
39 Twin
63 Double

B&B per person
from £77.00 Single
from £104.00 Dbl/Twn
Room only from
£195.00

Open Jan-Dec
B&B + Eve.Meal
from £95.00 pp

★★

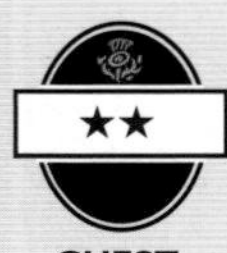

GUEST
HOUSE

Reidholme Guest House
36 Regent Park Square, Glasgow, G41 2AG
Tel: 0141 423 1855

B Listed terraced town house in quiet residential area on south side of city centre near Queens Park. Under 2 miles (3kms) from the Burrell Collection and Pollok Park. Convenient bus and rail connections to city centre on street park available, evening meals by prior arrangement.

1 Single 2 Pub Bath/Show
3 Twin
1 Double
1 Family

B&B per person
from £22.00 Single
from £44.00 Dbl/Twn

Open Jan-Dec
B&B + Eve.Meal
from £30.00

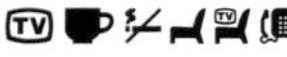

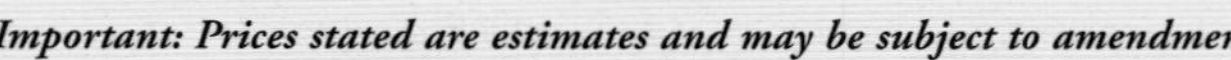

Important: Prices stated are estimates and may be subject to amendments

Glasgow

Map Ref: 1H5

HOTEL
★★★

Sherbrooke Castle Hotel
11 Sherbrooke Avenue, Glasgow, G41 4PG
Tel: 0141 427 4227 Fax: 0141 427 5685
E-mail: mail@sherbrooke.co.uk
Web: www.sherbrooke.co.uk

Situated in the leafy, up-market suburb of Pollokshields. This magnificent baronial building crafted in rich red sandstone, combines traditional grace with modern efficiency. The fully air conditioned restaurant serves fresh local produce, prepared by award winning chefs, complimented with an interesting wine cellar. Some annexe accommodation.

4 Single	All En Suite	B&B per person
5 Twin		from £65.00 Single
10 Double		from £42.50 Dbl/Twn
2 Family		

Open Jan-Dec

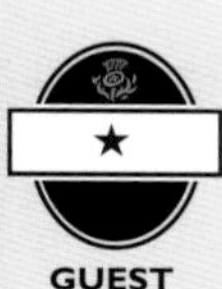

**GUEST
HOUSE**
★

Smiths Hotel
963 Sauchiehall Street, Glasgow, G3 7TQ
Tel: 0141 339 7674 Fax: 0141 334 1892

Family run bed and breakfast hotel ¾ mile (1 km) from city centre. On main bus routes. Near to Kelvin Hall, Art Gallery and SECC.

10 Single	9 En Suite fac	B&B per person
11 Twin		from £20.00 Single
6 Double		from £19.00 Dbl/Twn
6 Family		

Open Jan-Dec excl
Xmas/New Year

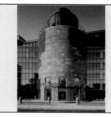

University of Strathclyde Graduate School of Business
199 Cathedral Street, Glasgow G4 0QU
Tel: 0141-553 6000   Fax: 0141-553 6137
e.mail: sgbs.reception@strath.ac.uk Web: www.sgbs.strath.ac.uk/hotel

Strathclyde Graduate Business School Hotel is a modern establishment with 107 fully appointed ensuite bedrooms, conveniently located in the heart of Glasgow City Centre – only 5 mins walk from Buchanan Galleries. It is the perfect choice of accommodation for that special shopping spree, weekend break or theatre trip.

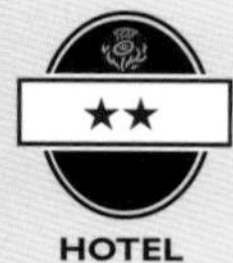

HOTEL
★★

Strathclyde Graduate Business School
Hotel-Conference Centre, 199 Cathedral Street,
Glasgow, G4 0QU
Tel: 0141 553 6000 Fax: 0141 553 6137
Web: www.sgbs.strath.ac.uk/hotel

Very central, modern residential business school with conference facilities. All ensuite. Private parking. 5 minute walk from the Concert Hall and Buchanan Galleries shopping complex.

73 Single	All En Suite	B&B per person
Standard		from £39.00 Single
22 Single		from £34.50 Dbl/Twn
Executive		
10 Double		
2 Twin		

Open Jan-Dec excl
Xmas/New Year

All properties graded by VisitScotland, formerly known as the Scottish Tourist Board.   Key to symbols is on back flap.

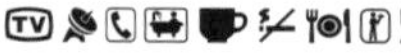

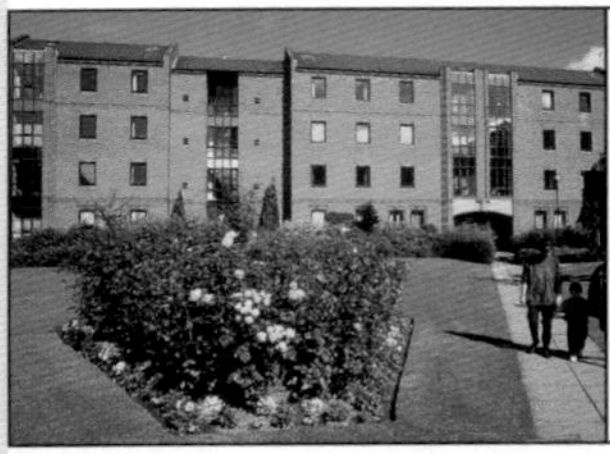

University of Strathclyde

Residence and Catering Services, 50 Richmond St., Glasgow G1 1XP
Tel: 0141-553 4148   Fax: 0141-553 4149
e.mail: rescat@mis.strath.ac.uk Web: www.rescat.strath.ac.uk

Strathclyde University offers a range of attractive accommodation in Glasgow city centre at affordable prices. En-suite and standard single rooms are located in the modern campus village adjacent to the Lord Todd bar/restaurant and twins and singles are available at Baird Hall in Sauchiehall Street.

★

CAMPUS
ACCOMMODATION

University of Strathclyde
Residence and Catering Services, 50 Richmond St.,
Glasgow, G1 1XP.
Tel: 0141 553 4148 Fax: 0141 553 4149
E-mail: rescat@mis.strath.ac.uk
Web: www.rescat.strath.ac.uk

Modern, purpose-built halls of residence on campus. Ideal centre for exploring the city.

912 Single	285 Ensuite singles
135 Twin	627 Standard singles
15 Double	
2 Family	

B&B per person
from £25.00 Single
from £21.50 Dbl/Twn

Open Jun-Sep

★★★

HOTEL

Swallow Hotel
517 Paisley Road West, Glasgow, G51 1RW
Tel: 0141 427 3146 Fax: 0141 419 1602

Modern city centre hotel with a leisure complex including pool. Extensive conference and banqueting facilities. Spacious, free car parking.

7 Single   All En Suite
53 Twin
57 Double

B&B per person
from £45.00 Single
from £35.00 Dbl/Twn
Room only
from £60.00

Open Jan-Dec
B&B + Eve.Meal
from £45.00

★★★

GUEST
HOUSE

The Town House
4 Hughenden Terrace, Glasgow, G12 9XR
Tel: 0141 357 0862 Fax: 0141 339 9605
E-mail: hospitality@thetownhouseglasgow.com
Web: www.thetownhouseglasgow.com

Glasgow's original and long established town house, located in the desirable West End, provides all the comforts one would expect for a relaxing holiday or a hectic business trip. Relax in front of the coal fire with a refreshment, enjoy the quality accommodation and legendary seafood breakfast in the morning. Parking is free and ample.

4 Twin   All En Suite
4 Double
2 Family

B&B per person
from £60.00 Single
from £36.00 Dbl/Twn

Open Jan-Dec

★★

SMALL
HOTEL

Wickets Hotel
52 Fortrose Street, Glasgow, G11 5LP
Tel/Fax: 0141 334 9334
E-mail: wicketshotel@hotmail.com
Web: www.wicketshotel.com.uk

Privately owned, overlooks cricket ground. Close to Clydeside.Expressway to city. Near Scottish Exhibition Centre and Glasgow Airport. Beer garden and conservatory for dining and drinking.

4 Single   All En Suite
3 Twin
4 Double

B&B per person
from £35.00 Single
from £45.00 Dbl/Twn

Open Jan-Dec excl
Xmas/New Year

Important: Prices stated are estimates and may be subject to amendments

Glasgow Airport, Renfrewshire · Map Ref: 1H5

HOTEL ★★★★

Lynnhurst Hotel
Park Road, Johnstone, Renfrewshire, PA5 8LS
Tel: 01505 324331 Fax: 01505 324219
E-mail: enquiries@lynnhurst.co.uk
Web: www.lynnhurst.co.uk

Friendly family run hotel in residential area. Conservatory, function and conference facilities. Glasgow Airport 5 miles (8kms). Many Victorian features of the original mansions sympathetically retained.

11 Single   All En Suite
1 Twin
7 Double
2 Family

B&B per person
from £40.00 Single
from £35.00 Dbl/Twn

Open Jan-Dec excl
Xmas/New Year

Howwood, Renfrewshire · Map Ref: 1G5

Bowfield Hotel & Country Club
HOWWOOD · RENFREWSHIRE · PA9 1DB
Tel: 01505 705225   Fax: 01505 705230
Web: www.bowfieldcountryclub.co.uk

A refreshingly different country hotel offering a wealth of facilities including swimming pool, sauna, jacuzzi, squash courts, gymnasium and health and beauty spa. This perfect country retreat is only 20 minutes from Glasgow Airport.
B&B from £50.00 per person per night sharing a twin or double room.
Two RAC Dining Awards.
AA ★★★ RAC ★★★   ★★★★ Hotel

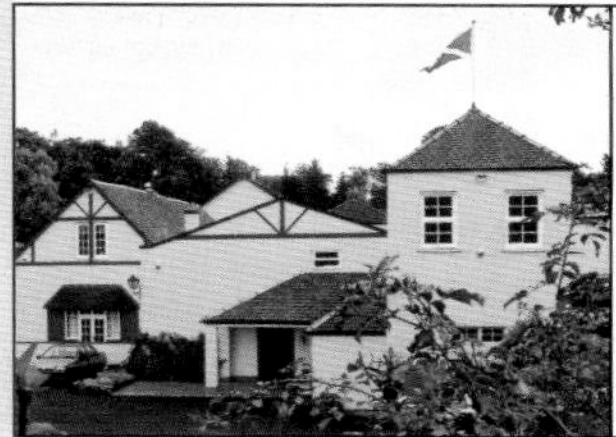

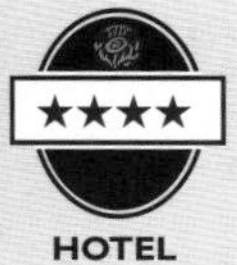

HOTEL ★★★★

Bowfield Hotel & Country Club
Howwood, Renfrewshire, PA9 1DB
Tel: 01505 705225 Fax: 01505 705230

A refreshingly different country retreat close to town and city attractions. A comprehensive leisure club with swimming pool and health & beauty spa and awarded restaurants.

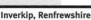

8 Twin   All En Suite
12 Double
3 Family

B&B per person
£68.00 Single
£48.00 Dbl/Twn

Open Jan-Dec
T.d.H £19.50
Bar snacks + meals

Inverkip, Renfrewshire · Map Ref: 1F5

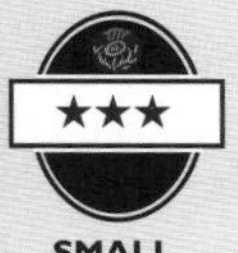

SMALL HOTEL ★★★

Inverkip Hotel
Main Street, Inverkip, Renfrewshire, PA16 0AS
Tel: 01475 521478 Fax: 01475 522065
E-mail: enquiries@inverkip.co.uk
Web: www.inverkip.co.uk

Family run hotel, on main tourist route adjacent to Scotland's No 1 yachting marina. Reputation for good food. Sports can be arranged. Busy restaurant and bars. Ideally positioned for the Clyde ferries to Dunoon and beyond or trips to Loch Lomond, Stirling and the Trossachs. 45 mins drive to Royal Troon.

2 Twin   All En Suite
2 Double
1 Family

B&B per person
from £40.00 Single
from £33.00 Dbl/Twn
Room only from £33.00

Open Jan-Dec

Lanark, Lanarkshire · Map Ref: 2A6

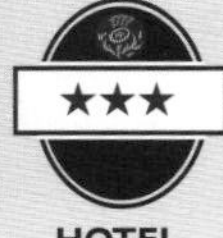

HOTEL ★★★

Cartland Bridge Hotel
Glasgow Road, Lanark, ML11 9UF
Tel: 01555 664426 Fax: 01555 663773
E-mail: sales@cartlandbridge.co.uk
Web: www.cartlandbridge.co.uk

Country house hotel, built in the Scottish Baronial style, set in 20 acres of woodland and garden. Easy access to all routes. 11 miles off the M74 and 1 mile from the historic market town of Lanark. Conference and function facilities with small and large rooms.

2 Single   All En Suite
1 Twin
12 Double
3 Family

B&B per person
from £58.00 Single
from £70.00 Dbl/Twn
Room only from £50.00

Open Jan-Dec

All properties graded by VisitScotland, formerly known as the Scottish Tourist Board. | *Key to symbols is on back flap.*

Lochwinnoch, Renfrewshire — Map Ref: 1G5

B&B

East Lochhead Country House & Cottages
Largs Road, Lochwinnoch, Renfrewshire, PA12 4DX
Tel/Fax: 01505 842610
E-mail: eastlochhead@aol.com
Web: www.eastlochhead.co.uk

1 Twin	All En Suite	B&B per person	Open Jan-Dec
1 Double		from £35.00 Single	B&B + Eve.Meal
1 Family		from £60.00 Dbl/Twn	£50.00-£55.00
		Room only from £25.00	

Spacious Victorian country house overlooking Barr Loch. Easy access to Glasgow Airport and motorway network. Convenient for Ayrshire Coast, Burns Country, Loch Lomond and Glasgow. Taste of Scotland member, evening meals available and breakfasts a speciality. All rooms en-suite.

B&B

Glenshian
Newton of Beltree, Lochwinnoch, Renfrewshire, PA12 8JL
Tel: 01505 842823

1 Double	All En Suite	B&B per person	Open Apr-Oct
1 Family		from £25.00 Single	
		from £28.00 Dbl/Twn	

200 year old Grade B listed house in tiny conservation hamlet, 15 minutes from Glasgow Airport and half an hour from Glasgow city centre and its famous shopping centres. Aileen the co-owner has been a Blue Badge guide for 12 years and is registered to drive her guests around Scotland should they wish.

**GUEST
HOUSE**

Westview
1 Dougalston Gardens South, Milngavie, Glasgow, G62 6HS
Tel: 0141 956 5973

1 Twin	All En Suite	B&B per person	Open Jan-Dec
1 Double		from £24.00 Single	
1 Family		from £40.00 Dbl/Twn	

Detached house in elevated position in quiet residential area yet only 6 miles from centre of Glasgow. Regular train service. All bedrooms ensuite with tea-making facilities. Private guests' lounge with tv. Ample private parking. At start of West Highland Way. Walkers welcome.

Motherwell, Lanarkshire — Map Ref: 2A5

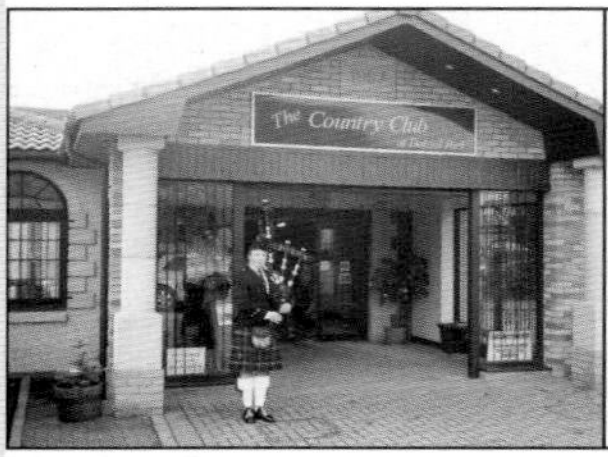

DALZIEL PARK HOTEL,
GOLF & COUNTRY CLUB
100 HAGEN DRIVE, DALZIEL PARK, MOTHERWELL ML1 5RZ
TEL: 01698 862862 FAX: 01698 862863
WEB: www.dalzielpark.co.uk

Situated in pleasant countryside estate 4 miles from Motherwell with good access to M74 and M8 at junction 6 and midway between Glasgow and Edinburgh. Convenient base for touring and relaxation. Facilities include country club with 18-hole course and floodlit driving range. Good food, modern, comfortable and excellent value for money.

**SMALL
HOTEL**

Dalziel Park Golf & Country Club
100 Hagen Drive, Motherwell, ML1 5RZ
Tel: 01698 862862 Fax: 01698 862863
Web: www.dalzielpark.co.uk

1 Single	All En Suite	B&B per person	Open Jan-Dec
4 Double		from £45.00 Single	
4 Family		from £25.00 Dbl/Twn	
		Room only	
		from £39.95	

Newly built accommodation opposite the Clubhouse offering traditional contemporary en-suite bedrooms. Set in picturesque clubhouse woodland setting. Offering 15-bay floodlight driving range, hairdresser and 18 hole golf course. Approximately 20 mins drive to Glasgow and Edinburgh.

Important: Prices stated are estimates and may be subject to amendments

---

Motherwell, Lanarkshire

Map Ref: 2A5

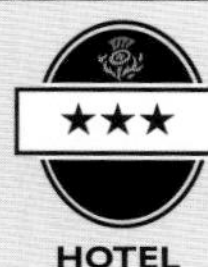

CAMPUS ACCOMMODATION ★

Stewart Hall of Residence
Motherwell College, Dalzell Drive, Motherwell,
Lanarkshire, ML1 2PP
Tel: 01698 261890 Fax: 01698 232527
E-mail: mcol@motherwell.co.uk
Web: www.motherwell.co.uk

On college campus and all on one level. Close to Strathclyde Park and M8/M74 motorway link for Glasgow and Edinburgh.

47 Single	1 En Suite fac	B&B per person	Open Jan-Dec excl
	15 Pub Bath/Show	from £20.00 Single	Xmas/New Year
	45 Priv.NOT ensuite	Room only per person	B&B + Eve.Meal
	1 Limited ensuite	from £17.00	from £24.00

Renfrew

Map Ref: 1H5

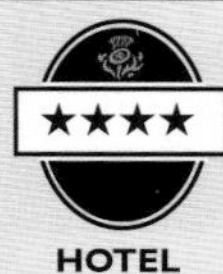

HOTEL ★★★

Normandy Cosmopolitan Hotel
Inchinnan Road, Renfrew, PA4 9EJ
Tel: 0141 886 4100 Fax: 0141 885 2366
E-mail: nres@cosmopolitan-hotels.com
Web: www.cosmopolitan-hotels.com

Conveniently located for both Glasgow Airport and City Centre. 141 en suite bedrooms with ample parking and courtesy airport transport for guests. Comprehensive Conference/Banqueting facilities ensure delegates needs are met in our air conditioned suites. Juliana's Restaurant serves a traditional Carvery daily accompanied by a fine selection of wines. Guests have complimentary use of the David Lloyd Leisure Club nearby.

9 Single	All En Suite	B&B per person	Open Jan-Dec
41 Twin		from £40.00 Single	
88 Double		from £55.00 Dbl/Twn	
3 Family			

Rosebank, Lanarkshire

Map Ref: 2A6

HOTEL ★★★★

Popinjay Hotel
Lanark Road, Rosebank, Clyde Valley, ML8 5QB
Tel: 01555 860441 Fax: 01555 860204
E-mail: popinjayhotel@attglobal.net
Web: www.popinjayhotel.co.uk

Built in Tudor style in 1882 set in 8 acres of private grounds with beautiful picturesque gardens reaching down to the banks of the River Clyde. Fishing rights and free golfing facilities nearby.

3 Single	All En Suite facs	B&B per person	Open Jan-Dec
5 Twin		from £59.00 Single	
30 Double			

Strathaven, Lanarkshire

Map Ref: 2A6

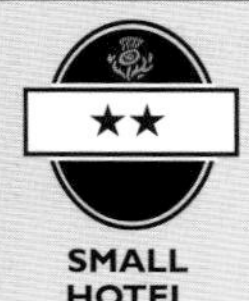

SMALL HOTEL ★★

Springvale Hotel
18 Lethame Road, Strathaven, Lanarkshire, ML10 6AD
Tel: 01357 521131

Informal, friendly family run hotel in quiet residential area close to town centre, with interesting public park at rear. Home cooking, baking and High Teas a speciality. Full evening meal not available. Restricted license.

5 Single	12 En Suite facs	B&B per person	Open Jan-Dec excl
2 Twin	1 Pub Bath/Show	from £27.00 Single	Xmas/New Year
3 Double		from £20.00 Dbl/Twn	B&B + Eve.Meal
2 Family			£28.00-£35.00

Uplawmoor, Renfrewshire

Map Ref: 1G6

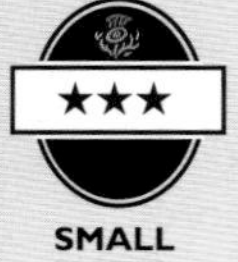

SMALL HOTEL ★★★

Uplawmoor Hotel
Neilston Road, Uplawmoor, Glasgow, G78 4AF
Tel: 01505 850565 Fax: 01505 850689
E-mail: enquiries@uplawmoor.co.uk
Web: www.uplawmoor.co.uk

Quality eighteenth century Coaching Inn situated in quiet picturesque village just thirty minutes from Glasgow City Centre and airport, gateway to Burns Country.

1 Single	All En Suite	B&B per person	Open Jan-Dec excl
3 Twin		from £35.00 Single	Xmas/New Year
9 Double		from £27.50 Dbl/Twn	B&B + Eve.Meal from
1 Family			£45.50

All properties graded by VisitScotland, formerly known as the Scottish Tourist Board.   **Key to symbols is on back flap.**

welcome to scotland

WEST HIGHLANDS AND ISLANDS, LOCH LOMOND, STIRLING AND TROSSACHS

From the green slopes of the Ochil Hills in the east to the far-flung Hebridean Islands on the western seaboard, you will discover a remarkably diverse region where history is set within a glorious natural environment.

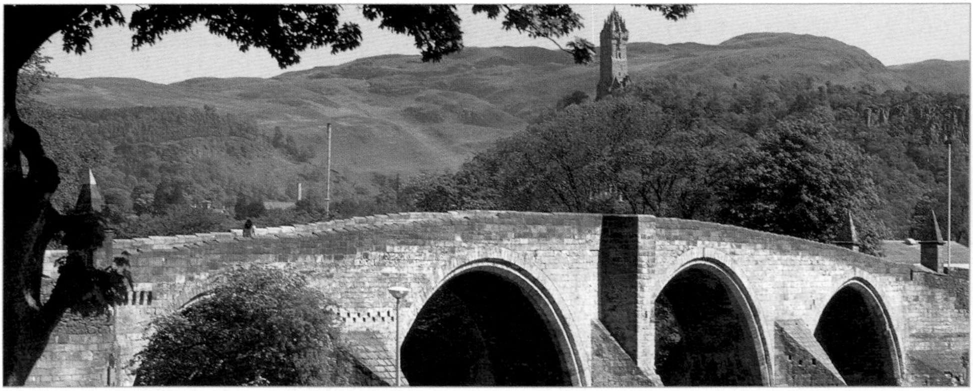

"Old Brig", Stirling, with the Wallace monument in the distance

IT is here that the geological Highland boundary fault divides the lowland south from the mountainous north. Scenically, this area has everything, from the bonny banks of Loch Lomond, a playground for generations of visitors, to the bustling town of Stirling and western coastal resort of Oban.

A good place to begin is the Royal Burgh of Stirling. As a gateway to the Highlands and an important centre, Stirling has played a leading role in Scotland's story. Today, the castle with its recently restored Great Hall and the historic Old Town are just one of its many attractions. Nearby is the National Wallace Monument, telling the real story of Scotland's first freedom-fighter, William Wallace.

In the early days of tourism, the location of Loch Lomond and the Trossachs, a highly scenic area just beyond the Highland line, made them easy to reach. Often described as "The Highlands in Miniature", the Trossachs is still easy to reach with its gateway being the bustling and friendly town of Callander.

At the Rob Roy and Trossachs Visitor Centre, you can uncover the legend of this celebrated folk hero. An excellent way to enjoy the captivating beauty of this area is on board the SS Sir Walter Scott which makes regular cruises across the placid waters of Loch Katrine. There are also plenty of cruising options on Loch Lomond, Scotland's largest loch (by surface area), which will shortly become part of Scotland's first national park. The story of the loch is interpreted at the new Lomond Shores Centre, opening in the summer of 2002.

WEST HIGHLANDS AND ISLANDS, LOCH LOMOND, STIRLING AND TROSSACHS

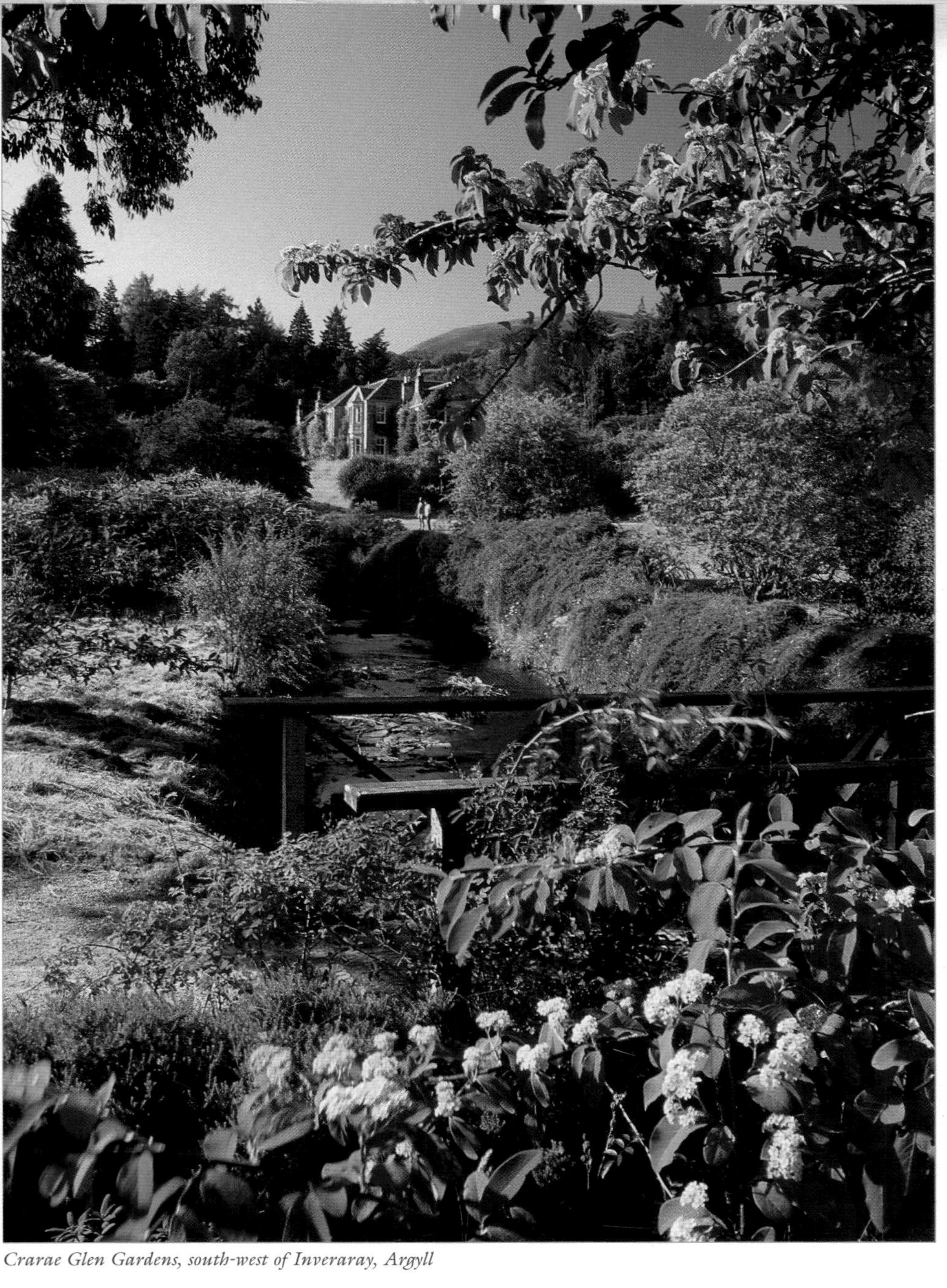

Crarae Glen Gardens, south-west of Inveraray, Argyll

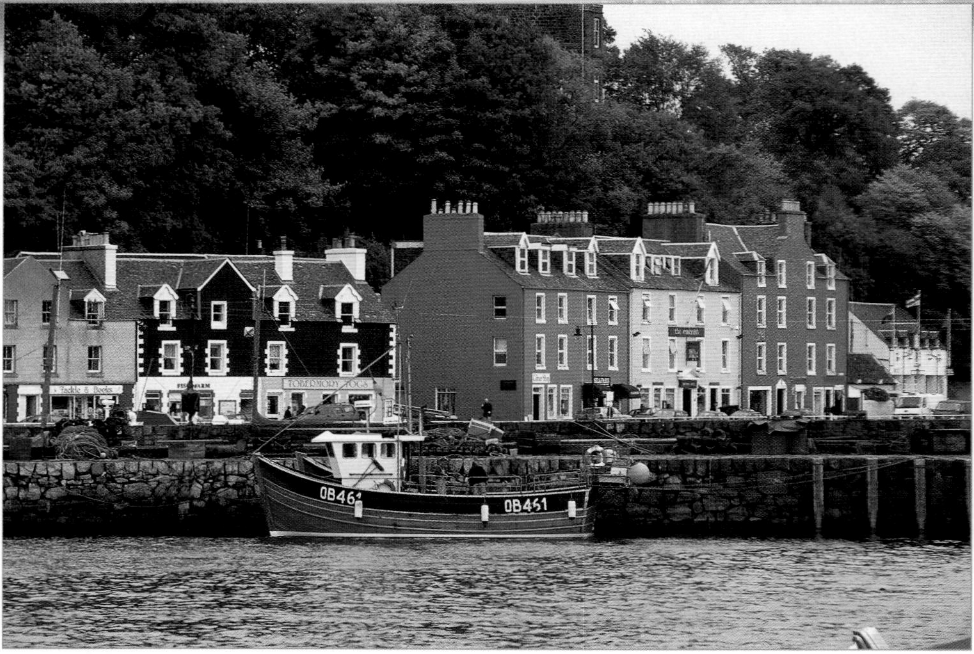

Tobermory, Isle of Mull

Further west is the delightful Cowal Peninsula with the fine Victorian resort of Dunoon and the lovely Isle of Bute with its magnificent Victorian gothic mansion, Mount Stuart and pleasant seaside resort of Rothesay. Across the sheltered waters of Loch Fyne sits the Georgian planned village of Inveraray and to the south the beautiful peninsula of Kintyre offering miles of shoreline and beaches with unsurpassed views of the islands. Regular ferry services cross to the lively island of Islay, world-famous for its peaty malt whiskies and then to Jura, which in contrast, has one road, one distillery, one hotel and lots of space.

The road west will take you through a panorama of dramatic mountains which sweep down to the coastal resort of Oban. Romantic names and places such as Tobermory with its picture postcard harbour await the visitor to Mull and the island of Iona and Staffa are close by. You could venture further west for a real experience of island life and visit Colonsay, Tiree or Coll, but wherever you choose, you can be sure you will find a warm welcome in the heartland of Scotland.

Events
West Highlands and Islands, Loch Lomond, Stirling and Trosscahs

2-6 May
15th Isle of Bute Jazz Festival
Isle of Bute, Various Venues
The 15th year of this popular festival featuring national and international jazz stars.
Contact: Rothesay Tourist Information Centre
Tel: 01700 502151
Web: www.isle-of-bute.com

26-27 May
Loch Fyne Seafood Fair
Loch Fyne, Argyllshire
A feast of west coast sea food, plus live entertainment.
Contact: Loch Fyne Oysters
Tel: 01499 600264
Web: www.loch-fyne.co.uk

14-16 June
Royal Rothesay Regatta and Carnival
Isle of Bute, Various Venues
Regatta–including round Bute race and various dingy races. Carnival, craft fair, farmers market, fancy dress parade etc.
Contact: Robert Alexander
Tel: 01700 50714

6 July
Stirling Highland Games
Stirling,
Stirling County Rugby Club
Highland games with pipe band competition, solo piping, drum major competition, heavyweight competition, wrestling competition and tug of war.
Contact: Irene Ponton
Tel: 01259 761735

11-14 July
Scottish Open Golf
Luss,
Loch Lomond Golf Club
Professional golf tournament, forming part of the PGA European tour.
Contact: Loch Lomond Golf Club
Tel: 01436 655555

27-28 July
World Championship Highland Games
Callander, Games Field
Traditional Highland games and Highland dancing.
Contact: Mr D McKirgan
Tel: 01877 330919

26 July-2 August
West Highland Yachting Week
Oban & Tobermory,
Various Venues
Yachts of all shapes and sizes race up the West Coast, with much on-shore festivities in the towns visited.
Contact: Miss Julia Heap
Tel: 01631 563309

30-31 August
Cowal Highland Gathering
Dunoon, The Stadium
Largest Highland games in the world, featuring Highland dancing championship and pipe band championship.
Contact:
Cowal Highland Gathering
Tel: 01369 703206
Web: www.cowalgathering.com

11-13 October
Phillips Tour of Mull Rally
Isle of Mull, Various Venues
Exciting car rally using the demanding roads on Mull.
Contact: Neil Molyneux
Tel: 01254 826564
Web: www.2300club.org

* *denotes provisional date, please check before attending.*

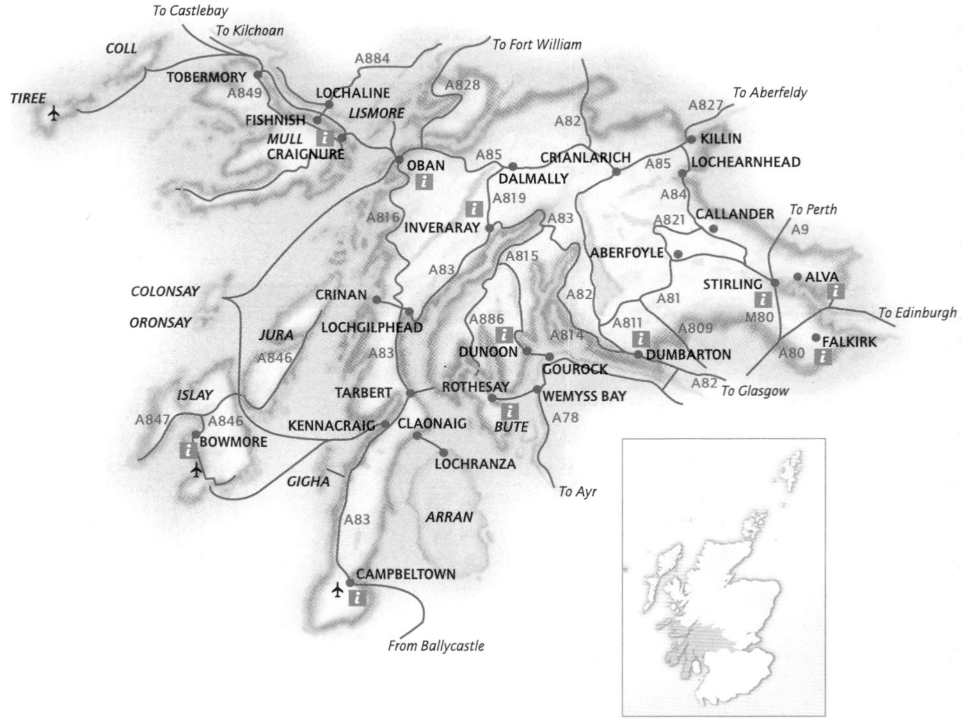

ARGYLL, THE ISLES,
LOCH LOMOND, STIRLING
AND TROSSACHS TOURIST
BOARD
Dept. SOS
7 Alexandra Parade
Dunoon
PA23 8AB

Tel: 01369 703785
Fax : 01369 706085
E-mail: info@scottishheartlands.org
Web: www.scottishheartlands.org

Tourist Information Centres
West Highlands and Islands,
Loch Lomond, Stirling and Trossachs

**WEST HIGHLANDS,
LOCH LOMOND,
STIRLING AND
TROSSACHS
TOURIST BOARD**

Aberfoyle
Trossachs Discovery
Centre
Main Street
Tel: (01877)
382352
*Jan-Dec, Nov-Mar
weekends only*

Alva
Mill Trail Visitor
Centre
Tel: (01259)
769696
Jan-Dec

Ardgartan
Arrochar
Tel: (01301)
702432
April-Oct

Balloch
Balloch Road
Tel: (01389)
753533
April-Oct

Bo'ness
Seaview Car Park
Tel: (01506)
826626
April-Sept

Bowmore
Isle of Islay
Tel: (01496)
810254
Jan-Dec

Callander
Rob Roy and
Trossachs
Visitor Centre
Ancaster Square
Tel: (01877)
330342
Mar-Dec
*Jan and Feb weekends
only*

Campbeltown
Mackinnon House
The Pier
Argyll
Tel: (01586)
552056
Jan-Dec

Craignure
The Pier
Isle of Mull
Tel: (01680)
812377
Jan-Dec

Drymen
Drymen Library
The Square
Tel: (01360)
660068
May-Sept

Dumbarton
Milton
A82 Northbound
Tel: (01389)
742306
Jan-Dec

Dunblane
Stirling Road
Tel: (01786)
824428
May-Sept

Dunoon
7 Alexandra Parade
Argyll
Tel: (01369)
703785
Jan-Dec

Falkirk
2-4 Glebe Street
Tel: (01324)
620244
Jan-Dec

Helensburgh
The Clock Tower
Tel: (01436)
672642
April-Oct

Inveraray
Front Street
Argyll
Tel: (01499)
302063
Jan-Dec

Killin
Breadalbane Folklore
Centre
Tel: (01567)
820254
March-end Oct

Lochgilphead
Lochnell Street
Argyll
Tel: (01546)
602344
April-Oct

Oban
Argyll Square
Argyll
Tel: (01631)
563122
Jan-Dec

Rothesay
Isle of Bute
Discovery Centre,
Winter Gardens
Tel: (01700)
502151
Jan-Dec

Stirling
Dumbarton Road
Tel: (01786)
475019
Jan-Dec

**Stirling (Royal
Burgh)**
The Esplanade
Tel: (01786)
479901
Jan-Dec

Stirling
Pirnhall Motorway
Service Area
Juntion 9, M9
Tel: (01786)
814111
April-Oct

**Tarbert,
Loch Fyne**
Harbour Street
Argyll
Tel: (01880)
820429
*Jan-Dec, Nov-Mar
weekends only*

**Tarbet-
Loch Lomond**
Main Street
Tel: (01301)
702260
April-Oct

Tobermory
Isle of Mull
Tel: (01688)
302182
April-Oct

Tyndrum
Main Street
Tel: (01838)
400246
April-Oct

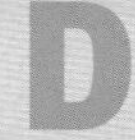

Aberfoyle, Perthshire　　　　　　　　　　　Map Ref: 1H3

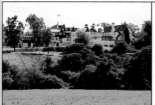

Inchrie Castle &
The Covenanters Inn

THE TROSSACHS · ABERFOYLE · PERTHSHIRE · FK8 3XD
Telephone: 01877 382347 Fax: 01877 382785
Web: www.inchriecastle.co.uk   ★★★ INN

Steeped in history and standing in the beautiful surroundings of The Trossachs
in the heart of Scotland's first National Park. Traditional charm and warmth of
welcome in a hotel that's proud to be all that is Scottish. **From £55.00 per
person per night DB&B.**

★★★

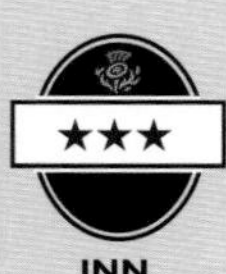

INN

Inchrie Castle and The Covenanters Inn
Duchray Road, Aberfoyle, Perthshire, FK8 3XD
Tel: 01877 382347 Fax: 01877 382785

5 Single	50 En Suite fac
24 Twin	2 Priv.NOT ensuite
18 Double	
5 Family	

Open Jan-Dec
B&B + Eve.Meal
£43.00-£65.00

Overlooking Aberfoyle, on the edge of Queen Elizabeth Park. Ideal base
for touring. Traditional coaching inn.

★★★★

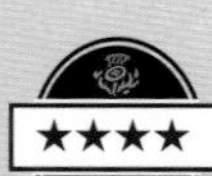

GUEST
HOUSE

Creag-Ard House
Aberfoyle, Stirling, FK8 3TQ
Tel/Fax: 01877 382297
E-mail: cara@creag-ardhouse.co.uk
Web: www.creag-ardhouse.co.uk

2 Twin	All En Suite
4 Double	

B&B per person
from £38.00 Single
from £28.00 Dbl/Twn

Open March-Oct
B&B + Eve.Meal
from £50.00

Welcoming Guest House with superb views over Loch Ard 3kms from the
centre of Aberfoyle Village in the heart of Trossachs. A haven of peace
and tranquility. Delicious breakfast with homebaking. Evening meals by
arrangement.

Acharacle, Argyll　　　　　　　　　　　Map Ref: 3F12

★★

SMALL
HOTEL

Loch Shiel House Hotel
Acharacle, Argyll, PH36 4JL
Tel: 01967 431224 Fax: 01967 431200
E-mail: info@lochshielhouse.fsnet.co.uk
Web: www.lochshielhouse.fsnet.co.uk

1 Single	All En Suite
3 Twin	
5 Double	
1 Family	

B&B per person
from £37.50 Single
from £32.50 Dbl/Twn

Open Jan-Dec

Friendly and relaxed hotel on shores of Loch Shiel. All bedrooms en suite
and recently refurbished to high standard. Cosy bar with real fire and
separate lounge. Local seafood a speciality on menus. Ideal location for
fishing, birdwatching, walking and touring Ardnamurchan Peninsula.
Flaming fires, friendly faces and fine food.

Ardchattan, Argyll　　　　　　　　　　　Map Ref: 1E2

★★★★

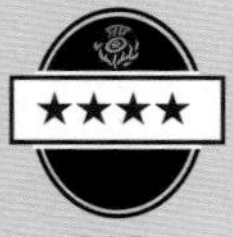

B&B

Blarcreen Farm Guest House
Ardchattan, Argyll, PA37 1RG
Tel/Fax: 01631 750272
E-mail: j.lace@blarcreenfarm.demon.co.uk
Web: www.blarcreenfarm.com

1 Dbl/Twin	All En Suite
2 Double	

B&B per person
from £28.50 Dbl/Twn

Open Mar-Dec
B&B + Eve.Meal from
£42.50

Victorian farmhouse overlooking Loch Etive and the hills beyond. Ideal
location for a quiet break. Quality, comfort, stunning views, excellence in
accommodation and food. King four-poster beds.

Important: Prices stated are estimates and may be subject to amendments

---

Ardfern, Argyll   Map Ref: 1E3

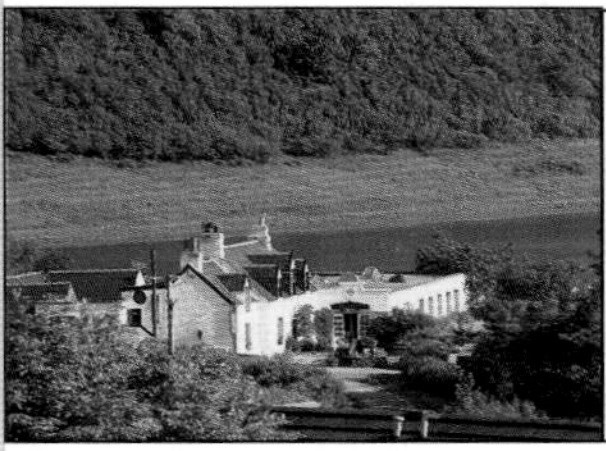

The Galley of Lorne Inn
by Lochgilphead, Argyll PA31 8QN
Telephone: 01852 500284 Fax: 01852 500284
Charming traditional inn, beautifully situated on the shores of Loch Craignish. Highest standards of comfort and service complemented by excellent food, with local seafood a speciality. Friendly pub with log fires, good company and a wide selection of malt whiskies. Bird and seal watching, riding, walking.

★★★

INN

Galley of Lorne Inn
Ardfern,by Lochgilphead, Argyll, PA31 8QN
Tel/Fax: 01852 500284

2 Twin	6 En Suite fac
5 Double	1 Priv.NOT ensuite

B&B per person
from £35.00 Single
from £33.50 Dbl/Twn

Open Jan-Dec

Lively traditional Highland Inn, with open fires. Emphasis on charcoal grilled steaks and local seafood. Most bedrooms with loch views.

Ardlui, Argyll   Map Ref: 1G3

★★

SMALL HOTEL

Ardlui Hotel
Ardlui, Loch Lomomd, Argyll, G83 7EB
Tel: 01301 704243 Fax: 01301 704268
E-mail: info@ardlui.co.uk
Web: www.ardlui.co.uk

2 Twin	All En Suite
4 Double	
2 Family	
1 Triple	
1 Single	

B&B per person
from £45.00 Single
from £35.00 Dbl/Twn

Open Jan-Dec

Former shooting lodge on A82 and on the banks of Loch Lomond with private gardens to shore. Caravan site adjacent. Moorings available. 1 hour from Glasgow or Oban & 1 ¹/₂ hours from Fort William via Glencoe.

Ardrishaig, by Lochgilphead, Argyll   Map Ref: 1E4

★★★

GUEST HOUSE

Allt-Na-Craig
Tarbert Road, Ardrishaig, Argyll, PA30 8EP
Tel: 01546 603245
Web: www.smoothhound.co.uk/hotels/alltnacr.html

1 Single	All En Suite
2 Twin	
2 Double	
1 Family	

B&B per person
from £32.00 Single
from £32.00 Dbl/Twn
Room only per person
from £27.00

Open Jan-Dec excl
Xmas/New Year
B&B + Eve.Meal
from £48.00

A Victorian Mansion set in picturesque grounds, with magnificent views across Loch Fyne. Entrance to Crinan Canal nearby. Home cooking. Hill-walking, bird-watching, fishing, golf, riding, diving, wind-surfing and many other outdoor activities are available in the area.

All properties graded by VisitScotland, formerly known as the Scottish Tourist Board.   **Key to symbols is on back flap.**

Arduaine, Argyll

Map Ref: 1E3

LOCH MELFORT HOTEL

ARDUAINE, BY OBAN, ARGYLL PA34 4XG
Telephone: 01852 200233 Fax: 01852 200214
e.mail: lmhotel@aol.com Web: www.loch-melfort.co.uk

The finest location for uninterrupted views of the west coast islands located on A816
between Oban and Inveraray beside the National Trust Gardens. Join our regular guests
and enjoy excellent award winning cuisine in our 2AA Rosette restaurant or in the
'Skerry' Bistro and Bar. *SEASONAL BREAKS AVAILABLE*
B&B from £39.00 per person per night

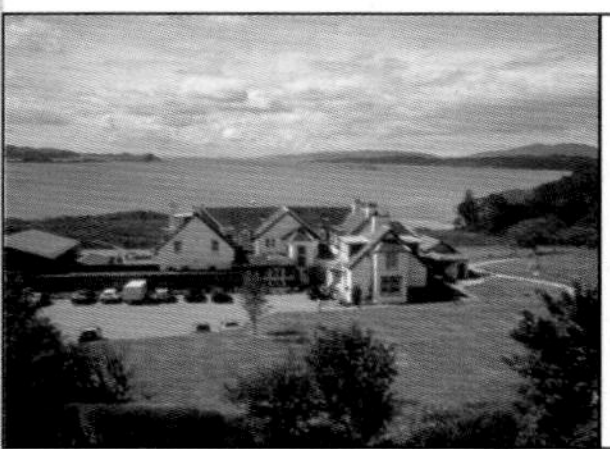

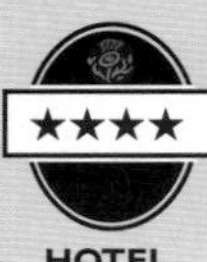

HOTEL

Loch Melfort Hotel
Arduaine, by Oban, Argyll, PA34 4XG
Tel: 01852 200233 Fax: 01852 200214
E-mail: lmhotel@aol.com
Web: www.loch-melfort.co.uk

Family run hotel located 20 miles south from Oban in a magnificent location overlooking
the Sound of Jura and many small islands. Spectacular views from all bedrooms, lounge
and restaurant. Emphasis on locally caught seafood and shellfish and enjoying an excellent
reputation for home cooking and fresh produce. Arduaine Gardens adjacent with many
other glorious gardens in the area. Pony trekking and watersports available. Some annexe
bedrooms.

13 Twin	All En Suite	B&B per person	Open Jan-Dec
13 Double		from £49.00 Single	B&B + Eve.Meal
2 Family		from £39.00 Dbl/Twn	from £45.00

Balloch, Dunbartonshire

Map Ref: 1G4

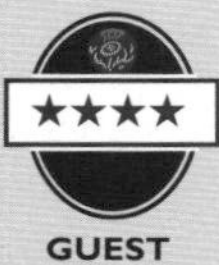

**GUEST
HOUSE**

Gowanlea Guest House
Drymen Road, Balloch, Dunbartonshire, G83 8HS
Tel: 01389 752456 Fax: 01389 710543
E-mail: gowanlea@aol.com
Web: http://members.aol.com/gowanlea/gowanlea.htm

Situated in residential area of Balloch, close to world famous Loch
Lomond. Friendly welcome. All rooms ensuite.

1 Twin	All En Suite	B&B per person	Open Jan-Dec
2 Double		£20.00-£30.00 Single	
		£20.00-£24.00 Dbl/Twn	

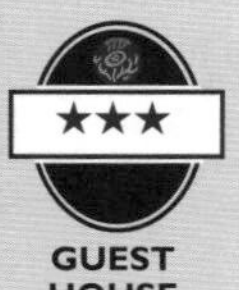

**GUEST
HOUSE**

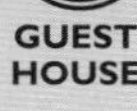

Heathpete Guest House
24 Balloch Road, Balloch, G83 8LE
Tel: 01389 752195
E-mail: sheathpete@aol.com

Extended family bungalow in heart of village with all amenities close by.
A few minutes walk to bus/rail stations, boat cruises and Country Park.

2 Double	All En Suite	B&B per person	Open Jan-Dec
2 Family		from £15.00 Single	
		from £15.00 Dbl/Twn	
		Room only from £14.00	

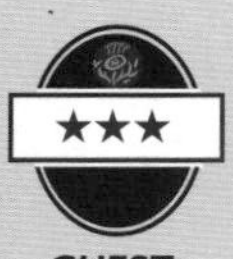

**GUEST
HOUSE**

Norwood Guest House
60 Balloch Road, Balloch, Loch Lomond,
Dunbartonshire, G83 8LE
Tel: 01389 750309 Fax: 01389 710469
E-mail: norwoodgh@aol.com

Centrally located overlooking Balloch Castle Country Park. Close to all
local amenities including restaurants and shops. A short stroll to Loch
Lomond and the Railway Station with its frequent service to Glasgow City
Centre.

2 Twin	All En Suite	B&B per person	Open Nov-Oct
3 Double		from £18.00 Single	
		from £18.00 Dbl/Twn	

Important: Prices stated are estimates and may be subject to amendments

Balloch, Dunbartonshire · Map Ref: 1G4

★★★★
B&B

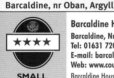

Sheildaig Farm

Upper Stoneymollen Road, Balloch, Alexandria
Dunbartonshire, G83 8QY
Tel: 01389 752459 Fax: 01389 753695
Mobile: 07711 317966
E-mail: sheildaigfarm@talk21.com
Web: www.scotland2000.com/sheildaig

Totally refurbished farm courtyard buildings in secluded setting. Conveniently situated for touring Loch Lomond and the Trossachs. Easy access to A82 and Glasgow Airport. Candlelit dinners, Taste of Scotland member with table license. 5 minutes from Balloch station with its service into Glasgow city centre.

1 Twin	All En Suite	B&B per person	Open Jan-Dec
3 Double		from £40.00 Single	B&B + Eve.Meal
1 Family		from £25.00 Double	from £40.00
		Room only from £22.50	

Barcaldine, nr Oban, Argyll · Map Ref: 1E2

★★★★
SMALL
HOTEL

Barcaldine House Hotel

Barcaldine, Nr Oban, Argyll, PA37 1SG
Tel: 01631 720219 Fax: 01631 720219
E-mail: barcaldine@breathe.co.uk
Web: www.countrymansions.com

Barcaldine House, the building of which started in 1709 by 'Red Patrick' is set into the foot of Ben Vreck and at the edge of the Barcaldine Forest. Dinner, using fresh local produce in season, is served in the impressive dining room. Guests can relax after dinner with a game of snooker on the full sized snooker table. Good base from which to visit Argylls' many attractions including sailings to the islands.

3 Twin	All En Suite	B&B per person	Open Jan-Dec
4 Double		from £50.00-£60.00	
		Single	
		from £40.00-£50.00	
		Dbl/Twn	

Bo'ness, West Lothian · Map Ref: 2B4

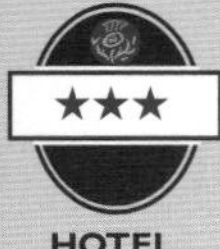

★★★
HOTEL

Richmond Park Hotel

26 Linlithgow Road, Bo'ness, West Lothian,
EH51 0DN
Tel: 01506 823213 Fax: 01506 822717
Web: www.richmondparkhotel.co.uk

Privately owned hotel, overlooking the river Forth centrally located between Stirling and Edinburgh. A la carte restaurant and popular lounge-diner. Residents conservatory and fitness room. Occasional Scottish entertainment.

1 Single	All En Suite	B&B per person	Open 3 Jan- 31 Dec
22 Twin		from £55.00 Single	
17 Double		from £75.00 Dbl/Twn	
6 Family			

Bridge of Orchy, Argyll · Map Ref: 1G1

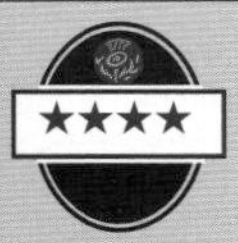

★★★★
SMALL
HOTEL

Bridge of Orchy Hotel

Bridge of Orchy, Argyll, PA36 4AD
Tel: 01838 400208 Fax: 01838 400313
E-mail: info@bridgeoforchy.co.uk

A hotel of character offering high quality rooms and service, conveniently located on the main A82 trunk road, 6 miles north of Tyndrum. Popular with walkers and outdoor enthusiasts. Spectacular scenery surrounds. Bar full of adventurous spirit. One AA rosette for food.

2 Twin	All En Suite	B&B per person	Open Jan-Nov
6 Double		£25.00-£55.00 Single	
2 Family		£20.00-£55.00 Dbl/Twn	

Rothesay, Isle of Bute · Map Ref: 1F5

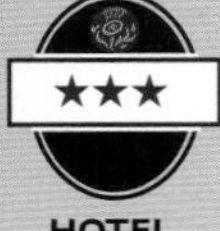

★★★
HOTEL

The Ardyne-St Ebba Hotel and Restaurant

37-38 Mountstuart Road, Rothesay, Isle of Bute, PA20 9EB
Tel: 01700 502052
E-mail: ardyne.hotel@virgin.net
Web: www.rothesay-scotland.com

Elegant, licensed Victorian hotel, with spectacular seafront views. All bedrooms en-suite. Growing reputation for comfortable accommodation and excellent restaurant.

1 Single	All En Suite	B&B per person	Open Jan-Dec excl
7 Twin	1 Pub Bath	from £30.00 Single	Xmas
5 Double		from £27.50 Dbl/Twn	B&B + Eve.Meal
5 Family		Room only from £25.00	from £42.00

All properties graded by VisitScotland, formerly known as the Scottish Tourist Board. | **Key to symbols is on back flap.**

Rothesay, Isle of Bute

Map Ref: 1F5

HOTEL ★★

Glenburn Hotel
Mount Stuart Road, Rothesay, Isle of Bute, PA20 9JP
Tel: 01786 436600 Fax: 01786 436650
E-mail: l.graig@shearingsholidays.co.uk
Web: www.shearingsholidays.com

Fine Victorian building in an outstanding position above its own terraced
gardens overlooking the sea.

10 Single	All En Suite
88 Twin	
29 Double	

Open Feb-Dec

**GUEST
HOUSE** ★

Lyndhurst Guest House
29 Battery Place, Rothesay, Isle of Bute, PA20 9DU
Tel: 01700 504799

Lyndhurst Guest House is pleasantly situated 5 minutes from Pier on the
Promenade overlooking Rothesay Bay. Most of the rooms enjoy
spectacular views across Rothesay Bay and to the Cowal Hills and Loch
Striven. Some private parking, Plenty free on street parking.

1 Single	B&B per person
2 Twin	from £18.00 Single
2 Double	from £18.00 Dbl/Twn
2 Family	Room only from £16.00

Opne Jan-Dec
B&B + Eve.Meal from
£22.00

Cairndow, Argyll

Map Ref: 1F3

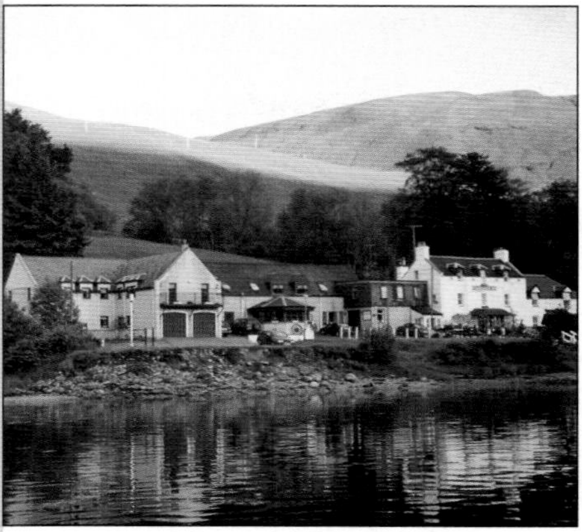

Cairndow Stagecoach Inn

Cairndow, Argyll PA26 8BN
Tel: 01499 600286 Fax: 01499 600220
e.mail: cairndowinn@aol.com

Across the 'Arrochar Alps' on Loch Fyne this
historic coaching inn enjoys a delightful situation
just off the A83. It is a haven of sparkling views,
high mountains and magnificent woodlands and
rivers.
We offer excellent accommodation in 14 bedrooms,
all en-suite, in a relaxed country atmosphere.
All have TV, radio, telephone, central heating etc.
Two deluxe bedrooms with two-person spa baths.
Stables Restaurant with conservatory and bar meals
served all day. Ideal centre for touring the Western
Highlands from Glencoe to Kintyre and
Loch Lomond and The Trossachs. Lochside beer
garden, sauna and solarium, half price golf.

INN ★★★

Cairndow Stagecoach Inn
Cairndow, Argyll, PA26 8BN
Tel: 01499 600286 Fax: 01499 600220
E-mail: cairndowinn@aol.com

Old Coaching Inn on Loch Fyne. Ideal centre for touring Western
Highlands. 9 bedrooms with loch view - all en-suite - all fully appointed.
2 rooms with 2 person spa baths. Stables restaurant and lounge meals
all day. Half-price golf at Inveraray. Beer garden. Sauna, solarium and
multi-gym.

6 Twin	All En Suite
6 Double	
2 Family	

B&B per person
from £28.00-£45.00
Single
from £24.00-£50.00
Dbl/Twn

Open Jan-Dec
B&B + Eve.Meal
from £35.00-£50.00

Important: Prices stated are estimates and may be subject to amendments

Callander, Perthshire Map Ref: 1H3

★★★

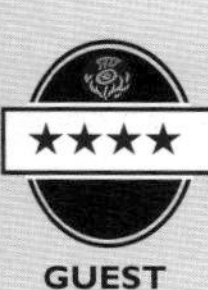

GUEST HOUSE

Annfield Guest House
North Church Street, Callander, Perthshire, FK17 8EG
Tel: 01877 330204 Fa: 01877 330674
E-mail: annfield@hotmail.com

Centrally situated in a quiet area of the town in close proximity to shops and restaurants. Stepping stone to the Highlands.

2 Twin	4 En Suite fac
4 Double	1 Priv.NOT ensuite
1 Family	2 Pub Bath/Show

B&B per person
from £25.00 Single
from £21.00 Dbl/Twn

Open Jan-Dec excl
Xmas/New Year

★★★★

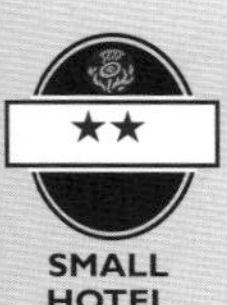

GUEST HOUSE

Arden House
Bracklinn Road, Callander, Perthshire, FK17 8EQ
Tel/Fax: 01877 330235
E-mail: ardenhouse@onetel.net.uk
Web: www.SmoothHound.co.uk/hotels/arden.html

Elegant Victorian country house, peacefully set in attractive gardens with marvellous views of hills and countryside. Home of BBC TV's 'Dr Finlay's Casebook'. Ideal base for touring the Trossachs and western highlands.

1 Single	All En Suite
2 Twin	
3 Double	

B&B per person
from £30.00 Single
from £27.50 Dbl/Twn

Open end Mar-end Oct

★★

SMALL HOTEL

Coppice Hotel
Leny Road, Callander, Perthshire, FK17 8AL
Tel: 01877 330188

Personally run hotel with emphasis on cuisine using fresh local produce when available.

1 Twin	All En Suite
3 Double	
1 Family	

B&B per person
from £23.00 Dbl/Twn

Open Jan-Dec
B&B + Eve.Meal from
£32.00

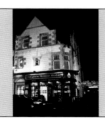

dalgair house hotel
113-115 MAIN STREET, CALLANDER, FK17 8BQ
TEL: 01877 330283 FAX: 01877 331114
E.MAIL: nieto@btinternet.com WEB: www.dalgair-house-hotel.co.uk

Family run small hotel with a friendly atmosphere. Superb a la carte restaurant, well stocked, characterful lounge bar/diner. In the heart of Callander's busy shopping centre, the gateway to the beautiful Trossachs. All rooms are fully en-suite with bath and shower and mainly king size beds. Fishing and golf arranged.

★★

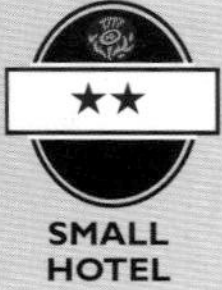

SMALL HOTEL

Dalgair House Hotel
113-115 Main Street, Callander, FK17 8BQ
Tel: 01877 330283 Fax: 01877 331114
E-mail: nieto@btinternet.com
Web: www.dalgair-house-hotel.co.uk

Family run, main street hotel of character with informal friendly service. Good food using local ingredients; Bistro and Restaurant. Ample car parking.

3 Twin	All Ensuite fac
4 Double	
1 Family	

B&B per person
from £35.00 Single
from £55.00 Dbl/Twn

Open Jan-Dec

All properties graded by VisitScotland, formerly known as the Scottish Tourist Board. | *Key to symbols is on back flap.* |

Callander, Perthshire — Map Ref: 1H3

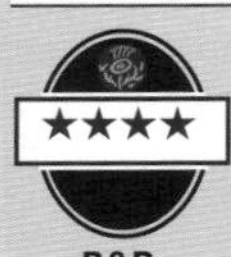

B&B ★★★★

Invertrossachs Country House
by Callander, Perthshire, FK17 8HG
Tel: 01877 331126 Fax: 01877 331229
E-mail: res@invertrossachs.co.uk
Web: www.invertrossachs.co.uk

Comfortable large rooms and suites within an Edwardian mansion
offering country house bed and breakfast and enjoying privacy and
seclusion by the shores of Loch Venachar. Spacious accommodation with
outstanding loch or mountain views.

1 Twin	All En Suite	B&B per person	Open Jan-Dec excl
2 Double		from £40.00 Single	Xmas/New Year
		from £40.00 Dbl/Twn	B&B + Eve.Meal from
			£62.50

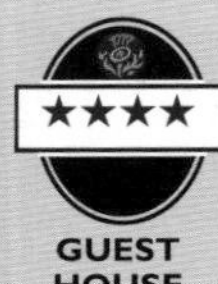

GUEST HOUSE ★★★★

Lubnaig Hotel
Leny Feus, Callander, Perthshire, FK17 8AS
Tel/Fax: 01877 330376
E-mail: reception@lubnaighotel.co.uk
Web: www.lubnaighotel.co.uk

Enhanced by its secluded location, large garden, private parking and
within easy walking distance of the town centre. A genuine Scottish
welcome awaits all guests. Why not stay longer, see Scotland and pay
less.

| 4 Twin | All En Suite | B&B per person | Open Apr-Oct |
| 6 Double | | from £30.00 Dbl/Twn | |

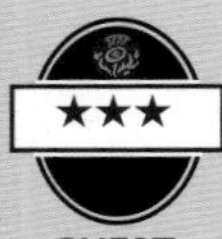

GUEST HOUSE ★★★

Riverview Guest House
Leny Road, Callander, Perthshire, FK17 8AL
Telex: 01877 330635 Fax: 01877 339386
E-mail: auldtoll@netscapeonline.co.uk
Web: www.nationalparksscotland.co.uk

Detached stone built Victorian house set in its own garden with private
parking. Close to town centre, leisure complex and local amenities.
Within easy walking distance of pleasant riverside park and cycle track.
Ideal base for exploring the beautiful Trossachs.

1 Single	All En Suite	B&B per person	Open Feb-Nov
2 Twin		from £20.00 Single	B&B + Eve.Meal
2 Double		from £20.00 Dbl/Twn	from £32.00

Campbeltown, Argyll — Map Ref: 1D7

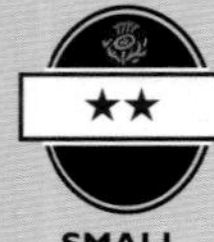

SMALL HOTEL ★★

Ardshiel Hotel
Kilkerran Road, Campbeltown, Argyll, PA28 6JL
Tel: 01586 552133 Fax: 01586 551422
E-mail: ardshiel@aol.com

Built in 1877 for a Campbeltown Whiskey Baron, The Ardshiel is now a
very comfortable and welcoming personally run hotel with a strong local
reputation for quality meals to suit all tastes. Real ales and a selection of
160 malt whiskies. Quiet location but only minutes walk from town
centre and Irish ferry terminal.

5 Twin	7 En Suite fac	B&B per person	Open Jan-Dec
2 Double	1 Pub Bath/Show	from £30.00 Single	
2 Family		from £30.00 Dbl/Twn	

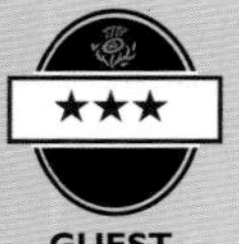

GUEST HOUSE ★★★

Westbank Guest House
Dell Road, Campbeltown, PA28 6JG
Tel/Fax: 01586 553660

A well maintained Victorian villa in a quiet residential area, near to
Machrihanish Golf Course. An ideal base for touring. 3 minutes walk to
all town centre restaurants, shops and attractions.

1 Single	6 En Suite fac	B&B per person	Open Jan-Dec
2 Twin	1 Priv.NOT ensuite	from £20.00 Single	
2 Double		from £18.00 Dbl/Twn	
2 Family			

Important: Prices stated are estimates and may be subject to amendments

Carradale, Argyll   Map Ref: 1E6

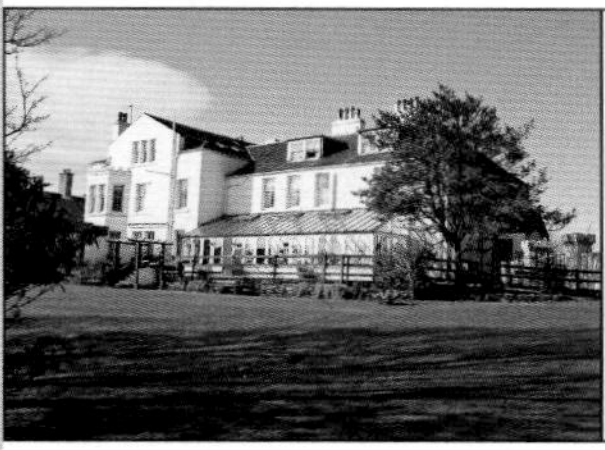

Carradale Hotel

Carradale, Nr. Campbeltown, Argyll PA28 6RY
Telephone and Fax: 01583 431223
e.mail: carradaleh@aol.com Web: www.carradalehotel.com

Overlooking Arran, this Taste of Scotland recommended family run hotel specialises in local fish and game, fine wines, local malts and cask ales. Golf on the adjacent course, sauna, bikes, fishing, riding, forest walks and sandy beaches. We provide an ideal base for exploring Kintyre and the Islands.

★★★

**SMALL
HOTEL**

Carradale Hotel
Carradale, Argyll, PA28 6RY
Tel/Fax: 01583 431223
E-mail: carradaleh@aol.com
Web: www.carradalehotel.com

Family run hotel, overlooking Arran. Beautiful scenery, golf, fishing, beaches, mountain bikes, hillwalking and sauna. Taste of Scotland recommended.

3 Twin	All En Suite	B&B per person	Open Jan-Dec
6 Double		from £25.00 Single	B&B + Eve.Meal
		from £25.00 Dbl/Twn	from £41.50

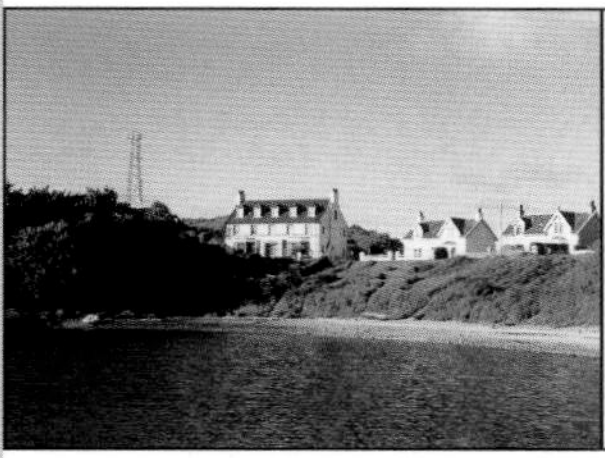

Dunvalanree

Port Righ Bay, Carradale, Campbeltown, Argyll PA28 6SE
Tel: 01583 431226 Fax: 01583 431339
e.mail: stay@dunvalanree.com Web: www.dunvalanree.com

Built in 1938, Dunvalanree is situated above the bay where Robert the Bruce landed in 1306. Follow in his footsteps, eat the best of Argyll produce then fall asleep to the sound of the sea. Ideal centre for visiting Kintyre - experience the history and natural wildlife at "the water's edge".

★★★★

**SMALL
HOTEL**

Dunvalanree House
Portrigh Bay, Carradale, Argyll, PA28 6SE
Tel: 01583 431226 Fax: 01583 431339
E-mail: stay@dunvalanree.com
Web: www.dunvalanree.com

Traditional 1930's guest house with many original features in idyllic location overlooking Portrigh Bay with views to Arran. Recently refurbished to a high standard with most rooms now ensuite.

1 Single	5 En Suite	B&B per person	Open Jan-Dec
6 Double	2 Priv.NOT ensuite	from £22.00-£36.00	B&B + Eve.Meal from £37.00-£50.00

Clachan, by Tarbert, Argyll

★★★

HOTEL

Balinakill Country House Hotel
Clachan, by Tarbert, Argyll, PA29 6XL
Tel: 01880 740206 Fax: 01880 740298
E-mail: info@balinakill.com
Web: www.balinakill.com

Located on the edge of the small hamlet of Clachan, 10 miles south of Tarbert, Balinakill is a fine family-run country home set within its own grounds offering its guests an excellent home for enjoying the delights of this beautiful and peaceful part of Scotland. Ferries to Ireland, Islay, Jura, Arran and Cowal.

2 Twin	All En Suite	B&B per person	Open Jan-Dec
6 Double		from £35.00 Single	B&B + Eve.Meal from £50.00
2 Family		from £35.00 Dbl/Twn	

Colintraive, Argyll　　　　　　　　　　Map Ref: 1F5

★★

SMALL
HOTEL

The Colintraive Hotel
Colintraive, by Dunoon, Argyll, PA22 3AS
Tel/Fax: 01700 841207
E-mail: kyleshotel@aol.com

A small family run hotel offering comfort and informality with
magnificent views of the Kyles of Bute. Built as a hunting lodge over 100
years ago, The Colintraive Hotel offers tranquility and remoteness which
belies a mere 2 hour journey time from Glasgow. The road to Colintraive
goes no further, so the rumble of passing traffic quickly becomes a distant
memory, with only the bleating of sheep to disturb the silence.

2 Twin	All En Suite	B&B per person	Open Jan-Dec
1 Double		from £24.00 Single	B&B + Eve.Meal
1 Family		from £20.00 Dbl/Twn	from £28.00
		Room only per person	
		from £20.00	

Coll, Isle of, Argyll　　　　　　　　　　Map Ref: 1B1

★★★

SMALL
HOTEL

Coll Hotel
Arinagour, Isle of Coll, Argyll, PA78 6SZ
Tel: 01879 230334 Fax: 01879 230317
E-mail: collhotel@aol.com

17c building with panoramic sea views across Mull and the Treshnish
Isles. Under 1 mile (2kms) from the ferry terminal. Bar and restaurant
meals available, specialising in seafood and using the best of fresh local
produce.

1 Single	All En Suite fac	B&B per person	Open Jan-Dec excl
1 Twin	2 Pub/Show	from £25.00 Single	Xmas/New Year
2 Double		from £25.00 Dbl/Twn	
2 Family			

Connel, Argyll　　　　　　　　　　Map Ref: 1E2

★★★★

GUEST
HOUSE

Ronebhal Guest House
Connel, by Oban, Argyll, PA37 1PJ
Tel: 01631 710310/813 Fax: 01631 710310
E-mail: ronebhal@btinternet.com
Web: www.ronebhal.co.uk

Victorian Villa set in beautiful gardens with magnificent views of Loch
Etive and the mountains beyond. Superior standard of hospitality and
comfort with a hearty breakfast served at individual tables. Within
walking distance of two restaurants. Ideal touring base. Private parking.
Oban 5 miles (8kms).

1 Twin	4 En Suite fac	B&B per person	Open Feb-Nov
3 Double	1 Priv.NOT ensuite	£20.00-£30.00 Single	
1 Family		£20.00-£30.00 Dbl/Twn	
		Room only per person	
		£18.00-£27.00	

Crianlarich, Perthshire　　　　　　　　　　Map Ref: 1G2

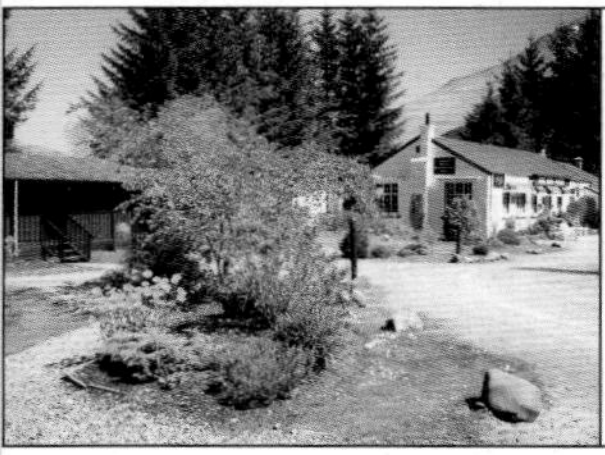

Ben More Lodge Hotel

Crianlarich, Perthshire FK20 8QS Tel: 01838 300210 Fax: 01838 300218
e.mail: info@ben-more.co.uk Web: www.ben-more.co.uk

Surrounded by spectacular scenery, adjacent to the road to the North West
Highlands. This family run lodge hotel offers ensuite accommodation with colour
TV and hospitality trays. Enjoy a drink or a meal prepared by our chef from the
finest Scottish game and fish from either table d'hôte or extensive bar meal
menus. An ideal centre for touring, walking, skiing, golf or simply relaxing.
B&B from £25, D,B&B from £35.

★★

INN

Ben More Lodge Hotel
Crianlarich, Perthshire, FK20 8QS
Tel: 01838 300210 Fax: 01838 300218
E-mail: info@ben-more.co.uk
Web: www.ben-more.co.uk

Pine lodges of a high standard with restaurant and bar adjacent. Ideal
base for touring, hillwalking and fishing.

1 Twin	All En Suite	B&B per person	Open Jan-Dec
7 Double		from £30.00 Single	B&B + Eve.Meal
2 Family		from £25.00 Dbl/Twn	from £35.00

Important: Prices stated are estimates and may be subject to amendments

Crianlarich, Perthshire

Map Ref: 1G2

★★★
GUEST HOUSE

Glenardran House
Crianlarich, Perthshire, FK20 8QS
Tel/Fax: 01838 300236
E-mail: john.glenardran@tesco.net
Web: www.championinternet.com/glenardran/

Situated in the centre of the village, close to the West Highland Way, this late Victorian house has 4 very comfortable en suite bedrooms each with a RcTV and hospitality tray. Excellent base for touring, walking or climbing. Non smoking.

2 Twin	All En Suite	B&B per person from £30.00 Single from £20.00 Dbl/Twn	Open Jan-Dec
2 Double			

Dalmally, Argyll

Map Ref: 1F2

★★★
GUEST HOUSE

Craig Villa Guest House
Dalmally, Argyll, PA33 1AX
Tel/Fax: 01838 200255
E-mail: tonycressey@craigvilla.fsnet.co.uk
Web: www.craigvilla.co.uk

Personally run guest house in own grounds amidst breathtaking scenery. Good touring base. Home cooking. Evening meal by arrangement. Ground floor en-suite.

2 Twin	5 En Suite fac	B&B per person from £25.00 Single from £19.00 Dbl/Twn	Open Mar-Nov
2 Double	1 Priv.NOT ensuite		B&B + Eve.Meal from £31.50
2 Family			

Dalmally, Argyll

Map Ref: 1F2

★★
GUEST HOUSE

Orchy Bank Guest House
Orchy Bank, Dalmally, Argyll, PA33 1AS
Tel: 01838 200370
E-mail: aj.burke@talk21.com

Victorian house situated on the banks of the River Orchy and surrounded on 3 sides by mountains over 3000 feet. Fishing, golf, walking and bird watching. Within 2 hours of Stirling, Glasgow, Fort William, Perth and Campbeltown and half an hour of Oban and Inveraray. Pets welcome.

2 Single	2 Pub Bath/Show	B&B per person from £20.00 Single from £19.00 Dbl/Twn	Open Jan-Dec excl Xmas/New Year
2 Twin	2 Priv.NOT ensuite		
1 Double			
2 Family			

Doune, Perthshire

Map Ref: 2A3

★★★★
B&B

Glenardoch House
Castle Road, Doune, Perthshire, FK16 6EA
Tel: 01786 841489

Charming traditional 18th century stone built house by historical Doune Castle. Set in its own riverside gardens, with views of the old bridge. Peaceful location. Excellent base for exploring the Trossachs and Western Highlands.

2 Double	All En Suite	B&B per person from £35.00 Single from £22.50 Dbl/Twn	Open May-Sept

All properties graded by VisitScotland, formerly known as the Scottish Tourist Board. | *Key to symbols is on back flap.*

Drymen, Stirlingshire

Map Ref: 1H4

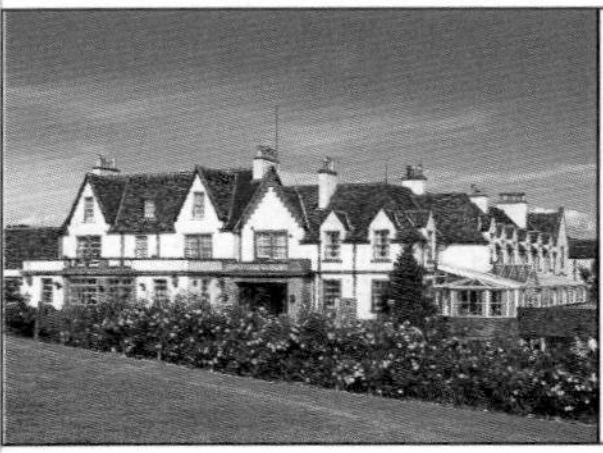

The Buchanan Arms Hotel & Leisure Club

Drymen, by Loch Lomond, Stirlingshire G63 0BQ
Tel: 01360 660588 Fax: 01360 660943
Web: www.buchananarms.co.uk

In the heart of a conservation village near picturesque Loch Lomond, the hotel seems to soak up the mood of the beautiful surrounding countryside. Comfort, fine dining and modern leisure facilities. DB&B from £59.00 per person per night. STB ★★★ AA ★★★ RAC ★★★. RAC Dining Award.

HOTEL

Buchanan Arms Hotel & Leisure Club
Drymen, Loch Lomond, Stirlingshire, G63 0BQ
Tel: 01360 660588 Fax: 01360 660943

Refurbished Coaching Inn in picturesque village close to Loch Lomond and Trossachs. Leisure facilities with swimming pool and squash courts.

9 Single	All En Suite	Open Jan-Dec
26 Twin		B&B + Eve.Meal
15 Double		£55.00-£80.00
2 Family		

HOTEL

Winnock Hotel
The Square, Drymen, Loch Lomond, G63 0BL
Tel: 01360 660245 Fax: 01360 660267
E-mail: winnockhotel@ic24.net
Web: www.winnockhotel.com

Traditional coaching Inn, dating in parts from early 18th C, situated centrally on the village green.

4 Single	All En Suite	B&B per person	Open Jan-Dec
12 Twin		from £49.00 Single	B&B + Eve.Meal from
26 Double		from £39.00 Dbl/Twn	£44.00
6 Family			

Dunoon, Argyll

Map Ref: 1F5

**SMALL
HOTEL**

The Ardtully Hotel
297 Marine Parade, Hunters Quay, Dunoon, Argyll PA23 8HN
Tel: 01369 702478

Friendly hotel, set in own grounds in an elevated position, affording us outstanding views of the Estuary and surrounding hills. Meals prepared using fresh produce. Some chalet bedrooms.

1 Twin	All En Suite	B&B per person	Open Jan-Dec
4 Double		from £35.00-£40.00	
2 Family		Single	
		from £25.00-£30.00	
		Dbl/Twn	

HOTEL

Argyll Hotel
Argyll Street, Dunoon, Argyll, PA23 7NE
Tel: 01369 702059 Fax: 01369 704483
E-mail: info@argyll-hotel.co.uk
Web: www.argyll-hotel.co.uk

Enjoying panoramic views over the Clyde; centrally located and close to the Ferry Terminal. Family run hotel offering a friendly atmosphere with facilities ideally suited to both businessmen and holidaymakers. Full bar and restaurant facilities available, serving meals all day. Children welcome. Conference/function facilities. DBB Packages.

4 Single	All En Suite	B&B per person	Open Jan-Dec
13 Twin		from £45.00 Single	B&B + Eve.Meal
12 Double		from £65.00 Dbl/Twn	from £45.00
3 Family			

Important: Prices stated are estimates and may be subject to amendments

Dunoon, Argyll

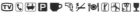

Map Ref: 1F5

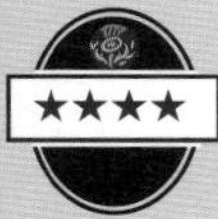

HOTEL

★★★★

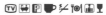

Enmore Hotel

Marine Parade, Dunoon, Argyll, PA23 8HH
Tel: 01369 702230 Fax: 01369 702148
E-mail: enmorehotel@btinternet.com
Web: www.enmorehotel.co.uk

Personal attention assured at this elegant Georgian House set in its own garden overlooking the Firth of Clyde. Each room tastefully decorated and furnished to create a relaxing atmosphere. Award winning restaurant and Taste of Scotland member. Squash courts and games room.

1 Single	All En Suite
3 Twin	
4 Double	
1 Family	

B&B per person
from £45.00 Single
from £35.00 Dbl/Twn

Open mid Dec-mid Feb
excl Xmas/New Year
B&B + Eve.Meal from £50.00

HOTEL

★★★

Esplanade Hotel

West Bay Promenade, Dunoon, Argyll, PA23 7HU
Tel: 01369 704070 Fax: 01369 702129
E-mail: relax@ehd.co.uk
Web: www.ehd.co.uk

Situated by the shores of the noble river Clyde, this family owned and run hotel offers excellent value breaks with a warm welcome, appetising meals, friendly service and comfortable well appointed bedrooms. Entertainment on most evenings. An ideal base to explore the South West Highlands and Islands or just relaxing and watching the world go by.

14 Single	All En Suite
27 Twin	
18 Double	
4 Family	

B&B per person
from £25.00 Single
from £22.50 Dbl/Twn
Room only from £20.00

Open April-Oct
B&B + Eve.Meal from £30.00

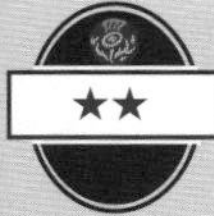

HOTEL

★★

Glenmorag Hotel

3 Kilbride Road, West Bay, Dunoon, Argyll, PA23 7QH
Tel: 01786 436600 Fax: 01786 436650
E-mail: l.graig@shearingsholidays.co.uk
Web: www.shearingsholidays.com

Large hotel in extensive grounds with panoramic views across Firth of Clyde.

3 Single	All En Suite
58 Twin	
8 Double	

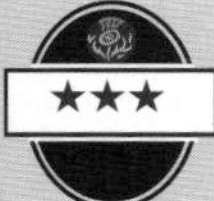

SMALL HOTEL

★★★

Lyall Cliff Hotel

141 Alexandra Parade, East Bay, Dunoon, Argyll, PA23 8AW
Tel/Fax: 01369 702041
E-mail: lyallcliff@talk21.com
Web: www.smoothhound.co.uk/hotels/lyall.html

Beautifully situated, family-run hotel on the sea-front, with lovely garden and private car-park. 3 ground-floor bedrooms, marvellous sea-views, and excellent food. Short breaks and music/themed weekends available spring and autumn. German spoken.

4 Twin	All En Suite
4 Double	
2 Family	

B&B per person
from £22.00 Single
from £40.00 Dbl/Twn
Room only per person
from £19.00

Open Jan-Oct
B&B + Eve.Meal
from £32.00

Fintry, Stirlingshire　　　　　　　　　　**Map Ref: 1H4**

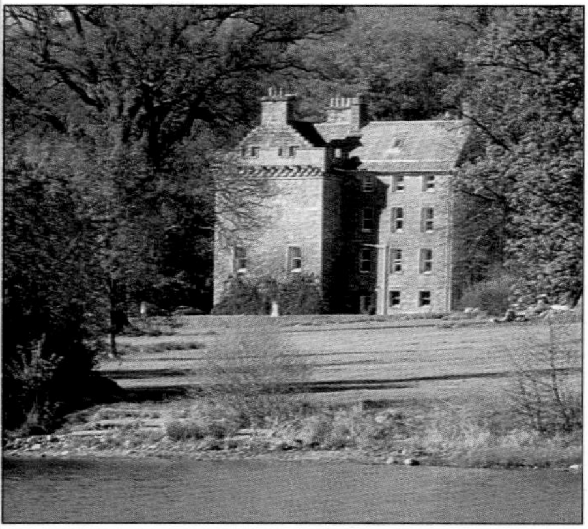

Culcreuch Castle Hotel and Country Park

Culcreuch Castle, Fintry, Stirlingshire G63 0LW
Telephone: 01360 860555 Fax: 01360 860556
e.mail: reservations@culcreuch.com Web: www.culcreuch.com

Magnificent 1600-acre parkland estate in breathtaking scenery. 700-year-old Culcreuch is a unique opportunity to sample the historic atmosphere of Central Scotland's oldest inhabited castle. Comfortable accommodation, cosy bar, licensed restaurant, free fishing, adjacent squash courts, log fires, warm welcome. Central for all Scotland's attractions, including Edinburgh (55 minutes by road). For free accommodation brochure, free fishing and golf brochures:– Contact: Laird of Culcreuch, Culcreuch Castle Hotel, Fintry, Stirlingshire G63 0LW.
Tel: (01360) 860555 Fax: (01360) 860556

HOTEL

Culcreuch Castle Hotel & Country Park
Culcreuch Castle, Fintry, Stirlingshire, G63 0LW
Tel: 01360 860555 Fax: 01360 860556
E-mail: reservations@culcreuch.com
Web: www.culcreuch.com

Romantic 14th century castle immersed in 1600 acre parkland estate surrounded by spectacular Highland scenery. Myriads of places to visit – discovered and undiscovered.

2 Twin	All En Suite	B&B per person	Open Jan-Dec
7 Double		from £58.00 Single	B&B + Eve.Meal
4 Family		from £38.00 Dbl/Twn	from £63.00

Isle of Gigha, Argyll　　　　　　　　　　**Map Ref: 1D6**

B&B

Post Office House
Isle of Gigha, Argyll, PA41 7AA
Tel: 01583 505251 Fax: 01583 505335
E-mail: postoffice@gigha.net Web: www.gigha.net

Built in the 1850's this Victorian stone built house, formerly the school, is now the island post office and shop. Dinner, bed and breakfast is available using fresh local produce. Ideal base for a visit to this picturesque island and enjoy peace and tranquility, sandy beaches, nature spotting, wild flowers and the famous Achamore Gardens. Cycles available for hire. Self catering also available.

1 Single	Pub Bath/Shower	B&B per person	Open Jan-Dec excl
1 Twin		from £20.00 Single	Xmas/New Year
2 Family		from £20.00 Dbl/Twn	B&B + Eve.Meal from
			£32.00

Helensburgh, Argyll　　　　　　　　　　**Map Ref: 1G4**

**GUEST
HOUSE**

Kirkton House
Darleith Road, Cardross, Argyll, G82 5EZ
Tel: 01389 841951 Fax: 01389 841868
E-mail: stbh@kirktonhouse.co.uk
Web: www.kirktonhouse.co.uk

Converted 18/19th Century farmstead commanding panoramic views of the Clyde from a tranquil country setting, yet only 25 mins drive from Glasgow Airport. Easy access to Loch Lomond, Glasgow, The Trossachs and West Highland routes. All rooms en suite with TV, telephone/modem terminal, ironing facilities, desk, tea/coffee, etc. A Taste of Scotland member - wine and dine at individual tables by oil lamplight. Open fire in lounge.

6 Twin	All En Suite	B&B per person	Open Feb-Nov excl
4		from £38.50 Single	Xmas/New Year
Double		from £28.50 Twin	B&B + Eve.Meal
4 Family			from £39.75

Important: Prices stated are estimates and may be subject to amendments

Helensburgh, Argyll — Map Ref: 1G4

★★★ B&B

Ravenswood
32 Suffolk Street, Helensburgh, Argyll, G84 9PA
Tel: 01436 672112
E-mail: ravenswood@breathemail.net
Web: www.stayatlochlomond.com/ravenswood or
www.visitscotland.com

2 Single / 2 En Suite fac
1 Twin / 1 Priv.NOT ensuite
1 Double

B&B per person
from £25.00 Single
from £25.00 Dbl/Twn
Room only from £25.00

Open Jan-Dec excl
Xmas/New Year

Relax in the garden or our elegant lounge after breakfasting from an extensive selection that concentrates on fresh, local produce. The town is a stroll away and has a range of shops, restaurants and pubs. A sample selection of menus is kept handy for guests to peruse. Sailing and golf are available locally. Local walkers and cycle routes are covered in our extensive area information available to all guests.

Inveraray, Argyll — Map Ref: 1F3

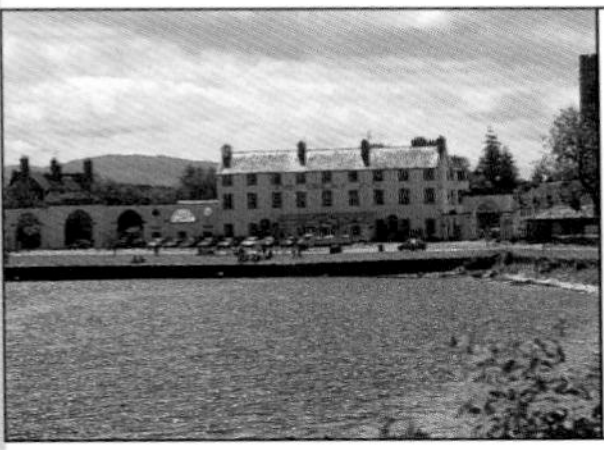

THE ARGYLL
FRONT STREET, INVERARAY PA32 8XB
Tel: 01499 302466 Fax: 01499 302389
e.mail: reception@the-argyll-hotel.co.uk Web: www.the-argyll-hotel.co.uk

With spectacular views over Loch Fyne, this impressive Grade A listed hotel offers modernised, luxurious rooms. Comfortable public areas with traditional log fires. Fully licensed with a wide range of malt whiskies. Our quality restaurant features the best of local produce.

★★★★ HOTEL

Argyll Hotel
Front Street, Inveraray, Argyll, PA32 8XB
Tel: 01499 302466 Fax: 01499 302389
E-mail: reception@the-argyll-hotel.co.uk
Web: www.the-argyll-hotel.co.uk

5 Single / All En Suite
13 Twin
12 Double
1 Family

B&B per person
from £58.00 Single
from £43.00 Dbl/Twn
Room only from £37.00

Open Jan-Dec excl
Xmas/New Year
B&B + Eve.Meal
from £61.00

Designed in 1750 by the famous Scottish builder John Adam, The Argyll formed part of the total rebuilding of Inveraray commissioned by the 3rd Duke of Argyll. Originally built to accommodate guests to the Castle, The Argyll today offers standards of hospitality that more than live up to its illustrious past.

Inverbeg, Argyll — Map Ref: 1G4

★★★★ SMALL HOTEL

Inverbeg Inn
Luss, Loch Lomomd, Dunbartonshire, G83 8PD
Tel: 01436 860678 Fax: 01436 860686
E-mail: info@inverbeginn.co.uk

4 Twin / All En Suite
15 Double
1 Family

B&B per person
from £45.00 Single
from £25.00 Dbl/Twn

Open Jan-Dec excl
Xmas

The Inverbeg Inn enjoys one of the most spectacular settings in Scotland. The hotel has 20 ensuite bedrooms. 8 luxury bedrooms are located by the shore of Loch Lomond. The dining room offers a fine selection of dishes prepared from fresh local produce. Outstanding location. A warm welcome awaits you. Some annexe accommodation.

Iona, Isle of, Argyll — Map Ref: 1B2

★★ SMALL HOTEL

Argyll Hotel
Isle of Iona, Argyll, PA76 6SJ
Tel: 01681 700334 Fax: 01681 700510
E-mail: reception@argyllhoteliona.co.uk
Web: www.argyllhoteliona.co.uk

6 Single / 14 En Suite fac
2 Twin / 1 Pub Bath/Show
8 Double
1 Family

B&B per person
from £37.00 Single
from £20.00-£50.00
Dbl/Twn

Open Apr-Oct
B&B + Eve.Meal
from £37.00-£67.00

Built in 1868 as the village Inn and extended, this small personally-run hotel has a growing reputation for quality food. Excellent view from frontage towards Isle of Mull. Short stroll to ferry.

All properties graded by VisitScotland, formerly known as the Scottish Tourist Board.   **Key to symbols is on back flap.**

Iona, Isle of, Argyll

Map Ref: 1B2

HOTEL ★★

St Columba Hotel
Isle of Iona, Argyll, PA76 6SL
Tel: 01681 700304 Fax: 01681 700688
E-mail: columba@btconnect.com
Web: www.stcolumba-hotel.co.uk

A haven for total freedom and relaxation on this exquisite Hebridean
island. Close to Abbey. Outstanding views from our sunlounges and
dining room, warm welcome, friendly staff, log fire. Our chef's provide
imaginative home baking and delicious home-cooked meals using fresh
Scottish produce, some from our own organically cultivated garden.
Children welcome. Ideal setting for a relaxing holiday for young and old.

9 Single	All En Suite	B&B per person	Open Apr-Oct
11 Twin		from £44.00 Single	B&B + Eve.Meal
3 Double		from £38.00 Dbl/Twn	from £48.00
4 Family		Room only per person	
		from £33.00	

Ballygrant, Isle of Islay, Argyll

Map Ref: 1C5

GUEST HOUSE ★★★★★

Kilmeny Country Guest House
Ballygrant, Isle of Islay, Argyll, PA45 7QW
Tel/Fax: 01496 840668
E-mail: info@kilmeny.co.uk
Web: www.kilmeny.co.uk

Traditional farmhouse on 300 acre beef farm. Comfort, friendliness and
peace. Emphasis on personal service, in a country house atmosphere.
Non-smoking.

1 Twin	All En Suite	B&B per person	Open Jan-Feb
2 Double		from £47.00 Single	B&B + Eve.Meal from
		from £37.00 Dbl/Twn	£61.00

Bowmore, Isle of Islay, Argyll

Map Ref: 1C6

INN ★★★

The Harbour Inn
The Square, Bowmore, Isle of Islay, Argyll, PA43 7JR
Tel: 01496 810330 Fax: 01496 810990
E-mail: harbour@harbour-inn.com
Web: www.harbour-inn.com

Welcoming, traditional, Islay Inn with award winning restaurant. Scottish
Tourist Board Thistle Award winners 1998. Good Food Guide
recommended. We use the best Islay seafood, shellfish, beef and lamb.
Lighter Bistro style lunch-time alternative. Friendly, cosy bar, popular
with locals and visitors. One or two Islay malts can often lead to a fine
sing-a-long evening.

6 Double	All En Suite	B&B per person	Open Jan-Dec
1 Family		from £42.50 Single	
		from £75.00 Double	

Port Charlotte, Isle of Islay, Argyll

Map Ref: 1B6

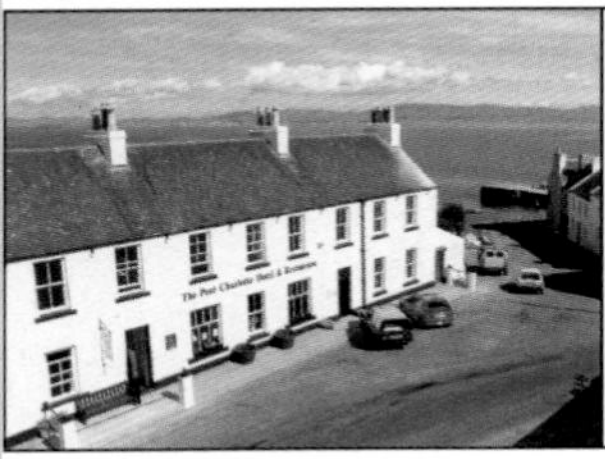

The Port Charlotte Hotel & Restaurant
Main Street, Port Charlotte, Isle of Islay, Argyll PA48 7TU
Tel: 01496 850360 Fax: 01496 850361
e.mail: carl@portchartottehot.demon.co.uk
Web: www.milford.co.uk/go/portcharlotte.html

Tastefully restored Victorian hotel with great sea views in attractive
conservation village. Ten ensuite rooms beautifully decorated and furnished
with antiques. Excellent restaurant featuring local seafood, beef and lamb.
Sandy beach. *Rooms from £55-£100.* **Please call for full colour brochure.**

SMALL HOTEL ★★★★

Port Charlotte Hotel
Main Street, Port Charlotte, Isle of Islay,
Argyll, PA48 7TU
Tel: 01496 850360 Fax: 01496 850361
E-mail: carl@portcharlottehot.demon.co.uk

Restored Victorian hotel offering all modern facilities in an informal,
relaxed atmosphere, situated in this picturesque conservation village on
the west shore of Loch Indaal. Fresh local seafood, lamb and beef.
Distillery visits, fishing and golfing can be arranged.

2 Single	All En Suite	B&B per person	Open Jan-Dec
2 Twin		£59.00 Single	
5 Double		£47.50 Dbl/Twn	
1 Family		£110.00 Family	

Important: Prices stated are estimates and may be subject to amendments

Port Ellen, Isle of Islay, Argyll

Map Ref: 1C6

★★★

SMALL HOTEL

Machrie Hotel & Golf Links
Port Ellen, Isle of Islay, Argyll, PA42 7AN
Tel: 01496 302310 Fax: 01496 302404
E-mail: machrie@machrie.com Web: www.machrie.com

Built over 250 years ago as a farmhouse, the Machrie combines the relaxed tradtional atmosphere of that period with modern service and comfort. It is an ideal place to relax and unwind from the stresses of the everyday world, be it sitting in front of a peat fire or playing golf, pool, snooker, carpet bowls, tennis or croquet. The hotel also boasts a hairdressing salon.

11 Twin	All En Suite
5 Double	

B&B per person
from £27.00 Single
from £54.00 Dbl/Twn

Open Jan-Dec
B&B + Eve.Meal from £50.00

★★

GUEST HOUSE

The Trout-Fly Guest House
8 Charlotte Street, Port Ellen, Isle of Islay, Argyll, PA42 7DF
Tel: 01496 302204 Fax: 01496 300076

Guest house in town centre. Evening meals on request. Convenient for ferry terminal, airport, golf-course and fishing. Restaurant for guests only B.Y.O.B. 3 distilleries within 3 miles.

1 Single	1 Pub Bath/Show
2 Twin	1 Priv.NOT ensuite
1 Double	

B&B per person
from £20.50

Open Jan-Dec excl Xmas/New Year

Craighouse, Isle of Jura, Argyll

Map Ref: 1D5

★★

SMALL HOTEL

Jura Hotel
Craighouse, Isle of Jura, Argyll, PA60 7XU
Tel: 01496 820243 Fax: 01496 820249
E-mail: jurahotel@aol.com
Web: http://stay.at/jurahotel

Family run hotel with gardens, overlooking Small Isles Bay and close to famous distillery. Showers, drying room and laundry facilities for sailors and walkers.

7 Single	9 En Suite fac
6 Twin	6 Pub Bath/Show
4 Double	
1 Family	

B&B per person
from £35.00 Single
from £70.00 Dbl/Twn

Open Feb-Nov

Kilchrenan, by Taynuilt, Argyll

Map Ref: 1F2

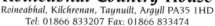

Roineabhal Country House
Roineabhal, Kilchrenan, Taynuilt, Argyll PA35 1HD
Tel: 01866 833207 Fax: 01866 833474
e.mail: maria@roineabhal.com Web: www.roineabhal.com

Country house offering luxury accommodation in a picturesque Highland village. Dinners, fine food suiting all diets. Home baked bread, muffins and kedgeree are just a few items you'll find for breakfast. House parties. Long weekend breaks. Pub nearby. Walking. Fishing. Log fires. STB ★★★★

★★★★

B&B

Roineabhal Country House
Kilchrenan, by Taynuilt, Argyll, PA35 1HD
Tel: 01866 833207 Fax: 01866 833474
E-mail: maria@roineabhal.com
Web: www.roineabhal.com

Traditional country house, centrally situated within easy reach of Oban, Fort William and Inveraray. Evening meals by arrangement utilising local produce, organic meals also available. Well behaved pets are welcome. Ensuring you of a warm West Highland welcome from the owners and family.

1 Twin	All En Suite
2 Double	

B&B per person
from £50.00 Single
from £35.00 Dbl/Twn

Open Jan-Dec excl Xmas
B&B + Eve.Meal from £65.00

All properties graded by VisitScotland, formerly known as the Scottish Tourist Board. | Key to symbols is on back flap. |

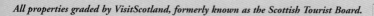

Kilchrenan, by Taynuilt, Argyll — Map Ref: 1F2

HOTEL
★★★★

Taychreggan Hotel
Kilchrenan, Taynuilt, Argyll, PA35 1HQ
Tel: 01866 833211/366 Fax: 01866 833244
E-mail: info@taychregganhotel.co.uk
Web: www.taychregganhotel.co.uk

Set at water's edge of Loch Awe, this former cattle drovers Inn boasts
good food, comfort and friendly staff: tranquility, seclusion and
relaxation.

11 Twin   All En Suite
8 Double

B&B per person
from £105.00 Single
£65.00-£105.00
Dbl/Twn

Open Jan-Dec
B&B + Eve.Meal from
£100.00

Killin, Perthshire — Map Ref: 1H2

**GUEST
HOUSE**
★★★

Breadalbane House
Main Street, Killin, FK21 8UT
Tel: 01567 820134 Fax: 01567 820798
E-mail: stay@breadalbane48.freeserve.co.uk
Web: www.smoothhound.co.uk/hotels/breadalbane

At the foot of the Tarmachan Ridge surrounded by Munroes, this well appointed guest
house featured in "Hidden Places of Scotland", provides excellent accommodation in well
equipped, centrally heated en-suite rooms. Private parking, secure cycle storage, drying
and ironing facilities and a ground floor room with bath are all available. Fishing, walking,
hill climbing, cycling, golfing, watersports and horse riding are all on the doorstep. Enjoy a
welcome as warm as the scenery is breathtaking.

2 Twin   All En Suite
3 Double
2 Family

B&B per person
from £25.00-£30.00
Single
from £20.00-£25.00
Double

Open Jan-Dec excl
Xmas/New Year
B&B + Eve.Meal from
£35.00-£40.00

Killin, Perthshire — Map Ref: 1H2

Dall Lodge Country House Hotel
Main Street, Killin, Perthshire FK21 8TN
Tel: 01567 820217 Fax: 01567 820726
e.mail: wilson@dalllodgehotel.co.uk Web: www.dalllodgehotel.co.uk

*Century-old mansion modernised, commanding stunning views of mountains on
outskirts of scenic Highland village. Perfect base for outdoor activities, golfing,
fishing, touring. Hotel offers home cooking, ensuite rooms, colour TV, hairdryers,
tea/coffee makers, four-poster bed. Conservatory, lounge, ground-floor rooms for
families or wheelchair or guests finding stairs difficult. Dinner served.*

HOTEL
★★★★

Dall Lodge Country House Hotel
Main Street, Killin, Perthshire, FK21 8TN
Tel: 01567 820217 Fax: 01567 820726
E-mail: wilson@dalllodgehotel.co.uk
Web: www.dalllodgehotel.co.uk

Century old mansion recently modernised with old world charm retained.
On outskirts of scenic Highland village commanding stunning views of
mountain and moorland. Scottish home cooking with fresh local produce.
Perfect base for outdoor activities, golf, fishing and hillwalking. Ground
floor rooms available.

1 Single   All En Suite
3 Twin
4 Double
2 Family

B&B per person
£45.50-£52.50 Single
£35.50-£49.50 Dbl/Twn

Open Mar-Oct
B&B + Eve.Meal
£59.00-£76.00

Killin, Perthshire

Map Ref: 1H2

FAIRVIEW HOUSE

Main Street, Killin, Perthshire FK21 8UT
Telephone: 01567 820667 Fax: 01567 820667
e.mail: info@fairview-killin.co.uk Web: www.fairview-killin.co.uk

Rick and Joan offer a warm welcome to their friendly, comfortable guest house set in a picturesque village. Relax by an open fire in the residents lounge with breathtaking views of the central highlands. Excellent off-street parking, good drying facilities, and home-cooked evening meals are also on offer.

★★★
GUEST HOUSE

Fairview House
Main Street, Killin, Perthshire, FK21 8UT
Tel/Fax: 01567 820667
E-mail: info@fairview-killin.co.uk
Web: www.fairview-killin.co.uk

Family run guest house specialising in home cooking. Excellent touring centre, good walking and climbing area.

1 Single	5 En Suite fac	B&B per person	Open Jan-Dec
2 Twin	2 Priv.NOT ensuite	£20.00-£24.00 Single	B&B + Eve.Meal
4 Double		£20.00-£24.00 Dbl/Twn	from £35.00

★★★
GUEST HOUSE

Invertay House
Killin, Perthshire, FK21 8TN
Tel: 01567 820492 Fax: 01567 820013
E-mail: invertay@btinternet.com

A very warm welcome in our listed, former Manse with walled gardens on outskirts of village and enjoying magnificent views. The emphasis is on comfort, (each room has en suite facilities, a RcTV and a well stocked hospitality tray), and fresh food including seasonal garden produce.

2 Twin	All En Suite	B&B per person	Open Mar-Nov
4 Double		from £28.00 Single	B&B + Eve.Meal
		from £23.00 Dbl/Twn	from £37.00

★★
HOTEL

Killin Hotel
Main Street, Killin, Perthshire, FK21 8TP
Tel: 01567 820296 Fax: 01567 820647
E-mail: killinhotel@btinternet.com
Web: www.killinhotel.com

Family run hotel in the village of Killin and overlooking the western end of Loch Tay. Trout and salmon fishing by arrangement. Come and experience our new Riverside Bistro.

5 Single	All En Suite	B&B per person	Open Jan-Dec
12 Twin		from £35.00 Single	B&B + Eve.Meal
12 Double		from £26.00 Dbl/Twn	from £42.00
3 Family			

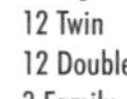

by Killin, Perthshire

Map Ref: 1H2

★★★
SMALL HOTEL

Morenish Lodge Hotel
Morenish, Killin, Perthshire, FK21 8TX
Tel/Fax: 01567 820258
E-mail: thomas@morenishlodgehotel.co.uk
Web: www.morenishlodgehotel.co.uk

Former shooting lodge enjoying superb views over Loch Tay in an area famed for natural history and outdoor pursuits.

1 Single	12 En Suite fac	B&B per person	Open Mar-Nov
6 Twin	1 Priv.NOT ensuite	from £33.00 Single	B&B + Eve.Meal
10 Double	1 Pub Bath/Show	from £33.00 Dbl/Twn	from £43.00
1 Family			

All properties graded by VisitScotland, formerly known as the Scottish Tourist Board. | Key to symbols is on back flap.

Kilmelford, by Oban, Argyll Map Ref: 1E3

CUILFAIL HOTEL
KILMELFORD, BY OBAN PA34 4XA

Charming old Scottish Hotel, 14 miles south of Oban. Dine in the
'Tartan Puffer' restaurant – indoor barbecue and grill. Rare collection of
old and valuable malt whiskies on display with many more to sample.
B&B from £20, with discounts for longer stays.
Catch the West Highland atmosphere!
For full details call (01852) 200274   Fax (01852) 200264
e.mail: david@cuilfail.co.uk

★★

**SMALL
HOTEL**

Cuilfail Hotel
Kilmelford, nr Oban, Argyll, PA34 4XA
Tel: 01852 200274 Fax: 01852 200264
E-mail: david@cuilfail.co.uk
Web: www.cuilfail.co.uk

Old coaching Inn situated in small village. Emphasis on traditional
Scottish fare based on local produce. 'Tartan Puffer' restaurant with
indoor barbecue and grill. Collection of rare malt whiskies on display,
over 100 available in bar.

4 Twin	All En Suite	B&B per person	Open Jan-Dec
6 Double		from £25.00 Single	B&B + Eve.Meal
2 Family		from £25.00 Dbl/Twn	from £40.00

Loch Lomond, Argyll Map Ref: 1G3

★★

**GUEST
HOUSE**

Greenbank Guest House
Arrochar, Argyll, G83 7AA
Tel: 01301 702305

By road and lochside in village of Arrochar with superb loch and
mountain views. Family run with licensed restaurant. Open all day for
meals & snacks. Rock garden. Private parking.

1 Single	B&B per person	Open Jan-Dec excl
2 Double	from £20.00 Single	Xmas/New Year
1 Family	from £18.50 Dbl/Twn	

Lochearnhead, Perthshire Map Ref: 1H2

Lochearnhead Hotel
Lochearnhead, Perthshire FK19 8PU
Tel: 01567 830229 Fax: 01567 830364

Family run hotel with stunning views over Loch Earn. Excellent golf
and touring centre with water sports on our doorstep. Seven golf
courses within 14 miles. All rooms have colour Sky TV and central
heating. Some with loch views. Try our popular bar and dining room
menus. Families and pets welcome.

★★

HOTEL

Lochearnhead Hotel
Lochearnhead, Perthshire, FK19 8PU
Tel: 01567 830229 Fax: 01567 830364

Privately owned, in elevated position overlooking Loch Earn. Water
sports centre and sailing facilities adjacent. Ideal centre for touring,
golfing, fishing and hillwalking.

1 Single	8 En Suite fac	B&B per person	Open Mar-Nov
6 Twin	2 Pub Bath/Show	from £30.00 Single	B&B + Eve.Meal
6 Double		from £35.00 Dbl/Twn	from £49.00

Important: Prices stated are estimates and may be subject to amendments

Lochgair, by Lochgilphead, Argyll

Map Ref: 1E4

★★

SMALL HOTEL

Lochgair Hotel
Lochgair, by Lochgilphead, Argyll, PA31 8SA
Tel/Fax: 01546 886333
E-mail: LochgairHotel@aol.com

3 Twin	All En Suite
6 Double	
1 Family	

B&B per person
£28.00-£30.00 Single
£22.00-£50.00 Dbl/Twn
Room only from £20.00

Open Jan-Dec
B&B + Eve.Meal
£32.00-£50.00

Lovely lochside village family run hotel, comfortable rooms. Good bar food, quality A la Carte menu. Restaurant. Residents lounge. 2 bars. Log fires, malt whiskies. Stunning scenery, walking, fishing, riding, golf. Special Offers.

Lochgilphead, Argyll

Map Ref: 1E4

★

INN

Argyll Hotel (Lochgilphead)
69 Lochnell Street, Lochgilphead, Argyll, P31 8JN
Tel: 01546 602221 Fax: 01546 603915
E-mail: argyll.hotel@bushinternet.com

4 Single	7 En Suite fac
4 Twin	5 Pub Bath/Show
4 Double	

B&B per person
from £19.00 Single
from £18.00 Dbl/Twn
Room only from £17.00

Open Jan-Dec

Traditional Highland Inn in town centre. Regular live entertainment including weekly disco. Recently refurbished steak house specialising in steak sizzlers. Large screen TV with satellite channels.

---

by Lochgilphead, Argyll

Map Ref: 1E4

Cairnbaan Hotel

CAIRNBAAN, NR LOCHGILPHEAD, ARGYLL PA31 8SJ
Telephone: 01546 603668   Fax: 01546 606045
E-mail: cairnbaan.hotel@virgin.net Web: www.cairnbaan.com
Delightful 18th century coaching inn overlooking Lock 5 on the Crinan Canal. Superb food served by our friendly team in relaxed and unhurried environment, close to Inveraray, Oban and ideal for discovering Argyll and the islands.

★★★★

HOTEL

Cairnbaan Hotel
by Lochgilphead, Argyll, PA31 8SJ
Tel: 01546 603668 Fax: 01546 606045

1 Single	All En Suite
3 Twin	
6 Double	

B&B per person
£55.00-£65.00 Single
£45.00-£55.00 Dbl/Twn

Open Jan-Dec

Privately owned, family run hotel in tranquil surroundings overlooking the Crinan Canal at Lock 5.

All properties graded by VisitScotland, formerly known as the Scottish Tourist Board. | *Key to symbols is on back flap.*

Luss

Map Ref: 1G4

The Lodge on Loch Lomond Hotel & Restaurant

Tel: 01436 860201   www.loch-lomond.co.uk

★★★

HOTEL

The Lodge on Loch Lomond Hotel & Restaurant

Luss, Loch Lomond, Argyll & Bute, G83 8PA
Tel: 01436 860201 Fax: 01436 860203
E-mail: lusslomond@aol.com
Web: www.loch-lomond.co.uk

14 Twin	All En Suite	B&B per person	Open Jan-Dec
25 Double		£37.50-£75.00 Dbl/Twn	

Modern pine lodge situated on the serene banks of Loch Lomond close to
Luss village. Modern pine panelling character reflects the tranquility of
the surrounding scenery. All bedrooms ensuite with a sauna. Informal
Brasserie style restaurant with magnificent views across Loch Lomond.

Machrihanish, by Campbeltown, Argyll

Map Ref: 1D7

★★★

**GUEST
HOUSE**

Ardell House

Machrihanish, by Campbeltown, Argyll, PA28 6PT
Tel/Fax: 01586 810235

7 Twin	All En Suite	B&B per person	Open Mar-Oct
2 Double		£32.00-£42.00 Single	
		£26.00-£32.00 Dbl/Twn	

Detached Victorian house within its own grounds, overlooking the golf
course and Machrihanish bay with views of Islay, Jura, Gigha and Kintyre
peninsula. Some annex accommodation available.

Calgary, Isle of Mull, Argyll

Map Ref: 1C1

★★★

**SMALL
HOTEL**

Calgary Hotel (formerly Calgary Farmhouse Hotel)

Calgary, by Dervaig, Isle of Mull, Argyll, PA75 6QW
Tel/Fax: 01688 400256
E-mail: calgary.farmhouse@virgin.net
Web: www.calgary.co.uk

1 Single	All En Suite	B&B per person	Open Mar-Nov
2 Twin		£28.80-£36.00 Single	B&B + Eve.Meal from
4 Double		£28.80-£36.00 Dbl/Twn	£45.00-£65.00
2 Family			

Converted farmhouse and steading, close to the beautiful white sands of
Calgary Beach. Taste of Scotland restaurant. Our menu consists of local
Scottish produce skilfully prepared by our award-winning chef and served
in our original Dovecote restaurant. All bedrooms tastefully and
individually decorated. Some with TV's. Radio available.

Craignure, Isle of Mull, Argyll

Map Ref: 1D2

★★★

INN

Craignure Inn

Craignure, Isle of Mull, Argyll, PA65 6AY
Tel: 01680 812305 Fax: 01680 812306
E-mail: janice@craignureinn-freeserve.co.uk
Web: www.craignure-inn.co.uk

1 Twin	All En Suite	B&B per person	Open Jan-Dec excl
1 Double		from £45.00 Single	Xmas/New Year
1 Family		from £29.50 Dbl/Twn	
		Room only per person	
		from £25.00	

Completely refurbished 17th century former drover's inn, conveniently
situated for ferry and bus tours. Characterful, friendly bars (including
non-smoking) popular with local trade. Bar meals available, non
residents welcome.

Important: Prices stated are estimates and may be subject to amendments

Craignure, Isle of Mull, Argyll

Map Ref: 1D2

★★

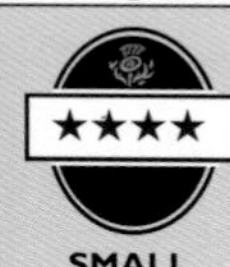

GUEST HOUSE

Pennygate Lodge
Craignure, Isle of Mull, Argyll, PA65 6AY
Tel: 01680 812333

1 Single	4 En Suite fac
4 Twin	2 Pub Bath/Show
2 Double	4 Priv.NOT ensuite
1 Family	

B&B per person
from £15.00 Single
from £18.00 Dbl/Twn
Room only from £11.00

Open Jan-Dec

Former Georgian manse set in 4.5 acres of landscaped garden with magnificent views of the Sound of Mull. Ideal base for touring, near main bus route and ferry terminal. Three night special breaks available. Evening meals on request.

Dervaig, Isle of Mull, Argyll

Map Ref: 1C1

★★★★

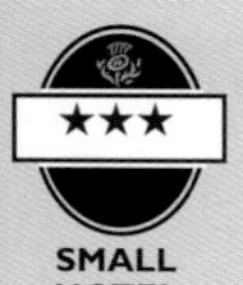

SMALL HOTEL

Druimard Country House
Dervaig, by Tobermory, Isle of Mull, PA75 6QW
Tel/Fax: 01688 400345
E-mail: druimard.hotel@virgin.net
Web: www.druimard.co.uk

2 Single	6 En Suite fac
3 Twin	1 Priv.NOT ensuite
4 Double	
2 Family	

D.B&B per person
from £77.00 Single
from £62.00 Dbl/Twn

Open Apr-Oct

Small Victorian country house hotel, with elegant restaurant,(2 AA Rosettes) Emphasis on using local produce. Adjacent to Mull Little Theatre. One room has a private bathroom, not en suite. 2 brand new ground floor bedrooms with separate entrance.

★★★

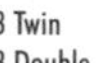

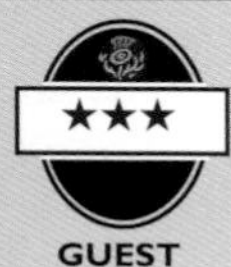

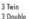

SMALL HOTEL

Druimnacroish Hotel
Dervaig, Isle of Mull, Argyll, PA75 6QW
Tel/Fax: 01688 400274
E-mail: stay@druimnacrosh.co.uk Web: www.druimnacroish.co.uk

3 Twin	All En Suite
3 Double	

B&B per person
from £35.00 Single
from £64.00 Dbl/Twn

Open Jan-Dec
B&B + Eve.Meal
from £49.50

Converted water mill set on a tranquil and secluded hillside offering a relaxed, friendly atmosphere, spacious accommodation, extensive gardens, good food, home made bread, superb views from every room. Put your feet up by the fire or enjoy the view from the conservatory. Well situated for Mull's many attractions including boat trips, wildlife, walking and the Mull Little Theatre. Taste of Scotland Award.

Fionnphort, Isle of Mull, Argyll

Map Ref: 1C2

★★★

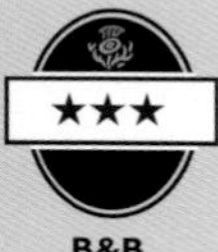

GUEST HOUSE

Achaban House
Fionnphort, Isle of Mull, Argyll, PA66 6BL
Tel: 01681 700205 Fax: 01681 700649
E-mail: camilla@achabanhouse.ndo.co.uk
Web: www.achabanhouse.com

1 Single	5 En Suite fac
2 Twin	1 Priv.NOT ensuite
2 Double	
1 Family	

B&B per person
from £25.00 Single
from £22.00 Dbl/Twn

Open Jan-Dec excl
Xmas/New Year
B&B + Eve.Meal from
£34.00

This is a delightful former manse which is set within its own grounds just a short distance inland from the village of Fionnphort and the ferry to Iona. Peaceful, relaxing away-from-the-road location with views towards Loch Pottie. Your hosts will afford you a very warm welcome and help you to enjoy the very best this beautiful part of Mull has to offer.

★★★

B&B

Seaview
Fionnphort, Isle of Mull, PA66 6BL
Tel: 01681 700235 Fax: 01681 700669
E-mail: john@seaviewmull.f9.co.uk
Web: www.iona.bed.breakfast.mull.com

2 Twin	4 En Suite fac
3 Double	1 Priv.NOT ensuite

B&B per person
£20.00-£25.00 Single
£18.00-£22.00 Dbl/Twn

Open Jan-Dec

Recently refurbished Scottish granite house with views over the Sound of Iona towards the Abbey. A minutes walk to Iona and Staffa Ferries.

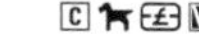

Tobermory, Isle of Mull, Argyll | Map Ref: 1C1

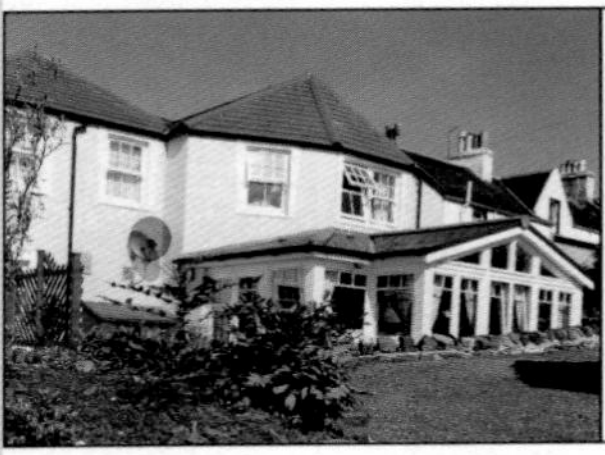

Highland Cottage
Breadalbane Street, Tobermory, Isle of Mull PA75 6PD
Telephone: 01688 302030 Fax: 01688 302727
e.mail: davidandjo@highlandcottage.co.uk
Web: www.highlandcottage.co.uk

Intimate friendly family run hotel in quiet location in Upper Tobermory with reputation for hospitality and good food. 4-poster beds, satellite TV and books galore. Plentiful parking and only minutes from bustling main street and fisherman's pier. Come and relax. Colour brochure from David and Josephine Currie – resident owners.

**SMALL
HOTEL**

&

Highland Cottage
Breadalbane Street, Tobermory, Isle of Mull, PA75 6PD
Tel: 01688 302030 Fax: 01688 302727
E-mail: davidandjo@highlandcottage.co.uk
Web: www.highlandcottage.co.uk

Newly built, family-run 'country house in the town' hotel located in the heart of upper Tobermory in conservation area. Well appointed bedrooms themed after local islands and including 2 with 4 poster beds. Imaginative cuisine using fresh, local ingredients served in our attractive, homely, dining room. High level of personal attention from resident owners. AA two rosettes.

1 Twin   All En Suite
5 Double

B&B per person
from £55.00 Single
from £43.50 Dbl/Twn

Open Jan-Dec excl mid-
Oct - mid-Nov
B&B + Eve.Meal
from £70.00

**SMALL
HOTEL**

The Tobermory Hotel
Tobermory, Isle of Mull, Argyll, PA75 6NT
Tel: 01688 302091 Fax: 01688 302254
E-mail: tobhotel@tinyworld.co.uk
Web: www.thetobermoryhotel.com

Under new ownership, this small family-run hotel is superbly sited on the waterfront overlooking the bay. The restaurant promotes fresh local produce and non-residents are welcome. There are fifteen en-suite rooms, two of which are on the ground floor and one room with separate bathroom. Ample street parking is available.

2 Single   All En Suite
4 Twin
8 Double
2 Family

B&B per person
from £40.00 Single
from £36.00 Dbl/Twn

Open Jan-Dec excl Xmas
B&B + Eve.Meal from
£53.00

Important: Prices stated are estimates and may be subject to amendments

Tobermory, Isle of Mull, Argyll   Map Ref: 1C1

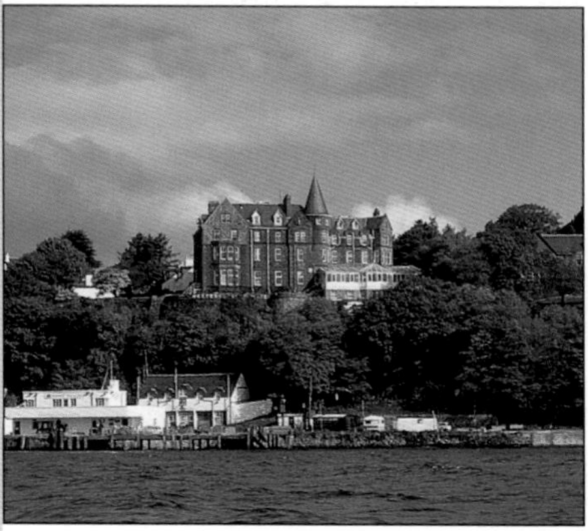

The Western Isles Hotel

Tobermory, Isle of Mull, Argyllshire PA75 6PR
Tel: 01688 302012 Fax: 01688 302297
e.mail: wihotel@aol.com Web: www.mullhotel.com

This 28 bedroomed Victorian Hotel, built in 1883 majestically stands against the skyline overlooking picturesque Tobermory Bay and the Sound of Mull. With its backdrop of the Morven Hills and Tobermory's brightly coloured houses, the hotel has arguably one of the finest views in the Hebridean Islands. Offering standard, master and deluxe bedrooms, the hotel is a haven of comfort.

The dining room serves a four-course dinner and coffee in a formal atmosphere, plus a more casual form of dining, the Conservatory bar, offering an interesting range of bar meals for both lunch and evening. Non-residents most welcome.

HOTEL ★★★★

The Western Isles Hotel	3 Single	B&B per person	Open Jan-18 Dec
Tobermory, Isle of Mull, Argyll, PA75 6PR	13 Twin	from £41.00 Single	B&B + Eve.Meal
Tel: 01688 302012 Fax: 01688 302297	12 Double	from £41.00 Double	from £54.50
E-mail: wihotel@aol.com	All En Suite		

Superbly situated overlooking Tobermory Bay, the hotel is a haven of peace and tranquility. Good food and comfort. Conservatory bar, serving bar meals. Non-residents very welcome. Small conferences, weddings and parties catered for.

📺 📞 🍳 🅿 🍽 🎣 🍴 ⓕ 🍸

Ⓒ 🐕 ♿ 🅦 🆅 ⊛

Uisken, by Bunessan, Isle of Mull, Argyll   Map Ref: 1C3

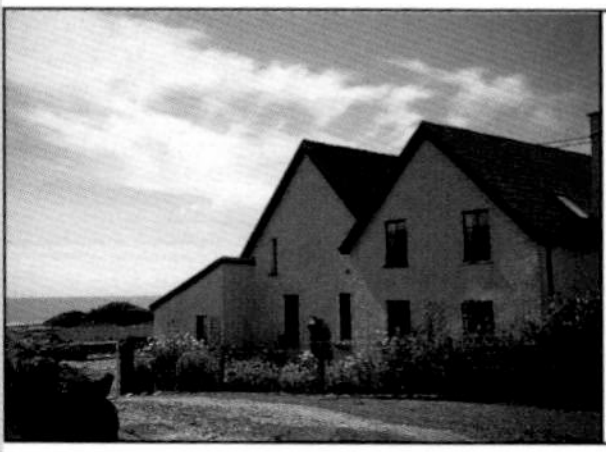

ARDACHY HOUSE HOTEL

Uisken, by Bunessan, Isle of Mull PA67 6DS
Tel/Fax: 01681 700505
e.mail: ardachy@talk21.com
Web: http://members.xoom.com/ardachy

Beautifully presented and quietly located but only 20 minutes drive from Iona and Staffa ferries. Overlooking the white sands of Ardalanish to the Isles of Colonsay, Jura and Islay. Dinner is by reservation. Prices for D,B&B £50-£59.50.

SMALL HOTEL ★★★

Ardachy House Hotel	3 Single	7 En Suite fac	B&B per person	Open Apr-Sep
Uisken, by Bunessan, Isle of Mull, Argyll, PA67 6DS	1 Twin	1 Pub Bath/Show	from £34.00 Single	B&B + Eve.Meal
Tel/Fax: 01681 700505	3 Double		from £34.00 Dbl/Twn	from £53.00
E-mail: ardachy@talk21.com	1 Family			
Web: http://members.xoom.com/ardachy				

Small, secluded, family-run hotel, 7 miles (11 kms) from Iona. Safe access to white sands of Ardalinish Beach. Spectacular views to Colonsay, Jura and Islay. 1 room without en-suite. Dinner by reservation only.

✉ 🍳 🅿 🍽 ✂ 🍴 🍸

♿ 🅦 🆅

All properties graded by VisitScotland, formerly known as the Scottish Tourist Board.   Key to symbols is on back flap.

Oban, Argyll

Map Ref: 1E2

★★

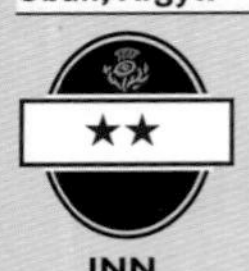

INN

Balmoral Inn

4 Craigard Road, Oban, Argyll, PA34 4NP
Tel: 01631 562731 Fax: 01631 566810
E-mail: balmoral@west-highland-holidays.co.uk
Web: www.oban.org.uk/accommodation/balmoral

Personally run and centrally situated close to shops, ferry and rail terminal. Incorporates a popular bistro restaurant.

2 Single	9 En Suite fac	B&B per person	Open Jan-Dec excl
2 Twin	1 Pub Bath/Show	from £25.00 Single	Xmas/New Year
7 Double		from £35.00 Dbl/Twn	
1 Family		Room only from £20.00	

★★★★

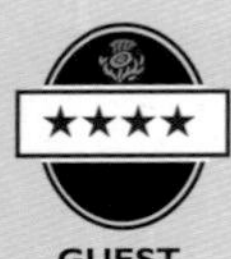

GUEST HOUSE

Don-Muir Guest House

Pulpit Hill, Oban, Argyll, PA34 4LX
Tel: 01631 564536 Fax: 01631 563739

Set in quiet residential area, high up on Pulpit Hill and close to public transport terminals. Parking available.

1 Single	3 En Suite fac	B&B per person	Open Apr-Oct
1 Twin	1 Pub Bath/Show	from £19.00 Single	
3 Double	1 Limited En Suite	from £20.00 Dbl/Twn	
		Room only from £15.00	

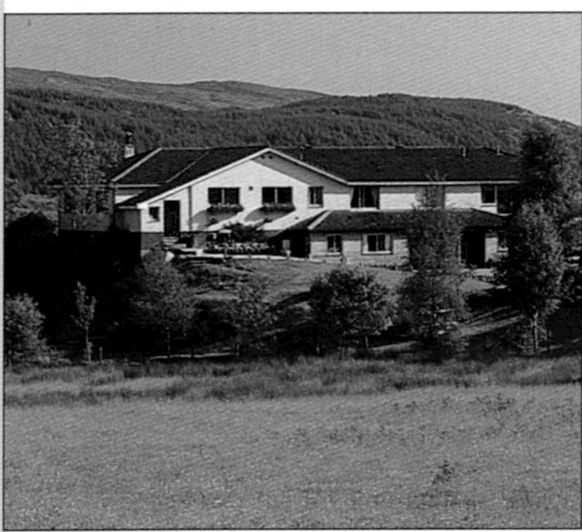

Foxholes Hotel

Cologin, Lerags, Oban, Argyll PA34 4SE
Tel: 01631 564982 Fax: 01631 570890
e.mail: shirley.foxholes@tesco.net
Web: www.hoteloban.com

Enjoy peace and tranquility at Foxholes, situated in its own grounds in a quiet glen 3 miles south of Oban, with magnificent views of the surrounding countryside. An ideal spot for those who wish to "get away from it all". Enjoy our superb five-course table d'hote menu and large selection of wines and spirits. All bedrooms ensuite, colour TV and tea/coffee-making facilities.
Send for colour brochure and tariff to Mrs S Dowson-Park at the above address.
Prices from £44.00 D,B&B pp per night. B&B from £29.00 pp per night. Single supplement £12 extra per night.
OPEN MARCH TO NOVEMBER.

★★★★

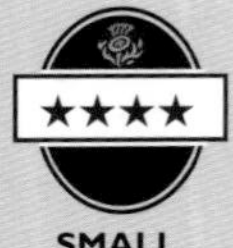

SMALL HOTEL

Foxholes Country Hotel

Lerags, Oban, Argyll, PA34 4SE
Tel: 01631 564982 Fax: 01631 570890
E-mail: shirley.foxholes@tesco.net
Web: www.hoteloban.com

Peacefully situated in a quiet glen with magnificent views yet a mere 3 miles (5kms) south of Oban. Ideally placed for the ferries for day trips to the islands of the inner Hebrides, Mull and Iona in particular. Many scenic drives including Fort William are within an hour of the Hotel and gardens. Fresh local produce used in our Table D'Hote dinners.

2 Twin	All En Suite	B&B per person	Open Mar-Nov excl
5 Double		from £41.00 Single	Xmas/New Year
		from £29.00 Dbl/Twn	B&B + Eve.Meal
			from £44.00

Important: Prices stated are estimates and may be subject to amendments

Oban, Argyll

Map Ref: 1E2

★★★★
GUEST HOUSE

Glenara Guest House
Rockfield Road, Oban, Argyll, PA34 5DQ
Tel: 01631 563172 Fax: 01631 571125
E-mail: glenara_oban@hotmail.com
Web: www.smoothhound.co.uk/hotels/glenara.html

Family run guest house close to the town centre and all amenities.
Tastefully and comfortably appointed rooms. No detail spared in caring
for guests individual needs. Excellent area for hillwalking, sailing, boat
cruising, archaeology and simply enjoying outstanding scenery. Non-
smoking.

1 Twin/
Triple
3 Double

B&B per person
from £30.00 Single
from £23.00 Dbl/Twn

Open Jan-Dec

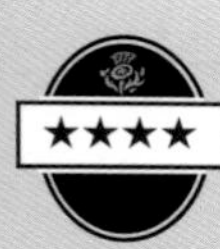

★★★★
GUEST HOUSE

Glenburnie House
Esplanade, Oban, Argyll, PA34 5AQ
Tel: 01631 562089
E-mail: Graeme.Strachan@btinternet.com
Web: www.glenburnie.co.uk

Convenient for town centre and all amenities, this family run hotel has
magnificent views of the bay and islands. Recently refurbished superior
rooms.

2 Single
4 Twin
8 Double

12 En Suite fac
2 Priv.NOT ensuite

B&B per person
£28.00-£35.00 Single
£28.00-£35.00 Dbl/Twn

Open Mar-Nov excl
Xmas/New Year

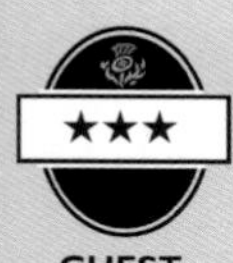

★★★
GUEST HOUSE

Glenrigh Guest House
Corran Esplanade, Oban, Argyll, PA34 5AQ
Tel/Fax: 01631 562991
E-mail: glenrigh@tesco.net

Family-run Victorian house with excellent views across Oban Bay. Short
walk from town centre and all amenities. Ample private parking.

3 Single
5 Twin
7 Double
4 Family

All En Suite

B&B per person
from £25.00-£30.00 Single
from £23.00-£30.00 Dbl/Twn
Room only per person
from £23.00-£30.00

Open Jan-Dec

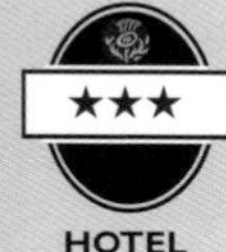

★★★
HOTEL

Great Western Hotel
Corran Esplanade, Oban, Argyll, PA34 5PP
Tel: 01786 436600 Fax: 01786 436650
E-mail: l.graig@shearingsholidays.co.uk
Web: www.shearingsholidays.com

Situated right on the seafront with fine views over Oban Bay.

18 Single
42 Twin
20 Double

All En Suite

Open Feb-Dec

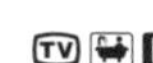

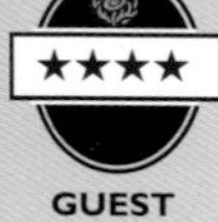

★★★★
GUEST HOUSE

Greencourt Guest House
Benvoulin Lane, Oban, Argyll, PA34 5EF
Tel: 01631 563987 Fax: 01631 571276
E-mail: stay@greencourt-oban.fsnet.co.uk
Web: www.greencourt-oban.fsnet.co.uk

Spacious family run property in quiet situation overlooking outdoor
bowling green, a short stroll to town centre and adjacent to leisure
centre. Attractive rooms, wholesome breakfasts, private parking. Ideal
touring base.

1 Single
1 Twin
4 Double

5 Ensuite fac
1 Priv.NOT ensuite

B&B per person
£22.00-£29.00 Single
£22.00-£29.00 Dbl/Twn

Open Jan-Dec

All properties graded by VisitScotland, formerly known as the Scottish Tourist Board. | *Key to symbols is on back flap.*

Oban, Argyll

Map Ref: 1E2

★★★★

GUEST HOUSE

Hawthornbank Guest House
Dalriach Road, Oban, Argyll PA34 5JE
Tel: 01631 562041
E-mail: hawthornbank@aol.com
Web: www.SmoothHound.co.uk/hotels/hawthorn.html

Brian and Valerie look forward to welcoming you to Hawthornbank, a tastefully refurbished Victorian villa set in a quiet location yet only a short stroll from the town centre. Comfortable well equipped rooms some with stunning views over Oban Bay. How can you resist?

1 Single	All En Suite	B&B per person
1 Twin		from £20.00 Single
6 Double		from £20.00 Dbl/Twn

Open Jan-Dec

★★★

B&B

Kathmore Guest House
Soroba Road, Oban, Argyll, PA34 4JF
Tel: 01631 562104
E-mail: wkathmore@aol.com

Kathmore guest house is just outside Oban Town Centre. A short walk from the bus, train and ferry terminals. Trouble-free parking is provided by our spacious private car park. All rooms well-furnished and equipped with colour TV's Tea/Coffee trays, hairdryer etc. Most are ensuite. Within walking distance of many restaurants and pubs.

1 Twin	4 En Suite fac	B&B per person
3 Double	1 Pub Bath/Show	£20.00-£35.00 Single
1 Family		£16.00-£22.00 Dbl/Twn

Open Jan-Dec excl Xmas

★★★★

SMALL HOTEL

The Kimberley Hotel
13 Dalriach Road, Oban, Argyll, PA34 5EQ
Tel: 01631 571115 Fax: 01631 571008
E-mail: info@kimberley-hotel.com
Web: www.kimberley-hotel.com

Victorian building of character set in an elevated position with open outlook over Oban, harbour and islands. Rooms are furnished in the Victorian style with modern comforts. The town centre with rich choice of shops and restaurants is only 5 minutes walk. Truly a choice location.

4 Single	All En Suite	B&B per person
10 Double		£55.00-£70.00 Single
		£110 -£130.00 Double

Open May-Oct

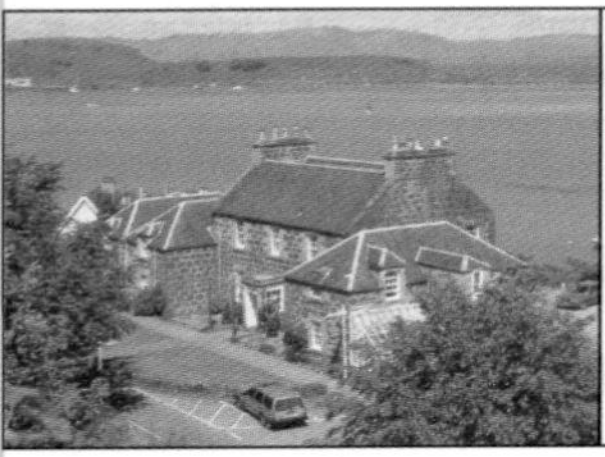

The Manor House
Gallanach Road, Oban, Argyll PA34 4LS
e.mail: manorhouseoban@aol.com
Web: www.manorhouseoban.com
In an enviable position on the foreshore of Oban Bay, The Manor House has long held the reputation for high quality in the comfort of its accommodation and the excellence of its Scottish cuisine. One AA Rosette.

All bedrooms have ensuite facilities.
Special weekends and breaks available.
For Reservations or Brochure and Tariff: Tel: 01631 562087/562611 Fax: 01631 563053

★★★★

SMALL HOTEL

Manor House Hotel
Gallanach Road, Oban, Argyll, PA34 4LS
Tel: 01631 562087 Fax: 01631 563053
E-mail: manorhouseoban@aol.com
Web: www.manorhouseoban.com

Family run Georgian house on the foreshore on the south side of Oban with extensive views across the Bay, close to the town centre.

3 Twin	All En Suite	DB&B per person
8 Double		from £70.00 Single
		from £100.00 Dbl/Twn

Open Jan-Dec excl Xmas

Important: Prices stated are estimates and may be subject to amendments

Oban, Argyll Map Ref: 1E2

GUEST HOUSE

★★★★

The Old Manse Guest House
Dalriach Road, Oban, Argyll, PA34 5JE
Tel: 01631 564886 Fax: 01631 570184
E-mail: oldmanse@obanguesthouse.co.uk
Web: www.obanguesthouse.co.uk

Victorian detached Villa set in beautiful gardens, with views of sea and islands. Superior standard of hospitality and comfort. Only minutes walk to town centre. Private parking. Family suite available.

1 Twin	All En Suite
3 Double	
1 Family	

B&B per person
£20.00-£32.00 Dbl/Twn

Open Mar-Nov incl. New Year

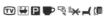

GUEST HOUSE

★★★★

Roseneath Guest House
Dalriach Road, Oban, Argyll, PA34 5EQ
Tel: 01631 562929 Fax: 01631 567218
E-mail: quirkers@aol.com
Web: www.oban.org.uk/accommodation/roseneath

Roseneath, a fine Victorian villa with views over Oban Bay towards the islands of Kerrera and Mull. An ideal touring base for visitors to Lorn and the Isles. Quiet location, yet less than a five minute walk from town centre, train and ferry terminals and convenient to all amenities, nearby

2 Twin	All En Suite
6 Double	

B&B per person
£25.00-£30.00 Single
£20.00-£27.00 Dbl/Twn

Open Feb-Nov

GUEST HOUSE

★★★

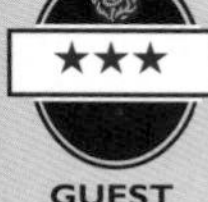

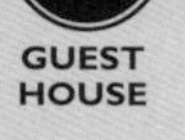

Sutherland Hotel
Corran Esplanade, Oban, Argyll, PA34 5PN
Tel/Fax: 01631 562539
E-mail: suthotel@aol.com
Web: www.smoothhound.co.uk/hotels/sutherland.html

Traditional Victorian house situated in the centre of Corran Esplanade overlooking Oban Bay with excellent views towards the islands. Conveniently situated close to the seafront with access to all town centre amenities. Good comfortable rooms. Evening meals by arrangement.

1 Single	9 En Suite fac
2 Twin	1 Pub Bath/Show
7 Double	2 Priv.NOT ensuite
3 Family	

B&B per person
£18.00-£25.00 Single
£18.00-£24.00 Dbl/Twn
Room only per person
£16.00-£22.00

Open Apr-Nov
B&B + Eve.Meal
from £28.00

GUEST HOUSE

★★★

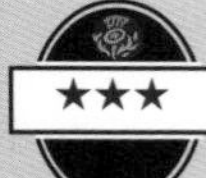

Thornloe Guest House
Albert Road, Oban, Argyll, PA34 5JD
Tel/Fax: 01631 562879
E-mail: thornloeoban@aol.com
Web: www.SmoothHound.co.uk/hotels/thornloe

Completely modernised Victorian semi-detached house with garden, in centrally situated residential area with fine views over Oban Bay towards the Isle of Mull. Within easy walking distance from town centre, leisure facilities and other amenities.

1 Single	7 En Suite fac
2 Twin	1 Priv.NOT ensuite
4 Double	
1 Family	

B&B per person
from £20.00 Single
from £20.00 Dbl/Twn
Room only from £20.00

Open Jan-Dec

B&B

★★★

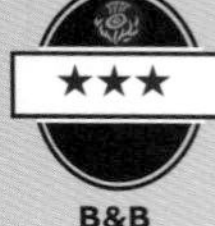

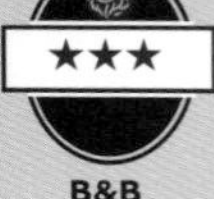

The Torrans
Drummore Road, Oban, Argyll, PA34 4JL
Tel: 01631 565342 Fax: 01631 565342

Comfortable family home in quiet residential cul-de-sac. 1 mile (2kms) from town centre and all amenities. Excellent views across Oban and the Islands.

1 Twin	2 En Suite fac
2 Double	1 Pub Bath/Show
	1 Priv.NOT ensuite

B&B per person
from £25.00 Single
from £16.20 Dbl/Twn

Open Jan-Dec

All properties graded by VisitScotland, formerly known as the Scottish Tourist Board. | *Key to symbols is on back flap.* |

Oban, Argyll

Map Ref: 1E2

★★★

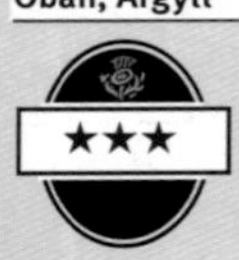

**GUEST
HOUSE**

Wellpark House
Esplanade, Oban, Argyll, PA34 5AQ
Tel: 01631 562948 Fax: 01631 565808
E-mail: enquiries@wellparkhouse.co.uk
Web: www.wellparkhouse.co.uk

Family run establishment in a quiet position on the esplanade.
Magnificent views over the bay to Isles of Kerrera and Mull.

5 Single	All En Suite	B&B per person	Open Apr-Oct
4 Twin		from £25.50 Single	
10 Double		from £20.50 Dbl/Twn	
2 Family		Room only per person	
		from £18.50	

---

by Oban, Argyll

Map Ref: 1E2

★★★

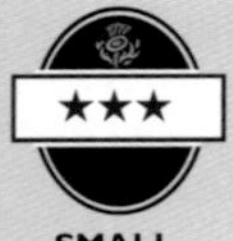

**SMALL
HOTEL**

Ards House
Connel, by Oban, Argyll, PA37 1PT
Tel: 01631 710255
E-mail: jb@ardshouse.com
Web: www.ardshouse.com

Warm friendly atmosphere in this family run house where husband is a
keen cook. Large relaxing lounge, table licence, superb sea and sunset
views. Taste of Scotland.

1 Single	6 En Suite fac	B&B per person	Open Mar-mid Nov
3 Twin	1 Priv.NOT ensuite	from £45.00 Single	B&B + Eve.Meal from
3 Double		from £90.00 Dbl/Twn	£55.00

The Falls of Lora Hotel

**Connel Ferry, by Oban, Argyll PA37 1PB
Telephone: 01631 710483   Fax: 01631 710694**

Overlooking Loch Etive this fine owner-run Hotel has 30 rooms –
from luxury to inexpensive family! Relax in the super Cocktail Bar
with open log fire and over 100 brands of whisky, there is an
extensive Bistro menu featuring local produce.
Oban is only 5 miles – the "Gateway to the Highlands & Islands".

★★★

HOTEL

Falls of Lora Hotel
Connel Ferry, by Oban, Argyll, PA37 1PB
Tel: 01631 710483 Fax: 01631 710694

Oban 5 miles, only 2 1/2 to 3 hours drive north-west of
Glasgow/Edinburgh. A fine owner-run Victorian hotel with a modern
extension.

6 Single	All En Suite	B&B per person	Open Feb-mid Dec
9 Twin		from £29.50 Single	
11 Double		from £19.50 Dbl/Twn	
4 Family			

Port of Menteith, Perthshire   Map Ref: 1H3

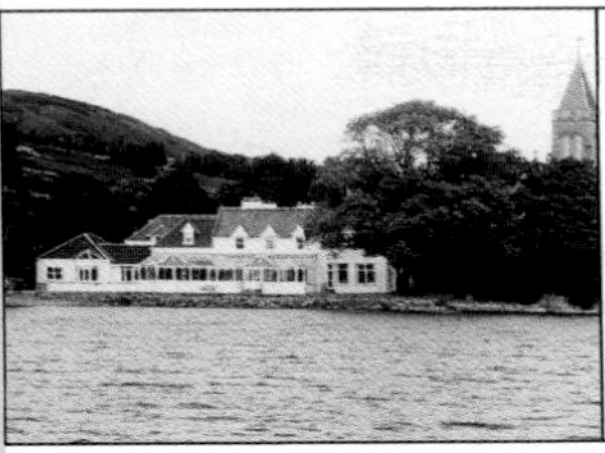

THE LAKE HOTEL – TROSSACHS
PORT OF MENTEITH, PERTHSHIRE FK8 3RA
Telephone: 01877 385258   Fax: 01877 385671
e.mail: enquiries@lake-of-menteith-hotel.com
Web: *www.lake-of-menteith-hotel.com*

*Outstanding situation on the shore of the Lake of Menteith. Bordering the Highlands
and within one hour of Edinburgh and Glasgow. All rooms with ensuite facilities.
Our cuisine emulates the restaurant with its spectacular lakeside setting.
Special weekends and breaks available.*
Reservations and brochure from above address.

★★★

**SMALL
HOTEL**

The Lake of Menteith Hotel
Port of Menteith, Perthshire, FK8 3RA
Tel: 01877 385258 Fax: 01877 385671
E-mail: enquiries@lake-of-menteith-hotel.com
Web: www.lake-of-menteith-hotel.com

Situated beside the Lake of Menteith with long views to the Isle of
Inchmahome and the hills beyond. Wonderful opportunities for
hillwalking, fishing, golf or just touring the marvellous countryside of the
Trossachs.

7 Twin   All En Suite
9 Double

B&B per person
from £55.00 Single
from £45.00 Dbl/Twn
Room only from £45.00

Open Feb-Dec
B&B + Eve.Meal from
£65.00

Stirling   Map Ref: 2A4

★★★★

**GUEST
HOUSE**

Castlecroft
Ballengeich Road, Stirling, FK8 1TN
Tel: 01786 474933 Fax: 01786 466716
E-mail: billsalmond@aol.com
Web: www.castlecroft.uk.com

Nestling on elevated site under Stirling Castle, this comfortable modern
house offers a warm welcome. Private facilities. Lounge with panoramic
view of the surrounding countryside. Large landscaped garden and
private lit parking area.

2 Twin   All En Suite
3 Double
1 Family

B&B per person
£35.00-£45.00 Single
£20.00-£25.00 Dbl/Twn

Open Jan-Dec excl
Xmas/New Year

All properties graded by VisitScotland, formerly known as the Scottish Tourist Board.   Key to symbols is on back flap.

Stirling

Stirling | Map Ref: 2A4

★★★★

GUEST HOUSE

Forth Guest House
23 Forth Place, Riverside, Stirling, FK8 1UD
Tel: 01786 471020 Fax: 01786 447220
E-mail: loudon@forthguesthouse.freeserve.co.uk
Web: www.forthguesthouse.freeserve.co.uk

Georgian terraced house within 5 minutes walking distance of railway station, town centre and swimming pool. Good location for touring, to either Glasgow or Edinburgh by car or train. Close to Stirling Castle and Wallace monument. Private parking.

1 Single
2 Twin
2 Double
1 Family

All En Suite

B&B per person
from £25.00 Single
from £19.50 Dbl/Twn

Open Jan-Dec

★★★

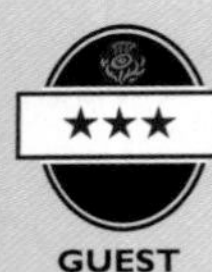

GUEST HOUSE

Garfield House
12 Victoria Square, Stirling, FK8 2QZ
Tel/Fax: 01786 473730

Family run guest house in traditional stone built Victorian house overlooking quiet square close to the town centre, castle and all local amenities. Ideal base for exploring historic Stirling, Loch Lomond and the Trossachs. Non smoking.

2 Twin
3 Double
3 Family

All En Suite

B&B per person
£22.00-£24.00 Dbl/Twn

Open Jan-Dec excl
Xmas/New Year

★★★

HOTEL

&

Express by Holiday Inn
Springkerse Business Park, Stirling, FK7 7XH
Tel: 01786 449922 Fax: 01786 449932
E-mail: info@hiex-stirling.com
Web: www.hiex-stirling.com

Designed for the business and leisure traveller alike, offering well equipped rooms and a range of business services. Situated on the eastern outskirts of the town with open views towards the Ochil Hills. Complimentary continental buffet breakfast.

38 Twin
4 Double
38 Family

All En Suite

Room + Cont.B/fast
from £49.50 Single
from £49.50 Dbl/Twn

Open Jan-Dec

★★★

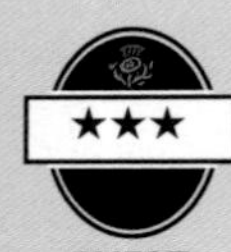

GUEST HOUSE

Whitegables B&B
112 Causewayhead Road, Stirling, FK9 5HJ
Tel/Fax: 01786 479838
E-mail: whitegables@b-j-graham.freeserve.co.uk

Tudor-style detached house in residential area located midway between Stirling Castle and the Wallace Monument. Easily accessible to motorway links. Private off road car parking available. Non smoking house.

1 Twin
1 Double
2 Family

All En Suite

B&B per person
from £25.00 Single
from £44.00 Double

Open Jan-Dec excl
Xmas/New Year

Important: Prices stated are estimates and may be subject to amendments

---

Strachur, Argyll　　　　　　　　　　　　　　　　**Map Ref: 1F3**

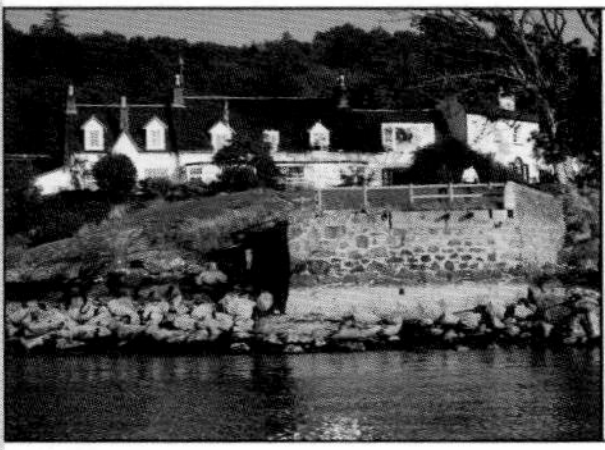

THE CREGGANS INN
Strachur, Argyll, PA27 8BX
Tel: 01369 860279 Fax: 01369 860637
e.mail: info1creggans-inn.co.uk Web: www.creggans-inn.co.uk

Overlooking Loch Fyne, this historic country hotel offers award winning food, an enthusiasts wine list and stylishly refurbished rooms. Relaxing at Creggans couldn't be simpler whether you walk the hills and glens, explore the coastline or just sit back with one of our malt whiskies and watch the sun set.

★ ★ ★

SMALL
HOTEL

The Creggans Inn
Strachur, Argyll, PA27 8BX
Tel: 01369 860279 Fax: 01369 860637
E-mail: info@creggans-inn.co.uk Web: www.creggans-inn.co.uk

Country Hotel, steeped in history, with magnificent views of Loch Fyne. An excellent reputation for fine food. 20 miles from Dunoon or Inveraray and only an hour from Glasgow Airport, Creggans is renowned for its food, wine and quality of local produce. Our restaurant overlooking Loch Fyne offers guests the best view in Scotland. Good walking for all abilities.

5 Twin	All En Suite	B&B per person	Open Jan-Dec
9 Double		from £55.00 Single	B&B + Eve.Meal
		from £55.00 Dbl/Twn	from £70.00
		Room only from £45.00	

Strathyre, Perthshire　　　　　　　　　　　　　　**Map Ref: 1H3**

★ ★ ★ ★

RESTAURANT
WITH
ROOMS

Creagan House Restaurant with Accommodation
Strathyre, Callander, Perthshire, FK18 8ND
Tel: 01877 384638 Fax: 01877 384319
E-mail: eatandstay@creaganhouse.co.uk
Web: www.creaganhouse.co.uk

A peaceful little gem of comfort surrounded by beautiful scenery. Five charming bedrooms with many thoughtful extras and a growing collection of antiques, friendly perfection is our aim. The baronial dining hall helps make each evening a special occasion, using meat from Perthshire, fruits and vegetables grown locally, herbs from our garden, all complemented by fine wines. Recently awarded two AA Rossettes and Red Star.

1 Twin	All En Suite	B&B per person	Open Mar-Jan
3 Double		from £52.50 Single	B&B + Eve.Meal
1 Family		from £42.50 Dbl/Twn	from £62.25

Tarbert, Loch Fyne, Argyll   Map Ref: 1E5

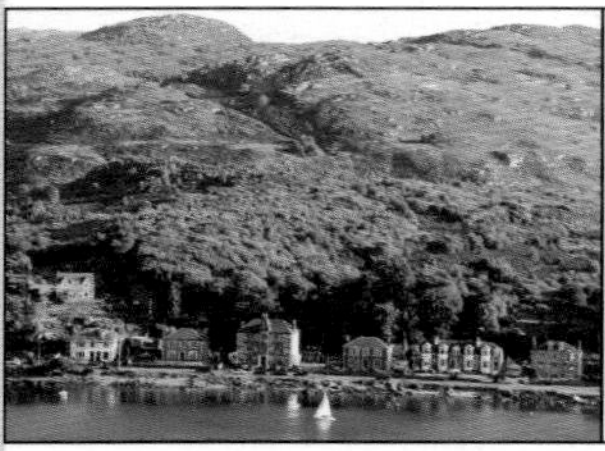

The Columba Hotel

Tarbert, Loch Fyne, Argyll PA29 6UF
Tel: 01880 820808   Fax: 01880 820808
e.mail: columbahotel@FSBDial.co.uk
Web: www.columbahotel.com

★★★ SMALL HOTEL

AA ✿

2 RAC dining awards

In a peaceful lochside setting within the fishing village of Tarbert
with superb views across Loch Fyne. Rooms are ensuite.
Log fires, bars, wholesomely different bar food and a restaurant
serving only the best of Scottish produce, imaginatively prepared.
BRONZE Ideally placed for touring Kintyre and the Islands of Argyll.

SMALL
HOTEL

The Columba Hotel
East Pier Road, Tarbert, Loch Fyne, Argyll,
PA29 6UF
Tel/Fax: 01880 820808
Web: www.columbahotel.com

2 Single   All En Suite

B&B per person
from £36.95 Single
Room only per person
from £36.95

Open Jan-Dec excl
Xmas
B&B + Eve.Meal
from £54.95

Tranquilly situated overlooking Loch Fyne within walking distance of
Tarbert. Warm welcome, open fires, local produce imaginatively prepared.

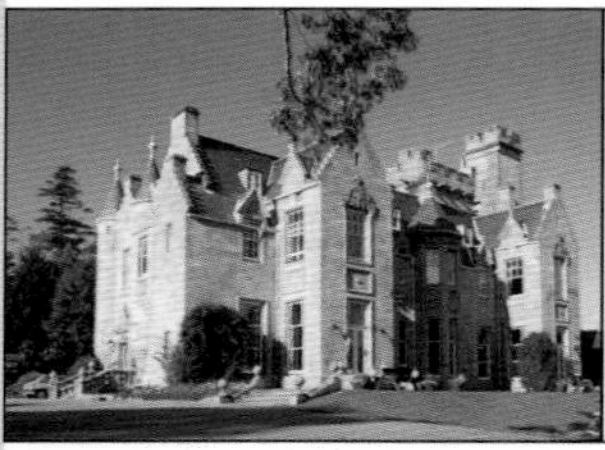

Stonefield Castle Hotel

Tarbert, Loch Fyne, Argyll PA29 6YJ
Tel: 01880 820836   Fax: 01880 820929
Web: www.stonefieldcastle.co.uk

★★★★
HOTEL

Breathtaking natural beauty surrounds the castle standing high on the Kintyre
peninsula. The awarded restaurant has one of the finest views on the West Coast,
while the gardens are renowned for their rare Rhododendrons, and exotic plants
and shrubs. Dinner, Bed & Breakfast from £75-£110 per person per night.
Taste of Scotland. Two RAC Dining Awards. **AA ★★★ RAC ★★★**

★★★★

HOTEL

Stonefield Castle Hotel
Loch Fyne, Tarbert, Loch Fyne, Argyll, PA29 6YJ
Tel: 01880 820836 Fax: 01880 820929

4 Single   32 En Suite fac
16 Twin   Suites avail
12 Double 1 Priv.NOT ensuite

Open Jan-Dec
B&B + Eve.Meal
£45.00-£90.00

Breathtaking natural beauty surrounding the baronial elegance of the
Castle with spectacular views over Loch Fyne and awarded restaurant.

Important: Prices stated are estimates and may be subject to amendments

Tarbet, Arrochar, Argyll

Map Ref: 1G3

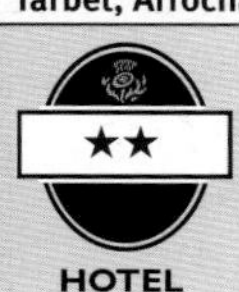

★★
HOTEL

Tarbet Hotel

Tarbet, Arrochar, Loch Lomond, Argyll & Bute, G83 7DE
Tel: 01786 436600 Fax: 01786 436650
E-mail: l.graig@shearingsholidays.co.uk
Web: www.shearingsholidays.com

Large touring hotel on the banks of Loch Lomond, central for visiting the Trossachs, the West Coast and West Highlands. Fishing available.

11 Single   All En Suite
35 Twin
26 Double
1 Family

Open Feb-Dec

---

by Tarbet, by Arrochar, Dunbartonshire

Map Ref: 1G3

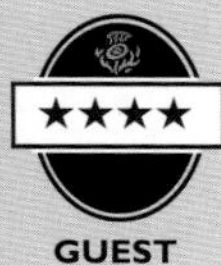

★★★★
GUEST HOUSE

Bonniebank House

Tarbet, by Arrochar, Loch Lomond, G83 7DJ
Tel: 01301 702300 Fax: 01301 702946
E-mail: info@bonniebank.f9.co.uk
Web: www.bonniebank.com

Bonniebank truly lives up to its name, being situated on the lochside with magnificent views across the water to Ben Lomond. Friendly Scottish welcome; well appointed rooms. Weather permitting, breakfast on the terrace right by the lochside.

4 Double   All En Suite

B&B per person
from £45.00 Single
from £30.00 Double

Open Jan-Dec excl Xmas/New Year

Tighnabruaich, Argyll

Map Ref: 1E5

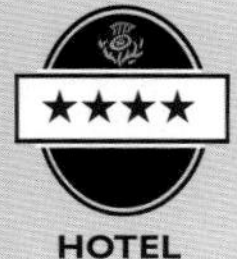

★★★★
HOTEL

Royal Hotel

Shore Road, Tighnabruaich, Argyll, PA21 2BE
Tel: 01700 811239 Fax: 01700 811300
E-mail: info@royalhotel.org.uk
Web: www.royalhotel.org.uk

A warm welcome and traditional Scottish hospitality awaits you at this hotel situated on the waters edge of the Kyles of Bute in one of the most scenic and unspoilt areas of Scotland's west coast. Personally run, chef-owner specialising in local seafood, venison and game. Taste of Scotland member.

9 Double   All En Suite
2 Family

B&B per person
from £57.00 Single
from £37.00 Double

Open Jan-Dec excl Xmas
B&B + Eve.Meal
from £55.00

Tillicoultry, Clackmannanshire

Map Ref: 2A3

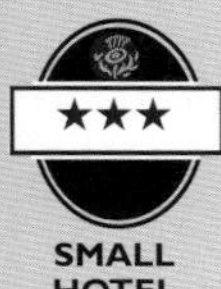

★★★
SMALL HOTEL

Harviestoun Country Hotel & Restaurant

Dollar Road, Tillicoultry, Clackmannanshire,
FK13 6PQ
Tel: 01259 752522 Fax: 01259 752523
Web: www.harviestouncountryhotel.com

Originally a 19th century farm steading sympathetically converted into well appointed bedrooms, courtyard restaurant, function suite, coffee house and gifts. Centrally situated for business, touring and golfing breaks with Glasgow and Edinburgh 45 mins approx by car.

8 Double   All En Suite
2 Family

B&B per person
from £50.00 Single
from £32.50 Dbl/Twn

Open Jan-Dec

All properties graded by VisitScotland, formerly known as the Scottish Tourist Board.   Key to symbols is on back flap.

Tiree, Isle of, Argyll — Map Ref: 1A1

★★★

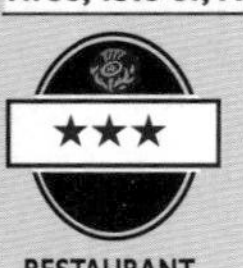

RESTAURANT
WITH ROOMS

The Glassary Restaurant with Rooms
Sandaig, Isle of Tiree, Argyll, PA77 6XQ
Tel/Fax: 01879 220684
E-mail: glassary@hotels.activebooking.com
Web: www.glassary-activebooking.com

2 Single	4 En Suite fac	B&B per person	Open Jan-Dec excl
1 Twin	1 Priv.NOT ensuite	from £28.00 Single	Xmas/New Year
2 Double		from £28.00 Dbl/Twn	B&B + Eve.Meal from £28.00

Bungalow with adjacent converted byre and Conservatory which serves as a licensed restaurant, specialising in local produce. 7 miles (11 km) from ferry and 4 miles (7 km) from airport. Panoramic view over islands and Atlantic Ocean. Satellite TV in the lounge.

Tyndrum, by Crianlarich, Perthshire — Map Ref: 1G2

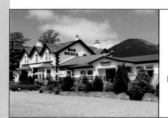

THE INVERVEY HOTEL

TYNDRUM, PERTHSHIRE FK20 8RY
TEL: 01838 400219 FAX: 01838 400280
E.MAIL: info@inverveyhotel.co.uk WEB: www.inverveyhotel.com

Family run hotel situated on the A82/85 at Tyndrum. It snuggles below some of the finest mountain scenery in Scotland and is ideally situated for the West Highland Way, hill-walking, climbing and ski-ing. Large lounge bar, restaurant, conservatory and games room, wonderful meeting places for guests and locals. Open all year.

★★

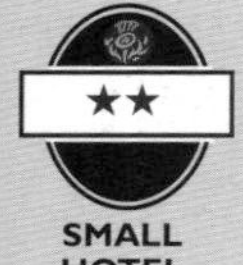

SMALL
HOTEL

The Invervey Hotel
Tyndrum, Perthshire, FK20 8RY
Tel: 01838 400219 Fax: 01838 400280
E-mail: info@inverveyhotel.co.uk
Web: www.inverveyhotel.com

5 Single	All En Suite	B&B per person	Open Jan-Dec excl New
7 Twin		from £20.00-£25.00	Year
6 Double		Single	B&B + Eve.Meal
3 Family		from £25.00 Dbl/Twn	from £36.00

Family hotel on main tourist route, surrounded on all sides by mountain scenery. An ideal base for fishing, shooting, walking. Climbing and ski-ing with ½ an hour drive.

Important: Prices stated are estimates and may be subject to amendments

welcome to Scotland

PERTHSHIRE, ANGUS & DUNDEE
AND THE KINGDOM OF FIFE

Plenty of contrasts here: From the white-walled harbourfront houses of the East Neuk fishing villages to the heathery silence of Rannoch Moor, from the arts and culture of Dundee to the tranquillity of the Angus Glens. This area makes a good place for a break, with a little of everything within easy reach.

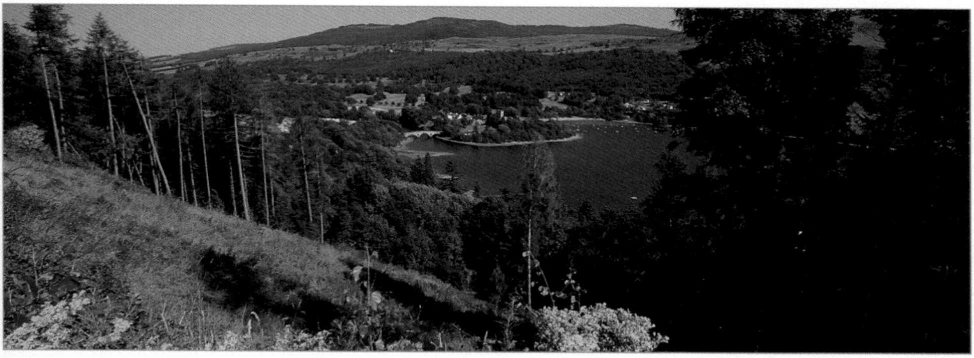

Village of Kenmore at the end of Loch Tay, Perthshire

PERTH is an important commercial centre for its hinterland both above and below the Highland line. Another Perthshire speciality are the little resort towns such as Dunkeld, Pitlochry or Aberfeldy, with their good range of visitor attractions such as the Scottish Plant Collectors Garden (Pitlochry) open 2002 and Dewar's World of Whisky at Aberfeldy.

The Kingdom of Fife has plenty of character, with St Andrews noted as Scotland's oldest university and also often called 'the home of golf'. The town offers excellent shopping and is within easy reach of attractive East Neuk villages like Crail southwards and also the city of Dundee across the Tay Bridge to the north.

Dundee is the city of Discovery, with Discovery Point one of Scotland's top attractions while its new Science Centre, 'Sensation' provides the whole family with hands-on fun. The Angus Glens are special places, with roads running deep into the hills through Glens Isla, Prosen, Clova or Esk – great country for walkers, birdwatchers and botanists. The coastline of Angus also offers plenty of interest, with spectacular cliffs and coves and small fishing ports such as Arbroath, home of the 'Arbroath smokie' – a fishy treat! Between hills and coast lie attractions such as Glamis Castle, birthplace of HM Queen Elizabeth the Queen Mother, and Edzell Castle with its unique garden.

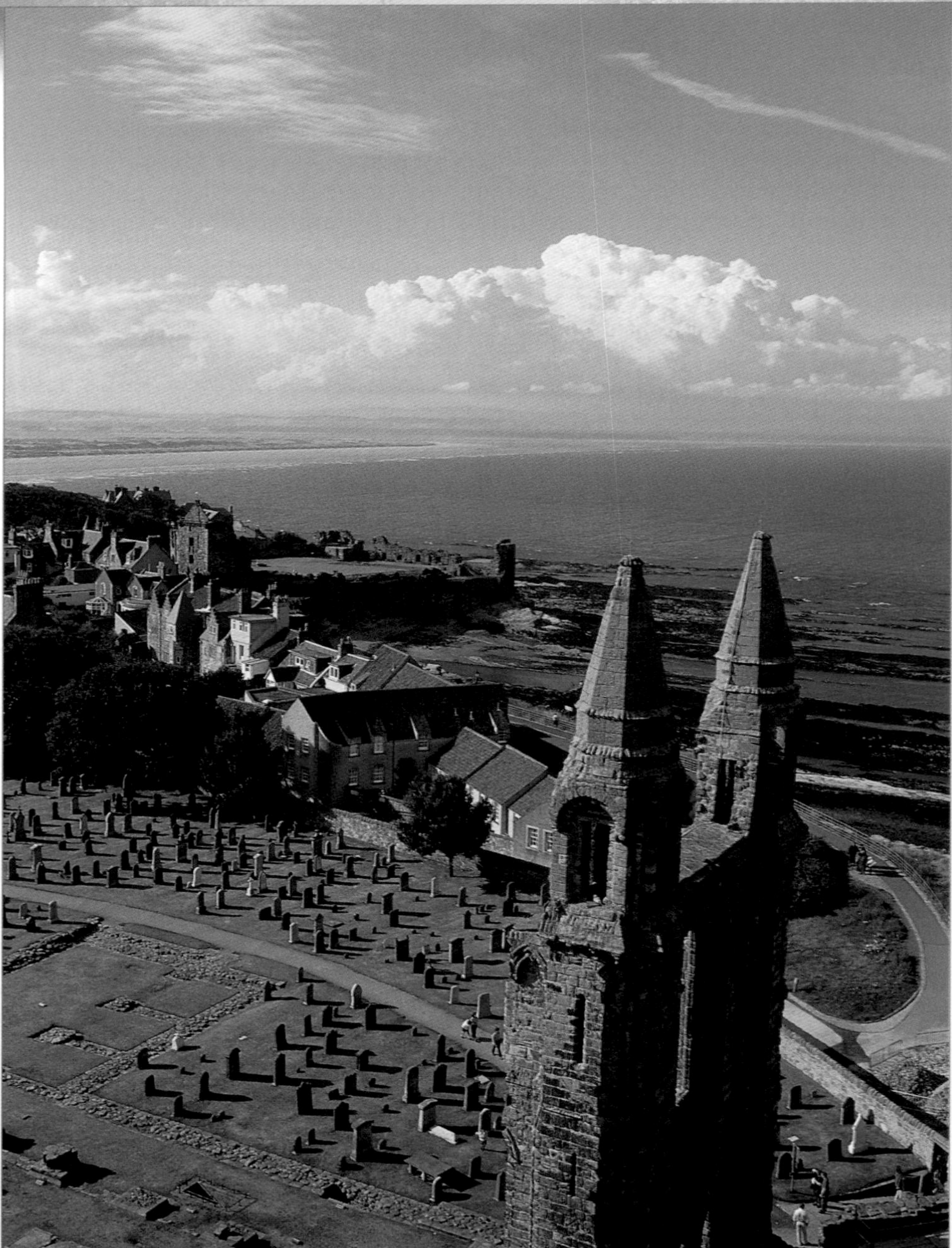

Looking north from the St Rules Tower across the town of St Andrews

Perthshire, Angus & Dundee and the Kingdom of Fife

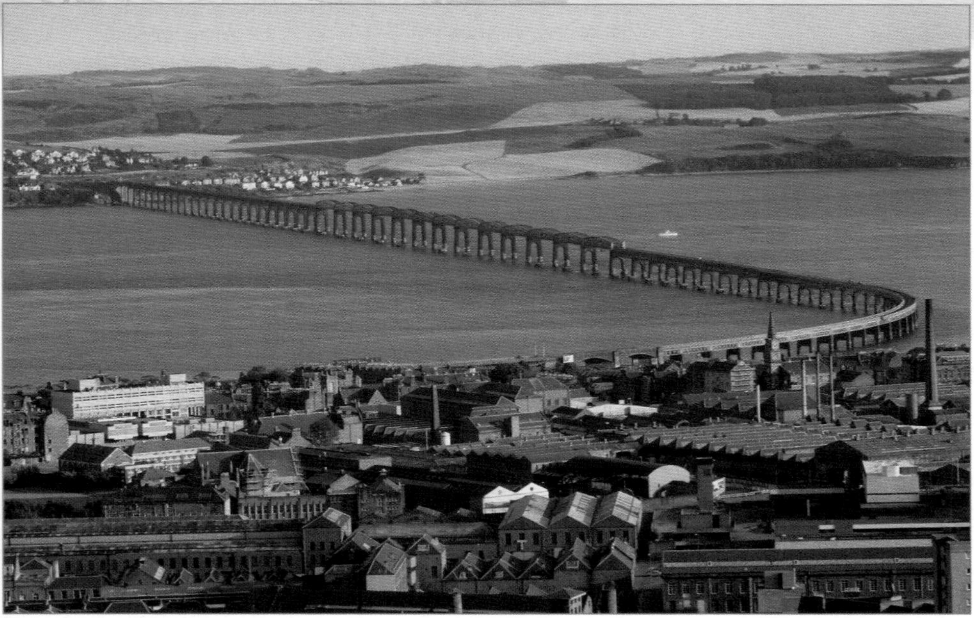

Looking across Dundee and the Firth of Tay towards Fife

Scattered across the whole area are a wide range of other attractions, such as Deep Sea World by North Queensferry (an aquarium featuring the world's largest walk-through tunnel), the birthplace cottage of the playwright JM Barrie in Kirriemuir, and also Scotland's National Garden at Perth and Bells Cherrybank Centre.

14-22 APRIL
Kirkcaldy Links Market
Kirkcaldy, Esplanade
The longest street fair in
Europe, which attracts most
of the biggest and best new
fair ground, rides in the
country.
Contact: John Haggart
Tel: 01592 417846

21-27 APRIL
St Andrews Golf Week
St Andrews,
Links Golf Courses
Annual golf week including
guaranteed golf on the
famous courses.
Contact:
Links Golf St Andrews
Tel: 01334 478639
Web:
www.links-golf-standrews.com

16-26 MAY
Perth Festival of the Arts
Perth, Various Venues
Festival of music, dance and
drama.
Contact:
Perth Festival Box Office
Tel: 01738 472706
Web: www.perthfestival.co.uk

25 & 26TH MAY
Atholl Highlanders Parade,
Atholl Gathering &
Highland Games
Blair Atholl, Blair Castle
Annual parade on the 25th
and traditional Highland
games on the 26th
Contact:
Atholl Estates Office
Tel: 01796 481355
Web:
www.atholl-estates.co.uk

* 6-7 JULY
Game Conservancy Fair
Perth, Scone Palace
Scottish Game Fair held in
the beautiful surroundings
of Scone Palace.
Contact: Mr Wolfe Murray
Tel: 01620 850577

* 27 JULY
Grand Scottish Prom
Forfar, Glamis Castle
Outdoor concert of classical
music with traditional
Scottish ballads and
fireworks finale.
Contact: Glamis Castle
Tel: 01307 840393
Web: www.great-houses-
scotland.co.uk

* 11 AUGUST
Perth Highland Games
Perth, Scone Palace
Traditional highland games
Contact: Andrew Rettie
Tel: 01738 627782

* 6-8 SEPTEMBER
Dundee Flower
and Food Festival
Dundee, Camperdown
Country Park
The largest horticultural
show on the East Coast of
Scotland.
Contact: Peter Sandwell
Tel: 01382 433815
Web: www.dundeecity.gov.uk

14 SEPTEMBER
RAF Leuchars Air Show
Fife, RAF Leuchars Airfield
One day air show with
events including flying
display, static display, craft
fair, classic car rally, funfair
and much more.
Contact: Air Show Office
Tel: 01334 838599
Web: www.airshow.co.uk

* denotes provisional date,
please check before arrival

AREA TOURIST BOARDS
PERTHSHIRE, ANGUS & DUNDEE AND THE KINGDOM OF FIFE

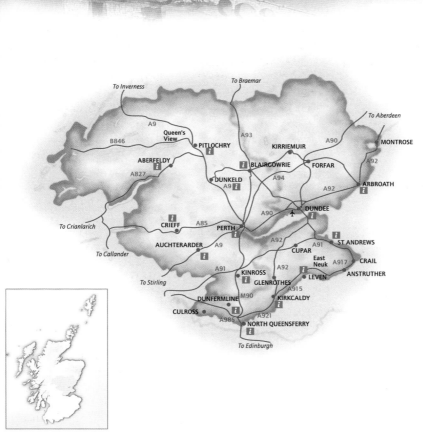

PERTHSHIRE TOURIST BOARD
Lower City Mills
West Mill Street
Perth
PH1 5QP

Tel: 01738 627958/9
Fax: 01738 630416
E-mail:
info@ptb.ossian.net
Web:
www.perthshire.co.uk

ANGUS AND DUNDEE TOURIST BOAD
21 Castle Street
Dundee
DD1 3AA

Tel: 01382 527527
Fax: 01382 527550
E-mail: enquiries@
angusanddundee.co.uk
Web:
www.angusanddundee.co.uk

KINGDOM OF FIFE TOURIST BOARD
70 Market Street
St Andrews
KY16 9NU

Tel: 01334 472021
Fax: 01334 478422
E-mail: standrewsstic@
KFTB.ossian.net
Web:
www.standrews.com/fife

Tourist Information Centres
Perthshire, Angus & Dundee and the Kingdom of Fife

ANGUS & CITY OF DUNDEE TOURIST BOARD

Arbroath
Market Place
Tel: (01241) 872609
Jan-Dec

Brechin
Brechin Castle Centre
Tel: (01356) 623050
April-Sept

Carnoustie
1b High Street
Tel: (01241) 852258
April-Sept

Dundee
21 Castle Street
Tel: (01382) 527527
Jan-Dec

Forfar
45 East High Street
Tel: (01307) 467876
April-Sept

Kirriemuir
Cumberland Close
Tel: (01575) 574097
April-Sept

Montrose
Bridge Street
Tel: (01674) 672000
April-Sept

KINGDOM OF FIFE TOURIST BOARD

Anstruther
Scottish Fisheries Museum
Tel: (01333) 311073
Easter-Sept

Crail
Crail Museum
and Heritage Centre
Marketgate
Tel: (01333) 450869
Easter-Sept

Dunfermline
1 High Street
Tel: (01383) 720999
Jan-Dec

Forth Bridges
North Queensferry
Tel: (01383) 417759
Jan-Dec

Kirkcaldy
19 Whytescauseway
Tel: (01592) 267775
Jan-Dec

St Andrews
70 Market Street
Tel: (01334) 472021
Jan-Dec

PERTHSHIRE TOURIST BOARD

Aberfeldy
The Square
Tel: (01887) 820276
aberfeldytic@perthshire.co.uk
Jan-Dec

Auchterarder
90 High Street
Tel: (01764) 663450
auchterardertic@perthshire.co.uk
Jan-Dec

Blairgowrie
26 Wellmeadow
Tel: (01250) 872960
blairgowrietic@perthshire.co.uk
Jan-Dec

Crieff
Town Hall
High Street
Tel: (01764) 652578
criefftic@perthshire.co.uk
Jan-Dec

Dunkeld
The Cross
Tel: (01350) 727688
dunkeldtic@perthshire.co.uk
Jan-Dec

Kinross
Adjacent to Kinross Service
Area, off Junction 6, M90
Tel: (01577) 863680
kinrosstic@perthshire.co.uk
Jan-Dec

Perth
Lower City Mills
West Mill Street
Tel: (01738) 450600
perthtic@perthshire.co.uk
Jan-Dec

Pitlochry
22 Atholl Road
Tel: (01796)
472215/472751
pitlochrytic@perthshire.co.uk
Jan-Dec

Aberdour, Fife

Map Ref: 2C4

★★★

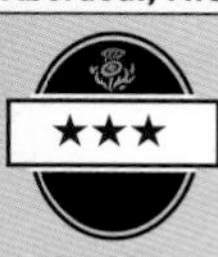

SMALL HOTEL

The Aberdour Hotel
38 High Street, Aberdour, Fife, KY3 0SW
Tel: 01383 860325 Fax: 01383 860808
E-mail: reception@aberdourhotel.co.uk
Web: www.aberdourhotel.co.uk

6 Twin	All En Suite	B&B per person	Open Jan-Dec
6 Double		from £35.00 Single	B&B + Eve.Meal
4 Family		from £25.00 Dbl/Twn	from £35.00

Personally run hotel specialising in traditional cooking and real ales on Fife coast in Conservation village 6 miles (10kms) from Forth Bridges. Convenient for touring and golf. Recently converted stables annexe furnished to a high standard. Non residents welcome.

Aberfeldy, Perthshire

Map Ref: 2A1

★★

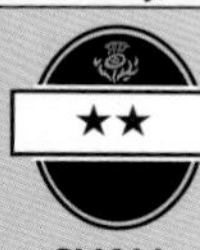

SMALL HOTEL

Fortingall Hotel
Fortingall, by Aberfeldy, Perthshire, PH15 2NQ
Tel: 01887 830367 Fax: 01887 830867
E-mail: hotel@fortingall.com
Web: www.fortingall.com

4 Twin	All En Suite	B&B per person	Open Mar-Dec excl
4 Double		from £25.00 Single	Xmas/New Year
2 Family		from £25.00 Dbl/Twn	B&B + Eve.Meal from £45.00

Independent Country Hotel offering comfortable en-suite rooms with excellent locally sourced cuisine. Located in the beautiful conservation village of Fortingall, the hotel is a superb centre for touring, walking and fishing.

★★★★

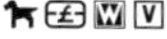

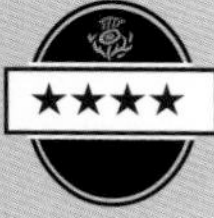

B&B

Tigh'n Eilean
Taybridge Drive, Aberfeldy, Perthshire, PH15 2BP
Tel/Fax: 01887 820109
Mobile: 07889 472248
E-mail: tigheilean@btinternet.com
Web: http://member.visitscotland.com/tighneilean

1 Single	All En Suite	B&B per person	Open Jan-Dec
1 Twin		from £25.00 Single	B&B + Eve.Meal
2 Double		from £20.00 Dbl/Twn	from £36.00

Elegant Victorian house overlooking the river. Warm and comfortable, home cooking. One room with jacuzzi.

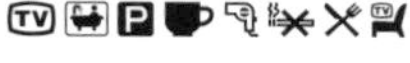

Alyth, Perthshire

Map Ref: 2C1

★★

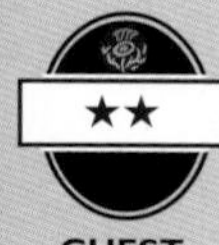

GUEST HOUSE

Airlie Mount Mansion House
2 Albert Street, Alyth, PH11 8AX
Tel: 01828 632986 Fax: 01828 632563
E-mail: airliemh@aol.com
Web: www.smoothhound.co.uk/hotels/airlie.html

1 Single	All En Suite	B&B per person	Open Jan-Dec
1 Twin		from £25.00 Single	B&B + Eve.Meal from
1 Double		from £45.00 Dbl/Twn	£35.00
4 Family			

A warm welcome at this Victorian mansion, quietly located in peaceful Alyth. Evening meals by arrangement. Ideal for golfers - 3 courses within 2 mile radius.

★★★★

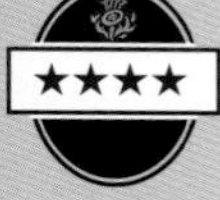

SMALL HOTEL

Drumnacree House
St Ninians Road, Alyth, Perthshire, PH11 8AP
Tel/Fax: 01828 632194
E-mail: derek@drumnacreehouse.co.uk
Web: www.drumnacreehouse.co.uk

5 Twin	All En Suite	B&B per person	Open Jan-Dec
5 Double		from £45.00 Single	B&B + Eve.Meal
1 Family		£35.00-£40.00 Dbl/Twn	£50.00-£65.00

Family run country house hotel, 5 miles (8 kms) from Blairgowrie. Emphasis on comfort and food, using seasonal garden produce.

All properties graded by VisitScotland, formerly known as the Scottish Tourist Board.   Key to symbols is on back flap.

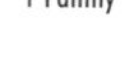

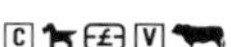

Anstruther, Fife

Map Ref: 2D3

★★★★

B&B

Laggan House

The Cooperage, Cellardyke, Anstruther, Fife, KY10 3AW
Tel/Fax: 01333 311170
E-mail: LagganHouse@Qwista.net.uk

2 Double	1 En Suite fac 1 Priv.NOT ensuite	B&B per person £22.00-£25.00 Dbl	Open Mar-Oct

Originally a cooperage servicing the fishing industry, the house is
situated 6 metres from the beach. The garden, patio and breakfast rooms
all overlook the sea with fantastic views. Direct access to coastal path. 9
miles from St Andrews, one hour from Edinburgh. Ideal for golfing or
touring Scotland.

Arbroath, Angus

Map Ref: 2D1

★★★

INN

Colliston Inn

Colliston, by Arbroath, Angus, DD11 3RP
Tel/Fax: 01241 890232
E-mail: collistoninn@hotmail.com

1 Twin 1 Double 1 Family	2 En Suite fac 1 Priv.NOT ensuite	B&B per person from £30.00 Single from £25.00 Dbl/Twn	Open Jan-Dec excl Xmas/New Year

Colliston Inn, a former manse is situated on the A933 west of the historic
Scottish fishing town of Arbroath. The Inn has an interesting varied menu
using local fresh produce to create good honest, up to date traditional
Scottish food. Many highly successful functions have taken place at
Colliston. We pride ourselves in giving a very personal service. Attending
to all organisation etc personally.

Auchterarder, Perthshire

Map Ref: 2B3

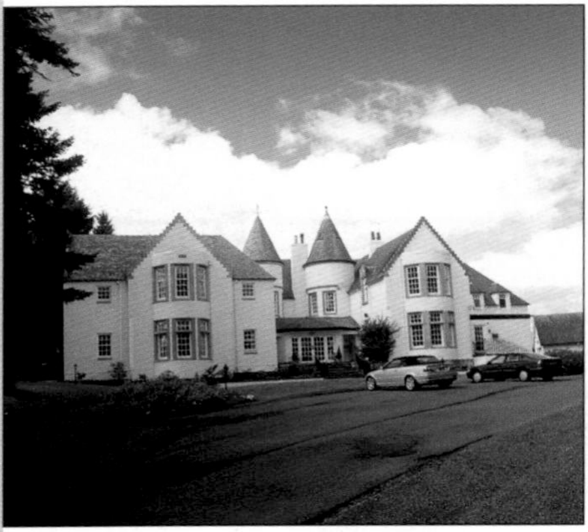

Cairn Lodge Hotel

Orchil Road, Auchterarder, PH3 1LX
Tel: 01764 662634/662431
Fax: 01764 664866
e.mail: email@cairnlodge.co.uk
Web: www.cairnlodge.co.uk

Sitting proudly in beautiful gardens and fronted
by Queen Victoria's Commemorative Jubilee
Cairn, the Cairn Lodge neighbours the world
famous Gleneagles complex on the edge of
Auchterarder. Beautiful and luxuriously
appointed en-suite accommodation, the elegant
'Capercaille' à la carte restaurant and the new
Jubilee Lounge, all add up to Perthshire's
premier country house hotel and restaurant.
B&B from £60-£85 per person per night.

Short breaks 3 nights for the price of 2.

★★★★

HOTEL

Cairn Lodge Hotel

Orchil Road, Auchterarder, PH3 1LX
Tel: 01764 662634 Fax: 01764 664866
E-mail: email@cairnlodge.co.uk
Web: www.cairnlodge.co.uk

1 Single 7 Twin 6 Double 3 Family	All En Suite	B&B per person from £60.00 Single from £100.00 Dbl/Twn	Open Jan-Dec excl Xmas/New Year B&B + Eve.Meal from £75.00

Personally run country house hotel, with large garden and putting green,
on outskirts of Auchterarder. Fine dining, prepared from fresh local
produce.

Important: Prices stated are estimates and may be subject to amendments

E

Auchterarder, Perthshire

Map Ref: 2B3

★★★

SMALL
HOTEL

Dunearn House Hotel
High Street, Auchterarder, Perthsire, PH3 1DB
Tel: 01764 664774 Fax: 01764 663242
E-mail: dunearnhouse@talk21.co.uk

2 Single	5 En Suite fac	B&B per person	Open Jan-Dec excl
2 Twin	3 Priv.NOT ensuite	from £50.00 Single	Xmas/New Year
3 Double		from £35.00 Dbl/Twn	
1 Family		Room only from £30.00	

Large Victorian country house in centre of excellent golfing country. All rooms have ensuite. Most country pursuits on the doorstep. Edinburgh, Glasgow, Stirling and Perth all within one hour by car.

Auchtermuchty, Fife

Map Ref: 2C3

★★

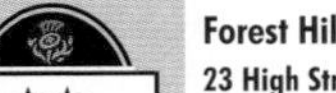

INN

Forest Hills Hotel
23 High Street, Auchtermuchty, KY14 7AP
Tel: 01337 828318

2 Single	4 En Suite fac	B&B per person	Open Jan-Dec
3 Double	1 Pub Bath/Show	from £30.00 Single	B&B + Eve.Meal from
1 Family		from £50.00 Dbl/Twn	£43.00

Privately owned 18th century hostelry (featured in 'Dr Finlay' TV series), with restaurant and bar meals, set in the heart of village.

Ballingry, nr Loch Leven, Fife

Map Ref: 2C3

★★

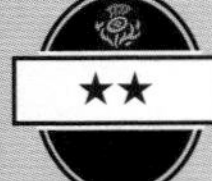

GUEST
HOUSE

Navitie House
nr Ballingry, Lochgelly, Fife, KY5 8LR
Tel: 01592 860295 Fax: 01592 869769
E-mail: navitie@aol.com
Web: http://navitiehouse.co.uk

1 Single	All En Suite	B&B per person	Open Jan-Dec
1 Twin		from £25.00 Single	B&B + Eve.Meal
1 Double		from £22.00 Dbl/Twn	from £32.00
4 Family		Room only from £22.00	

Detached 200-year-old house in its own grounds overlooking Ballingry village. Only 4 miles (6kms) from the Edinburgh to Perth motorway. Centrally located only 30/40 minutes drive from Edinburgh, Stirling, Perth and St Andrews. Evening meal by arrangement.

Birnam, by Dunkeld, Perthshire

Map Ref: 2B1

★★★

GUEST
HOUSE

Birnam Guest House
4 Murthly Terrace, Birnam, Dunkeld, PH8 0BG
Tel/Fax: 01350 727201
E-mail: enquiries@thebirnamguesthouse.co.uk
Web: www.thebirnamguesthouse.co.uk

2 Twin	All En Suite	B&B per person	Open Jan-Dec excl Xmas
2 Double		from £22.00 Single	
1 Family		from £22.00 Dbl/Twn	
		Room only from £20.00	

Looking onto the Birnam Hill famous for Shakespeare's Macbeth and opposite the new Birnam Theatre and Beatrix Potter Exhibition Garden, this friendly guest house is a mid-terraced Victorian villa recently refurbished to a high standard. All rooms ensuite. New conservatory lounge. Private parking. Residential licence.

Blair Atholl, Perthshire

Map Ref: 4C12

★★★

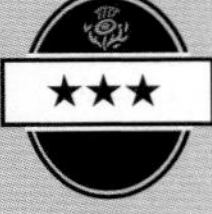

GUEST
HOUSE

Dalgreine Guest House
off St Andrews Crescent, Bridge of Tilt
Blair Atholl, Perthshire, PH18 5SX
Tel/Fax: 01796 481276

1 Single	2 En Suite fac	B&B per person	Open Jan-Dec
2 Twin	1 Pub Bath/Show	from £18.00 Single	B&B + Eve.Meal
2 Double	1 Priv.NOT ensuite	from £36.00 Dbl/Twn	from £27.00
1 Family			

Well appointed guest house, convenient for Blair Castle, Pitlochry Festival Theatre and the many local activities and attractions, including golf, pony-trekking, mountain bike hire, hill walks and river walks. Evening meals by arrangement.

All properties graded by VisitScotland, formerly known as the Scottish Tourist Board.   Key to symbols is on back flap.

Blair Atholl, Perthshire

Map Ref: 4C12

★★★

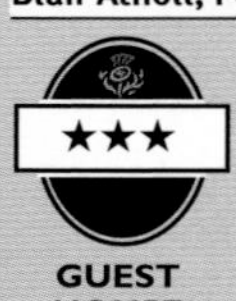

**GUEST
HOUSE**

Ptarmigan House
Blair Atholl, Perthshire, PH18 5SZ
Tel: 01796 481269
E-mail: gordon@ptarmiganhouse.co.uk
Web: www.ptarmiganhouse.co.uk

Former Victorian shooting lodge in great setting, overlooking the 1st
Fairway. Not to be missed.

| 2 Twin | All En Suite | B&B per person | Open Jan-Dec |
| 3 Double | | from £22.00 Dbl/Twn | |

Blairgowrie, Perthshire

Map Ref: 2B1

★★★

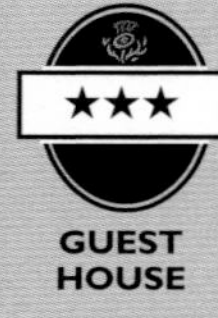

**GUEST
HOUSE**

The Laurels
Golf Course Road, Rosemount, Blairgowrie,
Perthshire, PH10 6LH   Tel/Fax: 01250 874920
E-mail: laurels-blairgowrie@talk21.com
Web: http://members.visitscotland.com/laurelsguesthouse

Originally a farmhouse dating from 1873, set back from main road, on outskirts of
Blairgowrie with own large garden and ample parking. Rosemount Golf Course is a short
walk away with a selection of 20 golf courses nearby. Ideal base for touring the beautiful
Perthshire countryside. Fishing, shooting, mountaineering, ski-ing, pony trekking all in the
local area.

1 Single	4 En Suite fac	B&B per person	Open mid Jan - mid
3 Twin	1 Pub Bath/Show	£19.00-£20.00 Single	Nov excl Xmas/New Year
2 Double		£19.00-£20.00 Dbl/Twn	

---

by Brechin, Angus

Map Ref: 4F12

★★★

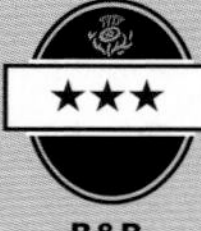

B&B

Blibberhill Farmhouse
by Brechin, Angus, DD9 6TH
Tel/Fax: 01307 830323
E-mail: wendysstewart@aol.com

Large well-appointed 18th century farmhouse, peacefully situated
between the glens and coast. Ideal touring/golfing base. Aberdeen and
Perth (one hour), St Andrews (40 minutes). Directions: first right after
Pictavia Visitor Centre onto B9134 for three miles, shortly after phone
box on left, farm sign on left.

1 Twin	All En Suite	B&B per person	Open Jan-Dec
1 Double		from £20.00 Single	B&B + Eve.Meal from
1 Family		from £17.00 Dbl/Twn	£28.00

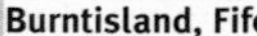

Burntisland, Fife

Map Ref: 2C4

★★★

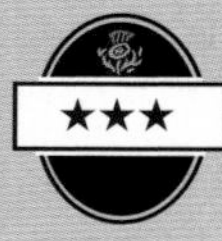

INN

Inchview Hotel
69 Kinghorn Road, Burntisland, Fife, KY3 9EB
Tel: 01592 872239 Fax: 01592 874866
E-mail: inchviewhotel@msn.com.uk

Family run hotel overlooking Burntisland Links and Pettycur Bay to the
Islands of the Forth Estuary. Flambe cooking in restaurant. Good
selection of real ales and continental beers in the lounge bar. Convenient
road and rail links to Edinburgh.

2 Single	All En Suite	B&B per person	Open Jan-Dec
3 Twin		from £42.50 Single	B&B + Eve.Meal from
6 Double		from £35.00 Dbl/Twn	£55.00
1 Family		Room only from £30.00	

★★★

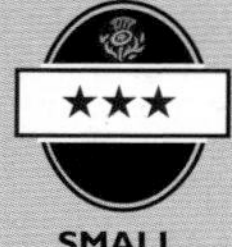

**SMALL
HOTEL**

Kingswood Hotel
Kinghorn Road, Burntisland, Fife, KY3 9LL
Tel: 01592 872329 Fax: 01592 873123
E-mail: rankin@kingswoodhotel.co.uk
Web: www.kingswoodhotel.co.uk

Privately owned, set in 2 acres of garden and woodland with fine views
across the Firth of Forth. Comfortable, modern bedrooms. Function and
conference facilities.

5 Twin	All En Suite	B&B per person	Open Jan-Dec excl
3 Double		from £52.00 Single	Xmas/New Year
1 Family		from £38.25 Dbl/Twn	B&B + Eve.Meal
			from £51.75

Important: Prices stated are estimates and may be subject to amendments

Carnoustie, Angus — Map Ref: 2D2

SMALL HOTEL ★★

Station Hotel
Station Road, Carnoustie, Angus, DD7 6AR
Tel: 01241 852447 Fax: 01241 855605
E-mail: ivorfarmer@aol.com

1 Single   All En Suite
9 Twin
1 Double
1 Family

B&B per person
from £35.00 Single
from £55.00 Dbl/Twn

Open Jan-Dec excl
Xmas/New Year

Long established family run hotel, short walk from the beach. 5 minutes walk to world famous championship course and many others within 30 minutes drive.

Comrie, Perthshire — Map Ref: 2A2

SMALL HOTEL ★★★★

The Royal Hotel
Melville Square, Comrie, Perthshire, PH6 2DN
Tel: 01764 679200 Fax: 01764 679219
E-mail: reception@royalhotel.co.uk
Web: www.royalhotel.co.uk

3 Twin   All En Suite
8 Double

B&B per person
from £70.00 Single
from £55.00 Dbl/Twn

Open Jan-Dec
B&B + Eve.Meal from £75.00

A hotel of natural elegance reflecting the simple charm and relaxed atmosphere of the village of Comrie and the surrounding area.

Coupar Angus, Perthshire — Map Ref: 2C1

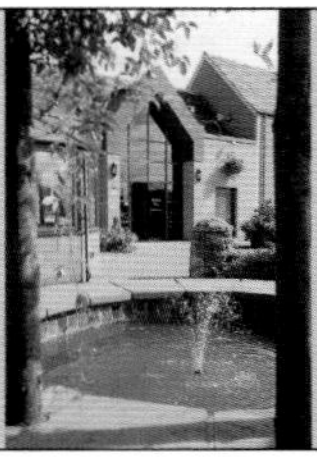

Red House Hotel

Station Road, Coupar Angus, PH13 9AL
Tel: 01828 628500 Fax: 01828 628574
e.mail: stay@red-house-hotel.co.uk
Web: www.red-house-hotel.co.uk
A warm welcome awaits you in our family owned and managed hotel. An ideal base for golfers, hill walkers, fishers and shooters. A relaxed atmosphere prevails within our restaurant which serves food all day. Snooker, squash and gymnasium all available for our residents use.

HOTEL ★★★

Red House Hotel
Station Road, Coupar Angus, Perthshire, PH13 9AL
Tel: 01828 628500 Fax: 01828 628574
E-mail: stay@red-house-hotel.co.uk
Web: www.red-house-hotel.co.uk

7 Twin   All En Suite
10 Double
3 Family

B&B per person
from £35.00 Single
from £60.00 Dbl/Twn

Open Jan-Dec excl
Xmas/New Year

Dating back to Victorian times the building was originally the Railway Hotel. Trains have long ceased to run through Coupar Angus and in its place is the vibrant Red House, a magnet for locals, visitors and business traveller. Family owned and managed you can be sure of a friendly team and genuine hospitality. The accommodation has a separate entrance.

Cowdenbeath, Fife — Map Ref: 2B4

GUEST HOUSE ★

The Crown Hotel
6 High Street, Cowdenbeath, Fife, KY4 9NA
Tel: 01383 610540 Fax: 01383 610540

4 Single
3 Twin
4 Double

B&B per person
from £21.50 Single
from £43.00 Dbl/Twn
Room only from £16.00

Open Jan-Dec excl
Xmas/New Year
B&B + Eve.Meal from £29.50

Family run town centre hotel, 100 metres from Railway Station. Indian Restaurant. Spacious Car park.

All properties graded by VisitScotland, formerly known as the Scottish Tourist Board.   *Key to symbols is on back flap.*

Crail, Fife
Map Ref: 2D3

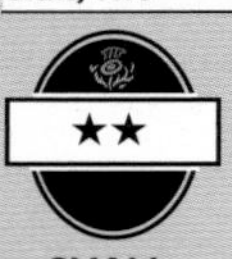

SMALL HOTEL
★★

Balcomie Links Hotel
Balcomie Road, Crail, Fife, KY10 3TN
Tel: 01333 450237 Fax: 01333 450540

3 Single	13 En Suite fac	B&B per person	Open Jan-Dec
7 Twin	2 Priv.NOT ensuite	from £35.00 Single	B&B + Eve.Meal
3 Double		from £47.50 Dbl/Twn	from £50.00
2 Family		Room only from £30.00	

Recently refurbished hotel close by picturesque harbour village. 9 miles (14kms) St Andrews. Ideal golfing base. Families and groups welcome. Wide choice of dishes available in either the lounge or the non-smoking dining room. Picturesque harbour and shoreline within a few minutes walk.

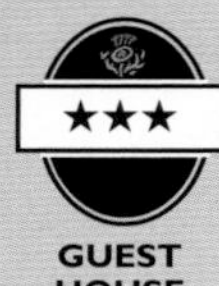

GUEST HOUSE
★★★

Denburn House
1 Marketgate North, Crail, Fife, KY10 3TQ
Tel: 01333 450253
Web: www.s-h-systems.co.uk/hotels/denburnh.html

1 Single	5 Ensuite fac	B&B per person	Open Jan-Dec
3 Twin	1 Priv.NOT ensuite	from £18.00 Single	
2 Double		from £20.00 Dbl/Twn	

18th century town house in small fishing village in the East Neuk of Fife. 15 minutes from St Andrews.

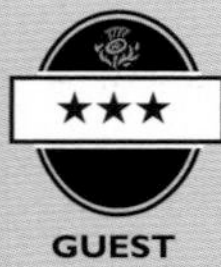

GUEST HOUSE
★★★

Selcraig House
47 Nethergate, Crail, Fife, KY10 3TX
Tel: 01333 450697 Fax: 01333 451113
E-mail: margaret@selcraighouse.co.uk
Web: www.selcraighouse.co.uk

2 Single	5 En Suite fac	B&B per person	Open Jan-Dec
2 Twin	1 Priv.NOT ensuite	from £20.00 Single	
1 Double		from £40.00 Dbl/Twn	
1 Family			

200-year-old Listed house in quiet street close to seashore. Convenient for touring the East Neuk of Fife and very close to coastal path walk. Non-smoking. Ample quiet village parking.

Crieff, Perthshire
Map Ref: 2A2

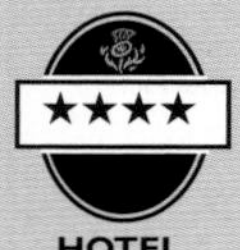

HOTEL
★★★★

Crieff Hydro
Crieff, Perthshire, PH7 3LQ
Tel: 01764 655555 Fax: 01764 653087
E-mail: enquiries@crieffhydro.com
Web: www.crieffhydro.com

44 Single	225 En Suite fac	B&B per person	Open Jan-Dec
60 Twin	Suites available	from £35.00 Single	B&B + Eve.Meal from
30 Double		from £35.00 Dbl/Twn	£54.00
88 Family			

Beautifully appointed Victorian resort hotel on edge of Highlands. Maintaining much of its original character. Exceptional for family holidays. Unrivalled leisure faciliites. Excellent food. Personal service.

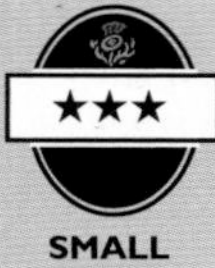

SMALL HOTEL
★★★

Gwydyr House Hotel
Comrie Road, Crieff, Perthshire, PH7 4BP
Tel/Fax: 01764 653277
E-mail: enquiries@gwdyrhouse.co.uk
Web: www.gwdyrhouse.co.uk

3 Twin	All En Suite	B&B per person	Open Jan-Dec excl
4 Double		from £40.00 Single	Xmas
1 Family		from £30.00 Dbl/Twn	B&B + Eve.Meal
			from £45.00

Personally run Country House Hotel with large garden sitting in an elevated position adjacent to Macrosty Country Park. Gwydyr House is situated near to various Perthshire Golf courses including the famous Gleneagles Golf Resort (see web site for full list of activities).

Important: Prices stated are estimates and may be subject to amendments

---

Crieff, Perthshire | Map Ref: 2A2

★★

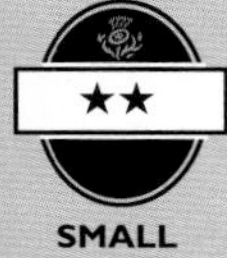

SMALL HOTEL

Leven House Hotel
Comrie Road, Crieff, Perthshire, PH7 4BA
Tel: 01764 652529

1 Single	8 En Suite fac	B&B per person	Open Feb-Nov
3 Twin	2 Pub Bath/Show	from £20.00 Single	B&B + Eve.Meal
6 Double		from £20.00 Dbl/Twn	from £36.00

Small family run hotel near town centre serving dinners and Scottish high teas. Ideally situated for touring and golf. Spacious car park.

★★★

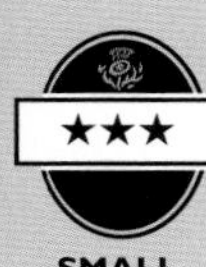

SMALL HOTEL

Roundelwood Health Spa
Drummond Terrace, Crieff, Perthshire, PH7 4AN
Tel: 01764 653806 Fax: 01764 655659
E-mail: health@roundelwood.freeserve.co.uk
Web: www.roundelwood.org

5 Single	All En Suite	D,B&B per person per	Open Jan-Dec
12 Twin		5 day prog incl of spa	
1 Double		treatments	
		from £560.00 Single	
		from £560.00 Dbl/Twn	
		Room only from	

Roundelwood Health Spa and Fitness Centre is set in beautiful Perthshire, overlooking the picturesque town of Crieff and surrounded by glorious mountains, rivers and lochs. It is the ideal setting for a health holiday.

★★★

HOTEL

The Murraypark Hotel
Connaught Terrace, Crieff, Perthshire, PH7 3DS
Tel: 01764658000 Fax: 01764 655311
E-mail: enquiries@murraypark.com
Web: www.murraypark.com

10 Twin	All En Suite	B&B per person	Open Jan-Dec
9 Double		£37.00-£50.00 Dbl/Twn	B&B + Eve.Meal from
1 Family			£37.50

Close to Crieff Hydro and enjoying a quiet environment and views across the Strathearn Valley, from some bedrooms. Recently refurbished to a high standard. Comfortable bar and restaurant facilities where you can enjoy our informal or formal dining. Our guests enjoy access to the extensive recreational, swimming pool and garden facilities of the Hydro.

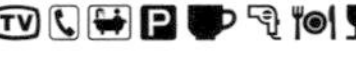

Dundee, Angus | Map Ref: 2C2

★★★

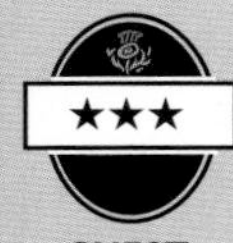

GUEST HOUSE

Aberlaw Guest House
230 Broughty Ferry Road, Dundee, Tayside, DD4 7JP
Tel/Fax: 01382 456929

2 Single	1 En Suite facs	B&B per person	Open Jan-Dec excl
1 Twin	1 Pub Bath/Show	from £20.00 Single	Xmas/New Year
2 Double	1 Limited ensuite	from £40.00 Dbl/Twn	

Family run Victorian house with private parking. Close to city centre, overlooking River Tay. Five mins on commuter bus to town centre. Ideal for golfing at Carnoustie and St. Andrews. Spacious ensuite room with view over River to Fife. Comfortable lounge available for guests use.

★★

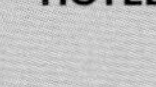

HOTEL

Dunlaw House Hotel
10 Union Terrace, Dundee, DD3 6JD
Tel/Fax: 01382 221703
E-mail: mail@dunlawhousehotel.co.uk
Web: www.vacations-in-scotland.co.uk

1 Single	6 Ensuite fac	B&B per person	Open Jan-Dec
5 Twin	1 Pub Bath/Show	from £28.00 Single	B&B + Eve.Meal
2 Double		from £48.00 Dbl/Twn	from £40.50
2 Family			

Hotel is situated in quiet conservation area of the city, but only 5 minutes down to the city centre. We are on the South side of the Lawhill, with views over the River Tay and very close to Dundee University and the colleges.

All properties graded by VisitScotland, formerly known as the Scottish Tourist Board. | Key to symbols is on back flap.

Dundee, Angus   Map Ref: 2C2

**GUEST
HOUSE**

Errolbank Guest House
9 Dalgleish Road, Dundee, Angus, DD4 7JN
Tel/Fax: 01382 462118

1 Single	5 En Suite fac	B&B per person	Open Jan-Dec excl
3 Twin	1 Priv.NOT	from £26.00 Single	Xmas/New Year
2 Double	en suite	from £22.00 Dbl/Twn	

Family-run Victorian villa. Comfortable bedrooms with TV, tea trays and central heating. All double and twin rooms en suite. Single room with private facilities adjacent. 1.2 miles east of city centre and Tay Bridge. Off main road near river and bus routes. Off street parking and garden. No smoking throughout.

HOTEL

Hilton Dundee
Earl Grey Place, Dundee, Angus, DD1 4DE
Tel: 01382 229271 Fax: 01382 200072
E-mail: reservations@dundee.stakis.co.uk
Web: www.dundee.hilton.com

74 Twin	All En Suite	B&B per person	Open Jan-Dec
54 Double		from £65.00 Single	B&B + Eve.Meal
1 Suite		from £45.00 Dbl/Twn	£15 Supplement per
		Room only from £60.00	person

Modern hotel with leisure facilities situated on the banks of the River Tay with views of the Kingdom of Fife. Easy access by road, rail and air. Conference facilities. Riverside Caffè Cino facility and restaurant and bar with views of the river. 24 hour room service. 90 Car Parking spaces.

**GUEST
HOUSE**

Restalrig Guest House
69 Clepington Road, Dundee, Angus, DD4 7BQ
Tel: 01382 455412 Fax: 01382 459864

1 Twin	All En Suite	B&B per person	Open Jan-Dec
2 Family		from £23.00 Single	
		from £18.00 Dbl/Twn	

Close to ring road yet within walking distance of Dundee city centre, this traditional stone built guest house is a good base for both business and touring. Close to the new international indoor sports centre. Run by great, great grandaughter of William McGonagall. Vegetarians catered for. Private off-street parking.

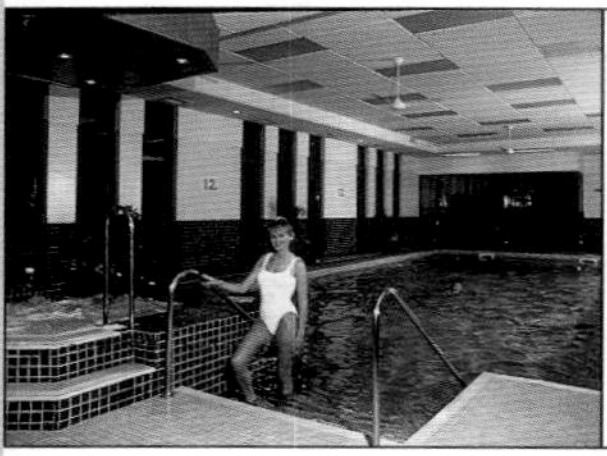

Woodlands Hotel

13 Panmure Terrace, Barnhill, Broughty Ferry, DD5 2QL
Tel: 01382 480033 *Fax:* 01382 480126
e.mail: woodlandshotel@bettinns.co.uk *Web:* www.bettinns.co.uk

Set in landscaped grounds within picturesque village. Individually designed bedrooms. Swimming pool, gym, sauna, spa, solarium. Near Carnoustie and ideal for golfing breaks. £36 per person per night sharing twin/double room.
Special golf and weekend rates available.

HOTEL

Woodlands Hotel
**13 Panmure Terrace, Barnhill, Dundee, Angus,
DD5 2QL**
Tel: 01382 480033 Fax: 01382 480126
Web: www.bettinns.co.uk

3 Single	All En Suite	B&B per person	Open Jan-Dec
13 Twin		£37.50-68.00 Single	
21 Double		£32.00-£45.00 Dbl/Twn	
1 Family			

Set in 4 acres of private grounds in quiet residential area. Close to the village of Broughty Ferry. Leisure facilities, satellite TV.

Important: Prices stated are estimates and may be subject to amendments

Dunfermline, Fife

Map Ref: 2B4

SMALL HOTEL

Abbey Park Hotel
5 Abbey Park Place, Dunfermline, Fife, KY12 7PT
Tel: 01383 739686 Fax: 01383 722801

Built around 1825, a Georgian town house set in the shadow of the Abbey, with its own rear gardens, yet close to the town centre. Ample private parking. Good rail and road links to Edinburgh - 15 miles (25km). No evening meals.

2 Single	8 En Suite fac	B&B per person	Open Jan-Dec excl
6 Twin	1 Priv.NOT ensuite	from £32.00 Single	Xmas/New Year
2 Double	2 Pub Bath/Show	from £23.00 Dbl/Twn	
1 Family			

GUEST HOUSE

Clarke Cottage Guest House
139 Halbeath Road, Dunfermline, Fife, KY11 4LA
Tel: 01383 735935 Fax: 01383 623767
E-mail: clarkecottage@ukonline.co.uk

Situated 1 mile West of Junction 3 (M90) and only a 2 minute walk to Queen Margaret Railway Station, this 19th century Victorian house has been tastefully extended to provide comfortable en-suite accommodation with independent access. Ample off-street parking. Ideally situated for visiting Edinburgh and surrounding areas in Fife.

6 Twin	All En Suite	B&B per person	Open Jan-Dec
3 Double		from £27.00 Single	
		from £23.00 Dbl/Twn	

SMALL HOTEL

Davaar House Hotel and Restaurant
126 Grieve Street, Dunfermline, Fife, KY12 8DW
Tel: 01383 721886 Fax: 01383 623633
Web: www.tasteofscotland.co.uk/davaar_house_hotel.html

Comfortable, tastefully furnished hotel retaining original Victorian features. Personally run with friendly individual attention. Taste of Scotland. Within easy access to M90 and only 14 miles from Edinburgh. One bedroom on the ground floor.

2 Single	All En Suite	B&B per person	Open Jan-Dec excl
4 Twin		£48.00-£55.00 Single	Xmas/New Year
3 Double		£35.00-£45.00 Dbl/Twn	B&B + Eve.Meal
1 Family			from £68.00-£88.00

SMALL HOTEL

Halfway House Hotel
35 Main Street, Kingseat, Fife, KY12 0TS
Tel: 01383 731661 Fax: 01383 621274

Privately owned hotel, close to junction 3 (M90). Easy access to Edinburgh and Fife coast. Trout fishing, golfing, water ski-ing, and Knockhill racing circuit close by. Childrens activity area.

5 Twin	All En Suite	B&B per person	Open Jan-Dec
3 Double		from £37.00 Single	B&B + Eve.Meal from
4 Family		from £22.50 Dbl/Twn	£30.00

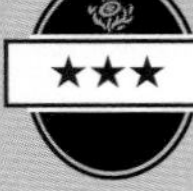

LODGE

The Hideaway Lodge & Restaurant
Kingseat Road, Halbeath, Dunfermline, Fife, KY12 0UB
Tel: 01383 725474 Fax: 01383 622821
E-mail: enquiries@thehideaway.co.uk
Web: www.thehideaway.co.uk

Recently built lodge alongside long established restaurant on outskirts of Dunfermline in quiet location close to M90 motorway. Adjacent restaurant serves lunches and dinners and is popular for food and drinks.

1 Twin	All En Suite	Room only from £45.00	Open Jan-Dec excl
7 Double			Xmas/New Year

All properties graded by VisitScotland, formerly known as the Scottish Tourist Board.

Key to symbols is on back flap.

Dunfermline, Fife — Map Ref: 2B4

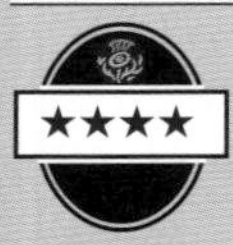

Keavil House Hotel
Main Street, Crossford, by Dunfermline, Fife, KY12 8QW
Tel: 01383 736258 Fax: 01383 621600
E-mail: keavil@queensferryhotels.co.uk
Web: www.keavilhouse.co.uk

HOTEL

Historic country house, including extensive leisure facilities, is set in 12 acres of grounds and gardens, making it a ideal location for relaxing. The Hotel offers 2 restaurants - awarded AA Rosette and member of Taste of Scotland. Within easy access of Edinburgh - only 20 minutes by train.

5 Single	All En Suite	B&B per person	Open Jan-Dec excl
19 Twin		£71.95-£99.95 Single	Xmas/New Year
19 Double		£62.25-£74.75 Dbl/Twn	B&B + Eve.Meal
4 Family		Room only from £62.00	from £90.95

Roscobie Farmhouse
Roscobie Farm, Dunfermline, Fife, KY12 0SG
Tel/Fax: 01383 731571

B&B

Traditional farmhouse, set on a 400 acre upland Beef and Sheep farm. Extensive rural views over Fife and South ward to the Lothians. Ideal location for exploring central Scotland, only 3 miles from junction 4 on the M90 motorway, and close to Knockhill Race Track (approx. one mile).

1 Twin	1 Pub Bath/Show	B&B per person	Open Jan-Dec
1 Family		from £20.00 Single	
		from £20.00 Dbl/Twn	

Dunkeld, Perthshire — Map Ref: 2B1

Royal Dunkeld Hotel
Atholl Street, Dunkeld, PH8 0AR
Tel: 01350 727322 Fax: 01350 728989
E-mail: reservations@royaldunkeld.co.uk
Web: www.royaldunkeld.co.uk

HOTEL

Personally run, early 19c coaching inn, situated in centre of historic town of Dunkeld. Golfing breaks and fishing packages a speciality. Some annexe bedrooms.

18 Twin	All En Suite	B&B per person	Open Jan-Dec
10 Double		from £45.00 Single	B&B + Eve.Meal from
7 Family		from £30.00 Dbl/Twn	£45.00
		Room only from £20.00	

---

by Dunkeld, Perthshire — Map Ref: 2B1

Tigh-Na-Braan
Amulree, by Dunkeld, Perthshire, PH8 0BZ
Tel: 01350 725247 Fax: 01350 725219
E-mail: tighnabraan@tesco.net

B&B

Formerly a manse, this Victorian house is now a comfortable B&B. It has 3 bedrooms - 2 with ensuite bathrooms and 1 with a private bathroom. Each room has a RcTV, radio and hospitality tray. The house is peacefully situated in a small village surrounded by hills. This is an ideal base for touring and walking. Guests can relax in the lounge in front of a real fire. Non-smoking house.

1 Twin	All En Suite	B&B per person	Open Jan-Dec
2 Double		from £22.00 Single	
		from £22.00 Dbl/Twn	

Edzell, Angus — Map Ref: 4F12

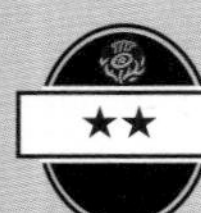

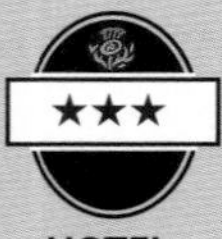

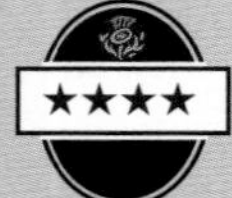

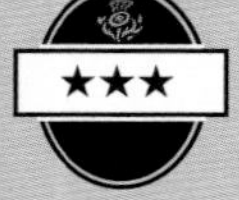

Panmure Arms Hotel
52 High Street, Edzell, DD9 7TA
Tel: 01356 648950 Fax: 01356 648000
E-mail: david@panmurearmshotel.co.uk
Web: www.panmurearmshotel.co.uk

HOTEL

A recently refurbished family run hotel with the emphasis on quality and service. Set in the picturesque village of Edzell with very easy access for golfing, shooting and fishing. A perfect holiday destination for exploring the beautiful Angus glens.

6 Twin	All En Suite	B&B per person	Open Jan-Dec
6 Double		from £42.50 Single	B&B + Eve.Meal from
3 Family		from £30.00 Dbl/Twn	£52.50

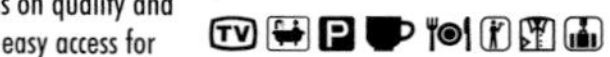

Important: Prices stated are estimates and may be subject to amendments

Falkland, Fife

Map Ref: 2C3

★★

INN

Hunting Lodge Hotel
High Street, Falkland, Fife, KY15 7BZ
Tel: 01337 857226 Fax: 01337 857978
Web: www.huntinglodgehotel.com

1 Twin	1 En Suite fac	B&B per person	Open Jan-Dec
1 Double	1 Pub Bath/Show	from £25.00 Single	
1 Family		from £38.00 Dbl/Twn	

17th century traditional family-run inn in centre of Falkland opposite the Palace. Handy for golf courses and touring north east Fife.

Freuchie, Fife

Map Ref: 2C3

★★

INN

Lomond Hills Hotel
Lomond Road, Parliament Square, Freuchie, Fife,
KY15 7EY
Tel: 01337 857498 Fax: 01337 857329
E-mail: lomondhilshotel@aol.com
Web: www.lomondhillshotel.co.uk

2 Single	All En Suite	B&B per person	Open Jan-Dec
7 Twin		from £40.00 Single	B&B + Eve.Meal
12 Double		from £60.00 Dbl/Twn	from £50.00
3 Family		Room only from £30.00	

Set in rolling countryside, hotel with leisure facilities, in the centre of the village which won the 1995 and 1996 'Village in Bloom' award.

Glenfarg, Perthshire

Map Ref: 2B3

★★

INN

Bein Inn
Glenfarg, Perth, Perthshire, PH2 9PY
Tel: 01577 830216 Fax: 01577 830211
E-mail: enquiries@beininn.com
Web: www.beininn.com

9 Twin	All En Suite	B&B per person	Open Jan-Dec
2 Double		from £25.00 Single	B&B + Eve.Meal from
		from £25.00 Dbl/Twn	£38.00

Drovers Inn dating from 1861 with a mixture of old and new. There are 11 bedrooms, all with ensuite facilities, RcTV, radio, direct dial telephone and a hospitality tray - 4 of the bedrooms have their own separate entrance. The Inn is ideally located for golfing, fishing, shooting and touring with easy access to the motorway system.

Glenisla, Perthshire

Map Ref: 4D12

★★★★

GUEST
HOUSE

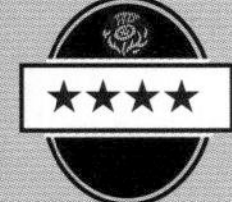

Glenmarkie Guest House, Health Spa and Riding Centre

Glenisla, Perthshire, PH11 8QB
Tel: 01575 582295
E-mail: holidays@glenmarkie.freeserve.co.uk

1 Twin	All En Suite	B&B per person	Open Jan-Dec
2 Double		from £23.00 Dbl/Twn	B&B + Eve.Meal
			£38.00

Situated in the the glen, a horse riding and walkers paradise offering peace and relaxation. A holiday for all seasons with top-to-toe beauty therapy.

Glenrothes, Fife

Map Ref: 2C3

★★★

HOTEL

Express by Holiday Inn
Leslie Roundabout, Leslie Road, Glenrothes, KY7 6XX
Tel: 01592 745509 Fax: 01592 743377
Reservations: 0800 897121
Web: www.hiexpress.co.uk

6 Twin	All En Suite	B&B per person	Open Jan-Dec
20 Double		from £21.25 Dbl/Twn	B&B + Eve.Meal
20 Family		Room only from £42.50	£35.00 pp
3 Disabled Rooms			

Comfortable modern rooms in convenient location in Glenrothes. Close to Dundee, Perth and St Andrews with good road links also to Edinburgh and Glasgow. Situated in the heart of Fife it makes a good base for time off being close to the many golf courses and historic sites throughout Fife.

All properties graded by VisitScotland, formerly known as the Scottish Tourist Board. | *Key to symbols is on back flap.*

Glenshee, Perthshire   Map Ref: 4D12

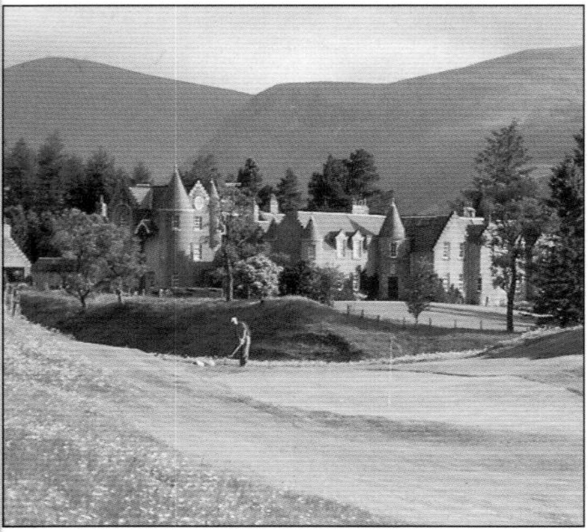

Dalmunzie House Hotel

SPITTAL OF GLENSHEE, BLAIRGOWRIE, PERTHSHIRE PH10 7QG
Tel: 01250 885224 Fax: 01250 885225
e.mail: dalmunzie@aol.com Web: www.dalmunzie.com

This family run Country House Hotel "in the hills", situated 1½ miles off the main A93 Perth-Braemar road, offers an ideal base for touring Royal Deeside and the Highlands. A relaxed, informal atmosphere, where roaring log fires, personal service, traditional Scottish cooking and 16 bedrooms all with private bathrooms are our hallmarks.

Golf, tennis, fishing and shooting are available on our 6,000-acre estate, and in winter months, skiing is on our doorstep – only 5 miles away.

HOTEL

Dalmunzie House Hotel
Spittal of Glenshee, Blairgowrie, Perthshire, PH10 7QG
Tel: 01250 885224 Fax: 01250 885225
E-mail: dalmunzie@aol.com
Web: www.dalmunzie.com

Referred to as the 'hotel in the hills', a warm and friendly family run hotel with log fires, games room, tennis, shooting and golfing.

9 Twin	All En Suite fac	B&B per person	Open 28 Dec-Nov
6 Double	1 Pub Bath/Show	from £32.00-£58.00	

Inchture, Perthshire   Map Ref: 2C2

SMALL HOTEL

Inchture Hotel
Main Street, Inchture, Perthshire, PH14 9RN
Tel: 01828 686298 Fax: 01828 686000
E-mail: info@inchture-hotel.co.uk
Web: www.inchture-hotel.co.uk

Set in a quiet village just off the A90 Perth to Dundee road this B listed small Hotel provides comfortable accommodation and is a popular local food stop. 9 miles to Perth 4 miles to Dundee. Rooms with Sky TV. Good base for golf, shooting and fishing.

3 Twin	All En Suite	B&B per person	Open Jan-Dec
3 Double		from £35.00 Single	
2 Family		from £25.00 Dbl/Twn	

Inverkeithing, Fife   Map Ref: 2B4

GUEST HOUSE

Forth Craig Private Hotel
90 Hope Street, Inverkeithing, Fife, KY11 1LL
Tel: 01383 418440

All ensuite rooms in this modern purpose built private hotel overlooking the Firth of Forth. Convenient road access to Edinburgh, St. Andrews & Stirling. Excellent train service to Edinburgh, only 15 minutes travel time.

2 Single	All En Suite	B&B per person	Open Jan-Dec
1 Twin		from £28.00 Single	
2 Double		from £24.00 Dbl/Twn	

Important: Prices stated are estimates and may be subject to amendments

Inverkeithing, Fife

Map Ref: 2B4

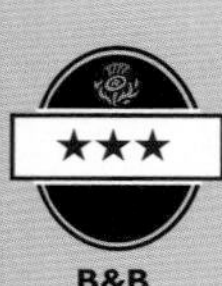

HOTEL

Queensferry Lodge Hotel
St Margarets Head, North Queensferry, Inverkeithing, Fife, KY11
1HP
Tel: 01383 410000 Fax: 01383 419708
E-mail: queensferry@corushotels.com
Web: www.corushotels.co.uk/queensferrylodge

21 Twin   All En Suite facs
56 Double

B&B per person
from £50.00 Single
from £30.00 Dbl/Twn
Room only from £45.00

Open Jan-Dec
B&B + Eve.Meal from
£42.00

Built in 1989 among landscaped hillside gardens on North shore of Firth
of Forth overlooking famous bridges. 77 contemporary style bedrooms
designed for travelling executive with modern communication facilities.
Extensive conference and banqueting facilities.

B&B

The Roods Guest House
16 Bannerman Avenue, Inverkeithing, Fife, KY11 1NG
Tel/Fax: 01383 415049
E-mail: bookings@theroods.com
Web: www.theroods.com

1 Twin   All En Suite
1 Double

B&B per person
from £23.00 Single
from £23.00 Dbl/Twn

Open Jan-Dec

Quietly secluded family home. Close to rail station and M90. Well
appointed bedrooms offering mini office and direct dial telephones.
Evening meal by arrangement. Both rooms on ground floor.

Killiecrankie, Perthshire

Map Ref: 4C12

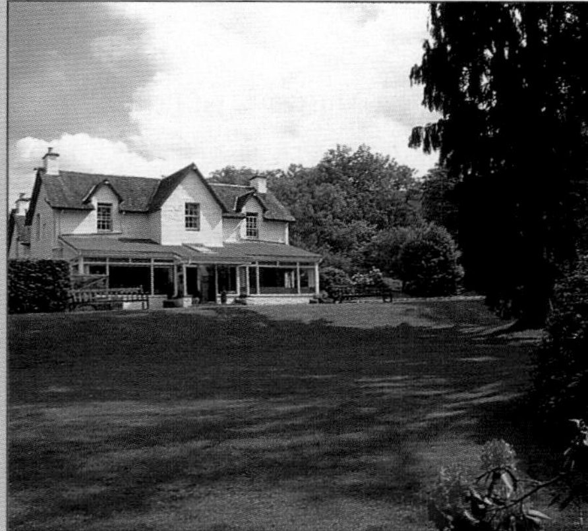

The Killiecrankie Hotel

**Killiecrankie, By Pitlochry, Perthshire PH16 5LG
Tel: 01796 473220 Fax: 01796 472451
e.mail: enquiries@killiecrankiehotel.co.uk
web: www.killiecrankiehotel.co.uk**

The Killiecrankie Hotel enjoys a fine setting in peaceful gardens
overlooking the beautiful Pass of Killiecrankie. There are 10
attractive bedrooms, including a ground-floor suite, with views of
the surrounding gardens and woodland. Exceptional food (Good
Food Guide, 2 AA Rosettes for dinner), and a congenial
atmosphere help make guests feel at home. All rooms have bath
and/or shower, colour television, radio, telephone and tea trays.
The area offers walking to suit everyone, is a photographer/
artist's paradise, a golfer's delight and is well located for touring.
Pitlochry and Blair Atholl 3 miles. Closed Jan. (and Mon/Tues in
December, February and March).
Also special breaks, Christmas and Hogmanay breaks.

AA ★★ (76%) ◉◉   ★★★★ HOTEL

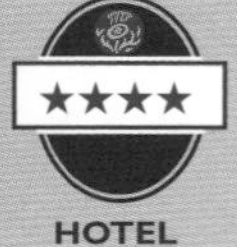

HOTEL

The Killiecrankie Hotel
Killiecrankie, by Pitlochry, Perthshire, PH16 5LG
Tel: 01796 473220 Fax: 01796 472451
E-mail: enquiries@killiecrankiehotel.co.uk
Web: www.killiecrankiehotel.co.uk

2 Single   All En Suite
3 Twin
4 Double
1 Family

Open Feb-Dec
B&B + Dinner
£69.00-£89.00

Personally run country hotel with warm and friendly atmosphere set in 4
acres of grounds, overlooking Pass of Killiecrankie.

All properties graded by VisitScotland, formerly known as the Scottish Tourist Board.   *Key to symbols is on back flap.*

by Kinross, Perthshire

Map Ref: 2B3

Nivingston Country House Hotel

Cleish, near Kinross, Kinross-shire KY13 0LS
Tel: 01577 850216   Fax: 01577 850238
e.mail: info@nivingstonhousehotel.co.uk
Web: www.nivingstonhousehotel.co.uk

★ ★ ★
SMALL HOTEL

You will find Nivingston Country House Hotel an ideal base from which to explore Tayside, Fife and Edinburgh or for a relaxing golfing or fishing break. You can enjoy superb comfort and food in a traditional environment where you will be spoiled by our attentive and caring team.

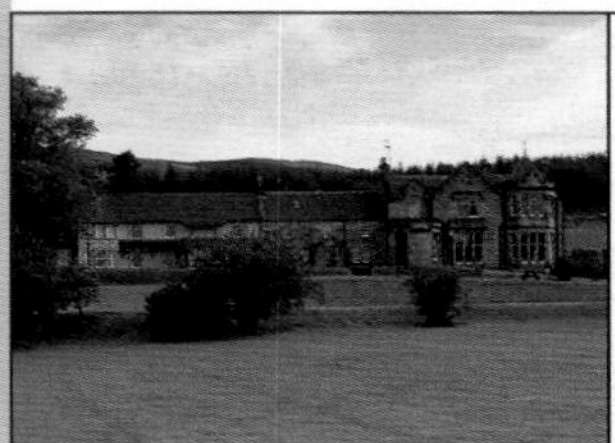

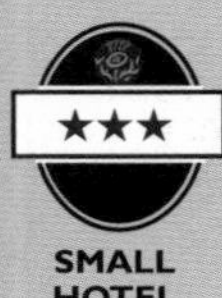

★ ★ ★
SMALL
HOTEL

Nivingston Country House Hotel
Cleish, Kinross-shire, KY13 0LS
Tel: 01577 850216 Fax: 01577 850238
E-mail: info@nivingstonhousehotel.co.uk
Web: www.nivingstonhousehotel.co.uk

2 Single	All En Suite
5 Twin	
10 Double	

B&B per person
from £75.00 Single
from £50.00 Dbl/Twn

Open Jan-Dec
B&B + Eve.Meal from
£85.00

Kirkcaldy, Fife

Map Ref: 2C4

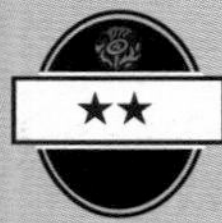

★ ★
HOTEL

Belvedere Hotel
Coxstool, West Wemyss, Kirkcaldy, Fife, KY1 4SL
Tel: 01592 654167 Fax: 01592 655279
E-mail: info@thebelvederehotel.com
Web: www.thebelvederehotel.com

Set in the picturesque Fife village of West Wemyss, dynamic view across the Firth of Forth, we pride ourselves on delivering the highest standards of service in relaxed and friendly surroundings. Ample free car parking. 30 minutes from St Andrews, Edinburgh and Perth, 15 minutes to Lundin Links and it's 18 hole golf course.

1 Single	All En Suite
9 Twin	
9 Double	
2 Family	

B&B per person
from £40.00 Single
from £25.00 Dbl/Twn

Open Jan-Dec excl
Xmas/New Year
B&B + Eve.Meal
from £37.00

Ladybank, Fife

Map Ref: 2C3

**AWAITING
INSPECTION**

Fernie Castle Hotel
Letham, by Cupar, Fife, KY15 7RU
Tel: 01337 810381 Fax: 01337 810422
Web: www.ferniecastle.demon.co.uk

16th century castle with 17 acres of mature grounds and small loch. Dungeon Bar, Wallace Lounge and Auld Alliance Room for formal dining. Situated in the heart of the Kingdom of Fife with all its golf courses including St Andrews within easy reach. Ground floor rooms available. Very popular venue for weddings and functions.

3 Single	All En Suite
8 Twin	
7 Double	
2 Mini-suites	

B&B per person
from £55.00 Single
from £110.00 Dbl/Twn

Open Jan-Dec
Eve.Meal from £23.95

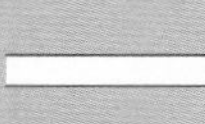

★ ★ ★ ★
GUEST
HOUSE

Redlands Country Lodge
Pitlessie Road, Ladybank, Cupar, Fife, KY15 7SH
Tel/Fax: 01337 831091
E-mail: redlandscountrylodge@btinternet.com
Web: www.SmoothHound.co.uk/hotels/redcount.html

Redlands is an attractive country cottage, with an adjacent Norwegian pine lodge, set in attractive gardens, with acres of woodland and fields all around. Good home cooking and baking. Only 14 miles from St Andrews and an ideal base for golfing and touring.

| 2 Twin | All En Suite |
| 2 Double | |

B&B per person
from £25.00 Dbl/Twn

Open Jan-Dec

Important: Prices stated are estimates and may be subject to amendments

Loch Earn, Perthshire   Map Ref: 1H2

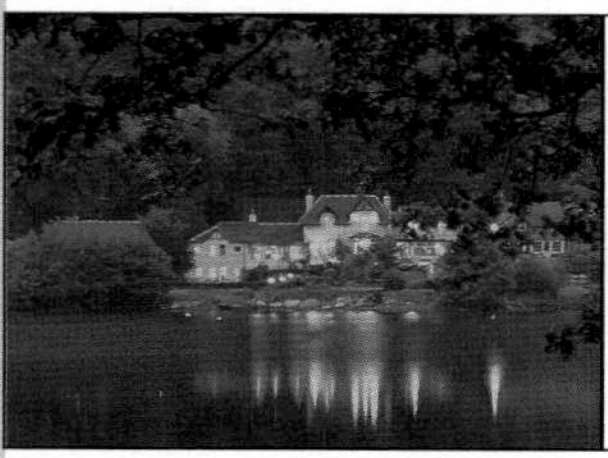

Achray House Hotel ★★★
Small Hotel

Loch Earn, St Fillans, Perthshire PH6 2NF
Telephone: 01764 685231 Fax: 01764 685320
e.mail: achrayhotelsltd@btinternet.com Web: www.achray-house.co.uk

AA ★★

Stunning lochside position in St Fillans – an area of outstanding natural beauty. Well-established, family run hotel, known for its wide selection of good food, service and a caring attitude that brings people back year after year. The perfect base for sightseeing, golf, walking, field and watersports.

★★★

**SMALL
HOTEL**

Achray House Hotel
Loch Earn, St Fillans, Perthshire, PH6 2NF
Tel: 01764 685231 Fax: 01764 685320
Web: www.achray-house.co.uk

Small, personally run hotel with extensive bar and restaurant menu. Picturesque village with magnificent views over Loch Earn.

3 Twin	8 En Suite fac	B&B per person	Open Feb-Jan
5 Double	1 Priv.NOT ensuite	from £32.00 Single	B&B + Eve.Meal
1 Family		from £20.00 Dbl/Twn	from £32.00

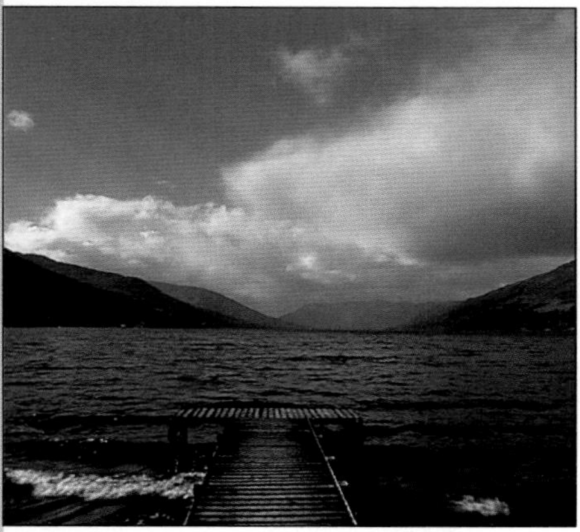

The Four Seasons Hotel

St Fillans, Perthshire PH6 2NF
Tel: 01764 685333 Fax: 01764 685444
e.mail: info@thefourseasonshotel.co.uk
Web: www.thefourseasonshotel.co.uk

The finest lochside location in the Southern Highlands
with views down Loch Earn.

Meall Reamhar Restaurant and Tarken Rum
offer imaginative cuisine using the best fresh local produce whilst considering both the adventurous and the traditional diner. Well placed in Scotland to enjoy many day trips including the scenic West Coast, Stirling Castle, Edinburgh, Blair Atholl and the Trossachs to name a few. For the energetic there are 26 golf courses within an hour, scenic walks, Munros to climb, fishing and shooting. Spectacular views with food to match, a warm welcome and friendly service.
What more could you wish for.

AA ★★★ RAC ★★★

THE TASTE
OF SCOTLAND

★★★

**SMALL
HOTEL**

The Four Seasons Hotel
St Fillans, Perthshire, PH6 2NF
Tel: 01764 685333 Fax: 01764 685444
Web: www.thefourseasonshotel.co.uk

The finest lochside location in the Southern Highlands with views over Loch Earn. To dine... you can choose between the Meall Reamhar Restaurant or the more informal Tarken Rum. In both we serve contemporary Scottish Cuisine, ranging from the imaginative to the traditional. Chef uses only the best ingredients from Scotland's natural larder which in many cases are supplied locally to produce a truly memorable meal.

4 Twin	All En Suite	B&B per person	Open Mar-Jan
8 Double		from £35.00 Single	B&B + Eve.Meal from
6 Family		from £70.00 Dbl/Twn	£58.00

All properties graded by VisitScotland, formerly known as the Scottish Tourist Board.   **Key to symbols is on back flap.**

Loch Rannoch, Perthshire — Map Ref: 1H1

★★★

GUEST HOUSE

Talladh-A-Bheithe Lodge
Loch Rannoch, by Pitlochry, Perthshire, PH17 2QW
Tel/Fax: 01882 633203
E-mail: ludwig@schottlandfreunde.mainz-online.de
Web: www.schottlandfreunde.de

Former shooting lodge overlooking Loch Rannoch. International cuisine.
Emphasis on German home baking.

3 Single	13 En Suite fac	B&B per person	Open May-Nov
8 Twin	1 Priv.NOT ensuite	from £27.00 Single	B&B + Eve.Meal
4 Double	2 Pub Bath/Show	from £24.00 Dbl/Twn	from £39.50
1 Family		Room only per person	
		from £18.00	

Lower Largo, Fife — Map Ref: 2D3

CRUSOE HOTEL

Main Street, Lower Largo KY8 6BT
Tel: 01333 320759   Fax: 01333 320865
e.mail: relax@crusoehotel.co.uk   Web: www.crusoehotel.co.uk

Family run hotel on the harbour front of historical Lower Largo.
Variety of golf courses close by including St Andrews only 20 minutes
drive. Good selection of home cooked bar food with extensive
a la carte dinner menu complemented by a reasonably priced wine list.
All served with a smile!

★★★

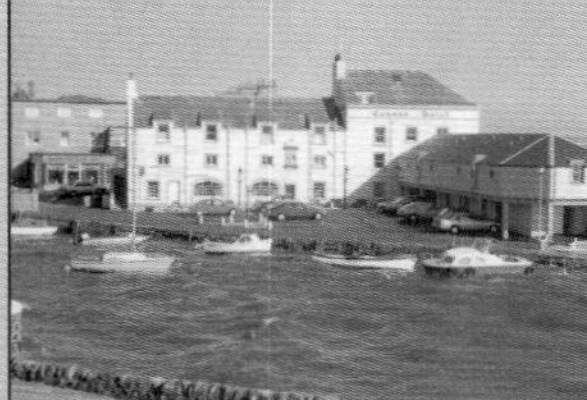

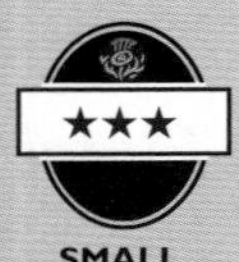

SMALL HOTEL

The Crusoe Hotel
2 Main Street, Lower Largo, Fife, KY8 6BT
Tel: 01333 320759 Fax: 01333 320865
E-mail: relax@crusoehotel.co.uk Web: www.crusoehotel.co.uk

The Crusoe enjoys an excellent seafront situation with its own harbour
and beach in the picturesque village of Lower Largo, the birthplace of
Alexander Selkirk who inspired the Robinson Crusoe Story. Home cooked
bar meals as well as an extensive à la carte menu in the restaurant,
where the meals are all served with a smile. A good centre for a family
holiday or a golfing break with numerous attractions and courses nearby.

2 Single	All En Suite	B&B per person	Open Jan-Dec
13		from £45.00 Single	B&B + Eve.Meal
Dbl/Twn		from £35.00 Dbl/Twn	from £50.00
2 Family			

Lundin Links, Fife — Map Ref: 2C3

★★★★

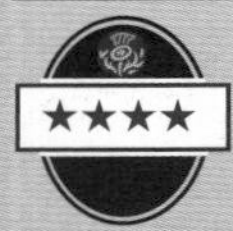

HOTEL

Old Manor Country House Hotel
Leven Road, Lundin Links, Fife, KY8 6AJ
Tel: 01333 320368 Fax: 01333 320911
E-mail: enquiries@oldmanorhotel.co.uk
Web: www.oldmanorhotel.co.uk

Late 19c house with excellent views across Lundin Links golf course,
Largo Bay and the Firth of Forth. Function room for
conferences/banqueting. Taste of Scotland and Scotch Beef Club.
Membership of Scotland's Hotels of Distinction. Only 35 miles from
Edinburgh, 12 miles St Andrews.

2 Single	All En Suite	B&B per person	Open Jan-Dec
9 Twin		from £60.00 Single	B&B + Eve.Meal
10 Double		from £120.00 Dbl/Twn	from £79.50
2 Family			

Markinch, Fife — Map Ref: 2C3

★★★

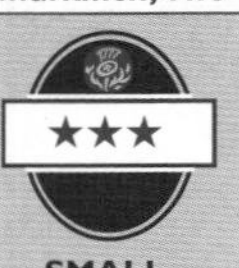

SMALL HOTEL

Laurel Bank Hotel
Balbirnie Street, Markinch, Fife, KY7 6DB
Tel/Fax: 01592 611205
E-mail: lesley@laurelbankhotel.fsnet.co.uk
Web: www.laurelbankhotel.com

Friendly family run hotel, 1 mile from Glenrothes and convenient for the
business traveller visiting the many commercial centres. Fax and office
services available. Good home cooking.

2 Single	All En Suite	B&B per person	Open Jan-Dec
4 Twin		from £32.00 Single	B&B + Eve.Meal
3 Double		from £21.00 Dbl/Twn	from £32.50
2 Family			

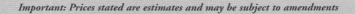

Important: Prices stated are estimates and may be subject to amendments

Montrose, Angus

Map Ref: 4F12

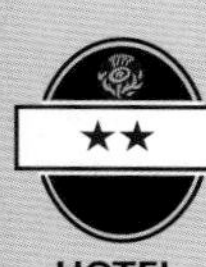

HOTEL

Best Western Links Hotel
Mid Links, Montrose, Angus, DD10 8RL
Tel: 01674 671000 Fax: 01674 672698
E-mail: reception@linkshotel.com
Web: www.linkshotel.com

Friendly hotel in quiet location yet close to town centre, golf course and beach.

5 Single	All En Suite	B&B per person	Open Jan-Dec
12 Twin		from £39.50 Single	B&B + Eve.Meal
8 Double		from £29.50 Dbl/Twn	from £49.50

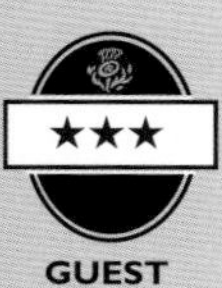

HOTEL

George Hotel Montrose
22 George Street, Montrose, Angus, DD10 8EW
Tel: 01674 675050 Fax: 01674 671153
E-mail: thegeorge@talk21.com
Web: www.thegeorge-montrose.co.uk

A privately owned stone-built hotel located in the centre of Montrose providing a central base for exploring this interesting part of Eastern Scotland with its championship golf courses sandy beaches and beautiful glens. There are some bedrooms on the third floor and no lift available.

11 Single	All En Suite	B&B per person	Open Jan-Dec
4 Twin		from £30.00 Single	
9 Double		from £30.00 Dbl/Twn	
1 Family			

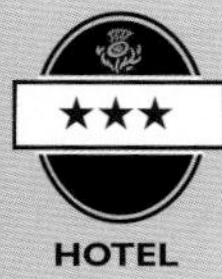

GUEST HOUSE

The Limes Guest House
15 King Street, Montrose, Angus, DD10 8NL
Tel/Fax: 01674 677236
E-mail: thelimes@easynet.co.uk
Web: http://easyweb.easynet.co.uk/thelimes/

Family run, centrally situated in quiet, residential part of town. A few minutes walk from the centre, railway station, beach and two golf courses. Private parking.

2 Single	4 En Suite fac	B&B per person	Open Jan-Dec
4 Twin	3 Pub Bath/Show	from £22.00 Single	
4 Double	2 Priv.NOT ensuite	from £18.00 Dbl/Twn	
2 Family	4 Limited ensuite	Room only from £20.00	

HOTEL

Montrose Park Hotel
61 John Street, Montrose, Angus, DD10 8RJ
Tel: 01674 663400 Fax: 01674 677091
E-mail: recep@montrosepark.co.uk
Web: www.montrosepark.com

Family run hotel with attractive mature gardens situated in residential area at Mid Links, close to town centre. Conference and function suites (200 people).

8 Single	All En Suite	B&B per person	Open Jan-Dec
29 Twin		from £30.00 Single	B&B + Eve.Meal from
20 Double		from £50.00 Dbl/Twn	£39.50
2 Family			

Perth

Map Ref: 2B2

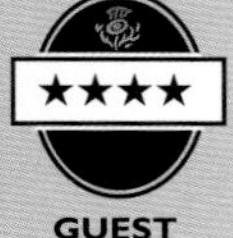

GUEST HOUSE

Achnacarry Guest House
3 Pitcullen Crescent, Perth, PH2 7HT
Tel: 01738 621421 Fax: 01738 444110
E-mail: info@achnacarry.co.uk
Web: www.achnacarry.co.uk

We offer warm hospitality in true Scottish tradition, in tastefully decorated surroundings. En suited rooms, including one on ground floor. Off street parking. An ideal base for visiting the many attractions in the area.

1 Single	4 En Suite fac	B&B per person	Open Jan-Dec
1 Twin	1 Priv.NOT ensuite	£25.00-£30.00 Single	
2 Double		£20.00-£25.00 Dbl/Twn	
1 Family			

All properties graded by VisitScotland, formerly known as the Scottish Tourist Board. | *Key to symbols is on back flap.*

Perth	Map Ref: 2B2

Ackinnoull Guest House
5 Pitcullen Crescent, Perth, PH2 7HT
Tel: 01738 634165

1 Twin	All En Suite	B&B per person	Open Jan-Dec
2 Double		from £20.00 Single	
1 Family		from £18.00 Dbl/Twn	

GUEST HOUSE

Beautifully decorated Victorian semi-villa on the outskirts of town. Private parking on premises. "Perth in Bloom" winners, as picturesque outside as in. Special rates for bookings of 3 days or more.

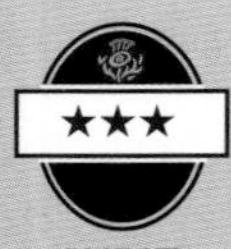

☒ ☐ ☐ P ☐ ☐ ☐ ☐ ☐ ☐

C ☐ V

Albert Villa Guest House
63 Dunkeld Road, Perth, PH1 5RP
Tel: 01738 622730 Fax: 01738 451182
E-mail: caroline@albertvilla.co.uk
Web: www.albertvilla.co.uk

4 Single	7 En Suite fac	B&B per person	Open Jan-Dec
2 Twin	3 Pub Bath/Show	from £22.00 Single	
2 Double		from £22.00 Dbl/Twn	
2 Family		Room only from £20.00	

GUEST HOUSE

Family guest house with ample car parking, close to sports centre and swimming pool. Ground floor bedrooms each have their own entrance.

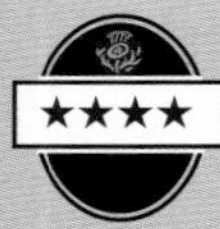

☒ ☐ P ☐ ☐ ☐ ☐

C ☐ ☐ W V

Almond Villa Guest House
51 Dunkeld Road, Perth, PH1 5RP
Tel: 01738 629356 Fax: 01738 446606
E-mail: almondvilla@compuserve.com

1 Single	All En Suite	B&B per person	Open Jan-Dec
2 Twin		from £20.00 Single	
1 Double		from £20.00 Double	
1 Family			

GUEST HOUSE

Semi-detached Victorian villa, close to town centre, Gannochy Trust Sports Complex, the North Inch and River Tay. Non smoking house.

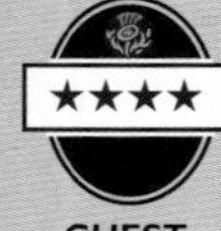

☒ ☐ ☐ P ☐ ☐ ☐ ☐

C ☐ ☐ W V

Ardfern Guest House
15 Pitcullen Crescent, Perth, PH2 7HT
Tel: 01738 637031

1 Twin	2 En Suite fac	B&B per person	Open Jan-Dec
1 Double	1 Priv.NOT ensuite	from £20.00 Single	
1 Family		from £18.00 Dbl/Twn	

GUEST HOUSE

Victorian semi-villa on outskirts of city within easy access to all amenities. Non-smoking throughout. Off road parking. Many original features of the house sympathetically restored and retained.

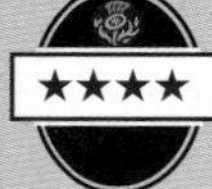

☒ ☐ ☐ ☐ P ☐ ☐ ☐ ☐ ☐

C V

Arisaig Guest House
4 Pitcullen Crescent, Perth, PH2 7HT
Tel/Fax: 01738 628240
E-mail: enquiries@arisaigguesthouse.co.uk
Web: www.arisaigguesthouse.co.uk

1 Single	All En Suite	B&B per person	Open Jan-Dec
1 Twin		from £22.50 Single	
2 Double		from £20.00 Dbl/Twn	
1 Family		Room only from £15.00	

GUEST HOUSE

Comfortable family run guest house, with off street parking. Close to city's many facilities. Local touring base. Ground floor bedroom.

☒ ☐ P ☐ ☐ ☐ ☐ ☐

C ☐ W

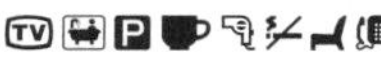

Important: Prices stated are estimates and may be subject to amendments

Perth

Map Ref: 2B2

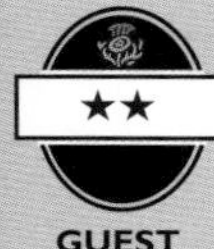

GUEST HOUSE ★★★★

Beechgrove Guest House
Dundee Road, Perth, PH2 7AQ
Tel/Fax: 01738 636147
E-mail: beechgroveg.h@sol.co.uk
Web: www.smoothhound.co.uk/hotels/beechgr or
www.beechgrove.uk.com

Listed building, former manse (Rectory) set in extensive grounds.
Peaceful, yet only a few minutes walk from the city centre. Non-smoking establishment.

1 Single	All En Suite	B&B per person	Open Jan-Dec
2 Twin		from £25.00 Single	
3 Double		from £20.00 Dbl/Twn	
2 Family			

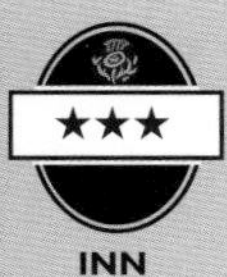

GUEST HOUSE ★★

Castleview Guest House
166 Glasgow Road, Perth, PH2 0LY
Tel/Fax: 01738 626415

Victorian house with private parking close to Cherrybank Heather Collection, yet only minutes from all amenities. The house has open views at the front and is minutes from the by pass.

1 Twin	All En Suite	B&B per person	Open Feb-Dec excl
1 Double		from £38.00 Dbl/Twn	Xmas/New Year
1 Family			

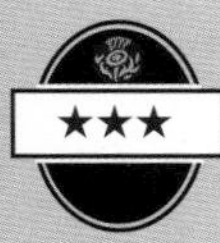

INN ★★★

Cherrybank Inn
210 Glasgow Road, Oakbank, Perth, PH2 0NA
Tel: 01738 624349
Fax: 01738 444962

Cherrybank Inn is situated on the outskirts of Perth, 2 miles off the motorway, offering accommodation in twin bedded ensuite rooms. Bar meals available. Continental breakfast only served in rooms and full breakfast available.

6 Twin	All En Suite	B&B per person	Open Jan-Dec
1 Double		from £28.00 Single	B&B + Eve.Meal
		from £40.00 Dbl/Twn	negotiable

GUEST HOUSE ★★★

Clunie Guest House
12 Pitcullen Crescent, Perth, PH2 7HT
Tel: 01738 623625 Fax: 01738 623238
E-mail: ann@clunieperth.freeserve.co.uk
Web: www.clunieguesthouse.co.uk

A warm welcome awaits you at Clunie Guest House which is situated on the A94 Coupar Angus road. There is easy access to the city centre with all its amenities including a variety of eating establishments. Alternatively, an evening meal can be provided if it is booked in advance. All rooms ensuite.

1 Single	All En Suite	B&B per person	Open Jan-Dec
1 Twin		£19.00-£25.00 Single	B&B + Eve.Meal
2 Double		£19.00-£23.00 Dbl/Twn	£30.00-£34.00
3 Family			

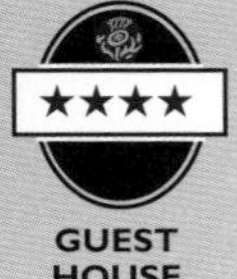

GUEST HOUSE ★★★★

Dunallan Guest House
10 Pitcullen Crescent, Perth, PH2 7HT
Tel/Fax: 01738 622551

Family run, conveniently located on A94 tourist route, within easy reach of town centre. All rooms with TV. All rooms en-suite. Ground floor bedroom with level access to house from private car park.

3 Single	All En Suite	B&B per person	Open Jan-Dec
2 Twin		from £23.00 Single	B&B + Eve.Meal
2 Double		from £22.00 Dbl/Twn	from £32.00
		Room only from £19.00	

All properties graded by VisitScotland, formerly known as the Scottish Tourist Board.

Key to symbols is on back flap.

Perth

Map Ref: 2B2

HOTEL

Huntingtower Hotel

Crieff Road, Perth, PH1 3JT
Tel: 01738 583771 Fax: 01738 583777
E-mail: reservations@huntingtowerhotel.co.uk
Web: www.huntingtowerhotel.co.uk

Country house hotel situated in its own grounds 2 miles West of Perth
City centre. A fine reputation for Scottish and continental cuisine in a
choice of restaurants. With facilities for conference and banqueting.

3 Single	All En Suite	B&B per person	Open Jan-Dec
24 Twin		from £89.50 Single	B&B + Eve.Meal
6 Double		from £55.00 Dbl/Twn	£75.50 Dbl/Twn
1 Family			

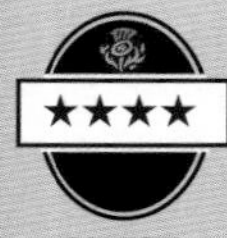

**GUEST
HOUSE**

Kinnaird Guest House

5 Marshall Place, Perth, PH2 8AH
Tel: 01738 628021 Fax: 01738 444056
E-mail: tricia@kinnaird-gh.demon.co.uk
Web: www.kinnaird-guesthouse.co.uk

Georgian house, centrally situated overlooking park. Private parking.
Short walk to town centre and convenient for railway and bus stations.
Personally run. Attentive owners.

1 Single	All En Suite	B&B per person
3 Twin		from £27.00 Single
3 Double		from £23.00 Dbl/Twn

Open Jan-Dec excl
Xmas/New Year

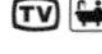

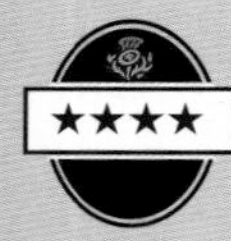

**SMALL
HOTEL**

Parklands Hotel

2 St Leonards Bank, Perth, PH2 8EB
Tel: 01738 622451 Fax: 01738 622046
E-mail: parklands.perth@virgin.net

Overlooking South Inch Park the beautifully decorated rooms within this
classical town house offer the amenities you would expect in a hotel of
this quality. Our Colourists bistro offers informal dining whilst the
Acanthus restaurant offers excellent cuisine imaginatively presented by
our award winning chef in elegant surroundings.

14 Single	All En Suite	B&B per person	Open Jan-Dec
6 Twin		from £69.00 Single	B&B + Eve.Meal from
8 Double		from £40.00 Dbl/Twn	£60.00
1 Family		Room only from £30.00	

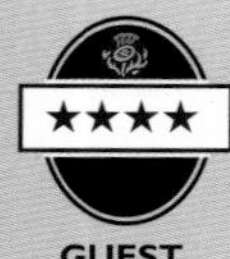

**GUEST
HOUSE**

Rowanlea Guest House

87 Glasgow Road, Perth, PH2 0PQ
Tel: 01738 621922 Fax: 01738 621922
E-mail: reception@rowanlea.fsbusiness.co.uk
Web: www.members.visitscotland.com/rowanlea

Victorian semi-detached family run home, recently refurbished. Off street
parking. Friendly personal attention. Non smoking house.

1 Single	All En Suite	B&B per person
2 Twin		from £25.00 Single
3 Double		from £45.00 Dbl/Twn
		Room only £20.00-£40.00

Open Jan-Dec

Perth   Map Ref: 2B2

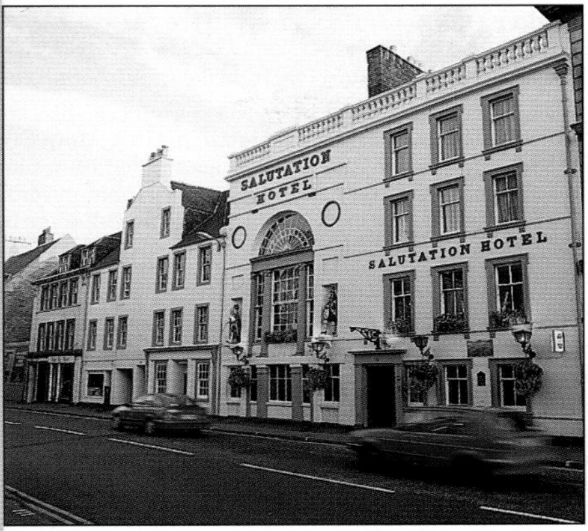

Salutation Hotel

*34 South Street, Perth PH2 8PH
Tel: 01738 630066 Fax: 01738 633598
e.mail: salessalutation@strathmorehotels.com
Web: www.strathmorehotels.com*

*The Salutation is one of Scotland's oldest established
hotels (1699). It is reputed Bonnie Prince Charlie
made his headquarters here during the '45.
The Salutation has recently been modernised. All 84
bedrooms are ensuite with colour television, tea/coffee
making facilities and direct dial telephones. Lift.
The Salutation is the place to stay if you are visiting
Perth on business or on holiday – The Adam
Restaurant with its feature window has a reputation
for fine food and efficient friendly service.*

★★
HOTEL

Salutation Hotel

34 South Street, Perth, PH2 8PH
Tel: 01738 630066 Fax: 01738 633598
E-mail: salessalutation@stathmorehotels.com
Web: www.strathmorehotels.com

Town centre hotel with refurbished bedrooms conveniently situated for
shops and theatre. Leisure centre within 0.5 miles (1km). Lift.

13 Single	All En Suite	B&B per person	Open Jan-Dec
45 Twin		from £55.00 Single	B&B + Eve.Meal
22 Double		from £35.00 Dbl/Twn	from £48.00
4 Family		from £30.00 room only	

---

by Perth   Map Ref: 2B2

★★★★
HOTEL

Ballathie House Hotel

Kinclaven, Stanley, Perth, Perthshire, PH1 4QN
Tel: 01250 883268 Fax: 01250 883396
E-mail: email@ballathiehousehotel.com
Web: www.ballathiehousehotel.com

Victorian Country House within its own grounds overlooking the River
Tay. 12 miles from historic city of Perth. New riverside rooms and suites
with balconies overlooking the river.

6 Single	All En Suite	B&B per person	Open Jan-Dec
18 Twin		from £75.00 Single	B&B + Eve.Meal
18 Double		from £75.00 Dbl/Twn	from £95.00

Pitlochry, Perthshire | Map Ref: 2A1

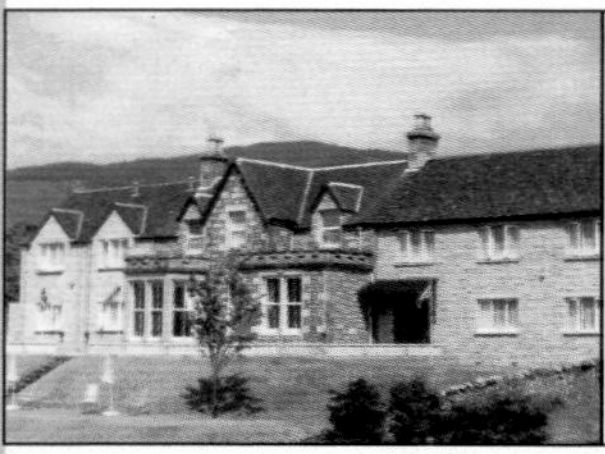

BALROBIN HOTEL
Higher Oakfield, Pitlochry, PH16 5HT
Tel: 01796 472901 Fax: 01796 474200
e.mail: info@balrobin.co.uk Web: www.balrobin.co.uk

Scottish country house in elevated grounds with truly majestic panoramic views only two streets up from Main Street. A blend of Victorian charm and modern accommodation making for a restful holiday. Personally run by the Hohman family (for 20 years) offering the highest standards at value for money prices.

SMALL HOTEL

Balrobin Hotel
Higher Oakfield, Pitlochry, Perthshire, PH16 5HT
Tel: 01796 472901 Fax: 01796 474200
E-mail: info@balrobin.co.uk Web: www.balrobin.co.uk

Situated in residential yet central part of town with most bedrooms (12-4 on ground floor) with superb panoramic views. Traditional home cooked food from a varied choice menu changing daily accompanied by a selection of fine wines. Residents only bar. Our central location affords easy access to 60% of Scotland making it a perfect base for long & short stays. Special short break & advance booking rates. To find us follow the brown tourist signs.

1 Single	All En Suite	B&B per person	Open Mar-Oct
3 Twin		£26.00-£42.00 Single	B&B + Eve.Meal
10 Double		£26.00-£38.00 Dbl/Twn	£36.00-£49.00
1 Family			

GUEST HOUSE

Bendarroch House
Strathtay, Pitlochry, Perthshire, PH9 0PG
Tel: 01887 840420 Fax: 01887 840438
E-mail: bendarrochhouse@netscape.net
Web: www.bendarroch-house.de

Fully refurbished Victorian house set in landscaped grounds with panoramic views of the River Tay which turns past the estate. Situated between Aberfeldy and Pitlochry. Golfing, fishing and canoeing only 2 minutes away, other sports available in the vicinity. Evening meal by prior arrangement, freshly cooked using local produce. Coffee and liqueurs found in the conservatory lounge.

3 Twin	All En Suite	B&B per person	Open Jan-Dec
1 Double		from £28.00 Single	
		from £25.00 Dbl/Twn	
		Room only from £20.00	

GUEST HOUSE

Buttonboss Lodge
25 Atholl Road, Pitlochry, PH16 5BX
Tel/Fax: 01796 472065 Evening: 01796 473000

Traditional Victorian house in centre of Pitlochry. Within walking distance of all facilities. Private parking. Nederlands, Deutch and Francais spoken.

1 Single	7 En Suite facs	B&B per person	Open Jan-Dec
2 Twin	1 Priv.NOT ensuite	£18.00-£22.00	
4 Double			
1 Family			

GUEST HOUSE

Carra Beag Guest House
16 Tobergargan Road, Pitlochry, Perthshire, PH16 5HG
Tel/Fax: 01796 472835
E-mail: visitus@carrabeag.oik.co.uk
Web: www.carrabeag.co.uk

Whatever your pursuits a friendly enjoyable stay is assured at Carra Beag. Enjoy magnificent uninterrupted views of the surrounding hills or stroll through our garden directly to Pitlochry's main street. We offer full facilities for walkers and cyclists. Private car park, and value for money.

2 Single	9 En Suite fac	B&B per person	Open Feb-Dec
3 Twin	1 Pub Bath/Show	from £16.00 Single	
3 Double		from £16.00 Dbl/Twn	
2 Family			

Important: Prices stated are estimates and may be subject to amendments

Pitlochry, Perthshire — Map Ref: 2A1

★★★

GUEST HOUSE

Dalshian House
Old Perth Road, Pitlochry, Perthshire, PH16 5TD
Tel: 01796 472173
E-mail: dalshianhouse@pitlochry.fsworld.co.uk

1 Twin	All En Suite	B&B per person	Open Mar-Oct
4 Double		from £20.50 Single	B&B + Eve.Meal
2 Family		from £20.50 Dbl/Twn	from £34.00

A warm welcome awaits you at this listed property situated on outskirts of Pitlochry. Set in picturesque parkland. An 18th century farmhouse retaining its original style but with all bedrooms en-suite and well equipped.

★★★★

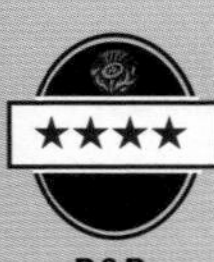

B&B

Dun-Donnachaidh
9 Knockard Road, Pitlochry, Perthshire, PH16 5HJ
Tel: 01796 474018 Fax: 01796 474218

1 Twin	All En Suite	B&B per person
2 Double		£24.50-£28.00
		Open Apr-Oct

Situated in an elevated position with superb views over the town, down the Glen & across to the surrounding hills. A substantial stonebuilt house with a very high standard of accommodation. Lovely cornices original ceiling roses, and wood doors all lovingly restored. Generous size rooms, all rooms have en suite facilities. No pets.

★★★★

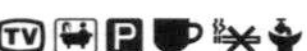

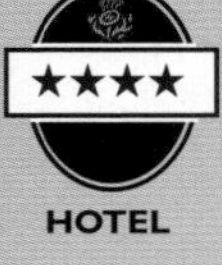

HOTEL

The Green Park Hotel
Clunie Bridge Road, Pitlochry, Perthshire, PH16 5JY
Tel: 01796 473248 Fax: 01796 473520
E-mail: bookings@thegreenpark.co.uk
Web: www.thegreenpark.co.uk

6 Single	All En Suite	B&B per person	Open Jan-Dec
15 Twin		£30.00-£44.00 Single	B&B + Eve.Meal
16 Double		£30.00-£44.00 Dbl/Twn	£42.00-£69.00
2 Family			

Family run country house hotel enjoying spectacular views over Loch Faskally. Within strolling distance of the shops and a pleasant walk from the Festival theatre, the hotel has become a well known landmark of the town. The hotel has a Red Rossette for food, and is a Taste of Scotland member.

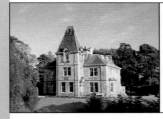

KNOCKENDARROCH HOUSE
Higher Oakfield, Pitlochry, Perthshire PH16 5HT
Telephone: 01796 473473 Fax: 01796 474068
e.mail: info@knockendarroch.co.uk
web: www.knockendarroch.co.uk

★★★★ SMALL HOTEL

THE TASTE OF SCOTLAND

The warmest of welcomes, with first-class food, wines and personal service complement this elegant Victorian mansion. Surrounded by mature oaks and beeches with glorious views over Pitlochry and the Tummel Valley, yet within walking distance of the town centre. Stay at Knockendarroch once and we're confident you'll want to return. AA ★★ 76% Rosette.

★★★★

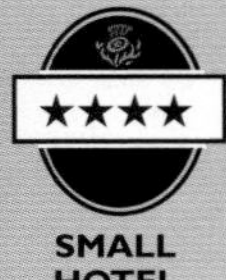

SMALL HOTEL

Knockendarroch House Hotel
Higher Oakfield, Pitlochry, Perthshire, PH16 5HT
Tel: 01796 473473 Fax: 01796 474068
E-mail: info@knockendarroch.co.uk
Web: www.knockendarroch.co.uk

6 Twin	All En Suite	Open Feb-Nov
6 Double		B&B + Eve.Meal
		£42.00-£65.00

An oasis of tranquillity in the heart of the town. Knockendarroch a gracious Victorian mansion, with glorious views over Pitlochry and Tummel valley. Set in it's own grounds surrounded by mature oaks, Knockendarroch with resident proprietors Jane & Tony Ross, combines a relaxed atmosphere, high standards in food, wines and personal attention. Lots to do locally and a perfect base for sightseeing and touring. Non-smoking hotel.

All properties graded by VisitScotland, formerly known as the Scottish Tourist Board. | Key to symbols is on back flap.

| Pitlochry, Perthshire | | | | Map Ref: 2A1 |

B&B
★★

Lonaig
28 Lettoch Terrace, Pitlochry, Perthshire, PH16 5BA
Tel: 01796 472422

| 2 Double | 1 Pub Bath/Show | B&B per person £15.50-£16.00 Dbl | Open Easter-mid Oct |

Semi detached house, with most attractive, well-tended, colourful garden. Set in a peaceful cul-de-sac with some views over the town. Non-smoking house.

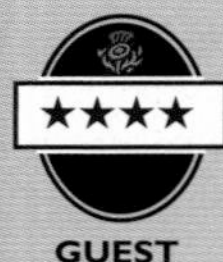

GUEST HOUSE
★★★★

Number 10
10 Atholl Road, Pitlochry, Perthshire, PH16 5BX
Tel: 01796 472346 Fax: 01796 473519
E-mail: num10pit@tinyonline.co.uk
Web: www.pitlochry-guesthouse.co.uk

2 Single	9 En Suite fac	B&B per person £18.00-£30.00 Single	Open Jan-Dec excl Xmas/New Year
3 Twin	1 Pub Bath/Show	£18.00-£30.00 Dbl/Twn	
5 Double		Room only £15.00-£27.00	
2 Family			

The relaxed warm atmosphere, and friendly hospitality of experienced hosts Fran and Alan will make you want to return regularly to this cosy retreat. The guest house has comfortable bedrooms, a snug bar, quiet lounge and a dining room serving only fresh food based on Scottish produce. In easy walking distance of the town centre, with a lovely ten minute walk over the river to Pitlochry Theatre.

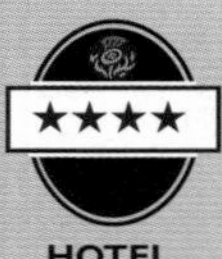

HOTEL
★★★★

Pine Trees Hotel and Garden Restaurant
Strathview Terrace, Pitlochry, Perthshire, PH16 5QR
Tel/Fax: 01796 472121
E-mail: info@pinetreeshotel.co.uk
Web: www.pinetreeshotel.co.uk

2 Single	All En Suite	B&B per person from £47.00 Single	Open Jan-Dec B&B + Eve.Meal
8 Twin		from £32.00 Dbl/Twn	from £49.00
10 Double			

Personally run Victorian country house in elevated position, with 10 acres of garden and woodland yet close to town centre. Neighbouring golf course and all amenities.

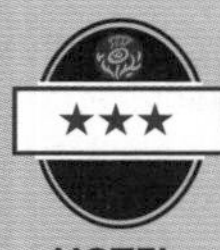

HOTEL
★★★

Pitlochry Hydro Hotel
Knockard Road, Pitlochry, Perthshire, PH16 5JH
Tel: 01786 436600 Fax: 01786 436650
E-mail: l.graig@shearingsholidays.co.uk
Web: www.shearingsholidays.com

10 Single	All En Suite		Open Feb-Dec
29 Twin			
17 Double			
4 Family			

The hotel and health club stand in their own grounds overlooking the town.

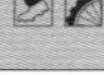

SMALL HOTEL
★★★

The Poplars
27 Lower Oakfield, Pitlochry, Perthshire, PH16 5DS
Tel: 01796 472129 Fax: 01796 472554
E-mail: enquiries@poplars-hotel.co.uk
Web: www.poplars-hotel.co.uk

4 Twin	10 En Suite fac	B&B per person from £26.00 Dbl/Twn	Open Jan-Dec B&B + Eve.Meal
4 Double	1 Priv.NOT ensuite		from £42.00
3 Family			

An imposing Victorian house with a rather unique atmosphere, beautifully situated in a very quiet yet convenient near town-centre location. Tastefully modernised to retain its traditional ambience. True Scottish hospitality personally and caringly provided by experienced Scottish owners Kathleen and Ian, whose local area and activity knowledge can greatly enhance your stay. Glenturret tourism award winner 'Most Enjoyable Hotel in Perthshire' 1999.

Important: Prices stated are estimates and may be subject to amendments

Pitlochry, Perthshire — Map Ref: 2A1

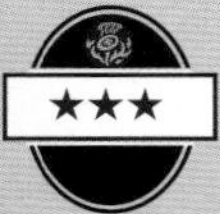

Rosemount Hotel
12 Higher Oakfield, Pitlochry, Perthshire, PH16 5HT
Tel: 01796 472302 Fax: 01796 474216
E-mail: info@scottishhotels.co.uk
Web: www.scottishhotels.co.uk

Personally run fully licencend hotel with friendly atmosphere, situated in elevated position overlooking Tummel Valley.

2 Single
7 Twin
13 Double
3 Family

All En Suite

B&B per person
from £30.00 Single
from £30.00 Dbl/Twn
Room only from £24.00

Open Jan-Dec
B&B + Eve.Meal
from £42.00

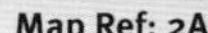

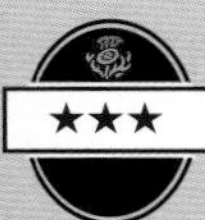

The Well House
11 Toberargan Road, Pitlochry, Perthshire, PH16 5HG
Tel: 01796 472239
E-mail: enquiries@wellhouseandarrochar.co.uk
Web: www.wellhouseandarrochar.co.uk

Personally run, centrally situated in residential area. Easy access to shops, amenities and theatre.

1 Twin
4 Double
1 Family

All En Suite

B&B per person
from £19.00 Dbl/Twn

Open Feb-Nov excl
Xmas/New Year
B&B + Eve.Meal
from £32.00

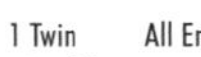

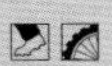

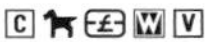

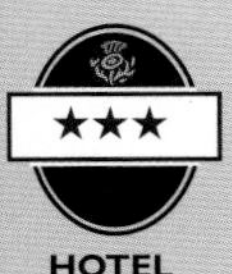

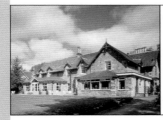

Westlands of Pitlochry ★★ AA
THE TASTE OF SCOTLAND

160 Atholl Road, Pitlochry, PH16 5AR
Telephone: 01796 472266 Fax: 01796 473994
e.mail: info@westlandshotel.co.uk Web: www.westlandshotel.co.uk

Beautifully situated and enjoying wonderful views, Westlands has been carefully extended and refurbished throughout. All rooms ensuite with TV/radio, tea/coffee tray, telephone, hairdryer and central heating.
Outstanding bistro restaurant/bar food. Special rates for Spring, Winter and Theatre Breaks.
We look forward to welcoming you!

Westlands Hotel
160 Atholl Road, Pitlochry, Perthshire, PH16 5AR
Tel: 01796 472266 Fax: 01796 473994
E-mail: info@westlandshotel.co.uk
Web: www.westlandshotel.co.uk

Recently refurbished, the hotel is pleasantly situated on the edge of town. The new Garden Room Restaurant uses fresh produce. Taste of Scotland.

1 Single
5 Twin
7 Double
2 Family

All En Suite

B&B per person
from £33.75 Single
from £28.75 Dbl/Twn

Open Jan-Dec excl
Christmas Day and
Boxing Day

St Andrews, Fife — Map Ref: 2D2

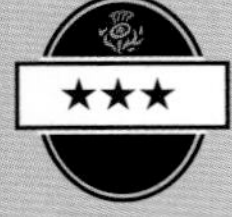

The Albany Hotel
56-58 North Street, St Andrews, KY16 9AH
Tel: 01334 477737 Fax: 01334 477742
E-mail: enqu@standrewsalbany.co.uk
Web: www.standrewsalbany.co.uk

Peacefully situated in the heart of St Andrews, close to shops, restaurants, golf courses and historic buildings, this elegant Georgian town house has been cleverly and sympathetically converted for use as an hotel. 21 rooms, all en suite, the Albany Hotel is able to maintain high standards in accommodation and service.

6 Single
4 Twin
8 Double
3 Family

All En Suite

B&B per person
from £75.00 Single
from £110.00 Dbl/Twn

Open Jan-Dec

All properties graded by VisitScotland, formerly known as the Scottish Tourist Board. | *Key to symbols is on back flap.*

St Andrews, Fife | **Map Ref: 2D2**

★★★★

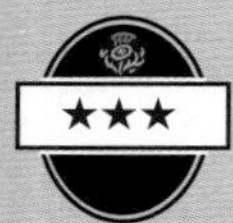

GUEST HOUSE

Aslar House
120 North Street, St Andrews, Fife, KY16 9AF
Tel: 01334 473460 Fax: 01334 477546
E-mail: enquiries@aslar.com
Web: www.aslar.com

Victorian family run terraced house furnished to a high standard with period features. Centrally situated for shops, golf courses, restaurants and cultural pursuits.

1 Single	All En Suite	B&B per person	Open Jan-Dec excl
2 Twin		from £29.00 Single	Xmas/New Year
2 Double		from £58.00 Dbl/Twn	

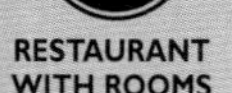

AWAITING INSPECTION

Burness House
1 Murray Park, St Andrews, Fife, KY16 9AW
Tel/Fax: 01334 474314
E-mail: marie&david@burnesshouse.com
Web: www.burnesshouse.com

2 Twin	All En Suite	B&B per person	Open Jan-Dec
3 Family		from £30.00 Single	
		from £30.00 Dbl/Twn	

★★★

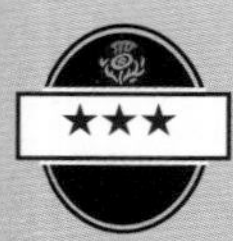

RESTAURANT WITH ROOMS

The Grange Inn
Grange Road, St Andrews, KY16 8LJ
Tel: 01334 472670 Fax: 01334 472604

17th century restaurant with rooms located within two miles of the historic town of St Andrews. In a pleasant rural position with panoramic views across St Andrews Bay it is the ideal place to relax in front of a log fire. Imaginatively prepared and presented food using fresh local produce.

1 Twin	All En Suite	B&B per person	Open Jan-Dec excl
1 Double		from £30.00 Single	Xmas/New Year
		from £25.00 Dbl/Twn	

★★★

HOTEL

New Hall, University of St Andrews
North Haugh, St Andrews, KY16 9XW
Tel: 01334 462000 Fax: 01334 462500
E-mail: holidays@st-andrews.ac.uk
Web: www.st-andrews.ac.uk

Modern accommodation in parkland setting for conferences and groups, as well as short breaks for individuals and families. Breakfast, lunch and dinner are served in the restaurant. The bar provides informal meals throughout the day. There is ample car parking. New Hall is within walking distance of the old town, the golf courses and the beach.

48 Double	All En Suite	B&B per person	Open Jun-Sep
24 Family		from £40.90 Single	B&B + Eve.Meal
		from £32.70 Double	from £42.50

★★★★★

HOTEL

Rufflets Country House
Strathkinness Low Road, St Andrews, Fife, KY16 9TX
Tel: 01334 472594 Fax: 01334 478703
E-mail: reservations@rufflets.co.uk
Web: www.rufflets.co.uk

Country house with relaxing ambience, set in 10 acres of beautiful gardens. Fresh seasonal produce served in the restaurant. 1.5 miles (3kms) from golf courses and coast.

5 Single	All En Suite	B&B per person	Open Jan-Dec
9 Twin		from £100.00 Single	
7 Double		from £95.00 Dbl/Twn	
1 Family			

Important: Prices stated are estimates and may be subject to amendments

St Andrews, Fife

Map Ref: 2D2

Rusacks Hotel
Pilmour Links, St Andrews, Fife, KY16 9JQ
Tel: 01334 474321 Fax: 01334 477896
E-mail: rusacks@heritage-hotels.co.uk
Web: www.heritage-hotels.com

This traditional hotel dating from c1887 has been extensively refurbished and 20 new bedrooms have recently been created with magnificent views of West Sands from many bedrooms. The bar and restaurant overlook the 18th hole of the famous Old Course. Close to town centre and University. Modern conference facilities available and non-residents also very welcome.

HOTEL

6 Single
41 Twin
18 Double
3 Family

All En Suite facs

B&B per person
from £45.00 Single
from £105.00 Dbl/Twn

Open Jan-Dec

St Andrews Golf Hotel

40 The Scores, St Andrews KY16 9AS
Tel: 01334 472611 Fax: 01334 472188
e.mail: reception@standrews-golf.co.uk
Web: www.standrews-golf.co.uk

This beautifully restored Victorian house sits on the cliffs overlooking St Andrews Bay and Links, 200 metres from the 1st tee of the 'Old Course'. The hotel is owned and operated by the Hughes family. The 22 individually styled ensuite bedrooms are rich in fabrics and textures. Enjoy the elegant lounges and the oak-panelled, candlelit restaurant with its stunning sea view. Here chef Colin Masson creates mouthwatering dishes from the best of local produce complemented by a wine list of rare quality. More casual dining is found in Ma Bells Bistro Bar, serving food all day and grills in the evening. Golf is central to our business and we specialise in tailoring holidays to your particular needs.

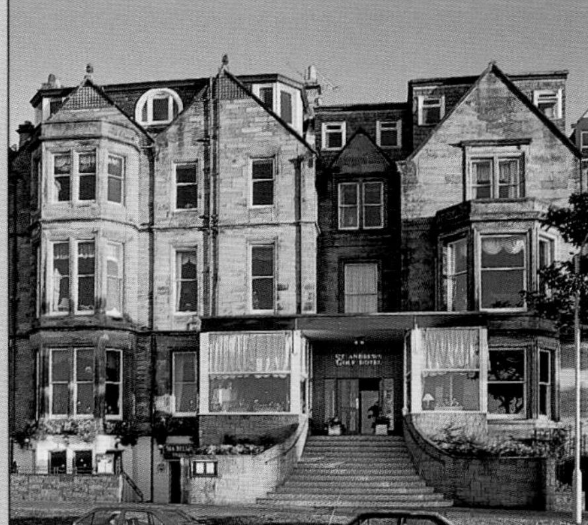

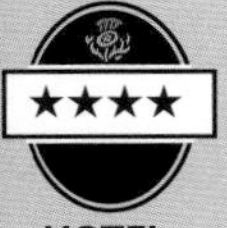

St Andrews Golf Hotel
40 The Scores, St Andrews, Fife, KY16 9AS
Tel: 01334 472611 Fax: 01334 472188
E-mail: reception@standrews-golf.co.uk

Privately owned hotel, situated 200 yards from the Old Course, overlooking St Andrews Bay. Imaginative use of local ingredients.

HOTEL

1 Single
10 Dbl/Twin
5 Double
6 Family

All En Suite

B&B per person
£107.00 Single
£80.00-£90.00
Dbl/Twn/Fam

Open Jan-Dec

West Park House
5 St Marys Place, St Andrews, Fife, KY16 9UY
Tel: 01334 475933 Fax: 01334 476634
E-mail: rosemary@westparksta.freeserve.co.uk
Web: www.westpark.standrews.co.uk

Beautiful Listed Georgian house c1830 in heart of historic town. Close to Old Course and all amenities. Sandy beaches close by and within easy reach of the pretty East Neuk fishing villages (approx 10 miles).

GUEST HOUSE

1 Twin
3 Double
1 Family

3 En Suite fac
2 Priv.NOT ensuite

B&B per person
from £32.00 Single
from £50.00 Dbl/Twn

Open Jan-Dec excl Xmas/New Year

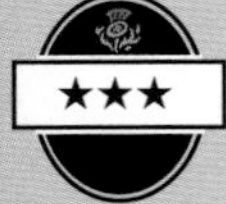

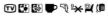

by St Andrews, Fife — Map Ref: 2D2

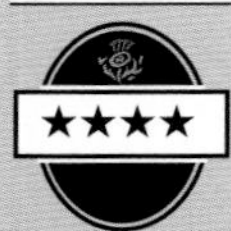

Greenacres Lodge
Fordelhill, Leuchars, by St Andrews, Fife, KY16 0BT
Tel: 01334 838242

2 Twin / 1 Double — All En Suite — B&B per person from £35.00 Single from £20.00 Dbl/Twn — Open Feb-Nov, B&B + Eve.Meal from £34.50

Country cottage with panoramic views over Eden Estuary. Open fire in the comfortable lounge. Candlelit dinners using fresh local produce.

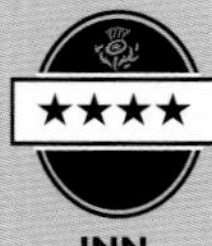

The Inn at Lathones
by Largoward, St Andrews, Fife, KY9 1JE
Tel: 01334 840494 Fax: 01334 840694
E-mail: Lathones@theinn.co.uk
Web: www.theinn.co.uk

2 Single / 5 Twin / 5 Double / 2 Family — All En Suite — B&B per person from £70.00 Single from £55.00 Dbl/Twn — Open 23 Jan - 6 Jan

Charming 400 year old Coaching Inn, just 5 miles from St Andrews. Sympathetically restored and enlarged. Offering modern comfort, great food and friendly people to look after your every need. Award winning chef - two AA Rosettes - using freshest of local Scottish produce.

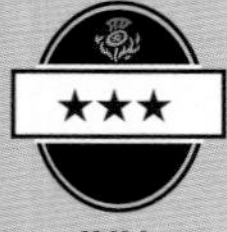

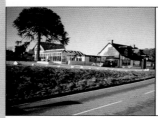

St Michael's Inn
**Leuchars, by St Andrews, Fife KY16 0DU
Tel: 01334 839220 e.mail: grahame@stmichaelsinn.com
Fax: 01334 838299 Web: www.stmichaelsinn.com**

This 18th-century inn has 8 well-appointed bedrooms with self-control heating, colour television, complimentary tea/coffee. Ideally situated for golfing breaks. There is an abundance of sightseeing in the area with good walks and beaches. 10 minutes from St Andrews, rail link is one mile, airport five miles.

St Michaels Inn
Leuchars, by St Andrews, Fife, KY16 0DU
Tel: 01334 839220 Fax: 01334 838299
Web: www.stmichaelsinn.com

1 Single / 2 Twin / 3 Double / 2 Family — All En Suite — B&B per person from £39.50 Single from £70.00 Dbl/Twn — Open Jan-Dec excl Xmas/New Year

Totally refurbished 200 year old former coaching Inn. Ideally located for golfing and St Andrews. Convenient for touring the Central Belt. Good reputation for traditional bar food, cooked to order. Easy access to train station and Dundee Airport. Good local bus service.

Scotlandwell, by Kinross, Perthshire — Map Ref: 2C3

The Well Country Inn
Lochgelly Road, Scotlandwell, by Kinross, KY13 9JA
Tel: 01592 840444
E-mail: thewellcountryinn@fsbdial.co.uk
Web: www.thewellcountryinn.com

1 Single / 6 Twin / 1 Double / 2 Family — All En Suite — B&B per person from £30.00 Single from £55.00 Dbl/Twn — Open Jan-Dec

The well country Inn is a family run business and is situated in one of the most beautiful areas of Scotland, renowned for its natural beauty and wealthy of sporting and leisure interest. Game shooting is popular sport in this area and our annexe bedrooms are fitted with gun safes and we have kennel facilities.

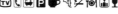

Important: Prices stated are estimates and may be subject to amendments

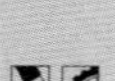

Stanley, Perthshire

Map Ref: 2B2

★★★

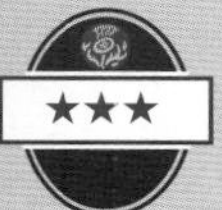

HOTEL

The Tayside Hotel

Mill Street, Stanley, Perthshire, PH1 4NL
Tel: 01738 828249 Fax: 01738 827216
E-mail: reservations@tayside-hotel.co.uk
Web: www.tayside-hotel.co.uk

Edwardian Hotel in historic village of Stanley surrounded by beautiful
scenery. Freshly prepared food using local produce and awards for its
legendary Tayside Roast. An hour from Edinburgh, ideally located for
golfing and fishing.

1 Single	All En Suite	B&B per person	Open Jan-Dec
6 Twin		from £25.00 Single	B&B + Eve.Meal from
6 Double		from £22.50 Dbl/Twn	£47.50
2 Family		Room only from £39.00	

Tayport, Fife

Map Ref: 2D2

★★★

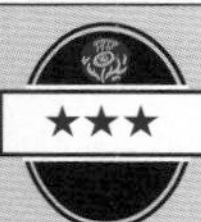

B&B

Forgan's B&B

23 Castle Street, Tayport, Fife, DD6 9AE
Tel/Fax: 01382 552682
E-mail: m.forgan@talk21.com   Web: www.forgan.ukf.net/

Truly Scottish welcome awaits you here. Situated in centre of Tayport, just
a short walk from picturesque harbour. Easy commuting to Dundee and
St Andrews. Good bus service. Near to Dundee and Leuchars Railway
Station. Many golf courses nearby. 1 hour drive from Edinburgh. Good
home cooking. Full Scottish breakfast, evening meals on request. Special
diets catered for. Children free when sharing with adults.

2 Twin	1 Pub/Bath Show	B&B per person	Open Jan-Dec
1 Double		£16.00-£19.00 Single	B&B + Eve.Meal
		£16.00-£19.00 Dbl/Twn	£22.00-£25.00

All properties graded by VisitScotland, formerly known as the Scottish Tourist Board. | *Key to symbols is on back flap.*

welcome to scotland

SCOTLAND'S CASTLE AND WHISKY COUNTRY – ROYAL DEESIDE TO SPEYSIDE

Between the granite of the high Cairngorms and a dramatic unspoilt coastline, lie hills, moors and wooded farmlands, river valleys and characterful towns, as well as Aberdeen, Scotland's third city, noted for its unique silver granite architecture and its floral displays.

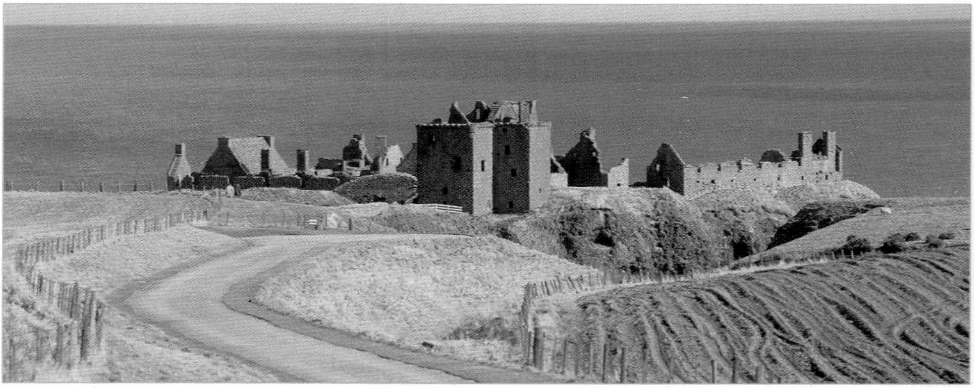

Dunottar Castle, south of Stonehaven, Aberdeenshire

ABERDEEN offers plenty for visitors: museums, art gallery, great shopping plus an expanding range of leisure attractions along its extensive promenade. The city is also the gateway to Royal Deeside, noted not just for Balmoral Castle and royal family connections, but beautiful scenery with plenty of walking, climbing and castles to visit nearby, plus Royal Lochnagar Distillery. The new Old Royal Station at Ballater portrays the areas association with Queen Victoria.

Malt whisky is most strongly associated with Moray and its unique Malt Whisky Trail, offering a wide choice of distilleries to visit many of which are located along the beautiful birchwood setting of the River Spey. The third major river in this area, the River Don, is associated with the Castle Trail, where some of the finest castles in Scotland are linked in a signposted trail, which range from the medieval fortress of Kildrummy to the Adam revival grandeur of Haddo House.

The coastline offers yet more delights, not just in the coastal links golf courses, endless beaches and spectacular cliffs and coves, but also in a further range of visitor attractions, including the unique Museum of Scottish Lighthouses at Fraserburgh, the site of Scotland's first lighthouse, and also the equally unique displays at Macduff Marine Aquarium, where a natural kelp reef – seen through one of the largest viewing windows in any British aquarium – shelters a community of fish and other sea creatures usually only seen by divers.

SCOTLAND'S CASTLE AND WHISKY COUNTRY – ROYAL DEESIDE TO SPEYSIDE

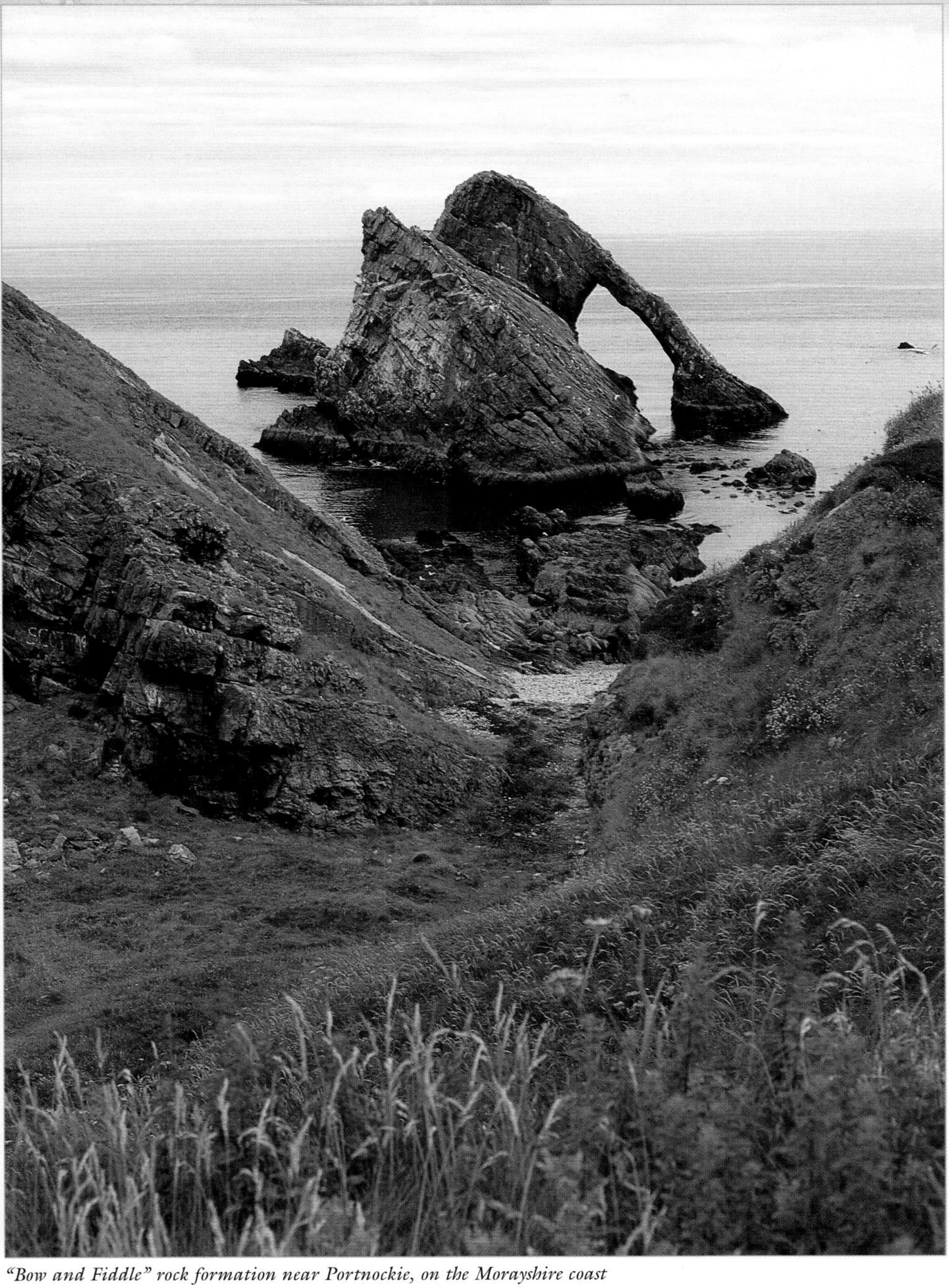

"Bow and Fiddle" rock formation near Portnockie, on the Morayshire coast

SCOTLAND'S CASTLE AND WHISKY COUNTRY –
ROYAL DEESIDE TO SPEYSIDE

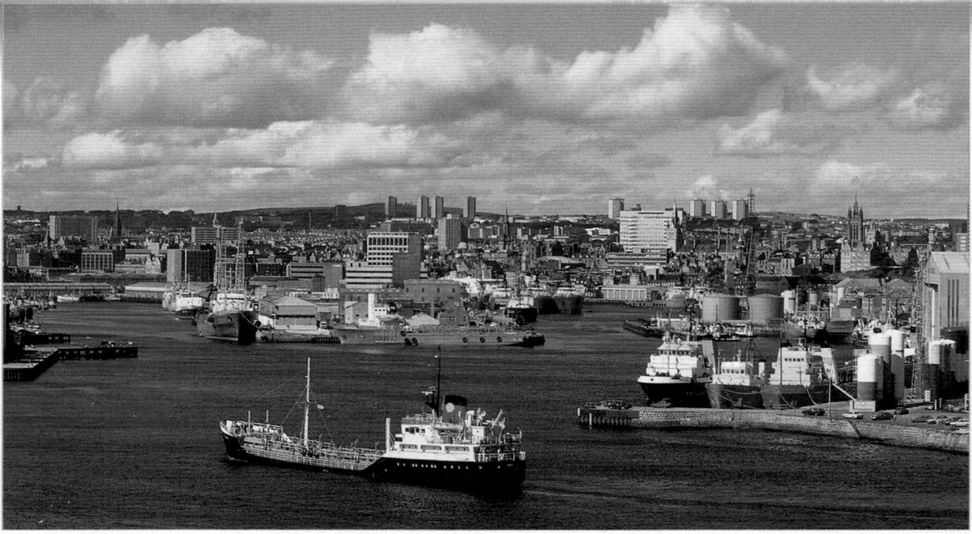

The Harbour, city of Aberdeen

Grampian is certainly full of surprises –
including the chance to see Britain's largest
resident colony of bottle-nose dolphins,
which turn up close to land anywhere on
the Moray Firth coast between Findhorn
and Banff.

Events
Scotland's castle and whisky country – Royal Deeside to Speyside

* 8 -10 March
Braemar Telemark Festival
Glenshee, Glenshee Ski Area
A unique event attracting
many top names from the
world of telemarking.
Contact: Rob Edmonds
Tel: 01339 741242
Web: www.ski-glenshee.co.uk

3-6 May
*Spirit of Speyside
Whisky Festival*
Speyside, Various Venues
Enjoy tastings, distillery
visits, music and many other
themed activities.
Contact: Elgin Tourist
Information Centre
Tel: 01343 542666
Web:
www.spiritofspeyside.com

* 8 June
Taste of Grampian
Inverurie,
Thainstone Centre
A celebration of the diversity
and richness of the local
larder.
Contact: Events Manager
Tel: 01467 623760
Web:
www.tasteofgrampian.co.uk

29-30 June
*Scottish Traditional
Boat Festival*
Portsoy, The Harbour
Sailing races and shoreside
craft demonstrations on
traditional Scottish boats.
Contact: Ian Bright
Tel: 01261 842951

31 July-10 August
*Aberdeen International
Youth Festival*
Aberdeenshire,
Various Venues
International multi-arts
festival.
Contact: Nicola Wallis
Tel: 0208 946 2995
Web: www.aiyf.org

1-4 August
Speyfest
Fochabers, Various Venues
A pan Celtic festival of
music and dance.
Contact: Gavin Hillson
Tel: 01343 821193
Web: www.speyfest.com

7 September
Braemar Gathering
Braemar, Princess Royal
Memorial Park
One of the most famous
Highland games featuring
traditional events.
Contact: Mr W.M. Meston
Tel: 01339 755377
Web:
www.braemargathering.org

**30 September-
3 October**
Speyside Golf Classic
Speyside, Various Venues
The Speyside Golf Classic
offers a unique golfing
experience set in some of
the most spectacular scenery
in Scotland.
Contact:
Scottish Golf Classics
Tel: 0800 027 1070 (UK)
or 01292 671500
Web:
www.scottishgolfclassics.com

31 December
*Stonehaven
Fireball Festival*
Stonehaven, High Street
The stroke of midnight see
balls of fire being swung
down the high street in this
dramatic New Year display.
Contact: Lynn Callaghan
Tel: 01569 764009
(after 6pm)

** denotes provisional date,
please check before attending.*

Area tourist boards
Scotland's castle and whisky country –
Royal Deeside to Speyside

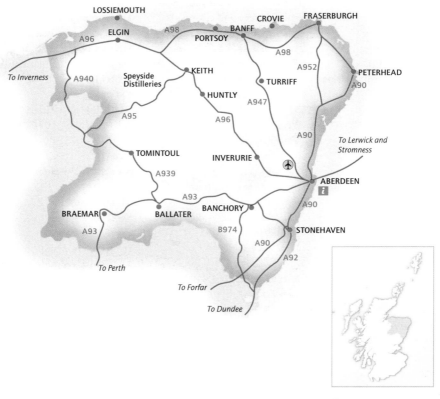

ABERDEEN AND
GRAMPIAN TOURIST
BOARD
27 Albyn Place
Aberdeen
AB10 1YL

Tel: 01224 288828
Fax: 01224 581367
E-mail:
info@castlesandwhisky.com
Web:
www.castlesandwhisky.com

TOURIST INFORMATION CENTRES
SCOTLAND'S CASTLE AND WHISKY COUNTRY –
ROYAL DEESIDE TO SPEYSIDE

ABERDEEN AND GRAMPIAN TOURIST BOARD

Aberdeen
Provost Ross's House
Shiprow
Tel: (01224) 288828
Jan-Dec

Alford
Railway Museum
Station Yard
Tel: (019755) 62052
Easter-Sept

Ballater
Station Square
Tel: (013397) 55306
Jan-Dec

Banchory
Bridge Street
Tel: (01330) 822000
Easter-Oct

Banff
Collie Lodge
Tel: (01261) 812419
Easter-Sept

Braemar
The Mews
Mar Road
Tel: (013397) 41600
Jan-Dec

Crathie
The Car Park
Balmoral Castle
Tel: (013397) 42414
Easter-Oct

Dufftown
The Clock Tower
The Square
Tel: (01340) 820501
Easter-Oct

Elgin
17 High Street
Tel: (01343) 542666/543388
Jan-Dec

Forres
116 High Street
Tel: (01309) 672938
Easter-Oct

Fraserburgh
Saltoun Square
Tel: (01346) 518315
Easter-Sept

Huntly
The Square
Tel: (01466) 792255
Easter-Oct

Inverurie
18 High Street
Tel: (01467) 625800
Jan-Dec

Stonehaven
66 Allardice Street
Tel: (01569) 762806
Easter-Oct

Tomintoul
The Square
Tel: (01807) 580285
Easter-Oct

Aberdeen

Map Ref: 4G10

GUEST HOUSE

Aberdeen Nicoll's Guest House

63 Springbank Terrace, Ferryhill, Aberdeen, AB11 6JZ
Tel/Fax: 01224 572867
E-mail: aberdeennicollsguesthouse@btinternet.com
Web: www.aberdeennicollsguesthouse.com

Family run, granite terraced guest house. Centrally located within ¼ mile
(½km) of city centre shops, 1 mile (2kms) from Duthie Park.

| 3 Twin | 3 En Suite fac |
| 3 Family | 2 Pub Bath/Show |

B&B per person
from £22.00 Single
from £34.00 Dbl/Twn

Open Jan-Dec

GUEST HOUSE

Aberdeen Springdale Guest House

404 Great Western Road, Aberdeen, AB10 6NR
Tel: 01224 316561 Fax: 01224 316561
E-mail: jamesestirling@msn.com
Web: www.aberdeenguesthouse.co.uk

Attractive granite house 2 miles (3kms) from city centre. On main bus
routes, 5 miles (8kms) from the airport and on route to Royal Deeside.

| 1 Single |
| 1 Twin |
| 2 Double |
| 2 Family |

B&B per person
£22.00-£35.00 Single
£40.00-£46.00 Dbl/Twn

Open Jan-Dec

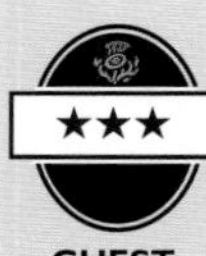

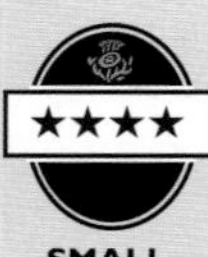

SMALL HOTEL

Aberdeen Craiglynn Hotel

36 Fonthill Road, Aberdeen, AB11 6UJ
Tel: 01224 584050 Fax: 01224 212225
E-mail: info@craiglynn.co.uk
Web: www.craiglynn.co.uk

A small family run hotel renowned for its Victorian elegance with modern
comforts. Ideally situated for business or leisure. Taste of Scotland
member. Car park. Residential licence.

| 5 Single | 7 En Suite fac |
| 1 Twin | 2 Priv.NOT ensuite |
| 2 Double |
| 1 Family |

B&B per person
from £30.00 Single
from £30.00 Dbl/Twn

Open Jan-Dec
B&B + Eve.Meal from
£47.50

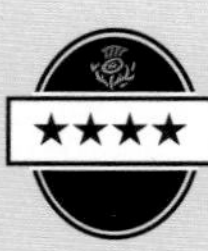

GUEST HOUSE

Allan Guest House

56 Polmuir Road, Ferryhill, Aberdeen, AB11 7RT
Tel: 01224 584484 Fax: 01224 595988
E-mail: stbbookings@camtay.co.uk
Web: www.camtay.co.uk

A Victorian terraced house situated on a bus route to the city centre. A
free parking area close to Duthie Park and Winter Gardens. Sociable
owners who are keen to offer comfortable accommodation and warm
hospitality. Home cooked suppers available by arrangement at time of
booking, with a wide choice available at breakfast. Special diets can be
catered for. Scotland's Best member.

| 3 Single | 6 En Suite fac |
| 3 Twin | 1 Priv.NOT ensuite |
| 4 Double |
| 2 Family |

B&B per person
from £27.00 Single
from £54.00 Dbl/Twn

Open Jan-Dec
B&B + Eve.Meal
from £36.50

Aberdeen		Map Ref: 4G10	

★★★

GUEST HOUSE

The Angel Islington Guest House
191 Bon Accord Street, Aberdeen, AB11 6UA
Tel/Fax: 01224 587043

Semi-detached granite built Victorian house in residential area on south side of city. Shops, railway station and Duthie Park within 1 mile (2kms).

2 Single	7 En Suite fac	B&B per person	Open Jan-Dec
2 Twin	2 Pub Bath/Show	£20.00-£28.00 Single	
2 Double		£17.00-£20.00 Dbl/Twn	
2 Family			

TV 🛩 🛏 ☕ 🖐 📱

C 🐕 V

★★

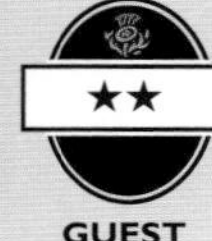

GUEST HOUSE

Balvenie Guest House
9 St Swithin Street, Aberdeen, AB10 6XB
Tel: 01224 322559 Fax: 01224 322773
E-mail: balveniegh@aol.com
Web: http://members.aol.com/balveniegh

Late Victorian granite built house in residential area in West End, close to city centre. Parking. Convenient for local and airport buses.

2 Single	2 Pub Bath/Show	B&B per person	Open Jan-Dec
2 Twin		from £18.00 Single	B&B + Eve.Meal from
1 Double		from £16.00 Dbl/Twn	£25.50

TV 🛩 ☕ ✕ 📱

C 🐕 ⊞ W V

★★★

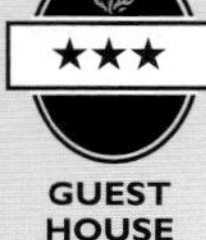

GUEST HOUSE

Beeches Private Hotel
193 Great Western Road, Aberdeen, AB10 6PS
Tel: 01224 586413 Fax: 01224 596919
E-mail: beeches-hotel@talk21.com
Web: www.beeches-hotel.com

Victorian detached granite house in residential area close to city centre. Private car parking. Beauty salon and Fitness Suite.

3 Single	All En Suite	B&B per person	Open Jan-Dec excl
2 Twin		from £30.00 Single	Xmas/New Year
2 Double		from £22.50 Dbl/Twn	
2 Family		Room only from £20.00	

TV 📞 🛏 P ☕ 🖐 ✕ 📱

C 🐕 ⊞

★★★

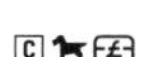

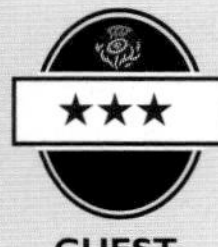

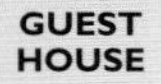

GUEST HOUSE

Belhaven Private Hotel
152 Bon Accord Street, Aberdeen, AB11 6TX
Tel/Fax: 01224 588384
E-mail: belhaven@aol.com

Late Victorian granite house in residential area, close to city centre and local park. Rail and bus station nearby. Small private sauna with adjoining Jacuzzi and shower available for guests use.

2 Single	4 En Suite fac	B&B per person	Open Jan-Dec
1 Twin	4 Pub Bath/Show	from £22.00 Single	
4 Double		from £19.00 Dbl/Twn	
1 Family			

TV 🛏 ☕ 🖐 ✕ 🖥 📱

C 🐕 ⊞ W V

★★★

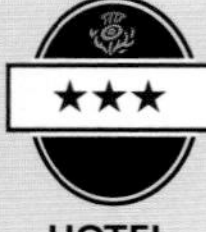

HOTEL

Brentwood Hotel
101 Crown Street, Aberdeen, AB11 6HH
Tel: 01224 595440 Fax: 01224 571593
E-mail: reservation@brentwood-hotel.demon.co.uk
Web: www.brentwood-hotel.demon.co.uk

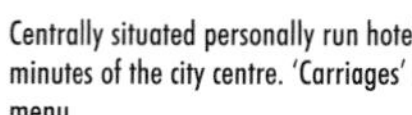

Centrally situated personally run hotel, recently refurbished and within minutes of the city centre. 'Carriages' Brasserie and Bar with A la carte menu.

24 Single	All En Suite	B&B per person	Open Jan-Dec excl
5 Twin		£35.00-£70.00 Single	Xmas/New Year
31 Double		£25.00-£40.00 Dbl/Twn	B&B + Eve.Meal
5 Family			£40.00-£55.00

TV 📞 🛏 P ☕ 🖐 ✕ 🍽 📮 🎱 🏆

⊞ W V

All properties graded by VisitScotland, formerly known as the Scottish Tourist Board. | Key to symbols is on back flap.

Aberdeen		Map Ref: 4G10		

★★

CAMPUS
ACCOMMODATION

Craibstone Estate
Scottish Agricultural College, Bucksburn, Aberdeen
AB21 9YA
Tel: 01224 711195 Fax: 01224 711298
Web: www.craibstone.com

Halls of Residence, set in extensive country park on outskirts of
Aberdeen, with easy access to all amenities.

79 Single
20 Twin

En Suite facs

B&B per person
from £20.00 Single
from £50.00 Twin

Open 21 Mar-21
Apr/July-Sept

★★★

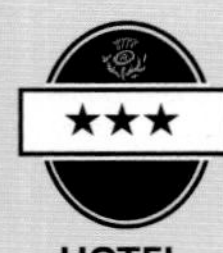

HOTEL

&

The Craighaar Hotel
Waterton Road, Bucksburn, Aberdeen, AB21 9HS
Tel: 01224 712275 Fax: 01224 716362
E-mail: info@craighaar.co.uk
Web: www.craighaarhotel.com

A charming hotel nestling in pleasant surroundings only 5 minutes from
the airport and 15 minutes from the city centre. All 55 bedrooms are well
appointed with satellite TV and trouser press. The restaurant is renowned
for quality cuisine and the hotel atmosphere is informal and relaxed. A
courtesy bus to the airport is available by arrangement.

3 Single
8 Twin
44 Double
2 Family

All En Suite

B&B per person
from £79.00 Single
from £44.50 Dbl/Twn

Open Jan-Dec excl
Xmas/New Year
B&B + Eve.Meal
from £57.00

★★★

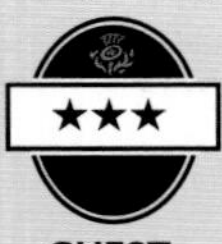

GUEST
HOUSE

Dunrovin Guest House
168 Bon-Accord Street, Aberdeen, AB11 6TX
Tel: 01224 586081 Fax: 01224 586081
E-mail: dellanzo@hotmail.com
Web: www.dunrovin.freeservers.com

Family run Victorian guest house situated in quiet tree-lined street midway between town centre and park on the river. A selection of
cosmopolitan restaurants within walking distance.

3 Single
3 Twin
1 Double
1 Family

2 En Suite fac
2 Pub Show Rms

B&B per person
from £20.00 Single
from £17.50 Dbl/Twn

Open Jan-Dec excl
Xmas/New Year

★

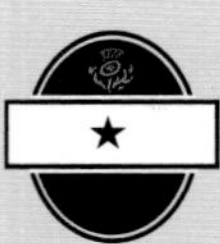

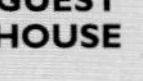

GUEST
HOUSE

Four Bees Guest House
356 Holburn Street, Aberdeen, AB10 7GX
Tel: 01224 585110

Traditional granite house with long garden, set back from the road.
Convenient for city centre and all amenities. On main bus routes.

1 Single
2 Twin
1 Double
2 Family

1 En Suite fac
3 Pub Bath/Show

B&B per person
from £15.00 Single
from £15.00 Dbl/Twn

Open Jan-Dec

★★★

GUEST
HOUSE

Furain Guest House
92 North Deeside Road, Peterculter, Aberdeen,
AB14 0QN
Tel: 01224 732189 Fax: 01224 739070
E-mail: furain@btinternet.com

Late Victorian house built of red granite. Family run. Convenient for
town, Royal Deeside and the Castle Trail. Private car parking. Dinner
available on Wednesday, Friday and Saturday.

1 Single
3 Twin
2 Double
2 Family

All En Suite

B&B per person
from £30.00 Single
from £21.00 Dbl/Twn
Room only per person
from £29.00

Open Jan-Dec excl
Xmas/New Year
B&B + Eve.Meal
from £36.00

Important: Prices stated are estimates and may be subject to amendments

Aberdeen

Map Ref: 4G10

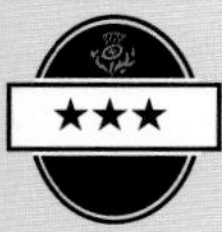

HOTEL ★★★

Jarvis Aberdeen
448 Great Western Road, Aberdeen, AB10 2NP
Tel: 01224 318724 Fax: 01224 312716
E-mail: sales.jaberdeen@jarvis.co.uk
Web: www.jarvis.co.uk

Modern hotel close to town centre. Informal atmosphere. A la carte menu, carvery and bar meals. Ample car parking. Function suites.

13 Single	All En Suite
9 twin	
31 Double	

B&B per person
from £45.00 Single
from £25.00 Dbl/Twn

Open Jan-Dec
B&B + Eve.Meal
from £35.00

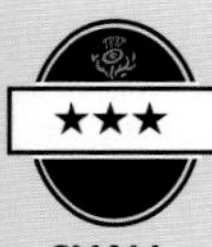

SMALL HOTEL ★★★

Mannofield Hotel
447 Great Western Road, Aberdeen, AB10 6NL
Tel: 01224 315888 Fax: 01224 208971
E-mail: mannofieldhotel@btconnect.com
Web: www.procona.co.uk

The Mannofield Hotel was built around 1880, in the traditional granite style, it is situated in Aberdeen's West End. Offering visitors the best of both worlds. Aberdeen's Airport and Exhibition Centre is only a 15 minute drive, whilst the city's excellent shopping, theatres and our universities are also just minutes away. On the main route to Royal Deeside, Castles, Whisky Trail and glorious scenery are also to be enjoyed.

2 Single	All En Suite
1 Twin	
4 Double	
2 Family	

B&B per person
£30.00-£49.00 Single
£54.00-£65.00 Dbl/Twn
Room only £25.00-£44.00

Open Jan-Dec excl Xmas/New Year
B&B + Eve.Meal from £64.00

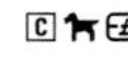

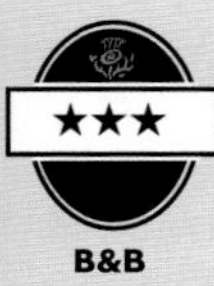

B&B ★★★

Manorville
252 Great Western Road, Aberdeen, AB10 6PJ
Tel/Fax: 01224 594190
E-mail: manorvilleabz@aol.com

Granite dwelling house in close proximity to town centre. On main bus route to Deeside. All rooms ensuite.

1 Twin	All En Suite
1 Double	
1 Family	

B&B per person
from £25.00 Single
from £20.00 Dbl/Twn

Open Jan-Dec excl Xmas/New Year

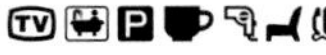

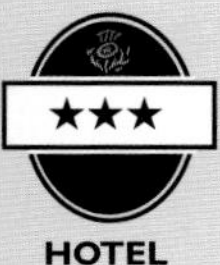

HOTEL ★★★

Northern Hotel
1 Great Northern Road, Aberdeen, AB24 3PS
Tel: 01224 483342 Fax: 01224 276103
E-mail: northern@bestwestern.co.uk

Category A listed Art Deco style building unique in the North East. 5 minutes to city centre and only 10 minutes from airport.

4 Single	All En Suite
11 Twin	
14 Double	
3 Family	

B&B per person
from £30.00 Single
from £40.00 Dbl/Twn

Open Jan-Dec excl Xmas/New Year

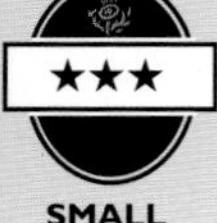

SMALL HOTEL ★★★

Old Mill Inn
South Deeside Road, Maryculter, Aberdeenshire, AB12 5FX
Tel: 01224 733212 Fax: 01224 732884
E-mail: info@oldmillinn.co.uk
Web: www.oldmillinn.co.uk

A friendly and informal family run country inn under the personal attention of the owners Mr Victor Sang and Mr Michael French. Conveniently located only 5 miles from Aberdeen on the edge of the River Dee and well-known for its wholesome dishes using fresh local produce.

1 Single	All En Suite
2 Twin	
3 Double	
1 Family	

B&B per person
from £45.00 Single
from £27.50 Dbl/Twn

Open Jan-Dec excl New Year

All properties graded by VisitScotland, formerly known as the Scottish Tourist Board.   *Key to symbols is on back flap.*

Aberdeen   **Map Ref: 4G10**

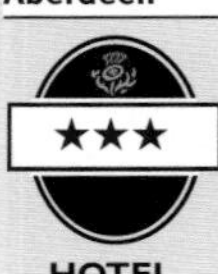

HOTEL

The Palm Court Hotel
81 Seafield Road, Aberdeen, AB15 8YU
Tel: 01224 310351 Fax: 01224 312707
E-mail: info@palmcourt.co.uk

Popular hotel with themed bar and restaurant situated in quiet
residential area in West End of city. Convenient for city bypass, airport 5
miles (8kms).

3 Single	All En Suite	B&B per person	Open Jan-Dec excl
1 Twin		from £30.00 Single	Xmas/New Year
19 Double		from £20.00 Dbl/Twn	B&B + Eve.Meal
1 Family			from £37.50

HOTEL

The Queen's Hotel
51-53 Queen's Road, Aberdeen, AB15 4YP
Tel: 01224 209999 Fax: 01224 209009
E-mail: thequeens@vagabond-hotels.com
Web: www.the-queens-hotel.com

Occupying an enviable location in the heart of the West End of Aberdeen,
this family run city centre hotel offers modern comforts in the traditional
style. All bedrooms have ensuite bath and shower and there is ample
parking. A range of function suites and conference facilities.

6 Single	All En Suite	B&B per person	Open Jan-Dec excl
5 Twin		from £40.00 Single	Xmas/New Year
14 Double		from £25.00 Dbl/Twn	B&B + Eve.Meal from
2 Family			£45.00

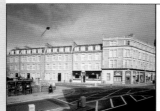

Skene House Suites, Aberdeen
96 Rosemount Viaduct, Aberdeen, AB25 1NX
Tel: 01224 645971 Fax: 01224 626866
e.mail: reservations@skene-house.co.uk Web: www.skene-house.co.uk

Skene House Rosemount, Skene House Holburn and Skene House Whitehall are
located in the centre of Aberdeen and provide our clients with "much more than
just a room" as each suite has 1-3 bedrooms, lounge, kitchen and bathroom(s).
Full Scottish breakfast is available at Skene House Holburn and Whitehall, and
continental breakfast is provided at Skene House Rosemount. Services include
daily maid service, free car parking and a partner restaurant scheme.

**SERVICED
APARTMENTS**

Skene House Rosemount
96 Rosemount Viaduct, Aberdeen, AB25 1NX
Tel: 01224 645971 Fax: 01224 626866
E-mail: rosemount@skene-house.co.uk
Web: www.skene-house.co.uk

A 'home away from home' located in the heart of Aberdeen, Skene
House provides a range of 1 to 3 bedrooms. Suites individually furnished
and decorated offering comfort and space with independence. Daily maid
service and off street parking. Shops and restaurants nearby.

61 Suites	All En Suite	Rates on application	Open all year

**SERVICED
APARTMENTS**

Skene House Holburn
6 Union Grove, Aberdeen, AB10 6SY
Tel: 01224 580000 Fax: 01224 585193
E-mail: holburn@skene-house.co.uk
Web: www.skene-house.co.uk

A 'home away from home' located in the heart of Aberdeen, Skene
House provides a range of 1 - 3 bedroom suites individually furnished
and decorated offering comfort and space with independance. Daily maid
service, off street parking, shops and restaurants nearby.

39 Suites	All En Suite	Rates on application	Open all year

Important: Prices stated are estimates and may be subject to amendments

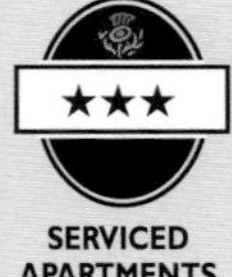

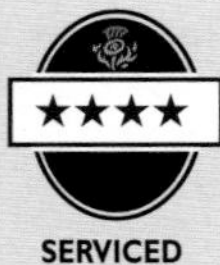

Aberdeen   Map Ref: 4G10

★★★★

SERVICED APARTMENTS

Skene House Whitehall
2 Whitehall Place, Aberdeen, Aberdeenshire, AB25 2NX
Tel: 01224 646600 Fax: 01224 218208
E-mail: whitehall@skene-house.co.uk
Web: www.skene-house.co.uk

A 'home away from home' located in the heart of Aberdeen, Skene House provides a range of 1 - 3 bedroom suites individually furnished and decorated offering comfort and space with independence. Daily maid service, off-street parking, shops and restaurants nearby.

29 Suites   All En Suite   Rates on application   Open all year

---

★★★

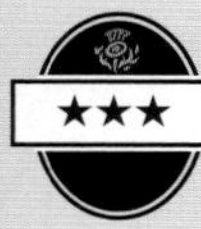

HOTEL

♿

Speedbird Inn
Argyll Road, Dyce, Aberdeen, AB21 0AF
Tel: 01224 772883 Fax: 01224 772560
E-mail: reception@speedbirdinns.co.uk
Web: www.speedbirdinns.co.uk

Modern comfortably furnished airport hotel offering facilities expected by todays traveller. Free seven channel TV in all rooms. Courtesy transport for surrounding area and airport terminals.

46 Twin   All En Suite   B&B per person   Open Jan-Dec
45 Double   £39.50-£50.45 Single
8 Family   £23.00-£27.70 Dbl/Twn

★★★

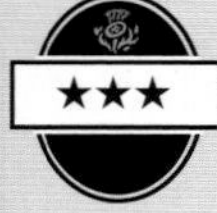

HOTEL

Westhill Hotel
Westhill, Aberdeenshire, AB32 6TT
Tel: 01224 740388 Fax: 01224 744354
E-mail: info@westhillhotel.co.uk
Web: www.westhillhotel.co.uk

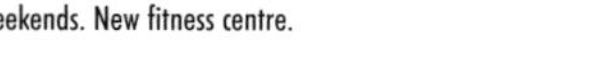

Modern style hotel in suburbs of Aberdeen, 6 miles (11kms) from city centre. Banqueting and conference facilities. Live entertainment at weekends. New fitness centre.

7 Single   All En Suite   B&B per person   Open Jan-Dec
22 Twin   from £35.00 Single   B&B + Eve.Meal
21 Double   from £25.00 Dbl/Twn   from £37.50
4 Family   Room only per person
                          from £30.00

★★★

HOTEL

The White Horse Inn
Old Road, Balmedie, Aberdeenshire, AB23 8XR
Tel/Fax: 01358 742404
E-mail: bookings@whitehorseinn.co.uk
Web: www.whitehorseinn.co.uk

Modern hotel, 7 miles (10kms) north of Aberdeen on main A90 Aberdeen - Ellon road. Nearby sandy beach and local golf courses. Function suite for 120. Golf packages can be arranged. Large car park adjacent to bedrooms.

17 Double   All En Suite   B&B per person   Open Jan-Dec
3 Family   from £32.00 Single
                           from £21.00 Double

Archiestown, Morayshire   Map Ref: 4D8

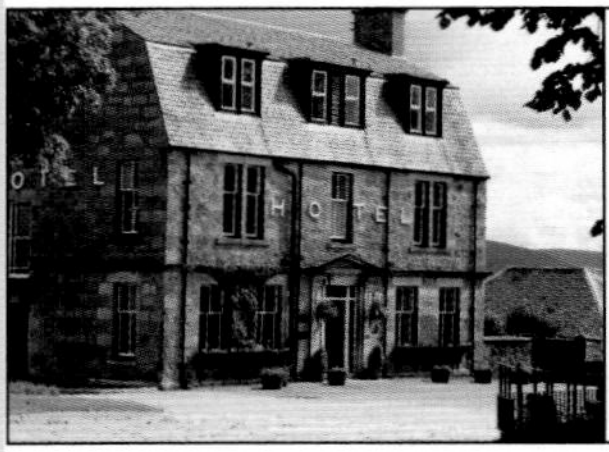

ARCHIESTOWN HOTEL
ARCHIESTOWN, BY ABERLOUR, MORAY AB38 7QL
TEL: 01340 810218 FAX: 01340 810239
WEB: www.archiestownhotel.co.uk

Attractive village hotel in charming square with pretty garden in the heart of Speyside. Golf, the Whisky Trail and many other attractions close by. One hour Inverness/Aberdeen. Personally run with friendly and attentive service, comfortable en-suite accommodation and award winning cooking in the bistro. Spring and autumn breaks available.

★★★★

**SMALL
HOTEL**

Archiestown Hotel
The Square, Archiestown, Morayshire, AB38 7QL
Tel: 01340 810218 Fax: 01340 810239
Web: www.archiestownhotel.co.uk

Recently upgraded village hotel, specialising in local seafood served in Bistro. 6 miles from Aberlour. Non residents welcome.

| 8 Twin | All En Suite | B&B per person | Open Feb-Dec excl. |
| 3 Single | | from £37.00 | Xmas and Boxing Day |

Ballater, Aberdeenshire   Map Ref: 4E11

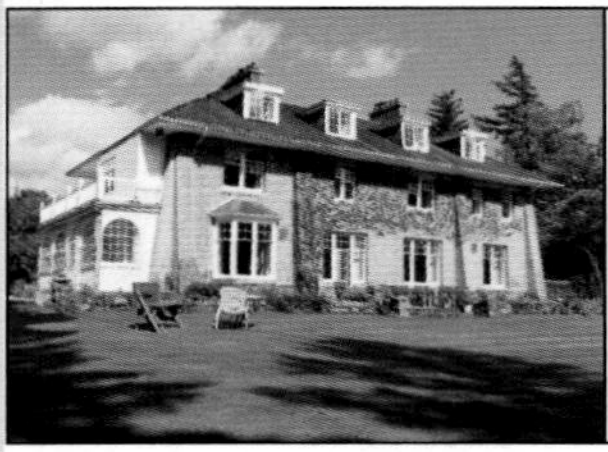

Balgonie Country House
Braemar Place, Ballater AB35 5NQ
Telephone: 013397 55482   Fax: 013397 55482
e.mail: balgoniech@aol.com Web: www.royaldeesidehotels.com

This charming Edwardian country house is set in three acres of tranquil gardens, overlooking Ballater Golf Course towards the hills beyond. Our attentive service to each guest ensures a relaxing and enjoyable stay. An idyllic base from which to explore an area of outstanding beauty.

★★★★

HOTEL

Balgonie Country House Hotel
Braemar Place, Ballater, Aberdeenshire, AB35 5NQ
Tel/Fax: 013397 55482
E-mail: balgoniech@aol.com
Web: www.royaldeesidehotels.com

In heart of Royal Deeside, secluded Edwardian country house set in 4 acres overlooking golf course. Fine Scottish cuisine and attentive service.

1 Single	All En Suite	B&B per person	Open Feb-Dec
3 Twin		from £69.50 Single	B&B + Eve.Meal
6 Double		from £59.50 Dbl/Twn	from £90.00

★★★★

HOTEL

Darroch Learg Hotel
Braemar Road, Ballater, Aberdeenshire, AB35 5UX
Tel: 013397 55443 Fax: 013397 55252
E-mail: nigel@darrochlearg.co.uk
Web: www.darrochlearg.co.uk

Country house charm and sophisticated food yet only minutes from picturesque Ballater. Stunning views south across Royal Deeside from wooded grounds. The restaurant is also popular with non residents.

1 Single	All En Suite	B&B per person	Open Feb-Dec excl
17		from £55.00 Single	Xmas
Dbl/Twn		from £110.00 Dbl/Twn	B&B + Eve.Meal
			from £72.55

Important: Prices stated are estimates and may be subject to amendments

Ballater, Aberdeenshire — Map Ref: 4E11

SMALL HOTEL

Deeside Hotel
Braemar Road, Ballater, Aberdeenshire, AB35 5RQ
Tel: 013397 55420 Fax: 013397 55357
E-mail: deesidehotel@btconnect.com
Web: www.deesidehotel.co.uk

4 Twin	All En Suite	B&B per person	Open Feb-Dec
4 Double		from £28.00 Single	B&B + Eve.Meal
1 Family		from £23.00 Dbl/Twn	from £39.00

Comfortable family hotel in a quiet location serving good freshly prepared food in an informal atmosphere. Our menu changes daily to reflect the availability of fresh local produce. Real Ale and interesting malt whiskies are available in our cosy bar. Two ground floor bedroooms, large garden and conservatory. Ample off road parking.

HOTEL

Glen Lui Hotel
Invercauld Road, Ballater, Royal Deeside, AB35 5RP
Tel: 013397 55402 Fax: 013397 55545
E-mail: infos@glen-lui-hotel.co.uk
Web: www.glen-lui-hotel.co.uk

2 Single	All En Suite	B&B per person	Open Jan-Dec
10 Twin		from £34.00 Single	B&B + Eve.Meal
5 Double		from £29.00 Dbl/Twn	from £45.00
2 Family			

A small friendly Country House Hotel situated in a quiet corner of this picturesque Highland village with views over the golf course to the dark mountains beyond. Separate pine terrace accommodation available in the garden grounds, particularly suited for the more independent traveller. A wide range of outdoor activities available in this spectacular

by Ballater, Aberdeenshire — Map Ref: 4E11

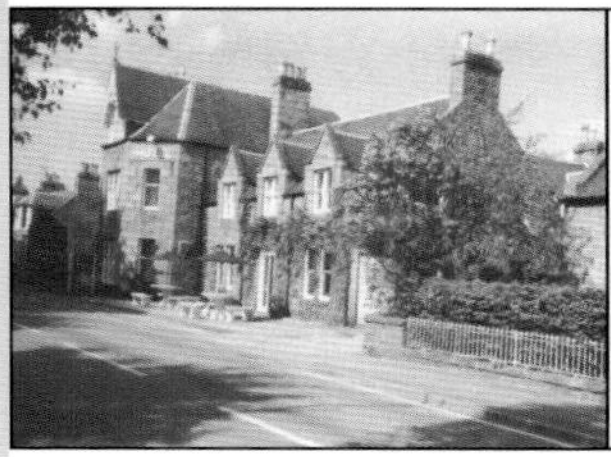

Loch Kinord Hotel

Ballater Road, Dinnet, Royal Deeside, Aberdeenshire AB34 5JY
Tel: 013398 85229   Fax: 013398 87007
e.mail: info@lochkinord.com   Web: www.lochkinord.com
Set in the heart of Royal Deeside, this Victorian Hotel offers an ideal location to explore the many tourist and sporting activities. Whisky distilleries, Highland Games, castles, golf, fishing, shooting, skiing, walking etc. Afterwards enjoy good food and a fine selection of malt whisky in front of real log fires.

HOTEL

Loch Kinord Hotel
Ballater Road, Dinnet, Aberdeenshire, AB34 5JY
Tel: 013398 85229 Fax: 013398 87007
E-mail: info@lochkinord.com
Web: www.lochkinord.com

1 Single	9 En Suite fac	B&B per person	Open Jan-Dec
1 Twin	2 Pub Bath/Show	£30.00-£65.00 Single	B&B + Eve.Meal
6 Double		£20.00-£40.00 Dbl/Twn	£35.00-£80.00
3 Family			

Under the enthusiastic new ownership of Jenny and Andrew Cox the hotel has undergone some refurbishment. Situated in the centre of this small village it makes a great base for exploring Royal Deeside, skiing, walking, and playing golf. Non-residents very welcome and popular in the area for excellent food.

Banchory, Aberdeenshire — Map Ref: 4F11

B&B

Primrose Hill Guest House
North Deeside Road, Silverbank, Banchory, Kincardineshire
AB31 5PY
Tel: 01330 823007

1 Single	B&B per person	Open Jan-Dec
1 Twin	from £22.00 Single	
2 Double	from £22.00 Dbl/Twn	
	Room only per person	
	from £18.00	

A traditional granite cottage built from local stone. Set back from the road with a good sized garden. Well presented bedrooms and a good supply of ensuite bathrooms. On outskirts of this Deeside town with a wide range of sporting activities in the area. Evening meal on request.

All properties graded by VisitScotland, formerly known as the Scottish Tourist Board. | *Key to symbols is on back flap.*

Banchory, Aberdeenshire | **Map Ref: 4F11**

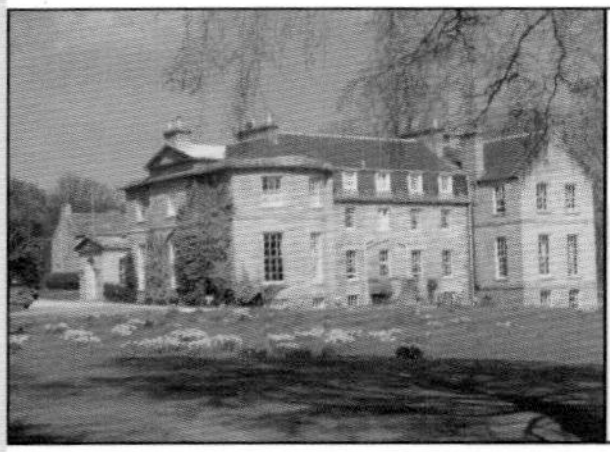

**★★★★
HOTEL**

Raemoir House Hotel
Raemoir, Banchory, Aberdeen AB31 4ED
Tel: 01330 824884 Fax: 01330 822171
e.mail: raemoirhse@aol.com Web: www.raemoir.com

Beautiful and timeless, a Scottish Baronial Manor set in 3,500 acres of parkland and forest in Royal Deeside. Filled with a fine collection of antiques. Raemoir is famed and has prestigious awards for its hospitality and food. A host of activities available - including romantic castles and whisky trails. AA ◎◎

**★★★★
HOTEL**

Raemoir House Hotel
Raemoir, Banchory, Kincardineshire, AB31 4ED
Tel: 01330 824884 Fax: 01330 822171
E-mail: raemoirhse@aol.com
Web: www.raemoir.com

Dating from 16c, country house on a 3,500 acre estate. We offer salmon fishing, tennis, shooting and 9 hole mini-golf. Self catering apartments available.

5 Single	All En Suite	B&B per person	Open All Year
7 Twin		from £50.00 Single	B&B + Eve.Meal
8 Double		from £45.00 Dbl/Twn	from £65.00

Banff | **Map Ref: 4F7**

**★★★
HOTEL**

Banff Springs Hotel
Golden Knowes Road, Banff, AB45 2JE
Tel: 01261 812881 Fax: 01261 815546
Web: www.banffspringshotel.co.uk

A warm welcome awaits you in this family run hotel overlooking the golden sands of the Moray Firth, a beautiful and unexploited part of Scotland. Thirty one en-suite bedrooms. Restaurant and Brasserie, with the prestigious 'Taste of Scotland' award. Ideal venue for golfing, fishing, art galleries, aquarium, antiques, equestrian centres, castles and whisky trails.

5 Single	All En Suite	B&B per person	Open Jan-Dec excl Xmas
20 Twin		from £35.00 Single	B&B + Eve.Meal from
6 Double		from £50.50 Dbl/Twn	£46.75

**★★
GUEST
HOUSE**

Carmelite House Hotel
Low Street, Banff, AB45 1AY
Tel/Fax: 01261 812152
E-mail: CarmeliteHoHo@aol.com
Web: www.northeastscotlandhotels.com

Family run Georgian town house in central location. Convenient for golf and all amenities. Evening meals available. Cosy residents bar. Private parking.

3 Single	3 En Suite fac	B&B per person	Open Jan-Dec
1 Twin	3 Pub Bath/Show	£22.00 Single	B&B + Eve.Meal
1 Double	1 Priv.NOT ensuite	from £20.00-£25.00	from £27.50
4 Family		Dbl/Twn	

Braemar, Aberdeenshire | **Map Ref: 4D11**

**★★★★
GUEST
HOUSE**

Callater Lodge
9 Glenshee Road, Braemar, Aberdeenshire, AB35 5YQ
Tel: 013397 41275 Fax: 013397 41345
E-mail: maria4@hotel-braemar.co.uk
Web: www.hotel-braemar.co.uk

A warm welcome awaits you at this pleasant Victorian house in its own spacious grounds. Ideal centre for touring and walking. Village centre nearby. 8 miles to Balmoral Castle and Glenshee Ski Centre. All home cooking using fresh local produce. Evening meal by arrangement.

1 Single	All En Suite	B&B per person	Open Jan-Dec
3 Twin		from £24.00 Single	B&B + Eve.Meal
3 Double		from £24.00 Dbl/Twn	from £39.00

Important: Prices stated are estimates and may be subject to amendments

Braemar, Aberdeenshire — Map Ref: 4D11

★★★

B&B

Mayfield House
11 Chapel Brae, Braemar, Aberdeenshire, AB35 5YT
Tel: 013397 41238
E-mail: info@mayhouse.co.uk
Web: www.mayhouse.co.uk

1 Single	2 Pub Bath/Show
1 Family/Tw in	
2 Double	

B&B per person
£19.00-£20.00 Single
from £19.00 Dbl/Twn

Open Mar-Nov

Situated in a quiet, peaceful situation with views over the site of the Royal Highland gathering to the mountains beyond. A guest house since Victorian times the present owners continue the family tradition with highland hospitality and all modern comforts.

🅿 ☕ 🍽 ✕ 🛏 ♣

Ⓥ

★★★

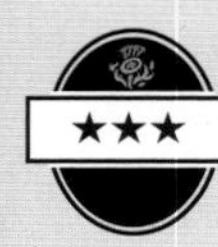

**GUEST
HOUSE**

Schiehallion House
10 Glenshee Road, Braemar, Aberdeenshire, AB35 5YQ
Tel: 013397 41679

1 Single	5 En Suite fac
3 Twin	1 Pub Bath/Show
3 Double	
2 Family	

B&B per person
from £20.00 Single
from £19.00 Dbl/Twn

Open Jan-Oct excl
New Year

Comfortable, tastefully decorated, Victorian house with attractive garden at gateway to Royal Deeside. Offering personal service and log fires. One ground floor annexe room. All nationalities welcome.

 🅿 ☕ ✕ 🛏 🍷 🛏 ▯

🐕 £

Buckie, Banffshire — Map Ref: 4E7

★★★

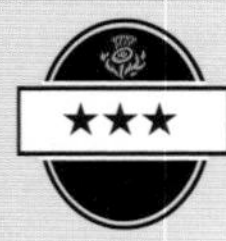

**SMALL
HOTEL**

Cluny Hotel
2 High Street, Buckie, Banffshire, AB56 1AQ
Tel/Fax: 01542 832922
E-mail: clunyhotel@tinyworld.co.uk

1 Single	
2 Twin	
2 Double	
1 Family	

B&B per person
from £26.00 Single
from £43.00 Dbl/Twn

Open Jan-Dec excl
Xmas/New Year
B&B + Eve.Meal from
£32.00

Victorian building recently refurbished with access from 1st floor. Conveniently situated in town centre. Food served all day.

📺 📞 🖥 ☕ 🍴 🍷

🐕 £ Ⓥ

All properties graded by VisitScotland, formerly known as the Scottish Tourist Board. | *Key to symbols is on back flap.*

Cullen, Banffshire   Map Ref: 4E7

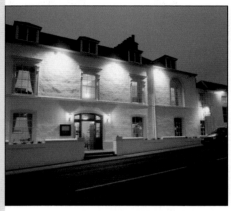

SEAFIELD HOTEL

19 SEAFIELD STREET,
CULLEN, BUCKIE, BANFFSHIRE AB56 4SG
TEL: 01542 840791   FAX: 01542 840736
E.MAIL: accom@theseafieldhotel.com
WEB: www.theseafieldhotel.com

The Seafield Hotel, owned by Alison and
Herbert Cox, is situated in the historic town of
Cullen. It provides excellent accommodation
and service for those requiring peace and
quiet. Enjoy a classic menu specialising in
local produce, and sample from a selection of
over 130 malt whiskies while relaxing in the
open fire lounge.

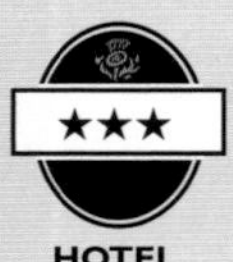

HOTEL

The Seafield Hotel
Seafield Street, Cullen, Banffshire, AB56 4SG
Tel: 01542 840791 Fax: 01542 840736
E-mail: accom@theseafieldhotel.com
Web: www.theseafieldhotel.com

A warm friendly welcome at this family run hotel in the centre of a small
town on the Moray coast. Ideal location for golfing, walking and
exploring the whisky trail. Midway between Inverness and Aberdeen.

4 Single	All En Suite	B&B per person	Open 1 Jan - 12 Dec
8 Twin		from £50.00 Single	B&B + Eve.Meal from
6 Double		from £35.00 Dbl/Twn	£55.00
2 Family		Room only from £30.00	

Dufftown, Banffshire   Map Ref: 4E9

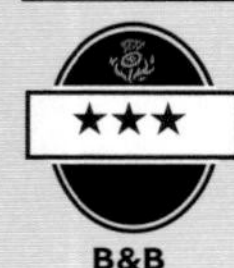

B&B

Gowan Brae Guest House
19 Church Street, Dufftown, Keith, Banffshire, Ab55 4AR
Tel/Fax: 01340 820461
E-mail: gowanbrae@breathemail.net
Web: www.gowanbrae-dufftown.co.uk

Family run bed & breakfast in small Speyside town. Ideal location for
touring the whisky trail, touring and walking.

1 Twin	All En Suite	B&B per person	Open Jan-Dec excl
2 Double		from £16.00 Dbl/Twn	Xmas/New Year
1 Family			B&B + Eve.Meal from
			£25.00

Elgin, Moray   Map Ref: 4D8

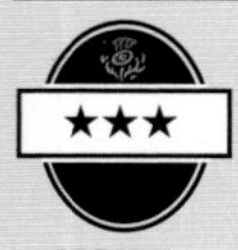

HOTEL

Laichmoray Hotel
Maisondieu Road, Elgin, Morayshire, IV30 1QR
Tel: 01343 540045 Fax: 01343 540055
E-mail: enquiries@laichmorayhotel.co.uk
Web: www.laichmorayhotel.co.uk

Family-run hotel with large car park, close to Railway Station and town
centre. Whisky Theme Bar and new conservatory/family room. Serving
quality lunch, high tea, supper and dinner. Conference & function
facilities also available.

12 Single	All En Suite	B&B per person	Open Jan-Dec excl
10 Twin		from £38.00 Single	Xmas/New Year
12 Double		from £30.00 Dbl/Twn	
4 Family			

Important: Prices stated are estimates and may be subject to amendments

Elgin, Moray   **Map Ref: 4D8**

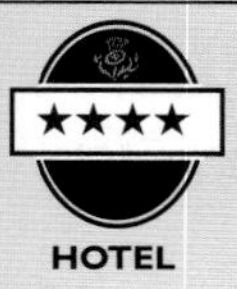

HOTEL

Mansefield House Hotel
Mayne Road, Elgin, Moray, IV30 1NY
Tel: 01343 540883 Fax: 01343 552491
E-mail: reception@mansefieldhousehotel.com
Web: www.mansefieldhousehotel.com

Completely refurbished former manse with a la carte restaurant conveniently situated near centre of Elgin. 4 poster rooms available. Ideal base for both business and leisure. Member of Taste of Scotland.

5 Single	All En Suite	B&B per person	Open Jan-Dec
4 Twin		£55.00-£70.00 Single	B&B + Eve.Meal
10 Double		£90.00-£110.00	from £68.00
2 Family		Dbl/Twn	

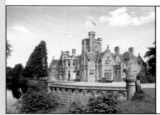

The Mansion House Hotel

The Haugh, Elgin, Moray IV30 1AW
Tel: 01343 548811 Fax: 01343 547916
e.mail: reception@mhelgin.co.uk

The charm of the past in a peaceful riverside setting, minutes from Elgin. Many bedrooms with four-poster beds. Country club facilities, indoor pool, spa, sauna, Turkish bath, gymnasium, snooker. Ideal base for Whisky, Castle and Golf Trails.

Weekends and weekly packages available from £60 B&B per person per night.

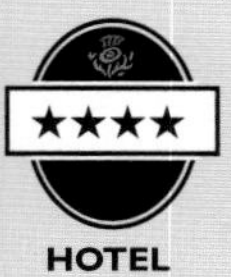

HOTEL

The Mansion House Hotel & Country Club
Stirrat's Ltd, The Haugh, Elgin, Moray, IV30 1AW
Tel: 01343 548811 Fax: 01343 547916
E-mail: reception@mhelgin.co.uk
Web: www.mansionhousehotel.co.uk

19c Scots baronial mansion with a castellated tower set in a quiet situation overlooking the River Lossie. Tastefully restored and decorated. Centrally situated for the castle and whisky trails and within easy reach of numerous excellent golf courses.

6 Twin	All En Suite	B&B per person	Open Jan-Dec
16 Double		£70.00-£95.00 Single	
		£60.00-£75.00 Dbl/Twn	

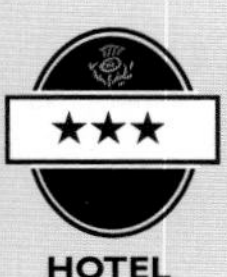

HOTEL

Sunninghill Hotel
Hay Street, Elgin, Moray, IV30 1NH
Tel: 01343 547799 Fax: 01343 547872
E-mail: wross94063@aol.com
Web: www.hotelselgin.co.uk

Victorian house, modern extension with annexe accommodation. Near centre of historic Cathedral town. Many golf courses. Sandy beaches 5 miles (8kms).

3 Single	All En Suite	B&B per person	Open Jan-Dec
12 Twin		from £38.00 Single	
1 Double		from £27.50 Dbl/Twn	
3 Family		Room only from £44.00	

★★★

GUEST HOUSE

West End Guest House
282 High Street, Elgin, Moray, IV30 1AG
Tel: 01343 549629
E-mail: westend.house@virgin.net

Traditional Victorian villa with garden, close to A96. 10 minute walk from city centre and all amenities.

3 Twin	5 En Suite fac	B&B per person	Open Jan-Dec
1 Double	1 Priv.NOT ensuite	from £18.50 Single	
2 Family		from £19.50 Dbl/Twn	

All properties graded by VisitScotland, formerly known as the Scottish Tourist Board. | **Key to symbols is on back flap.**

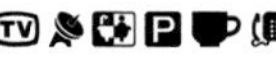

Garmouth, Moray — Map Ref: 4E7

★★

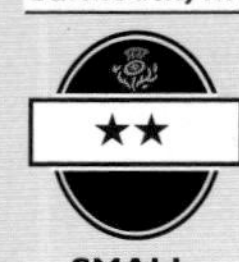

**SMALL
HOTEL**

The Garmouth Hotel

South Road, Garmouth, Fochabers, Moray, IV32 7LU
Tel: 01343 870226 Fax: 01343 870632

Family run hotel in listed village at mouth of River Spey. Ideal for
walking the Speyside Way, fishing, golfing and riding. 2 annexe
bedrooms.

1 Single	All En Suite	B&B per person	Open Jan-Dec excl
3 Twin		from £30.00 Single	Xmas/New Year
1 Double		from £22.50 Dbl/Twn	B&B + Eve.Meal
2 Family			from £32.00

TV 🖨 P 🍵 ⚒ 🍽 🍷

C 🐕 ♿ V

Glenlivet, Banffshire — Map Ref: 4D9

★★★★

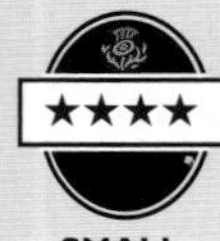

**SMALL
HOTEL**

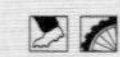

Minmore House Hotel

Glenlivet, Banffshire, AB37 9DB
Tel: 01807 590378 Fax: 01807 590472
E-mail: minmorehouse@ukonline.net
Web: www.fishinscotland.net

A warm welcome awaits you in this comfortable, family-run hotel,
situated amidst splendid scenery of Glenlivet, in the heart of whisky
country. Log fires, large garden, fine food and wine.

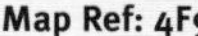

2 Single	9 En Suite fac	B&B per person	Open Mar-Dec
3 Twin		from £55.00 Single	B&B + Eve.Meal from
4 Double		from £55.00 Dbl/Twn	£82.50
1 Family			

✉ 📞 🖨 P 🍷 🚰 ⚒ 🍽 🎿 🏠 🍷

🐕 ♿ V 🐄

Huntly, Aberdeenshire — Map Ref: 4F9

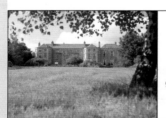

CASTLE HOTEL

Huntly, Aberdeenshire AB54 4SH
Telephone: 01466 792696 Fax: 01466 792641
e.mail: castlehot@enterprise.net Web: www.castlehotel.uk.com

17th-century former home of the Dukes of Gordon situated in its own
grounds above the River Deveron. Comfortable well-appointed ensuite
accommodation. Good Scottish food served in our dining room and
bar. An ideal base for touring, hillwalking, castle and whisky trails.
Golf courses abound in the area.

★★★

HOTEL

Castle Hotel

Huntly, Aberdeenshire, AB54 4SH
Tel: 01466 792696 Fax: 01466 792641
E-mail: castlehot@enterprise.net
Web: www.castlehotel.uk.com

Formerly the ancient family home of the Gordons. Standing in own
grounds overlooking Huntly. Open fires in dining room and lounge. Local
fishing.

12 Twin	All En Suite	B&B per person	Open Jan-Dec
5 Double		from £45.00 Single	B&B + Eve.Meal from
3 Family		from £37.50 Dbl/Twn	£45.00

TV 📞 🖨 P 🍷 🚰 ⚒ 🍽 🏠 🍷

C 🐕 ♿ V

★★

**SMALL
HOTEL**

Gordon Arms Hotel

The Square, Huntly, Aberdeenshire, AB54 8AF
Tel: 01466 792288 Fax: 01466 794556
E-mail: reception@gordonarms.demon.co.uk
Web: www.gordonarms.demon.co.uk

19th Century former coaching inn, situated in the central square of the
market town of Huntly. Lounge bar and separate 'Cheers Bar'. Plenty to
see and do in the area, including visiting castles, Royal Deeside,
exploring the coastline and fishing villages, and much more.

1 Single	All En Suite	B&B per person	Open Jan-Dec
2 Twin		from £35.00 Single	
7 Double		from £45.00 Dbl/Twn	
3 Family		from £30.00 room only	

TV 📞 🖨 🍵 🍷

C 🐕 ♿ V

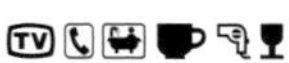

Important: Prices stated are estimates and may be subject to amendments

Inverurie, Aberdeenshire

Map Ref: 4G9

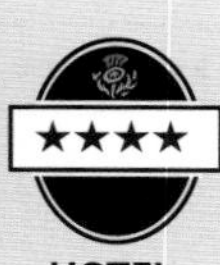

★★
SMALL HOTEL

Kintore Arms Hotel
83 High Street, Inverurie, AB51 3QJ
Tel: 01467 621367 Fax: 01467 625620
E-mail: kintore@fsbdial.co.uk
Web: www.kintorearmshotel.co.uk

8 Single	16 En Suite fac	B&B per person	Open Jan-Dec
4 Twin		from £45.00 Single	B&B + Eve.Meal from
6 Double		from £35.00 Dbl/Twn	£55.00
2 Family			

Listed building dating from 1855, situated in the town of Inverurie, 18 miles from Aberdeen and 13 miles from Aberdeen airport. Good base for the business or leisure traveller; much to see and do in the area - golf, fishing, castles and historic sites and more.

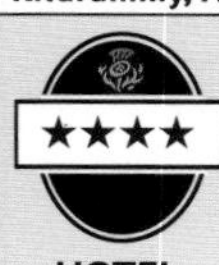

★★★★
HOTEL

Strathburn Hotel
Burghmuir Drive, Inverurie, Aberdeenshire, AB51 4GY
Tel: 01467 624422 Fax: 01467 625133
E-mail: strathburn@btconnect.com
Web: www.strathburn-hotel.co.uk

6 Single	All En Suite	B&B per person	Open Jan-Dec excl
4 Twin		from £55.00 Single	Xmas/New Year
14 Double		from £45.00 Dbl/Twn	B&B + Eve.Meal
1 Family			from £65.00

Modern hotel and restaurant with friendly atmosphere, overlooking Strathburn Park in Inverurie. Personally run.

Kildrummy, Aberdeenshire

Map Ref: 4E10

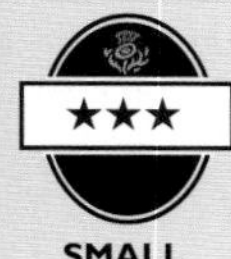

★★★★
HOTEL

Kildrummy Castle Hotel
Kildrummy, Alford, Aberdeenshire, AB33 8RA
Tel: 019755 71288 Fax: 019755 71345
E-mail: bookings@kildrummycastlehotel.co.uk
Web: www.kildrummycastlehotel.co.uk

1 Single	All En Suite	B&B per person	Open Feb-Dec
5 Twin		from £80.00 Single	B&B + Eve.Meal
8 Double		from £67.50 Dbl/Twn	from £69.00
2 Family			

Traditional Scottish mansion house set amidst acres of gardens and woodland overlooking the original 13th century castle ruins. Tastefully furnished and decorated retaining original features. A la carte restaurant using finest local ingredients.

Lossiemouth, Moray

Map Ref: 4D7

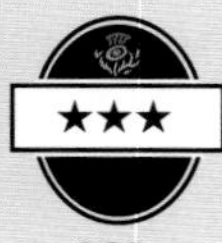

★★★
SMALL HOTEL

Laverock Bank Hotel
St Gerardines Road, Lossiemouth, Moray, IV31 6RA
Tel: 01343 812350 Fax: 01343 812255
E-mail: mail@laverockbankhotel.com
Web: www.laverockbankhotel.com

2 Single	8 En Suite facs	B&B per person	Open Jan-Dec
3 Twin	2 Priv.NOT ensuite	from £30.00 Single	B&B + Eve.Meal from
4 Double		from £25.00 Dbl/Twn	£35.00
1 Family			

Centrally situated a few yards from the famous Moray golf course and beautiful sandy beaches. Some rooms enjoy seaviews. Four poster beds with jaccuzi. Families are always very welcome. Our Seaview Restaurant offers a wide selection of meal and snack options and our popular well prepared a la carte menu is available each evening. Conference facilities for up to 100 people. Competitive prices on application.

★★★
B&B

Norland Bed & Breakfast
Norland, Stotfield Road, Lossiemouth, Moray, IV31 6QP
Tel: 01343 813570

2 Twin	1 En Suite fac	B&B per person	Open Jan-Dec excl
1 Double	1 Pub Bath/Show	from £18.00 Single	Xmas/New Year
		from £19.00 Dbl/Twn	

Victorian villa situated in spacious garden with panoramic views over the Moray Firth to Cromarty and Caithness; next to championship links course of Moray Golf Club. Private parking.

All properties graded by VisitScotland, formerly known as the Scottish Tourist Board.   **Key to symbols is on back flap.**

Newburgh, Aberdeenshire — Map Ref: 4H9

★★★

HOTEL

Udny Arms Hotel
Main Street, Newburgh, Aberdeenshire, AB41 6BL
Tel: 01358 789444 Fax: 01358 789012
E-mail: enquiry@udny.demon.co.uk
Web: www.udny.co.uk

5 Single	All En Suite	B&B per person	Open Jan-Dec
8 Twin		from £35.00 Single	B&B + Eve.Meal
12 Double		from £42.50 Dbl/Twn	from £60.00
1 Family			

Modernised Victorian hotel, featuring antique furniture, overlooking River Ythan Estuary. Overlooks local golf course and Forvie nature reserve. Home of the famous Sticky Toffee Pudding. Award winning restaurant. Visit us at our website www.udny.co.uk

Oldmeldrum, Aberdeenshire — Map Ref: 4G9

★★★★

B&B

Cromlet Hill Guest House
Cromlet Hill, South Road, Oldmeldrum, Aberdeenshire, AB51 0AB
Tel: 01651 872315 Fax: 01651 872164

1 Twin	All En Suite fac	B&B per person	Open Jan-Dec excl Xmas
1 Double		from £28.00 Single	
1 Family		from £22.00 Dbl/Twn	

Spacious, elegant, Listed Georgian mansion, in large secluded gardens within conservation area. Airport 20 minutes. On the castle trail and close to many well known National Trust properties. Including Fyvic Castle, Hodds and Pitmeddon Gardens.

★★★★

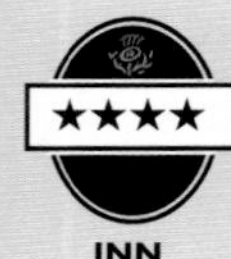

INN

The Redgarth
Kirk Brae, Oldmeldrum, AB51 0DJ
Tel: 01651 872353
E-mail: redgarth1@aol.com

1 Twin	All En Suite	B&B per person	Open Jan-Dec excl
2 Double	3 Pub Bath/Show	from £40.00 Single	Xmas/New Year
		from £25.00 Dbl/Twn	

Detached, granite-built house with large gardens & car park, with fine views towards Bennachie. Non-smoking bedrooms. Home-cooking, including vegetarian choice. Selection of ales (cask conditioned).

Peterhead, Aberdeenshire — Map Ref: 4H8

★★★

HOTEL

Palace Hotel
Prince Street, Peterhead, Aberdeenshire, AB42 1PL
Tel: 01779 474821 Fax: 01779 476119
E-mail: info@palacehotel.co.uk   Web: www.palacehotel.co.uk

3 Single	All En Suite	B&B per person	Open Jan-Dec
3 Twin	Suite avail	£60.00 Single	
62 Double		£25.00-£30.00 Dbl/Twn	
1 Family			

Friendly and welcoming privately owned hotel, centrally situated in Peterhead, but with ample private parking. Dining options include the Brasserie and the more informal Diner; choice of bars, with live music some nights. Excellent base for both business and leisure traveller. Much to see and do in the area, including golf, watersports, fishing, pony trekking, or exploring the fascinating coastline.

Portsoy, Banffshire — Map Ref: 4F7

★★

SMALL HOTEL

The Boyne Hotel
2 North High Street, Portsoy, Banffshire, AB45 2PA
Tel/Fax: 01261 842242
E-mail: enquiries@boynehotel.co.uk
Web: www.boynehotel.co.uk

4 Single	All En Suite	B&B per person	Open Jan-Dec
4 Twin		£20.00-£25.00 Single	B&B + Eve.Meal
4 Double		£20.00-£25.00 Dbl/Twn	£27.00-£50.00
		Room only per person	
		£15.00-£20.00	

Refurbished 18c building on Square in seaside town, close to harbour and sandy seaside. Home cooking. Under personal supervision.

Important: Prices stated are estimates and may be subject to amendments

| Stonehaven, Kincardineshire | | | Map Ref: 4G11 |

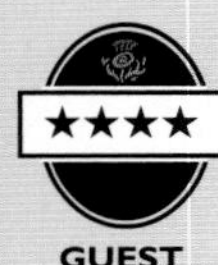

GUEST HOUSE
★★★

Alexander Guest House

36 Arduthie Road, Stonehaven, AB39 2DD
Tel: 01569 762265 Fax: 0870 1391045
E-mail: marion@alexanderguesthouse.com
Web: www.alexanderguesthouse.com

Family run guest house situated five minutes walk from town centre, beach, stonebuilt harbour, restaurant and shops. TV lounge, licence, and some ensuite rooms available. Non-smoking household. Scotland's Best member.

2 Single	5 En Suite fac	B&B per person	Open Jan-Dec
1 Twin	1 Pub Bath/Show	from £22.00 Single	
2 Double		from £24.00 Dbl/Twn	
2 Family			

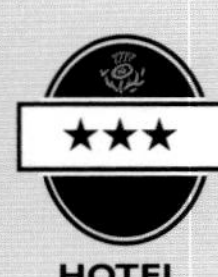

GUEST HOUSE
★★★★

Arduthie House

Ann Street, Stonehaven, Kincardineshire, AB39 2DA
Tel: 01569 762381 Fax: 01569 766366
E-mail: arduthie@talk21.com

Centrally located elegant detached Victorian house with attractive garden. Spacious guests lounge, sun lounge and 4 poster bedroom available. Evening meals by arrangement.

1 Single	5 En Suite fac	B&B per person	Open Jan-Dec excl
2 Twin	1 Priv.NOT ensuite	from £18.00 Single	Xmas/New Year
2 Double		from £24.00 Dbl/Twn	B&B + Eve.Meal from
1 Family			£36.00

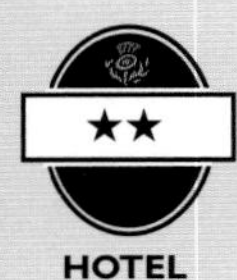

HOTEL
★★★

The Heugh Hotel

Westfield Road, Stonehaven, Kincardineshire, AB39 2EE
Tel: 01569 762379 Fax: 01569 766637
E-mail: kevin@heughhotel.com
Web: www.heughhotel.com

Granite baronial mansion, built at the turn of the century, with extensive original oak panelling; standing in its own grounds a short distance from the centre of Stonehaven. A family run hotel, with a friendly and relaxed atmosphere, providing an excellent base for exploring the east coast, Royal Deeside and beyond.

3 Single	All En Suite	B&B per person	Open Jan-Dec excl
2 Twin		from £45.00 Single	Xmas/New Year
1 Double		from £65.00 Dbl/Twn	

HOTEL
★★

Royal Hotel

44 Allardice Street, Stonehaven, B39 2BU
Tel: 01569 762979 Fax: 01569 763122
E-mail: royalhotelstonehaven@totalise.co.uk
Web: www.royalhotelstonehaven.co.uk

Situated at the centre of this small town yet on the beach front. All bedrooms are en-suite with some rooms having sea views. Popular for meals in the busy lounge bar.

1 Single	All En Suite facs	B&B per person	Open Jan-Dec
6 Twin		from £44.00 Single	
10 Double		from £29.00 Dbl/Twn	
1 Family			

All properties graded by VisitScotland, formerly known as the Scottish Tourist Board. | Key to symbols is on back flap. |

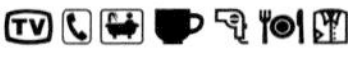

Stonehaven, Kincardineshire   Map Ref: 4G11

★★

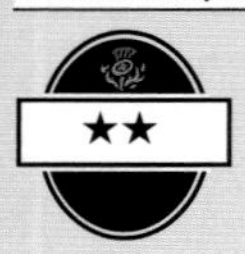

INN

Station Hotel
Arduthie Road, Stonehaven, Aberdeenshire, AB39 2NE
Tel: 01569 762277
Web: www.stationhotelstonehaven.co.uk

4 Single	5 En Suite fac	B&B per person	Open Jan-Dec excl
7 Twin	9 Pub Bath/Show	£24.00-£35.00 Single	Xmas/New Year
3 Double		£36.00-£46.00 Dbl/Twn	

Recently refurbished this well placed Station Hotel only 50 metres from the train offers some ensuite bedrooms and tea and coffee making facilities. A large lounge bar with separate public bar. Only a short distance to town centre, harbour and beach.

TV 🖾 🍵 ✕ ⛾ ⫯

C £ V

welcome to scotland

THE HIGHLANDS AND SKYE

Scenic variety is the keynote in this area – from the soaring craggy heights of Glencoe to the wide-skies and glittering lochans of the flow country of Caithness in the north. East-west contrasts are just as spectacular. This area takes in both the sunny, sandy shores of the inner Moray Firth around Nairn, with its coastal links golf courses, and the dazzling white beaches around Morar in the west, with the small isles filling the horizon.

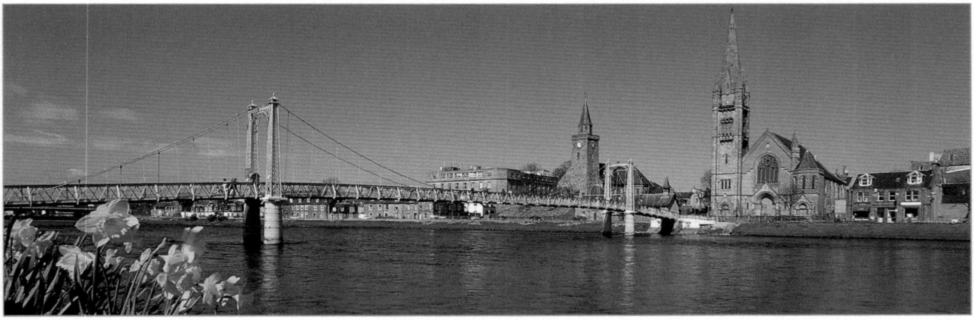

City of Inverness

WITH the Torridon mountains, Kintail and the peaks of Sutherland all adding to the spectacle, this area has more than simply scenic grandeur. There are substantial towns with everything for the visitor and the city of Inverness, sometimes called 'the capital of the Highlands' is a natural gateway to the northlands. At the western end of the Great Glen is Fort William, in the shadow of Britain's highest mountain, Ben Nevis. This town is another busy location, a natural route centre and meeting place with a whole range of facilities and attractions.

The eastern seaboard also has plenty of interesting towns: picturesque Cromarty, with the air of an old-time Scottish burgh, Dornoch with its cathedral and famous championship golf course.

Tain with Glenmorangie Distillery on its outskirts. Helmsdale with its evocation of Highland life in the Timespan Heritage Centre and Art Gallery. Further north, Wick and Thurso are major centres.

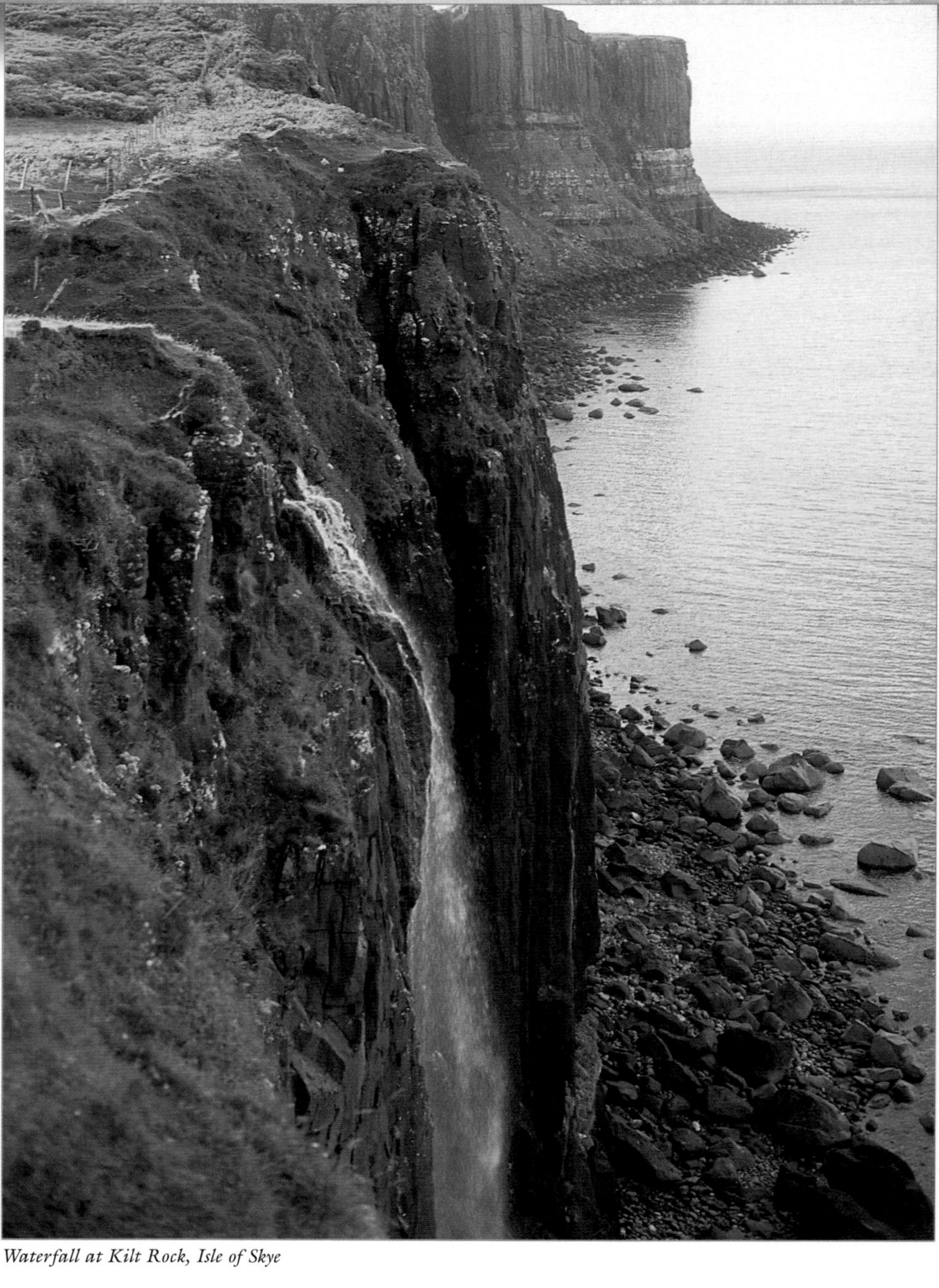

Waterfall at Kilt Rock, Isle of Skye

The Highlands and Skye

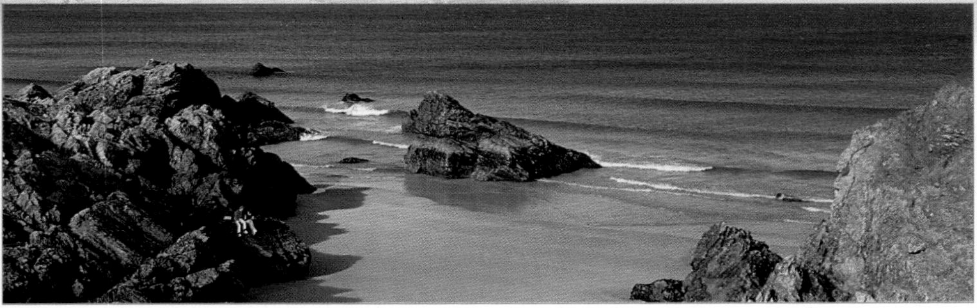

Sango Bay, North of Durness, Sutherland

The Isle of Skye is famed for the spectacle of the Cuillin Hills with their craggy ridges offering a serious climbing challenge. However, there are plenty of less active pursuits. Armadale Castle and the Museum of the Isles, Dunvegan Castle and the Aros Experience all tell the fascinating story of the island.

26-27 JANUARY
Sled Dog Rally
Aviemore,
Glenmore Forest Park
Sled dog racing, timed trials
taking place over two days
attracting many teams.
Contact:
John & Penny Evans
Tel: 01908 609796
Web:
www.siberianhuskyclub.com

16 FEBRUARY-
7 MARCH
Inverness Music Festival
Inverness, Various Venues
A series of events and
concerts taking place
throughout the city,
including music, dance,
piping, fiddling and
accordion.
Contact: Festival Office
Tel: 01463 716616

* 24 MAY-8 JUNE
Highland Festival
Highlands, Various Venues
Music, theatre, dance, visual
art and street events to
celebrate Highland culture.
Contact:
Highland Festival Office
Tel: 01463 711112
Web:
www.highlandfestival.org.uk

13-16 MAY
Highland Golf Classic
Highlands, Various Courses
The Highland golf classic
promises to become one of
the best new club golfer
events in Scotland.
Contact:
Scottish Golf Classics
Tel: 0800 027 1070 (UK)
or 01292 671500
Web:
www.scottishgolfclassics.com

13 JULY
Inverness
Highland Games
Inverness, Bught Park
The largest Highland games
in the Highlands.
Contact: Gerry Reynolds,
Highland Council
Tel: 01463 724 2626
Web: www.
invernesshighlandgames.com

22-27 JULY
Inverness Tattoo
Inverness,
Northern Meeting Park
Military and pipe bands,
display teams and Highland
dancing.
Contact: Bob Shanks
Tel: 01463 244395

7 AUGUST
Skye Highland Games
Portree, Games Field
Traditional Highland games.
Contact: Allan Stewart
Tel: 01478 612540
Web: www.highlandgames.
community.skye.co.uk

21-22 SEPTEMBER
Talisker Skye & Lochalsh
Food and Drink Festival
Skye & Lochalsh,
Various Venues
This food and drink festival
highlights the diversity and
quality of produce which
comes from the
world-renowned area.
Contact:
Skye & Lochalsh Enterprise
Tel: 01478 612841
Web:
www.foodfestival.skye.co.uk

12-20 OCTOBER
Highland
Archaeology Week
Highlands, Various Venues
Over 120 events throughout
the region with an
archaeology theme.
Contact: Archaeology Unit,
Highland Council
Tel: 01463 702502
Web:
www.higharch.demon.co.uk

** denotes provisional date,
please check before attending.*

AREA TOURIST BOARDS
THE HIGHLANDS AND SKYE

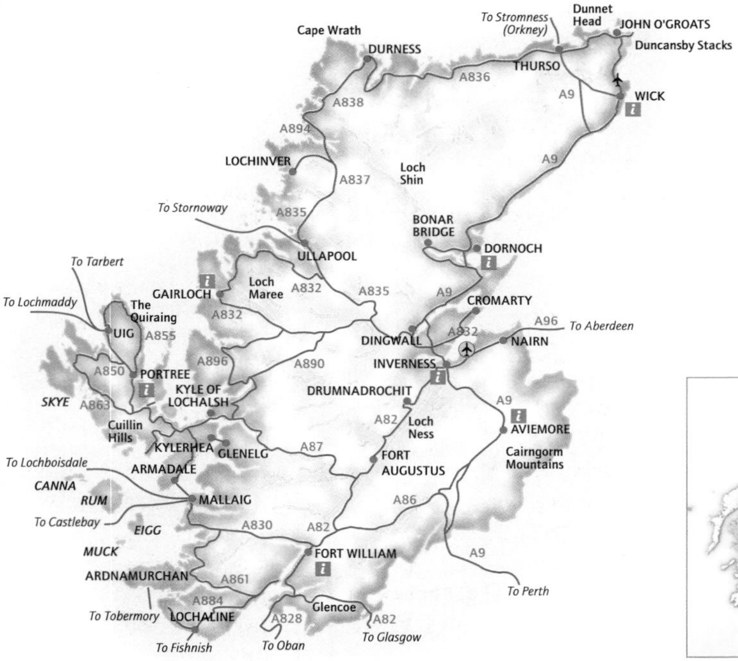

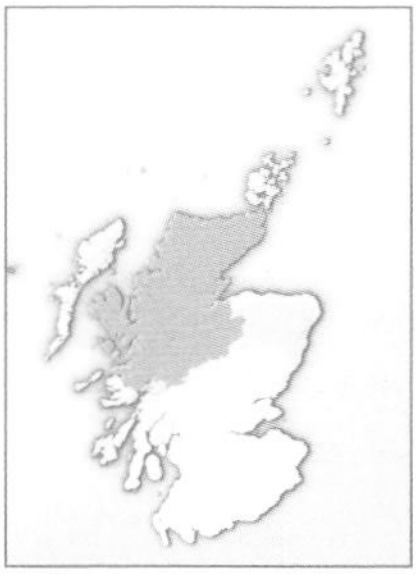

**THE HIGHLANDS OF
SCOTLAND TOURIST
BOARD**
Peffery House
Strathpeffer
Ross-shire
IV14 9HA

Tel: 08 70 5143070
Fax: 01997 421168
E-mail: info@host.co.uk
Web:
www.highlandfreedom.com

**THE HIGHLANDS OF
SCOTLAND TOURIST
BOARD**

Aviemore
Grampian Road
Inverness-shire
Tel: (01479) 810363
Jan-Dec

Ballachulish
Argyll
Tel: (01855) 811296
April-Oct

Bettyhill
Clachan
Sutherland
Tel: (01641) 521342
April-Sept

Broadford
Isle of Skye
Tel: (01471) 822361
April-Oct

Daviot Wood
A9 by Inverness
Tel: (01463) 772203
April-Oct

Dornoch
The Square
Sutherland
Tel: (01862) 810400
Jan-Dec

Dunvegan
2 Lochside
Isle of Skye
Tel: (01470) 521581
April-Sept

Durness
Sango
Sutherland
Tel: (01971) 511259
April-Oct

Fort Augustus
Car Park
Inverness-shire
Tel: (01320) 366367
April-Oct

Fort William
Cameron Square
Inverness-shire
Tel: (01397) 703781
Jan-Dec

Gairloch
Auchtercairn
Ross-shire
Tel: (01445) 712130
Jan-Dec

Glenshiel
Kintail
Kyle of Lochalsh
Ross-shire
Tel: (01599) 511264
April-Oct

Grantown on Spey
High Street
Morayshire
Tel: (01479) 872773
April-Oct

Helmsdale
Timespan
Sutherland
Tel: (01431) 821640
April-Sept

Inverness
Castle Wynd
Tel: (01463) 234353
Jan-Dec

John O'Groats
County Road
Caithness
Tel: (01955) 611373
April-Oct

Kilchoan
Pier Road
Argyll
Tel: (01972) 510222
Easter-Oct

Kingussie
King Street
Inverness-shire
Tel: (01540) 661297
May-Sept

Kyle of Lochalsh
Car Park
Inverness-shire
Tel: (01599) 534276
April-Oct

Lairg
Sutherland
Tel: (01549) 402160
April-Oct

Lochcarron
Main Street
Ross-shire
Tel: (01520) 722357
April-Oct

Lochinver
Main Street
Sutherland
Tel: (01571) 844330
April-Oct

Mallaig
Inverness-shire
Tel: (01687) 462170
April-Oct

Nairn
62 King Street
Nairnshire
Tel: (01667) 452753
April-Oct

North Kessock
Ross-shire
Tel: (01463) 731505
Jan-Dec

Portree
Bayfield House
Bayfield Road
Isle of Skye
Tel: (01478) 612137
Jan-Dec

Ralia
A9 North
by Newtonmore
Inverness-shire
Tel: (01540) 673253
April-Oct

Spean Bridge
Inverness-shire
Tel: (01397) 712576
April-Oct

Strathpeffer
The Square
Ross-shire
Tel: (01997) 421415
April-Nov

Strontian
Argyll
Tel: (01967) 402131
April-Oct

Thurso
Riverside
Tel: (01847) 892371
April-Oct

Uig
Ferry Terminal
Isle of Skye
Tel: (01470) 542404
April-Oct

Ullapool
Argyle Street
Ross-shire
Tel: (01854) 612135
April-Nov

Wick
Whitechapel Road
Caithness
Tel: (01955) 602596
Jan-Dec

Achiltibuie, Ross-shire — Map Ref: 3G6

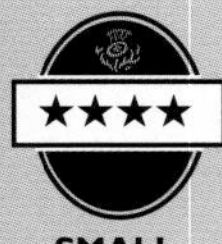

**SMALL
HOTEL**

★★★★

Summer Isles Hotel
Achiltibuie, nr Ullapool, Ross-shire, IV26 2YG
Tel: 01854 622282 Fax: 01854 622251
E-mail: summerisleshotel@aol.com
Web: www.summerisleshotel.co.uk

Personally run hotel, set amidst magnificent scenery. Annexe
accommodation available. Emphasis on cuisine using fresh local
ingredients and home baking.

3 Twin   All En Suite
10 Double

B&B per person
from £69.00 Single
from £52.00 Dbl/Twn

Open April-Oct excl
Xmas/New Year
B&B + Eve.Meal
from £92.00

Achnasheen, Ross-shire — Map Ref: 3H8

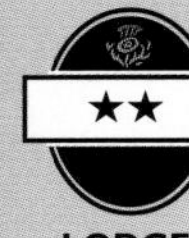

LODGE

★★

Ben Damph Lodges
Torridon, Achnasheen, IV22 2EY
Tel: 01445 791242 Fax: 01445 791296
E-mail: ben@lochtorridonhotel.com
Web: www.lochtorridonhotel.com

Comfortable lodge accommodation in the midst of Torridon Mountains,
restaurant and bar close by.

12 Family   All En Suite

B&B per person
from £30.00 Single
from £55.00 Dbl/Twn

Open Apr-Oct

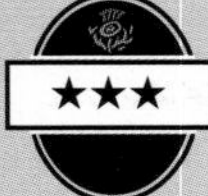

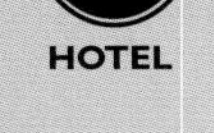

HOTEL

★★★

Ledgowan Lodge Hotel
Achnasheen, Ross-shire, IV22 2EJ
Tel: 01445 720252 Fax: 01445 720240
E-mail: info@ledgowanlodge.co.uk
Web: www.ledgowanlodge.co.uk

A personally run former hunting lodge, c1904, retaining much of its
original charm and character. All bedrooms have private facilities.

2 Single   All En Suite
4 Twin
3 Double
1 Family

B&B per person
from £34.00 Single
from £31.00 Dbl/Twn
Room only per person
from £25.00

Open Apr-Oct
B&B + Eve.Meal
from £49.00

Ardelve, by Dornie, Ross-shire — Map Ref: 3F9

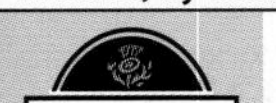

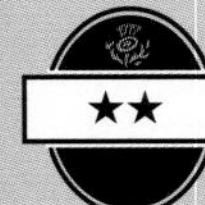

**GUEST
HOUSE**

★★

Caberfeidh House
Ardelve, by Kyle of Lochalsh, Ross-shire, IV40 8DY
Tel: 01599 555293
E-mail: info@caberfeidh.plus.com
Web: www.caberfeidh.plus.com

Substantial house, with open views to lochs and Eilean Donan Castle. Just
off main A87 on road to skye. Close to Five Sisters, Isle of Skye, Plockton
and Wester Ross Coastal Trail.

1 Single   3 En Suite fac
2 Twin   1 Pub Bath/Show
3 Double

B&B per person
from £18.00 Single
from £18.00 Dbl/Twn

Open Jan-Dec excl
Xmas/New Year

Arisaig, Inverness-shire — Map Ref: 3F11

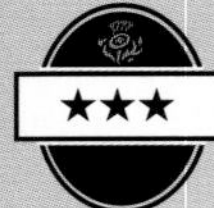

B&B

★★★

Kilmartin Guest House
Kinloid Farm, Arisaig, Inverness-shire, PH39 4NS
Tel: 01687 450366 Fax: 01687 450611

B & B on working farm (0.5 miles) 1 km from Arisaig attractively sited
on an elevated position commanding magnificent views overlooking the
sea and the islands of Skye, Rhum and Eigg. 5 mins car journey to
wonderful white sands. Evening meals available. Golf course 3 miles.

1 Twin   All En Suite
2 Double

B&B per person
from £24.00 Dbl/Twn

Open March-Oct

All properties graded by VisitScotland, formerly known as the Scottish Tourist Board. | Key to symbols is on back flap. |

Auldearn, by Nairn, Inverness-shire — Map Ref: 4C8

Boath House
Auldearn, Nairn, IV12 5TE
Tel: 01667 454896 Fax: 01667 455469
E-mail: wendy@boath-house.demon.co.uk
Web: www.boath-house.com

SMALL HOTEL

Grade A listed Georgian mansion set in 20 acres of lawns, woodland and streams. Award winning restaurant overlooking the lake. Facilities include fishing, gymnasium, Beauty salon and leisure area with sauna and Jacuzzi. Wonderful beaches, golf course, and some of Scotland's best loved castles all within minutes of this beautiful and historic house. Scottish Country House Hotel of the Year—Which? 2002.

7 Single	All En Suite	B&B per person	Open Jan-Dec
2 Twin		from £67.50 Single	B&B + Eve.Meal
7 Double		from £67.50 Dbl/Twn	from £102.50
2 Family			

Aultbea, Ross-shire — Map Ref: 3F6

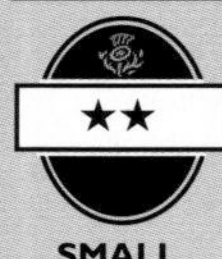

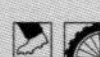

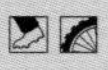

Aultbea Hotel & Restaurant
Aultbea, Ross-shire, IV22 2HX
Tel: 01445 731201 Fax: 01445 731214
E-mail: aultbeahotel@btconnect.com
Web: www.aultbeahotel.co.uk

SMALL HOTEL

Comfortable hotel situated on the shore of Loch Ewe with magnificent views. Fishing available. Inverewe Gardens, 5 miles (9kms). Food served in our Waterside Bistro, lounge bar & Zetland Restaurant.

1 Single	All En Suite	B&B per person	Open Jan-Dec
1 Twin		from £32.50 Single	
5 Double		from £32.50 Dbl/Twn	
1 Family			

Cartmel Guesthouse
Birchburn Road, Aultbea, Ross-shire, IV22 2HZ
Tel: 01445 731375

GUEST HOUSE

Comfortable bungalow guest house set in 1.5 acres of mature garden. Personally run. Evening meals by prior arrangement and vegetarians very welcome. Regret no smoking.

2 Twin	2 En Suite fac	B&B per person	Open Mar-Oct
2 Double	1 Pub Bath/Show	£25.00-£30.00 Single	B&B + Eve.Meal
		£20.00-£25.00 Dbl/Twn	£35.00-£40.00

Mellondale Guest House

47 Mellon Charles, Aultbea, Ross-shire IV22 2JL
Telephone: 01445 731326 Fax: 01445 731326
e.mail: mellondale@lineone.net

Enjoy the personal touch at Mellondale. From the warm welcome to the home cooking in a peaceful setting overlooking Lochewe, Mellondale is the perfect place to relax and take in the spectacular scenery. Ideal for walking, climbing and birdwatching. Inverewe Gardens 9 miles.

Mellondale Guest House
47 Mellon Charles, Aultbea, Ross-shire, IV22 2JL
Tel/Fax: 01445 731326
E-mail: mellondale@lineone.net

GUEST HOUSE

Comfortable family guest house set in 4 acres, with open views of Loch Ewe. 9 miles (14.4 Kms) from Inverewe Gardens. Ideal walking centre.

2 Twin	All En Suite	B&B per person	Open Mar-Oct
2 Double		from £23.00 Dbl/Twn	B&B + Eve.Meal
			from £37.00

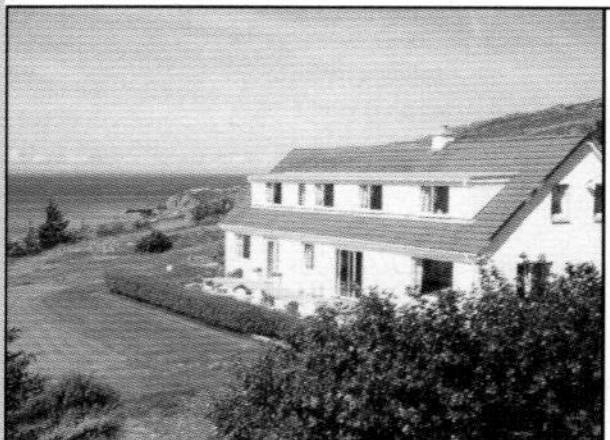

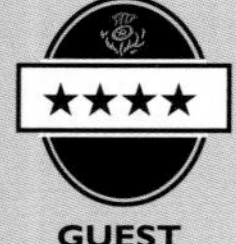

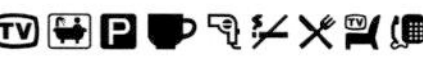

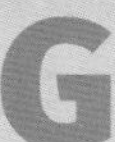

Aviemore, Inverness-shire   Map Ref: 4C10

Aviemore Highlands Hotel
Aviemore Centre, Aviemore, Inverness-shire,
PH22 1PJ
Tel: 01479 810771 Fax: 01479 811473
E-mail: sales@aviehighlands.demon.co.uk
Web: www.aviehighlnds.demon.co.uk

HOTEL

Modern hotel set close to the centre of Aviemore, facilities include the
Ben Macdui restaurant, the White lady bar and the Illicit Still. Lots of
activities available locally, for both the summer and winter visitor.

42 Twin	All En Suite	B&B per person	Open Jan-Dec
34 Double		from £47.00 Single	B&B + Eve.Meal
27 Family		from £32.00 Dbl/Twn	from £42.00

Aviemore Inn
Aviemore, Inverness-shire, PH22 1PH
Tel (Reservations) 01479 811811
Fax: (Reservations) 01479 811309
Web: www.hilton.com

HOTEL

Situated in the heart of the Aviemore Centre, this modern hotel offers
comfortable accommodation.

52 Twin	All En Suite	B&B per person	Open Jan-Dec
10 Double		from £70 room only	B&B + Eve.Meal
			£35.00-£45.00

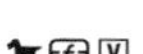

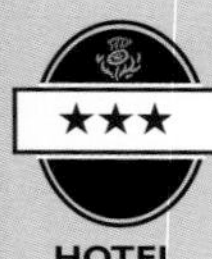

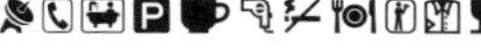

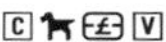

Cairngorm Guest House
Grampian Road, Aviemore, Inverness-shire, PH22 1RP
Tel/Fax: 01479 810630
E-mail: conns@lineone.net
Web: www.aviemore.co.uk/cairngormguesthouse

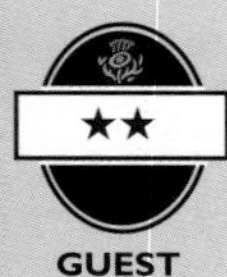

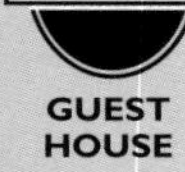

GUEST
HOUSE

Detached stone villa, within 5 minutes walk from the centre and 10
minutes from bus and rail stations.

3 Twin	All En Suite	B&B per person	Open Jan-Dec
5 Double		£20.00-£40.00 Single	
1 Family		£18.00-£25.00 Dbl/Twn	

Corrour House Hotel
Rothiemurchus, by Aviemore, Inverness-shire,
PH22 1QH
Tel: 01479 810220 Fax: 01479 811500
Web: www.corrourhousehotel.co.uk

SMALL
HOTEL

Friendly family run, country house hotel, standing in four acres of garden
and woodland, with views of Rothiemurchus and Cairngorm mountains.

1 Single	All En Suite	B&B per person	Open Jan-Oct
2 Twin		from £30.00 Single	B&B + Eve.Meal
4 Double		from £60.00 Dbl/Twn	from £50.00
1 Family			

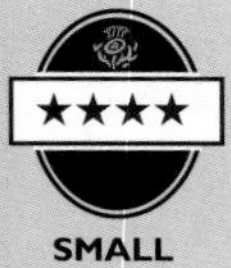

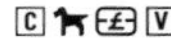

Ravenscraig Guest House
141 Grampian Road, Aviemore, Inverness-shire, PH22 1RP
Tel: 01479 810278 Fax: 01479 812742
E-mail: ravenscrg@aol.com

GUEST
HOUSE

Ravenscraig is centrally located in the village and an ideal base for
touring the Highlands. Popular with birdwatchers, golfers, walkers &
cyclists are our quiet ground floor garden rooms with their own front
doors allowing easy access as well as privacy. We also offer family rooms,
a comfortable guest lounge with a small library, drying facilities, ski/golf
locker, plentiful parking and legendary breakfasts!

1 Single	All En Suite	B&B per person	Open Jan-Dec
4 Twin		from £18.00 Single	
5 Double		from £18.00 Dbl/Twn	
2 Family			

All properties graded by VisitScotland, formerly known as the Scottish Tourist Board. | **Key to symbols is on back flap.** |

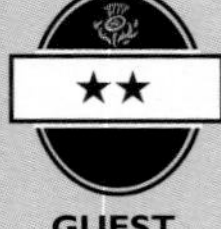

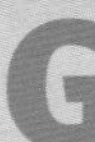

Aviemore, Inverness-shire | Map Ref: 4C10

★★★

**SMALL
HOTEL**

The Rowan Tree Country Hotel
Loch Alvie, by Aviemore, Inverness-shire, PH22 1QB
Tel/Fax: 01479 810207
E-mail: enquiries@rowantreehotel.com
Web: www.rowantreehotel.com

The hotel is set amid stunning scenery overlooking peaceful Loch Alvie and offers a calm, relaxing haven, ideally located for the area's many activities. Our 11 characterful, well equipped, bedrooms, cosy lounges with open fires, home cooked 4 course dinners and selection of superb wines all combine with our warm welcome to ensure that you enjoy your stay to the full.

1 Single	10 En Suite fac	B&B per person	Open Jan-Dec
3 Twin	1 Priv.NOT ensuite	from £29.50 Single	B&B + Eve.Meal
5 Double		from £29.50 Dbl/Twn	from £47.50
2 Family			

Ballachulish, Argyll | Map Ref: 1F1

★★★★

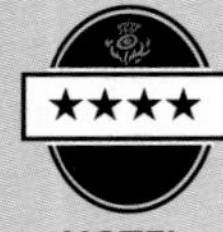

HOTEL

The Ballachulish Hotel
Ballachulish, nr Fort William, Argyll, PH49 4JY
Tel: 01855 821582 Fax: 01855 821463
E-mail: reservations@freedomglen.co.uk
Web: www.freedomglen.co.uk

Glide through dramatic Glencoe and the mountains divide to reveal this breathtaking lochside setting. Fulfill your dream of the historic Highland Hotel. Savour fine Scottish cuisine, relax to the welcoming log fires in the elegant lounge. Complimentary use of nearby indoor heated pool and leisure centre.

8 Single	All En Suite	B&B per person	Open Jan-Dec
23 Twin		£70.00-£90.00 Single	
19 Double		£70.00-£100.00	
4 Family		Dbl/Twn	

★★★

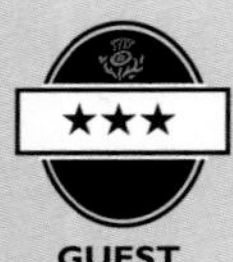

**GUEST
HOUSE**

Craiglinnhe House
Lettermore, Ballachulish, Argyll, PH49 4JD
Tel/Fax: 01855 811270
E-mail: craiglinnhe@ballachulish.sol.co.uk
Web: www.milford.co.uk/go/craiglinnhe.html

Lochside Victorian villa amid spectacular mountain scenery offering period charm with modern comfort. Warm, friendly atmosphere, good food and wine. Ideal base for exploring the Western Highlands.

2 Twin	All En Suite	B&B per person	Open Feb-Dec
3 Double		from £22.00 Dbl/Twn	B&B + Eve.Meal
			from £37.00

★★★

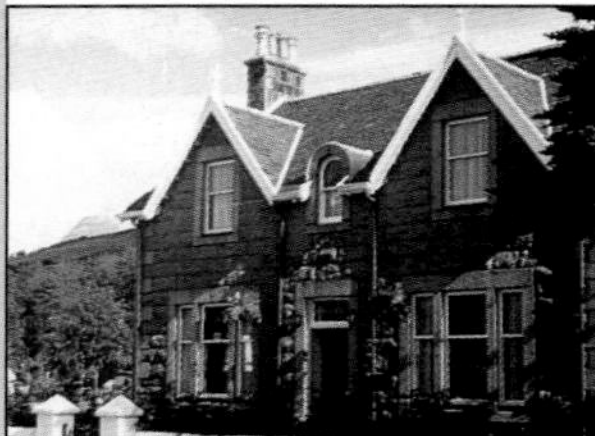

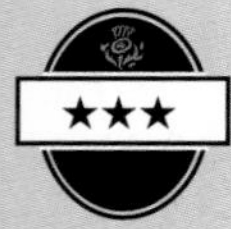

**GUEST
HOUSE**

Fern Villa Guest House
Loanfern, Ballachulish, Argyll, PH49 4JE
Tel: 01855 811393 Fax: 01855 811727
Web: www.fernvilla.com

A warm welcome awaits you in this fine Victorian granite built house in the lochside village amidst spectacular scenery. One mile from Glencoe, convenient for Fort William. Home baking and Natural Cooking of Scotland features on our dinner menu. Table licence. The perfect base for walking, climbing or touring in the West Highlands. Private parking.

2 Twin	All En Suite	B&B per person	Open Jan-Dec
3 Double		from £20.00 Dbl/Twn	B&B + Eve.Meal
			from £33.00

Important: Prices stated are estimates and may be subject to amendments

Escape to glorious Glencoe

Choose a hotel with a warm lochside welcome

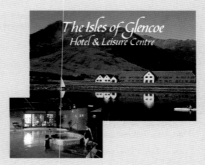

*"an irresistible mix of history and
style with modern comforts."*

- ◆ A Baronial Highland Home
- ◆ Fine Scottish Cuisine
- ◆ Log Fires
- ◆ Adjacent Golf Course

*"a really friendly place to go with a
great, relaxed family atmosphere."*

- ◆ A Friendly, Family Place to Go!
- ◆ Relaxed and convivial
- ◆ Kids Club
- ◆ Leisure Facilities

Special Offers on Selected Dates

£99 per person for 3 nights B&B, Dinner from £15 per night

Call Now 01855 821582
www.freedomglen.co.uk

The Freedom of the Glen Family of Hotels, Onich, Near Fort William, PH33 6RY
fax: 01855 821463 email reservations@freedomglen.co.uk

All properties graded by VisitScotland, formerly known as the Scottish Tourist Board. | *Key to symbols is on back flap.*

Beauly, Inverness-shire — Map Ref: 4A8

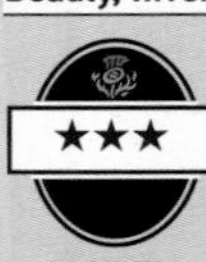

HOTEL

★★★

The Priory Hotel
The Square, Beauly, Inverness-shire, IV4 7BX
Tel: 01463 782309 Fax: 01463 782531
E-mail: reservations@priory-hotel.com
Web: www.priory-hotel.com

2 Single	All En Suite	B&B per person	Open Jan-Dec
15 Twin		from £39.50 Single	B&B + Eve.Meal
15 Double		from £30.00 Dbl/Twn	from £45.00
2 Family		Room only from £50.00	

Situated in the attractive village square of Beauly, this privately run hotel offers excellent facilities, coupled with friendly, efficient informal service. Enjoy the flexibility of early check-in's, late check out's, food available all day and best of all - breakfast available till lunchtime.

Boat of Garten, Inverness-shire — Map Ref: 4C10

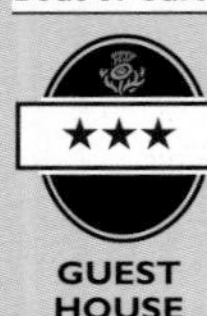

GUEST HOUSE

★★★

Avingormack Guest House
Boat of Garten, Inverness-shire, PH24 3BT
Tel: 01479 831614 Fax: 01479 831344
E-mail: avin.gormack@ukgateway.net

1 Twin	2 En Suite fac	B&B per person	Open Jan-Dec excl Xmas
2 Double	1 Pub Bath/Show	from £20.00 Dbl/Twn	B&B + Eve.Meal
1 Family			from £35.00

Rural guest house, 4 miles from Aviemore with stunning views. Within easy reach of all attractions. Award winning traditional and vegetarian breakfasts.

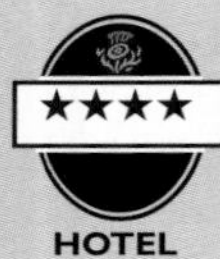

HOTEL

★★★★

The Boat Hotel
Deshar Road, Boat of Garten, Inverness-shire, PH24 2BH
Tel: 01479 831258 Fax: 01479 831414
E-mail: holidays@boathotel.co.uk
Web: www.boathotel.co.uk

4 Single	All En Suite	B&B per person	Open Jan-Dec
15 Twin		£65.00-£70.00 Single	B&B + Eve.Meal
11 Double		£50.00-£55.00 Dbl/Twn	£70.00-£80.00
2 Family		Room only from £45.00	

Privately owned Victorian hotel recently refurbished to a very high standard, overlooking the 18 hole championship golf course. Award winning 'Taste of Scotland' cuisine in "The Capercaillie" restaurant. Individual in style with friendly personalised service. Golf and fishing packages arranged.

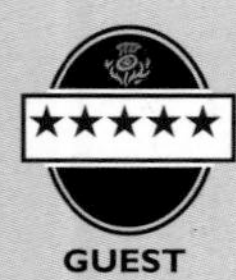

GUEST HOUSE

★★★★★

Glenavon House Hotel
Kinchurdy Road, Boat of Garten, Inverness-shire, PH24 3BP
Tel/Fax: 01479 831213

1 Single	All En Suite	B&B per person	Open Apr-Oct
2 Twin		from £35.00 Single,	B&B + Eve.Meal
2 Double		Dbl/Twn	from £60.00

Recently renovated Victorian mansion with the highest standard of personal care and cuisine. Ideal for small sporting house parties, or just relaxing in perfect central Highland location.

Brora, Sutherland — Map Ref: 4C6

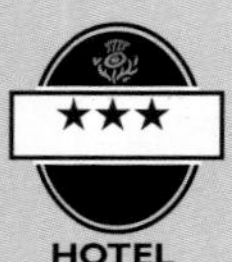

HOTEL

★★★

Links Hotel
Golf Road, Brora, Sutherland, KW9 6QS
Tel: 01408 621252 Fax: 01408 621181
E-mail: info@highlandescape.com
Web: www.highlandescape.com

4 Single	All En Suite	B&B per person	Open Apr-Oct
11 Twin		from £68.00 Single	
5 Double		from £49.00 Dbl/Twn	
2 Family			

Open outlook over the golf course to the sea beyond. Access to sandy beach. The hotel has a relaxed atmosphere and good food. It makes an excellent base for golfing or fishing holidays, or for touring the northern Highlands. Leisure facilities, including indoor swimming pool, are situated at our sister hotel 200 metres away and are available to guests.

Important: Prices stated are estimates and may be subject to amendments

Brora, Sutherland — Ref: 4C6

B&B

★★★★

Lynwood
Golf Road, Brora, Sutherland KW9 6QS
Tel/Fax: 01408 621226

1 Dbl/Twn	All En Suite	B&B per person	Open March-Dec excl
1 Double		from £28.00 Single	Xmas/New Year
1 Twin		from £23.00 Dbl/Twn	B&B + Eve.Meal from £38.00

Enjoy a warm welcome and relaxed atmosphere at this elegant Edwardian House. The perfect venue for small golfing and house parties. Lynwood is situated close to Brora Golf Club and overlooks the harbour and River Brora. Relax in the large secluded garden or take one of the many interesting local walks. Our enthusiasm for good food is reflected in the imaginative way, we prepare dishes from local highland produce.

HOTEL

★★★★

Royal Marine Hotel
Golf Road, Brora, Sutherland, KW9 6QS
Tel: 01408 621252 Fax: 01408 621181
E-mail: info@highlandescape.com
Web: www.highlandescape.com

1 Single	All En Suite	B&B per person	Open Jan-Dec
15 Twin		from £68.00 Single	B&B + Eve.Meal
5 Double		from £49.00 Dbl/Twn	from £69.00
1 Family			

Traditional country house hotel, offering excellent facilities and access to golfing, fishing and countryside. Recently completed leisure complex with indoor pool, sauna, steam room, jacuzzi and curling rink.

Carrbridge, Inverness-shire — Map Ref: 4C9

SMALL HOTEL

★★★

The Cairn Hotel
Main Road, Carrbridge, Inverness-shire, PH23 3AS
Tel: 01479 841212 Fax: 01479 841362
E-mail: cairn.carrbridge@talk21.com

2 Single	4 En Suite fac	B&B per person	Open Jan-Dec
1 Twin	1 Pub Bath/Show	from £19.00 Single	
2 Double		from £22.00 Dbl/Twn	
2 Family			

Enjoy the country pub atmosphere, log fire, malt whiskies, real ales and affordable food in this family owned village centre hotel. Close to the historic bridge a perfect base for touring the Cairngorms, Whisky Trail and Loch Ness.

Carrbridge, Inverness-shire — Map Ref: 4C9

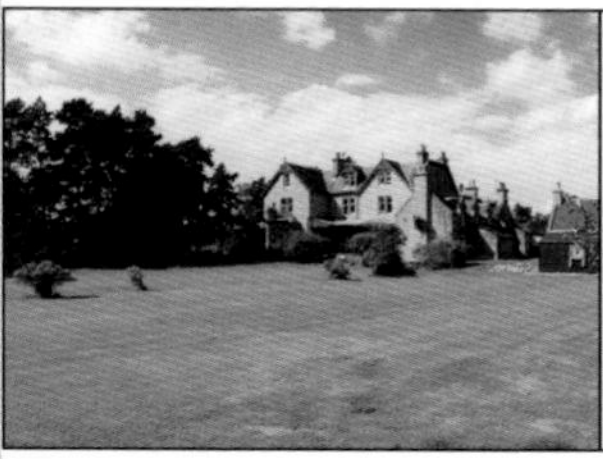

Dalrachney Lodge Hotel
CARRBRIDGE, INVERNESS-SHIRE PH23 3AT
Telephone: 01479 841252   Fax: 01479 841383
e.mail: stay@dalrachney.co.uk Web: www.dalrachney.co.uk

Situated in 16 acres with magnificent views of Cairngorms. This AA ★★★ former hunting lodge, just off the A9, makes an ideal base for your Highland holiday. Tastefully refurbished **Dalrachney** offers spacious very well-appointed rooms. Emphasis on good food complemented by fine selection of wines, malts and liqueurs. Easy access to many attractions.

SMALL HOTEL

★★★★

Dalrachney Lodge Hotel
Carrbridge, Inverness-shire, PH23 3AT
Tel: 01479 841252 Fax: 01479 841383
E-mail: stay@dalrachney.co.uk
Web: www.dalrachney.co.uk

1 Single	10 En Suite fac	B&B per person	Open Jan-Dec
3 Twin	1 Priv.NOT ensuite	from £40.00 Single	B&B + Eve.Meal
4 Double		from £30.00 Dbl/Twn	from £45.00
3 Family		Room only from £50.00	

Victorian former hunting lodge, with many antique and period furnishings, set in 16 acres of peaceful surroundings. Cuisine using local produce.

All properties graded by VisitScotland, formerly known as the Scottish Tourist Board. | **Key to symbols is on back flap.**

Carrbridge, Inverness-shire | **Map Ref: 4C9**

GUEST HOUSE

★★

The Pines Country House
Duthil, Carrbridge, Inverness-shire, PH23 3ND
Tel: 01479 841220 Fax: 01479 841220*51
E-mail: lynn@thepines-duthil.fsnet.co.uk
Web: www.thepines-duthil.fsnet.co.uk

Set in 2 acres of mature woodland, 2 miles (3kms) from village. Offering personal service and homely atmosphere. Ideal for all activities.

1 Twin	All En Suite	B&B per person	Open Jan-Dec
2 Double	1 Pub Bath/Show	from £21.50 Single	B&B + Eve.Meal
1 Family		from £19.00 Dbl/Twn	from £29.00

Contin, Ross-shire | **Map Ref: 4A8**

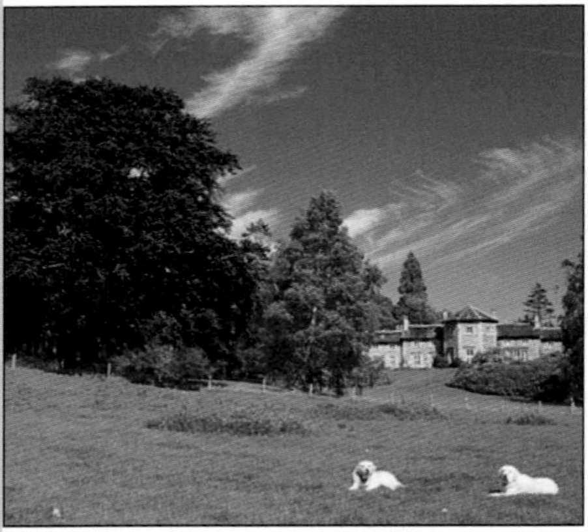

Coul House Hotel
by Strathpeffer, Ross-shire IV14 9ES
Tel: 01997 421487 Fax: 01997 421945
e.mail: coulhouse@bestwestern.co.uk
Web: www.milford.co.uk/go/coulhouse.html

Our views are breathtaking. The ancient "Mackenzies of Coul" picked a wonderful situation for their lovely home. Today, Ann and Martyn will give you a warm Highland welcome. You'll enjoy the "Taste of Scotland" food of Chefs Taylor and Maclean, log fires, summer evening piper and "Hamish", the hotel's loveable labrador. From Coul House it's so easy to cruise on Loch Ness, visit Cawdor Castle, sail to the Summer Isles...sample numerous distilleries (Glen Ord is only 5 miles), or visit the Wildlife Park, Culloden Battlefield...for golfers, there's a 5-course holiday including championship Royal Dornoch...for anglers, we can arrange salmon and trout fishing...there's pony trekking too. **Ring or write for our colour brochure.**

HOTEL

★★★★

Coul House Hotel
Contin, by Strathpeffer, Ross-shire, IV14 9ES
Tel: 01997 421487 Fax: 01997 421945
E-mail: coulhouse@bestwestern.co.uk
Web: www.milford.co.uk/go/coulhouse.html

Personally run, secluded country house with fine views over surrounding countryside. 4-Poster room and suite available. Taste of Scotland.

3 Single	All En Suite	B&B per person	Open Jan-Dec
7 Twin		from £54.00 Single	B&B + Eve.Meal from
7 Double		from £39.00 Dbl/Twn	£54.50
3 Family			

Dalwhinnie, Inverness-shire | **Map Ref: 4B11**

INN

★

The Inn at Loch Ericht
Dalwhinnie, Inverness-shire, PH19 1AF
Tel: 01528 522257 Fax: 01528 522270
E-mail: reservations@priory-hotel.com
Web: www.priory-hotel.com

Friendly hotel in small Highland village. All rooms with ensuite facilities. Meals served all day. Walkers and Cyclists welcome.

15 Twin	All En Suite	B&B per person	Open Jan-Dec
10 Double		from £19.50 Single	B&B + Eve.Meal from
2 Family		from £17.50 Dbl/Twn	£30.00
		Room only from £29.50	

Important: Prices stated are estimates and may be subject to amendments

Dornie, by Kyle of Lochalsh, Ross-shire

Map Ref: 3G9

★★★

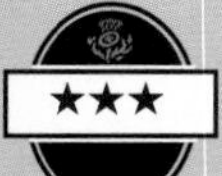

SMALL HOTEL

Dornie Hotel
7/10 Francis Street, Dornie, Rossshire, IV40 8DT
Tel: 01599 555205 Fax: 01599 555429
E-mail: dornie@madasafish.com

2 Single	8 En Suite fac	B&B per person	Open Jan-Dec
3 Twin	2 Pub Bath/Show	£25.00-£35.00 Single	
4 Double		£25.00-£35.00 Dbl/Twn	
3 Family			

Occupying one of the most scenic areas in Scotland, this family run 13 bedroom hotel is situated in the village of Dornie, & is only a short walk from the magnificent Eilean Donan Castle. Rooms are well equipped & the hotel offers an excellent selection of modern cuisine specializing in local seafood. Castle weddings attractively catered for. We look forward to welcoming you to a relaxing & peaceful stay.

Dornoch, Sutherland

Map Ref: 4B6

★★

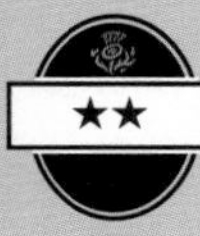

HOTEL

Dornoch Hotel
Grange Road, Dornoch, IV25 3LD
Tel: 01786 436600 Fax: 01786 436650
E-mail: l.graig@shearingsholidays.co.uk
Web: www.shearingsholidays.com

14 Single	All En Suite	Open Feb-Dec
68 Twin		
28 Double		

Close to famous golf course and overlooking Dornoch Firth, this hotel has some refurbished rooms, and a pitch and putt on front lawn.

★★★

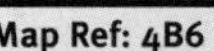

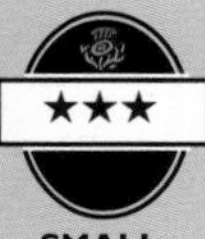

SMALL HOTEL

The Eagle Hotel and Bank House
Castle Street, Dornoch, Sutherland, IV25 3SR
Tel: 01862 810008 Fax: 01862 811355
E-mail: irene@eagledornoch.co.uk
Web: www.eagledornoch.co.uk

4 Twin	All En Suite	B&B per person	Open Jan-Dec excl
4 Double		from £30.00 Single	Xmas/New Year
4 Family		from £24.00 Dbl/Twn	

Paul and Irene welcome you to the Eagle Hotel where personal attention is guaranteed. 'Every customer is a new friend'. Meals - all day, every day in a friendly pub atmosphere where families are welcome. Three new bedrooms are located in the nearby Bank House and are furnished to an excellent standard.

★★

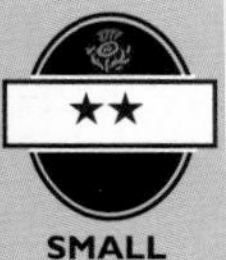

SMALL HOTEL

Mallin House Hotel
Church Street, Dornoch, Sutherland, IV25 3LP
Tel: 01862 810335 Fax: 01862 810810
E-mail: mallin.house.hotel@zetnet.co.uk
Web: www.users.zetnet.co.uk/mallin-house

3 Single	All En Suite	B&B per person	Open Jan-Dec
3 Twin		from £35.00 Single	
3 Double		from £29.00 Dbl/Twn	
1 Family		Room only from £25.00	

Friendly family run hotel, situated close to the centre of the charming and historic town of Dornoch. A choice of menus available. Carefully prepared by the chef/patron and his wife. Excellent sandy beaches close by. Ideal base for golfing, fishing, shooting and birdwatching or for exploring the varied scenic splendours of Sutherland.

★★★★

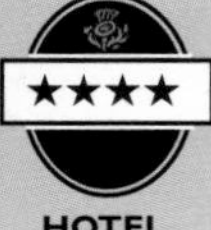

HOTEL

The Royal Golf Hotel
1st Tee, Dornoch, Sutherland, IV25 3LG
Tel: 01667 452301 (ext 247/259) Fax: 01667 455267
E-mail: rooms@morton-hotels.com
Web: www.morton-hotels.com

5 Single	All En Suite	B&B per person	Open Jan-Dec
18 Twin	Suites avail	from £85.00 Single	
2 Double		from £54.00 Dbl/Twn	

Previously a family mansion, the hotel overlooks the golf course and the Dornoch Firth. 5 minutes walk to town. Taste of Scotland. Golf packages available. Extensively refurbished. Car park and golf club storage.

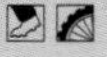

All properties graded by VisitScotland, formerly known as the Scottish Tourist Board. | **Key to symbols is on back flap.**

Dornoch, Sutherland | Map Ref: 4B6

★★

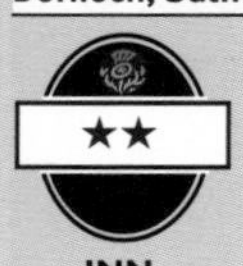

INN

The Trentham Hotel
The Poles, Dornoch, Sutherland, IV25 3HZ
Tel: 01862 810551 Fax: 01862 811426
Web: http://thetrenthamhotel.co.uk/side.htm

18c coaching inn on main Inverness - Wick road, under 2 miles (5kms) from Dornoch. Good base for the golf courses of East Sutherland. Ideal stopover on road to Orkney. Extensive bar menu available, wide selection of malt whiskies. Beauty salon.

1 Single	2 Pub Bath/Show
3 Twin	
1 Double	
1 Family	

B&B per person
from £20.00 Single
from £17.50 Dbl/Twn
Room only per person
from £12.50

Open Jan-Dec excl
Xmas/New Year

Drumnadrochit, Inverness-shire | Map Ref: 4A9

★★★

HOTEL

Loch Ness Lodge Hotel
Drumnadrochit, Inverness-shire, IV63 6TU
Tel: 01456 450342 Fax: 01456 450429
E-mail: info@lochness-hotel.com
Web: www.lochness-hotel.com

Set in 8 acres of varied woodland above Loch Ness. The Lodge has 2 modern bedroom wings. Visitor Centre and organised boat cruises on Loch Ness.

1 Single	All En Suite
37 Twin	
6 Double	
6 Family	

B&B per person
from £40.00 Single
from £30.00 Dbl/Twn
Room only from £25.00

Open May-Oct
B&B + Eve.Meal from
£45.00

Drumnadrochit, Inverness-shire | Map Ref: 4A9

★★★

SMALL
HOTEL

Polmaily House Hotel
Drumnadrochit, Inverness-shire, IV63 6XT
Tel: 01456 450343 Fax: 01456 450813
E-mail: polmaily@btinternet.com
Web: www.polmaily.co.uk

A country house in extensive grounds with a restaurant using fresh local ingredients. Leisure facilities with a wide range of organised activities for children. Fishing, sailing and horse riding activities can also be arranged for children. Indoor pool included. The grounds include large outdoor play area, rabbits, guinea pigs to pet and indoor play areas for wet weather.

1 Twin	All En Suite
3 Double	
6 Family	

B&B per person
from £38.00 Single
from £38.00 Dbl/Twn
per room

Open Jan-Dec

Dulnain Bridge, by Grantown-on-Spey, Inverness-shire | Map Ref: 4C9

★★★★

SMALL
HOTEL

Auchendean Lodge Hotel
Dulnain Bridge, by Grantown-on-Spey,
Inverness-shire, PH26 3LU
Tel/Fax: 01479 851347
E-mail: hotel@auchendean.com Web: www.auchendean.com

Edwardian former shooting lodge, retaining character and style, with panoramic views of the Cairngorm mountains, the River Spey and Abernethy forest. Extensive wine list; interesting cuisine, using home grown and locally sourced vegetables and produce, including wild mushrooms. A friendly welcome and an informal relaxing atmosphere.

1 Single	All En Suite
2 Twin	
2 Double	
1 Family	

B&B per person
from £36.00 Single
from £36.00 Dbl/Twn

Open Jan-Dec
B&B + Eve.Meal
from £61.00

Dundonnell, Ross-shire | Map Ref: 3G7

★★★★

HOTEL

Dundonnell Hotel
Dundonnell, Little Loch Broom, nr Ullapool, Ross-shire,
IV23 2QR
Tel: 01854 633204 Fax: 01854 633366
E-mail: selbie@dundonnellhotel.co.uk
Web: www.dundonnellhotel.com

Family run hotel with emphasis on personal service. Interesting cuisine with use of fresh local produce. Situated at end of Little Loch Broom.

1 Single	All En Suite
15 Twin	
12 Double	
2 Family	

B&B per person
from £35.00 Single
from £70.00 Dbl/Twn

Open Mar-Nov +
festive season
B&B + Eve.Meal from
£45.00

Duror, Argyll | Map Ref: 1E1

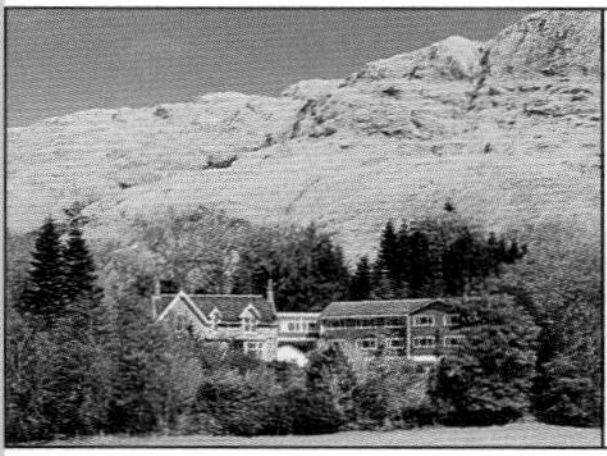

Stewart Hotel
Duror, by Appin, Argyll PA38 4BW
Tel: 01631 740268 Fax: 01631 740549
e.mail: thestewarthotel@hotmail.com Web: www.thestewarthotel.co.uk

A friendly family run country hotel, set amongst 5 acres of woodland gardens beside the river Duror. Spectacular views over Loch Linnhe to the Morvern Hills. Refurbished to a high standard and under new ownership, the ideal destination for any short break or longer stay.

★★★

SMALL
HOTEL

Stewart Hotel
Duror, by Appin, PA38 4BW
Tel: 01631 740268 Fax: 01631 740549
E-mail: thestewarthotel@hotmail.com
Web: www.thestewarthotel.co.uk

Family run hotel set in 5 acres of beautiful gardens 15 miles from Fort William and 25 miles from Oban. The hotel which has been recently refurbished, offers a friendly, relaxed, informal style of service in both the bar and the restaurant.

2 Family	All En Suite
12 Double	
11 Twin	

B&B per person from
£20.00-£27.00 +
£5.00 single
supplement

Open all year
B&B + Eve.Meal
£35.00-£40.00 per
person + £5.00 single
supplement

All properties graded by VisitScotland, formerly known as the Scottish Tourist Board. | Key to symbols is on back flap. |

Durness, Sutherland   Map Ref: 4A3

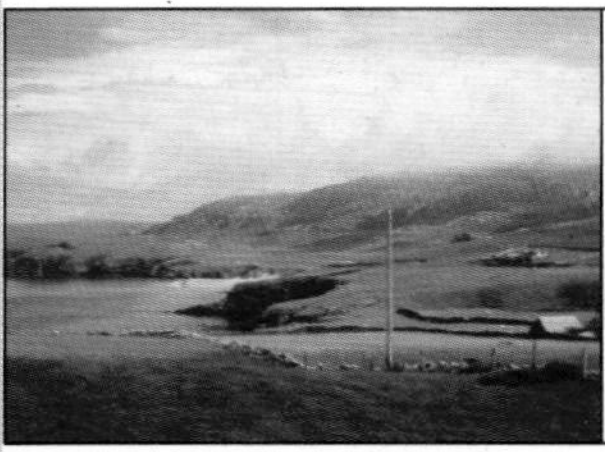

Smoo Cave Hotel

Lerin, Durness, Sutherland IV27 4QB
Tel/Fax: 01971 511227   e.mail: smoo.hotel@virgin.net
The most north westerly hotel in mainland Scotland, where you will
find a warm and friendly welcome, with comfortable accommodation
and the very best of food. Excellent base for enjoying a golf, fishing,
walking or touring holiday with wonderful sandy beaches and of course
the famous Smoo Caves and Cape Wrath.

★

INN

Smoo Cave Hotel			
Durness, Sutherland, IV27 4QB			
Tel/Fax: 01971 511227			

1 Twin	2 En Suite fac	B&B per person	Open Jan-Dec
1 Double	1 Pub Bath/Show	from £16.50 Dbl/Twn	
1 Family			

Accommodation provided in this local inn with open fires. Close to the
Smoo Cave, which is open to visitors to walk and look at the cave.
Ground floor room available.

📺 📻 🅿 ✕ 🍸 📟

🅲 🐾 ♿ 🅦 🆅

Fort Augustus, Inverness-shire   Map Ref: 4A10

★★

**SMALL
HOTEL**

Caledonian Hotel			
Fort Augustus, Inverness-shire, PH32 4BQ			
Tel: 01320 366256			
E-mail: hotel@lochness-scotland.co.uk			
Web: www.lochness-scotland.co.uk			

3 Twin	8 En Suite fac	B&B per person	Open Easter-Sep
6 Double	1 Pub Bath/Show	from £25.00 Single	B&B + Eve.Meal
2 Family	1 Priv.NOT ensuite	from £22.50 Dbl/Twn	from £40.00

Warm welcome at this family run hotel overlooking Benedictine Abbey.
32 miles (53 kms) from Inverness and Fort William.

📺 📻 🅿 🍺 🍴 🍸

🅲 ♿ 🆅

★★★

**SMALL
HOTEL**

Inchnacardoch Lodge Hotel			
Loch Ness, by Fort Augustus, Inverness-shire,			
PH32 4BL			
Tel: 01320 366258 Fax: 01320 366248			
E-mail: lochness97@aol.com			
Web: www.smoothhound.co.uk/hotels/inchna.html			

3 Twin	All En Suite	B&B per person	Open Jan-Dec
7 Double		from £45.00 Single	
5 Family		from £35.00 Dbl/Twn	

Country house hotel on north side of Fort Augustus with fine views of
Loch Ness and surrounding hills. Ideal base for touring and outdoor
activities.

📺 📞 📻 🅿 🍺 ✂ 🍴 🍸

Fort William, Inverness-shire   Map Ref: 3H12

★★★

**GUEST
HOUSE**

Ben View Guest House			
Belford Road, Fort William, Inverness-shire,			
PH33 6ER			
Tel: 01397 702966			
E-mail: benview@gowanbrae.co.uk			
Web: www.benviewguesthouse.co.uk			

2 Single	All En Suite	B&B per person	Open Mar-Nov
2 Twin		from £18.00 Single	
6 Double		from £18.00 Dbl/Twn	
1 Family			

Family run guest house conveniently situated for bus and train stations,
town centre and leisure centre. All rooms with ensuite or private
bathrooms. Tastefully decorated lounges for guests use. Ample private
parking available.

📺 📻 📺 🅿 🍺 ✂ 🛏 🏠 📟

🅲 🆅

Important: Prices stated are estimates and may be subject to amendments

Fort William, Inverness-shire   Map Ref: 3H12

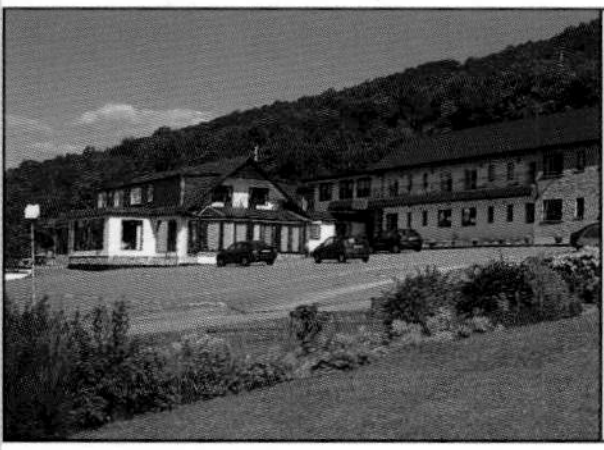

Clan MacDuff Hotel

Achintore Road, Fort William, Inverness-shire PH33 6RW
Telephone: 01397 702341   Fax: 01397 706174
e.mail: reception@clanmacduff.co.uk Web: www.clanmacduff.co.uk

Situated overlooking Loch Linnhe, with outstanding views of magnificent Highland scenery. Well-appointed en-suite bedrooms with colour television, hospitality tray etc. Large choice dinner menu. Delicious bar suppers. Fine selection of malt whiskies. Large car-park. This friendly family-run hotel is dedicated to providing good quality and value hospitality.

★★

HOTEL

Clan MacDuff Hotel

Achintore Road, Fort William, Inverness-shire, PH33 6RW
Tel: 01397 702341 Fax: 01397 706174
E-mail: reception@clanmacduff.co.uk
Web: www.clanmacduff.co.uk

This family run hotel overlooks Loch Linnhe, 2 miles south of Fort William. The Hotel is situated in its own grounds with large car park. Enjoy the highland scenery from the conservatory or patio. All public rooms have magnificent views of the Loch and the mountains beyond. Dinner is a traditional menu with varied choice. We offer the comfort and freedom of a hotel at economic prices. Brochure on request.

2 Single	All En Suite	B&B per person	Open Apr-Nov excl
15 Twin		from £26.00 Single	Xmas/New Year
15 Double		from £22.00 Dbl/Twn	B&B + Eve.Meal
4 Family			from £35.00

★★

GUEST HOUSE

Craig Nevis Guest House

Belford Road, Fort William, Inverness-shire,
PH33 6BU
Tel/Fax: 01397 702023
Web: www.craignevis.co.uk

Personally run guest house. Offering comfortable reasonably priced accommodation short distance from town centre, swimming pool and all amenities. 2 mins walk from railway station. Off-street parking. 3 rooms in adjacent bungalow.

2 Single	6 En Suite fac	B&B per person	Open Jan-Dec excl
3 Twin	1 Pub Bath/Show	from £18.00 Single	Xmas/New Year
2 Double		from £18.00 Dbl/Twn	
2 Family			

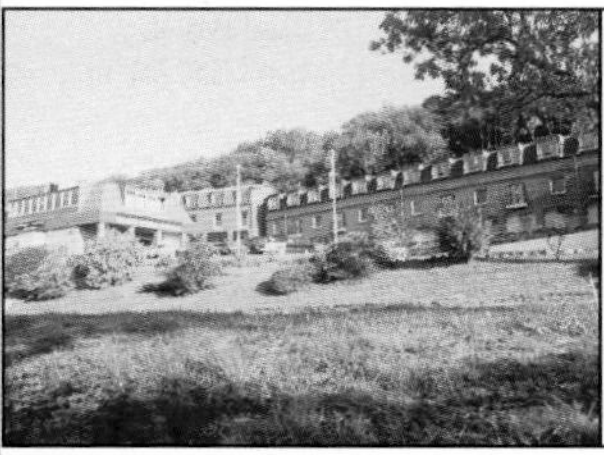

Croit Anna Hotel

Situated three miles south of Fort William on the shores of Loch Linnhe, has all rooms with private facilities, colour TV/Sky TV and hospitality trays. We have the ideal location for touring the magnificent West Highlands of Scotland. B&B from as little as £25.00 per person.

Send for full brochure: Croit Anna Hotel,   **★★★ HOTEL**
Achintore Road, Fort William PH33 6RR
Tel: 01397 702268 e.mail: croitanna@compuserve.com
Fax: 01397 704099 Web: www.croitanna.co.uk

★★★

HOTEL

Croit Anna Hotel

Achintore Road, Fort William, Inverness-shire,
PH33 6RR
Tel: 01397 702268 Fax: 01397 704099
Web: www.croitanna.co.uk

Situated on the shores of Loch Linnhe, overlooking the hills of Morven. Quality En-Suite accommodation with SKY TV and Hospitality tray. Menus feature the best of fresh Scottish fare. Traditional Hospitality from a Family run Hotel with regular entertainment.

12 Single	All En Suite	B&B per person	Open mid Mar-mid Nov
28 Twin		from £30.00 Single	
15 Double		from £25.00 Double	
5 Family			

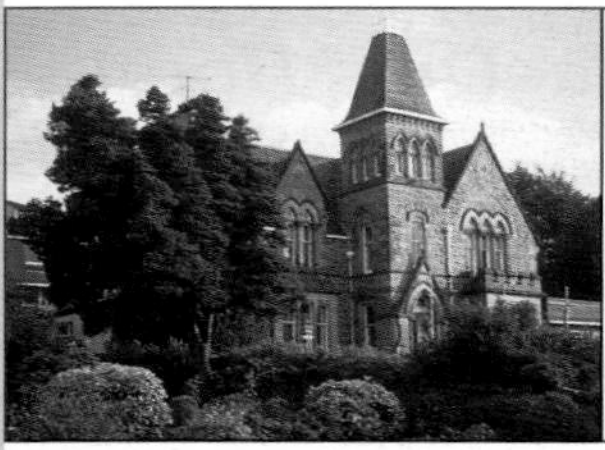

CRUACHAN HOTEL

Achintore Road, Fort William PH33 6RQ
Tel: 01397 702022 Fax: 01397 702239
e.mail: reservations@cruachan-hotel.co.uk
Web: www.cruachan-hotel.co.uk
Family run hotel with warm friendly atmosphere. 200 yards from
Fort William on main A82. Large car park next to main road.
Magnificent views from our sun terrace. Ideal base for touring the
Highlands and islands. Scottish entertainment most nights.

★★

HOTEL

Cruachan Hotel

Achintore Road, Fort William, Inverness-shire,
PH33 6RQ
Tel: 01397 702022 Fax: 01397 702239
E-mail: reservations@cruachan-hotel.co.uk
Web: www.cruachan-hotel.co.uk

Victorian villa, modern wing attached, standing in own grounds
overlooking Loch Linnhe and only 400 yards from Fort William's main
shopping street.

7 Single	All En Suite	B&B per person	Open Feb-Nov
25 Twin		from £25.00 Single	
20 Double		from £22.00 Dbl/Twn	
5 Family			

📺 🅿 ☕ 🍽 🍷

🄫 🐕 Ⓥ

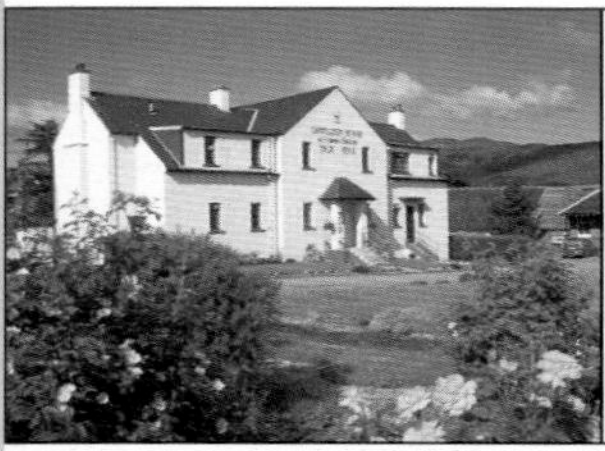

Distillery Guest House

Nevis Bridge, North Road, Fort William PH33 6LR
Telephone: 01397 700103   Fax: 01397 702980
e.mail: disthouse@aol.com
Web: www.fort-william.net/distillery-house
Situated at the entrance to Glen Nevis just 5 minutes from the
Town Centre. *Distillery House* has been upgraded to high standards.
Set in the extensive grounds of the *Glenlochy Distillery* with views over the
River Nevis, all bedrooms are ensuite. New Self-Catering Apartments now
available. *Bed & Breakfast from £22.50 per person.*

★★★★

GUEST
HOUSE

Distillery House

Nevis Bridge, North Road, Fort William, Inverness-shire,
PH33 6LR
Tel: 01397 700103 Fax: 01397 702980
E-mail: disthouse@aol.com

Distillery house at old Glenlochy Distillery in Fort William beside A82,
road to the Isles. Situated at the entrance to Glen Nevis just 5 minutes
from the town centre. Distillery House has been upgraded to high
standards. Set in the extensive grounds of the Glenlochy Distillery with
views over the River Nevis. All bedrooms are ensuite with TV, telephone
and hospitality tray.

1 Single	All En Suite	B&B per person	Open Jan-Dec
2 Twin		from £25.00 Single	
2 Double		from £22.50 Dbl/Twn	
1 Family			

📺 📞 🖨 🅿 ☕ 🥃 ⚗ 🛏

🄫 💷 🅦

Important: Prices stated are estimates and may be subject to amendments

Fort William, Inverness-shire | Map Ref: 3H12

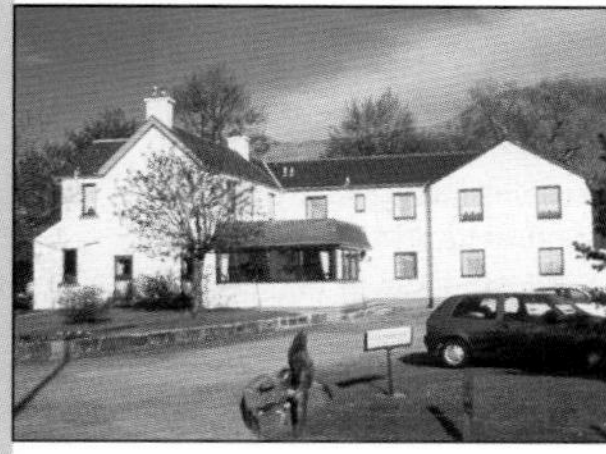

Glenlochy Guest House

Nevis Bridge, Fort William, Inverness-shire PH33 6PF
Telephone: 01397 702909
e.mail: glenlochyguesthouse@hotmail.com

Situated in its own spacious grounds within walking distance of town centre and Ben Nevis. At entrance to Glen Nevis. Recommended by *"Which Best B&B Guide"*. Special rates for 3 or more nights. Large private car park. 8 of 10 bedrooms are ensuite. Phone for reservations or colour brochure. B&B from £18.

★★★

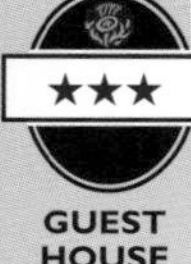

GUEST HOUSE

Glenlochy Guest House and Apartments
Nevis Bridge, North Road, Fort William,
Inverness-shire, PH33 6PF
Tel: 01397 702909
E-mail: glenlochyguesthouse@hotmail.com

Detached house with garden situated at Nevis Bridge, midway between Ben Nevis and the town centre. 0.5 miles (1km) to railway station. 2 annexe rooms.

3 Twin	8 En Suite fac	B&B per person	Open Jan-Dec
5 Double	2 Pub Bath/Show	from £20.00 Single	
2 Family		from £18.00-£28.00	
		Dbl/Twn	

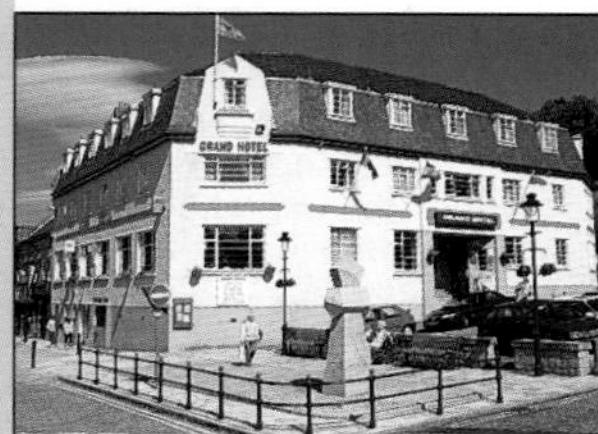

Grand Hotel ★★★
HOTEL

○ INVESTOR IN PEOPLE

FORT WILLIAM,
INVERNESS-SHIRE PH33 6DX
Tel/Fax: 01397 702928 e.mail: enquiries@grandhotel-scotland.co.uk
Web: www.grandhotel-scotland.co.uk

This popular town centre hotel enjoys an excellent local reputation with its clientele for friendly service and award winning cuisine. The hotel is an ideal base to tour the scenic West Highlands. Experience the Highlands whilst relaxing in comfortable surroundings. Special 2 and 3 night rates available. Visit our website.

★★★

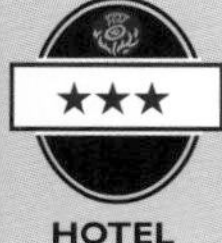

HOTEL

Grand Hotel
Gordon Square, Fort William, Inverness-shire,
PH33 6DX
Tel/Fax: 01397 702928
E-mail: enquiries@grandhotel-scotland.co.uk
Web: www.grandhotel-scotland.co.uk

Conveniently located in the town centre, our family run hotel offers good food and accommodation at competitive prices. Excellent base from which to explore the scenic West Highlands by car or by foot. Children welcome. Baby listening service as well as highchairs and cots. Our chef is happy to assist with all your dietary requests.

3 Single	All En Suite	B&B per person	Open Feb-Dec excl
13 Twin		from £25.00 Single	Xmas
10 Double		from £22.00 Dbl/Twn	B&B + Eve.Meal
4 Family			from £38.00

Key to symbols is on back flap.

Fort William, Inverness-shire | Map Ref: 3H12

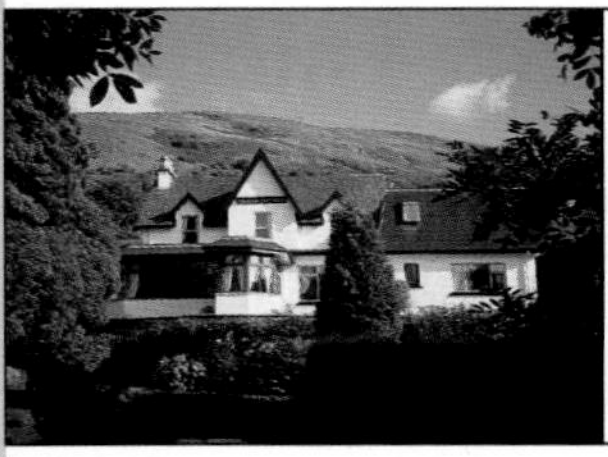

GUISACHAN HOUSE

Alma Road, Fort William, Inverness-shire PH33 6HA
Telephone: 01397 703797 Fax: 01397 703797
e.mail: info@stablesrooms.fsnet.co.uk
Web: www.fort-william.net/guisachan-house

★★★
GUEST HOUSE

Beautifully situated overlooking Loch Linnhe and Ardgour Hills, within 5 mins walking distance of town centre, rail and bus stations. All rooms have private facilities, TV, tea-making. There is a comfortable lounge where you can enjoy a drink from our well-stocked bar. Private parking.

★★★

GUEST HOUSE

Guisachan House
Alma Road, Fort William, Inverness-shire, PH33 6HA
Tel/Fax: 01397 703797
E-mail: info@stablesrooms.fsnet.co.uk
Web: www.fort-william.net/guisachan-house

Family run establishment situated in its own grounds within easy walking distance of town centre, rail and bus stations. There is a comfortable lounge and well-stocked private bar. Open all year round.

2 Single	15 En Suite fac	B&B per person	Open Jan-Dec excl
5 Twin	1 Pub Bath/Show	from £18.00 Single	Xmas/New Year
6 Double	1 Priv.NOT ensuite	from £28.00 Dbl/Twn	
3 Family			

IMPERIAL HOTEL

FRASER SQUARE, FORT WILLIAM PH33 6DW
Telephone: 01397 702040 Fax: 01397 706277
e.mail: reception@the-imperial-hotel.co.uk
Web: www.the-imperial-hotel.co.uk

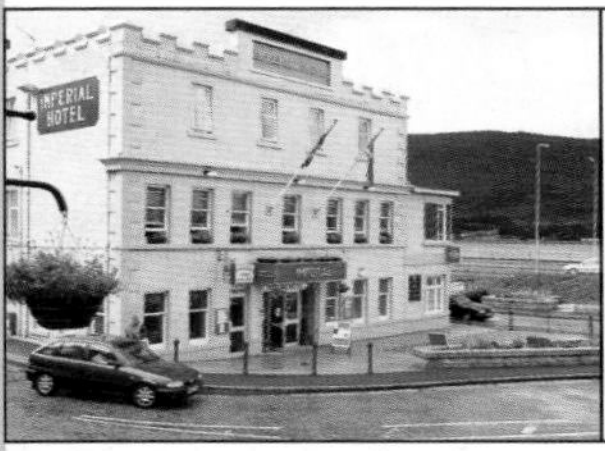

Quality town-centre hotel with some fine views over Loch Linnhe and surrounding countryside. Good food and modern luxurious rooms offer the discerning traveller and businessman an ideal base in Fort William. Fully licensed, A La Carte menu, buffet, servery, conference facilities, executive rooms.

★★★

HOTEL

Imperial Hotel
Fraser Square, Fort William, Inverness-shire,
PH33 6DW
Tel: 01397 702040 Fax: 01397 706277
E-mail: reception@the-imperial-hotel.co.uk
Web: www.the-imperial-hotel.co.uk

Town centre hotel with some fine views over Loch Linnhe and surrounding countryside. Good food and modern rooms offer the discerning traveller and businessman, an ideal base in Fort William. Fully licensed, a la carte menu, buffet, servery, conference facilities.

5 Single	All En Suite	B&B per person	Open Jan-Dec excl
13 Twin		from £45.00 Single	Xmas/New Year
13 Double		from £38.00 Dbl/Twn	B&B + Eve.Meal
		Room only from £30.00	from £53.00

Important: Prices stated are estimates and may be subject to amendments

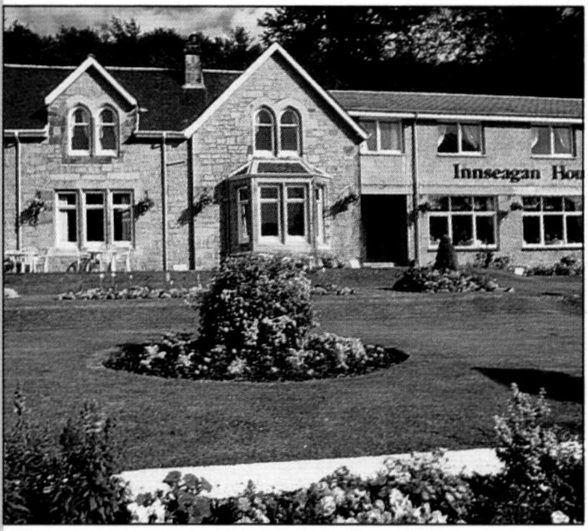

Innseagan House Hotel
Achintore Road, Fort William PH33 6RW

Tel: 01397 702452 Fax: 01397 702606
e.mail: frontdesk@innseagan-holidays.com
Web: www.innseagan-holidays.com

"The Lochside Hotel where standards matter"
Innseagan is spectacularly located in its own grounds on the shores of Loch Linnhe only one and a half miles from Fort William town centre. With 24 en-suite bedrooms we are large enough to provide the facilities, privacy and services of a hotel yet small enough to give each guest personal attention. Our new casual dining has proved highly popular with our guests.
The owners and staff take pride in our high standards of service, comfort and cleanliness. Phone now for our brochure or to book.
Two large car parks. **Sorry no coach parties.**

★★★

HOTEL

Innseagan House Hotel
Achintore Road, Fort William, Inverness-shire, PH33 6RW
Tel: 01397 702452 Fax: 01397 702606
E-mail: frontdesk@innseagan-holidays.com
Web: www.innseagan-holidays.com
This Victorian house, situated in its own grounds has been tastefully extended and fully modernised. It now offers all the facilities and comfort of a modern hotel whilst maintaining the character of the original building. Only 1.5 miles from Fort William and overlooking Loch Linnhe to the mountains. Cleanliness and efficiency are the watchwords of the management and staff.

2 Single	All En Suite	B&B per person	Open Jan-Dec
7 Twin		from £32.50 Single	
15 Double		from £23.50 Dbl/Twn	

★★★

GUEST HOUSE

Mansefield House
Corpach, Fort William, Inverness-shire, PH33 7LT
Tel/Fax: 01397 772262
E-mail: mansefield@aol.com
Web: www.fortwilliamaccommodation.com
This traditional Scottish Guest House is situated on the 'Road to the Isles' and set in mature gardens with views of the surrounding mountains. We specialise in relaxation, comfort and home cuisine. Being small and select the ambience is special and attention personal and friendly.

1 Twin	All En Suite	B&B per person	Open Jan-Dec excl
2 Double		from £20.00 Dbl/Twn	Xmas
2 Family			B&B + Eve.Meal
			from £34.00

All properties graded by VisitScotland, formerly known as the Scottish Tourist Board. | Key to symbols is on back flap.

Fort William, Inverness-shire   Map Ref: 3H12

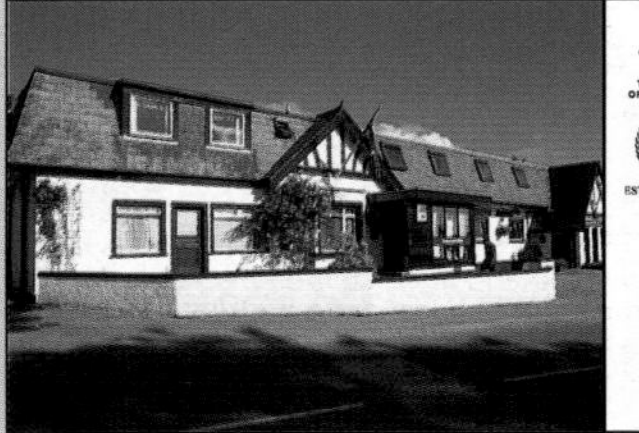

The Moorings Hotel

BANAVIE, FORT WILLIAM PH33 7LY
Telephone: 01397 772797 Fax: 01397 772441
e.mail: reservations@moorings-fortwilliam.co.uk
Web: www.moorings-fortwilliam.co.uk
Relaxing countryside hotel, 5 minutes from Fort William, beside the
Caledonian Canal with views of Ben Nevis. Excellent Restaurant with AA
Rosette and RAC Merit Awards. Bar meals are served in the Mariners Bar and
the Upper Lounge. 28 en-suite bedrooms, friendly, personal service –
an ideal base for your Highland holiday. AA ⊛   AA/RAC ★★★.

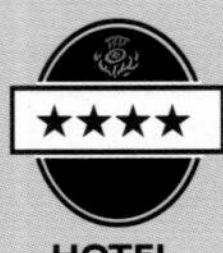

HOTEL

Moorings Hotel
Banavie, by Fort William, Inverness-shire,
PH33 7LY
Tel: 01397 772797 Fax: 01397 772441
E-mail: reservations@moorings-fortwilliam.co.uk
Web: www.moorings-fortwilliam.co.uk

Privately owned hotel situated beside the Caledonian Canal and
Neptune's Staircase. Many rooms have views of the Ben Nevis mountain
range and canal locks. Restaurant and Mariners bar serving interesting
and well presented meals using local produce where available.

2 Single	All En Suite	B&B per person	Open Jan-Dec
6 Twin		from £34.00 Single	B&B + Eve.Meal from
19 Double		from £34.00 Dbl/Twn	£57.00
1 Family			

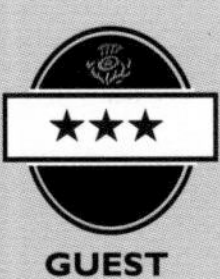

GUEST
HOUSE

Stronchreggan View Guest House
Achintore Road, Fort William, PH33 6RW
Tel/Fax: 01397 704644
E-mail: patricia@apmac.freeserve.co.uk
Web: www.stronchreggan.co.uk

Stronchreggan View is family run by Archie and Pat McQueen. Modern
double glazed house overlooking Loch Linnhe with views of the Ardgour
Hills and surrounding countryside. Excellent centre for visiting Oban,
Mull, Skye, Aviemore and many other spots.

1 Twin	All En Suite	B&B per person	Open Mar-Nov
4 Double		from £20.00 Dbl/Twn	B&B + Eve.Meal from
			£30.00

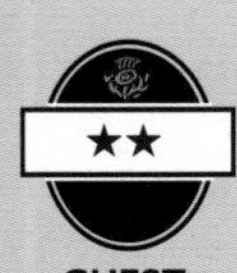

GUEST
HOUSE

Viewfield
Alma Road, Fort William, Inverness-shire, PH33 6HD
Tel: 01397 704763

Family house in elevated location set above Fort William yet within
walking distance of town centre. Private parking available.

1 Single	2 En Suite fac	B&B per person	Open Jan-Dec
3 Family	2 Priv.NOT ensuite	from £16.00 Single	
		from £16.00 Dbl/Twn	
		Room only from £15.00	

Fort William, Inverness-shire   Map Ref: 3H12

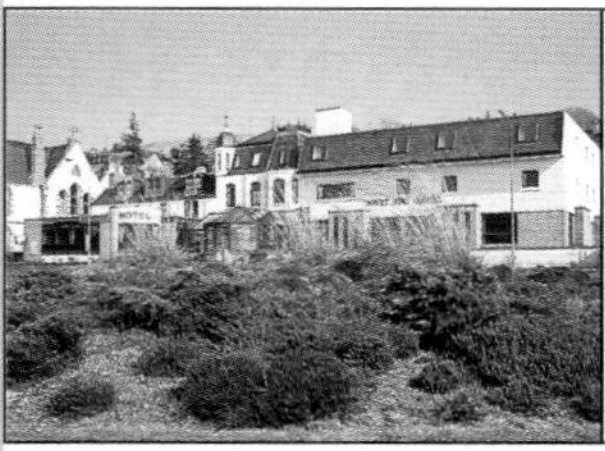

West End Hotel
Achintore Road, Fort William PH33 6ED
Telephone: 01397 702614   Fax: 01397 706279
e.mail: welcome@westend-hotel.co.uk
Web: www.westend-hotel.co.uk

Family run hotel overlooking Loch Linnhe on main road into town,
3 minutes walk from shops. All rooms ensuite with colour television,
telephone and tea-making facilities. Table d'hôte menu/bar meals.
Entertainment 3/4 nights during summer season. Enjoys breathtaking
views of Loch Linnhe and the Ardgour mountains.

★★★

HOTEL

West End Hotel
Achintore Road, Fort William, Inverness-shire,
PH33 6ED
Tel: 01397 702614 Fax: 01397 706279

Family run hotel in the centre of Fort William overlooking Loch Linnhe.
Ideal base for touring the West Highlands.

7 Single	51 En Suite fac	B&B per person	Open Feb-Dec
21 Twin		£25.00-£40.00 Single	
17 Double		£20.00-£35.00 Dbl/Twn	
5 Family			

---

by Fort William, Inverness-shire   Map Ref: 3H12

★★★★

RESTAURANT
WITH ROOMS

Old Pines Restaurant with Rooms
Spean Bridge, by Fort William, PH34 4EG
Tel: 01397 712324 Fax: 01397 712433
E-mail: handgh@oldpines.co.uk
Web: www.oldpines.co.uk

Masterchef Proprietor and Restaurant of the year 2000 award in Good
Food guide. Taste of Scotland Macallan Award Winner 1998. Winner -
Best Breakfast in Scotland 2001. (AA). A rare combination of relaxed
informality and seriously good food.

1 Single	All En Suite	Open Jan-Dec excl
2 Twin		Xmas/New Year
3 Double		B&B + Eve.Meal
2 Family		£62.00-£82.00

Foyers, Inverness-shire   Map Ref: 4A10

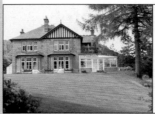

Foyers Bay House

Foyers, Loch Ness, Inverness IV2 6YB
Tel: 01456 486624 Fax: 01456 486337
e.mail: panciroli@foyersbay.freeserve.co.uk
Web: www.foyersbay.freeserve.co.uk
Splendid Victorian villa overlooking Loch Ness. Lovely grounds adjoining famous
falls of Foyers. Conservatory cafe-restaurant with breathtaking views of Loch
Ness. Ideal base for touring the many historical and tourist attractions in this
beautiful region. Also six self-catering units within grounds.

★★★

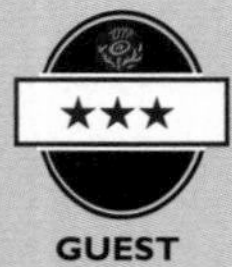

**GUEST
HOUSE**

Foyers Bay House
Foyers, Loch Ness, Inverness, IV2 6YB
Tel: 01456 486624 Fax: 01456 486337
E-mail: panciroli@foyersbay.freeserve.co.uk
Web: www.foyersbay.freeserve.co.uk

Set in its own 4 acres of wooded pine slopes, rhododendrons and apple
orchard, Foyers Bay House offers 5 rooms all with ensuite facilities. Just
500 yards from the famous Falls of Foyers and situated just by Loch Ness,
home of the famous monster.

3 Twin	All En Suite	B&B per person	Open Jan-Dec
2 Double		from £29.00 Single	B&B + Eve.Meal
		from £25.00 Dbl/Twn	from £31.00

Gairloch, Ross-shire   Map Ref: 3F7

★★★

HOTEL

Gairloch Hotel
Gairloch, Highland Region, IV21 2BL
Tel: 01786 436600 Fax: 01786 436650
E-mail: l.graig@shearingsholidays.co.uk
Web: www.shearingsholidays.com

Victorian hotel overlooking the Gairloch . Recently refurbished
throughout. Ideal centre for touring west coast. Golf and sailing nearby.

8 Single	All En Suite	Open Mar-Nov
51 Twin		
13 Double		

★★

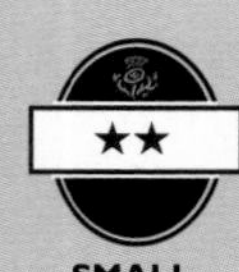

**SMALL
HOTEL**

Millcroft Hotel
Strath, Gairloch, Ross-shire, IV21 2BT
Tel: 01445 712376 Fax: 01445 712091
E-mail: enquiries@millcroft-hotel.co.uk
Web: www.millcroft-hotel.co.uk

Elevated position, close to shops, overlooking loch to mountains and
islands. Family run with good reputation for food using fresh local
produce.

5 Double	All En Suite	B&B per person	Open Jan-Dec
		from £28.00 Single	B&B + Eve.Meal
		from £26.00 Dbl/Twn	from £42.00

★

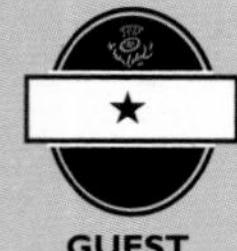

**GUEST
HOUSE**

The Mountain Restaurant & Lodge
Strath Square, Gairloch, Ross-shire, IV21 2BX
Tel: 01445 712316

In Gairloch's main square. Unique themed restaurant and lodge. Views
across bay to mountains. 4 poster beds and ocean views. Mountaineering
memorabilia donated by Chris Bonnington and others. Candlelit dinners
during H/S. Daytime speciality coffee shop featuring cappucino and
espresso drinks and over 60 different teas and coffees. Mountain style
home baking, snacks and lunches. All in an informal atmosphere.
Lochside sun terrace. Nature shop/ Bookstore.

1 Twin	All En Suite	B&B per person	Open Mar-Nov + New
2 Double		from £25.00 Single	Year
		from £19.95 Dbl/Twn	

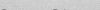

Important: Prices stated are estimates and may be subject to amendments

Gairloch, Ross-shire   Map Ref: 3F7

MYRTLE BANK HOTEL

Low Road, Gairloch, Ross-shire IV21 2BS
Telephone: 01445 712004   Fax: 01445 712214
e.mail: myrtlebank@msn.com   Web: www.myrtlebankhotel.com

Newly extended and refurbished, this family run hotel offers an ideal base for touring Wester Ross. Our widely recommended 'Taste of Scotland' restaurant serves local seafood and enjoys panoramic views to the Isle of Skye. Golf, sailing, sandy beaches and the world-famous Inverewe Garden are all nearby.

★★★

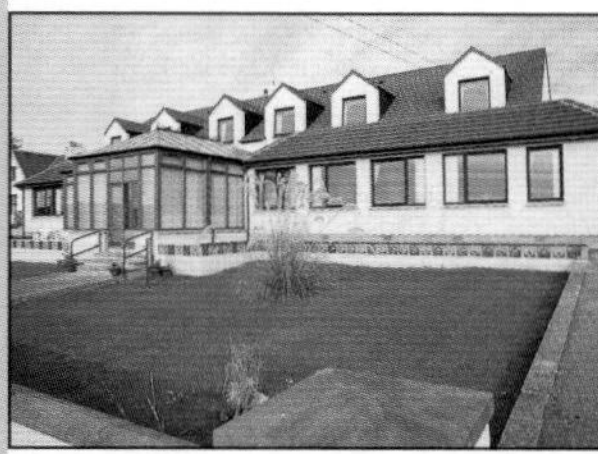

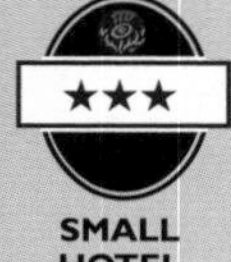

SMALL
HOTEL

Myrtle Bank Hotel
Low Road, Gairloch, Ross-shire, IV21 2BS
Tel: 01445 712004 Fax: 01445 712214
E-mail: myrtlebank@msn.com
Web: www.myrtlebankhotel.com

This family run hotel, recently refurbished and extended is situated on waterfront with views over Gairloch towards Isle of Skye. Restaurant and bar meals available, using fresh local produce.

1 Single	All En Suite	B&B per person	Open Jan-Dec excl
5 Twin		from £35.00 Single	Xmas/New Year
4 Double		from £70.00 Dbl/Twn	
2 Family			

THE OLD INN

GAIRLOCH, ROSS-SHIRE IV21 2BD
TEL: 01445 712006 FAX: 01445 712445
WEB: www.theoldinn.co.uk

Coaching Inn overlooking the harbour. Specialising in local seafood, game and real ales. Comfortable ensuite rooms, ideal base for walking, fishing, birdwatching, beaches, Inverewe Gardens and Torridon. Highland safaris and wildlife tours, pony trekking and golf close by. Off-season rates. Taste of Scotland accredited.

★★★

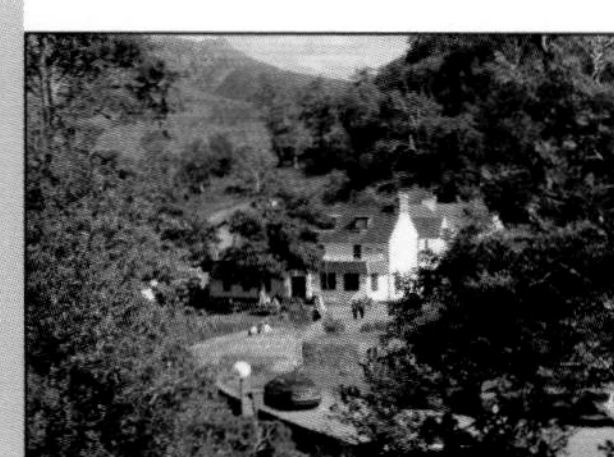

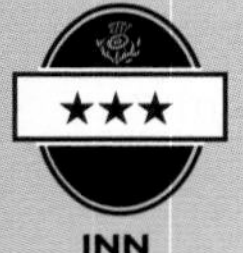

INN

The Old Inn
Gairloch, Ross-shire, IV21 2BD
Tel: 01445 712006 Fax: 01445 712445
Web: www.theoldinn.co.uk

18c coaching Inn in picturesque setting near sea-loch and hills. All rooms ensuite with colour TV. Specialities include Real Ale and the menu includes special dishes using the best of freshly caught seafood prepared on the premises.

1 Single	All En Suite	B&B per person	Open Jan-Dec
4 Twin		from £27.50 Single	
6 Double		from £25.00 Dbl/Twn	
3 Family			

★★★

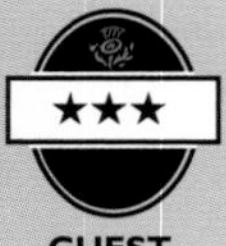

GUEST
HOUSE

Whindley Guest House
Auchtercairn Brae, Gairloch, Ross-shire, IV21 2BN
Tel/Fax: 01445 712340
E-mail: whindleygairloch@tinyworld.co.uk
Web: www.whindley.co.uk

Modern bungalow with large garden in elevated position, with fine views overlooking Gairloch Bay, and across to Skye. Beach and golf course nearby. Evening meals by arrangement. Non smoking house.

1 Twin	All En Suite	B&B per person	Open Jan-Dec excl
1 Double		from £19.00 Single	Xmas/New Year
1 Family		from £19.00 Dbl/Twn	B&B + Eve.Meal
			from £33.00

All properties graded by VisitScotland, formerly known as the Scottish Tourist Board.   Key to symbols is on back flap.

Garve, Ross-shire | **Map Ref: 4A8**

★★★

SMALL
HOTEL

Inchbae Lodge Hotel
by Garve, Ross-shire, IV23 2PH
Tel: 01997 455269 Fax: 01997 455207
E-mail: info@inchbae-lodge-hotel.co.uk
Web: www.inchbae-lodge-hotel.co.uk

Victorian former hunting lodge, now a family run hotel situated half way between Inverness and Ullapool, on the River Blackwater. Some ground floor rooms are available in a separate block; these are particularly suitable for the less mobile, and for guests with dogs. Activities available in the area include walking, climbing, cycling; excellent base for exploring the NorthWest and East Highlands.

1 Single	All En Suite	B&B per person	Open Jan-Dec excl
6 Twin		from £35.00 Single	Xmas
4 Double		from £29.00 Dbl/Twn	B&B + Eve.Meal
4 Family		Room only	from £52.00
		from £42.00	

Glencoe, Argyll | **Map Ref: 1F1**

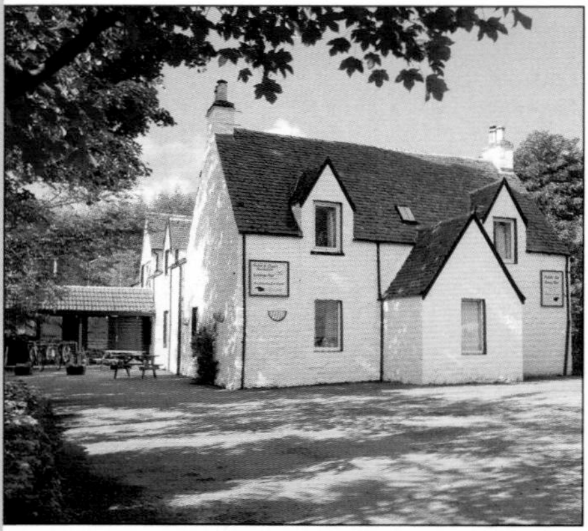

CLACHAIG INN
Glencoe, Argyll PH49 4HX
Tel: 01855 811252 Fax: 01855 811679
e.mail: inn@clachaig.com
web: www.clachaig.com

Set in the heart of this awe-inspiring glen with glorious mountain views, the Clachaig has been a source of hospitality to visitors to the glen for over 300 years. A magnificent Highland setting ideal for your holiday to relax unwind and adjust to a slower pace. A perfect base for touring and sightseeing the beautiful West Coast or local walking and bird watching. Mountain sports, water sports and fishing available locally. Comfortable accommodation in en-suite rooms with TV. Imaginative freshly prepared food. Great range of cask conditioned ales and malt whiskies. Good Beer Guide listed. Luxury chalets also available.
B&B from £22-£36 with D,B&B from £33-£46.

★

INN

Clachaig Inn - Glencoe
Glencoe, Argyll, PH49 4HX
Tel: 01855 811252 Fax: 01855 811679
E-mail: inn@glencoescotland.com
Web: www.glencoescotland.com

Set in the heart of Glencoe with magnificent views, a unique atmosphere and a warm family welcome. Comfortable accommodation and interesting menus specialising in local produce and a large selection of cask conditioned ales. Your ideal holiday base. Some annexe accommodation. Some non-smoking bedrooms.

2 Single	16 En Suite fac	B&B per person	Open Jan-Dec
7 Twin	1 Pub Bath/Show	£25.00-£35.00 Single	B&B + Eve.Meal
5 Double		£22.00-£35.00 Dbl/Twn	£33.00-£46.00
5 Family			

★★★

GUEST
HOUSE

Dorrington Lodge
Tigh-Phuirt, Glencoe, Argyll, PH49 4HN
Tel: 01855 811653 Fax: 01855 811995
E-mail: info@dorrington-lodge.com
Web: www.dorrington-lodge.com

Comfortable, modern house just off main road, with excellent views over Loch Leven. Home cooked meals using quality local produce.

2 Twin	3 En Suite fac	B&B per person	Open Jan-Dec excl
2 Double	1 Priv.NOT ensuite	from £20.00 Single	Xmas/New Year
		from £18.00 Dbl/Twn	B&B + Eve.Meal
			from £28.00

Important: Prices stated are estimates and may be subject to amendments

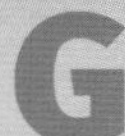

Glencoe, Argyll

Map Ref: 1F1

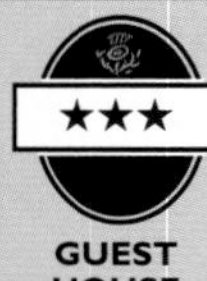

GUEST HOUSE

★★★

Dunire Guest House
Glencoe, Argyll, PH49 4HS
Tel: 01855 811305 Fax: 01855 811671

| 2 Twin | All En Suite | B&B per person | Open 27 Dec-Nov |
| 3 Double | | from £17.00 Dbl/Twn | excl Xmas |

Modern bungalow in centre of Glencoe Village. Ideal base for touring, climbing and hill walking, in fact all outdoor pursuits. All bedrooms tastefully furnished with TV's, radio's and tea-making facilities. Cosy guests lounge. Ample private parking. Drying facilities for walkers.

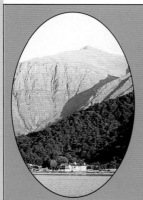

Glencoe hotel

GLENCOE • SCOTLAND • PH49 4HW
Tel: 01855 811245 Fax: 01855 811687
e.mail: glencoehotel@hotmail.com
web: http://www.GlencoeHotel-Scotland.com

Experience the romance and drama of Scotland's West Highlands where the mountains meet the sea and an air of mystery still shrouds the remote glens. The Glencoe Hotel is the natural choice for holiday satisfaction where we will tempt you with the quality of our cuisine and the extensive selection of Scotch Whiskies in our cosy cocktail bar. All rooms have private facilities. An ideal base for both the outdoor enthusiast and the adventurous motorist and traveller. Full colour brochure and current tariff available on request. Open All Year.

Special **GLENCOE STOPOVER** Holiday

Any five consecutive nights, Full Breakfast and Table d'Hote Dinner, complimentary 'Dram' on arrival and complimentary Wine with Dinner on last evening.

From **£145** per person

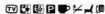

Glencoe hotel

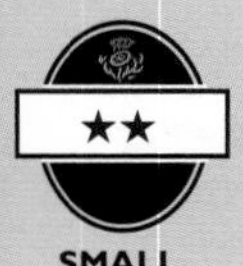

SMALL HOTEL

★★

Glencoe Hotel
Glencoe, West Highlands, PH49 4HW
Tel: 01855 811245 Fax: 01855 811687
E-mail: glencoehotel@hotmail.com
Web: www.GlencoeHotel-Scotland.com

2 Single	All En Suite	B&B per person	Open Jan-Dec excl
3 Twin		from £36.00 Single	Xmas
7 Double		from £24.00 Dbl/Twn	
3 Family		Room only per person	
		from £20.00	

In the same family for over 60 years this hotel offers a warm and friendly atmosphere with superb views over Loch Leven and beyond.

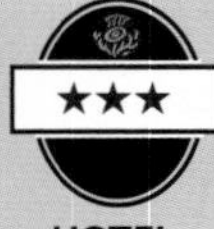

HOTEL

★★★

Isles of Glencoe Hotel & Leisure Centre
Ballachulish, nr Fort William, Argyll, PH49 4HL
Tel: 01855 821582 Fax: 01855 821463
E-mail: reservations@freedomglen.co.uk
Web: www.freedomglen.co.uk

21 Twin	All En Suite	B&B per person	Open Jan-Dec
22 Double		£75.00-£85.00 Single	
16 Family		£75.00-£95.00 Dbl/Twn	

Almost afloat, nestling on the lochside, this friendly, family hotel offers everything for which you dream on holiday; spacious loch and mountain-view bedrooms and a relaxed, convivial ambience. Luxuriate in the Leisure Centre - heated pool, sauna, steam room, jacuzzi, exercise room and solarium. Enjoy the casual lochside conservatory restaurant. Special breaks.

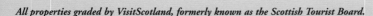

Glencoe, Argyll

Map Ref: 1F1

★★★

GUEST HOUSE

Scorrybreac Guest House
Glencoe, Argyll, PH49 4HT
Tel/Fax: 01855 811354
E-mail: john@scorrybeac.freeserve.co.uk
Web: www.scorrybreac.cwc.net

Scorrybreac is a comfortable single storey guest house in beautiful woodland surroundings, overlooking Loch Leven, in a quiet secluded location on the edge of village, near local forest walks. Ideal base for exploring Glencoe and Ben Nevis area or for a shorter stay on a more extended tour of the Highlands. Colourful garden. Ample parking.

3 Twin	5 En Suite fac
3 Double	1 Priv.NOT ensuite

B&B per person
from £20.00 Single
from £18.00 Dbl/Twn

Open 26 Dec - 31 Oct

★★★

GUEST HOUSE

Strathlachlan - The Glencoe Guest House
Upper Carnoch, Glencoe, PH49 4HU
Tel: 01855 811244 Fax: 01855 811873
E-mail: bookings@glencoeguesthouse.com
Web: www.glencoeguesthouse.com

Strathlachlan is a modern, whitewashed bungalow standing on former croft land in a quiet, peaceful setting overlooking the River Coe. The guest house lies at the end of a cul-de-sac on the edge of Glencoe Village and only two minutes walk from the monument marking the site of the infamous massacre. Popular with walkers, climbers and skiers who tell interesting stories round the fireside at the end of the day.

1 Single	All En Suite
1 Twin	
2 Double	
2 Family	

B&B per person
from £17.00 Single
from £17.00 Dbl/Twn

Open Jan-Dec
B&B + Eve.Meal from £29.00

Glenfinnan, Inverness-shire

Map Ref: 3G12

★★★

SMALL HOTEL

The Prince's House
Glenfinnan, near Fort William, Inverness-shire PH37 4LT
Tel: 01397 722246
E-mail: princeshouse@glenfinnan.co.uk
Web: www.glenfinnan.co.uk

Set in historic "Bonnie Prince Charlie" country on the romantic Road to the Isles this former coaching inn has been tastefully modernised to provide all the facilities of modern day. We pride ourselves on giving individual attention and quality food in a relaxed atmosphere. Awarded an AA red rosette. Taste of Scotland member.

1 Single	All En Suite
2 Twin	
5 Double	
1 Family	

B&B per person
from £40.00 Single
from £35.00 Dbl/Twn

Open Mid Feb-Dec
B&B + Eve.Meal from £50.00

Grantown-on-Spey, Moray

Map Ref: 4C9

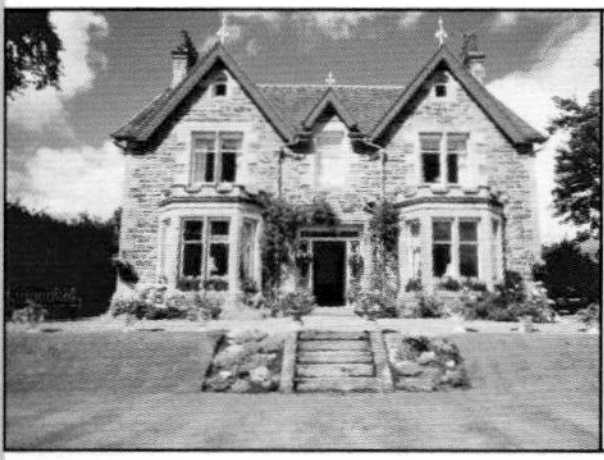

Ardconnel House

Woodlands Terrace, Grantown-on-Spey, Moray PH26 3JU
Tel/Fax: 01479 872104   e.mail: enquiry@ardconnel.com
Web: www.ardconnel.com

*An elegant and comfortable Victorian house furnished with antiques and pine.
All bedrooms are ensuite offering colour TV, hairdryer and hospitality tray.
Excellent "Taste of Scotland" dinner prepared by french owner/chef. Licensed.
No smoking throughout. 2001/2002 AA Guest Accommodation of the Year for Scotland.*

AA ◆◆◆◆◆   RAC ◆◆◆◆◆

★★★★★

GUEST HOUSE

Ardconnel House
Woodlands Terrace, Grantown-on-Spey, Moray, PH26 3JU
Tel/Fax: 01479 872104
E-mail: enquiry@ardconnel.com
Web: www.ardconnel.com

Splendid Victorian villa with private car parking. All rooms ensuite. No smoking throughout. Taste of Scotland selected member. Warm welcome assured. Peaceful friendly ambience. French and German spoken.

1 Single	All En Suite
1 Twin	
2 Double	
2 Family	

B&B per person
from £35.00 Single
from £30.00 Dbl/Twn

Open Easter-Nov
B&B + Eve.Meal from £52.50

Important: Prices stated are estimates and may be subject to amendments

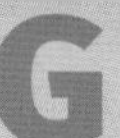

Grantown-on-Spey, Moray | **Map Ref: 4C9**

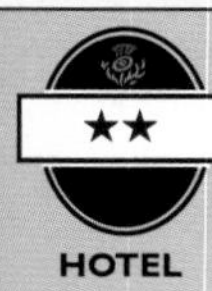

★★
HOTEL

Coppice Hotel
Grant Road, Grantown-on-Spey, PH26 3LD
Tel/Fax: 01479 872688

4 Single	All En Suite fac	B&B per person	Open Feb-Jan
2 Family	1 Pub Bath/Show	from £25.00 Single	B&B + Eve.Meal from
		from £25.00 Family	£35.00

The Coppice Hotel is privately owned and stands in it's own woodlands, in the heart of the Scottish Highlands, an area renowned for its scenic beauty. A warm welcome awaits.

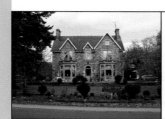

Culdearn House

Woodlands Terrace, Grantown-on-Spey, Moray PH26 3JU
Telephone: 01479 872106 Fax: 01479 873641
e.mail: culdearn@globalnet.co.uk Web: www.culdearn.com

Elegant country house with friendly Scottish hosts.
Comfortable rooms with every facility. Log fires.
Excellent cuisine with fine wine list and 80 malt whiskies.
Superb location for all manner of activities.
3 and 7 day breaks available. Taste of Scotland recommended.
On the Whisky and Castle Trails.

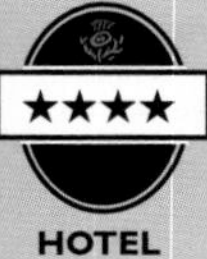

★★★★
HOTEL

Culdearn House Hotel
Woodlands Terrace, Grantown-on-Spey, Moray-shire
PH26 3JU
Tel: 01479 872106 Fax: 01479 873641
E-mail: culdearn@globalnet.co.uk
Web: www.culdearn.com

1 Single	All En Suite	DB&B per person	Open Mar-Nov
3 Twin		from £65.00 Single	B&B + Eve.Meal
5 Double		from £65.00 Dbl/Twn	£65.00

Elegant Victorian house, retaining many original features and caringly restored to include all modern comforts. Warm and friendly atmosphere. All rooms ensuite facilities. Taste of Scotland member. Award winning kitchen. Interesting wine list and unique collection of malt whisky.

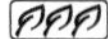

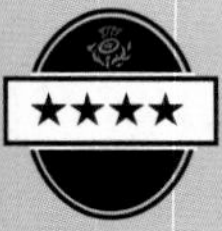

★★★★
GUEST HOUSE

Dunallan House
Woodside Avenue, Grantown-on-Spey, PH26 3JN
Tel/Fax: 01479 872140
E-mail: dunallan@cwcom.net
Web: www.dunallan.mcmail.com

1 Single	6 En Suite fac	B&B per person	Open Jan-Dec
2 Twin	1 Priv.NOT ensuite	from £25.00 Single	B&B + Eve.Meal
3 Double		from £22.00 Dbl/Twn	from £39.00
1 Family			

Dunallan is a splendid example of Victorian elegance oozing with the charm of a bygone era. Original period fireplaces are in the residents lounge and dining room, giving extra warmth to cheer you on those cooler evenings. Home cooking, featuring fresh local produce, by prior arrangement. All rooms are tastefully furnished, Victorian Room and Honeymoon Suite are also available.

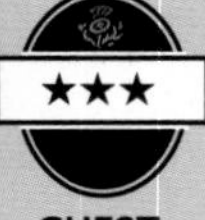

★★★
GUEST HOUSE

Firhall Guest House
Grant Road, Grantown-on-Spey, PH26 3LD
Tel: 01479 873097 Fax: 01479 873097
E-mail: firhall@cs.com
Web: www.SmoothHound.co.uk/hotels/firhall.html

1 Single	3 En Suite fac	B&B per person	Open Jan-Dec excl Xmas
1 Twin	1 Pub Bath/Show	£17.00-£19.00 Single	
1 Double	1 Priv. Bathroom	£17.00-£25.00 Dbl/Twn	
3 Family			

Firhall is a fine example of victorian elegance, retaining much of the original character of this period. Particular features include the beautifully preserved pitched pine woodwork, ornate cornices and marble fireplaces. Home cooking. Family run.

All properties graded by VisitScotland, formerly known as the Scottish Tourist Board. | **Key to symbols is on back flap.**

| Grantown-on-Spey, Moray | | | | Map Ref: 4C9 |

★★★★

GUEST HOUSE

Garden Park Guest House
Woodside Avenue, Grantown-on-Spey, Moray, PH26 3JN
Tel: 01479 873235

Victorian, stone built house set in own colourful garden, quietly located a short walk from the centre of Grantown on Spey. Guests' lounge with log-burning stove; home cooked meals made with fresh produce served in the dining room with its individual tables. A short selection of wines is available. Five ensuite rooms, one of which is on the ground floor. A friendly and relaxing base for exloring the area. French spoken.

3 Twin	All En Suite	B&B per person	Open Mar-Oct
2 Double		from £24.00 Single	B&B + Eve.Meal
		from £48.00 Dbl/Twn	£36.50

★★

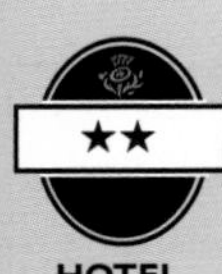

HOTEL

Grant Arms Hotel
The Square, Grantown on Spey, PH26 3HF
Tel: 01786 436600 Fax: 01786 436650
E-mail: l.graig@shearingsholidays.co.uk
Web: www.shearingsholidays.com

Victorian hotel (Queen Victoria stayed here in 1860) overlooking spacious town square. Ideal for touring the Highlands and Balmoral.

4 Single	All En Suite	Open Feb-Dec
33 Twin		
11 Double		
4 Family		

★★★★

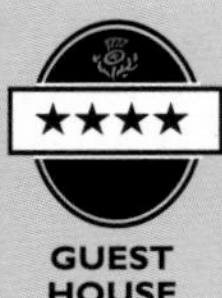

GUEST HOUSE

Kinross House
Woodside Avenue, Grantown-on-Spey, Moray, PH26 3JR
Tel: 01479 872042 Fax: 01479 873504
E-mail: milne@kinrosshouse.freeserve.co.uk
Web: www.kinrosshouse.freeserve.co.uk

Attractive Victorian villa in peaceful area. Welcoming and relaxed atmosphere with open fires. Traditional home-cooking using fresh local produce. Free use of sauna and cycles/mountain bikes. No smoking house. Ground floor rooms. Laundry service.

2 Single	6 Ensuite fac	B&B per person	Open Jan-Dec
2 Twin	1 Private Bath	from £24.00 Single	B&B + Eve.Meal
2 Double		from £46.00 Dbl/Twn	from £40.00
1 Family			

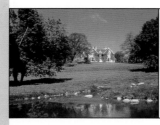

Muckrach Lodge Hotel & Restaurant
Dulnain Bridge, Grantown-on-Spey, Inverness-shire PH26 3LY
Tel: 01479 851257 Fax: 01479 851325
e.mail: info@muckrach.co.uk Web: www.muckrach.co.uk
Victorian Lodge in the heart of The Highlands. Cairngorms and Strathspey provides an unspoilt environment for recreation and rare wildlife, or tour Royal Deeside, Loch Ness, Skye and The Malt Whisky Trail. Lovely rooms, hospitable service, fine dining and a distinguished cellar turn a pleasant stay into a memorable experience. AA ❀❀

★★★★

HOTEL

Muckrach Lodge Hotel & Restaurant
Dulnain Bridge, Grantown on Spey, Inverness-shire, PH26 3LY
Tel: 01479 851257 Fax: 01479 851325
E-mail: info@muckrach.co.uk
Web: www.muckrach.co.uk

Victorian sporting lodge in peaceful setting with 10 secluded acres overlooking river Dulnain with views to Strathspey and the Cairngorms. Spacious bedrooms, open fires and public rooms with fine dining and distinguished cellar. Dedicated business suite for small conferences. Aromatherapy and beautician services.

2 Single	13 En Suite fac	B&B per person	Open Jan-Dec
2 Twin	1 Priv.NOT ensuite	from £25.00 Single	
7 Double		from £25.00 Dbl/Twn	
3 Family			

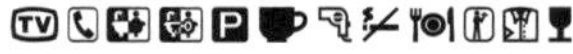

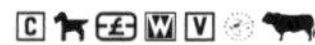

Important: Prices stated are estimates and may be subject to amendments

Grantown-on-Spey, Moray

Map Ref: 4C9

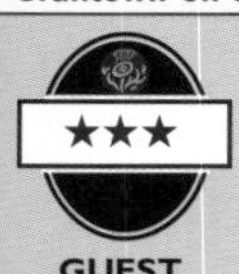

★★★
GUEST HOUSE

Parkburn Guest House
High Street, Grantown-on-Spey, Moray, PH26 3EN
Tel: 01479 873116

2 Single	4 En Suite fac	B&B per person	Open Jan-Dec
1 Twin	2 Pub Bath/Show	from £20.00 Single	
3 Double		from £20.00 Dbl/Twn	

Semi detached Victorian villa standing back from main road with ample parking available. Fishing and fishing tuition can be arranged.

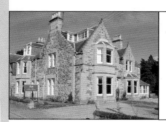

THE TASTE OF SCOTLAND

The Pines

18 Woodside Avenue, Grantown-on-Spey PH26 3JR
Telephone/Fax: 01479 872092
e.mail: info@thepinesgrantown.co.uk
Web: www.thepinesgrantown.co.uk

A stylish ancestral Highland home now used as a small hotel. The elegant lounges and dining rooms are filled with family portraits, other paintings, objets d'art and antiques. Outside, wander through the spacious, tranquil garden with its beautiful woodland backdrop leading to the River Spey. Golfing. Bird watching. Fishing. Walking. Whisky. Castles.

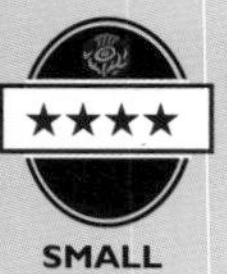

★★★★
SMALL HOTEL

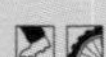

The Pines
Woodside Avenue, Grantown-on-Spey, Moray, PH26 3JR
Tel/Fax: 01479 872092
E-mail: info@thepinesgrantown.co.uk
Web: www.thepinesgrantown.co.uk

1 Single	7 En Suite fac	B&B per person	Open Mar-Oct
3 Twin	1 Priv.NOT ensuite	from £40.00 Single	B&B + Eve.Meal
4 Double		from £35.00 Dbl/Twn	from £60.00

Beautiful 19th century country house, totally re-furbished and restored to the highest standards. All rooms en-suite or private. Two lounges and small library. Choice of dining room or conservatory. Taste of Scotland members. Large, secluded garden in woodland setting. Rare birds, deer and red squirrel.

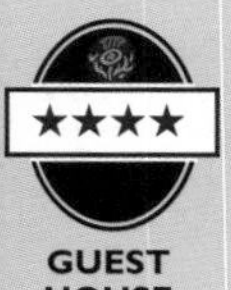

★★★★
GUEST HOUSE

Rossmor Guest House
Woodlands Terrace, Grantown-on-Spey, Moray,
PH26 3JU
Tel/Fax: 01479 872201
E-mail: dennis.day@vigin.net
Web: http://freespace.virgin.net/dennis.day/rossmor.html

2 Twin	All En Suite	B&B per person	Open Mar-Nov
4 Double		from £25.00 Single	
		from £22.00 Dbl/Twn	

Spacious Victorian detached house with original features and large garden. A warm welcome. Parking. Panoramic views. No smoking throughout.

Invergarry, Inverness-shire

Map Ref: 3H11

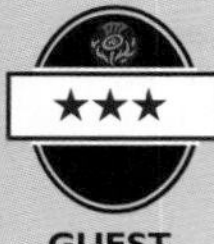

★★★
GUEST HOUSE

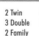

Forest Lodge
South Laggan, Invergarry, by Spean Bridge, Inverness-shire,
PH34 4EA
Tel: 01809 501219 Fax: 01809 501476
E-mail: info@flgh.co.uk   Web: www.flgh.co.uk

2 Twin	6 En Suite fac	B&B per person	Open Jan-Dec excl
3 Double	1 Priv.NOT ensuite	from £21.00 Dbl/Twn	Xmas/New Year
2 Family			B&B + Eve.Meal
			from £34.00

Staying in the Great Glen for one night or more? Situated where the Caledonian Canal joins Loch Lochy and Oich. We offer pleasant, ensuite accommodation and home cooking in our relaxed and friendly home. Open all year for touring, walking or just to relax. Please call for a brochure.

All properties graded by VisitScotland, formerly known as the Scottish Tourist Board. | Key to symbols is on back flap. |

Glengarry Castle Hotel

Invergarry, Inverness-shire PH35 4HW
Tel: 01809 501254   Fax: 01809 501207
e.mail: castle@glengarry.net
Web: www.glengarry.net

Country House Hotel privately owned and personally
run by the MacCallum family for over 40 years.
Situated in the heart of the Great Glen, this is a
perfect centre for touring both the West Coast and
Inverness/Loch Ness area. Magnificently situated in
60 acres of wooded grounds overlooking Loch Oich.
Recently refurbished, 4 rooms with 4-poster beds,
all rooms have ensuite bathrooms, TV, radio and
telephone. Private tennis court, trout and pike fishing
in Loch Oich. Children and dogs welcome.

For brochure please contact Mr D MacCallum.

HOTEL

Glengarry Castle Hotel
Invergarry, Inverness-shire, PH35 4HW
Tel: 01809 501254 Fax: 01809 501207
E-mail: castle@glengarry.net
Web: www.glengarry.net

Privately owned country mansion, some rooms with four-poster beds.
Extensive wooded grounds to loch with impressive hill and forest views.

2 Single	25 En Suite fac	B&B per person	Open 22 Mar-11 Nov
10 Twin	1 Priv.NOT ensuite	£50.00-£55.00 Single	B&B + Eve.Meal
11 Double	2 Pub Bath/Show	£40.00-£70.00 Dbl/Twn	from £66.00
2 Family			

**SMALL
HOTEL**

Invergarry Hotel
Invergarry, Inverness-shire, PH35 4HJ
Tel: 01809 501206 Fax: 01809 501400
E-mail: hotel@invergarry.net
Web: www.invergarry.net

Our family owned and managed hotel is the ideal touring base. See
Skye, Ben Nevis, Loch Ness and much much more or just relax in front of
an open fire with your favourite tipple and good book. The choice is
yours. Real ales and a lot of malt whiskies.

1 Single	All En Suite	B&B per person	Open Jan-Dec
3 Twin		from £30.00 Single	
5 Double		from £25.00 Dbl/Twn	
1 Family			

**SMALL
HOTEL**

Glenmoriston Arms Hotel & Restaurant
Loch Ness, Inverness-shire, IV63 7YA
Tel: 01320 351206 Fax: 01320 351308
E-mail: scott@lochness-glenmoriston.co.uk
Web: www.lochness-glenmoriston.co.uk

18c hotel in Highland village, offering a wide range of fine malt
whiskies. Fishing available. Easy access for touring Skye, Torridon and
Loch Ness area.

3 Twin	All En Suite	B&B per person	Open Mar-Dec excl
4 Double		from £55.00 Single	Xmas/New Year
1 Family		from £35.00 Dbl/Twn	B&B + Eve.Meal from
			£65.00

Important: Prices stated are estimates and may be subject to amendments

Inverness **Map Ref: 4B8**

★★★ GUEST HOUSE

Aberfeldy Lodge Guest House

11 Southside Road, Inverness, IV2 3BG
Tel: 01463 231120 Fax: 01463 234741
E-mail: class@algh.freeserve.co.uk
Web: www.SmoothHound.co.uk/hotels/aberfeld.html

Comfortable Guest House close to city centre. All rooms ensuite. Hearty breakfast, vegetarians catered for and children welcome. Private car park.

2 Twin, 3 Double, 4 Family — All En Suite
B&B per person from £25.00 Single, from £19.00 Dbl/Twn
Open Jan-Dec

★★★★ GUEST HOUSE

Ach Aluinn Guest House

27 Fairfield Road, Inverness, IV3 5QD
Tel/Fax: 01463 230127

Newly refurbished, detached Victorian house with private parking in quiet residential road. 5 minutes walk from town centre, restaurants, Eden Court Theatre and Railway Station. All rooms ensuite, with bath and shower. Lock-up facilities for motor and pedal cycles.

2 Twin, 1 Double, 2 Family — All En Suite
B&B per person from £25.00 Single, from £45.00 Dbl/Twn
Open Jan-Dec

★★★ GUEST HOUSE

Ardmuir House

16 Ness Bank, Inverness, IV2 4SF
Tel/Fax: 01463 231151
E-mail: hotel@ardmuir.com
Web: www.ardmuir.com

Family run guest house on the bank of the River Ness close to town centre and Ness Islands. Conveniently situated for exploring the Highlands.

1 Single, 4 Twin, 3 Double, 2 Family — All En Suite
B&B per person from £34.50 Single, from £57.00 Dbl/Twn
Open Jan-Dec excl Xmas/New Year

★★★★ GUEST HOUSE

Avalon Guest House

79 Glenurquhart Road, Inverness, IV3 5PB
Tel: 01463 239075 Fax: 01463 709827
E-mail: avalonhouse79@hotmail.com

Recently built, family run Guest House, situated on A82 road to Loch Ness and Fort William. A 10 minute walk takes you into the town centre and all its amenities such as restaurants, Eden Court Theatre, cinemas and many more. Close to Sports Centre and Aquadome. Ideal base for touring the Highlands.

2 Single, 2 Twin, 1 Double, 1 Family — 5 En Suite fac, 1 Pub Bath/Show
B&B per person from £30.00 Single, from £25.00 Dbl/Twn, Room only from £23.00
Open Feb-Dec

★★★★★ GUEST HOUSE

Ballifeary House Hotel

10 Ballifeary Road, Inverness, IV3 5PJ
Tel: 01463 235572 Fax: 01463 717583
E-mail: info@ballifearyhousehotel.co.uk
Web: www.ballifearyhousehotel.co.uk

Attractive detached Victorian villa situated in quiet residential area, and just a short walk to the Eden Court Theatre, River Ness and many excellent restaurants. The house is tastefully decorated and furnished throughout and has a very relaxed and friendly atmosphere. Lovely sitting room with wealth of tourist information. Large car park in the grounds. Establishment not suitable for families as minimum age is 15 years.

2 Twin, 3 Double — All En Suite
B&B per person from £48.00 Single, from £36.00 Dbl/Twn
Open Apr-Oct

Inverness | Map Ref: 4B8

Brae Ness Hotel
17 Ness Bank, Inverness, IV2 4SF
Tel: 01463 712266 Fax: 01463 231732
E-mail: braenesshotel@aol.com
Web: www.braenesshotel.co.uk

SMALL HOTEL

Family run hotel on River Ness close to town centre. Home cooking using fresh local produce a speciality. No smoking in dining room and most bedrooms.

1 Single	9 En Suite fac	B&B per person	Open May-Oct
4 Twin	1 Priv.NOT ensuite	from £35.00 Single	B&B + Eve.Meal
3 Double		from £29.00 Dbl/Twn	from £51.00
2 Family			

Cedar Villa Guest House
35 Kenneth Street, Inverness, IV3 5DH
Tel/Fax: 01463 230477
E-mail: cedarvilla@guesthouseinverness.co.uk
Web: www.guesthouseinverness.co.uk

GUEST HOUSE

Centrally situated with easy access to theatre, bus and railway.

2 Twin	3 En Suite	B&B per person	Open Jan-Dec excl Xmas
1 Double	1 Priv.NOT ensuite	from £18.00 Single	
3 Family		from £34.00 Dbl/Twn	

Craigmonie Hotel & Leisure Sportif
ANNFIELD ROAD, INVERNESS IV2 3HX
Telephone: 01463 231649   Fax: 01463 233720
e.mail: info@craigmonie.com   Web: www.craigmonie.com
Comfortable Town House style hotel, informal relaxed atmosphere, ensuite accommodation, including poolside suites and 4-poster deluxe double bedrooms. Full leisure facilities including heated pool, choice of fine dining in the Chardonnay restaurant, or al fresco Conservatory Wine Bar. Every taste and dining style is catered for. Room and breakfast, single from £76, twin/double from £96. **STB ★★★★   AA ★★★**

Craigmonie Hotel
Annfield Road, Inverness, IV2 3HX
Tel: 01463 231649 Fax: 01463 233720
E-mail: info@craigmonie.com
Web: www.craigmonie.com

HOTEL

Privately owned family run hotel, situated just a short distance from the city centre, ample car parking is available. Facilities include the "Leisure Sportif" - heated pool, sauna, solarium, mini gymnasium, a choice of formal or informal dining is available whether in the Chardonnay Restaurant, the Conservatory or Bistro.

4 Single	All En Suite	B&B per person	Open Jan-Dec
14 Twin	Suites avail	£70.00-£78.00 Single	
14 Double	7 Pub Bath/Show	£48.00-£58.00 Dbl/Twn	
3 Family			

Crown Court Hotel
25 Southside Road, Inverness, IV2 3BG
Tel: 01463 234816 Fax: 01463 714900
E-mail: reception@crowncourt.co.uk
Web: www.crowncourt.co.uk

SMALL HOTEL

Lying in a quiet residential area close to Inverness town centre, the Crown Court Hotel has the ambience of a country house hotel in the town.

3 Twin	All En Suite	B&B per person	Open Jan-Dec
5 Double		from £37.50 Dbl/Twn	
1 Family			

Important: Prices stated are estimates and may be subject to amendments

Inverness | Map Ref: 4B8

SMALL HOTEL

Cuchullin Lodge Hotel
43 Culduthel Road, Inverness, IV2 4HQ
Tel: 01463 231945 Fax: 01463 231613
E-mail: culduthel@aol.com
Web: www.cuchullinlodge-culduthel.com

Victorian house with many original features and large garden with mature trees, in residential area on south side of town centre. Some annexe bedrooms.

3 Single All En Suite
5 Twin
3 Double
1 Family

B&B per person
from £45.00 Single
from £38.00 Dbl/Twn

Open Feb-Oct

TV ⊞ P 🍴 ⬚ ⬚ ⬚

⬚ V

CULDUTHEL LODGE
14 Culduthel Road, Inverness IV2 4AG
Tel: 01463 240089   Fax: 01463 240089
e.mail: STB@culduthel.com
Web: www.culduthel.com

Overlooking the River Ness stands Culduthel Lodge, an elegant Georgian residence of architectural interest. Caringly restored, furnished and decorated with great attention to detail and comfort, we offer a warm and relaxed atmosphere. In fine weather, aperitifs are enjoyed on the garden terrace. In cooler months the drawing room beckons with crackling log fires. The dining room provides an inviting setting in which to enjoy a daily changing menu of imaginative cooking with good wines. Our guest rooms provide more than one would expect: television, CD/Radio cassette player, hospitality tray, telephone, flowers, fruit, sherry, umbrella, luxury toiletries, hairdryer and complimentary newspaper.

SMALL HOTEL

Culduthel Lodge
14 Culduthel Road, Inverness, IV2 4AG
Tel/Fax: 01463 240089
E-mail: stb@culduthel.com
Web: www.culduthel.com

An elegant Georgian residence built c1840 set in attractive gardens on elevated site above the River Ness. Quiet location a few minutes walk from town centre.

1 Single All En Suite
2 Twin
8 Double
1 Family

B&B per person
from £45.00 Single
from £45.00 Dbl/Twn

Open Jan-Dec
B&B + Eve.Meal
from £65.00

TV ☏ ⊞ P 🍴 ⬚ ✕ ⬚ ⬚ ⬚ ⬚ ⬚

🐕 ⬚ V

HOTEL

Drumossie Hotel
Old Perth Road, Inverness, IV2 2BE
Tel: 01786 436600 Fax: 01786 436650
E-mail: l.graig@shearingsholidays.co.uk
Web: www.shearingsholidays.com

Hotel standing in its own grounds 3 miles (5kms) South of Inverness with easy access to A9. Ideal for touring. Facilities for meetings and conferences.

19 Single All En Suite
45 Twin
6 Double
2 Family

Open Feb-Dec

TV ☏ ⊞ P 🍴 ⬚ ⬚

⬚ W V

All properties graded by VisitScotland, formerly known as the Scottish Tourist Board. | Key to symbols is on back flap.

Inverness   Map Ref: 4B8

GUEST HOUSE
★★★★★

Eden House
8 Ballifeary Road, Inverness, IV3 5PJ
Tel/Fax: 01463 230278
E-mail: edenhouse@btinternet.com
Web: www.edenhouse.btinternet.co.uk

Eden House is a lovely Victorian Villa set in a quiet residential part of the City yet only minutes from City Centre and local attractions. Eden House has been personally run for many years by the resident proprietors Les and Christina Hunter who ensure all guests are warmly welcomed into their home and enjoy Five Star accommodation for their holiday in the Highlands.

2 Twin	All En Suite	B&B per person	Open Apr-Nov
2 Double		from £40.00 Single	
1 Family		from £30.00 Dbl/Twn	

GUEST HOUSE
★★★★

Felstead Guest House
18 Ness Bank, Inverness, IV2 4SF
Tel/Fax: 01463 231634
E-mail: felsteadgh@aol.com
Web: www.jafsoft.com/felstead/felstead.html

Overlooking the River Ness, 5 mins walk from the town centre, Felstead, an elegant Georgian house, offers a high standard of comfort and service with a homely, relaxing and friendly touch by its owners.

2 Single	5 En Suite fac	B&B per person	Open Jan-Dec excl
3 Twin/	1 Priv.NOT ensuite	£28.00-£35.00 Single	Xmas/New Year
Family	1 Pub Bath/Show	£25.00-£35.00 Dbl/Twn	
2 Double			

Glendruidh House Hotel
Tel: 01463 226499   Fax: 01463 710745
e.mail: wts@cozzee-nessie-bed.co.uk
Web: www.cozzee-nessie-bed.co.uk/intro.html
Glendruidh House specialises in good old-fashioned hospitality. Situated amongst extensive grounds adjacent to Loch Ness golf course. Savour the superb traditional cuisine prepared from the very best fresh local produce. Relax in the circular drawing room or enjoy a dram in the sumptuous bar. **Individual oasis well worth finding!**

SMALL HOTEL
★★★★

Glendruidh House Hotel
by Castle Heather, Old Edinburgh Road South, Inverness, IV2 6AR
Tel: 01463 226499 Fax: 01463 710745
E-mail: wts@cozzee-nessie-bed.co.uk
Web: www.cozzee-nessie-bed.co.uk/intro.html

Mainly 19th century house set amongst large grounds consisting of woods and rolling lawns. Unique circular drawing room and elegant dining room serving excellent traditional cuisine prepared from the very best local produce. With a superb wine list and an excellent selection of malt whiskies you can be sure of a very pleasant stay. A wonderful base for many activity holidays, touring or just taking things easy. No smoking throughout.

2 Twin	All En Suite	B&B per person	Open Jan-Dec
3 Double		from £49.00 Single	B&B + Eve.Meal
		from £36.00 Dbl/Twn	from £65.00

Inverness	Map Ref: 4B8

Glen Mhor Hotel & Restaurants
9-12 Ness Bank, Inverness IV2 4SG
Tel: 01463 234308 Fax: 01463 713170
e.mail: glenmhor@ukonline.co.uk Web: www.glen-mhor.com

Beautifully and quietly situated on River Ness near stations, parks, sports facilities, theatre and shops. All bedrooms ensuite. Plenty of car parking. Great Scottish and international cuisine in 2 restaurants. Resident beautician. Golf, fishing, shooting by arrangement. Ideal base for activity holidays and touring Loch Ness, coastal beaches and the Highlands.

★★★

HOTEL

Glen Mhor Hotel & Restaurants
9-12 Ness Bank, Inverness, IV2 4SG
Tel: 01463 234308 Fax: 01463 713170
E-mail: glenmhor@ukonline.co.uk
Web: www.glen-mhor.com

Traditional stone built house in quiet residential area, overlooking River Ness. Only 5 minutes walk to town centre and Eden Court Theatre on opposite side of river. Adjacent cottage/annexe accommodation. Choice of restaurant and Nicos Bistro.

9 Single	42 En Suite fac	B&B per person	Open Jan-Dec excl New
23 Twin	3 Priv.NOT ensuite	from £49.00 Single	Year
10 Double		from £35.00 Dbl/Twn	B&B + Eve.Meal
3 Family			from £49.00

Inverness Marriott Hotel
Culcabock Road, Inverness IV2 3LP
Tel: 01463 237166   e.mail: inverness@marriotthotels.co.uk
Fax: 01463 225208 Web: www.marriotthotels.com/invkm

4-star hotel only one mile from town. All 82 rooms are luxuriously furnished and very spacious. Extensive leisure complex with large indoor pool. Hotel has fine restaurant, large comfortable lounge areas and a south-facing conservatory. Excellent Weekend Breaks and 5 and 7 night luxury holidays available all year. ★★★★ HOTEL

★★★★

HOTEL

Inverness Marriott Hotel
Culcabock Road, Inverness, IV2 3LP
Tel: 01463 237166 Fax: 01463 225208
E-mail: inverness@marriotthotels.co.uk
Web: www.marriotthotels.com/invkm

Original manor house dating back to the 18th century set in 4 acres of gardens. Leisure club with indoor swimming pool, jacuzzi, sauna, steam room, exercise room, hairdresser, beauty treatments and pitch and putt. 1 mile (2kms) from town centre, 7 miles (11kms) from airport.

2 Single	All En Suite	B&B per person	Open Jan-Dec
39 Twin		Room only from £76.00	B&B + Eve.Meal
30 Double			from £113.50
11 Family			

★★★

GUEST HOUSE

Larchfield House
15 Ness Bank, Inverness, IV2 4SF
Tel: 01463 233874 Fax: 01463 711600
E-mail: info@larchfieldhouse.com
Web: www.larchfieldhouse.com

Peacefully situated on the banks of the River Ness and yet within five minutes pleasant walk to the town centre, rail and coach terminals. Larchfield House offers quality accommodation at a reasonable price. All rooms are fully ensuite and prices include a traditional cooked breakfast. All produce is sourced locally.

1 Single	All En Suite	B&B per person	Open Jan-Dec excl
1 Twin		from £25.00 Single	Xmas/New Year
3 Double		from £25.00 Dbl/Twn	
1 Family			

All properties graded by VisitScotland, formerly known as the Scottish Tourist Board.   **Key to symbols is on back flap.**

Inverness				Map Ref: 4B8

SMALL HOTEL

Lochardil House Hotel
Stratherrick Road, Inverness, IV2 4LF
Tel: 01463 235995 Fax: 01463 713394
E-mail: lochardil@ukonline.co.uk

3 Single	All En Suite
2 Twin	
7 Double	

B&B per person
from £78.00 Single
from £108.00 Dbl/Twn

Open Jan-Dec excl
Xmas/New Year

18c castellated country house in 5 acres of private gardens with extensive parking. Under 2 miles (3kms) from centre. Former home of the Macdonalds. Popular venue for large and small meetings and conferences. Day delegate rates. Conservatory restaurant. Serving lunch and dinner and open to non-residents.

HOTEL

MacDougall Clansman Hotel
103 Church Street, Inverness, IV1 1ES
Tel/Fax: 01463 713702
E-mail: macdougallhotel@aol.com
Web: www.host.co.uk

3 Single	14 En Suite fac
4 Twin	1 Priv.NOT ensuite
3 Double	
5 Family	

B&B per person
from £27.00 Single
from £24.00 Dbl/Twn

Open Jan-Dec excl
Xmas/New Year
B&B + Eve.Meal
from £33.00

Family-run hotel in convenient town centre location, close to Rail & Bus stations, Tourist Information Centre and all shops. On street parking and limited private parking available. French, German and Spanish spoken. Non-smoking rooms available.

MOYNESS HOUSE
6 BRUCE GARDENS, INVERNESS IV3 5EN
Telephone/Fax: 01463 233836
e.mail: stay@moyness.co.uk   Web: www.moyness.co.uk
This fine Victorian villa has been sympathetically restored with elegant decoration and furnishings enhancing the many beautiful original features. The delightful bedrooms (all en-suite) offer modern comfort and period charm. All are no smoking. Pretty garden and ample parking. Located in quiet area near town centre, theatre and lovely riverside.
Brochure from Jenny and Richard Jones or book on 01463 233836.

GUEST HOUSE

Moyness House
6 Bruce Gardens, Inverness, IV3 5EN
Tel/Fax: 01463 233836
E-mail: stay@moyness.co.uk
Web: www.moyness.co.uk

1 Single	All En Suite
2 Twin	
4 Double	

B&B per person
£33.00-£37.00 Single
£33.00-£37.00 Dbl/Twn

Open Jan-Dec excl
Xmas/New Year

Gracious Victorian villa with attractive walled garden. Family run, in quiet area. Short walk to town centre, river, Eden Court Theatre and many sporting amenities. Moyness House is totally non-smoking.

GUEST HOUSE

Oakfield Guest House
1 Darnaway Road, Kingsmills, Inverness, IV2 3LF
Tel/Fax: 01463 237926
E-mail: oak@btinternet.com

1 Single	6 En Suite fac
2 Twin	
3 Double	

B&B per person
from £20.00 Single
from £18.00 Dbl/Twn

Open Jan- Dec excl
Xmas/New Year

Detached house with private parking in peaceful residential area within easy walking distance of restaurants, shops and all amenities. Credit cards accepted. Ideal for touring the Highlands Loch Ness and the Moray Coast.

Important: Prices stated are estimates and may be subject to amendments

Inverness Map Ref: 4B8

★★★
GUEST
HOUSE

Rotherwood Guest House
7 Midmills Road, Inverness, IV2 3NZ
Tel: 01463 225732
E-mail: junejim.taylor@lineone.net
Web: www.rotherwoodguesthouse.co.uk

Traditional red sandstone house with a warm relaxing environment. In a quiet residential area yet only a few minutes walk from town centre and station. All rooms ensuite. Non-smoking house. 30 minutes by car to the famous Loch Ness.

| 1 Twin | All En Suite |
| 2 Double | |

B&B per person
from £25.00 Single
from £20.00 Dbl/Twn

Open Jan-Dec

★★★
GUEST
HOUSE

St Ann's House
37 Harrowden Road, Inverness, IV3 5QN
Tel: 01463 236157 Fax: 01463 236157
E-mail: stannshous@aol.com
Web: www.hotelinverness.co.uk

19c traditional stone built house in quiet residential area. Small comfortable family run, assuring a friendly welcome. Tranquil well planted garden available for guests enjoyment.

1 Single	5 En Suite fac
2 Twin	1 Priv.NOT ensuite
2 Double	
1 Family	

B&B per person from £22.00 Single
fom £25.00 Dbl/Twn

Open Mar-Oct

★★★
B&B

Tamarue
70A Ballifeary Road, Inverness, IV3 5PE
Tel: 01463 239724

Situated in quiet residential area, close to town centre, River Ness, golf course, Eden Court Theatre, Aquadome and Sports Centre. Off street parking.

| 1 Twin | 1 En Suite fac |
| 2 Double | 1 Pub Bath/Show |

B&B per person
£16.00-£25.00 Single
£15.00-£20.00 Dbl/Twn
Room only £12.00-
£15.00

Open Jan-Dec excl
Xmas/New Year

★★★
GUEST
HOUSE

Whinpark Guest House
17 Ardross Street, Inverness, IV3 5NS
Tel/Fax: 01463 232549
E-mail: whinparkhotel@talk21.com.uk
Web: www.whinparkhotel.co.uk

Family run stone built house in quiet location close to town centre, Eden Court Theatre. Some private parking.

1 Single	All En Suite
3 Twin	
4 Double	
2 Family	

B&B per person
from £25.00 Single
from £19.00 Dbl/Twn

Open Jan-Dec excl
Xmas/New Year

John o'Groats, Caithness Map Ref: 4E2

★★
GUEST
HOUSE

Caber Feidh Guest House
John O'Groats, Wick, Caithness, KW1 4YR
Tel: 01955 611219

Centrally situated in John O' Groats and 2 miles (3kms) from Duncansby Head. It is well situated for exploring the north east, including the north coast of Sutherland, the inland Flow Country, and more. Day trips to Orkney are a popular choice.

2 Single	7 En Suite fac
4 Twin	7 Pub Bath/Show
4 Double	
4 Family	

B&B per person
from £20.00 Single
from £17.00 Dbl/Twn

Open Jan-Dec excl
Xmas/New Year
B&B + Eve.Meal
from £26.00

All properties graded by VisitScotland, formerly known as the Scottish Tourist Board. | Key to symbols is on back flap.

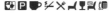

John o'Groats, Caithness — Map Ref: 4E2

★

SMALL HOTEL

Seaview Hotel
John o'Groats, Caithness, KW1 4YR
Tel/Fax: 01955 611220
E-mail: seaviewhotel@barbox.net
Web: www.mywebpage.net/seaview

1 Single	5 En Suite fac	B&B per person	Open Jan-Dec
4 Twin	4 Pub Bath/Show	from £20.00 Single	B&B + Eve.Meal
8 Double		from £14.50 Dbl/Twn	from £25.00
4 Family		Room only per person	
		from £14.50	

Comfortable range of accommodation. 5 mins walk or 2 mins drive from Orkney Passenger Ferry. Secure facilities for bikes/cycles. Off-road parking. John 'O' Groats Visitor/Craft Centre, Stacks of Duncansby, cliff walks and puffins, fine views of the sea and nearby Orkney.

★★

INN

Sinclair Bay Hotel
Main Street, Keiss, by Wick, Caithness, KW1 4UY
Tel: 01955 631233 Fax: 01955 631492
E-mail: sinclairbayhotel@yahoo.com
Web: www.sinclairbayhotel.co.uk

1 Single	3 En Suite fac	B&B per person	Open Jan-Dec excl
1 Twin	1 Pub Bath/Show	from £16.00 Single	Xmas/New Year
3 Double	1 Priv.NOT ensuite	from £15.00 Dbl/Twn	
2 Family			

A small popular family fun hotel, The Sinclair Bay offers a warm Caithness welcome to everyone, including children and pets. Lying 8 miles south of John O Groats, in the fishing village of Keiss, we provide the ideal base for the summer ferry to the Orkney Isles or for touring the north coast of Scotland.Wick is only 8 mile away, where you can enjoy shops, swimming, golf, tennis, squash, etc.The hotel can arrange loch and sea fishing.

Kingussie, Inverness-shire — Map Ref: 4B11

★★★★

GUEST HOUSE

Avondale House
Newtonmore Road, Kingussie, Inverness-shire, PH21 1HF
Tel/Fax: 01540 661731
E-mail: avondalehouse@talk21.com
Web: www.avondalehouse.com

3 Twin	3 En Suite fac	B&B per person	Open Jan-Dec
1 Double	1 Priv. Bath/Show	from £19.00 Dbl/Twn	B&B + Eve.Meal
			from £31.50

A splendid example of an Edwardian Home nr. centre of village, this family run Guest House is attractively furnished and equipped with all we hope you could need for a comfortable, relaxing stay. Excellent home cooking. A beautiful part of Scotland. Ideal for outdoor pursuits, ski-ing, walking, sauna, birdwatching, cycling.

Columba House Hotel & Garden Restaurant
Manse Road, Kingussie, Inverness-shire PH21 1JF
W
Telephone: 01540 661402 Fax: 01540 661652
e.mail: reservations@columbahousehotel.com
web: www.columbahousehotel.com

★★★
SMALL HOTEL

Nestling in large grounds. Candlelit Garden Restaurant, with patio onto landscaped walled garden, ideal for summertime dining, offers superb traditional Scottish cuisine. Cosy bar. Open fire in comfortable and homely lounge. Beautiful ensuite bedrooms, views, romantic four-poster rooms. Friendly atmosphere, your comfort and enjoyment is our priority. Ample parking. AA ◆◆◆◆

★★★

SMALL HOTEL

Columba House Hotel & Garden Restaurant
Manse Road, Kingussie, Inverness-shire, PH21 1JF
Tel: 01540 661402 Fax: 01540 661652
E-mail: reservations@columbahousehotel.com
Web: www.columbahousehotel.com

3 Twin	All En Suite	B&B per person	Open Jan-Dec
3 Double		from £35.00 Single	B&B + Eve.Meal
2 Family		from £30.00 Dbl/Twn	from £45.00
		Room only per person	
		from £25.00	

Nestling in large grounds. Excellent cuisine in Garden Restaurant in the landscaped, walled garden. Warm, cosy bar, open fire in lounge. Friendly atmosphere. Romantic Four-Poster rooms. Ample parking.

Important: Prices stated are estimates and may be subject to amendments

Kingussie, Inverness-shire	Map Ref: 4B11

HOTEL ★★★

Duke of Gordon Hotel
Newtonmore Road, Kingussie, Inverness-shire, PH21 1HE
Tel: 01540 661302 Fax: 01540 661989
E-mail: dukegor@dial.pipex.com
Web: www.cairngorm-travel.co.uk

Victorian hotel on main street with golf and fishing available locally in summer and skiing in winter. Facilities may vary depending on season. Hotel recently re-furbished to high standard of fabric.

10 Single
39 Twin
11 Double
5 Family

All En Suite

B&B per person
from £35.00-£70.00
Single
from £33.00-£62.00
Dbl/Twn
Room only from

Open Jan-Dec
B&B + Eve.Meal from
£40.00-£86.00

SMALL HOTEL ★★★

The Osprey Hotel
Ruthven Road, Kingussie, Inverness-shire, PH21 1EN
Tel/Fax: 01540 661510
E-mail: aileen@ospreyhotel.co.uk
Web: www.ospreyhotel.co.uk

Personally run hotel in centre of village, imaginative cuisine including vegetarian meals using fresh produce. Taste of Scotland member.

1 Single
3 Twin
4 Double

All En Suite

B&B per person
from £24.00 Single
from £24.00 Dbl/Twn

Open Jan-Dec
B&B + Eve.Meal from
£39.00

Scot House Hotel
Kingussie, Inverness-shire PH21 1HE
Tel: 01540 661351 Fax: 01540 661111
e.mail: enquiries@scothouse.com Web: www.scothouse.com

Award-winning small hotel set amid the magnificent scenery of The Cairngorms. Relaxing, friendly atmosphere, personal service. Superb restaurant and cosy bar (bar meals). Close to golf, fishing, skiing, sailing, R.S.P.B., distilleries, castles, historic sites, forests, gliding, pony-trekking and more! Central location makes ideal base for touring The Highlands.

SMALL HOTEL ★★★★

Scot House Hotel
Newtonmore Road, Kingussie, Inverness-shire, PH21 1HE
Tel: 01540 661351 Fax: 01540 661111
E-mail: enquiries@scothouse.com
Web: www.scothouse.com

Award-winning family-run small hotel, situated in centre of Kingussie. Restaurant and bar meals. Ample car parking.

5 Twin
3 Double
1 Family

All En Suite

B&B per person
from £30.00 Single
from £30.00 Dbl/Twn

Open Feb-Dec

Kinlochbervie, Sutherland	Map Ref: 3H3

HOTEL ★★★

Old School Hotel
Inshegra, Kinlochbervie, Sutherland, IV27 4RH
Tel/Fax: 01971 521383

Restaurant with comfortable rooms in converted bungalow and bothy. Superb views of sea and surrounding countryside. All annexe accommodation.

1 Single
3 Twin
1 Double
1 Family

4 En Suite fac
2 Pub Bath/Show

B&B per person
from £29.00 Single
from £24.00 Dbl/Twn

Open Jan-Dec excl
Xmas/New Year

All properties graded by VisitScotland, formerly known as the Scottish Tourist Board. | **Key to symbols is on back flap.**

Kinlochleven, Argyll | Map Ref: 3H12

MacDonald Hotel
Fort William Road, Kinlochleven, Argyll, PH50 4QL
Tel: 01855 831539 Fax: 01855 831416
E-mail: martin@macdonaldhotel.co.uk
Web: www.macdonaldhotel.co.uk

SMALL HOTEL

A modern, yet traditional, hotel set beside a tidal creek at the head of Loch Leven. Mid-way between Glen Nevis and Glencoe at the foot of the Mamores, the Macdonald Hotel is the perfect base to enjoy the best of west Highland walking or touring. Personally managed by the proprietors who pride themselves on providing a relaxed, informal, environment and the very best of Highland foods from fresh local

5 Twin	All En Suite	B&B per person
4 Double		from £28.00 Single
1 Family		from £28.00 Dbl/Twn

Open Mar-Dec
B&B + Eve.Meal from £40.00

Tailrace Inn
Riverside Road, Kinlochleven, Argyll, PH50 4QH
Tel: 01855 831777 Fax: 01855 831291
E-mail: tailrace@btconnect.com
Web: www.tailraceinn.co.uk

INN

The Tail Race Inn is situated in the centre of the scenic village of Kinlochleven. Surrounded by the Mamore Mountains midway between Glencoe and Ben-Nevis. An ideal stopover for walkers, climbers or those who enjoy the outdoors. Excellent drying room facilities. Lively, atmospheric bar with wide-screen satellite TV. All rooms comfortably furnished with TV's and tea trays.

3 Twin	All En Suite	B&B per person
2 Double		from £27.00 Single
1 Family		from £40.00 Dbl/Twn
		Room only from £30.00

Open Jan-Dec

Kyle of Lochalsh, Ross-shire | Map Ref: 3F9

Kyle Hotel
Main Street, Kyle of Lochalsh, Ross-shire, IV40 8AB
Tel: 01599 534204 Fax: 01599 534932
E-mail: thekylehotel@btinternet.com
Web: www.btinternet.com/~thekylehotel

HOTEL

Recently modernised hotel, 5 minutes walk from the railway station, in the centre of the village. 8 bedrooms on the ground floor. Close to Skye Bridge.

9 Single	All En Suite	B&B per person
14 Twin		from £38.00 Single
8 Double		from £32.00 Dbl/Twn

Open Jan-Dec
B&B + Eve.Meal from £47.00

Kylesku, Sutherland | Map Ref: 3H4

KYLESKU HOTEL
KYLESKU, BY LAIRG, SUTHERLAND IV27 4HW
Tel: 01971 502231   Fax: 01971 502313
e.mail: kylesku.hotel@excite.co.uk

Comfortable friendly hotel with wonderful lochside views. Cosy bedrooms ensuite. Excellent restaurant and bar meals, local seafood a speciality. Log fires, relaxation, fishing, bird life, boating, hill walking, seals, wildlife, Great Britain's highest waterfall, boat trips to Handa Island, sandy beaches and lots more exciting interests to discover.

Kylesku Hotel
Kylesku, by Lairg, Sutherland, IV27 4HW
Tel: 01971 502231 Fax: 01971 502313
E-mail: kylesku.hotel@excite.co.uk

SMALL HOTEL

Converted former ferry house at water's edge, spectacular views over Loch Glendhu to mountains beyond. Fresh produce, seafood a speciality. Annexed room available and some rooms without television.

2 Twin	6 En Suite fac	B&B per room
6 Double	2 Priv.NOT ensuite	£30.00-£35.00 Single
1 Family		£55.00-£65.00 Dbl/Twn
		£75.00 Family

Open Mar-Oct

Important: Prices stated are estimates and may be subject to amendments

Kylesku, Sutherland
Map Ref: 3H4

★★★★
SMALL HOTEL

Newton Lodge
Newton, Kylesku, Sutherland
Tel/Fax: 01971 502070
E-mail: newtonlge@aol.com
Web: www.smoothhound.co.uk/hotels.newtonlo.html

A small comfortable private hotel, surrounded by an inspiring panorama of mountains and lochs. Ample car parking available. Non-smoking establishment, seal colony can be seen from lounge and conservatory. Four poster room available. Ideal base for Britains highest waterfall and Handa Island bird sanctuary.

3 Twin	All En Suite	B&B per person	Open May-Sep
4 Double		from £28.00 Dbl/Twn	B&B + Eve.Meal
			from £43.00

TV 🖨 P 🍵 🗝 🏋 🍴 ▨ 🍷
Ⓥ

Lairg, Sutherland
Map Ref: 4A6

★★★
B&B

Park House
Station Road, Lairg, Sutherland, IV27 4AU
Tel: 01549 402208 Fax: 01549 402693
E-mail: dwalkerparkhouse@tinyworld.co.uk
Web: www.host.co.uk

A warm welcome awaits you in this Victorian style house overlooking Loch Shin. Friendly and relaxed atmosphere. Emphasis on home cooking. Stalking, rough shooting, salmon and trout fishing available for guests by arrangement.

2 Twin	All En Suite	B&B per person	Open Jan-Dec excl
1 Double		from £28.00 Single	Xmas/New Year
		from £23.00 Dbl/Twn	B&B + Eve.Meal from
			£36.00

TV 🖨 P 🍵 🗝 ✕ 🍽 (🎱
🐕 ⓔ Ⓦ Ⓥ

Lochcarron, Ross-shire
Map Ref: 3G9

★★★
SMALL HOTEL

Rockvilla Hotel & Restaurant
Main Street, Lochcarron, Ross-shire, IV54 8YB
Tel: 01520 722379 Fax: 01520 722844
E-mail: rockvillahotel@btinternet.com
Web: www.smoothhound.co.uk/hotels/rockvill

Personally run small hotel at centre of this coastal village. Restaurant with sea views. Emphasis on fresh fish in season.

1 Twin	2 En Suite fac	B&B per person	Open Jan-Dec
2 Double	2 Pub Bath/Show	from £34.00 Single	B&B + Eve.Meal from
1 Family		from £24.00 Dbl/Twn	£42.00

TV 🌀 🍵 ✂ 🍴 🍷
Ⓒ ⓔ Ⓥ

Lochinver, Sutherland
Map Ref: 3G5

★★★★
SMALL HOTEL

The Albannach
Baddidarroch, Lochinver, Sutherland, IV27 4LP
Tel: 01571 844407 Fax: 01571 844285
E-mail: the.albannach@virginnet.co.uk

19c house of great character. Spectacular views across Lochinver Bay to Suilven. Original style cooking, emphasis on fresh produce.

2 Twin	All En Suite	DB&B per person	Open Mar 20-Nov
3 Double		from £87.00 Single	
		from £82.50 Dbl/Twn	

📞 🖨 P 🗝 🏋 🍴 🍷
ⓔ Ⓥ 🐄

Lochinver, Sutherland   Map Ref: 3G5

INVER LODGE HOTEL
Lochinver, Sutherland IV27 4LU
Tel: 01571 844496 Fax: 01571 844395
e.mail: stay@inverlodge.com
Web: www.inverlodge.com

Loch Inver and the western sea is its foreground, its backdrop the great peaks of Sutherland – Suilven and Canisp.
Inver Lodge offers high standards of accommodation and cuisine making the most of locally caught and landed fish.
The restaurant and all bedrooms have superb sea views. We offer fishing on three salmon rivers. **For further details please contact Nicholas Gorton.**

★★★★

HOTEL

Inver Lodge Hotel
Iolaire Road, Lochinver, Sutherland, IV27 4LU
Tel: 01571 844496 Fax: 01571 844395
E-mail: stay@inverlodge.com
Web: www.inverlodge.com

Modern hotel with accent on comfort and friendliness. Restaurant and all bedrooms can enjoy sea-scape and setting sun over Lochinver harbour.

11 Twin	All En Suite	B&B per person	Open Apr-Nov
9 Double		from £80.00 Single	B&B + Eve.Meal from
		from £65.00 Dbl/Twn	£90.00

★★★★

GUEST HOUSE

Polcraig Guest House
Lochinver, Sutherland, IV27 4LD
Tel/Fax: 01571 844429
E-mail: cathelmac@aol.com

A warm, friendly welcome awaits you here at Polcraig. Ideally situated in a quiet location with views across Lochinver Harbour. A short walk takes you to a choice of places for eating out. Your hosts Jean and Cathel will provide you with a hearty breakfast before you set out for your day. Explore the Highlands, taking in the spectacular views and an abundance of wildlife.

3 Twin	All En Suite	B&B per person	Open Jan-Dec
2 Double		from £20.00-£40.00 Single	
		from £20.00-£25.00 Dbl/Twn	
		Room only per person from £40.00	

Lybster, Caithness   Map Ref: 4D4

★★★★

SMALL HOTEL

The Portland Arms Hotel
Lybster, Caithness, KW3 6BS
Tel: 01593 721721 Fax: 01593 721722
E-mail: info@portlandarms.co.uk
Web: www.portlandarms.co.uk

Former staging inn, some rooms with four poster beds or half testers. Local 9 hole golf course. Fishing available. Courtesy transport to/from airport. Ideal base to explore Caithness, convenient stopover en-route to Orkney.

5 Single	All En Suite	B&B per person	Open Jan-Dec
3 Twin		£40.00-£55.00 Single	B&B + Eve.Meal
11 Double		£35.00-£40.00 Dbl/Twn	£50.00-£60.00
3 Family			

Important: Prices stated are estimates and may be subject to amendments

Mallaig, Inverness-shire | Map Ref: 3F11

Marine Hotel
MALLAIG INVERNESS-SHIRE PH41 4PY
Tel: 01687 462217
Fax: 01687 462821

At the end of the Road to the Isles. A warm welcome awaits you at our family run hotel which is conveniently situated for rail and Skye ferry terminals. Ideal base for day trips to neighbouring lochs and islands. All rooms ensuite. Enjoy fresh, local seafood and our Highland cuisine. **B&B from £26-£36 pppn.**

e.mail: marinehotel@btinternet.com
Web: www.road-to-the-isles.org.uk/marine-hotel.html
For brochure and tariff contact: Tanya Ironside.
AA ★★ ★★★ **Hotel**

★★★
HOTEL

Marine Hotel
Mallaig, Inverness-shire, PH41 4PY
Tel: 01687 462217 Fax: 01687 462821
E-mail: marinehotel@btinternet.com
Web: www.road-to-the-isles.org.uk/marine-hotel.html

Family run hotel situated in the centre of a fishing village close to the railway station and ferry terminal. Taste of Scotland scheme member. Mallaig is still an important West Coast fishing port which enables us to source and serve an abundance of fresh seafood. Visitor attractions include heritage centre, marine world, swimming pool, 9 hole golf course (5 miles).

3 Single	18 En Suite fac	B&B per person	Open Jan-Dec excl
10 Twin	1 Priv.NOT ensuite	from £30.00 Single	Xmas/New Year
5 Double		from £26.00 Dbl/Twn	B&B + Eve.Meal from
1 Family			£40.00

falte to West Highland hotels
Lochaber

AA & RAC ★★

West Highland Hotel
Mallaig, Inverness-shire PH41 4QZ
Tel: 01687 462210   Fax: 01687 462130
e.mail: westhighland.hotel@virgin.net
Web: www.westhighlandhotel.co.uk

Family run hotel on the famous Road to the Isles. Ideal for visiting the Isle of Skye and Western Isles by ferry, also steam train trips to Fort William. Locally caught fish on our menu daily, all rooms ensuite, colour TV and tea-making. Fully licensed. Own large car park.

★★★
HOTEL

West Highland Hotel
Mallaig, Inverness-shire, PH41 4QZ
Tel: 01687 462210 Fax: 01687 462130
E-mail: westhighland.hotel@virgin.net
Web: www.westhighlandhotel.co.uk

Hotel with recent conservatory extension. Stands above the village of Mallaig with views over the harbour to the Isle of Skye beyond. All public areas recently upgraded to high standard. Bar meals served and non-residents welcome. 4 annexe bedrooms.

6 Single	All En Suite	B&B per person	Open Apr-Nov excl
17 Twin		from £32.00 Single	Xmas/New Year
11 Double		from £30.00 Dbl/Twn	B&B + Eve.Meal
5 Family			from £45.00

Morar, Inverness-shire Map Ref: 3F11

Morar Hotel
Morar, Mallaig PH40 4PA
Tel: 01687 462346 Fax: 01687 462212
e.mail: enquiries@morarhotel.co.uk
Web: www.morarhotel.co.uk

*Family run hotel on the romantic Road to the Isles 3 miles from Mallaig,
the southern gateway to Skye and the Inner Hebrides. The Hotel overlooks the
silver sands of Morar. Venison, salmon/sea trout. 50% reduction for children.
Hotel offers salmon/sea trout fishing on Loch Morar.*

★★

HOTEL

Morar Hotel
Morar, by Mallaig, Inverness-shire, PH40 4PA
Tel: 01687 462346 Fax: 01687 462212
E-mail: enquiries@morarhotel.co.uk
Web: www.morarhotel.co.uk

Family run hotel on 'Road to the Isles' with magnificent views over Silver
Sands of Morar and islands of Rhum and Eigg. Some ground floor
annexe accommodation. Only 3 miles from Mallaig and car ferry to Isle
of Skye.

3 Single	All En Suite	B&B per person	Open Apr-Nov
10 Twin		from £30.00 Single	
10 Double		from £30.00 Dbl/Twn	
3 Family			

★★

B&B

Sunset Guest House
Morar, Mallaig, Inverness-shire, PH40 4PA
Tel: 01687 462259 Fax: 01687 460085
E-mail: sunsetgh@aol.com
Web: www.sunsetguesthouse.co.uk

Small family house in West Highland village, close to Morar sands.
Mallaig 3 miles (5kms) with ferries to Skye and Small Isles. Authentic
Thai cuisine.

1 Twin	1 En Suite fac	B&B per person	Open Jan-Dec
1 Double	2 Pub Bath/Show	from £13.50 Single	B&B + Eve.Meal from
1 Family		from £27.00 Dbl/Twn	£20.00

Muir of Ord, Ross-shire Map Ref: 4A8

★★★★

SMALL
HOTEL

The Dower House
Highfield, Muir of Ord, Ross-shire, IV6 7XN
Tel/Fax: 01463 870090
E-mail: STB@thedowerhouse.co.uk
Web: www.thedowerhouse.co.uk

More a private house than a hotel, this highly individual conversion from
a former dowagers house has created a warm and comfortable
ambience. The food is excellent and memorable. The house is situated in
5 acres of mature grounds in the countryside between the Rivers Beauly
and Conon, some 14 miles west of Inverness.

3 Twin	All En Suite	B&B per person	Open Jan-Dec excl
1 Double		from £55.00 Single	Xmas
1 Suite		from £110.00 Dbl/Twn	

★★

SMALL
HOTEL

Ord House Hotel
Muir of Ord, Ross-shire, Highlands, IV6 7UH
Tel/Fax: 01463 870492
E-mail: eliza@ord-house.com
Web: www.ord-house.com

Country house dating from 1637, set in extensive grounds of both formal
garden and park and woodland. Taste of Scotland with emphasis on
fresh food. Friendly and informal service in comfortable surroundings - a
relaxing environment.

6 Twin	All En Suite	B&B per person	Open May-Oct excl
4 Double		from £48.00 Dbl/Twn	Xmas/New Year
			B&B + Eve.Meal
			from £67.00

Important: Prices stated are estimates and may be subject to amendments

Nairn	Map Ref: 4C8

Braeval Hotel
Crescent Road, Nairn, IV12 4NB
Tel: 01667 452341

2 Single — All En Suite
2 Twin
2 Double
1 Family

B&B per person
from £30.00 Single
from £25.00 Dbl/Twn
Room only from £20.00

Open Jan-Dec excl
Xmas/New Year
B&B + Eve.Meal from
£35.00

A small family run hotel, a Scottish experience with traditional Scottish fayre in a relaxed and friendly atmosphere.

Claymore House Hotel
Seabank Road, Nairn, IV12 4EY
Tel: 01667 453731 Fax: 01667 455290
E-mail: ClaymoreNairnScotland@compuserve.com
Web: www.claymorehousehotel.com

1 Single — All En Suite
5 Twin
5 Double
2 Family

B&B per person
from £42.50 Single
from £85.00 Dbl/Twn

Open Jan-Dec
B&B + Eve.Meal
from £55.00

Family run hotel with the emphasis on friendliness, traditional food and flexibility and customer care.

Golf View Hotel & Leisure Club
The Seafront, Nairn, IV12 4HD
Tel: 01667 452301 Fax: 01667 455267
E-mail: rooms@morton-hotels.com
Web: www.morton-hotels.com

4 Single — All En Suite
25 Twin
15 Double
3 Family

B&B per person
from £86.00 Single
from £54.00 Dbl/Twn

Open Jan-Dec

Victorian hotel with modern leisure centre overlooking the sea and the hills of the Black Isle. Championship golf course nearby. Headquarters hotel for 1999 Walker Cup. Function suite (up to 120 persons) for private functions, weddings and conferences. Many rooms refurbished 2001.

Greenlawns
13 Seafield Street, Nairn, IV12 4HG
Tel/Fax: 01667 452738
E-mail: greenlawns@cali.co.uk
Web: www.greenlawns.uk.com

1 Single — All En Suite
3 Twin
3 Double

B&B per person
from £20.00 Single
from £20.00 Dbl/Twn
Room only from £17.50

Open Jan-Dec
excl Xmas
B&B + Eve.Meal
from £30.00

Comfortable Victorian house with a relaxed atmosphere. Quiet situation near to the town centre and beach.

Havelock House Hotel
Crescent Road, Nairn, IV12 4HB
Tel/Fax: 01667 455500
E-mail: gordonmclaughlan@hotmail.com
Web: www.havelockhousehotel.co.uk

2 Twin 3
Double

B&B per person
from £20.00 Single
from £20.00 Double
Room only per person
from £18.00

Open Jan-Dec
B&B + Eve.Meal from
£25.00

Discover the delights and tranquility of Nairn. Nestling on the south shore of the Moray Firth. Nairn enjoys a remarkable amount of sunshine which blends well with the sandy beaches and safe sea swimming, golf, tennis, bowling and heated swimming pool, all within the town.

All properties graded by VisitScotland, formerly known as the Scottish Tourist Board. | *Key to symbols is on back flap.*

| Nairn | | | | | Map Ref: 4C8 | | |

Invernairne Hotel

Thurlow Road, Nairn, IV12 4EZ
Tel: 01667 452039 Fax: 01667 456760
E-mail: invernairne@hotmail.com
Web: www.golf-vacations.co.uk

SMALL HOTEL

Former Victorian mansion house, now a family run hotel situated in landscaped grounds, with a private path down to a safe beach. Swimming pool and golf are both within walking distance. Meals are served in the dining room or in the panelled lounge bar, with it's open fire. There is now also a small gift shop on the premises.

2 Single	All En Suite	B&B per person	Open Jan-Dec excl
1 Twin		from £40.00 Single	Xmas/New Year
3 Double		from £30.00 Dbl/Twn	B&B + Eve.Meal
3 Family			from £45.00

Newton Hotel & Highland Conference Centre

Inverness Road, Nairn, IV12 4RX
Tel: 01667 453144 Fax: 01667 454026
E-mail: rooms@morton-hotels.com
Web: www.morton-hotels.com

HOTEL

The Newton Hotel is an elegant Georgian building set in over 20 acres of secluded grounds & overlooks the Nairn Championship Course. Guests are able to use the leisure facilities at our sister hotel (500 yards) The Golf View. Local attractions include: Cawdor Castle, Malt Whisky Trail, Loch Ness, Culloden Battlefield and there are 20 golf courses within an hours drive. Golf inclusive packages available. Free car parking. 1 AA Rosette for food.

6 Single	All En Suite	B&B per person	Open Jan-Dec excl Xmas
31 Twin		from £86.00 Single	
18 Double		from £54.00 Dbl/Twn	
2 Family			

Rhyden House

7 Cumming Street, Nairn, IV12 4NQ
Tel: 01667 453736
E-mail: rhyden.house@which.net
Web: www.rhydenhouse.com

GUEST HOUSE

Victorian sandstone house of character. 2 minutes level walk to beach. Secluded garden. Lunches and evening meals available in our restaurant, always using local produce.

1 Single	3 En Suite fac	B&B per person	Open Mar-Nov
1 Twin	2 Pub Bath/Show	from £24.00 Single	B&B + Eve.Meal
2 Double	1 Priv.NOT ensuite	from £22.00 Dbl/Twn	from £34.00
2 Family			

Sunny Brae Hotel

Marine Road, Nairn, IV12 4EA
Tel: 01667 452309 Fax: 01667 454860
E-mail: reservations@sunnybraehotel.com
Web: www.sunnybraehotel.com

SMALL HOTEL

Small friendly family run hotel, offering personal attention to guests. Dinners emphasising fresh local produce. Located close to the town centre and all it's amenities, yet with uninterrupted sea views towards the Moray Firth. Plenty of advice available on what to do - golf, trips to Speyside, the Moray Coast or over to the West and the Far North.

1 Single	All En Suite	B&B per person	Open Mar-Nov
4 Twin		from £39.00 Single	B&B + Eve.Meal
4 Double		from £35.00 Dbl/Twn	from £49.00

The Windsor Hotel

Albert Street, Nairn, IV12 4HP
Tel: 01667 453108 Fax: 01667 456108
E-mail: windsornairnscotland@btinternet.com
Web: www.windsor-hotel.co.uk

HOTEL

Set within residential area of Nairn and within 3 mins walk of town centre, close to the beach, many sporting activities, including the town's two championship golf courses. It has retained much of its character, whilst being sympathetically refurbished in line with the owners commitment to a continual upgrade. Ideal base for touring the Inverness Highlands. Fort George, Culloden Battlefield, Cawdor and Brodie Castles and Loch Ness.

8 Single	All En Suite	B&B per person	Open Jan-Dec
22 Twin		from £45.00 Single	B&B + Eve.Meal from
16 Double		from £40.00 Dbl/Twn	£45.00
6 Family			

Important: Prices stated are estimates and may be subject to amendments

Onich, by Fort William, Inverness-shire

Map Ref: 3G12

Allt-nan-Ros Hotel

Onich, by Fort William, Inverness-shire PH33 6RY
Tel: 01855 821210 Fax: 01855 821462
e.mail: bookings@allt-nan-ros.co.uk
web: www.allt-nan-ros.co.uk

AA ★★★ ◎◎, RAC ★★★ (3 diningroom awards), Minotel "Classic Gold" hotel, Ashley Courtenay and Taste of Scotland are all testimonies to the quality and atmosphere of this acclaimed, friendly and family run West Highland hotel. All bedrooms, lounge and restaurant, with its panoramic windows, look south down Loch Linnhe towards the hills of Appin and Morvern.

★★★★

HOTEL

Allt-nan-Ros Hotel

Onich, nr Fort William, Inverness-shire, PH33 6RY
Tel: 01855 821210 Fax: 01855 821462
E-mail: bookings@allt-nan-ros.co.uk
Web: www.allt-nan-ros.co.uk

One of the most highly acclaimed family run hotels in the West Highlands. The "burn of the roses" aptly describes the hotel which faces south down Loch Linnhe to the hills of Ardgour and Appin. All rooms share the same superb view and the 2 AA rosette cuisine is enjoyed by all. James and Fiona MacLeod and their staff ensure that the ambience is always relaxing and friendly and the facilites exquisite.

2 Single	All En Suite
7 Twin	
11 Double	

B&B per person
from £45.00 Single
from £45.00 Dbl/Twn

Open Jan-Dec excl Xmas
B&B + Eve.Meal from £67.50

Camus House Lochside Lodge

ONICH, BY FORT WILLIAM, INVERNESS-SHIRE PH33 6RY
Tel/Fax: 01855 821200
e.mail: Young@CamusHouse.Freeserve.co.uk
Web: www.SmoothHound.co.uk/hotels/camushouse.html

In extensive lochside gardens, midway between Ben Nevis and Glencoe. Ideal base for touring, walking, mountain biking, climbing and ski-ing. Most rooms are ensuite with central heating, TV and teasmaid. We provide excellent cooking, friendly service and are fully licensed. **Dinner, Bed & Breakfast – £36-£45.** **Weekly – £200-£280. Open from February to November. Brochure available.**

★★★

GUEST HOUSE

Camus House Lochside Lodge

Onich, by Fort William, Inverness-shire, PH33 6RY
Tel/Fax: 01855 821200
E-mail: young@camushouse.freeserve.co.uk
Web: www.smoothhound.co.uk/hotels/camushouse.html

Large well appointed house, comfortably furnished, superb views of the sea loch and hills. In extensive lochside gardens, midway between Ben Nevis and Glencoe. Ideal base for touring, walking, mountain biking, climbing and ski-ing. Most rooms are ensuite with central heating and teasmaid. We provide excellent cooking, friendly service and restricted licence.

2 Twin	6 En Suite fac
3 Double	1 Priv.NOT ensuite
2 Family	1 Pub Bath/Show

B&B per person
from £28.00 Single
from £24.00 Dbl/Twn

Open Feb-Nov
B&B + Eve.Meal from £36.00

★★★★

SMALL HOTEL

Cuilcheanna House

Onich, Inverness-shire, PH33 6SD
Tel: 01855 821226
E-mail: relax@cuilcheanna.freeserve.co.uk
Web: www.cuilcheanna.co.uk

Russell and Linda Scott invite you to stay at their small country hotel, peacefully situated some 300m from the main road overlooking Loch Linnhe, amidst breathtaking scenery. We pride ourselves on the standard of food we serve - freshly prepared from the best locally sourced ingredients. Set 4 course meal but alternatives include vegetarian and special diets. Fully licensed with personally selected wine and malt whisky lists. Taste of Scotland.

2 Twin	All En Suite
5 Double	

B&B per person
from £44.50 Single
from £29.50 Dbl/Twn

Open Easter-Oct
B&B + Eve.Meal from £47.00

All properties graded by VisitScotland, formerly known as the Scottish Tourist Board. | *Key to symbols is on back flap.*

Onich, by Fort William, Inverness-shire		Map Ref: 3G12		

HOTEL

The Lodge On The Loch Hotel
Onich, nr Fort William, Inverness-shire, PH33 6RY
Tel: 01855 821237 Fax: 01855 821463
E-mail: reservations@freedomglen.co.uk
Web: www.freedomglen.co.uk

Discover seclusion and serenity - enjoy one of the West Coast's finest panoramas. 'The lodge' is a perfect Highland retreat. Relax in peaceful lounges. Savour memorable evenings in the charming loch view Taste of Scotland restaurant - renowned for the freshest produce. Choice of individually designed rooms available with many personal touches.

2 Single	16 En Suite fac	D.B&B only	Open Mar-Nov,
4 Twin		from £73.00 Single	Xmas/New Year
13 Double		£73.00-£105.00	
		Dbl/Twn	

INN

Nether Lochaber Hotel
Corran, by Fort William, Inverness-shire, PH33 6SE
Tel: 01855 821235 Fax: 01855 821545

The original Inn is one of the oldest in the Highlands and was last extended in 1880, retaining its original character to offer peace and comfort in 5 warm, cosy bedrooms most with private facilities. The old bar is an antique in its own right and every room in the Inn is different.

1 Single	All En Suite	B&B per person	Open Jan-Dec excl
2 Twin		from £22.00 Single	Xmas/New Year
1 Double		from £25.00 Dbl/Twn	
1 Family		Room only from £30.00	

B&B

Old Manse
Onich, Inverness-shire, PH33 6RY
Tel: 01855 821202 Fax: 01855 821312
E-mail: marymichie.OldManse.Onich@btinternet.com
Web: www.onich.co.uk

Early 19c former manse, a Listed Thomas Telford building, set in its own garden in the village of Onich, with loch and mountain views. Pets welcome. Substantial continental breakfast provided. Laundry and drying facilities available. Swimming and leisure facilities free of charge at a nearby hotel. Wide choice of eating places in the area. Twixt Ben Nevis and Glencoe.

1 Twin	2 En Suite fac	B&B per person	Open Apr-Oct
1 Double	1 Priv.NOT ensuite	from £25.00 Single	
1 Family		from £15.00 Dbl/Twn	

THE ONICH HOTEL ★★★ AA/RAC

ONICH, Nr FORT WILLIAM, INVERNESS-SHIRE PH33 6RY
Tel: 01855 821214   Fax: 01855 821484
e.mail: enquiries@onich-fortwilliam.co.uk
Web: www.onich-fortwilliam.co.uk

★★★★
SMALL HOTEL   AA ◉

Located in glorious gardens on the shores of Loch Linnhe, all public rooms enjoy the marvellous view over to Glencoe. You can choose from our award winning restaurant which serves local cuisine and our Deerstalker lounge bar serves tasty meals throughout the day. Children and families welcome.

**SMALL
HOTEL**

Onich Hotel
Onich, Fort William, Inverness-shire, PH33 6RY
Tel: 01855 821214 Fax: 01855 821484
E-mail: enquiries@onich-fortwilliam.co.uk
Web: www.onich-fortwilliam.co.uk

Personally run hotel with gardens extending to lochside. Superb all season views across Loch Linnhe to mountains. Interesting menu, local produce.

4 Single	All En Suite	B&B per person	Open Jan-Dec
5 Twin		from £34.00 Single	B&B + Eve.Meal
11 Double		from £34.00 Dbl/Twn	from £57.00
7 Family			

Important: Prices stated are estimates and may be subject to amendments

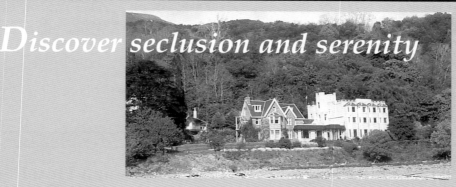

Discover seclusion and serenity

the **Lodge** *on the* **Loch**

Enjoy one of the West Coast's finest panoramas. Spellbinding luxury makes "the Lodge" a perfect highland retreat. Choose from individual luxury bedrooms with many personal touches. Relax in peaceful lounges and savour memorable evenings in the charming lochview restaurant.

Call for room details, price list, complimentary area guide and sample menus or visit our website to view every stunning bedroom.

Call Now 01855 821237
www.freedomglen.co.uk/ll

The Lodge On The Loch Hotel, Onich, Near Fort William, PH33 6RY
fax: 01855 821463 email reservations@freedomglen.co.uk

All properties graded by VisitScotland, formerly known as the Scottish Tourist Board. | *Key to symbols is on back flap.*

Poolewe, Ross-shire

Map Ref: 3F7

★★★

SMALL
HOTEL

Poolewe Hotel
Poolewe, Achnasheen, IV22 2JX
Tel: 01445 781241 Fax: 01445 781405
E-mail: reservations@poolewehotel.com
Web: www.poolewehotel.com

2 Single	8 En Suite fac	B&B per person	Open Jan-Dec
3 Twin	1 Priv.NOT ensuite	from £32.00 Single	B&B + Eve.Meal
3 Double		from £27.50 Dbl/Twn	from £38.00
1 Family			

Former inn dating in part from 18c. Now a family run hotel recently refurbished. Situated in village and close to Inverewe Gardens. Good food at reasonable prices.

Portmahomack, Ross-shire

Map Ref: 4C7

The Caledonian Hotel

Main Street, Portmahomack, Ross-shire IV20 1YS
Tel: 01862 871345 Fax: 01862 871757
e.mail: info@caleyhotel.co.uk Web: www.caleyhotel.co.uk

Friendly, family run hotel on an exceptional beach-front location in a truly picturesque village. Enjoy spectacular sunsets across the Dornoch Firth from the comfort of the restaurant or sun lounge. Ideal touring or golfing base. Children welcome. Regular live music in the bar. 3 nights D,B&B for the price of 2.

★★

HOTEL

Caledonian Hotel
Main Street, Portmahomack, Ross-shire, IV20 1YS
Tel: 01862 871345 Fax: 01862 871757

9 Twin	All En Suite	B&B per person	Open Jan-Dec
1 Double		£27.00-£35.00 Single	B&B + Eve.Meal
5 Family		£45.00-£59.00 Dbl/Twn	£33.00-£49.00

Family run Hotel overlooking sandy beach. Magnificent views across the Dornoch Firth. Watersports and golf close by. Regular live music.

Raasay, Isle of, Ross-shire

Map Ref: 3E9

★★

SMALL
HOTEL

Isle of Raasay Hotel
Raasay, by Kyle, Ross-shire, IV40 8PB
Tel/Fax: 01478 660222

1 Single	All En Suite	B&B per person	Open Jan-Dec
8 Twin		from £25.00 Single	B&B + Eve.Meal
1 Double		from £25.00 Dbl/Twn	from £40.00
2 Family			

Family run hotel, overlooking Sound of Raasay towards Cuillin Hills. Hill and forest walks, trout fishing, interesting local geology/archeology. Ideal base for artists and nature watchers. Groups catered for.

Roy Bridge, Inverness-shire

Map Ref: 3H12

★★★

INN

The Inn at Roybridge
Roy Bridge, Inverness-shire, PH31 4AG
Tel: 01397 712253 Fax: 01397 712641
E-mail: stay@stronlossit.co.uk
Web: www.stronlossit.co.uk

1 Single	All En Suite	B&B per person	Open Jan-Dec
2 Twin		from £30.00 Single	B&B + Eve.Meal
7 Double		from £27.50 Dbl/Twn	from £40.00
1 Family		Room only from £22.50	

Family run, in a small village amidst beautiful Highland scenery. Centrally situated for touring the Scottish Highlands. 12 miles (19km) to Fort William. Bar meals and recently refurbished a la carte restaurant.

Important: Prices stated are estimates and may be subject to amendments

---

Scourie, Sutherland — Map Ref: 3H4

★★★

SMALL HOTEL

Scourie Hotel
Scourie, Sutherland, IV27 4SX
Tel: 01971 502396 Fax: 01971 502423
E-mail: patrick@scourie-hotel.co.uk
Web: www.scourie-hotel.co.uk

Personally run, ideally situated for touring this rugged area of North West Scotland. Hotel specialises in fishing for brown trout and salmon. Some boats available. Four course dinner with local produce.

6 Single	All En Suite	B&B per person
6 Twin		from £34.00 Single
6 Double		from £29.00 Double
2 Family		

Open Apr-Oct
B&B + Eve.Meal from £46.00

Ardvasar, Sleat, Isle of Skye, Inverness-shire — Map Ref: 3E11

★★★

SMALL HOTEL

Ardvasar Hotel
Ardvasar, Sleat, Isle of Skye, Inverness-shire, IV45 8RS
Tel: 01471 844223 Fax: 01471 844495
E-mail: christine@ardvasar-hotel.demon.co.uk
Web: www.ardvasarhotel.com

Under new ownership this historic 19th Century Inn has fine views across the sea to Mallaig. Established reputation for good food, member of Taste of Scotland.

4 Twin	All En Suite	B&B per person
5 Double		from £45.00 Single
3 Family		from £80.00 Dbl/Twn

Open Jan-Dec
B&B + Eve.Meal from £62.50

Broadford, Isle of Skye, Inverness-shire

★★

HOTEL

Broadford Hotel
Broadford, Isle of Skye, IV49 9AB
Tel: 01471 822204 Fax: 01471 822414
Web: www.granduk.com

Friendly welcome and relaxed atmosphere in traditional Hotel overlooking Broadford Bay. 15 mins from Skye bridge, good base for all Skye holidays.

6 Single	All En Suite	B&B per person
15 Twin		£25.00-£40.00 Single
6 Double		£25.00-£40.00 Dbl/Twn
2 Family		

Open Mar-Dec
B&B + Eve.Meal £35.00-£50.00

Duntulm, Isle of Skye, Inverness-shire — Map Ref: 3D7

Duntulm Castle Hotel
Duntulm, Isle of Skye IV51 9UF
Tel: 01470 552213 Fax: 01470 552292
e.mail: info@duntulmcastle.co.uk Web: www.duntulmcastle.co.uk

Unrivalled coastal setting at the Northernmost tip of Skye with views across the Minch. Homely and comfortable inn. Ensuite bedrooms, colour TV, hot drink facilities. Excellent Scottish cuisine. Ideal for outer isles ferry at Uig. Peaceful and secluded with wonderful coast and hill walks. Beautiful self-catering cottages adjacent.

★

HOTEL

Duntulm Castle Hotel
Duntulm, Isle of Skye, IV51 9UF
Tel: 01470 552213 Fax: 01470 552292
E-mail: info@duntulmcastle.co.uk
Web: www.duntulmcastle.co.uk

Friendly hotel enjoying outstanding location with unsurpassed views over the Minch to the outer Isles. Cosy and informal atmosphere on the secluded northern most point of Skye.

3 Single	23 En Suite fac	B&B per person
12 Twin	4 Pub Bath/Show	from £25.00 Single
12 Double	5 Priv.NOT ensuite	from £19.00 Dbl/Twn
1 Family		

Open Apr-Oct
B&B + Eve.Meal from £34.00

All properties graded by VisitScotland, formerly known as the Scottish Tourist Board.

Key to symbols is on back flap.

Dunvegan, Isle of Skye, Inverness-shire   Map Ref: 3D9

Dunvegan Hotel

Main Street, Dunvegan, Isle of Skye IV55 8WA Tel/Fax: 01470 521497
e.mail: dunveganhotel@freenetname.co.uk
Web: www.dunveganhotel.co.uk

A small family run hotel newly refurbished to a high standard.
Overlooking Loch Dunvegan we are situated half a mile from
Dunvegan Castle. We pride ourselves on home cooking and
live traditional music played in the bar on a regular basis.

★★★

SMALL
HOTEL

Dunvegan Hotel
Main Street, Dunvegan, Isle of Skye, IV55 8WA
Tel:/Fax: 01470 521497
E-mail: dunveganhotel@freenetname.co.uk
Web: www.dunveganhotel.co.uk

Under new family ownership this extensively upgraded small hotel is
enjoying a new lease of life. Popular locally for food and drink, non-
residents are also welcome. Occasional folk music and entertainment in
the pub.

2 Twin	All En Suite	B&B per person	Open Jan-Dec
1 Family		from £35.00	
3 Double			

ROSKHILL HOUSE

by Dunvegan, Isle of Skye IV55 8ZD
Telephone: 01470 521317 Fax: 01470 521761
e.mail: stay@roskhill.demon.co.uk
A home from home where quality is a price you can afford.
Relax, unwind and enjoy hearty and wholesome farmhouse style
food. Take in the clean air and stunning scenery. Special rates for
3 nights or more. Warm hospitality and relaxed friendly
surroundings provided by Gillian and John.
Full brochure on our website: www.roskhill.demon.co.uk.

★★★★

GUEST
HOUSE

Roskhill House
Roskhill, Dunvegan, Isle of Skye, Inverness-shire, IV55 8ZD
Tel: 01470 521317 Fax: 01470 521761
E-mail: stay@roskhill.demon.co.uk
Web: www.roskhill.demon.co.uk

This cosy crofthouse is beautifully situated 3 miles south of Dunvegan
Castle, ideal for touring this historic & romantic island, walking, climbing,
bird watching, etc. Delicious old fashioned home cooking prepared fresh
each day and served in the stone walled dining room with log fire &
resident's bar. High standards, peaceful surroundings and personal
attention assured. Your 'home away from home', stay a while.

1 Twin	3 En Suite fac	B&B per person	Open Jan-Dec excl
3 Double	1 Priv.NOT ensuite	from £32.00 Single	Xmas/New Year
		from £27.00 Dbl/Twn	B&B + Eve.Meal
			from £41.50

★★

SMALL
HOTEL

The Tables Hotel
Dunvegan, Isle of Skye, Inverness-shire, IV55 8WA
Tel/Fax: 01470 521404
E-mail: bookings@tables-hotel.co.uk
Web: www.tables-hotel.co.uk

100 year old house in village, 0.75 mile (1km) from castle. Fine views
over MacLeods Tables. Accent on relaxation, informality. Vegetarians
welcomed.

1 Single	4 En Suite fac	B&B per person	Open Mar-Dec
2 Twin	1 Priv.NOT ensuite	from £27.00 Single	B&B + Eve.Meal from
1 Double		from £27.00 Dbl/Twn	£45.00
1 Family			

Important: Prices stated are estimates and may be subject to amendments

Edinbane, by Portree, Isle of Skye, Inverness-shire — Map Ref: 3D8

★★★★
GUEST HOUSE

Shorefield Guest House
Edinbane, by Portree, Isle of Skye, IV51 9PW
Tel: 01470 582444 Fax: 01470 582414
E-mail: shorefield@aol.com
Web: www.shorefield.com

Award winning family run guest house offering quality ensuite accommodation. Disabled facilities category 1. Non-smoking. Excellent breakfasts using local produce. Some of Skye's finest restaurants nearby. Private parking.

1 Single   All En Suite
1 Twin
1 Double
2 Family

B&B per person
from £24.00 Single
from £24.00 Dbl/Twn

Open Jan-Dec excl Xmas

Elgol, Isle of Skye, Inverness-shire — Map Ref: 3E10

★
GUEST HOUSE

Strathaird House
Elgol Road, Strathaird, Isle of Skye,
Inverness-shire, IV49 9AX
Tel: 01471 866269 Fax: 01471 866320
E-mail: strathairdhouse@skye.co.uk
Web: www.strathairdhouse.skye.co.uk

Family run guesthouse above Kilmarie Bay on the Elgol road. Ideal for walks to Camasunary Bay, Blaven, the Cuillins, seashore exploring and boat trips to Loch Coruisk. Rambling house with glorious views, licensed 'Hayloft Restaurant', fireside library, drying room and garden.

2 Single   1 En Suite fac
1 Double   5 Pub/Bath Show
4 Family   1 Priv.NOT ensuite

B&B per person
£25.00-£30.00 Single
£25.00-£30.00 Dbl/Twn

Open Easter-Sep

Portnalong, Isle of Skye, Inverness-shire — Map Ref: 3D9

★★
SMALL HOTEL

Taigh Ailean Hotel
11 Portnalong, Carbost, Isle of Skye,
Inverness-shire, IV47 8SL
Tel: 01478 640271
E-mail: welcome@taigh-ailean-hotel.co.uk
Web: www.taigh-ailean-hotel.demon.co.uk

Small family hotel with lots of local flavour, situated at the north end of the scenically beautiful, unspoilt Minginish Peninsula.

2 Double   4 En Suite fac
3 Family   1 Priv.NOT ensuite

B&B per person
from £28.00 Single
from £40.00 Dbl/Twn

Open Jan-Dec

Portree, Isle of Skye, Inverness-shire — Map Ref: 3E9

★★★★
GUEST HOUSE

Almondbank
Viewfield Road, Portree, Isle of Skye, IV51 9EU
Tel: 01478 612696 Fax: 01478 613114
E-mail: jansvans@aol.com

Modern house on the outskirts of Portree. Well appointed lounge and dining room with panoramic views of Portree Bay.

2 Twin   3 En Suite fac
2 Double   1 Priv.NOT ensuite

B&B per person
from £25.00 Single
from £25.00 Dbl/Twn

Open Jan-Dec

★★★
GUEST HOUSE

Corran Guest House
Kensaleyre, Portree, Isle of Skye, IV51 9XE
Tel: 01470 532311

In a small country village overlooking Loch Snizort, 8 miles (10kms) from Portree and from Uig ferry terminal. Extensive gardens with lovely views.

1 Single
1 Double
2 Family

B&B per person
£22.00-£24.00 Single
from £48.00 Dbl/Twn

Open Jan-Dec
B&B + Eve.Meal from
£34.00

Cuillin Hills Hotel
Portree, Isle of Skye IV51 9QU
Tel: 01478 612003   Fax: 01478 613092
e.mail: office@cuillinhills.demon.co.uk
Web: www.cuillinhills.demon.co.uk

Superbly situated with breathtaking views over Portree Bay towards the grandiose Cuillin Mountain range. A very fine hotel open all-year-round enjoying an excellent location for exploring the island. Our chef uses the best of local produce wherever possible to create imaginative menus combining traditional favourites with Highland specialities in our award-winning restaurant and bar. Relax after dinner in front of a roaring log fire. Enjoy high standards of comfort, cuisine and service in a warm, friendly atmosphere with the very best of Highland hospitality.

From £35 per person per night.   AA ★★★ ❀

*Contact: **Mr Murray Mcphee***

HOTEL

Cuillin Hills Hotel
Portree, Isle of Skye, Inverness-shire, IV51 9QU
Tel: 01478 612003 Fax: 01478 613092
E-mail: office@cuillinhills.demon.co.uk
Web: www.cuillinhills.demon.co.uk

19th century former hunting lodge, set in 15 acres of grounds overlooking Portree Bay, with views towards the Cuillin Hills. Friendly staff, and an emphasis on good food, with a choice of formal or informal dining. Facilities available for conferences, functions and weddings. Open all year.

4 Single	All En Suite	B&B per person	Open Jan-Dec
10 Twin		from £35.00 Single	B&B + Eve.Meal
15 Double		from £35.00 Dbl/Twn	from £43.00
1 Family			

GUEST HOUSE

Givendale Guest House
Heron Place, Portree, Isle of Skye,
Inverness-shire, IV51 9GU
Tel: 01478 612183
E-mail: ctrayner@onetel.net.uk

Quiet area with outstanding views. 10 minutes walk from centre of Portree. Quality food and accommodation. Printed walks and maps available. Guided walks by arrangement. Please phone or write for details.

1 Twin	3 En Suite fac	B&B per person	Open Jan-Dec
3 Double	1 Priv.NOT ensuite	£20.00-£30.00 Single	
		£20.00-£27.00 Dbl/Twn	

Portree, Isle of Skye, Inverness-shire | Map Ref: 3E9

Rosedale Hotel
Portree, Isle of Skye IV51 9DB
Tel: 01478 613131   Fax: 01478 612531

Established family-run hotel. Unrivalled waterfront location with magnificent views. 23 ensuite bedrooms, cocktail bar and comfortable lounges. Harbour front restaurant featuring modern innovative cuisine using quality fresh ingredients served in a fine dining ambience of crisp linen, silver and crystal. Accolades include AA Rosette, RAC merit awards for hospitality and Taste of Scotland.

★★★

HOTEL

Rosedale Hotel
Beaumont Crescent, Portree, Isle of Skye,
Inverness-shire, IV51 9DB
Tel: 01478 613131 Fax: 01478 612531

5 Single	All En Suite	B&B per person	Open Apr-Oct
10 Twin		from £42.00 Single	B&B + Eve.Meal
7 Double		from £36.00 Dbl/Twn	from £57.00
1 Family			Bedrms/Restaurant
			Non-smoking.

Very comfortable and unusual hotel imaginatively created from former fishermens houses dating back to the reign of William IV. Award winning cuisine in an outstanding waterside location.

Sleat, Isle of Skye, Inverness-shire | Map Ref: 3F10

★★★

HOTEL

Hotel Eilean Iarmain
Isle Ornsay, Sleat, Isle of Skye, Inverness-shire, IV43 8QR
Tel: 01471 833332 Fax: 01471 833275
E-mail: hotel@eilean-iarmain.co.uk
Web: www.eileaniarmain.co.uk

4 Twin	All En Suite	B&B per person	Open Jan-Dec
6 Double		from £90.00 Single	B&B + Eve.Meal
2 Family		from £60.00 Dbl/Twn	from £91.00
4 Suites			

Over 100 years old with many original antiques Eilean Iarmain is idyllically located overlooking the picturesque Isle Ornsay harbour, having a unique character, being traditional, hospitable and homely. Award winning restaurant with menus featuring the very best of local seafood and game. Recently under new management, and 4 new superior suites alongside the hotel, all with mini bars.

Staffin, Isle of Skye, Inverness-shire | Map Ref: 3E8

FLODIGARRY COUNTRY HOUSE HOTEL
Staffin, Isle of Skye IV51 9HZ. Tel: 01470 552203 Fax: 01470 552301
e.mail: info@flodigarry.co.uk Web: www.flodigarry.co.uk

Taste of Scotland, Macallan Country House Hotel of the Year. Stunning sea and mountain views. Fine historic mansion in secluded wooded grounds. Superb ensuite bedrooms, central heating, log fires and old-world atmosphere. Award-winning restaurant, bar and conservatory meals. Open all year. Children welcome. Special low-season breaks.
Contact: Andrew or Pam Butler.   ★★★★

★★★★

HOTEL

Flodigarry Country House Hotel
Flodigarry, Staffin, Isle of Skye,
Inverness-shire, IV51 9HZ
Tel: 01470 552203 Fax: 01470 552301
E-mail: info@flodigarry.co.uk
Web: www.flodigarry.co.uk

1 Single	All En Suite	B&B per person	Open Jan-Dec
5 Twin		from £55.00 Single	B&B + Eve.Meal
9 Double		from £49.00 Dbl/Twn	from £74.00
4 Family			

Family-run Victorian house with strong Jacobite connections. Superb sea and mountain views, private grounds. Award winning cuisine.

All properties graded by VisitScotland, formerly known as the Scottish Tourist Board. | Key to symbols is on back flap.

Staffin, Isle of Skye, Inverness-shire | **Map Ref: 3E8**

★★

**SMALL
HOTEL**

Glenview Inn & Restaurant
Culnacnoc, Staffin, Isle of Skye, Inverness-shire, IV51 9JH
Tel: 01470 562248 Fax: 01470 562211
E-mail: valtos@lineone.net
Web: www.SmoothHound.co.uk/hotels/glenvi.html

Tastefully converted traditional island house, ideally situated for
exploring Northern Skye. Friendly atmosphere, good food. Adequate
parking available. The restaurant specialises in local fish and seafood
and a choice of traditional vegetarian and ethnic delicacies are offered.

1 Twin	4 En Suite fac	B&B per person	Open Mar-Oct
3 Double	1 Priv.NOT ensuite	from £20.00 Dbl/Twn	B&B + Eve.Meal
1 Family			from £33.50

Spean Bridge, Inverness-shire | **Map Ref: 3H12**

Corriegour Lodge Hotel

LOCH LOCHY, BY SPEAN BRIDGE,
LOCHABER, INVERNESS-SHIRE PH34 4EB
TEL: +44 (0)1397 712685 FAX: +44 (0)1397 712696
E.MAIL: info@corriegour-lodge-hotel.com
WEB: www.corriegour-lodge-hotel.com

*"Better food than the top London restaurants,
and a view to die for"* - THE MIRROR.

This former Victorian hunting lodge enjoys the very finest
setting in "The Great Glen". Dine in our Loch View
Conservatory enjoying the very best Scottish cuisine, fresh
seafood, Aberdeen Angus, homemade breads and puddings,
extensive selection of wines and malt whiskies. Our emphasis
is on your total relaxation and comfort. Log fires and big
comfy sofas. Come and be cushioned from the stresses of
everyday life. Walking, scenery, skiing, history. Private beach
and fishing school. Special spring/autumn breaks available.

★★★★

**SMALL
HOTEL**

Corriegour Lodge Hotel
Loch Lochy, by Spean Bridge, Inverness-shire,
PH34 4EB
Tel: 01397 712685 Fax: 01397 712696
Web: www.corriegour-lodge-hotel.com

Corriegour Lodge Hotel, a former hunting lodge, is set in nine acres of mature woodland
and garden with open views over Loch Lochy. Seventeen miles North of Fort William on the
road to Skye, many of Scotland's attractions are in easy reach. Local activities include
walking, cycling, climbing, pony trekking or fishing from the hotel jetty. The Loch
Restaurant is a distinct member of Taste of Scotland.

2 Single	All En Suite	B&B per person	Open Feb-Nov
2 Twin		from £55.50 Single	and New Year
4 Double		from £55.50 Dbl/Twn	B&B + Eve.Meal
1 Family			from £69.50

★★★★

**GUEST
HOUSE**

Corriechoille Lodge
Spean Bridge, Inverness-shire, PH34 4EY
Tel: 01397 712002
E-mail: enquiry@corriechoille.com
Web: www.corriechoille.com

An old fishing lodge set in a peaceful and secluded location with
breathtaking mountain views. Corriechoille is a family run guest house
where you can enjoy good food and drink in comfortable surroundings
with personal attention.

1 Twin	All En Suite	B&B per person	Open Apr-Oct
2 Double		from £30.00 Single	B&B + Eve.Meal from
2 Family		from £23.00 Dbl/Twn	£39.00

Important: Prices stated are estimates and may be subject to amendments

Spean Bridge, Inverness-shire   Map Ref: 3H12

★★

SMALL HOTEL

Letterfinlay Lodge Hotel
Loch Lochy, Spean Bridge, Inverness-shire,
PH34 4DZ
Tel: 01397 712622

1 Single	9 Ensuite fac	B&B per person	Open Mar-Oct
6 Twin	4 Priv.NOT ensuite	from £28.50 Single	
6 Double	4 Limited ensuite	from £57.00 Dbl/Twn	
2 Family			

Originally a Victorian shooting lodge this hotel stands on an enchanting site overlooking beautiful Loch Lochy in romantic Lochaber. Family run and owned by the Forsyth family for over 30 years. Popular for bar lunches and suppers. Ideal centre for touring the Highlands. Fishing and shooting by arrangement.

★★★

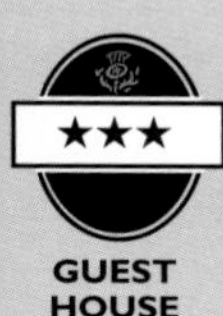

GUEST HOUSE

Smiddy House
Spean Bridge, Inverness-shire, PH34 4EU
Tel: 01397 712335 Fax: 01397 712043
E-mail: enquiry@smiddyhouse.com
Web: www.smiddyhouse.com

2 Twin	All En Suite	B&B per person	Open Jan-Dec
2 Double		from £30.00 Single	
1 Family		from £45.00 Dbl/Twn	

Completely refurbished family run guest house and licensed Bistro at the centre of this small Highland village, ideal for all local activities including touring, walking, climbing, fishing, horse riding, golf and winter skiing.

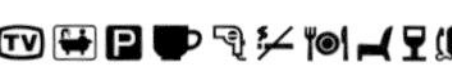

Strathpeffer, Ross-shire   Map Ref: 4A8

★★

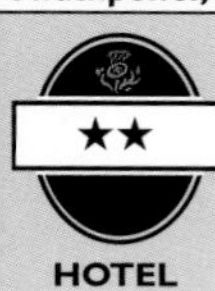

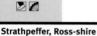

HOTEL

Highland Hotel
Strathpeffer, Highland Region, IV14 9AN
Tel: 01786 436600 Fax: 01786 436650
E-mail: l.graig@shearingsholidays.co.uk
Web: www.shearingsholidays.com

31 Single	All En Suite		Open Feb-Dec
72 Twin			
29 Double			

Large Victorian Hotel with oak panelled public areas. Hotel overlooks village square and pump room. 17 miles (27kms) west of Inverness.

Strontian, Argyll   Map Ref: 1E1

★★★★

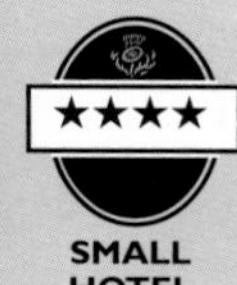

SMALL HOTEL

Kilcamb Lodge Hotel
Strontian, Argyll, PH36 4HY
Tel: 01967 402257 Fax: 01967 402041
E-mail: kilcamblodge@aol.com
Web: www.kilcamblodge.co.uk

1 Single	All En Suite	Rates per room	Open Mar-Nov plus
5 Twin		from £60.00 Single	New Year
5 Double		from £80.00 Dbl/Twn	
		Room only from £80.00	

The Good Hotel Guide "Scottish Hotel of the Year" Kilcamb Lodge is a stone built Georgian house situated in 20 acres of own grounds facing south across Loch Sunart with half a mile of private shoreline. Our daily changing menu uses the best local produce. AA 2 rosettes for fine cuisine. Each ensuite bedroom is furnished to a high standard each with their own individual style and character.

Tain, Ross-shire   Map Ref: 4B7

★★★★

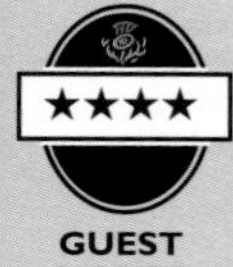

GUEST HOUSE

Golf View Guesthouse
13 Knockbreck Road, Tain, Ross-shire
Tel: 01862 892856 Fax: 01862 892172
E-mail: golfview@btinternet.com
Web: www.golf-view.co.uk

3 Twin	3 En Suite fac	B&B per person	Open Feb-end Nov
1 Double	1 Pub Bath/Show	from £25.00 Single	
1 Family		from £23.00 Dbl/Twn	

Secluded Victorian house with panoramic views over golf course and across the Dornoch Firth. Centrally situated in Scotland's oldest Royal Burgh.

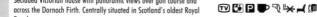

All properties graded by VisitScotland, formerly known as the Scottish Tourist Board.   **Key to symbols is on back flap.**

Tain, Ross-shire
Map Ref: 4B7

★★★★ HOTEL

Morangie House Hotel
Morangie Road, Tain, Ross-shire, IV19 1PY
Tel: 01862 892281 Fax: 01862 892872
E-mail: wynne@morangiehotel.com
Web: www.morangiehotel.com

Family run, recently extended former Victorian mansion, in own grounds on northern edge of Tain. A la carte restaurant, extensive bar meal menu. Taste of Scotland. Golfing can be arranged on several courses in the area.

4 Single	All En Suite	B&B per person	Open Jan-Dec
9 Twin		from £60.00 Single	B&B + Eve.Meal
10 Double		from £45.00 Dbl/Twn	from £65.00
3 Family			

Thurso, Caithness
Map Ref: 4D3

★★★ SMALL HOTEL

The Park Hotel
Thurso, Caithness, KW14 8RE
Tel/Fax: 01847 893251
E-mail: parkthurso@yahoo.co.uk
Web: www.parkhotelthurso.co.uk

Comfortable and friendly family run hotel fully licenced with 11 well appointed ensuite bedrooms all with TV, hairdryer, tea and coffee etc. All meals served. New conservatory lounge and dining room. Large private car park.

1 Single	All En Suite	B&B per person	Open Jan-Dec excl New
8 Twin		from £30.00 Single	Year
2 Double		from £25.00 Double	
8 Family		Room only	
		from £45.00	

★★★ SMALL HOTEL

Station Hotel
Princes Street, Thurso, Caithness, KW14 7DH
Tel: 01847 892003 Fax: 01847 891820
E-mail: stationhotel@lineone.net
Web: www.internet-promotions.co.uk/station

Personally run hotel, situated in the centre of Thurso, a short walk from the railway and bus stations. Good friendly base for the business traveller or for the visitor who is coming up to explore the coastline, archaeology and wildlife of the country of Caithness; not to mention a good base for making that trip to Orkney.

5 Single	All En Suite	B&B per person	Open Jan-Dec
9 Twin		from £30.00 Single	
6 Double			
3 Family			

Tongue, Sutherland
Map Ref: 4A3

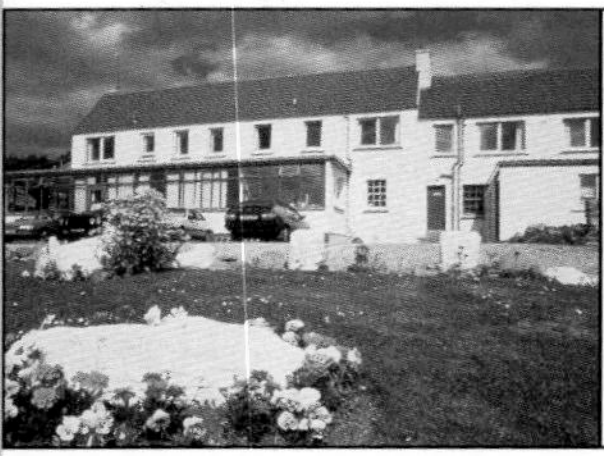

The Ben Loyal Hotel
TONGUE, SUTHERLAND IV27 4XE
Tel: 01847 611216 Fax: 01847 611212
e.mail: benloyalhotel@btinternet.com Web: www.benloyal.co.uk
"A Sanctuary from the Stress of Urban Living" ★★★ SMALL HOTEL AA ֍
Open all year, discover the clear sea and golden sands of this Highland oasis. Overlooking the Kyle and Ben Loyal we are renowned for our warm welcome, friendly staff and good food. Trout and salmon fishing can be arranged. Ashley Courtenay recommended hotel. 2 RAC Dining Awards. **£58.50-£64 for D,B&B or £287-£385 per week D,B&B.**

★★★ SMALL HOTEL

Ben Loyal Hotel
Tongue, Sutherland, IV27 4XE
Tel: 01847 611216 Fax: 01847 611212
Web: www.benloyal.co.uk

Stone built hotel with fine views of Ben Loyal and Kyle of Tongue. Friendly atmosphere. Fishing and real ale available.

2 Single	All En Suite	B&B per person	Open Jan-Dec excl
5 Twin		£38.00-£40.00 Single	Xmas/New Year
4 Double		£38.00-£40.00 Dbl/Twn	B&B + Eve.Meal
			from £58.50

Tongue, Sutherland
Map Ref: 4A3

**SMALL
HOTEL**

The Tongue Hotel
Tongue, Sutherland, IV27 4XD
Tel: 01847 611206 Fax: 01847 611345
Web: www.scottish-selection.co.uk

4 Twin
10 Double
2 Family

All En Suite

B&B per person
from £30.00 Single
from £30.00 Dbl/Twn

Open Mar-Oct

A traditional Victorian Highland hotel retaining original style and charm. Panoramic views over Kyle of Tongue, ideal base for nature enthusiasts.

Tore, Ross-shire
Map Ref: 4B8

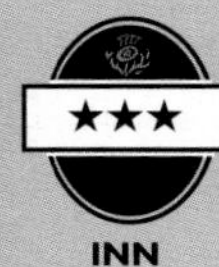

INN

Kilcoy Arms Hotel
Tore, Ross-shire, IV6 7RZ
Tel: 01463 811285 Fax: 01463 811285
E-mail: kilcoy@cali.co.uk
Web: www.cali.co.uk/users/freeway/kilcoy

2 Twin
1 Double

All En Suite

B&B per person
from £35.00 Single
from £55.00 Dbl/Twn

Open Jan-Dec
B&B + Eve.Meal from
£50.00

Recently renovated Victorian Inn close to A9 in the Black Isle. Popular bar serving lunches and suppers with all home cooked food. 8 miles (13kms) from Inverness centre. See leaflet

Ullapool, Ross-shire
Map Ref: 3G6

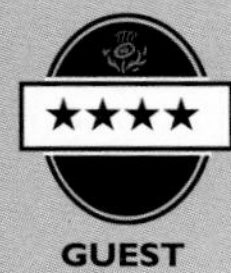

**GUEST
HOUSE**

Ardvreck Guest House
Morefield Brae, Ullapool, Ross-shire, IV26 2TH
Tel: 01854 612028 Fax: 01854 613000
E-mail: Ardvreck.Guesthouse@btinternet.com
Web: www.SmoothHound.co.uk/hotels/ardvreck.html

2 Single
2 Twin
4 Double
2 Family

All En Suite

B&B per person
from £23.00 Single
from £23.00 Dbl/Twn
Room only per person
from £20.00

Open Mar-Oct

Guest house set amidst some of the best hillwalking country and breathtaking scenery in Scotland. Elevated country position overlooking Ullapool and Lochbroom. Spacious, well appointed rooms most with spectacular sea view, all with ensuite shower room, T.V and tea/coffee facility. Residents lounge available at all times. Local facilities include a leisure centre, swimming pool, sauna, golf course, fishing and museum.

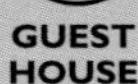

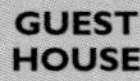

**GUEST
HOUSE**

Point Cottage Guest House
22 West Shore Street, Ullapool, Ross-shire, IV26 2UR
Tel: 01854 612494 Fax: 01854 613464
E-mail: stay@pointcottage.co.uk
Web: www.pointcottage.co.uk

1 Twin
2 Double

All En Suite

B&B per person
£25.00-£45.00 Single
£20.00-£26.00 Dbl/Twn

Open 1 Feb-31 Oct

Tastefully converted 18c fisherman's cottage where a warm welcome and a high level of local knowledge are assured. Marvellous lochside views to mountains beyond. Very quiet location but only 2 minutes walk to village centre. Vegetarian cooked breakfast available.

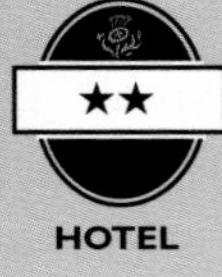

HOTEL

Royal Hotel
Ullapool, Highland Region, IV26 2SY
Tel: 01786 436600 Fax: 01786 436650
E-mail: l.graig@shearingsholidays.co.uk
Web: www.shearingsholidays.com

3 Single
30 Twin
12 Double
1 Family

All En Suite

Open Mar-Nov

Standing in its own grounds occupying a prominent position with several balcony rooms overlooking the harbour and Loch Broom.

All properties graded by VisitScotland, formerly known as the Scottish Tourist Board. | **Key to symbols is on back flap.**

Ullapool, Ross-shire

Map Ref: 3G6

★★★

**GUEST
HOUSE**

Strathmore House

Morefield, Ullapool, Ross-shire, IV26 2TH
Tel: 01854 612423 Fax: 01854 613485
E-mail: murdo@strathmore.fsnet.co.uk

Guest house enjoying panoramic views over Loch Broom and Ullapool.
Some bedrooms have separate front entrance. Ideal touring base for
north west coast. Comfortable TV lounge and reading room.

| 6 Double | All En Suite | B&B per person
from £25.00 Single
from £18.00 Double | Open Easter-Sep |

Whitebridge, Inveness-shire

Map Ref: 4A10

★★

**SMALL
HOTEL**

Whitebridge Hotel

Whitebridge, Inverness, Inverness-shire, IV2 6UN
Tel: 01456 486226 Fax: 01456 486413
E-mail: whitebridgehotel@southlochness.demon.co.uk
Web: www.southlochness.demon.co.uk

Personally run hotel, nestling in foothills of Monadhliath Mountains,
beside B862 on East side of Loch Ness, 24 miles (38kms) South of
Inverness.

| 3 Twin
6 Double
3 Family | 10 En Suite fac | B&B per person
from £28.00 Single
from £25.00 Dbl/Twn | Open Mar-Dec excl
Xmas/New Year
B&B + Eve.Meal from
£35.00 |

Important: Prices stated are estimates and may be subject to amendments

welcome to Scotland

THE OUTER ISLANDS:

Western Isles, Orkney, Shetland

The Outer Isles are for visitors seeking adventure, a sense of being outside Britain – yet still a part of it – and seeing a different culture. All three island groupings – the Western Isles, Orkney and Shetland – contrast with each other. Orkney and Shetland share a Norse heritage, while the Western Isles are the stronghold of the Gael. Excellent ferry and air links mean getting to any of these groups of islands is straight forward.

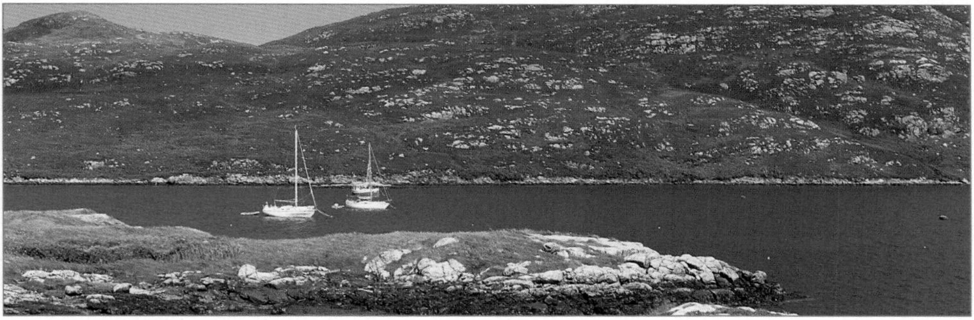

Loch Baghasdail, Lochboisdale, Outer Hebrides

THE Western Isles offer some of Scotland's finest seascapes and beaches, as well as the springtime flowers of the machair – the shell-sand coastal pasture. Ancient monuments such as the spectacular Callanais Standing Stones are a reminder of the heritage of prehistory on the islands. The preserved Black House at Arnol is a reminder of the more recent life of the crofters on these islands, and is one of many heritage museums on the islands.

Orkney's green islands, like the Western Isles, have a strong sense of continuity stretching back to ancient times. The past is all around at places like Skara Brae, a magnificently preserved Stone Age village, and Maes Howe, a unique burial chamber already more than a millennium old when pillaged by Vikings.

Kirkwall is the setting for St Magnus Cathedral, the most magnificent Norman work in Scotland. Another theme to explore is the seagoing tradition, including the recent history of Scapa Flow as a naval anchorage, portrayed at the fascinating museum at Lyness on Hoy. Orkney's wildlife includes spectacular seabird colonies along its dramatic coastline.

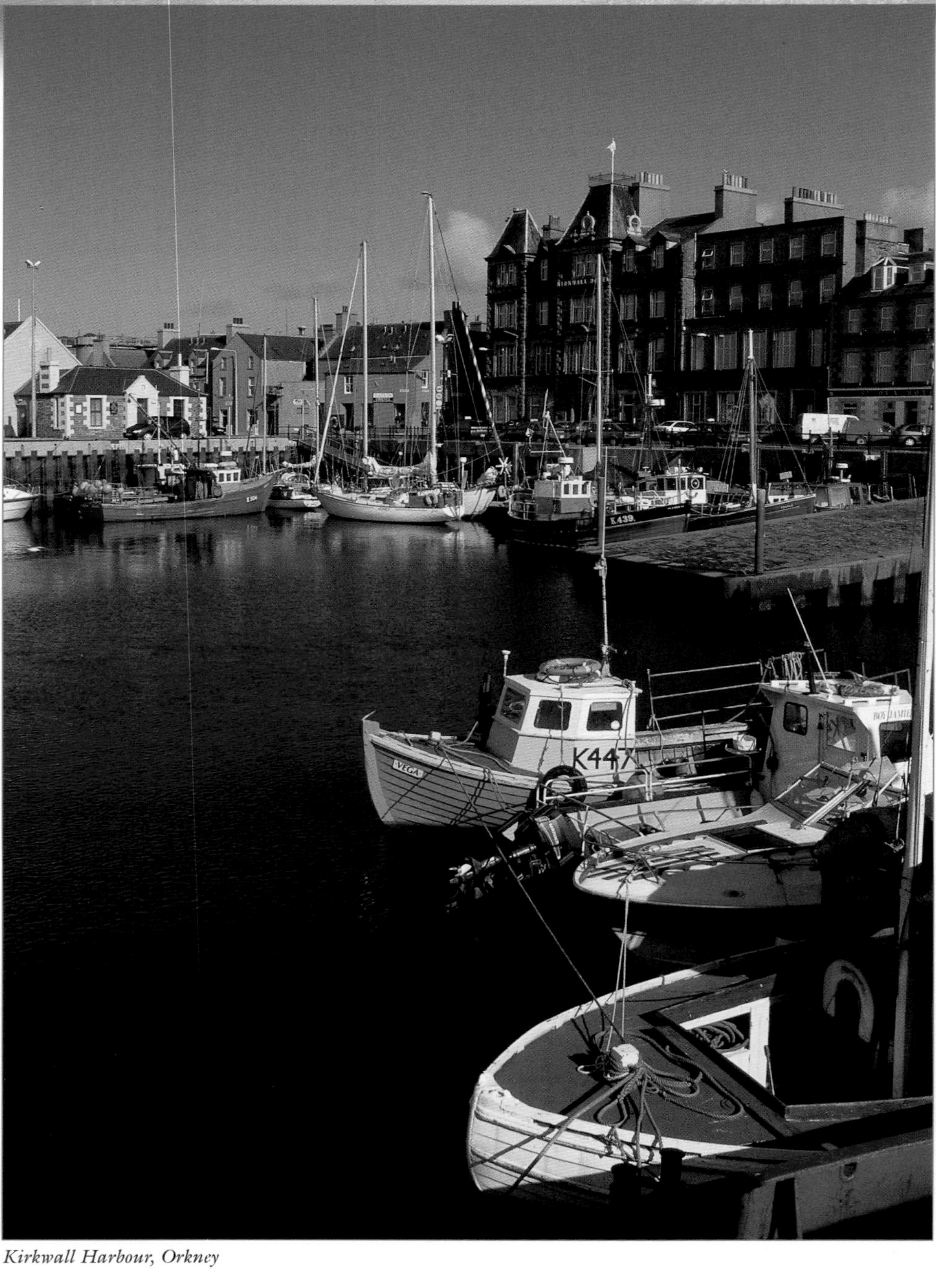

Kirkwall Harbour, Orkney

The Outer Islands:
Western Isles, Orkney, Shetland

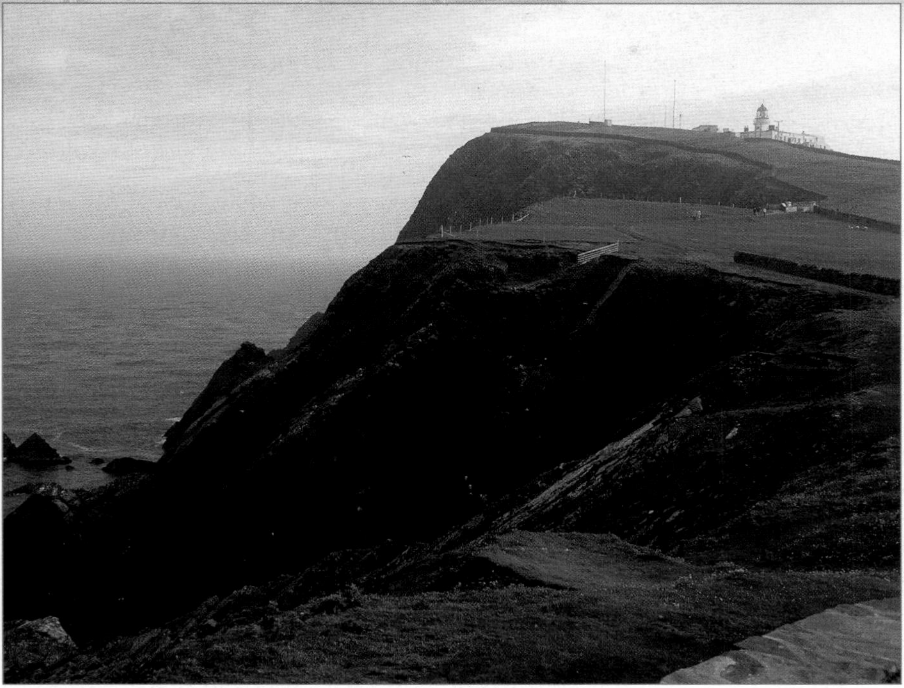

Sumburgh Head, Shetland

Shetland has the strongest sense of somewhere different. Here the Scandinavian influence is apparent – in dialect, music, even architecture and traditions. The sea pervades the way of life, with nowhere more than three miles from salt water.
Like Orkney, there is an abundance of wildlife – seals, otters and seabirds – from Sumburgh Head in the south of the islands past the national nature reserve at Herrmaness on Unst to Muckle Flugga at the most northerly point of Britain. Shetland is for adventurers, with long summer daylight hours in 'the land of the simmer dim' leaving even more time to enjoy the unique island ambience.

EVENTS
THE OUTER ISLANDS:
Western Isles, Orkney, Shetland

1 JANUARY &
25 DECEMBER
Men & Boy's Ba' Games
Kirkwall, Market Cross
Traditional game of street
football with around 400
players.
Contact: Bobby Leslie
Tel: 01856 872961
Web: www.visitorkney.com

29 JANUARY
Up Helly Aa
Lerwick, Harbourside
Traditional Viking fire
festival culminating in the
burning of a replica Viking
Galley
Contact: Lerwick Tourist
Information Centre
Tel: 01595 693434
Web: www.visitshetland.com

* 25-29 APRIL
Shetland Folk Festival
Shetland, Various Venues
Local and invited musicians
perform at venues
throughout the islands.
Contact:
Shetland Islands Tourism
Tel: 01595 693434
Web: www.visitshetland.com

16-21 JUNE
St Magnus Festival
Orkney, Various Venues
Annual midsummer
celebration of the arts.
Contact:
St Magnus Festival Office
Tel: 01856 871445
Web: www.visitorkney.com

* 8-12 JULY
Ceolas Music
Summer School
South Uist, Various Venues
Expert tuition in piping,
fiddling, singing, scotch
reels, step dancing and the
Gaelic language.
Contact: Mairi McInnes
Tel: 01870 620333
Web: www.ceolas.co.uk

* 10 - 13 JULY
Hebridean Celtic Festival
Isle of Lewis,
Various Venues
Gaelic music from
home-grown professional
and world class performers
from across the Celtic
nations.
Contact:
Hebridean Celtic Festival
Tel: 07001 878787
Web: www.hebceltfest.com

21-27 JULY
Stromness Shopping Week
Stromness, Various Venues
Gala week featuring a host
of events to entertain the
whole family.
Contact: Jacqueline Wishart
Tel: 01856 850939

1-3 AUGUST
Hebridean
Maritime Festival
Stornoway, Isle of Lewis,
Various Venues
Boat and sailing festival.
Contact: Ken Kennedy
Tel: 01851 703562
Web: www.sailhebrides.co.uk

* 30 AUGUST -
2 SEPTEMBER
Walk Shetland 2002
Shetland, Various Venues
A celebration of the islands
on foot.
Contact: Lerwick Tourist
Information Centre
Tel: 01595 693434
Web: www.visitshetland.com

* 14-21 SEPTEMBER
Taste of Orkney
Food Festival
Orkney, Various Venues
A feast of delicious
opportunities to sample
Orkney's finest food and
drink.
Contact: Kirkwall Tourist
Information Centre
Tel: 01856 872856
Web: www.visitorkney.com

* 26-29 SEPTEMBER
Shetland
Storytelling Festival
Shetland, Various Venues
Storytelling festival with
music, dance and drama as
the tales unfold.
Contact: Lerwick Tourist
Information Centre
Tel: 01595 693434
Web: www.visitshetland.com

** denotes provisional date,
please check before attending*

Area tourist boards
The Outer Islands:
Western Isles, Orkney, Shetland

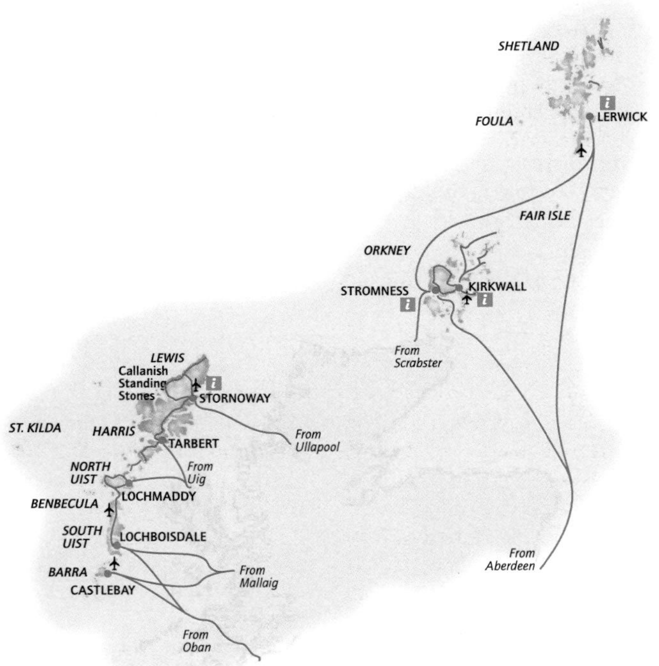

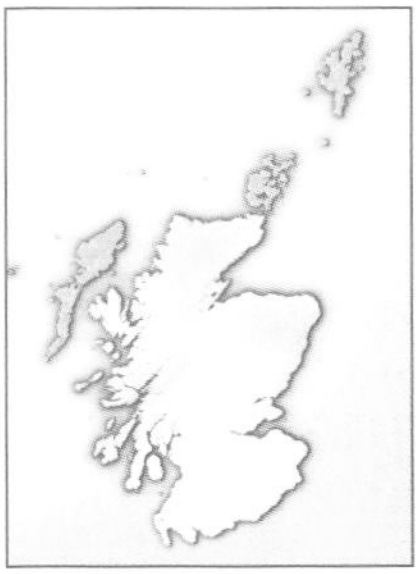

Western Isles
Tourist Board
26 Cromwell Street
Stornoway
Isle of Lewis
HS1 2DD

Tel: 01851 703088
Fax: 01851 705244
E-mail: stornowaytic@
witb.ossian.net
Web: www.witb.co.uk

Orkney Tourist
Board
6 Broad Street
Kirkwall
Orkney
KW15 1NX

Tel: 01856 872856
Fax: 01856 875056
E-mail:
info@otb.ossian.net
Web: www.visitorkney.com

Shetland Islands
Tourism
Market Cross
Lerwick
Shetland
ZE1 0LU

Tel: 01595 693434
Fax: 01595 695807
E-mail:
shetland.tourism@
zetnet.co.uk
Web: www.visitshetland.com

Tourist Information Centres
The Outer Islands:
Western Isles, Orkney, Shetland

Western Isles Tourist Board

Castlebay
Main Street
Isle of Barra
Tel: (01871) 810336
Easter-Oct

Lochboisdale
Pier Road
Isle of South Uist
Tel: (01878) 700286
Easter-Oct

Lochmaddy
Isle of North Uist
Tel: (01851) 500321
Easter-Oct

Stornoway
26 Cromwell Street
Isle of Lewis
Tel: (01851) 703088
Jan-Dec

Tarbert
Pier Road
Isle of Harris
Tel: (01859) 502011
Easter-Oct

Orkney Tourist Board

Kirkwall
6 Broad Street
Orkney
Tel: (01856) 872856
Jan-Dec

Stromness
Ferry Terminal Building
The Pier Head
Orkney
Tel: (01856) 850716
Jan-Dec

Shetland Tourist Board

Lerwick
The Market Cross
Shetland
Tel: (01595) 693434
Jan-Dec

Tangasdale, Isle of Barra, Western Isles
Map Ref: 3A11

★★★
HOTEL

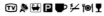

Isle of Barra Hotel
Tangasdale Beach, Isle of Barra, Western Isles,
HS9 5XW
Tel: 01871 810383 Fax: 01871 810385
E-mail: barrahotel@aol.com
Web: www.isleofbarra.com/iob.html

Family run hotel, with friendly local staff, specialising in fresh local
seafood, Aberdeen Angus beef and fine wines. Superbly situated
overlooking beautiful white sandy bay washed by the Atlantic Ocean.

26 Twin	All En Suite	B&B per person	Open end Mar-
4 Double		from £37.00 Single	begin Oct & Hogmanay
		from £32.00 Dbl/Twn	B&B + Eve.Meal
		Room only per person	from £48.00
		from £30.00	

Scarista, Isle of Harris, Western Isles

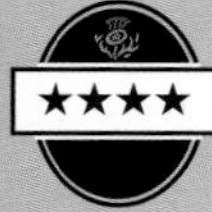

★★★★
**GUEST
HOUSE**

Scarista House
Scarista, Isle of Harris, HS3 3HX
Tel: 01859 550238 Fax: 01859 550277
E-mail: timandpatricia@scaristahouse.com
Web: www.scaristahouse.com

Former manse with a country house atmosphere. Inspiring views of ivory
sand and a turquoise sea. Emphasis on fresh produce and quiet
relaxation. Member of Taste of Scotland.

2 Twin	All En Suite	B&B per person	Open Jan-Dec excl New
3 Double		from £67.00 Single	Year
		from £61.00 Dbl/Twn	B&B + Eve.Meal from
			£86.00

Tarbert, Isle of Harris, Western Isles
Map Ref: 3C6

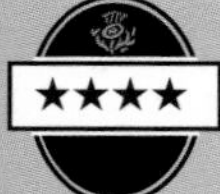

★★★★
**GUEST
HOUSE**

Allan Cottage Guest House
Tarbert, Isle of Harris, HS3 3DJ
Tel/Fax: 01859 502146
Web: www.witb.co.uk/links/allancottage.htm

Sympathetically converted Old Harris Telephone Exchange, offering very
high standard of comfort. We are ideally situated within easy reach of
any point on the island. We maintain the same high standard of service
and hospitality that has made Allan Cottage known and mentioned in
guidebooks worlwide.

1 Twin	2 En Suite fac	B&B per person	Open May-Sept
2 Double	1 Priv.NOT ensuite	£32.00-£38.00 Single	
		£32.00-£38.00 Dbl/Twn	

Achmore, Isle of Lewis, Western Isles
Map Ref: 3D5

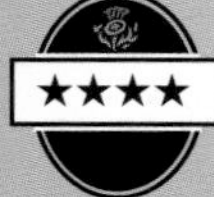

★★★★
**GUEST
HOUSE**

Cleascro Guest House
Achmore, Isle of Lewis, Western Isles, HS2 9DU
Tel/Fax: 01851 860302
E-mail: donna@cleascro.co.uk
Web: www.cleascro.co.uk

Modern family house, with attractive garden, in rural setting. Centrally
located for visits to all parts of the island. Home-cooked evening meal
available with fresh local produce.

1 Twin	All En Suite	B&B per person	Open Feb-Nov
2 Double		from £25.00 Single	B&B + Eve.Meal
		from £50.00 Dbl/Twn	from £45.00
		Room only from £17.00	

Callanish, Isle of Lewis, Western Isles
Map Ref: 3D4

★★★★
**GUEST
HOUSE**

Eshcol Guest House
21 Breasclete, Callanish, Lewis, Western Isles
HS2 9ED
Tel/Fax: 01851 621357
E-mail: neil@eshcol.com Web: www.eshcol.com

Modern detached house quietly situated in the crofting village of
Breasclete, with an open outlook over Loch Roag towards the Uig hills.
Good base to explore Lewis, or just to relax. Only 2 miles to the Callanish
standing stones. All bedrooms non-smoking. Local produce used where
possible in our highly recommended evening meals. B.Y.O.B.

2 Twin	2 En Suite fac	B&B per person	Open Mar-Oct
1 Double	1 Priv.NOT ensuite	from £29.00 Single	B&B + Eve.Meal from
		from £58.00 Dbl/Twn	£47.00

All properties graded by VisitScotland, formerly known as the Scottish Tourist Board.   **Key to symbols is on back flap.**

Stornoway, Isle of Lewis, Western Isles — Map Ref: 3D4

HOTEL ★★★

Cabarfeidh Hotel
Manor Park, Stornoway, Isle of Lewis,
HS1 2EU
Tel: 01851 702740 Fax: 01851 705572
E-mail: caberfeidh@calahotels.com
Web: www.calahotels.com

Recently refurbished hotel with a la carte restaurant offering interesting choice of dishes with emphasis on local produce. Lift to all floors.

10 Single	All En Suite	B&B per person	Open Jan-Dec
28 Twin		from £72.00 Single	B&B + Eve.Meal
8 Double		from £48.00 Dbl/Twn	from £92.00

HOTEL ★★

Royal Hotel
Cromwell Street, Stornoway, Isle of Lewis,
HS1 2DG
Tel: 01851 702109 Fax: 01851 702142
E-mail: royal@calahotels.com
Web: www.calahotels.com

This friendly and comfortable hotel has fine views of Stornoway's fishing harbour and castle. Our Boatshed Restaurant offers fine cuisine using fresh local produce.

6 Single	24 En Suite fac	B&B per person	Open Jan-Dec excl
71 Twin	2 Priv.NOT ensuite	from £57.00 Single	Xmas/New Year
12 Double		from £38.00 Dbl/Twn	B&B + Eve.Meal
1 Family			from £70.00

HOTEL ★★

Seaforth Hotel
11 James Street, Stornoway, Isle of Lewis, HS1 2QW
Tel: 01851 702740 Fax: 01851 703900
E-mail: seaforth@calahotels.com
Web: www.calahotels.com

Modern hotel, the largest on the island, situated in the centre of Stornoway, within walking distance of the ferry terminal. Local leisure and fitness centre is just across the road. The hotel makes an excellent base for exploring Lewis and Harris.

19 Single	All En Suite	B&B per person	Open Apr-Nov
28 Twin		from £50.00 Single	B&B + Eve.Meal from
17 Double		from £36.00 Dbl/Twn	£64.00
3 Family			

Locheport, Isle of North Uist, Western Isles — Map Ref: 3B8

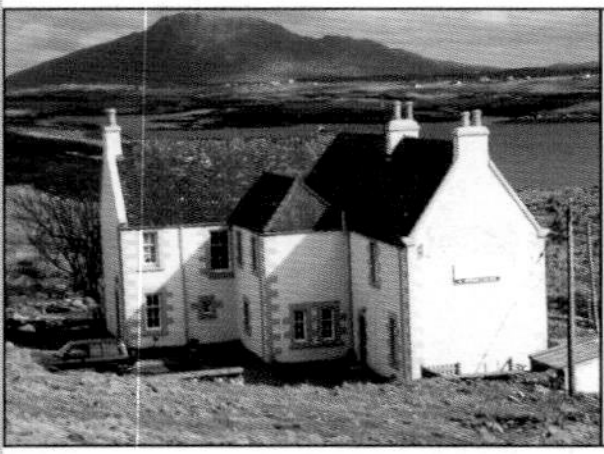

Langass Lodge

NORTH UIST, THE WESTERN ISLES HS6 5HA
Telephone: 01876 580285 Fax: 01876 580385
e.mail: langasslodge@btconnect.com

Commanding scenic views over a sea loch and situated beside a stone circle and neolithic burial chamber. This comfortable small hotel is the ideal base for exploring the Western Isles. All the well-appointed rooms have ensuite facilities and the excellent restaurant specialises in seafood and game.

Prices from £45 B&B.

**SMALL
HOTEL** ★★★

Langass Lodge Hotel
Locheport, North Uist, Western Isles, HS6 5HA
Tel: 01876 580285 Fax: 01876 580385

Traditional Inn, set in splendid isolation, overlooking Loch Eport and about 8 miles (13kms) from Lochmaddy ferry terminal. Popular retreat for anglers, ornithologists and lovers of the outdoors. Fishing available on all of the North Uists renouned lochs.

1 Single	All En Suite	B&B per person	Open Jan-Dec
4 Twin		from £45.00 Single	
2 Double		from £75.00 Dbl/Twn	

Important: Prices stated are estimates and may be subject to amendments

Lochmaddy, Isle of North Uist, Western Isles — Map Ref: 3B8

HOTEL ★★

Lochmaddy Hotel
Lochmaddy, North Uist, Western Isles, HS6 5AA
Tel: 01876 500331
Fax: 01876 500210
E-mail: info@lochmaddyhotel.co.uk
Web: www.lochmaddyhotel.co.uk

Providing Hebridean hospitality and good food situated 100 yards from ferry terminal. Free trout fishing for guests. Salmon and sea trout fishing also available to guests on reduced rate, priority permits.

8 Single	All En Suite	
2 Twin		
2 Double		
3 Family		

B&B per person
from £27.50 Single
from £55.00 Dbl/Twn

Open Jan-Dec
B&B + Eve.Meal from £37.50

Kirkwall, Orkney — Map Ref: 5B12

GUEST HOUSE ★★

Sanderlay Guest House
2 Viewfield Drive, Kirkwall, Orkney, KW15 1RB
Tel: 01856 875587 Fax: 01856 876350
E-mail: enquiries@sanderlay.co.uk
Web: www.sanderlay.co.uk

Comfortable modern house in quiet residential area on outskirts of town. Some ensuite and 3 self-contained family units. Private parking available. Credit cards accepted. Ideal base for exploring the Orkney mainland or for visiting the North Isles.

1 Single	4 En Suite fac	
1 Twin	1 Pub Bath/Show	
2 Double		
2 Family		

B&B per person
£18.00-£24.00 Single
£14.00-£22.00 Dbl/Twn
Room only per person
£11.00-£21.00

Open Jan-Dec

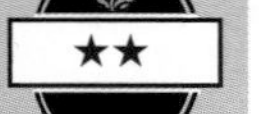

GUEST HOUSE ★★

St Ola Hotel
Harbour Street, Kirkwall, Orkney, KW15 1LE
Tel/Fax: 01856 875090

Friendly family run harbour front hotel. All rooms have private facilities. Convenient for North Isles ferries.

2 Single	All En Suite	
2 Twin		
1 Double		
1 Family		

B&B per person
from £32.00 Single
from £23.00 Dbl/Twn

Open Jan-Dec excl Xmas/New Year

Papa Westray, Orkney — Map Ref: 5B10

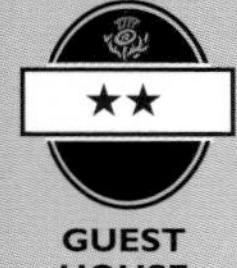

GUEST HOUSE ★★

Beltane House
Papa Westray, Orkney, KW17 2BU
Tel: 01857 644267 Fax: 01857 644282/250

Recently converted terraced cottages, modern and comfortable, with homecooking and community shop. Can collect from boat or plane.

3 Twin	All En Suite	
1 Double		

B&B per person
from £26.50 Single
from £23.50 Double

Open Jan-Dec excl Xmas/New Year
Eve.Meal from £16.50

Sanday, Orkney — Map Ref: 5D10

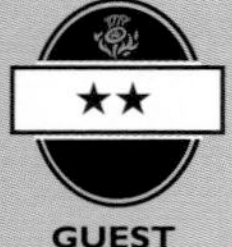

GUEST HOUSE ★★

Orkney Healing Retreat
The Belsair, Sanday, Orkney, KW17 2BJ
Tel: 01857 600206
E-mail: orkneyretreat@hotmail.com

Relax in this peaceful and comfortable island retreat. Warm welcome and home cooking. Beautiful beaches and ideal for walking. A complete break to renew mind, body and soul. Quiet Room and Healing Room available.

2 Single	3 En Suite fac	
1 Twin	1 Pub Bath/Show	
1 Double		

B&B per person
from £18.50 Single
from £37.00 Dbl/Twn

Open Jan-Dec excl Xmas/New Year
B&B + Eve.Meal from £27.50

All properties graded by VisitScotland, formerly known as the Scottish Tourist Board.   Key to symbols is on back flap.

Stenness, Orkney | Map Ref: 5B12

★★★

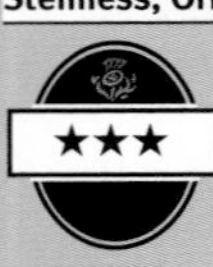

HOTEL

Standing Stones Hotel
Stenness, Orkney, KW16 3JX
Tel: 01856 850449 Fax: 01856 851262
E-mail: standingstones@sol.co.uk
Web: www.visitorkney

Situated on the shores of the Loch of Stenness, just off the main Kirkwall to Stromness road. This is an excellent central base for exploring Orkney's many historical and archaeological attractions, or for fishing or birdwatching.

4 Single	All En Suite
8 Twin	
2 Double	
3 Family	

B&B per person
from £33.00 Single
from £33.00 Dbl/Twn
Room only per person
from £27.00

Open Jan-Dec excl
Xmas/New Year
B&B + Eve.Meal
from £48.00

Stromness, Orkney | Map Ref: 5B12

★★

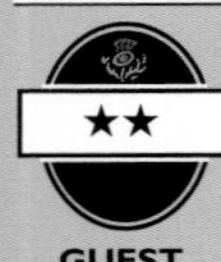

GUEST HOUSE

Orca Hotel
76 Victoria Street, Stromness, Orkney, KW16 3BS
Tel/Fax: 01856 850447
E-mail: info@orcahotel.com   Web: www.orcahotel.com

Centrally located in the historic town of Stromness, the perfect starting point to explore the scenery, wildlife and archaeology of the islands. Relax in the friendly, comfortable atmosphere of this harbourside guest house and start your day with a delicious breakfast. Spend the evening in the private lounge or savour an à la carte meal in the candlelit cellar bistro. Self-catering option for groups of 8 to 16.

1 Single	All En Suite
2 Twin	
1 Double	
2 Family	

B&B per person
from £19.00 Single
from £17.00 double
Room only £12.00

Open Jan-Dec

★★★

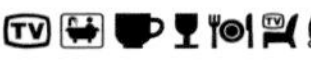

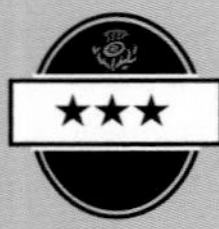

HOTEL

The Stromness Hotel
The Pier Head, Stromness, Orkney, KW16 3AA
Tel: 01856 850298 Fax: 01856 850610
E-mail: info@stromnesshotel.com
Web: www.stromnesshotel.com

Recently refurbished hotel, situated in the heart of the fishing port of Stromness. Overlooking the harbour, with views out towards Scapa Flow. Much to see and do locally, plus all of Orkney's famous archaeological sites. Fishing, golf, birdwatching are all available.

6 Single	All En Suite
21 Twin	
9 Double	
6 Family	

B&B per person
£30.00-£40.00 Single
£30.00-£40.00 Dbl/Twn
Room only per person
£24.00-£34.00

Open Jan-Dec
B&B + Eve.Meal
£42.00-£52.00

Lerwick, Shetland | Map Ref: 5G6

★★★

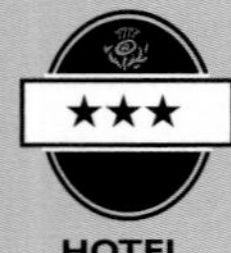

HOTEL

The Lerwick Hotel
15 South Road, Lerwick, Shetland, ZE1 0RB
Tel: 01595 692166 Fax: 01595 694419
E-mail: reception@Lerwickhotel.co.uk
Web: www.shetlandhotels.com

Modern hotel in Lerwick, on sea shore overlooking Breiwick Bay and Bressay Island. Catering for holiday and business travel. Tours organised.

9 Single	All En Suite
16 Twin	
6 Double	
4 Family	

B&B per person
from £69.00 Single
from £44.50 Dbl/Twn

Open Jan-Dec excl
Xmas/New Year

★★★

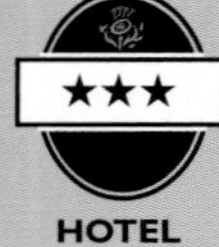

HOTEL

♿

The Shetland Hotel
Holmsgarth Road, Lerwick, Shetland, ZE1 0PW
Tel: 01595 695515 Fax: 01595 695828
E-mail: reception@shetlandhotel.co.uk
Web: www.shetlandhotels.com

Modern hotel with spacious bedrooms. Views to busy harbour and Isle of Bressay.

46 Twin	All En Suite
15 Double	
3 Family	

B&B per person
from £60.00 Single
from £44.00 Dbl/Twn

Open Jan-Dec excl
Xmas/New Year
B&B + Eve.Meal
from £55.95

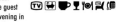

Important: Prices stated are estimates and may be subject to amendments

FACILITIES
For visitors with disabilities

VisitScotland, in conjunction with the English Tourism Council and Wales Tourist Board operates a national accessible scheme that identifies, acknowledges and promotes those accommodation establishments that meet the needs of visitors with disabilities.

The three categories of accessibility, drawn up in close consultation with specialist organisations concerned with the needs of people with disabilities are:

CATEGORY 1

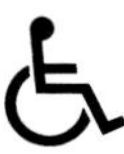

Unassisted wheelchair access for residents

CATEGORY 2

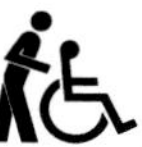

Assisted wheelchair access for residents

CATEGORY 3

Access for residents with mobility difficulties

CATEGORY 1

Achilty Hotel
Achilty, Contin, by Strathpeffer
Ross-shire, IV14 9EE
Tel: 01997 421355

Airlie Mount Holidays
2 Albert Street, Alyth, Blairgowrie
Perthshire, PH11 8AX
Tel: 01828 632986

Ardgarth Guest House
1 St Mary's Place, Portobello
Edinburgh, EH15 2QF
Tel: 0131 669 3021

Atholl Villa
29 Atholl Road, Pitlochry
Perthshire, PH16 5BX
Tel: 01796 473820

Balcary Bay Hotel
Auchencairn, by Castle Douglas
Kirkcudbrightshire, DG7 1QZ
Tel: 01556 640217

Battledown Bed & Breakfast
off Station Road, Forgandenny
Perthshire, PH2 9EL
Tel: 01738 812471

Beardmore Hotel
Beardmore Street, Clydebank
Greater Glasgow, G81 4SA
Tel: 041 9516000

Brae Lodge Guest House
30 Liberton Brae, Edinburgh
Lothian, EH16 6AF
Tel: 0131 6722876

**Burrastow House
Hotel & Restaurant**
Walls, Shetland, ZE2 9PD
Tel: 01595 809307

Carlogie House Hotel
Carlogie Road, Carnoustie
Angus, DD7 6LD
Tel: 01241 853185

Carlton George Hotel
44 West George Street
Glasgow, G2 1DH
Tel: 0141 353 6373

Ceilidh B&B
34 Clifton Road, Lossiemouth
Moray, IV31 6DP
Tel: 01343 815848

Claymore House Hotel
45 Seabank Road, Nairn
Inverness-shire, IV12 4EY
Tel: 01667 453731

Coille-Mhor House
20 Houston Mains Holdings
Uphall, Broxburn
West Lothian, EH52 6PA
Tel: 0506 854044

Copthorne Hotel
122 Huntly Street
Aberdeen, AB10 1SU
Tel: 01224 630404

Covenanters' Inn
High Street, Auldearn
Nairn, IV12 5TG
Tel: 01667 452456

Crossroads
Stoneybridge, South Uist
Western Isles, HS8 5SD
Tel: 01870 620321

Cruachan Guest House
Dalmally, Argyll, PA33 1AA
Tel: 01838 200496

Cuil-Na-Sithe
Lochyside, Fort William
Inverness-shire, PH33 7NX
Tel: 01397 702267

Dalhousie Courte Hotel
Cockpen Road, Bonnyrigg
Midlothian, EH19 3HS
Tel: 0131 660 3200

Days Inn
Welcome Break M74/A7
Abington, Lanarkshire, ML12 6RG
Tel: 01864 502782

Days Inn
80 Ballater Street
Glasgow, G5 0TW
Tel: 0141 429 4233

Dhailling Lodge
155 Alexandra Parade
Dunoon, Argyll, PA23 8AW
Tel: 01369 701253

FACILITIES
For visitors with disabilities

Dolly's B & B
33 Aignish Point,Lewis
Western Isles, HS2 0PB
Tel: 01851 870755

Drumoig Hotel & Golf Course
Drumoig, Leuchars
by St Andrews, Fife, KY16 0BE
Tel: 01382 541800

Dryburgh Abbey Hotel
St Boswells
Roxburghshire, TD6 0RQ
Tel: 01835 822261

Dunvalanree House
Portrigh Bay, Carradale
Argyll, PA28 6SE
Tel: 01583 431226

Empire Travel Lodge
Union Street, Lochgilphead
Argyll, PA31 8JS
Tel: 01546 602381

Forest Hills Hotel
Kinlochard, by Aberfoyle
Perthshire, FK8 3TL
Tel: 01877 387277

Fourpenny Cottage
Skelbo, Dornoch
Sutherland, IV25 3QF
Tel: 01862 810727

The Garden House Hotel
Sarkfoot Road, Gretna
Dumfriesshire, DG16 5EP
Tel: 0461 337621

Gattaway Farm
Abernethy
Perthshire, PH2 9LQ
Tel: 01738 850746

Glasgow Hilton
1 William Street
Glasgow, G3 8HT
Tel: 0141 204 5555

Glasgow Marriott
500 Argyle Street
Glasgow, G3 8RR
Tel: 0141 226 5577

The Gleneagles Hotel
Auchterarder, Perthshire, PH3 1NF
Tel: 01764 662231

The Glenholm Centre
Broughton, by Biggar
Lanarkshire, ML12 6JF
Tel: 01899 830408

Greenacre
Aberfeldy Road
by Killin, Perthshire, FK21 8TY
Tel: 01567 820466

Highland Cottage
Breadalbane Street, Tobermory
Isle of Mull, PA75 6PD
Tel: 01688 302407

Holiday Inn
161 West Nile Street
Glasgow, G1 2RL
Tel: 0141 332 0110

Holiday Inn Express – Stirling
Springkerse Business Park
Stirling, Stirlingshire, FK7 7XH
Tel: 01786 449922

Holiday Inn Express Livingston
Starlaw Road, Bathgate
West Lothian, EH48 1LQ
Tel: 01506 650650

Holiday Inn Glasgow City West
Bothwell Street
Glasgow, G2 7EN
Tel: 0870 4009032

Howard Johnson Hotel
Cartsburn
Greenock, PA15 4RT
Tel: 01475 786666

Hunters Lodge Hotel
Annan Road, Gretna
Dumfriesshire, DG16 5DL
Tel: 0461 338214

Inchyra Grange Hotel
Grange Road, Polmont
Stirlingshire, FK2 0YB
Tel: 0324 711911

The Invercauld Arms Hotel
Invercauld Road, Braemar
Aberdeenshire, AB35 5YR
Tel: 013397 41605

Inverness Marriott
Culcabock Road, Inverness
Inverness-shire, IV2 3LP
Tel: 01463 237166

Invernettie Guest House
South Road, Peterhead
Aberdeenshire, AB42 0YX
Tel: 01779 473530

Isle of Skye Hotel
Queensbridge
18 Dundee Road, Perth
Tayside, PH2 7AB
Tel: 01738 624471

**Isles of Glencoe Hotel &
Leisure Centre**
Ballachulish, Argyll, PA39 4HL
Tel: 01855 811602

James Watt College
Waterfront Campus
Customhouse Way, Greenock
Renfrewshire, PA15 1EN
Tel: 01475 731360

Jarvis International
Almondview, Livingston
West Lothian, EH54 6QB
Tel: 01506 431222

Jurys Edinburgh Inn
43 Jeffrey Street
Edinburgh, Lothian, EH1 1DH
Tel: 0131 200 3300

Kings Hall
University of Aberdeen
Aberdeen, AB24 3FX
Tel: 01224 273444

Lav'rockha Guest House
Inganess Road, Kirkwall
Orkney, KW15 1SP
Tel: 01856 876103

Loch Torridon Hotel
Torridon, Achnasheen
Ross-shire, IV22 2EY
Tel: 01445 791242

The Lodge at Daviot Mains
Daviot, Inverness-shire, IV2 5ER
Tel: 01463 772215

Marcliffe at Pitfodels
North Deeside Road
Pitfodels, Aberdeen, AB15 9YA
Tel: 01224 861000

Melville Guest House
2 Duddingston Crescent
Edinburgh, Lothian, EH15 3AS
Tel: 0131 669 7856

FACILITIES
For visitors with disabilities

Motherwell College Stewart Hall
Dalzell Drive, Motherwell
Lanarkshire, ML1 2DD
Tel: 01698 261890

North Lodge Guest House
Canonbie, Dumfriesshire, DG14 0TF
Tel: 013873 71409

Northbay House
Balnabodach
Castlebay, Isle of Barra
Outer Hebrides, HS9 5UT
Tel: 01871 890255

Old Pines Restaurant with Rooms
By Spean Bridge
Inverness-shire, PH34 4EG
Tel: 01397 712324

The Old Station
Stravithie Bridge
St Andrews, Fife, KY16 8LR
Tel: 01334 880505

Panmure Hotel
Tay Street, Monifieth
Angus, DD5 4AX
Tel: 01382 532911

Patio Hotel Aberdeen
Beach Boulevard, Aberdeen
Aberdeenshire, AB24 5EF
Tel: 01224 633339

Rathcluan
Carslogie Road, Cupar
Fife, KY15 4HY
Tel: 01334 650000

Rosslea Hall Hotel
Ferry Road, Rhu
Dunbartonshire, G84 8NF
Tel: 01436 439955

Rowantree Guest House
38 Main Street, Glenluce
Newton Stewart
Wigtownshire, DG8 0PS
Tel: 015813 300244

Ryrie
24 Lindsay Drive, Wick
Caithness, KW1 4PG
Tel: 01955 603001

Sheraton Grand Hotel
1 Festival Square
Edinburgh, EH3 9SR
Tel: 0131 229 9131

Shetland Hotel
Holmsgarth Road
Lerwick, Shetland, ZE1 0PW
Tel: 01595 695515

Shorefield
Edinbane
Isle of Skye, IV51 9PW
Tel: 01470 582444

Simpsons Hotel
79 Lauriston Place
Edinburgh, EH3 9HZ
Tel: 0131 622 7979

Speedbird Inn
Argyll Road, Dyce
Aberdeen
Aberdeenshire, AB21 0AF
Tel: 01224 772884

Stirling Management Centre
University of Stirling
Stirling, FK9 4LA
Tel: 01786 451666

Strathpeffer Hotel
Strathpeffer
Ross-shire, IV14 9DF
Tel: 0997 421200

Strathwhillan House
Brodick, Isle of Arran, KA27 8BQ
Tel: 01770 302331

Stronsay Hotel
Stronsay, Orkney, KW17 2AR
Tel: 01857 616213

Thistle Aberdeen Airport Hotel
Argyll Road, Aberdeen
Aberdeenshire, AB21 0AF
Tel: 01224 725252

Thistle Aberdeen Altens
Souterhead Road, Altens
Aberdeen, Aberdeenshire, AB12 3LF
Tel: 01224 877000

Thistle Edinburgh
107 Leith Street
Edinburgh, EH1 3SW
Tel: 0131 556 0111

Thistle Irvine
46 Annick Road
Irvine, Ayrshire, KA11 4LD
Tel: 01294 274272

Thorndale
Manse Road, Stonehouse
Lanarkshire, ML9 3NX
Tel: 01698 791133

Tigh-Na-Cheo
Garbhein Road, Kinlochleven
Argyll, PA40 4SE
01855 831434

Torr House Hotel
8 Moss Street, Elgin
Moray, IV30 1LU
Tel: 01343 542661

Travelodge Edinburgh South
46 Dreghorn Link
A720 City Bypass
Edinburgh, EH13 9QR
Tel: 0131 441 4296

Travelodge Glasgow Paisley Road
251 Paisley Road, Glasgow, G5 8RA
Tel: 0141 4203882

Travelodge Kinross Service Area
Turphills Tourist Centre
Kinross, Perthshire, KY13 7NQ
Tel: 08700 850950

The Trefoil Centre
Gorgarbank, Edinburgh, EH12 9DA
Tel: 0131 339 3148

Viewfield House Hotel
Portree, Isle of Skye, IV51 9EU
Tel: 0478 612217

Welcome Lodge
Welcome Break Service Area M74
Gretna Green
Dumfriesshire, DG16 5HQ
Tel: 01461 337566

West Park Villas
West Park Road, Dundee
Angus, DD2 1NN
Tel: 01382 667169

The Westin Turnberry Resort
Turnberry, Ayrshire, KA26 9LT
Tel: 01655 331000

Westwood House
Houndwood, by St Abbs
Berwickshire, TD14 5TP
Tel: 01361 850232

FACILITIES
For visitors with disabilities

Windsor Hotel
18 Albert Street, Nairn
Inverness-shire, IV12 4HP
Tel: 01667 453108

Woodland House
Torlundy, Fort William
Inverness-shire, PH33 6SN
Tel: 01397 701698

CATEGORY 2

**Aberdeen City Centre
Premier Lodge**
Invelair House, West North Street
Aberdeen, Aberdeenshire, AB24 5AR
Tel: 0870 700 1304

Aberdeen Marriott Hotel
Riverview Drive, Farburn, Dyce
Aberdeenshire, AB21 7AZ
Tel: 01224 770011

**Aberdeen South
West Premier Lodge**
Straik Road, Westhill
Aberdeenshire, AB32 6JN
Tel: 0870 700 1303

Aberdeen West Premier Lodge
North Anderson Drive
Aberdeen, Aberdeenshire, AB15 6DW
Tel: 0870 700 1300

Arden House
Newtonmore Road, Kingussie
Inverness-shire, PH21 1HE
Tel: 01540 661369

Ardencaple Hotel
Shore Road, Rhu
Dunbartonshire, G83 8LA
Tel: 01436 820200

Auchenskeoch Lodge
By Dalbeattie
Kirkcudbrightshire, DG5 4PG
Tel: 01387 780277

**Auchrannie Country
House Hotel**
Brodick, Isle of Arran, KA27 8BZ
Tel: 01770 302234

Balbirnie House Hotel
Balbirnie Park, Markinch
by Glenrothes, Fife, KY7 6NE
Tel: 01592 610066

The Ballachulish Hotel
Ballachulish, Argyll, PA39 4JY
Tel: 01855 811606

The Baltasound Hotel
Baltasound, Unst
Shetland, ZE2 9DS
Tel: 01957 711334

Barony Hotel
Birsay, Orkney, KW17 2LS
Tel: 01856 721327

Bewleys Hotel Glasgow
110 Bath Street
Glasgow, G2 2EN
Tel: 0141 353 0800

Burnside Apartments
19 West Moulin Road
Pitlochry, Perthshire, PH16 5EA
Tel: 01796 472203

Caledonian Hotel
Princes Street
Edinburgh, EH1 2AB
Tel: 0131 459 9988

Clan MacDuff Hotel
Achintore Road, Fort William
Inverness-shire, PH33 6RW
Tel: 01397 702341

Cloisters
Church Holme, Talmine
Sutherland, IV27 4YP
Tel: 01847 601286

Clonyard House Hotel
Colvend, Dalbeattie
Kircudbrightshire, DG5 4QW
Tel: 01556 630372

Clunebeg Lodge
Clunebeg Estate, Drumnadrochit
Inverness-shire, IV63 6US
Tel: 01456 450387

Comely Bank
32 Burrell Street, Crieff
Perthshire, PH7 4DT
Tel: 01764 653409

Crombie Johnston Hall
University of Aberdeen
Aberdeen, AB24 3TS

Dall Lodge Country House Hotel
Main Street, Killin
Perthshire, FK21 8TN
Tel: 01567 820217

Dryfesdale Hotel
Dryfebridge, Lockerbie
Dumfriesshire, DG11 2SF
Tel: 01576 202427

Dundee East Premier Lodge
115-117 Lawers Drive
Panmurefield Village
Broughty Ferry, Dundee, DD5 3TS
Tel: 0870 700 1360

Dundee North Premier Lodge
Camperdown Leisure Park
Dayton Drive, Kingsway
Dundee, DD2 3SQ
Tel: 0870 700 1362

Dyce Skean Dhu Hotel
Farburn Terrace, Dyce
Aberdeenshire, AB21 7DW
Tel: 01224 723101

East Kilbride Premier Lodge
Eaglesham Road, East Kilbride
Glasgow, G75 8LW
Tel: 0870 700 1398

Edinburgh East Premier Lodge
City Bypass, Newcraighall
Edinburgh, EH2 8SG
Tel: 0870 700 1372

Edinburgh Premier Lodge
94-96 Grassmarket
Edinburgh, Lothian, EH1 2JR
Tel: 0870 700 1370

Express by Holiday Inn
200 Dunkeld Road
Inveralmond, Perth
Perthshire, PH1 3AQ
Tel: 01738 636666

Falkirk Premier Lodge
Glenbervie Business Park
Bellsdyke Rd, Larbert
Falkirk, Stirlingshire, FK5 4EG
Tel: 0870 700 1386

Garvock House Hotel
St John's Drive, Transy
Dunfermline, Fife, KY12 7TU
Tel: 01383 621067

Glasgow Moat House
Congress Road
Glasgow, G3 8QT
Tel: 0141 306 9988

FACILITIES
For visitors with disabilities

Glenaveron
Golf Road, Brora
Sutherland, KW9 6QS
Tel: 01408 621601

Glentress Hotel & Country Inn
Innerleithen Road, Kirnlaw, Peebles
Peebles-shire, EH45 8NB
Tel: 01721 720100

The Gretna Chase Hotel
Sark Bridge, Gretna
Dumfriesshire, CA6 5JB
Tel: 01461 337517

Hilcroft Hotel
East Main Street, Whitburn
West Lothian, EH47 0JU
Tel: 01501 740818

Hilton Edinburgh Airport
Edinburgh International Airport
Edinburgh, EH28 8LL
Tel: 0131 519 4400

Hilton Edinburgh Grosvenor
7-21 Grosvenor Street
Edinburgh, EH12 5EF
Tel: 0131 226 6001

Holiday Inn Edinburgh
Corstorphine Road
Edinburgh, EH12 6UA
Tel: 0870 400 9026

Holiday Inn Edinburgh – North
107 Queensferry Road
Edinburgh, EH4 3HL
Tel: 0131 332 2442

Huntingtower Hotel
Crieff Road, Perth
Perthshire, PH1 3JT
Tel: 01738 583771

Ivory House
14 Vogrie Road, Gorebridge
Midlothian, EH23 4HH
Tel: 01875 820755

Jarvis Caledonian Hotel
Church Street, Inverness
Inverness-shire, IV1 1DX
Tel: 01463 235181

Keavil House Hotel
Crossford, Dunfermline
Fife, KY12 8QW
Tel: 01383 736258

Kinloch House Hotel
By Blairgowrie
Perthshire, PH10 6SG
Tel: 01250 884237

Kynachan Loch Tummel Hotel
Tummel Bridge
Perthshire, PH16 5SB
Tel: 01796 484848

Loch Fyne Hotel
Newtown, Inveraray
Argyll, PA32 8XT
Tel: 01499 302148

The Lodge on the Loch
Creag Dhu, Onich, by Fort William
Inverness-shire, PH33 6RY
Tel: 01855 821237

The Log Cabin Hotel
Glen Derby, Kirkmichael
Blairgowrie, Perthshire, PH10 7NB
Tel: 01250 881288

The Mill
Grahamshill
Kirkpatrick Fleming, by Lockerbie
Dumfriesshire, DG11 3BQ
Tel: 01461 800344

Moorings Hotel
114 Hamilton Road, Motherwell
Lanarkshire, ML1 3DG
Tel: 01698 258131

Morangie House Hotel
Morangie Road, Tain
Ross-shire, IV19 1PY
Tel: 01862 892281

Muckrach Lodge Hotel
Dulnain Bridge, Grantown-on-spey
Moray, PH26 3LY
Tel: 01479 851257

Murraypark Hotel
Connaught Terrace, Crieff
Perthshire, PH7 3DJ
Tel: 01764 653731

Nethybridge Hotel
Nethybridge
Inverness-shire, PH25 3DP
Tel: 01479 821203

New Lanark Mill Hotel
New Lanark
Lanarkshire, ML11 9DB
Tel: 01555 667200

New Weigh Inn Hotel
Burnside, Thurso
Caithness, KW14 7UG
Tel: 01847 893722

Oakbank Farm
Lamlash, Isle of Arran, KA27 8LH
Tel: 01770 600404

Observatory Guest House
North Ronaldsay
Orkney, KW17 2BE
Tel: 01857 633200

Orasay Inn
Lochcarnan, South Uist
Outer Hebrides, HS8 5PD
Tel: 01870 610298

Patio Hotel
1 South Avenue
Clydebank Business Park
Clydebank, Glasgow
Dunbartonshire, G81 2RW
Tel: 0141 951 1133

Plockton Hotel
Harbour Street, Plockton
Ross-shire, IV52 8TN
Tel: 01599 544274

Quality Hotel Central
Gordon Street, Glasgow, G1 3SF
Tel: 0141 221 9680

Queen Margaret College
36 Clerwood Terrace
Edinburgh, EH12 8TS
Tel: 0131 317 3314/3310

Roineabhal Country House
Kilchrenan, by Taynuilt
Argyll, PA35 1HD
Tel: 01866 833207

Stromabank
Hoy, Orkney, KW16 3PA
Tel: 01856 701404

Stronlossit Hotel
Roy Bridge
Inverness-shire, PH31 4AG
Tel: 01397 712253 *or*
0800 0155321

Travelodge Dumbarton A82
Milton, Dumbarton
Strathclyde, G82 2TY
Tel: 01389 765202

FACILITIES
For visitors with disabilities

Travelodge Dumfries
A75 Annan Road, Collin
Dumfries, DG1 3SE
Tel: 01387 750658

Travelodge Edinburgh Central
33 St Mary Street
Edinburgh, EH1 1TA
Tel: 0131 557 6281

Travelodge Stirling Service Area
Pirnhall, Stirling, FK7 8EU
Tel: 08700 850950

The Underwater Centre
Fort William
Inverness-shire, PH33 6LZ
Tel: 01397 703786

Whitchester Guest House
Hawick, Roxburghshire, TD9 7LN
Tel: 01450 377477

2 Mulindry Cottages
Bridgend, Isle of Islay
Argyll, PA44 7PZ
Tel: 01496 810397

CATEGORY 3

Aaron Glen Guest House
7 Nivenskowe Road
Loanhead, Midlothian, EH20 9AU
Tel: 0131 440 1293

Abbey Lodge Hotel
137 Drum Street, Gilmerton
Edinburgh, EH17 8RJ
Tel: 0131 6649548

Aberdour Hotel
38 High Street, Aberdour
Fife, KY3 0SW
Tel: 01383 860325

Aberfeldy Lodge
11 Southside Road, Inverness
Inverness-shire, IV2 3BG
Tel: 01463 231120

Alcorn Guest House
5 Hyndford Street, Dundee
Angus, DD2 3DY
Tel: 01382 668433

Anchorage Guest House
31 Balloch Road, Balloch
Dunbartonshire, G83 8SS
Tel: 01389 753336

The Anchorage Hotel
Shore Road, Sandbank
by Dunoon, Argyll
PA23 8QG
Tel: 01369 705108

Ardbeg Cottage
19 Castle Street, Lochmaben
Dumfries-shire, DG11 1NY
Tel: 01387 811855

Ardgowan Town House Hotel
94 Renfrew Road, Paisley
Renfrewshire, PA3 4BJ
Tel: 041 889 4763

Arnabhal
5 Gerraidh Bhailteas
Bornish, South Uist
Western Isles, HS8 5RY
Tel: 01878 710371

Ashbank
Lucklawhill, Balmullo
Fife, KY16 0BQ
Tel: 01334 870807

Avalon
12 West Side, Tarbert
Harris, Western Isles, HS3 3BG
Tel: 01859 502334

Avalon Guest House
79 Glenurquhart Road
Inverness, Inverness-shire, IV3 5PB
Tel: 01463 239075

Balavil Sport Hotel
Main Street, Newtonmore
Inverness-shire, PH20 1DL
Tel: 01540 673220

Ballathie House Hotel
Kinclaven, by Stanley
Perthshire, PH1 4QN
Tel: 01250 883268

Barn Lodge
Croftside
Pirnhall, Stirling
Stirlingshire, FK7 8EX
Tel: 01786 813591

Baxters Country Inn
Darvel Road, Strathaven
Lanarkshire, ML10 6QR
Tel: 01357 440341

Belvedere Guest House
Alma Road, Brodick
Isle of Arran, KA27 8AZ
Tel: 01770 302397

Birchbank Activity Lodge
Knockan, Elphin by Lairg
Sutherland, IV27 4HH
Tel: 01854 666203 *or* 666215

Blarglas
Luss, Dunbartonshire, G83 8RG
Tel: 01389 850278

Braefield Guest House
Braefield Road, Portpatrick
Wigtownshire, DG9 8TA
Tel: 0776 810255

Britannia Hotel
Malcolm Road, Aberdeen
Grampian, AB21 9LN
Tel: 01224 409988

Broomfield House
Thorn Street, Earlston
Berwickshire, TD4 6DR
Tel: 01896 848084

The Bungalow
81 High Street, Buckie
Banffshire, AB56 1BB
Tel: 01542 832367

Cambria Guest House
141 Bannockburn Road
Stirling, FK7 0EP
Tel: 01786 814603

Canon Court
20 Canonmills, Edinburgh
Mid Lothian, EH3 5LH
Tel: 0131 474 7000

Cherrybank Inn
210 Glasgow Road
Perth, PH2 0NA
Tel: 01738 624349

Chesterton House
Formaston Park, Aboyne
Aberdeenshire, AB34 5HF
Tel: 013398 86740

Clarke Cottage Guest House
139 Halbeath Road
Dunfermline, Fife, KY11 4LA
Tel: 01383 735935

FACILITIES
For visitors with disabilities

Cormiston Cottage
Cormiston Road, Biggar
Lanarkshire, ML12 6NS
Tel: 01899 220200

Corsewall Lighthouse Hotel
Kirkcolm, by Stranraer
Wigtownshire, DG9 0QG
Tel: 01776 853220

Coul House Hotel
Contin, by Strathpeffer
Ross-shire, IV14 9EY
Tel: 01997 421487

Craig Nevis West
Belford Road, Fort William
Inverness-shire, PH33 6BU
Tel: 01397 702023

Craigatin House
165 Atholl Road, Pitlochry
Perthshire, PH16 5QL
Tel: 01796 472478

Craiglynne Hotel
Woodlands Terrace
Grantown-on-Spey
Morayshire, PH26 3JX
Tel: 01479 872597

Craignethan House
Jedburgh Road, Kelso
Roxburghshire, TD5 8BZ
Tel: 01573 224818

Craigvrack Hotel
38 West Moulin Road
Pitlochry, Perthshire, PH16 5EQ
Tel: 01796 472399

Crannog
New Liston Road, Kirkliston
West Lothian, EH29 9EA
Tel: 0131 333 4621

Crieff Hydro Hotel
Crieff, Perthshire, PH7 3LQ
Tel: 01764 655555

Crofters Wayside Inn
Lochton of Durris
by Banchory
Aberdeenshire, AB31 6DB
Tel: 01330 844543

Croit Anna Hotel
Achintore Road, Fort William
Inverness-shire, PH33 6RR
Tel: 01397 702268

Cromasaig
Torridon Road, Kinlochewe
Ross-shire, IV22 2PE
Tel: 01445 760 234

Cross Keys Hotel
36-37 The Square, Kelso
Roxburghshire, TD5 7HL
Tel: 01573 223303

Dalerb
Craignavie Road, Killin
Perthshire, FK21 8SH
Tel: 01567 820961

Darroch Learg Hotel
Braemar Road, Ballater
Aberdeenshire, AB35 5UX
Tel: 03397 55443

Dinwoodie Lodge Hotel
Johnstone Bridge, by Lockerbie
Dumfriesshire, DG11 2SL
Tel: 01576 470289

Distant Hills Guest House
Roybridge Road, Spean Bridge
Inverness-shire, PH34 4DU
Tel: 01397 712452

Dreamweavers
Mucomir, By Spean Bridge
Inverness-shire, PH34 4EQ
Tel: 01397 712548

Dromnan Guest House
Garve Road, Ullapool
Ross-shire, IV26 2SX
Tel: 01854 612333

Druimard Country House
Dervaig, Tobermory
Isle of Mull, PA75 6QW
Tel: 01688 400345

Drumfork Farm
Helensburgh
Dunbartonshire, G84 7JY
Tel: 01436 672329

Drumnadrochit Hotel
Drumnadrochit
Inverness-shire, IV63 6TU
Tel: 01456 450218

Drumossie Park Cottage
Drumossie Brae, Inverness
Inverness-shire, IV2 5BB
Tel: 01463 224127

Dumfries & Galloway College
Heathhall, Dumfries, DG1 3QZ
Tel: 01387 265621

Dunallan House
Woodside Avenue
Grantown-on-Spey
Moray, PH26 3JN
Tel: 01479 872140

Dunedin
42 Strath, Gairloch
Ross-shire, IV21 2DB
Tel: 01445 712050

Dunlaverock
Coldingham Bay
Berwickshire, TD14 5PA
Tel: 01890 771450

Dunmore
19 Newton Street, Blairgowrie
Perthshire, PH10 6HT
Tel: 01250 874451

Dunroamin
South Keiss, Wick
Caithness, KW1 4XG
Tel: 01955 631283

East Haugh House
Country Hotel & Restaurant
East Haugh, by Pitlochry
Perthshire, PH16 5JS
Tel: 01796 473121

Edenmouth Farm
Kelso, Roxburghshire, TD5 7QB
Tel: 01890 830391

Enterkine House
Annbank, by Ayr
Ayrshire, KA6 5AL
Tel: 01292 521608

Erskine Bridge Hotel
Erskine, Renfrewshire, PA8 6AN
Tel: 0141 812 0123

Ettrickvale
33 Abbotsford Road, Galashiels
Selkirkshire, TD1 3HW
Tel: 01896 755224

Express by Holiday Inn
Stoneyfield, Inverness, IV2 7PA
Tel: 01463 732700

FACILITIES
For visitors with disabilities

Fairfield House Hotel
12 Fairfield Road, Ayr
Ayrshire, KA7 2AR
Tel: 01292 267461

Falls of Lora Hotel
Connel Ferry, by Oban
Argyll, PA37 1PB
Tel: 01631 710 483

Fendoch Guest House
Sma' Glen, Crieff
Perthshire, PH7 3LW
Tel: 0764 653446

Fenwick Hotel
Fenwick, by Kilmarnock
Ayrshire, KA3 6AU
Tel: 01560 600478

The Fernhill Hotel
Heugh Road, Portpatrick
Wigtownshire, DG9 8TD
Tel: 01776 810220

Finlay Ross (Iona) Ltd
Martyr's Bay, Isle of Iona
Argyll, PA76 6SP
Tel: 01681 700357

The Fishermans Tavern Hotel
10-16 Fort Street
Broughty Ferry, Dundee
Angus, DD5 2AD
Tel: 01382 775941

Fishers Hotel
75-79 Atholl Road, Pitlochry
Perthshire, PH16 5BN
Tel: 01796 472000

Forbes Arms Hotel
Milltown of Rothiemay
Huntly, Aberdeenshire, AB54 7LT
Tel: 0466 711248

Forss House Hotel
Forss, by Thurso
Caithness, KW14 7XY
Tel: 01847 861201

Freedom Inn
Aviemore Centre, Aviemore
Inverness-shire, PH22 1PF
Tel: 01479 810781

Gairloch View
3 Digg, Staffin
Isle of Skye, IV51 9LA
Tel: 01470 562718

Galley of Lorne Inn
Ardfern, by Lochgilphead
Argyll, PA31 8QN
Tel: 01852 500284

Glen Mhor Hotel
9-12 Ness Bank, Inverness
Inverness-shire, IV2 4SG
Tel: 01463 234308

Glen Orchy Guest House
20 Knab Road, Lerwick
Shetland, ZE1 0AX
Tel: 01595 692031

Glenmarkie Guest House
Glenisla, by Blairgowrie
Perthshire, PH11 8QB
Tel: 01575 582295

Goldenstones Hotel
Queens Road, Dunbar
East Lothian, EH42 1LG
Tel: 01368 862356

Gordon Hotel
Wellington Road, Nigg
Aberdeen, Aberdeenshire, AB12 3GH
Tel: 01224 873012

Green Park Hotel
Clunie Bridge Road, Pitlochry
Perthshire, PH16 5JY
Tel: 01796 473248

Greenlawns
13 Seafield Street, Nairn
Inverness-shire, IV12 4HG
Tel: 01667 452738

Hazeldean Guest House
4 Moffat Road
Dumfries, DG1 1NJ
Tel: 01387 266178

Heathpete
24 Balloch Road, Balloch
Dunbartonshire, G83 8LE
Tel: 01389 752195

Hetland Hall Hotel
Carrutherstown
Dumfriesshire, DG1 4JX
Tel: 01387 840201

Hideaway
Craigdarroch Drive, Contin
Ross-shire, IV14 9EL
Tel: 01997 421127

Hilton Strathclyde
Pheonix Crescent, Bellshill
North Lanarkshire, ML4 3JQ
Tel: 01698 395500

Holland House
Pollock Halls
18 Holyrood Park Road
Edinburgh, EH16 5AY
Tel: 0800 287118

Holly Tree Hotel
Kentallen, Appin
Argyll, PA38 4BY
Tel: 01631 740292

Holmrigg
Wester Essendy, Blairgowrie
Perthshire, PH10 6RD
Tel: 01250 884309

Holyrood Aparthotel
1 Nether Bakehouse, Holyrood
Edinburgh, EH8 8PE

Horizon Hotel
Esplanade, Ayr
Ayrshire, KA7 1DT
Tel: 01292 264384

Horseshoe Inn
Main Road, Eddleston
Peeblshire, EH45 8QP
Tel: 01721 730225

Kalmar
Balmaclellan
Kirkcudbrightshire, DG7 3QE
Tel: 01644 420685

Kelly's Guest House
3 Hillhouse Road, Edinburgh
Lothian, EH4 3QP
Tel: 0131 3323894

Kildonan Hotel
27 Queens Terrace, Ayr
Ayrshire, KA7 1DX
Tel: 01292 285122

Kilspindie House Hotel
High Street, Aberlady
Longniddry, EH32 0RE
Tel: 01875 870682

The Kimberley Hotel
Dalriach Road, Oban
Argyll, PA34 5EQ
Tel: 01631 571115

FACILITIES
For visitors with disabilities

Kingspark Llama Farm
Berriedale, Caithness, KW7 6HA
Tel: 01593 751202

Kinkell House Hotel
Easter Kinkell, by Conon Bridge
Ross-shire, IV7 8HY
Tel: 01349 861270

Kinross House Guest House
Woodside Avenue
Grantown-on-Spey
Moray, PH26 3JR
Tel: 01479 872042

Kirklands Hotel
Ruthwell, Dumfriesshire, DG1 4NP
Tel: 01387 870284

Kirkton Inn
1 Main Street, Dalrymple
Ayrshire, KA6 6DF
Tel: 01292 560241

The Knowe
5 Ancaster Road, Callander
Perthshire, FK17 8EL
Tel: 01877 330076

The Laurels
320 Gilmerton Road
Edinburgh, Midlothian
EH17 7PR
Tel: 0131 666 2229

Lilybank
Shore Road, Lamlash
Isle of Arran, KA27 8LS
Tel: 01770 600230

Lindsay Guest House
108 Polwarth Terrace
Edinburgh, EH11 1NN
Tel: 0131 337 1580

Links Hotel
Mid Links, Montrose
Angus, DD10 8RL
Tel: 01674 671000

Loch Tummel Inn
Strathtummel, Pitlochry
Perthshire, PH16 5RP
Tel: 01882 634272

Lochan Cottage Guest House
Lochyside,Fort William
Inverness-shire, PH33 7NX
Tel: 01397 702695

Lochside Guest House
Blackwaterfoot
Isle of Arran, KA27 8EY
Tel: 01770 860276

Lomond Country Inn
Main Street, Kinnesswood
Kinross, KY13 9HN
Tel: 01592 840253

Lyndale
Station Road, Beauly
Inverness-shire, IV4 7EH
Tel: 01463 783672

Lynedoch
7 Mayne Avenue, Bridge of Allan
Stirlingshire, FK9 4QU
Tel: 01786 832178

Mardon
37 Kenneth Street
Inverness, IV3 5DH
Tel: 01463 231005

Masson House
18 Holyrood Park Road
Edinburgh, EH16 5AY
Tel: 0131 667 0662

Moir Lodge
28 Linkfield Road, Musselburgh
East Lothian, EH21 7LL
Tel: 0131 653 2827

Moraydale
276 High Street, Elgin
Morayshire, IV30 1AG
Tel: 01343 546381

Moyness House
6 Bruce Gardens
Inverness, IV3 5EN
Tel: 01463 233836

Newbyres Cottage
8 Hunterfield Road, Gorebridge
Midlothian, EH23 4TR
Tel: 01875 821268

Northern Hotel
1 Great Northern Road
Aberdeen, AB24 3PS
Tel: 01224 483342

Novar
2 Home Street, Aberfeldy
Perthshire, PH15 2AJ
Tel: 01887 820779

The Old Mill Inn & Restaurant
Mill Lane, Pitlochry
Perthshire, PH16 5BH
Tel: 01796 474020

Piersland House Hotel
15 Craigend Road, Troon
Ayrshire, KA10 6HD
Tel: 0292 314747

Pitbauchlie House Hotel
Aberdour Road, Dunfermline
Fife, KY11 4PB
Tel: 01383 722282

Portpatrick Hotel
Heugh Road, Portpatrick
Wigtownshire, DG9 8TQ
Tel: 01776 810333

The Priory
Bracklinn Road, Callander
Perthshire, FK17 8EH
Tel: 01877 330001

Priory Lodge
8 The Loan, South Queensferry
West Lothian, EH30 9NS
Tel: 0131 331 4345

Quality Hotel Station Ayr
Burns Statue Square, Ayr
Ayrshire, KA7 3AT
Tel: 01292 263268

Quality Hotel Station Perth
Leonard Street, Perth
Perthshire, PH2 8HE
Tel: 01738 624141

Red House Hotel
Station Road, Coupar Angus
Perthshire, PH13 9AL
Tel: 01828 27216

The Reiver's Rest
81 High Street, Langholm
Dumfriesshire, DG13 0DJ
Tel: 01387 381343

Rhugarbh Croft
Appin, Argyll, PA38 4BA
Tel: 01631 730309

Richmond Park Hotel
26 Linlithgow Road, Bo'ness
West Lothian, EH51 0DN
Tel: 01506 823213

FACILITIES
For visitors with disabilities

Rob Roy Motel
Aberfoyle, Stirlingshire, FK8 3UX
Tel: 01877 382245

Rockmount Cottage
Dura Den Road, Pitscottie
Cupar, KY15 5TG
Tel: 01334 828164

Roman Camp Hotel
Main Street, Callander
Perthshire, FK17 8BG
Tel: 01877 330003

Rose Cottage Guest House
Gelston, Castle Douglas
Kircudbrightshire, DG7 1SH
Tel: 01556 502513

Royal Garden Apartments
York Buildings, Queen Street
Edinburgh, EH2 1HY

RSR Braeholm
31 East Montrose Street
Helensburgh, Argyll & Bute
G84 7HR
Tel: 01436 671880

Rufflets Country House Hotel
Strathkinness Low Road
St Andrews, Fife, KY16 9TX
Tel: 01334 472594

Scotties B&B
213 Nicol Street
Kirkcaldy, Fife
KY1 1PF
Tel: 0592 268596

Selkie B&B Sumandar Villa
Harbour Road, Brora
Sutherland, KW9 6QF
Tel: 01408 621717

Shawlands Hotel
Ayr Road, Canderside Toll
by Larkhall, Lanarkshire
ML9 2TZ
Tel: 01698 791111

Soluis Mu Thuath Guest House
Braeintra, Achmore
Stromeferry, Ross-shire, IV53 8UN
Tel: 01599 577219

Spinnaker Hotel
121 Albert Road, Gourock
Renfrewshire PA19 1BU
Tel: 01475 633107

Springvale Hotel
18 Lethame Road, Strathaven
Lanarkshire, ML10 6AD
Tel: 01357 521131

Strathburn Hotel
Burghmuir Drive, Inverurie
Aberdeenshire, AB51 4GY
Tel: 01467 624422

Sunbank House Hotel
50 Dundee Road, Perth
Perthshire, PH2 7BA
Tel: 01738 624882

Swallow Hotel
Kingsway West, Invergowrie
Dundee, Angus
DD2 5JT
Tel: 01382 641122

Theatre Hotel Ltd
25/27 Elmbank Street
Glasgow, Strathclyde, G2 4PB
Tel: 0141 227 2772

Tobermory Hotel
53 Main Street, Tobermory
Isle of Mull, PA75 6NT
Tel: 01688 302091

Tontine Hotel
6 Ardgowan Square, Greenock
Renfrewshire, PA16 8NG
Tel: 0475 723316

Torbay Lodge
31 Lovers Walk,
Dumfries, DG1 1LR
Tel: 01387 253922

Travelodge Glasgow Central
5 Hill Street, Glasgow, G3 6RP
Tel: 0141 3331515

Virdafjell
Shurton Brae, Gulberwick
Shetland, ZE2 9TX
Tel: 01595 694336

Wallamhill House
Kirkton, by Dumfries
Dumfriesshire, DG1 1SL
Tel: 01387 248249 *or*
0850 750150 *(mobile)*

Waverley
35 Strathspey Avenue, Aviemore,
Inverness-shire, PH22 1SN
Tel: 01479 811226

Whinrig
12 Burgh Road, Lerwick
Shetland, ZE1 0LB
Tel: 01595 693554

White House
Drumndrochit,
Inverness-shire, IV63 6TU
Tel: 01456 450337

INDEX
By location

INDEX
By location

INDEX
By location

INDEX

By location

INDEX
By location

BOOKS
To help you

VISITSCOTLAND produces a series of four accommodation guides to help you choose your holiday accommodation. The most comprehensive guides on the market, they give details of facilities, price, location and every establishment in them carries a quality assurance award from VisitScotland.

Scotland: **Hotels & Guest Houses 2002**
£9.50 (incl. p&p)

Over 800 entries, listing a variety of hotels and guest houses throughout Scotland. Also includes inns, lodges, restaurant with rooms, bed and breakfasts, campus accommodation, serviced apartments and international resort hotels. Comprehensive location maps. Completely revised each year. Full colour throughout.

Scotland: **Bed & Breakfast 2002**
£6.50 (incl. p&p)

Over 1,000 entries, listing a variety of bed and breakfast establishments throughout Scotland. Also includes hotels, guest houses, inns,
lodges, restaurant with rooms and campus accommodation. Comprehensive location maps. Completely revised each year.

Scotland: **Caravan & Camping 2002**
£4.50 (incl. p&p)

Over 180 entries, listing caravan parks and individual caravan holiday homes for hire. Includes self-catering properties. Comprehensive location maps. Completely revised each year.

Scotland: **Self Catering 2002**
£7.00 (incl. p&p)

Over 750 entries, listing cottages, flats, chalets, log cabins and serviced apartments to let. Many in scenic areas or bustling towns and cities. Caravan holiday homes included. Comprehensive location maps. Completely revised each year. Full colour throughout.

Touring Guide to Scotland
£6.00 (incl. p&p)

A new, fully revised edition of this popular guide which now lists over 1,500 things to do and places to visit in Scotland. Easy to use index and locater maps. Details of opening hours, admission charges, ageneral description and information on disabled access.

Touring Map of Scotland
£4.00 (incl. p&p)

A new and up-to-date touring map of Scotland. Full colour with comprehensive motorway and road information, the map details over 20 categories of tourist information and names over 1,500 things to do and places to visit in Scotland

You can order any of the above by filling in the coupon on the next page or by telephone.

PUBLICATIONS
Order form

Mail Order

Please tick the publications you would like, cut out this section and send it with your cheque, postal order (made payable to VisitScotland) or credit card details to:

VisitScotland, FREEPOST, Dunoon, Argyll PA23 8PQ

Scotland: **Hotels & Guest Houses 2002**	£9.50 (incl. p&p)	☐
Scotland: **Bed & Breakfast 2002**	£6.50 (incl. p&p)	☐
Scotland: **Caravan & Camping 2002**	£4.50 (incl. p&p)	☐
Scotland: **Self Catering 2002**	£7.00 (incl. p&p)	☐
Touring Guide to Scotland	£6.00 (incl. p&p)	☐
Touring Map of Scotland	£4.00 (incl. p&p)	☐

Block capitals please:

Name (Mr/Mrs/Ms)

Address

Post code Telephone No.

Total remittance enclosed £

Please charge my *Visa/Access account (*delete as appropriate)

Card no. ☐☐☐☐☐☐☐☐☐☐☐☐☐☐☐☐ Expiry date ☐☐☐☐

Signature

Date

Telephone orders

To order BY PHONE: simply call free 08705 511511 (national call rate) quoting the books you would like and give your credit card details.

NOTES

NOTES